IMMIGRANT ENTREPRENEURS

IMMIGRANT ENTREPRENEURS

KOREANS IN LOS ANGELES

1965–1982

IVAN LIGHT AND EDNA BONACICH

University of California Press

Berkeley · Los Angeles · London

University of California Press
Berkeley and Los Angeles, California

University of California Press, Ltd.
London, England

Copyright © 1988 by
The Regents of the University of California

Library of Congress Cataloging-in-Publication Data

Light, Ivan Hubert.
  Immigrant entrepreneurs.

  Bibliography: p.
  Includes index.
    1. Korean American business enterprises—California—
Los Angeles.   2. Korean Americans—California—Los
Angeles.   3. Koreans—California—Los Angeles.
1. Bonacich, Edna.   II. Title.
HD2346.U52L64   1988   338'.04'089957079493   87-25541
ISBN 0-520-06146-2 (alk. paper)

Printed in the United States of America

1 2 3 4 5 6 7 8 9

To Leah and Phil in grateful appreciation

Contents

Preface

Hegel once wrote that it would be possible in principle to reconstruct an entire civilization from a button. Korean entrepreneurship is our button. In studying this Korean case we have been led from the local details to war and peace, international trade and tariffs, unemployment and welfare, and immigration and labor law. Although we do not claim to have revealed the structure of world capitalism in a case study, we hope to have illuminated that big subject by close examination of this small subject.

We have made equal contributions to this text, but they have reflected task specialization as befits an effective partnership. Bonacich specialized in the external causes, and Light in the internal causes of Korean entrepreneurship. Therefore, although we discussed and critiqued each other's drafts, Light wrote and had final authority for chapters 1 and 5–12. Bonacich's sphere of responsibility and final authority was chapters 2–4, and 13–16. She also wrote chapter 17. A coin toss determined the order of authors' names on the title page.

SLIDE TRANSPARENCIES

The authors have produced a slide-assisted lecture—including maps and photographs—to accompany this text. For particulars, please write: Professor Ivan Light, Department of Sociology, University of California, 405 Hilgard Avenue, Los Angeles, CA 90024.

INTERVIEW NOTES

In completing this project, we conducted 138 interviews with Koreans and non-Koreans. Interviewees were persons deemed knowledgeable because of their job, organization membership, or reputation. We took notes on these interviews. We have preserved the anonymity of interview respondents as they were promised. However, a complete record of our interview notes will become available in the Library of the University of California, Los Angeles twenty-five years after publication of this book.

ACKNOWLEDGMENTS

In the period 1975–1976, the authors received help from the Institute for Social Science Research at UCLA. We express our special gratitude to the Director of the Institute, Howard Freeman, for his support and confidence. In the period 1976–1979, our research was supported by grant number SOC 76-12340 from the National Science Foundation, Sociology Division. We thank NSF for its confidence and financial support. Naturally, any errors of fact or opinion are the responsibility of the authors. The Institute for Social Science Research and the National Science Foundation bear no responsibility.

The Asian American Studies Center at UCLA made several small grants that enabled us to obtain documentation that would otherwise have been missing from this book. In this connection, we would like to thank Edward Chang, Eun-Jin Lee, Hye-Kyung Lee, Tara Sethia, and Sun-Bin Yim, all of whom obtained and organized information about Koreans in Los Angeles.

The University of California Academic Senates at Los Angeles and Riverside supported research assistance that the completion of this book absolutely required. We thank: Parvin Abyaneh, Yen Espiritu, Jonathan Fox, Mitchell Gelfand, Arlene Johnson, Im Jung-Kwuon, Lisa Lee, and Joe Weber.

Charles Choy Wong and Tae Hwan Jung provided invaluable assistance while completing their doctoral dissertations at UCLA and UC Riverside, respectively. Charles Wong contributed especially to the development of the initial research problem, in identifying and collecting relevant materials, and in conducting numerous interviews. Tae Hwan Jung provided computer expertise, while keeping us abreast of events reported in the Korean vernacular press, translating Korean language materials, and interpreting community events. Jung is coauthor of chapter 9.

During the course of the project several people volunteered help. An undergraduate at UCLA, Terry Chang, translated Korean documents. Richard Platkin and Peter Fonda-Bonardi helped us acquire valuable data on Los Angeles businesses. Im Jung-Kwuon completed some reinterviews of Korean business leaders. To all these we are very grateful.

We also thank members of the Korean community, and officers of the Department of Alcoholic Beverage Control, the International Ladies Garment Workers' Union, the Immigration and Naturalization Service, the United Way, and many others, who gave us their time, ideas, and help. Without such cooperation no sociological research is possible.

I. L.
E. B.

Los Angeles, California
June 30, 1987

PART ONE

INTRODUCTION

1

Immigrant Entrepreneurs in America

In the mid-1970s, the people of Los Angeles became aware that a large and rapidly growing Korean colony had formed along Olympic Boulevard about three miles west of the Civic Center. Anyone traveling this boulevard would notice many Hangul signs proclaiming the presence of Korean small businesses. The big Korean colony was the more striking because in 1970 hardly any Koreans had resided in Los Angeles. In recognition of the new Korean enclave, the City of Los Angeles proclaimed the Olympic Boulevard neighborhood "Koreatown" in 1980 and posted signs so stating on major streets and freeways. Representing by 1980 about eight-tenths of 1 percent of the total population of Los Angeles Country, the 60,618 Koreans were still a small minority even after a decade of immigration. Nonetheless, Koreans were conspicuous among those "persevering Asians" whom the *Los Angeles Times* editorially identified the city's "new middle class" chiefly on the basis of their visibility in small business.[1]

The extent of Korean entrepreneurship was remarkable. In 1982, the yellow pages of the Korean telephone directory enumerated 4266 Korean-owned business firms in Los Angeles County, approximately 2.6 percent of all firms (Oh, 1983: 10). In retail trade, Koreans operated nearly 5 percent of all firms in the County. Since Koreans numbered less than 1 percent of the County population, their overrepresentation in business was appreciable. Similarly, the 1980 U.S. Census disclosed that 22.5 percent of Koreans in Los Angeles were self-employed or unpaid family workers. Since only 8.5 percent of the Los Angeles County labor force found employment in these categories, Koreans were nearly three times more frequent in entrepreneurship than were non-Koreans. Additionally, as Yu (1982b: 51, 54) discovered, Korean entrepreneurs employed an additional 40 percent of coethnics in their firms so that about 62 percent of employed Koreans in Los Angeles County were either self-

3

employed or employees of Korean-owned firms, mostly service and retail proprietorships.

Korean entrepreneurship did not develop in what mainstream business corporations regarded as an attractive business climate.[2] Despite its glittering reputation, Los Angeles suffered many of the blighted conditions so common among big cities of the East and Midwest (Light, 1988; 1983: 421–429). Between 1972 and 1979, Los Angeles County's share of the region's manufacturing employment declined from 81.7 to 71.6 (Soja, Morales, and Wolff, 1983). Crime, unemployment, plant closings, residential crowding, time consumed in journey to work, and housing prices increased faster than national averages in the 1970s. Air quality improved, but remained poor relative to other big cities.

These changes accompanied demographic trends generally indicative of lower socioeconomic population in the urban core relative to the ring—and increased residential segregation of whites from blacks, Asians, and Hispanics. As a result of immigration from Mexico, the City of Los Angeles' Latino population increased 57.3 percent in the decade 1970–1980 compared to an increase of 5.5 percent in the City's total population (Oliver and Johnson, 1984: 74). Between 1960 and 1980 the aggregate population of the City and County of Los Angeles increased only half as fast as the aggregate population of the four surrounding counties. Additionally, the white population of the City of Los Angeles declined from 71.9 to 44.4 percent in this twenty-year period while Los Angeles County's white population declined from 79.0 to 49.4 percent of the total. Although the decrease in percentage of the white population began earlier, the pace of decline accelerated in the 1970s: the white population of the County of Los Angeles declined 13 percent in the 1960s and 26 percent in the 1970s (Light, 1988).

In the peak period of Korean influx, retail and service industries experienced least growth in central Los Angeles. Table 1 shows that in both retail and service industries, establishments and employees expanded most in the four adjacent counties that composed the outer ring of the metropolitan area; they expanded least in the City of Los Angeles, the region's core. However, small firms flourished in the core. In service industries, mean size of firms increased in the ring but decreased in the core. In retail industries, mean employees per firm increased less rapidly in the core than on the periphery.

Table 1. Retail and Service Establishments in Los Angeles and Four Adjacent Counties, 1967–1977

	Retail Trade			Selected Services		
	1967	1977	Index*	1967	1977	Index*
City of Los Angeles						
Establishments	24,587	25,033	102	25,692	40,829	159
Employees	157,025	183,668	117	134,210	173,582	129
Mean Employees/Establishment	6.4	7.3	114	5.2	4.3	83
County of Los Angeles						
Establishments	57,287	58,995	103	52,985	83,757	158
Employees	367,638	452,246	123	234,168	357,748	153
Mean Employees/Establishment	6.4	7.7	120	4.4	4.3	98
Four Adjacent Counties**						
Establishments	23,138	29,608	123	16,272	35,466	218
Employees	125,511	232,373	185	47,228	114,855	243
Mean Employees/Establishment	5.2	7.8	150	2.9	3.2	110

* (1977/1967) × 100
** Orange, Riverside, San Bernardino, Ventura
Sources: U.S. Bureau of the Census, County and City Data Book, 1983 (Washington, D.C.: USGPO, 1983); Idem., County and City Data Book, 1977 (Washington, D.C.: USGPO, 1978); Idem., County and City Data Book, 1971 (Washington, D.C.: USGPO, 1973).

These reductions in firm size confirm the general tendency for small business of flourish in slow-growth areas (Greene, 1982: 6). Since three-quarters of Korean-owned businesses concentrated in retail and service industries, the influx of small Korean firms owed something to the favorable conditions for small business that came into existence in central Los Angeles in the 1970s. Paradoxically, these favorable conditions for small business arose in generally unfavorable business environment.

ECONOMIC AND SOCIAL BENEFITS OF KOREAN IMMIGRATION

The influx of Korean-owned firms conferred obvious economic benefits on Los Angeles. Korean firms tended to service low income, nonwhite neighborhoods generally ignored and underserved by big corporations (Bernstein, 1977; Scott, 1981, 1983; Holley, 1985). As a result of Korean entrepreneurship, wheels of commerce turned where they would otherwise have been still, and the City of Los Angeles took a percentage in sales tax. Additionally, Koreans injected money and skill into the Los Angeles economy, thus stimulating employment and earnings. Since about 62 percent of Koreans found employment in the Korean ethnic economy, Koreans actually generated most of their jobs and wealth.

Korean entrepreneurship conferred social as well as economic benefits upon Los Angeles. First, the Korean influx restored the neighborhoods in which Koreans settled. Koreatown itself developed in a deteriorating, underutilized area on the northern boundary of the City's black ghetto. As Koreans moved in, this neighborhood's appearance and prosperity revived. Property values increased (Sherman, 1979: 1). In addition to Koreatown, residential home of about one-third of County Koreans, Koreans clustered in a handful of widely scattered locations, often associating with other Asians.

Second, their residential and commercial interests compelled Koreans to combat street crime, Los Angeles' most feared problem (Endicott, 1981). Admittedly, many acculturated Koreans moved to the suburbs (Yu, 1983: 32–33). This local migration encouraged the relocation of some Korean business firms, which followed their owners to the suburbs. However, Korean firms were generally less mobile than Korean households. Insofar as their economic niche tethered them to Los

Angeles—since suburban locations offered scant openings for mom and pop firms—Koreans had to face a crime problem that other populations had fled. Hard as it was for Koreatown residents to tolerate street crime, it was impossible for Koreatown merchants who required safe streets and parking lots in order to guarantee customer access to their business premises.

Third, Koreans valued public education and improved it. Indeed, many Korean families had emigrated to the United States because of this country's superior educational opportunities. As a result, Korean students won more than their share of honors, prizes, and college scholarships. In 1978, Koreans were 26 percent of the 675 honor students at five central Los Angeles secondary schools.[3] In 1982, Koreans represented 3.0 percent of the undergraduate student body at the University of California at Los Angeles even though Koreans numbered less than one percent of Los Angeles County's population from which two-thirds of UCLA's undergraduate students were recruited (University of California, 1984: 68).

KOREANS IN OTHER CITIES

The 1980 census reported that 13.5 percent of employed Koreans in the United States were self-employed or unpaid family workers (table 2). In contrast, only 7.3 percent of all employed persons were so occupied. The percentage of Koreans self-employed or unpaid family workers exceeded that of every other nationality origin group. Although uncorrected for rural or urban residence, a bias that minimizes Korean stature, these census results indicate that Korean entrepreneurship was a national phenomenon and not just a Los Angeles phenomenon. But Korean entrepreneurship was most in evidence in the seven metropolitan areas wherein resided 47 percent of the nation's 355,000 Korean immigrants. Of these seven, two were in Southern California. Outside Southern California, Koreans concentrated in New York, Honolulu, Chicago, Washington, D.C., and San Francisco. Wherever Koreans settled, their entrepreneurship attracted attention. Illsoo Kim (1981a: ch. 4; 1981b) has provided a descriptive account of Korean entrepreneurship in New York City where Koreans clustered in the fruit and vegetable business, wig stores, and garment factories. Koreans in Chicago attracted attention because of the many small retail and service proprietorships

Table 2.   Self-Employed Workers as a Percentage of
Employed Persons by Detailed Nationality Origin:
For the United States, 1980 (in percentages)

	Employees of Own Corporation	Self-Employed Workers	Unpaid Family Workers
All persons	2.1	6.8	0.5
Japanese	NA	7.9	0.6
Chinese	NA	7.2	1.0
Korean	NA	11.9	1.6
Vietnamese	NA	2.2	0.5
Mexican	NA	3.5	0.3
Cuban	NA	5.8	0.4
Irish	2.0	6.6	0.5
Italian	3.5	6.9	0.4
Polish	2.5	5.9	0.4

Source: U.S. Bureau of the Census. *Census of Population.* vol. 1. *Characteristics of the Population.* Ch. C. *General Social and Economic Characteristics.* Pt. 1. *United States Summary.* PC80-1-C1 (Washington, D.C.: USGPO, 1983), pp. 159, 165, 173.

 they operated in black neighborhoods (K. C. Kim and Hurh, 1984). Myers (1983: 83) found that three-quarters of Korean men in Philadelphia "succeeded in becoming small business entrepreneurs." Since Koreans were overrepresented in entrepreneurship nationally, the presumption is strong that Korean immigration had an entrepreneurial impact in other cities just as it had in Los Angeles.

OTHER ENTREPRENEURIAL IMMIGRANTS

In the 1980s the United States discovered that immigrant entrepreneurship, a phenomenon of immense historical importance, was still a potent economic force in big cities (Doerner, 1985; Greenwald, 1985). As it had been in every decennial census since 1980 (Higgs, 1977: 162–163; Conk, 1981: 711–712), the rate of self-employment among immigrants was higher than the rate among the native born in 1980. Case studies identified several new immigrant groups who heavily utilized entrepreneurship in identifiable industries and localities.[4]

North America was not distinctive in resurgent entrepreneurship.

According to Boissevain (1984: 20), Common Market countries registered an increase in self-employment in 1978, the first since 1945. This reversal of the trend occurred where unemployment was heaviest, and "increasing self-employment among migrants" was part of the cause. Research in Britain (Ward and Jenkins, 1984) called attention to the extensive self-employment among foreign-born Greeks, Italians, Gujerati Hindus, Sikhs, and Pakistanis. As in the United States, the entrepreneurship of immigrants in Britain mostly occurred in depressed cities (Aldrich et al., 1981).

Although many entrepreneurially inclined immigrant minorities came to attention during the 1970s, only the Cubans in Miami developed an ethnic economy that rivaled the Korean achievement in Los Angeles (Wilson and Martin, 1982; Portes and Bach, 1985: chs. 8–9). Cuban-owned enterprises in Miami increased from 919 in 1967 to 8000 in 1976 (Wilson and Portes, 1980: 303). Like Koreans, Cubans concentrated in identifiable industries rather than fanning out over the industrial spectrum. Textiles, leather, cigarmaking, construction, finance, and furniture became Cuban specialities. Cubans controlled 40 percent of the construction industry in Miami and 20 percent of the banks in 1980. Portes, Clark, and Lopez (1981–1982: 18) found that 20 percent of Cubans in Miami were self-employed in 1979, and 49 percent found employment in Spanish-speaking firms owned by coethnics. Employment in the ethnic economy increased to 49 percent in 1979 from 39 percent in 1976. Moreover, workers in the Cuban economy received returns on their human capital (education, knowledge, experience) equivalent to those paid in the "mainstream center economy" and far superior to those paid in the secondary labor market, a junkpile of deadend jobs (Wilson and Portes, 1980: 314). Enclave employment did not disadvantage immigrant workers and probably made better opportunities available than they would have found on the general labor market (Portes, 1981: 291).

Portes' Miami results confirmed those of Reitz (1980) who had studied the economic performance of Slavs, Italians, and Chinese in Toronto. About one-third of South Europeans and Chinese in Toronto worked in settings in which their native tongue was spoken. These settings included ethnic businesses as well as work groups "within Anglo-Saxon controlled organizations" (Reitz, 1980: 154–155). Among Toronto's immigrants, those who worked in the ethnic economy earned better returns on their human capital than did immigrants in the English-speaking economy. "For members of minority groups with low levels of education," Reitz (1980: 164) concluded, "work in settings controlled by their own group is quite attractive from the standpoint of income opportunity."

THE REVIVAL OF SMALL BUSINESS

The resurgence of immigrant entrepreneurship in Britain, Canada, and the United States undermined the position of social scientists who, following C. W. Mills (1951), widely believed that small business had provided an important avenue of social mobility in the past but, in an era of giant corporations, was no longer of economic or social consequence.[5] Admittedly, this negative expectation had firm grounding in historical evidence. Three decades ago, C. W. Mills showed that the proportion of proprietors in the labor force had decreased in every decennial census between 1880 and 1940. This process occurred, Mills (1951: 24) maintained, because big firms eliminated or incorporated small firms in the process of capitalist concentration. Projecting this trend into the future, Mills predicated that concentration would continue until self-employment passed into historical oblivion. Mills' analysis received impressive support from ensuing trends in the business population (see Light, 1974, 1984). Between 1950 and 1972 the proportion of self-employed in the nonfarm economy continued to decline just as Mills had predicted. In 1973 a slim majority of American farmers continued to be self-employed, but less than seven percent of nonfarm workers were self-employed (Ray, 1975).

Given this uninterrupted trend, most social scientists agreed with Mills (see Bottomore, 1966: 50; O'Connor, 1973: 29–30; Horvat, 1982: 11–15). Only a dissenting few found evidence of small business decline unpersuasive (Boissevain, 1984: 24–25). Giddens (1973: 78) described the postwar decline of small business as "a slowly declining curve rather than progressive approach to zero." Gagliani (1981: 267) found some evidence that small business owners had experienced "income reduction relative to wage earners," but these declines amounted to "missed opportunities at most" rather than "economic disaster." Stein (1974: 1, 90) criticized the prevailing assumption that large economic firms were more efficient than small ones, also noting presciently that recent changes in the American economy had *enhanced* "the benefits and opportunities for smaller enterprises when contrasted with those for larger ones."

By 1984, five empirical findings challenged the virtual consensus that had earlier developed around the concentration thesis. First, in 1972 nonagricultural self-employment in the United States ceased to decline as a percentage of the labor force (Fain, 1980). Indeed, in the period 1972–1984, nonagricultural self-employment actually increased 28 percent faster than the wage and salary labor force. Between 1972 and 1984, the self-employed increased from 6.8 to 8.3 percent of the nonfarm labor force. In 1978 the same surprising result appeared in Common Market countries where, for the first time since 1945, governments recorded "a net increase in the number of entrepreneurs and family workers" (Boissevain, 1984: 20).

A second surprise was how many jobs small business created during the 1970s and 1980s (Wells Fargo Bank, 1985: 4). Birch (1981) compared the number of jobs created in metropolitan areas by 5.6 million big and small business firms in the period 1969–1976. He found that metropolitan areas differed in respect to job creation rather than job loss. That is, cities that suffered net job loss in this period did so because their rates of job creation were too low to offset natural decrease rather than because departing firms eliminated jobs. Of all new jobs created, small firms with 20 or fewer employees created two-thirds, and firms with 100 or fewer employees created 80 percent (1981: 7). The biggest job producers were small firms in service industries. Confirming Birch's results, Teitz (1981) studied job creation in California between 1975 and 1979, the same period in which growth of self-employment outpaced growth of wage and salary employment. Teitz found that firms with fewer than 20 employees created 56 percent of jobs in this period. According to Greene (1982: 6), small business created 3 million jobs in the preceding decade whereas the 1000 largest firms in the U.S. economy "recorded virtually no net gains in employment."

Third, Granovetter (1984: 323) discovered that, contrary to the myth of bureaucratization, "size of the workplace" in the American economy hardly increased between 1920 and 1977. Even in manufacturing, bastion of large firms, Granovetter found no decrease in the proportion of workers in smaller establishments between 1923 and 1966. Between 1966 and 1977 that proportion actually increased. At no point in the twentieth century did more than one-third of manufacturing workers actually find employment in establishments larger than 1000 workers.

Fourth, new information indicates that previous estimates of the self-employed population systematically underestimated its size. The 1980 U.S. Census enumerated 8,641,000 self-employed persons in the United States.[6] Deriving its data from tax returns, the U.S. Internal Revenue Service published an enumeration of sole proprietors in 1980. The IRS reported 12,701,597 sole proprietorships in 1980.[7] Since some self-employed were partners, the number of self-employed reported ought to have been larger than the number of sole proprietors. In fact, it was only two-thirds as large. The disparity is known to result from different methods of enumeration, a problem discussed in the President's report to Congress.[8] U.S. government publications have acknowledged the undercounts of the self-employed and have pledged to develop a "small business data base" that tabulates the moonlighters, the no-employee firms, and the underground firms ignored by the census (U.S. Small Business Administration, 1980; Karsh, 1977).

Studies of the underground economy delivered a fifth blow to the assumption that small business had atrophied (Portes and Sassen-Koob, 1987). Narrowly defined, the underground economy consists of goods and services that change hands clandestinely, usually for purpose of tax evasion. More broadly defined, the underground economy includes illegal activities concealed for obvious reasons, and traditionally noncommodified work such as housework or child care (McDonald, 1984: 4–5). Utilizing a narrow definition, Guttman (1977: 27) estimated that the underground economy concealed 9.4 percent of the gross national product (GNP) from official enumeration and from taxation. Commissioner of the Internal Revenue Service, Jerome Kurtz (1980: 4, 15–17) declared Guttman's estimates compatible with IRS estimates. Since the units exchanging clandestine goods and services were mostly small firms, Guttman found, taking account of the underground economy magnified the economic importance of the small business sector.[9] The IRS estimated that $300 billion in income evaded taxation in the underground economy during 1981.[10] Moreover, Guttman (1977: 27) indicated that the underground economy had increased its importance in the postwar welfare state. That is, as the welfare state laid tax burdens on business, the underground economy took the form of tax evasion (Smith, 1981: 52).

IMMIGRATION AND BUSINESS POPULATION

The revival of small business and the resurgence of immigrant entrepreneurship were contemporaneous and compatible. Either might have caused the other. On the one hand, immigration began to increase in 1968 when the 1965 Amendment of the Immigration and Nationality Act took full effect. Small business turned upward in 1972. This sequence suggests that renewed immigration contributed to the resurgence of small business. On the other hand, a general growth of small business beginning in 1972 preceded the subsequent growth of immigrant entrepreneurship in the United States. Boissevain (1984: 20) has also treated the growth of ethnic entrepreneurship as "part of a wider growth" of small business in Europe generally. This order implies that reviving small business created opportunities for immigrant entrepreneurs.

Although these causal sequence might reinforce rather than exclude one another, with renewed self-employment spurring immigrant entrepreneurship and immigrants increasing self-employment, the magnitude of the two trends indicates the priority of small business growth, and, therefore, its claim to causal preeminence. After all, the nonfarm business population grew 2.5 million in the period 1972–1984. Assuming *twice* the Los Angeles 1977 rate of 4.0 nonfarm self-employed per 100 urban population, 28 million immigrants would have been necessary to produce an increase in self-employment of this magnitude. Yet in the period 1961–1978 only 6.8 million immigrants entered the United States. Even these rough calculations suffice to demonstrate that immigration could not have produced *all* the increased self-employment observed. Because growth of self-employment exceeded the immigration needed to explain it, one concludes that resurging self-employment created a favorable context for immigrant entrepreneurship, and, in this sense, caused it.

On the other hand, in view of the fact that immigrants have always exhibited rates of self-employment higher than native-born persons, increased immigration might also have boosted the level of

Table 3.   Self-employment and Foreign-born Population in
272 SMSAs, 1980: Regression Coefficients

Independent Variables	Dependent Variable: SEP	
	B	Beta
NBLF Native-born Labor Force	0.06	0.70*
FBLF Foreign-born Labor Force	0.13	0.34*
Constant	57.00	
R^2	0.97	

*$P < .01$
Source: U.S. Bureau of the Census, *Census of Population and Housing, 1980: Public-Use Microdata Sample A* (Washington, D.C.: Bureau of the Census, 1983).

self-employment by boosting the percentage of entrepreneurially inclined persons in the population. In 1970, 9.8 percent of foreign-born men age sixteen or older were self-employed in twenty-two large metropolitan areas for which the U.S. Census published data.[11] In the same year only 6.0 percent of native-born men of native parents were self-employed in the same metropolitan areas. Obviously, an increase in the foreign-born component of the labor force in the 1970s might have raised the general level of self-employment, possibly helping to reverse decades of decline.

Census data confirm this possibility. From the Public Use Sample of the 1980 U.S. Census, we developed a comprehensive file showing self-employment and nativity of the labor force in 272 Standard Metropolitan Statistical Areas (SMSAs). To establish the independent contribution of the foreign- and native-born components of the labor force to self-employment in these 272 SMSAs, we regressed self-employed persons (SEP) on native-born labor force (NBLF) and foreign-born labor force (FBLF). Table 3 displays the results. The unstandardized regression coefficients show that in these 272 SMSAs an increase of 100 native-born workers in the labor force of each SMSA caused an increase of 6 self-employed workers. However, an increase of 100 foreign-born workers caused an increase of 13 self-employed workers.[12]

Similar logic applies to Korean entrepreneurship in Los Angeles. In the period 1967–1977, the County of Los Angeles added 1,708 retail establishments and 30,772 service establishments (table 1). In 1977 the U.S. Census enumerated 1,089 Korean-owned retail stores in Los Angeles County and 693 Korean-service firms. In principle, Korean firms alone might have produced 64 percent of the entire decade's growth in retail firms, but they could not have produced more than 2 percent of total growth in service firms. Summing the two industries, one finds that Koreans produced 5.5 percent of total growth. Obviously, Korean influx did not produce all these new firms. Rather, Koreans obtained a share of the County's business growth which created a context for their entrepreneurship. On the other hand, numbering less than 1 percent of the population of Los Angeles County, Koreans alone accounted for 5.5 percent of new firm growth in this decade. Had Koreans produced retail and service firms at the same rate as the rest of the County's population, they would only have opened 260 firms instead of the 1,782 they actually opened. In this sense, the Korean influx caused the population of retail and service firms to exceed by 1,522 the size expected from an equivalent influx of non-Koreans. Therefore, Korean entrepreneurs did not simply fill existing vacancies: Korean influx increased the business population of Los Angeles County.

SUPPLY-SIDE SOCIOLOGY

These considerations expose two shortcomings of the concentration theory, still the orthodox explanation of small business population in developed market economies. First, the concentration theory operates strictly on the demand side, predicting progressive, irreversible decline of small business by reference to declining returns on invested capital. Even if correct as far as it goes, this doctrine overlooks the supply of entrepreneurs. Yet, as both Smelser (1976: 126) and Kilby (1971: 2–6) have observed, the market for entrepreneurs has a supply side as well as a demand side. If the supply of entrepreneurs increased, the number of small firms could increase *even though* return on invested capital decreased. Since immigrants have always had a higher propensity for self-employment than the native born, an increase in the proportion of immigrants in the general population might increase the supply of entrepreneurs, thus exerting upward pressure upon the number of small business enterprises (Boissevain, 1984: 33–36).

Second, as Giddens (1973: 283–284) has emphasized, the concentration theory assumes that only market influences affect the size of the business population. Marx (1965: 1, 763) had expected that the progressive reduction of small capital would be "accomplished by the action of the immanent laws of capitalistic production itself, by the centralization of capital." However, the United States government has persistently intervened to frustrate or retard market forces tending otherwise toward the progressive reduction of small capital. Four important interventions were ideology, taxation policy, antitrust policy, and immigration policy. With the exception of immigration policy, all other government interventions favored small business in the postwar era. Thus, the Small Business Act of 1958 celebrated the social value of small business and declared the desirability of public support for a population of business enterprises greater than what the unassisted market would otherwise provide.[13] Taxation policy supported small business by de facto toleration of tax evasion on the part of small business owners whom the Internal Revenue Service repeatedly identified as the most noncompliant section of the taxpaying public (Tanzi, 1980). Indeed, chronic tax evasion largely produced the underground economy whose discovery compelled authorities to raise their estimates of the business population. Finally, antitrust policy supported small business by reducing concentration of big firms, thus maintaining more competitive conditions in industry.

In contrast, restrictive immigration policies (1924–1965) did not support small business because immigration restriction reduced the proportion of foreign born in the total population. Restrictive immigration policy ended in 1965. The result was an abrupt increase in volume of immigration to the United States, an increase in the proportion of foreign born in the labor force, and an increase in the supply of entrepreneurs. Liberalization of the immigration law was an obvious prerequisite of Korean entrepreneurship in Los Angeles since Koreans would not have been permitted to enter the United States without this legal change.

The economic intervention of the state is axiomatic in Marxist sociology (O'Connor, 1973; Habermas, 1973: 33). Reviewing this literature, Gold, Lo, and Wright (1975: 48) even concluded that as capitalism matures, its development "depends more and more upon the active intervention of the state." But sociology did not apply this vision to the state's involvement in the "competitive sector." Indeed, the words "competitive sector" imply that here a real, market-based economy actually prevails. Although the competitive sector is competitive, this nomenclature implies more independence of politics than conditions warranted. In point of fact, the U.S. government intervened in the competitive sector in many effective ways just as it intervened in the monopoly sector. Restriction of immigration was an unforeseen but potent intervention in the competitive sector.

FROM MIDDLEMAN MINORITIES TO IMMIGRANT ENTREPRENEURS

Why were immigrants in general, and Koreans in particular, more frequently self-employed than native-born Americans? Explicating that question is a basic concern of this book. This issue is not new. The extensive literature on middleman minorities offers the starting point for this discussion.[14] Middleman minorities are entrepreneurial ethnic minorities who cluster in commercial occupations, especially in Third World societies. Examples include overseas Chinese, Japanese, Armenians, Greeks; Jews of the diaspora; East Indians in Uganda; Ibo of Nigeria; and certain religious minorities such as Jains and Parsees of India, or Quakers in eighteenth-century Britain (Light, 1980: 31; 1983: ch. 14).

The theory of middleman minorities offered an appealing handle with which to begin an investigation of Korean entrepreneurship. First, middleman literature addressed the problem of overrepresented ethnic minorities in business. Since Korean entrepreneurship was the key problem of this research, middleman theory spoke to the central issue. Second, middleman literature stressed the supply side of entrepreneurship, emphasizing the ability of entrepreneurial subgroups to develop firms in unpromising economic contexts. In view of the dilapidated inner city context in which Korean entrepreneurship emerged, middleman theory was readily applicable here. Third, the middleman literature explained the intergroup tensions that typically arise when alien business owners buffer elites and masses. This tension arose in Los Angeles as we document in chapter 12.

Nonetheless, middleman theory proved too restrictive, and we found it desirable to widen our terminology from middleman minorities to immigrant entrepreneurs. One problem was the orientation of middleman theory toward Third World contexts whereas

Korean immigrant entrepreneurship occurred in a developed society. Additionally, traditional societies disdained commercial roles and the minorities who filled them. However, the United States is not a traditional society. In the United States small business owners are cultural heroes—not pariahs—so the middleman theory offered no firm guidance to the American reality (Mayer, 1947, 1953). Finally, middleman theory stressed sojourning minorities (Jews, Chinese, Gypsies) whose commercial way of life developed as a historic response to pariah status. Koreans did not have a tradition of wandering through the world as commercial middlemen and, in this important respect, middleman theory offered no guidance to Korean entrepreneurship in Los Angeles.

The concept of immigrant or ethnic entrepreneurship offered a broader research framework than did the older concept of middleman minorities. *Immigrant entrepreneurship* means self-employment within the immigrant group at a rate much in excess of the general rate *Ethnic entrepreneurship* denotes ethnic minority specialization in self-employment without, however, imposing the requirement of foreign-born origin. Thus, immigrant entrepreneurship turns into ethnic entrepreneurship when a second, native-born generation continues the self-employment of the parental generation. Obviously, immigrant and ethnic entrepreneurship often accompany one another but for precision's sake, one should separate the two. In this sense, middleman minorities are a special case of ethnic entrepreneurship. Middleman minorities emerge from ethnic entrepreneurship when a succession of generations has forged a tradition of commercial specialization in a nonassimilating ethnic minority.

Immigrant entrepreneurship achieves conceptual breadth in contrast to the historic specificity that accompanies the concept of middleman minority. This breadth yields a more abstract analysis in which the entrepreneurship of immigrant groups is explained by their resources (Light, 1984). Ethnic resources support the competitive position of individual firms owned by coethnics. This bootstrapping method builds entrepreneurship from the elements of ethnic culture. *Ethnic resources* are social features of a group which coethnic business owners utilize in business or from which their business passively benefits. Ethnic resources include values, knowledge, skills, information, attitudes, leadership, solidarity, an orientation to sojourning, and institutions. If one observes, for example, that immigrants work long hours under harsh conditions, save most of their incomes, express satisfaction with skimpy money rewards, help one another with business skills and information, utilize nepotistic hiring and apprenticeship, follow one another into the same trades, combine easily in restraint of trade, or utilize rotating credit associations, one would be calling attention to the manner in which ethnic resources promoted immigrant entrepreneurship. After all, if nonimmigrants shared these resources, possession would confer no commercial advantage upon immigrants, and so confer no basis for explaining why immigrant self-employment exceeds that of nonimmigrants.

One must distinguish ethnic resources from class resources which may, however, be simultaneously present in the same immigrant group. *Class resources* are cultural and material. On the material side, class resources are private property in the means of production or distribution, personal wealth, and investments in human capital (Robinson, 1984: 184; Bates, 1985: 552). On the cultural side, class resources of entrepreneurship are bourgeois values, attitudes, knowledge, and skills transmitted intergenerationally in the course of primary socialization. As such, these cultural resources are class-specific rather than common to an entire immigrant group regardless of class level. Thus defined, class cultural resources of entrepreneurship resemble what DiMaggio (1982: 190, 191) has called "cultural capital." Although hard to differentiate at the margin, class and ethnic resources are different phenomena, each of which is capable of promoting entrepreneurship.

In the specific case of Koreans in Los Angeles, both ethnic resources and class resources supported the entrepreneurship of group members. That is, Koreans were highly educated in their country of origin, often well endowed with money upon arrival in the United States, and commonly middle or upper middle class in social origin. These were class resources. On the other hand, Koreans also passed business information among themselves; worked long hours; mobilized unpaid family labor; maintained expected patterns of nepotism and employer paternalism; praised a Calvinist diety; utilized alumni, family, and congregational solidarities; thought of themselves as sojourners; expressed satisfaction with poorly remunerated work; and utilized rotating credit associations in financing their businesses.

All of these ethnic characteristics also contributed to Korean entre-preneurship. In sum, Korean entrepreneurship simultaneously bene-fited from class resources and old-fashioned ethnic resources.

IMMIGRANT ENTREPRENEURS IN THE
WORLD SYSTEM

Since the separate contributions of ethnic and class resources to en-trepreneurship are still only partially understood, tracing and docu-menting their independent and joint effects represents an important task of this research. Chapters 5 to 12 contain the results. However, as originally conceived, the immediate causes and consequences of ethnic resources were to constitute the *whole* of this research. The readjustment of emphasis occurred because, as our middle-range research progressed, we became dissatisfied with the theoretical boundaries that had guided initial formulations. Narrow concentra-tion upon entrepreneurial resources left unanswered the world system context in which Korean immigration to Los Angeles had occurred. That is, the abrupt appearance of Korean immigrants in Los Angeles took the form of a historic wild card that collided with long-standing trends toward concentration in the domestic econ-omy. Yet, without Korean immigration, no Korean entrepreneur-ship would have occurred. Therefore, a complete explanation of Korean entrepreneurship in Los Angeles required an explanation of why Koreans had come to Los Angeles at all.

This requirement lodged Korean immigrant entrepreneurship squarely in the international realm because Korean immigration was itself the product of nearly a century of contact between Korea and the United States (Koo and Yu, 1981: 1). For Americans, the Korean War (1950–1953) was a distant "police action." For Koreans, this war was a historical watershed whose consequences were still un-raveling in the 1970s. These consequences included the displace-ment of the urban bourgeoisie from North Korea into South Korea during the Korean War, and the subsequent flight from South Korea of one part of the urban middle class among whom ex–North Koreans were prominent. In this sense, Korean entrepreneurs in American cities were products of the Korean War and of the subse-quent involvements of the United States in the economic, political, and military affairs of South Korea. Similar characterizations prob-

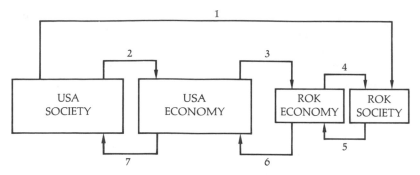

Figure 1 Interacting Spheres of Economy and Society in the United States and the Republic of Korea

ably apply, we believe, to Cubans in Miami, Vietnamese in Orange County, Lebanese Christians in Detroit and Toledo, Iranians in Los Angeles, and even to Pakistanis and East African Hindus in Britain. In all these cases, today's entrepreneurial immigrants were belated consequences of yesterday's foreign policies. Admittedly, a single-case study of Koreans could neither test nor prove generalizations about world system and immigrant entrepreneurship. Nonetheless, we undertook this study in the belief that an exploration of Korean entrepreneurs in Los Angeles would reduce the existing gap between a plenitude of world system theory and a poverty of empirical research (Portes and Walton, 1981: 4, 13).

Taking account of entrepreneurial labor in the world system requires new models linking internal dynamics of one society with those of another. A flow-chart diagram clarifies our argument (figure 1). Drawn to approximate scale of relative population size, the rectangles in this diagram represent interacting spheres of economy and society in the United States and the Republic of Korea. Numbered arrows are for reference.[15] Within the U.S. economy, concentration had reduced the proportion of the labor force self-employed. An influx of Korean immigrants (arrow 6) after 1968 increased the supply of entrepreneurs, thus increasing the number and percentage of self-employed in the Los Angeles labor force. Utilizing class and ethnic resources, Koreans in Los Angeles achieved overrepresentation in the business population. How they achieved this overrepresentation is the subject of part three of our text.

However, this resource mobilizing and conversion process should not hog the limelight because, in order to open small businesses in Los Angeles, Koreans had first to obtain the permission of the United States government to enter and work in the United States. This permission they obtained with the passage of the Immigration and Nationality Act of 1965. This law opened Los Angeles (arrow 2) to immigration, thus affecting the city's business population. In this sense, a political intervention of the U.S. government was partially effective in reversing or, at least, retarding the decline of small business.

Liberalization of U.S. immigration law would have exerted no effect upon the U.S. economy had there been no immigrants ready to enter the U.S. labor force. In fact, Korea presented the United States with an army of able-bodied workers wishing to enter. Why were Koreans available for immigration to the United States? Overlooking for the moment the sources of their desire to emigrate from their homeland—motivational issues—we turn first to the willingness of the Republic of Korea to tolerate emigration. As viewed from Korea, the emigration of Koreans to the United States was a labor export of the Korean economy. As Zolberg (1978: 268–269) has reminded us, governments need not permit emigration. Neither the Soviet Union nor North Korea, a Soviet ally, routinely tolerated emigration of citizens during the 1970s. Since the communists would have unified Korea in 1950 except for American military intervention (arrow 1), U.S. military intervention produced a non-communist Korean government that later (arrow 5) permitted labor emigration. Therefore, the entrepreneurship of Koreans in Los Angeles in 1975 really depended upon the U.S. military intervention in Korea a generation earlier.

If we now ask why Koreans wished to leave their homeland, volunteering for the hardships of an immigrant's life, attention turns to social conditions in South Korea. In the course of its accelerated export-led industrialization, South Korea suffered social dislocations during the 1960s and 1970s (arrow 4). Among these were rapid population growth, cultural crisis, overurbanization, urban primacy and marginality, housing shortages, air and water pollution, short supply of educational opportunities, inadequate medical care, unemployment, political and religious repression, danger and fear of war, police lawlessness, military dictatorship, and industrial despotism. Additionally, the country's real wages, although rising, began the decade at about 15 percent of those in the United States, thus rendering emigration to the United States economically attractive. As a result of these economic and social conditions (arrows 4, 5), many Koreans desired to leave their homeland.

However, we also maintain (see part two) that U.S. interventions in South Korea promoted these social conditions after 1953. United States interventions were both public and private. On the private side, U.S. capital sought out cheap labor in South Korea (arrow 3) in order to evade the wage demands of American workers (cf. Portes and Walton, 1981: 55). On the public side, the U.S. government propped up successive Korean dictatorships in order to bolster the world system's boundary with communism and to provide secure investment opportunities for multinational corporations. Without massive American interventions, South Korea would not have experienced the export-led economic growth and therewith the social conditions that prompted emigration. Therefore, the political and military interventions of the United States in South Korea are part of the explanation of Korean entrepreneurship in Los Angeles: no interventions, no immigrants; no immigrants, no entrepreneurs.

Part four explores the forces that brought immigrant Koreans into entrepreneurship as well as the economic benefits American big business derived from their employment in that occupation. Recruitment to entrepreneurship was not left to the marketplace. U.S. policy also shaped the Koreans' occupational concentrations. In general, immigrant entrepreneurs benefited big business. Korean entrepreneurs filled marketing gaps in central cities, supplied self-financing franchisees to assume the risks of central city investments, provided big firms with indirect access to cheap labor, and permitted big corporations to hire unregulated business satellites in order to evade the wage demands of organized labor. Additionally, Korean retailers distributed the products of big business in hard-to-access central city markets. In principle, Korean businesses accomplished nothing that big corporations could not have managed for themselves with wage workers. The advantage of the Koreans was their cheap labor. This conclusion suggests the desirability of treating Korean immigrant entrepreneurship as a disguised form of cheap labor conceptually analogous to traditional forms of cheap labor. If the general function of immigrant labor has always been, as Portes and Walton (1981: 49) have concluded, "to increase the supply of cheap labor," the immigration of entrepreneurial Koreans also satisfied this need.

SUMMARY

Between 1975 and 1982, Korean immigrants entered the business population of Los Angeles in great numbers. Korean influx stabilized neighborhoods, improved public education, counteracted street crime, and injected new capital and entrepreneurial vigor into the County's economy. Yet, this influx posed a challenge to social theory which long ago wrote off small business as an archaic survival. One source of this error was exclusive concentration upon the demand for small business entreprises to the entire neglect of factors, like immigration, which affect the supply of entrepreneurs. Underemployed in secondary labor markets, Korean immigrants had the motive, money, and education to open small business enterprises. Additionally, Koreans had ethnic resources that assisted them in business.

However, Korean immigrant entrepreneurship also developed in a historical world system. This world system engineered their immigration to the United States, thus creating the situation that eventuated in Korean immigrant entrepreneurship in Los Angeles and other American cities. When Korean immigrants in the United States turned to small business self-employment, they completed a domestic economic consequence of an international economic process set in motion decades earlier by the United States' export of capital, technology, and military power to their peninsula.

PART TWO

THE INTERNATIONAL CONTEXT AND THE ROOTS OF EMIGRATION

2

Cheap Labor in South Korea:
The U.S. Role

The purpose of this section of the volume is to examine the relations between the United States and South Korea in an attempt to understand why hundreds of thousands of Koreans left their homeland in the late 1960s and 1970s to come to the United States as immigrants. Our central thesis is that Koreans came to the United States as cheap labor and that Korean immigrant entrepreneurship was a disguised form of cheap labor utilization by U.S. capitalism. The cheapness of Korean immigrant labor was partially a product of the immigration experience itself, but its roots lay in conditions in South Korea.

The price of labor in South Korea was partly a function of the nation's level of economic development. During the 1960s and 1970s Korea was a poor, developing Third World country with a low standard of living. But the condition of workers in Korea was not solely a product of level of development. It was also a function of South Korea's position in the world capitalist system. In collaboration with certain classes in Korea, the United States helped to keep Korean labor cheap and controlled. In turn U.S. capital—along with the capitalists of other nations such as Japan—was able to take advantage of the cheapness of labor in that country through trade and investment there.

The movement of Korean labor to the United States was but one small manifestation of the utilization of Korean cheap labor by international capital. A fragment of the Korean labor force moved to the United States to be used there. Probably Korean labor that remained in South Korea was of greater significance to U.S. capitalists than were the migrants. Regardless of which group was more important, they were both sides of the same coin: in one case capital moved to cheap labor; in the other, cheap labor moved to capital.

In this chapter we begin by comparing the price of labor in South Korea with its price in the United States. Our purpose is to show the gross discrepancy that existed between the two countries which served to attract U.S. capital to Korea and provided an incentive for Koreans to move to the United States. The role of the U.S. government in the Korean peninsula is then examined in an effort to demonstrate that the U.S. contributed importantly to the low price of labor in Korea. In chapter 3 we turn to the role played by the Korean government in suppressing labor standards, in part, on behalf of international capital. Finally, in chapter 4 we turn to the causes and character of emigration from Korea to the United States.

The international system described in part two is time-bound, as is the large-scale emigration from South Korea to the United States. Even as we are writing, the price of labor is rising in South Korea, and the Korean position within the world capitalist system is shifting. These changes do not invalidate the processes analyzed in this section; they only show that processes do not continue indefinitely. We are describing a particular historical period, extending roughly from the early 1960s to 1980, in which the relations between South Korea and the United States generated considerable migration from one country to the other. If the relations between the two countries change drastically, and if South Korea ceases to be a source of cheap labor for world capitalism, we would expect that emigration, too, would taper off.

THE PRICE OF LABOR IN
SOUTH KOREA

The price of labor encompasses the total cost to an employer of utilizing a set of workers.[1] Wage payments make up the largest component of labor cost; however, labor cost also includes work conditions and fringe benefits such as health care and education for workers and their families. The price of labor is also affected by worker militance. Thus, production time lost during a strike raises employer costs, as do seniority rights and rigorous health and safety standards. In assessing the relative price of labor in two different countries one ought to take all these factors into account.

Adequate international comparisons of the price of labor are difficult to establish (ILO, 1977: 620). Even simple wage comparisons are plagued with such problems as different systems of measurement (for example, whether they are based on actual payroll

Table 4.   Monthly Wages in the Nonagricultural Sector,
United States and South Korea, 1969–1981, in $U.S.

	U.S.*	South** Korea	Korea as Percentage of U.S.
1969	$535	$40	7.5
1970	567	57	10.0
1971	605	59	9.8
1972	646	61	9.4
1973	690	68	9.9
1974	743	88	11.8
1975	799	95	11.9
1976	857	129	15.1
1977	925	170	18.4
1978	1001	230	22.9
1979	1084	295	27.2
1980	1276	267	22.9
1981	1350	328	24.3

*U.S. data are converted from hourly wages based on 176 hours per month.
**Korean data, which include family allowances and the value of payments in kind, are converted from Won to $U.S. using annual exchange rates. See ILO, 1977: 859; U.S. Monthly Bulletin of Statistics, 1980, 1981.
Source: International Labour Office, *Yearbook of Labour Statistics* (Geneva: International Labour Office, 1977, 1983).

data, or on negotiated wage rates which exclude bonuses and premium payment for overtime), variations in the inclusion of family allowances and other fringe benefits, and fluctuations in the value of currencies even if the official exchange rate is taken into account.[2]

Despite these problems, we have made an effort to compare the price of labor in South Korea and the United States. Three measures were employed. First, average wages provide the most important and direct component of labor costs. Second, hours worked is one indicator of work conditions, and shows the capacity of employers to maximize plant operating time. Third, strike activity indicates employer losses due to lost work time, but more importantly, suggests the degree to which employers, presumably backed by the state, are able to exercise coercive control over their work forces.

Comparative monthly wages in the nonagricultural sector for the United States and South Korea in the early 1970s are shown in table 4. From 1970 to 1975, Korean wages hovered around one-tenth of

U.S. wages. In 1976, Korean wages began to improve relative to the United States, a trend that continued into the 1980s. However, during the first decade of mass migration of Koreans to the United States, 1965–1975, the wage discrepancy between the two countries was immense.

Each country demonstrated considerable variation in average wages across different industries. In the United States, for instance, workers in the clothing industry averaged $3.41 an hour in 1976, compared to $6.57 in industrial chemicals, $5.43 in metal products, and so on (ILO, 1977: 677–678). South Korea showed similar internal variation, following more or less the same pattern as U.S. industries. Therefore the ratio of Korean to U.S. wages remained approximately the same, regardless of industry. For example, in the clothing industry, Koreans earned 12 percent of U.S. earnings. In industrial chemicals Koreans earned 19 percent, and in metal products they earned 11 percent of U.S. wages (ILO, 1977: 687–688). Thus low wages in Korea were not an artifact of differences in industrial concentration.

Not only did Korean workers earn low wages; they also worked long hours. The International Labor Organization (1977: 517–518) provides comparable data on twenty-one countries for 1976. Among these, South Korea ranked second, with an average workweek for nonagricultural workers of 50.7 hours. In contrast, the United States ranked nineteenth out of twenty-one, with an average of 36.2 hours worked per week. Two years later, in 1978, Korea ranked first out of twenty-five countries, with an average workweek of 51.3 hours. The United States, meanwhile, had dropped to 35.8 hours, ranking twenty-second out of twenty-five (ILO, 1979: 299–300).

A third indicator of labor cost to the employer is labor unrest. Table 5 contrasts the United States and South Korea on this dimension. The first two columns show that the United States had a considerably larger number of disputes than did Korea, on the order of 100 to 1 even in years of highest unrest in Korea. Of course the two countries differed in the size of their labor force: in 1977 the Korean civilian labor force numbered 12,929,000, compared to 90,564,000 for the United States (ILO, 1979: 178, 182). The remainder of the table takes this into account by assessing the rate of labor disputes and number of workdays lost per 1000 members of the civilian labor

Table 5. Industrial Disputes in the United States and
South Korea, 1969–1981

	Number of Disputes		Number of Workers Involved per 1000 in Labor Force		Working Days Lost per 1000 In Labor Force	
	U.S.	Korea	U.S.	Korea	U.S.	Korea
1969	5700	7	31.8	3.2	550.3	17.4
1970	5716	4	42.0	0.0	844.7	0.9
1971	5138	10	41.4	0.1	601.5	1.1
1972	5010	0	21.0	0.0	331.3	0.0
1973	5353	0	26.7	0.0	331.1	0.0
1974	6074	58	32.3	1.9	559.1	1.5
1975	5031	52	20.6	0.9	368.4	1.2
1976	5649	49	27.6	0.5	433.9	1.4
1977	5506	58	22.5	0.6	396.6	0.6
1978	4230	102	16.9	0.8	384.4	0.1
1979	4827	105	17.5	1.0	351.7	1.2
1980	3885	206	13.8	3.6	335.2	4.5
1981	2568	186	10.8	2.5	246.3	2.2

Source: International Labour Office, *Yearbook of Labour Statistics* (Geneva: International Labour Office, 1979), pp. 178, 182, 594–595; 1982, pp. 216–217, 678–679.

force. Clearly, a much higher proportion of U.S. than of Korean workers was involved in labor disputes, and the cost to employers in terms of lost workdays was much higher in the United States.

Two trends are of special interest. First, like the wages gap, during the period studied the disputes gap was decreasing so that the difference between South Korea and the United States was steadily diminishing. This diminution arose as much from declining numbers of disputes, declining worker involvement, and shorter length of labor disputes in the United States as from increases in all of the aforesaid in South Korea. But in 1981 the disputes gap between the United States and South Korea was still very large. Second, South Korea had a spurt of lengthy labor disputes which climaxed in 1980, the year of President Park's assassination. Thereafer, under Chun Doo Hwan, the country's labor turmoil slightly subsided (Sung, 1982: 188–189).

Although Korean labor was relatively cheap, educational standards were relatively high. About 90 percent of the population was literate, and 5 percent had college training. According to Lyman (1975: 248), "The nation's education system must rank among the most developed of the so called 'underprivileged' nations." Indeed Korea's level of education was comparable to a nation with three times its median GNP (Adelman and Robinson, 1978: 41). As a result "Korea has an abundant supply of trained or trainable educated labor at comparatively very low cost" (Lyman, 1975: 249; see also Koo, 1981b: 103; Clare, et al., 1969: 369). Put another way, Korean workers were "cheap skilled labor" (Balassa, 1971: 73). This feature distinguished South Korea from many other Third World countries where cheap labor was mainly unskilled.

It might be argued that the discrepancy in price of labor is a reflection of differences in the productivity of labor between the two countries. Perhaps Korean workers have been paid less because their output per hour is lower. Discrepancies in wage rates could, therefore, mask equal labor costs to the employer, who receives the same amount of output for a certain level of wages, even though both output and wages are spread over different time spans in the two countries.

We cannot test this notion directly since absolute rates of labor productivity are not provided in the ILO statistics. However, indices of productivity growth in the manufacturing sector reveal a 17 percent increase between 1970 and 1976 for the United States, whereas South Korea's labor productivity grew by 80 percent (ILO, 1977: 613). Indeed, among all the thirty-one countries for which ILO provided information, South Korea showed the greatest increase in productivity. Of course, there still could have been a gap in labor productivity, accounting for some of the price discrepancy throughout the 1970s. But any productivity gap was closing far more quickly than the wage gap, indicating that productivity could not be the main factor in the price differential.

During the 1980s the price of Korean labor appeared to be rising. Nevertheless, during the period of our study a marked international differential in the price of labor existed between the United States and South Korea. The discrepancy in price of labor contributed to a rise in exports and, as we shall see, to emigration to the United States.

INTERNATIONAL TRADE

The discrepancy in the price of labor between the two countries set up a pressure toward the displacement of high-priced labor and its products in the United States by cheaper labor and its products from South Korea. This pressure was reflected in changing trade relations between the two countries. Historically, manufacturing has typically been centralized in the developed economies, whereas less-developed nations have specialized in the production of raw materials. In the 1960s and 1970s, however, the availability of cheap labor in countries like South Korea shifted some manufacturing to the Third World, including manufacturing intended for markets in the developed countries. Thus, since the mid-1960s, South Korea emerged as a major exporter of manufactured goods to developed countries (Balassa, 1971; Helleiner, 1973).

From 1952 to 1963 South Korea averaged $34 million worth of annual exports, while annual imports averaged $358 million. In 1964 exports climbed to $119.1 million, to $175.1 million in 1965, and so on upward. Table 6 presents Korea's exports between 1967 and 1978. Looking at the totals first, we see a large annual increase every year. While some of the increases may be accounted for by changing exchange rates, there is no denying the tremendous rise in volume of exports. Over the whole period of 1967 to 1978, exports rose by an average of 35 percent per annum. Even the 1977–1978 growth was an astounding 26.5 percent.

South Korea's export mix did not change very much over the years, with the exception of a decline in crude materials (SITC or Standard International Trade Classification 3), and a rise in machinery and transport equipment (SITC 7). Manufactured exports, especially basic manufactures (SITC 6) and miscellaneous manufactured goods (SITC 8), dominated Korea's exports at least since 1967. However a real change occurred in the sheer volume of these exports. Korea moved, in a few short years, from the status of a very minor exporter, to that of one of the leading developing countries exporting manufactured goods.

A number of other developing countries demonstrated a similar pattern. Helleiner (1973: 24) found that in 1969 Korea ranked sixth among developing countries exporting manufactured products, be-

Table 6. Distribution of Exports from South Korea by Major Trade Classification, 1967–1978
(in thousands of dollars)

SITC Product		1967	1968	1969	1970	1971	1972	1973	1974	1975	1976	1977	1978
0. Food and Live Animals	$	37,928	44,492	50,279	65,537	69,661	106,988	245,588	299,735	602,339	508,331	945,001	932,598
	%	11.8	9.8	8.1	7.8	6.5	6.6	7.6	6.7	11.9	6.6	9.4	7.3
1. Beverages and Tobacco	$	7,019	8,621	14,850	14,231	15,277	14,006	22,947	47,514	67,565	78,279	108,390	119,969
	%	2.2	1.9	2.4	1.7	1.4	0.9	0.7	1.1	1.3	1.0	1.1	0.9
2. Crude Materials Excluding Fuels	$	58,005	61,506	73,042	99,973	94,875	119,200	196,102	198,429	150,494	195,800	299,885	328,674
	%	18.1	13.5	11.7	12.0	8.9	7.3	6.1	4.4	3.0	2.5	3.0	2.6
3. Mineral Fuels, Lubricants, etc.	$	1,772	2,298	4,837	8,761	11,278	18,176	35,424	107,731	104,477	144,611	116,766	40,617
	%	0.6	0.5	0.8	1.0	1.1	1.1	1.1	2.4	2.1	1.9	1.2	0.3
4. Animal and Vegetable Oils and Fats	$	119	113	68	59	80	275	631	1,775	936	1,169	4,474	11,413
	%	0.0	0.0	0.0	0.0	0.0	0.0	0.0	0.0	0.0	0.0	0.0	0.1
5. Chemicals	$	2,359	3,116	9,754	11,413	14,867	36,079	48,514	91,833	74,797	119,466	226,017	340,711
	%	0.7	0.7	1.6	1.4	1.4	2.2	1.5	2.1	1.5	1.5	2.2	2.7
6. Basic Manufactures	$	101,382	143,599	173,826	220,887	328,356	514,236	1,102,937	1,475,543	1,484,646	2,336,427	3,019,334	3,783,594
	%	31.7	31.5	27.9	26.4	30.8	31.7	34.2	33.1	29.2	30.3	30.0	29.8
7. Machinery, Transport Equipment	$	14,185	24,464	53,219	61,469	87,441	171,647	396,903	672,334	702,090	1,280,445	1,741,244	2,587,115
	%	4.4	5.4	8.5	7.3	8.2	10.6	12.3	15.1	13.8	16.6	17.3	20.4
8. Misc. Manufactured Goods	$	97,239	167,006	242,345	352,497	445,420	642,757	1,169,865	1,546,978	1,882,604	3,028,026	3,544,411	4,536,122
	%	30.4	36.7	38.9	42.2	41.7	39.6	36.3	34.7	37.0	39.2	35.3	35.7
9. Goods Not Classified by Kind	$	219	188	295	357	351	725	7,114	18,498	11,068	22,515	40,935	29,828
	%	0.1	0.0	0.0	0.0	0.0	0.0	0.2	0.4	0.2	0.3	0.4	0.2
TOTAL	%	100.0	100.0	100.0	100.0	100.0	100.0	100.0	100.0	100.0	100.0	100.0	100.0
	$	320,227	455,403	622,515	835,184	1,067,606	1,624,089	3,226,025	4,460,370	5,081,016	7,715,069	10,046,457	12,710,641
ORIGINAL TOTAL*	$	320,229	455,401	622,516	835,185	1,067,607	1,624,088	3,225,025	4,460,370	5,081,016	7,715,108	10,046,457	12,710,641

*There were minor discrepancies between the total figures presented and the summation of the ten categories. The original total is the one provided by the bank.
Source: Bank of Korea, *Economic Statistics Yearbook* (Seoul: Bank of Korea, 1979), p. 193.

hind Hong Kong, Taiwan, India, Yugoslavia, and Mexico. Close behind Korea were Brazil, Argentina, Pakistan, and the Philippines.
United Nations (1977: vol. 1) trade statistics for 1976 estimate the
percentage of total exports from each country that were manufactured. At that time Hong Kong still ranked number one, with $8386
million worth of manufactured exports.[3] South Korea ranked second,
close behind Hong Kong with $8160 million in manufactured ex-
ports. For Hong Kong, 98.4 percent of exports were manufactures;
for Korea, the figure was 93.1 percent. Coming next was Singapore,
with about $5.4 billion in manufactured exports, accounting for 82.3
percent of all exports. The ranking continues with Brazil, Yugoslavia, India, Mexico, Malaysia, Argentina, and the Philippines.
Clearly South Korea had become one of the leading "developing
nations" specializing in manufactured exports.[4]

The United States was Korea's largest export customer. In 1978
Korea exported $4.06 billion worth of goods to the United States,
accounting for 31.9 percent of all its exports. The proportion of exports going to the United States declined from a high of 51.7 percent in 1968. However, the dollar value of exports to the United
States continually climbed. For instance, between 1975 and 1978,
Korea's exports to the United States increased 164 percent (or $2.5
billion). Japan was Korea's second most important market, accounting for 20.7 percent of her exports in 1978 (Bank of Korea, 1979:
194–195).

The United States was less dependent on South Korean imports
than was Korea on exports to the United States. For a long time
over 70 percent of all imports to the United States came from developed countries, notably Canada and Japan. After 1972 there was
a marked shift toward imports from developing countries. Thus, in
1972, 25.6 percent of imports to the United States came from developing countries. Thereafter the figure rose to 29.0 percent in
1973, jumped sharply to 38.9 percent in 1974, continued to climb
gradually to a peak of 45.3 percent in 1977, and then dropped to
41.0 percent in 1978 (U.N., 1978: vol. 1, 1119). Despite the slippage
in 1978, there was a clear shift towards greater reliance on imports
from less-developed countries. Most of this shift was accounted for
by rising petroleum imports and prices, but an important component
was the rise in manufactured imports from cheap labor countries like
South Korea.

In 1978, South Korea accounted for 2.2 percent of total U.S. imports, representing a rise from 1970 when her contribution was almost nil. During that period, overall imports rose dramatically from just under $40 billion in 1970 to $172 billion in 1978, more than quadrupling. Thus the proportions conceal the extent to which the U.S. import market for Korean products grew. In 1972 the United States imported $708 million worth of goods from South Korea. By 1976 the figure had risen to $2.4 billion and by 1978 to $3.8 billion. In the latter year Korea ranked tenth as a source of imports and was the leading importer among non-oil-producing developing countries, according to the United Nations (1975: vol. 1, 957; 1977: vol. 1, 915; 1978: vol. 1, 1119).

The U.S. balance of payments with South Korea gradually deteriorated. In 1972, the United States imported $708 million worth of goods from Korea, but exported $735 million to that country, a surplus of $27 million. Imports and exports both increased over the years, but in 1976 imports from Korea overtook exports, with the United States importing $2.434 billion worth of goods while exporting only $2.015 billion, for a deficit of $419 million. By 1978 the deficit had climbed to over $1 billion.[5] However, South Korea was unable to improve her trade balance with Japan, her own major source of imports. In 1976, 35.3 percent of Korean imports came from Japan (compared with 22.4 percent from the United States), whereas only 23.4 percent of exports were destined for Japan (as opposed to 32.4 percent for the United States). Indeed Korea had a $1.3 billion trade deficit with Japan in 1976. This deficit was greater than her overall trade deficit (U.N., 1977: vol. 1, 526). By 1978 these trade balances had deteriorated still further to 39.8 percent of imports from Japan and 20.3 percent from the United States, and to 20.6 percent of exports to Japan and 32.1 percent to the United States (U.N., 1978: vol. 1, 674). In other words, Korea was able to make up some of the loss to Japan by a favorable export–import ratio with other countries, notably the United States. Korea's balance of trade was negative overall, but was positive with the United States, the principal relationship of concern here.

Although the overall dependence of the United States on imports from South Korea was modest, there was considerable variation by product. The most important imports from South Korea were clothing, veneers and plywood, footwear, and electrical machinery. Each of these exceeded $100 million. South Korea was the biggest U.S. supplier of veneers and plywood, travel goods and handbags, fur goods, plastic articles, and miscellaneous manufactures. South Korea was the second most important supplier of clothing, accounting for 14 percent of imports in this line in 1975.

Wigs deserve special mention because of this commodity's retail importance to the immigrant community in Los Angeles. Wigs were the third most important Korean export to the United States in 1966 behind only plywood and clothing. The 1966 figure of $10.6 million represented a tenfold rise from 1965 (Kim, 1970: 109) By 1974, total wig exports from Korea were valued at $72.9 million (U.N., 1975: vol. 1. 529) of which $51.2 million went to the United States. Wigs from Korea accounted for 89 percent of the import market in that year,[6] making up an important proportion of "other manufactured goods." In 1975, total wig exports rose again to $75.3 million, only to decline in 1976 to $69.5 million, and to continue declining to $60.2 million by 1978 (U.N., 1979: vol. 1, 680).

The huge rise in manufactured exports to the United States from South Korea reflected the utilization, by sectors of the American population, of the relatively cheaper labor power in South Korea. Commodities could be imported from that country at a fraction of the price for which they could by produced in the United States using American labor. The trade statistics thus reveal that, starting in the mid-1960s, Korean workers increasingly became a part of an international work force, the products of whose labor were consumed on an international market.

U.S. INVOLVEMENT IN SOUTH KOREA

Capitalists in the developed countries are attracted to cheap labor in the Third Word (Trajtenberg, 1977). By utilizing this labor, they are able to reduce costs, improve competitiveness, and increase profits. Especially if their own labor force is increasingly costly and militant and their national reserve army of labor inaccessible, they are likely to shift some operations overseas, in "runaway shops," to areas of the world where peasants are in the process of being transformed into a proletariat. Such was the case with the United States and South Korea.

Private U.S. capital was attracted to cheap Korean labor. U.S. corporations invested in Korean enterprises, subcontracted parts of the production process to Korean firms, and imported cheap Korean goods to the U.S. market. These processes received some political and economic support from the U.S. government. Therefore, the tremendous rise in manufactured imports from South Korea was not simply a product of internal developments in that country, but also reflected U.S. capitalist activity. In the process, the United States contributed to the creation and perpetuation of cheap labor in South Korea.

The United States did not play a direct role in suppressing Korean labor. Rather, the U.S. government supported an authoritarian regime in South Korea, which in turn suppressed Korean labor. Conceivably the United States never intended this result. In the early days of the U.S. presence, Korea was politically too unstable to attract private capital. United States support for Korea reflected the strategic goals of keeping South Korea free from communist control and containing the Soviet Union (Baldwin, 1974: 7). Indeed it seems likely that the United States would have preferred a more democratic government more concerned about the redistribution of accumulated wealth, thereby enhancing the stability of a noncommunist society on the peninsula. But whether intended or not, the United States helped to create and then supported governments that kept Korean labor cheap.

In 1945 Japan surrendered to the Soviet Union in northern Korea and to the United States in southern Korea. The two occupying powers were unable to agree upon a program of withdrawal and unification. Korea was divided and the United States set up military rule in the south from 1945 to 1948. Because there had been regional complementarity, with the North specializing in power generating and heavy industry, the division of the country undermined the South's economy (Frank, et al., 1975: 6–7). Combined with many other postwar problems, this weakness led to a heavy dependence on U.S. aid (Kuznets, 1977: 31).

To establish an anticommunist regime in the South, the United States had to suppress leftists. Communists had played the leading role in both the nationalist resistance to Japan and in the labor movement (K. Y. Lim, 1976a: 45–50) and now claimed the right to rule an independent, united Korea (Baldwin, 1974: 8–9). Unwilling to accede to such a demand, the United States attempted to establish a so-called democratic regime in the South, while eradicating the left.

The United States financed and armed rightists, while its army helped to suppress leftist protests (Baldwin, 1974: 10).

When the U.S. military government came to power the only labor federation in the country was the communist-led General Council of Korean Trade Unions (GCKTU). A new organization, the Federation of Korean Trade Unions (FKTU), was formed in 1946 and given U.S. recognition as the sole legitimate labor federation (K. Y. Lim, 1976a: 45–50). According to Lim (1976a: 56), "The FKTU had two main purposes: a) to support the conservative policies of the government, and b) to eliminate the Communists from the labor movement in South Korea." In 1946 the GCKTU called a nationwide strike to protest economic conditions. Police smashed the strike and the military government declared martial law, bringing in U.S. troops to restore order. Over a thousand people were arrested and sixteen were sentenced to death. In 1947 the GCKTU was outlawed (K. Y. Lim, 1976a: 57–59). As a result of these policies, by 1948, the left had been effectively destroyed, driven underground, or fled to the north (Baldwin, 1974: 10).

In 1948 the U.S. military government withdrew, leaving behind an anticommunist republic under Syngman Rhee. Rhee's regime was harshly repressive. Under the National Security Law he arrested opposition members of the National Assembly, closed down newspapers criticizing his government, manipulated the constitution, and rigged elections (Kuznets, 1977: 34–35; Lee, 1975: 21–24). Rhee's new republican government increased the suppression of labor unions and attempted to coopt the FKTU into the ruling Liberal Party (Lim, 1976a: 61) so that "any meaningful labor activity became impossible" (Kuznets, 1977: 33).

Under Rhee's regime, U.S. aid shifted from relief to the granting of aid for economic development. The dependence of South Korea on U.S. aid helped to keep Rhee in power. Despite conflicts with the U.S. government, Rhee had many supporters in the United States and therefore had better access to aid than other Korean politicians (Lovell, 1975: 167). The aid agreement had strings attached, including the provision that the Republic of South Korea facilitate foreign private investment (Kuznets, 1977: 36). Another important provision declared that aid would be immediately terminated if a coalition government were formed with even one Communist Party member (Choy, 1971: 361).

The Korean War broke out in 1950. The United Nations command was under the control of U.S. generals. Meanwhile, U.S. aid technicians went to South Korea advising the government on a wide variety of economic and political issues (Cole and Lyman, 1971: 23). No labor movement was permitted during the war (Lim, 1976a: 60).

An armistice was signed in 1953. The Mutual Defense Treaty with South Korea committed the United States to support the South against communist aggression (Y. Koo, 1975: 215). Rhee ruled until 1960. From 1953 to 1960 Korea received foreign aid, mainly from the United Nations Korean Reconstruction Agency (UNKRA) and the United States. UNKRA's aid totaled $120 million during the eight-year period, while U.S. aid amounted to $1.745 billion (Frank, et al., 1975: 12). Close to three-quarters of all South Korean investment at this time came from foreign aid (Frank, et al., 1975: 15).

The Rhee government was toppled by a student uprising in 1960, putting Chang Myon in office (Lee, 1975: 25–29). Chang's government was soon overthrown by a military coup d'etat led by Park Chung Hee. The military government lasted until the end of 1963, when elections were held and Park was returned to office as civilian president. He remained in this office until assassinated in 1979.

The 1961 military coup was intended, in part, to counter U.S. influence, especially in the military. Coup leaders were not friends of U.S. officials, who tried to prevent the coup and were critical of the military government throughout (Lovell, 1975: 171–173, 180). The new Korean leaders wanted to reduce Korea's dependence upon the United States, in part by normalizing relations with Japan (Cole and Lyman, 1971: 38). On the other hand, they realized that U.S. aid was essential and made efforts to ease the antagonism (Lovell, 1975: 181–182). From the U.S. point of view the military government's strong anticommunist stance was not displeasing.

When civilian rule was reestablished in 1963, a rapprochement with the United States followed (Cole and Lyman, 1971: 94–95). United States financial support continued to pour into the country in the form of aid grants and public loans. For example, between 1963 and 1971 when the program was terminated, $525.7 million worth of agricultural surplus was imported under U.S. Public Law 480. From 1963 to 1977, the U.S. Agency for International Development (AID) gave Korea $530.8 million. AID grants decreased over the years, from a high of $119 million in 1963, to a low of $948,000 in 1977 (Bank of Korea, 1978: 227). As AID grants declined, public loans became more important (Cole and Lyman, 1971: 90). The growth of such loans is shown in the following figures: in 1963 the United States loaned South Korea $9.1 million; in 1971 the sum was $120.7 million (Frank, et al., 1975: 103).

After the mid-1970s, Korea came to depend less on the United States for public loans (Kuznets, 1977: 77), though these loans were still substantial. Thus in 1977, Korea received $615.9 million in foreign public loans, of which $99.2 million or 16.1 percent came from the United States, the largest amount from any single country. The bulk of public loans, 54.4 percent, came from international banking institutions such as the International Bank for Reconstruction and Development (IBRD) (Hapdong News Agency, 1978: 120), most of which received substantial U.S. funding. Despite changes in the form of U.S. government financial support for South Korea, the level of U.S. support clearly remained high.

In addition to providing money, the United States played an active role in Korean economic planning. Early postwar planning was entirely in the hands of foreigners, especially from the United States (Cole and Lyman, 1971: 204). After Park came to power, the United States sent teams of experts to assist the Korean government in planning a development program (Cole and Lyman, 1971: 205; Baldwin, 1974: 20–21).

The United States gave South Korea military assistance. Between 1945 and 1975, U.S. military aid to South Korea totaled $6.5 to $7 billion, higher than that awarded any country except South Vietnam. Even in the first decade of Park's civilian regime, 1963–1973, U.S. military expenditure in Korea was $2.6 billion. And the military aid bill held at a rate of $160 million or more each year during the 1970s (Henderson, 1978: 179). For instance, in 1976 it totaled $196.8 million.[7] According to Henderson:

> Military inputs, both as incentives and as training and socialization, are inevitably political inputs as well. The overwhelming effects of such inputs on the institutional, social, and political developments of South Korea, thus inexorably smothered in our military embrace, have been starkly, if not ludicrously, clear in the political system and the governmental and legal values of the ... Park regime. (1978: 179)

Put simply, U.S. military support helped to keep a military government in power.

In the wake of the Vietnam War, the United States reduced its troop strength in South Korea. The reduction faced opposition both in Korea and the United States and was countered by assurances that U.S. military support would remain as reliable as ever.

When added together, U.S. economic and military aid to South Korea proved substantial. Between 1946 and 1976 the United States provided a total of $222.4 billion worth of economic and military assistance, loans, and grants worldwide. Of this amount, South Korea received $12.6 billion or 5.6 percent. The Korean total was the second largest, behind South Vietnam ($23.3 billion). After Korea came India ($9 billion), Israel, France, and Britain ($8 billion each), and so on.[8] In 1976, U.S. aid to the world totaled $6.99 billion, of which $345.6 million (or close to 5 percent) went to South Korea. Korea ranked third as a recipient at that time, behind Israel and Egypt.[9] Thus South Korea continued to rank high in U.S. overseas involvement.

United States influence on postwar South Korea was cultural as well as economic and military. The United States encouraged an ideology of parliamentary democracy and anticommunism. Sometimes the influence was exerted politically, by strings tied to aid agreements. Sometimes it was more subtle, by the establishment of missionary schools and churches in Korea and the provision of educational opportunities for Korean leaders in the United States (Cole and Lyman, 1971: 57–62). For example, the *Korea Annual*[10] reported that the U.S. military government "planted the American education system in Korea to provide the Korea people with democratic education under the principle of equal opportunity." This kind of institutional influence was found in many spheres, including labor law (K. Y. Lim, 1976a), as we shall see in the next chapter.

In sum, the influence of the United States on South Korea was massive. Although keeping Korean labor cheap was not their manifest goal, U.S. policies indirectly had this consequence in at least three major and interrelated ways. First, the United States supported right-wing dictatorships that suppressed dissent, including labor dissent. Without U.S. support it is questionable whether these regimes could have survived.

Second, in directly crushing and then aiding the South Korean government to crush communist dissidence, the United States helped destroy the most potent representative of labor. It seems likely that, at least on the surface, the United States wanted to create a moderate Korean democracy in which labor had as much voice as it did in the United States. But by destroying the Marxist left, U.S. policy handed hegemony to the authoritarian right, thereby crippling the Korean labor movement.

Third, and most important, the United States consistently supported the development of capitalism in South Korea. Capitalism drives people out of subsistence production and into selling their labor-power for a wage. In the early stages of this transition new proletarians compete with each other for limited jobs, thereby driving down wages. Because the drive for profits is the major engine of the system, little concern is given to the problem of redistributing accumulated wealth. The needs of workers are given a low priority; hence, the price of labor-power is kept low.

As capitalism develops, and workers begin to organize, the price of labor-power gradually rises. This rise was beginning to occur in South Korea, as we saw in table 4. However, the first two conditions, which the United States helped to induce, namely, dictatorship and the destruction of a communist movement, retarded this development.

Private U.S. Capital in South Korea

Once a cheap labor force had come into existence in Korea, foreign capital was attracted to it. United States capitalists made use of Korean cheap labor in four major ways: direct business investments in South Korea, commercial loans to Korean enterprises, subcontracting to Korean firms, and importing cheap Korean goods to sell in the United States. These methods are listed in order of decreasing control by U.S. capitalists.

Direct investments

Direct investment means a U.S. capitalist or parent company owned some or all of a South Korean firm and could influence its policies. Degree of control could vary from the establishment of a totally owned subsidiary of a U.S. multinational corporation, to a joint venture with a Korean company, or to a modest investment in an already existing firm. The investment required to obtain control or ownership varies among countries and authors disagree about criteria. Some consider a firm foreign-owned if 50 percent or more of its stock is in foreign hands. Some consider the degree of ownership necessary for control to be much smaller. Another variable is the nationality of management: a firm can have substantial foreign ownership but be managed by Koreans and therefore appear more Korean than American. These problems of definition make it difficult to determine the precise degree of U.S. direct investment in South Korea.

Before looking at the Korean case, we should note that U.S. multinational investment in Third World countries in general was rising in the 1970s (International Labour Organization, 1976b: 10–17; Trajtenberg, 1977). Until the mid-1960s most U.S. overseas corporate investments were in Canada or Western Europe. Investment in underdeveloped countries emphasized raw materials and food staples. But thereafter multinational corporations began to open manufacturing plants in Third World countries. Thus, 7 percent of all U.S. corporate profits came from overseas in 1960. Around 1967 the proportion began to rise, reaching 30 percent by the mid-1970s. In 1957 foreign investment was 9 percent of total U.S. corporate investments; by 1970 it had reached 25 percent, starting to climb in the mid-1960s (Müller, 1975: 24).

The reasons for this rise are not hard to uncover:

> The very rapid growth of foreign investments, particularly in the assembly of semi-finished products, which is highly labor-intensive, is explained by the presence of cheap labour in the developing countries, rising wages in the developed countries, and the need to remain competitive at home and abroad. The differences in wage levels between the two groups of countries are large enough to justify setting up production units abroad. (International Labour Office, 1976a: 11)

Earlier forms of capitalist involvement in underdeveloped countries took the form of the extraction of raw materials, or import-substitution (the development of local industries to produce goods that had previously been imported, for the local market). The new type of capitalist involvement was different: "What characterizes this form of internationalization is that the possibility of using cheap labor becomes the decisive factor ... The motivating factor is the low wages themselves" (Trajtenberg, 1977: 176). In turning to cheap labor, capitalists were able to turn back the clock to an earlier era in terms of the kind of labor force with which they had to deal:

"The effect is equivalent to what would happen in the central countries if hours and speed of work could be increased and, particularly, wages reduced" (Trajtenberg, 1977: 177).

Direct investments in South Korea took the form of projects approved by the Korean government. Some of these were joint ventures with Korean businesses. The first foreign investment project was approved in 1962. By 1977, Korea had approved 854 projects for a total foreign investment of $870,344,000. True, the largest single source of investments was Japan, with 668 projects; U.S. companies came second with 115, or 13.5 percent of the total. However, U.S. investments totaled $168,630,000, with an average investment per project of $1,466,000, compared to $771,000 for Japan. Thus, while there were fewer U.S. projects, they tended to be larger.[11]

A comprehensive picture of U.S. direct investments in particular is difficult to obtain. The *Korea Annual*[12] listed among major investors the following from the United States: General Motors, Ford, Caltex, Union Oil, Gulf Oil, and Dow Chemical. These firms were all engaged in joint ventures with Korean firms. General Motors and Ford were assembling cars; Gulf, Caltex, and Union Oil ran oil refineries; and Dow Chemical helped run a chemical plant. From the Overseas Private Investment Corporation (OPIC) we obtained a list of all the U.S. investments in South Korea that they had insured in 1976. Many of the 113 projects listed were in industries manufacturing for export.

In general, U.S. multinationals in South Korea made big profits on Korean cheap labor whether or not they produced for the export market (Buss, 1982: 124). However, when multinationals exported to the United States, the issue of displacing one labor force with a cheaper one became especially poignant. Not only did U.S. workers sustain job loss when local capital moved overseas, but they also faced the devastating competition of cheap imports produced to some extent by their own vanished capitalists.

The runaway shop was not limited to South Korea. Affiliate exports to the United States from all countries increased from $6.3 billion in 1966 to $31.7 billion in 1975. This change represented an increasing share of the U.S. import market, from 25 percent of total imports in 1962 to 32 percent in 1975 (Chung, 1977: 34). In other words, by 1975 one-third of all imports to the United States were produced by overseas affiliates of U.S. companies. This proportion varied by country and region. For Canada it was a huge 58 percent, for Japan a mere 1 percent, and for Europe, around 15 percent. For developing countries it was about one-third (Chung, 1977: 35). According to Helleiner (1978: 25), if one took account of all multinational linkages, such as minority ownerships, or licensing agreements, the degree of "related party" trade would climb substantially. Thus he estimates that, in 1977, "48 percent of all U.S. imports originated with a party related by ownership (5 percent of voting stock or more) to the buyer." About half of this intraparty importing was by U.S. parent companies from majority-owned U.S. foreign affiliates (Helleiner, 1981: 10–11).

The extent of U.S. multinational involvement in Korean exports to the United States was difficult to ascertain. Cohen (1975: 10) estimated that all foreign firms accounted for at least 15 percent of South Korea's maufactured exports in 1971, suggesting that the U.S. proportions were considerably less than 15 percent. Still, in some fields U.S. involvement appeared substantial. For example, in 1973, 31 percent of foreign investment in electronics came from U.S. corporations. In this industry about 80 percent of Korean production was for export. Big U.S. and Japanese assembly plants, subsidiaries of such corporations as Motorola, Signetics, American Micro Systems, Fairchild, Control Data, and Applied Magnetics, accounted for 25 percent of output, but 50 percent of exports. In addition, joint ventures produced 27 percent of output and 21 percent of exports (Hasan, 1976: 177–186). Although the proportion of such exports which went to the United States is unknown, it appears likely that most U.S. subsidiaries were producing for the U.S. market.

Some U.S. multinational investment in manufactured exports to the United States was concealed by the definition of affiliate. Cohen (1975: 61–62) found that cloth and yarn exports were almost all produced by Korean firms. However, although the board of directors was Korean, most of the capital was provided by foreign textile firms (Cohen, 1975: 9). It seems unlikely that this kind of investment would appear in the Korean government statistics as a project.

Commercial loans

Commercial loans are loans from private institutions, such as banks or insurance companies, whereas public loans are made by governments and international government-created agencies. Commercial

Table 7. Distribution of Foreign Loans and Investments in
South Korea, 1977 (in million dollars)

	Total $	U.S. $	U.S. %	Japan $	Japan %
Public Loans	615.7	99.2	16.1	53.5	8.7
Direct Investments	104.4	8.2	7.8	37.6	36.0
Commercial Loans	1,135.8	233.9	20.6	321.3	28.9
Total	1,855.9	341.3	18.4	412.4	22.2

Source: Korea Annual (Seoul: Hapdong News Agency, 1978), p. 120.

loans are distinguished from direct investments in that the lender exercises no working control over the capital. Still, commercial lending is a profit-making activity, and cheap labor means big profits. Thus, in terms of volume, commercial loans were the most important way in which foreign capital was invested in South Korea in the period under investigation. Table 7 shows the relative importance of public loans, direct investments, and commercial loans in 1977. Clearly commercial loans outstripped the other two categories.[13]

The table also shows the different investment patterns of the United States and Japan. The United States provided a higher proportion of public loans than Japan, had less direct investments, and had almost three-quarters as much invested in commercial loans in South Korea. Combining the three sources of financing one finds that the two countries were far more similar in total investment in Korea than the figures on direct investment would suggest.

In sum, considerably more U.S. capital went to South Korea in the form of commercial loans than direct investments. Since commercial loans were a less visible form of participation in the Korean economy, it might appear that U.S. capital had a less substantial investment in Korea than it actually did. But in fact, commercial loans seem to have been the most important way in which U.S. capital took advantage of Korean cheap labor.

Subcontracting

United States corporations and financial institutions did not need to invest directly in Korean enterprise in order to play an active role in the production and importation of cheap Korean products. A less direct form of involvement was subcontracting, in which U.S. companies arranged with Korean-owned and -operated firms for the production of certain commodities for the U.S. market.

Watanabe (1972b: 430–431) distinguishes three types of international subcontracting. The first is commercial subcontracting. This type involves a metropole firm's receiving orders for its products, then subcontracting the production to firms in developing countries like South Korea. The metropole firm acts as a trading company, delivering products under its brand name. In the second type, cross-border subcontracting, a metropole firm arranges for the manufacture of some parts and components by a Third World firm. The parts are then exported to the metropole for assembly and distribution. (One might add the opposite possibility, that is, the production of parts, the assembly of which is subcontracted to a foreign firm and then shipped back for distribution.) The third type, within-border subcontracting, involves a similar arrangement, but this time between a foreign subsidiary and indigenous subcontractors. For example, multinationals in South Korea could arrange with local manufacturers to perform elements of the production process, such as parts manufacture or assembly. The advantage to the parent firm is obvious: they "take advantage of the plentiful cheap labour in developing countries." (Watanabe, 1972b: 431–432).

An important type of international subcontracting is bonded processing. Here the government of the sub-contracting firm holds the tariff duties on the imported materials, remitting them when re-export is confirmed by the customs office. This system expedites overseas assembly. In 1962, when they were first introduced, bonded processing exports were evaluated at $1 million and accounted for 1.82 percent of all exports. In 1977 they had risen to $1.76 billion in value and accounted for 17.53 percent of exports. The most important items were garments and electrical appliances, accounting for 60 and 25 percent of the total, respectively, in 1968 (Watanabe, 1972b: 433).

In 1976, South Korea shipped $626,758,000 worth of bonded process exports to the United States. These exports accounted for one-quarter of all exports to the United States in that year. Bonded process exports to the United States made up 40 percent of all bonded process exports from South Korea.[14]

Not all bonded process exports were under the aegis of foreign firms. Some were accounted for by indigenous firms and some by subsidiaries of multinationals. In 1970, bonded process exports from South Korea in the electronics industry were valued at $55 million. Of this amount, $33 million was from 100 percent foreign-owned companies, $8 million from joint ventures, and $14 million (25 percent) from Korean-owned firms. The proportion of indigenous firms was higher in the textile and garment industries (Watanabe, 1972b: 433). These totals do not isolate the role of the United States.

Regardless of ownership, bonded processing bespeaks overseas assembly. It is a system whereby imported parts can be assembled for export without tying up capital in tariff payments or having to deal with bureaucratic requirements. Thus, although no U.S. capital need have been invested in an assembly plant, U.S. corporations could still make use of Korean cheap labor to assemble their products.

It is difficult to obtain statistics on the extent of all the various types of subcontracting between U.S. corporations and Korean firms so a few illustrations must suffice. The following item appeared in *Korea Business*:[15] "Dongnam Electric Ind. Co. has recently signed contracts for the supply of a total of 40,000 refrigerators to the United States. The firm also won contracts for the supply of TV sets, CB transceivers, electronic wristwatches, etc." In 1970, the Taehan Shipbuilding Corporation contracted with Gulf Oil Co. of the United States to export tankers of 20,000 to 30,000 G/T (gross ton, including weight of packaging).[16] Nine Korean firms, which participated in the International Toy Exhibition in New York in February 1976, won contracts worth $746,500. Further contracts with importers-wholesalers valued at $2.3 million were still being negotiated.[17] Helleiner notes

the emergence of large trading houses with the capacity and the initiative to search the world for low-cost sources of the products they sell. Several large American retailing firms already have permanent representatives in South-East Asia contracting with local firms to supply garments to quite precise quality and fashion specifications. (1973: 28)

Subcontracting masked the extent of U.S. capital's involvement in South Korea. United States capital could exercise a marked control over the production process through subcontracting without any capital having changed hands. It was even possible that U.S. contractors could fix prices, or set ceilings on prices, thereby setting constraints on Korean workers' aspirations. In addition, control of troublesome labor was left entirely in the hands of Korean middlemen. There are important parallels between international subcontracting and subcontracting within the United States among the immigrants, which will be considered in part four.

Importing

Fading almost imperceptibly into commercial subcontracting is simple importing. The difference between subcontracting and pure trade lies in the degree of control exercised by the buyer. In subcontracting, the purchaser specifies beforehand what he wants. In importing, the producer makes what he wants under conditions that he determines and then seeks a buyer. Of course he need not have literally completed production before marketing his commodities. The distinction is a fine one. Consider the following item from *Korea Business*:

> Martin Kramer, chairman of the board, and Elliot Stone, president of Gimbel Brothers, Inc., were in Seoul recently to appraise its import activities and buying procedures from Korea. They were accompanied by J. Mellon and D. Leavitt of Gimbels Corporate Buying Office. Gimbel Brothers is a major importer of Korean textile products and such hardware as toys and footware items, and supplies the goods to the U.S. market through a chain of 38 department stores.[18]

No mention is made of Gimbels contracting for items though they presumably made their specific wants known. Another example is the following report: "Union and Ilssin steel companies of Korea received, from the United States and European countries, order for 500,000 tons of steel products."[19] The degree of control exercised by the purchasers is unclear. Many such items appeared in *Korea Business*.

Hone (1974) contends that importing by the large retail buying and importing groups was of far greater significance than direct investments. These groups, including firms like Sears, J. C. Penney, and Montgomery Ward, occupied an oligopolistic position, giving them considerable power. Their buying offices in the Far East "are in a position to place enormous orders and are often able to book 60–100 percent of a unit's capacity for one or two years. In such a situation the loss of an order is much more serious than accepting a very low price" (Hone, 1974: 149). Thus they contributed to the cheapness of labor in these countries.

The extent of U.S. corporate involvement in importing from South Korea is difficult to determine. The *Korea Annual*[20] listed "foreign business firms" in Korea, of which 26 were from Japan, 24 from Germany, 10 from Britain, 20 from elsewhere, and 131 (62 percent of the total) from the United States. Some of these probably managed direct investments (such as Korea Gulf Oil Co., Motorola Korea, Ltd.), but others seemed to be mainly engaged in trade, for example, American Import Merchants Corporation, Associated Merchandising Corporation, J. C. Penney Purchasing Corporation, Sears Roebuck Overseas, Inc., and so on. Such firms may have been subcontracting or importing into the Korean market, but it seems highly likely that several of them were engaged in the import trade to the United States. Gimbels was one of those listed, suggesting that many of the importers may not have maintained a base in Korea.

United States capitalists gain by importing from cheap labor countries in three ways. First, cheap imports can undersell U.S. goods and still sustain a high mark-up from initial labor costs. Second, U.S. capitalists can use the import threat as a club to compel U.S. workers to limit their demands for higher wages and better work conditions. Third, cheap imports can be used to curb inflation in the United States, helping to keep down the wage bill. Thus even simple trade has implications for labor displacement if it occurs between countries with marked discrepancies in the price of labor.

During the period of our study, not all importing from South Korea occurred under the auspices of U.S. importers. Korean businesses also played a part. Korean importers and exporters constituted one important element in the Los Angeles immigrant community. When Korean capitalists dominated the import trade, the class alignments took a slightly different twist since some U.S. businesses shared with workers the threat of displacement by cheap Korean goods. However, the second and third aforementioned benefits would continue to accrue to U.S. capital, probably acting as sufficient incentive for some businesses to support such imports regardless of the nationality of the importer. In addition, local retailers could buy cheap goods from Korean importers, and still profitably undersell local competitors—even though they did not do the importing themselves. Widescale business and conservative political support for free trade and tariff reductions bespeak these interests.

In sum, U.S. businesses took advantage of Korean cheap labor in a variety of ways. Direct investments in South Korea were only the most obvious form. The tremendous increase in imports from Korea in the 1970s was probably a much better indicator of U.S. capital's stake in Korean cheap labor, though even that measure ignores the use of Korean labor by U.S. capital for production for non-U.S. markets.

U.S. GOVERNMENT INVOLVEMENT

The runaway shop and importation of cheap commodities from South Korea were not wholly in the hands of private capital. They received active support from the U.S. government. True, there were contradictory forces within the U.S. government which opposed these processes, but for now we concentrate on the more dominant political institutions and arrangements that supported them. Three U.S. laws specifically supported the development of the runaway shop and cheap imports. These were: tariff item 807, the Overseas Private Investment Corporation, and the Generalized System of Preferences.

Tariff item 807

There were actually two relevant tariff items: 806.30 and 807. The latter covered considerably more products, however, and was used as a shorthand in discussing tariff support for runaway shops. The U.S. Tariff Commission[21] described these items as follows:

> Tariff items 806.30 and 807.00 are provided for in schedule 8, part 1, subpart B, of the Tariff Schedules of the United States (TSUS). Pursuant to the provisions of item 806.30, articles of metal (except precious metal) that have been manufactured, or subjected to a process of manufacture, in the United States and exported for processing and return to the United States for further processing, are subject to duty only on the value of the foreign processing. Under tariff item 807.00, imported articles assembled in foreign countries with fabricated components that have been manufactured in the United States are subject to duty on the full value of the imported product less the value of the U.S. fabricated components contained therein. No further processing

in the United States is required for articles imported under item 807.00.

In other words, these items permitted duty-free reentry of U.S. components sent abroad for processing. Item 806.30 was limited to metal products (having originated in 1956 in a request by the automobile industry to be able to have certain processing done in contiguous areas of Canada in time of breakdowns and other emergencies) and required that these products go through further processing in the United States in order to qualify for duty-free treatment.[22] In contrast, item 807 was not limited to metal products, and the commodities did not need to undergo further processing on reentry. Indeed, it was strictly limited to assembly abroad of U.S.-manufactured components, specifying that the U.S. parts should not be significantly advanced or improved overseas in order to receive duty-free treatment.[23]

Item 807 originated in a Customs Court ruling in 1954. This ruling concerned installing a U.S.-built motor in a Canadian boat, which was then imported into the United States. It was written into law in 1963 and clarified through amendment by 1965.[24] The original intent was to support U.S. production by encouraging the use of U.S.-made components in foreign-made products, since overseas producers could benefit from the special treatment accorded to such components (Ericson, 1970: 35).

Original intent need not correspond to practice, however. Items 807 and 806.30 permitted U.S. corporations to set up assembly plants in cheap labor countries. Since corporations only had to pay duty on the value added to exported products, it was economically rational to move assembly to countries where labor was cheap. As Ericson noted: "An increasing share of Section 807 trade reflects the use by U.S. firms of low wage, unskilled labor in certain developing countries to assemble products for the U.S. market" (1970: 35).

Between 1966 and 1969 imports under these two tariff items increased from $953 million to $1.8 billion. In both years, item 807 accounted for most of the imports, with $890 million in the former year, and $1.6 billion in the latter.[25] In 1966, the combined value of item 806.30 and 807 imports equaled 6 percent of total dutiable imports, rising to 8 percent in 1969.[26] By 1975, imports under both items had risen to $5.16 billion, almost a fivefold increase from 1969.

Although the proportion of total imports did not change (since the United States began importing large quantities of oil), the proportion of manufactured goods entering under these provisions rose from 8 percent in 1969 to 10.2 percent in 1975.[27]

The Tariff Commission conducted a survey of firms using item 807 in 1969. They managed to contact the firms accounting for 92 percent of imports under this provision in that year and found that 40 percent of the imports were brought in by U.S. concerns with investments in overseas assembly facilities. About 60 percent of these were primarily oriented to item 807 assembly, that is, they were set up specifically to take advantage of the provision. The remainder was accounted for by foreign concerns that obtained U.S. components on their own. A small part, mainly in apparel, was composed of U.S. subcontractors or importers with no financial interest in the foreign firm in which assembly was done.[28] For item 806.30, involvement by U.S. firms was higher.

In 1966, only 6.8 percent of imports under item 807 came from developing countries. Most came from Canada, Japan, and Western European countries. However, by 1969, developing countries accounted for 22.2 percent of item 807 imports, an increase in dollar value of $306.4 million.[29] By 1974, less developed countries accounted for 39.9 percent of item 807 imports, totaling $1.93 billion in value. In the same year, 73.7 percent of item 806.30 articles came from developing countries.[30]

South Korea ranked tenth among the countries from which item 807 commodities were imported in 1974, and sixth in both the absolute duty-free value and the proportion of total value that entered duty-free. Among underdeveloped countries Korea ranked sixth in total value of item 807 imports, very close to Brazil. The $66.8 million worth of items imported under item 807 in 1974 represented a sharp rise from 1966, when the total was only a few thousand dollars. In 1974 South Korea exported $1.49 billion worth of goods to the United States. Thus about 4.5 percent of Korean exports to that country came under item 807. The U.S. House Ways and Means Committee[31] reported that, based on preliminary figures in 1977, item 807 imports from South Korea had risen to $80,179,000, pushing it ahead of Brazil ($69 million) into fifth place among developing countries. In 1977, $3.12 billion worth of exports from South Korea went to the United States.[32] Imports brought in under

Tariff items 806.30 and 807 thus made up 8.13 percent of total imports from South Korea in that year, a rise in the proportion (from 4.5 percent in 1974) as well as in absolute value.

There is no doubt that items 806.30 and 807 stimulated the use of cheap foreign labor. Indeed, the Tariff Commission[33] lists as one of the factors explaining the rapid growth of trade under these provisions "the disparity between U.S. and foreign labor costs of assembly and processing." The Tariff Commission listed three classes of beneficiary. First were U.S. manufacturers who used foreign plants that they owned, operated, or employed on a contract basis to assemble U.S. components: "Benefits derived from the domestic/foreign operations and from the provisions of item 807.00 accrue directly to them." Most firms manufactured their own components for overseas assembly but some purchased items from other U.S. producers. The second type consisted of U.S. entrepreneurs not engaged in manufacturing in either country who exported purchased U.S. components and contracted for their assembly abroad in plants operated by foreign nationals. Again benefits "accrue directly to such U.S. entrepreneurs." The third set of users consisted of foreign manufacturers and their U.S. importers: "The benefit of duty remission under Item 807.00 accrues directly to the U.S. importer," while the foreign manufacturer benefited indirectly if the importer kept prices sufficiently low to give the products a competitive edge.[34]

Overseas private investment corporation

Another way that the U.S. government supported U.S. capital in the Third World was the Overseas Private Investment Corporation. OPIC was set up by the U.S. government under Title IV of the Foreign Assistance Act of 1961, as amended in 1969 (Public Law 91–175). A wholly U.S. government-owned corporation, OPIC's administration was first delegated to the Agency for International Development (AID) until January 1971, when it was established as a separate agency.[35]

> With the creation of OPIC ... the government emphasized recognition of the private investment process as a key element in foreign economic policy, and its belief that a working partnership between the public and private sectors could help to maintain the U.S. competitive position in the new markets of the Third World.[36]

OPIC was the only U.S. government agency that directly promoted private investment in underdeveloped countries.[37]

OPIC had two chief functions: to provide financial support to companies wishing to invest in developing countries and to provide insurance for such companies when the political situation in the country of investment was defined as unstable. In fiscal 1978 OPIC supported eighty-four projects, ten of which were aided financially by loans or guarantees, and the remainder by insurance. The ten financed projects received an OPIC commitment of $17.9 million.[38]

Emphasis was placed on investments in the least developed countries. In 1978, thirty-six of the eighty-four supported projects were in countries with an annual per capita GNP of $520 or less (in 1975 dollars). OPIC also emphasized investments by smaller U.S. businesses, especially those smaller than the "Fortune 1000." Eighty-six percent of support for finance projects went to such firms, while 32 percent of the seventy-five new insurance projects supported in 1978 were for smaller firms.[39] Both of these policies were part of OPIC's congressional mandate and received increased emphasis in April 1978, when the agency was renewed until 1981. These policies suggest that part of the purpose of OPIC was the expansion of capitalism into peripheral areas. The effort to incorporate smaller businesses suggests an attempt to broaden internal political support for such policies, while penetration of the poorest countries made their cheap labor available.

In 1975, U.S. corporations directly invested about $4.2 billion in developing countries. The value of OPIC-assisted projects (including both finance and insurance) was $1.6 billion, just over one-third of total direct investments.[40] We cannot say whether these proportions held true for South Korea. Still, OPIC was not an inconsequential agency.

South Korea was among the more advanced developing nations and therefore not a top priority target for OPIC financial assistance. None of the OPIC projects supported between 1976 and 1978 was in Korea. However, in mid-1977, four projects were listed as "active finance projects," suggesting that they had been set up prior to 1976 and were receiving continuing support. They were: a $41 million guarantee for Kyung in Energy (Union Oil Company of California); a $3 million guarantee for Korea Nylon Company (Chemtex Fibers); a $700,000 loan to the Korea Capital Corporation; and a $1 million loan to Korea Semiconductors, Inc. (Integrated Circuits International).[41] Needless to say, these projects did not conform to the OPIC ideal of supporting small U.S. businesses.

OPIC offered three types of insurance for overseas private investors: insurance against inconvertibility of local currency to U.S. dollars; insurance against expropriation; and insurance against war, revolution, and insurrection. In other words, the U.S. government was providing a back-up for political difficulties that could arise for private investors in Third World countries. Without this guarantee, the cheap labor in these countries would have been unavailable for private exploitation because of political risk.

Shortly after it began operations, OPIC faced nationalizations in Chile. As a result, the Overseas Private Investment Corporation Amendment Act was passed in 1974. This act authorized OPIC to borrow up to $100 million from the U.S. Treasury to discharge insurance liabilities.[42] The Foreign Assistance Act was amended in 1975 and subsequently provided "that the full faith and credit of the United States of America is pledged for the full payments and performance of obligations incurred by the Overseas Private Investment Corporation under its insurance and guaranty contracts."[43] If OPIC did not have sufficient funds, "Congress would have to appropriate funds to fulfill the pledge of full faith and credit to which such obligations are entitled."[44] These laws laid the political risk for exploiting cheap labor abroad upon the U.S. taxpayer, while the whole profit accrued to private corporations.

South Korea was one of the most important countries for which U.S. investors demanded insurance from OPIC. In 1978, U.S. companies in Korea were insured for $350 million against war, revolution, or insurrection; $310 million against expropriation; and $270 million against inconvertibility. These amounts placed South Korea among the top three countries on all three types of insurance.[45]

The benefits of OPIC activity to U.S. capital were spelled out unambiguously in its publications: promoting U.S. manufactured exports and creating markets in the developing world; opening up new sources of raw materials needed for U.S. operations; and earning profits which would lead to a capital reflow exceeding the amount of initial capital outlay.[46] Unstated was the benefit of OPIC aid in gaining access to the cheap labor of the Third World. At the same time, OPIC supporters believed they were acting in the interests of Third

World countries by helping them to develop, and in the interests of U.S. workers, by helping to create jobs.[47] In other words, they believed that what was good for American business was also good for the world.

As a U.S. government agency, OPIC needed to appear to represent the public interest, not the profit-interest of multinational corporations. Hence its obligation was described as follows: "The Corporation is specifically prohibited from supporting 'runaway industries' and rejects any enterprise which might have adverse effects on the domestic job market or might create detrimental job conditions."[48] However, in the view of the AFL-CIO this mandate was not followed, and organized labor continuously urged Congress to terminate OPIC.[49]

Generalized System of Preferences

The GSP was a list of manufactured and semimanufactured commodities which the United States allowed to be imported free of duty from developing countries. The ostensible purpose of the GSP was to boost the manufactured exports of developing countries, thereby helping them to industrialize. The plan was promoted at a 1968 meeting of the United Nations Committee on Trade and Development (UNCTAD), an organization that was dominated by Third World countries, and was endorsed by the major industrialized nations late in 1970 (Bell, 1972: 299).[50] The United States was slow in implementing this scheme, presumably because of certain class conflicts with respect to the policy we shall consider later. Here we briefly describe the GSP and its impact on trade with South Korea.[51]

The U.S. GSP was incorporated into the Trade Act of 1974, which stipulated that it remain in operation for ten years. It went into effect January 1, 1976 and would remain in force until January 2, 1985. A GSP year operated from March 1 to the end of February to enable the government to publish a list of articles which became subject to limitations.

GSP imports were subject to a "clause of limitations" setting up two criteria for suspending duty-free treatment for an eligible item from a beneficiary country. First, the value of a product imported in one calendar year should not exceed $25 million. Second, the quantity of an item imported from a specific country should not exceed 50 percent of the value of total imports of that item to the United

States during a year. In addition, at least 35 percent of the value of the commodity at the time of entry was required to derive from the developing country, in the form of raw materials or processing. These limitations supposedly permitted the GSP to foster balanced growth of exports from developing countries.

Ninety-eight countries and thirty-nine dependent territories were designated "beneficiary developing countries" in 1976. South Korea was one of them. The GSP was, to some extent, a political weapon of the developed bloc in that OPEC (Organization of Petroleum Exporting Countries) members and "undesirable" political regimes were excluded.

GSP encouraged exporters to change their export mix to take advantage of the tariff gap. According to the *Los Angeles Times*,[52] in the first ten months of 1978, $4.2 billion of imports (from all countries) were brought in under GSP, more than $1 billion above the 1977 total. South Korea also responded to the incentive. We coded the 1977 Census of Imports for GSP as well as for tariff items 806.30 and 807 and found that $514,892,000 worth of imports from Korea came in under this provision, accounting for 16.5 percent of imports from that country. Using the *Los Angeles Times* estimate of GSP imports from all countries in 1977, Korea's proportion was about 16 percent.

Although GSP was not intended to aid runaway shops, at least one such case was uncovered. The discovery was made accidentally by the Ironworkers International Union. They found that Brown and Root, Inc., a construction company based in Houston, was building two multimillion-dollar oil drilling platforms in a Malaysia subsidiary, planning to import the rigs duty-free under GSP. Brown and Root justified its actions: "The Malaysian fabrication yard is ... precisely the kind of economic development Congress sought to encourage." But Congressman George Miller doubted that many members of Congress interpreted GSP as an "incentive for runaway U.S. corporations."[53]

The fact that only a minimum of 35 percent of value added needed to come from the developing country provided an obvious loophole for abuse. U.S. corporations could surreptitiously subcontract parts of the production process overseas, then import the results duty-free under GSP. Even without such linkages, segments of the U.S. capitalist class would benefit from GSP, notably: im-

porters and retailers of GSP goods who could undercut their competitors or sell products at the going rate while making huge profits;
and capitalists in complementary industries who could purchase inputs more cheaply. The latter benefit extended to employers whose
workers could buy imported consumer items more cheaply, enabling
them to lower the wage bill.

Cheap imports were of varying benefit to U.S. capitalists depending on their industry. Competitors facing cheap imports were hurt,
but businesses in complementary fields were aided. Government decisions regarding which products could enter duty-free under GSP
affected the structure of U.S. capitalism; some U.S. industries were
sacrificed and others were protected. We suspect that the losers
were smaller businesses. Multinational corporations could set up
subsidiaries abroad, buy stock in cheap labor corporations or lend
capital to them, or engage in the import trade themselves. Smaller
firms were less likely to be able to adjust to cheap foreign competition. Arrangements like GSP thus probably served to concentrate
the U.S. economy by driving out the small capitalist.

THE CONSEQUENCES FOR U.S. LABOR

The impact of rising trade and overseas investments by U.S. capital
on American workers is a subject that has been hotly debated (see,
for example, Kujawa, 1973; Flanagan and Weber, 1974).[54] The
findings differed widely, with some authors arguing that U.S.
workers were helped, and others that they were harmed by these
developments. The International Labour Office[55] found that studies
ranged from finding that about 500,000 jobs were lost to the United
States between 1966 and 1969, to an estimate that 600,000 U.S. jobs
had been created as a result of multinational activities.

We do not wish to enter the fray at this level. From our perspective, the new international economic order was an issue of class
struggle. Although the debate was phrased in scholarly terms, the
fancy econometric models often masked efforts to persuade people
to one particular class interest or another. Our purpose, then, is to
uncover what these class interests were, rather than to examine the
overall impact of the new order.[56]

Broadly speaking, the new international economic order served
the interests of U.S. capital and contradicted the interests of U.S.

labor. Using cheap labor in countries like South Korea—whether in the form of cheap imports, or investments abroad, or both combined—enabled U.S. capital to bypass high-priced labor at home.[57] Just as the immigration of cheap labor permits capital to act as though a labor movement had never existed, so too does capital's exodus abroad to the cheap labor countries of the world.

One can argue that the flow of capital abroad was, by the 1960s and 1970s, the major adaptation of capital to the rising price of labor at home. In the late nineteenth and early twentieth centuries the chief mechanism for dealing with the problem was massive immigration. But immigration law was drastically altered, as we shall see later (in chapter 13), to ensure that immigrant workers could not be used as a major reserve army of labor any more. The law had loopholes, however, and some cheap labor still entered the country. Rather than depend on this uncertain and somewhat inaccessible flow, U.S. capital preferred to move directly to its source. Not only was immigrant labor less available, but cheap labor could be more effectively exploited through the aid of military dictatorships in their own countries.

The new international economic order can thus be seen as a stratagem on the part of capital to deal with the domestic labor movement and its attendant state regulation of industries. Fleeing overseas enabled capital to employ a much more desirable labor force, one that was desperate for work, willing to work long hours, unused to labor militance, and subdued by paternalistic traditions and nationalist ideologies. Clearly such a labor force was preferable to the one they had at home. Thus overseas expansion can be seen as a form of displacement, with the cheap labor of the Third World used to undercut and displace U.S. workers.

The different class interests were clearly revealed in the Congressional debates about Tariff items 806.30 and 807. Capitalists almost universally favored these provisions and opposed their repeal. Labor, on the other hand, unanimously wanted to do away with them. Eight business associations, representing at least 3000 firms including many of the major corporations of the country, testified against the repeal of items 806.30 and 807 at Congressional hearings in 1976.[58] Only one business group testified in favor of repeal: the Apparel Industries Inter-Association Committee, representing garment industry firms, mainly in New York and other eastern and southern states.[59] The reasons given were the tremendous rise in imports from cheap labor countries, including South Korea. We assume this organization represented the smaller garment manufacturers who were unable to escape overseas in any form.

Interestingly, all government witnesses, representing the Nixon administration, favored retention of these tariff items. Only the Labor Department expressed doubts, and its position was essentially that the impact of these items could not be determined. Government and capital appeared united on this issue.

Labor's analysis of the situation was revealed in their testimony before various governmental agencies.[60] The U.S. Tariff Commission's 1970 study of items 806.30 and 807, for example, included a statement by the director of the AFL-CIO's department of research:

> The issue before the Commission, at this time, is merely one aspect of a continuing and growing problem—the mushrooming expansion of foreign subsidiary operations of U.S. firms. Continued delays in repeal of 807 and similar sections of the Tariff Code encourage the growth of these operations, with the displacement of U.S. production and employment. Item 807 is one small loophole in the tax structure for the advantage of U.S.-based multinational companies ... [It serves] to encourage the avoidance, by such companies, of U.S. wages, labor and social standards. The profit margins of such operations are thereby aided, to the detriment of American workers and communities ... [Repeal] would eliminate this specific type of federal inducement for the displacement of U.S. production and employment by runaway operations to countries whose wage levels are as much as 90% lower than ours.[61]

The testimony was lengthy and covered many points. One of the more trenchant observations was the high rate of unemployment and underemployment, especially among unskilled and marginal workers, who faced most keenly the competition from cheap labor overseas. The problem was not, however, restricted to this underclass. Semiskilled factory production workers in the economy's mainstream were increasingly threatened while, "as relatively sophisticated production is being exported, even highly skilled industrial workers are being displaced."

In 1976, the AFL-CIO again gave testimony against Items 806.30 and 807, and this time their language was even more direct:

> The AFL-CIO asks once more for repeal of two tariff loopholes that reward the export of U.S. jobs and the exploitation of foreign labor ... These provisions offer extra tax incentives for U.S. companies to

expand production abroad, for sweatshop jobbers to contract out work to the cheapest labor in the world, and extra preferences for foreign imports into impacted U.S. markets. These loopholes have cost at least 500,000 U.S. jobs directly. Indirectly, these loopholes have been a forerunner for the transfer of production abroad, at an additional loss of hundreds of thousands of jobs yearly.[62]

The representative went on to attribute high U.S. unemployment to the runaway shop.

The AFL-CIO saw these tariff items as only part of the problem, and their repeal was but one facet of their strategy to save U.S. jobs from being displaced overseas. Six other needed actions were mentioned: removal of all preferential tax treatment for multinationals' foreign operations, comprehensive federal monitoring of multinationals, regulation of the export of the most advanced U.S. productive equipment, regulation of the export of U.S. capital and technology, regulation of imports into the United States, and immediate enforcement of the Trade Act of 1974, which provided for U.S. government action against unfair competition.[63]

Organized labor was aware of GSP. The AFL-CIO described it as "special zero tariffs on imports of more than 2,700 products and parts of products from over 1,000 low-wage countries and territories." They saw it as an alternative to item 807. When GSP was removed from a commodity, the overseas producers turned to 807. When GSP was instated, the corporations dropped item 807.[64]

The AFL-CIO also called for an end to OPIC.[65] Charging that the Agency used taxpayers' money to insure multinational corporations as they set up runaway shops, the AFL-CIO provided evidence that OPIC was not limiting itself either to small U.S. firms or to the poorest countries. "The list of corporations [OPIC insures] is more representative of the Fortune 500 than small firms. The giants of agribusiness, banking, and manufacturing—Cargill, Bank of America, Dow, ITT—are on the lists." They provided several examples of OPIC-supported firms which resulted in layoffs or the closing of plants in the United States, for example, firms producing sheet glass and TV bulbs in South Korea, which were associated with shutdowns or layoffs in Ohio, Michigan, and West Virginia. In sum, labor saw OPIC as a device to get U.S. taxpayers to subsidize the risks taken by U.S. capital abroad—to the detriment of U.S. workers.[66]

Capitalists recognized that some workers might be temporarily dislocated by the new international economic order, but they argued that long-run readjustments would occur. From labor's point of view, however, the dislocations caused by reliance on cheap foreign labor appeared catastrophic. Labor, they argued, was not a mobile factor of production which could easily be shifted around.

> Workers are infinitely less mobile than capital. Labor is not an automatically interchangeable resource or statistic, as some economists believe. A displaced shoe worker in one state of the United States does not automatically become a clerical worker in another state, or even within the same state. With good fortune, the son of a displaced electronics production worker in Chicago may become a computer programmer in San Francisco. But the displaced worker will be unemployed for many months and probably will wind up with a job at lesser skill and pay, if he is fortunate enough to find a job. (Goldfinger, 1973: 34–35)

The adjustment assistance actually provided displaced workers under the Trade Act of 1974 was, in labor's view, totally inadequate. In 1976 the AFL-CIO estimated that at least 435,000 workers had filed petitions for assistance. Of these, 160,000 were certified as eligible, but only 106,000 were able to work their way through the bureaucratic maze to file a claim. Finally, only 58,000 had actually received any payments. The average aid amounted to $1200 per worker. Only twenty-three workers had received financial job search assistance, and twenty-three had received relocation assistance. One observer notes: "It is in fact a bandaid program, and a small one at that" (Finley, 1978: 131). As Watkins and Karlik (1978: 2) conclude: "The adjustment assistance provisions of the Trade Expansion Act have generally been conceded to be a failure ... The reasons for failure are diverse, but perhaps are best summed up by labor's oft repeated comment that adjustment assistance is essentially burial assistance."

Not only was labor concerned about direct displacement as jobs disappeared overseas, they also feared the "reverse multiplier effect," that is, the ricochetting of job loss to support and related lines of work (Shaw, 1971: 58). In other words, rather than accepting capital's argument that overseas investments and imports would create spinoff jobs, they expected the reverse: spinoff job losses.

In labor's view, even the consumer did not benefit from the new international economic order. Because of international oligopolies, according to U.S. labor, prices remained high. The benefits of cheap labor were not passed on to the consumer, but were retained by capital in the form of higher profits.

> [The international corporations] can produce overseas with low labor costs and sell in U.S. or foreign markets at or near domestic prices, retaining the profits. With the creation of vast "international oligopolies," there is little competition between firms. The unions note that earnings of U.S. foreign affiliates rose 13% in 1969 while the earnings of domestic companies barely inched forward. (Shaw, 1971: 58)

Similarly, Ericson (1970: 34) points out with regard to the Mexican border region: "Opponents claim that the prices paid by the American consumer for products made in the Mexican border areas do not reflect the lower wage costs of Mexican workers."

Chaikin of the ILGWU claimed that importers often sold garments at local prices. In testifying before the House Ways and Means Committee against tariff item 807, he presented examples of pairs of garments, one produced overseas and one locally, with identical price tags. A set of shirts sold under the Sears label for $8 included one made in South Korea and the other in the United States. Even when importers did not undersell local producers, they had an "unfair competitive edge" in that their greater profits permitted them to spend more on promotion.[67]

It seems highly likely that, in many instances, importers did undersell the local market. In the Sears case, the shirts were on sale for $4.99. While Sears could obviously not charge more for one of a pair of identical shirts, they probably lost money on the U.S.-made one. That prices were the same may have reflected U.S. manufacturers' efforts to meet foreign competition, rather than the lack of interest in underselling by importers. The latter had the tremendous advantage of being able to undersell the local market and still make a huge profit. It seems inconceivable, in a highly competitive industry, that they would not do so. If this was the case, then the U.S. consumer did benefit from lower prices. But a question can be raised as to whether the consumer was able to maintain his or her gain. Since most consumers were, in fact, also workers, employers in the United States would be able to translate lower consumer prices into lower wages, leaving the consumer with the same purchasing power he or she had before.

United States labor also challenged capital's contention that overseas investments aided workers in developing countries. Testifying at the hearings on items 806.30 and 807, a representative of the AFL-CIO stated:

> While the companies involved in these mass movements show little concern for the American workers made jobless, many of whom are blacks, Chicanos, other minorities, and women, and most with families, the companies often seek to justify their actions as improving the living standards in the other countries. Such claims simply don't square with the facts ... A story in the *New York Times* of March 20, 1976 reported that in South Korea where most workers are worse off because of inflation, multinational enterprises receive special favors in tax payments and labor laws despite the fact that such favors affect the basic rights of Korean laborers. An earlier *New York Times* story reported that South Korea is determined to keep wages low for U.S. investors, even to the point of stationing uniformed police and secret agents to watch over teenage girls manufacturing products for the U.S. market, at 11 hours a day, 7 days a week for $23 per week.[68]

In sum, free trade and overseas expansion might increase overall efficiency, but the benefits were not spread to everyone. Instead, in labor's view, capital kept them. The real effect of the internationalization of capital was larger—even grotesquely larger—profits.

Thus, while U.S. capital pursued cheap labor in South Korea, and received considerable U.S. government support in the process, not all sectors of American society benefited. In particular, the American working class saw itself as suffering as a consequence of these policies. Overseas trade and investment of the kind represented by U.S. involvement in South Korea was thus an issue of class struggle within the United States.

CONCLUSION

This chapter has attempted to show that cheap labor in South Korea, and cheap labor-based imports to the United States, resulted, in some part, from the interventions of the U.S. government and capitalist class. United States policies in South Korea helped keep Korean labor cheap; and U.S. capital took advantage of Korean cheap labor, through direct investments, loans, subcontracting, and participation in the importation of cheap goods. The U.S. government provided incentives for U.S. capital to make use of Korean cheap labor in the form of special tariff provisions, loans and insurance to overseas investors. Thus U.S. capital, backed by the government, played an active role in processes that harmed the American working class, whose spokespersons objected vociferously in Congress and elsewhere.

3

The Role of the Korean Government

The importing of cheap goods into the U.S. market was not only in the hands and interests of U.S. capital (backed by the state); it was also actively promoted by the South Korean government. South Korea supported the development of manufactured exports. It encouraged foreign capital to invest in Korean enterprises. And it played an important part in keeping the basis for both of these alive by helping to maintain the cheapness of Korean labor. In this chapter we briefly examine the Korean policies that encouraged exports and foreign investment. The bulk of the chapter deals with labor policies broadly conceived to include not only labor law and practice, but also the general distributive policies of the government, as well as nationalistic efforts to mobilize Korean workers to sacrifice for the good of the nation. In a final section we develop a general model of the interaction between class and national interests in complex situations like this.

ENCOURAGEMENT OF EXPORTS AND FOREIGN INVESTMENT

EXPORTS

The South Korean government developed a battery of export incentives. These incentives included tariff exemptions on imported raw materials, components, and capital equipment when these were to be used in exports; indirect tax exemptions; reduced prices on overhead items such as electricity and railroad transportation; a 50 percent reduction in taxes on income derived from exports; special accelerated depreciation; and preferential access to credit for financing both fixed investment and working capital (Frank, et al., 1975: 63–67; Hasan, 1976: 56; Westphal, 1978: 350).

A less standard subsidy was the "wastage allowance" under which exporters and their suppliers could import intermediate products up to stated limits free of duty. The limits exceeded normal wastage, and the excess not used for exports could be sold on the local market, typically at high profit. As one observer notes: "There is evidence that this subsidy grew in importance and that the allowances to many industries increased in the late sixties" (Hasan, 1976: 56). Plywood exports in particular benefited from the allowance on imported roundwood, which accounted for half the total subsidy from the wastage allowance system in the early 1970s (Hasan, 1976: 58).

Another support for exports was the "export–import link" system, entitling selected exporters to import certain popular items otherwise excluded. The purpose was to encourage marginal exports by allowing exporters to recoup possible losses through domestic sales. In the early 1970s this system came to be used less frequently —when it was necessary to offset temporary losses by exporters, or to foster the entrance into new export markets (Westphal, 1978: 350–351).

As South Korea's export position strengthened, some subsidies were removed or reduced. For example, in the early 1970s, Korea abolished the business income tax preference on export earnings. Duty-free import of machinery for the export sector was eliminated in 1974 and replaced by a more selective system of exemptions. In 1970 subsidies totaled over 30 percent of the value of exports. By 1975 they had declined to 15 percent (Hasan, 1976: 57, 94).

South Korea's export incentive system stressed manufactured goods. Using another measure of subsidy, Hasan (1976: 58) reports that, in 1968, the subsidy on total exports was 7 to 9 percent, but for manufactured exports, 9 to 12 percent. Balassa (1971: 62) considered this priority a distinguishing feature of South Korea (and Taiwan), compared to most developing countries.

In addition to financial incentives, the Korean government supported exports by establishing convenient locations for their production. By 1976, six export industrial estates had been set up on 920 acres around Seoul and Inchon. There was also a "special" export industrial estate of 2602 acres, the Gumi Electronics Industrial Estate: "All the industries located in an industrial estate enjoy general advantages such as low land costs, adequate power and water supplies, good road networks, various supporting facilities including special administrative support, and also property tax concessions including property acquisition and registration tax." [1]

Furthermore, the government set up two "free export zones," one in Masan, established in 1970, and the other, near Iri, in 1973: "These two zones are special administrative taxfree areas having the characteristics of bonded areas where the applications of various pertinent laws and regulations have been waived or relaxed altogether." [2] These zones made it easier and cheaper to import products intended as export components than to import goods for the Korean market (Cohen, 1975: 58–59).

In the mid-1970s, the government designated five Korean firms "general trading companies" in order to encourage the concentration of exports in a few large companies. This number had risen to thirteen by 1978.[3] Korea was consciously following the model of Japan's *zaibatsus*. General trading companies received special government support. By having large, heavily capitalized firms specializing in exports, Korea hoped further to boost its overseas trade.[4]

In 1964 the government founded the Korea Trade Promotion Corporation (KOTRA) and set up an overseas network to promote Korean exports (Frank, et al., 1975: 50). KOTRA published *Korea Business*, a bimonthly magazine that kept readers abreast of new economic developments. For example, the Korean government was anxious to take advantage of any tariff breaks the United States might offer. Thus, KOTRA's *Korea Business Special (For American Importers)*, No. 1, 1976, informed exporters which products could take advantage of the Generalized System of Preferences (GSP). They also pointed out where competing developing countries would suffer suspended eligibility because of the clause on limitations. South Korea was poised to move in on such products.

Korea's efforts to promote exports did not depend directly on the cheapness of Korean labor. Indeed, as Westphal (1978: 351) points out, the subsidies mainly gave support to Korean exports relative to domestic production. They did not particularly bolster the exports' position in the world market other than to permit Korean exporters to trade freely. Free trade, however, permitted Korean cheap labor to enter the world market.

The pattern of export sector increases after 1964 shows that the policies of the Park government developed world access to Korean cheap labor: virtually all were in labor intensive industries. Adelman and Robinson note: "Indeed, between 1966 and 1970 nearly one-half of the increase in the labor force (or some 320,000 persons) were absorbed directly in export-oriented employment" (1978: 45). Encouragement of exports enabled Korean business owners to exploit their country's greatest asset in the world market.

FOREIGN CAPITAL

Under the Foreign Capital Inducement Law of 1966, amended in 1973, South Korea offered four major incentives to foreign investors:

> (1) Complete exemption from corporate and property taxes for five years and 50 percent exemption for another three years, (2) complete exemption from customs duties for imported capital goods and for raw materials used in exports, (3) no limit on the remittance of foreign profits, and (4) no requirement on the proportion of foreign ownership. (Cohen, 1975: 72)

Under the first of these, *Korea Business*[5] listed six distinct forms of tax reduction and exemption. Foreign investors could also take advantage of several tax privileges under other tax laws.[6] In addition, the government guaranteed repayment of external debt (both principle and interest), including private loans from foreign private enterprises (S. H. Kim, 1970: xxi). This guarantee covered expropriation and nationalization.[7]

In addition to these inducements, the government of South Korea provided information and assistance to foreign investors through its Bureau of Foreign Investment Promotion of the Economic Planning Board. The bureau provided information on economic conditions, laws, and investment opportunities, and it received and reviewed investment applications in cooperation with other appropriate government agencies. It also provided assistance in obtaining import licenses, building materials, power and water facilities, and in dealing with other problems that might arise; also, it publicized and promoted opportunities and incentives.[8] KOTRA was also active in publicity.

Red tape hinders the efforts of many underdeveloped countries to attract foreign capital. Licenses are typically required for importing materials, exporting products, and capital investment in production facilities. If state-owned firms are involved, approval must pass through the legislature. Customs clearance may also cause delays. Investors can usually proceed more quickly and easily in the industrialized countries, where these processes are streamlined and rationalized. Fully aware of this problem, the South Korean government set up a "one-stop service" to expedite the processing of necessary paperwork, by gathering the relevant government officials in one room and cutting the required number of forms drastically (Watanabe, 1972b: 443–444). This bureaucratic streamlining increased Korea's ability to compete for foreign capital.

In addition to encouraging exports, the aforementioned "export industrial estates" and "free export zones" also served as inducements to foreign capital. The industrial estates granted tax concessions to foreign invested enterprises, and bonded warehouses could be established in them with the approval of the Customs Office.[9]

The free export zones at Masan and Iri were yet more important inducements to foreign capital. Similar zones have sprung up in other developing Asian countries, including Taiwan, the Philippines, Singapore, Indonesia, and Malaysia, and more recently, the People's Republic of China. They were also found in other areas of the world such as the U.S.–Mexican border region (Ericson, 1970; Fernandez, 1977: 131–148). These free trade zones (FTZs) were a relatively new phenomenon in the 1960s. Although free ports, allowing the bypassing of customs regulations, had existed for a long time, the new FTZs were intended for manufacturing rather than for commerce. Foreign investors were invited to set up manufacturing plants to produce goods for export. Customs freedom permitted components to enter for processing and reexport with minimum bureaucratic or financial inconvenience.[10]

The FTZ was like a country within a country. FTZs were often cut off from the rest of the nation by barbed wire or concrete walls. Usually goods produced there were not permitted to enter the home market; they were entirely for export (Takeo, 1977: 1). In other words, FTZs served as facilities for multinational corporations, enabling them to export part of their production process abroad. For instance, Ericson (1970) describes the Mexican border area as a zone where U.S. companies got products assembled cheaply for the U.S. market. Korean FTZs served the same purpose (Helleiner, 1973: 39), though not only for U.S. firms. By setting up such zones, the Korean government actively encouraged runaway shops from the advanced capitalist countries.

In sum, the Korean government provided a battery of supports and inducements to foreign capital. Essentially these concessions facilitated access to the fundamental resource South Korea had to offer foreign companies: its cheap labor.

LABOR POLICIES

Chapter 2 presented statistical evidence showing that labor was cheap in South Korea. We have suggested that the U.S. government and private capital helped to create a situation in which Korean labor remained cheap as well as politically available. However, the prime mover was the Korean government itself. While the United States shared responsibility, by helping to prop up a certain kind of regime, Korea's policies determined labor conditions.

The price of Korean labor was not entirely determined by political considerations. Even in fully equalitarian social systems, the gross output of an economy sets an upper limit on what can be distributed to the workers. Even if the South Korean government had decreed equal income to all, there would still have been a discrepancy in the price of labor between the United States and South Korea, with Korean workers earning considerably less than U.S. workers. Political factors exacerbated the discrepancy, however. The more the ruling class in South Korea could suppress the nation's workers, the cheaper would be Korea's labor-power.

LABOR STANDARDS

There was no minimum wage in South Korea in the 1970s, although, under the Labor Standards Law, a minimum wage could be established for specific industries by the director general of the Office of Labor Affairs (OLA). Wages were in fact very low. An OLA study reported in 1974 that the average wage earner's monthly income of $65 was $20 less than the Economic Planning Board's calculation of the expenses of an average household (K. Y. Lim, 1976a: 200–201). An unusually high proportion of the wage was paid in special "allowances," emphasizing paternalistic relations between employer and employee (K. Y. Lim, 1976a: 201–203). Lim (1976a: 204) concludes that the wage level was much lower in South Korea than in countries at a comparable level of economic development.

The standard work week was forty-eight hours: eight hours a day, six days a week. The work day could be extended by mutual agreement, and overtime was supposed to be paid at 150 percent of the standard hourly rate. However Korean law specified that workers could not claim payment for labor of less than one hour. Therefore, many companies required workers to arrive thirty to forty-five minutes early and released them thirty to forty-five minutes late, thereby gaining considerable additional labor without paying overtime (C. S. Kim, 1977: 33). A 1967 survey found that only 3 out of 103 firms actually paid an overtime allowance (K. Y. Lim, 1976a: 222).

Minors (thirteen to eighteen years) were permitted to work up to forty-two hours a week.[11] Children less than thirteen years old were not allowed to work, but numerous violations occurred. A 1969 government survey of 5000 big firms uncovered 1430 cases of hiring children under thirteen. Illegal child labor was far more frequent in smaller establishments not covered by the survey (Breidenstein, 1974: 269).

Korean law entitled employees to one paid holiday per month (apart from the standard one day per week), which could be accumulated. In other words, the worker received two weeks a year of paid vacation. If a worker had perfect attendance, the employer was required to grant eight more days of paid vacation; for those with 90 percent attendance, the reward was three extra days. Extra vacation benefits accrued to people who had been long-time employees of a firm.[12]

The retirement age was fifty-five, with exceptions for family-owned companies and some top management. The purposes of early retirement appear to have been twofold: to maintain a healthy, productive work force, and to minimize the number of highly paid workers with seniority. There were no pension plans, and the law required only severance pay. Firms with sixteen or more employees had to establish a severance pay plan whereby retired workers were paid one month's average wages for each year in continuous service.[13] Assuming a worker was employed thirty years for one company, an optimal condition, he or she would still have earned only two and one-half years' worth of severance pay on which to retire. Living frugally one might be supported by retirement benefits up to the age of sixty.

The weakness of retirement benefits was probably linked to the retention of some precapitalist social arrangements in South Korea. In all likelihood, employers assumed that the "elderly" would be supported by their families. Reliance on precapitalist forms to subsidize wage labor was a common means of keeping labor cheap, as in the South African Bantustans and other forms of "migrant labor" (Burawoy, 1976; Castells, 1975).

The only health benefit an employer was required to provide was an annual physical examination, and then only if the firm had sixteen or more workers. Safety provisions were equally minimal: an employee exposed to dangerous work conditions was not supposed to work more than six hours per day or thirty-six per week. This rule could be suspended with special permission from the OLA. In case of industrial accidents, the employer was required to pay 60 percent of the worker's ordinary wages during the period of medical treatment, plus compensation for handicaps resulting from on-the-job injuries. Death on the job required the payment of 1000 days' wages to the family plus funeral expenses. Employers with sixteen or more workers had to subscribe to Industrial Accident Compensation Insurance, provided by the OLA.[14]

Minimal as were these provisions, a 1973 survey found 96 percent of businesses in South Korea out of compliance. Older plants were likely to have inadequate lighting, ventilation, and sanitary facilities. Another report found that only one out of three plants was reasonably free of hazard. Forty-one percent were declared to be "bad," and 27 percent "poor" with respect to health and safety. Only 9 percent of plants were rated "good" (K. Y. Lim, 1976a: 224–225). As a result, in the 1960s, industrial accidents were four times more likely to occur in Korea than in the United States (Lim, 1976a: 226).

Breidenstein provides the following description of work conditions in Korean factories:

> A workday of ten to twelve hours with one short rest break is the rule and up to eighteen hours is quite common ... A survey of mining and manufacturing enterprises by the R.O.K. Industrial Health Association shows: an eight-hour workday in 43 percent; up to twelve hours in 23 percent; and more than twelve hours in 33 percent ... Extra pay for overtime or night work, though prescribed by law, is an exception. Many companies withhold wages and severance pay for several months. Illumination, ventilation, heating, and noise protection in most factories are so poor that the worker's health frequently suffers. Industrial accidents, due to the absence of safety precautions and overwork of the laborers, are frequent, and increasing annually; compensation pay, if given, is nominal. Assault, mistreatment of young workers, and sexual exploitation of female workers are common. (1974: 254, 268)

Another description comes from a worker at a textile company in Seoul:

> At our factory, we work three 8-hour shifts, but from when to when we do not know. We are forced to come 30—60 minutes early and work until the job is finished—however long it may take! If we are supposed to finish by 10 p.m. we often don't get home until just before curfew at 12 a.m. If we live in the dormitory we sometimes work until 1 a.m. or 2 a.m.... Because the machines run continuously we are so busy that we often cannot have a meal break ... We are ashamed to say that sometimes we cannot go to the toilet so must use the factory floor. (cited in C. S. Kim, 1977: 33—34)

In 1970, a twenty-three-year-old worker immolated himself in protest over sweatshop conditions in the garment industry. Earlier, he had been fired from a textile factory for trying to organize a union. Before his suicide, this worker exposed some of the conditions in the industry: half of the 27,000 garment workers in his district were under fifteen years old, and many worked thirteen to sixteen hours a day in overcrowded, poorly lit, and unventilated rooms, sometimes only five feet high (Breidenstein, 1974: 254; see also Valence, 1973: 85—86).

It is unclear whether labor standards were especially low in foreign-invested firms and/or plants manufacturing for export. Cohen (1975: 72—90) studied ten multinationals (four U.S. and six Japanese) producing for export. Comparing them with several Korean-owned firms in the same lines, he found no clear differences in 1970. Cohen believed foreign forms paid highly skilled workers more than local firms, but had fewer highly skilled workers, so the average wage balanced out (Cohen, 1975: 79—81). In other words, foreign firms did not force wages down. However, they did not push them up either. They seemed merely to take advantage of prevailing low standards.

In contrast, Kei (1977: 69) reported that, although the average wage in South Korea was 46,612 won ($96) as of June 1975, the average in the Masan free export zone was only 35,631 won ($74). In part this discrepancy arose because the majority of workers in the FTZ were young women paid much less than men. In 1975, for instance, the average wage of males in Masan was 67,634 won. Female earnings averaged only 45.9 percent of this amount. Women made up three-quarters of the Masan work force in that year. Eighty-four percent were under twenty-nine years of age, compared to 36 percent for the entire Korean work force (Kei, 1977: 71–72). Young women like this were the cheapest labor in the world (Fuentes and Ehrenreich, 1983). OLA conducted an investigation of the Masan free export zone in 1974 and found 88 percent of firms were violating the Labor Standards Law (Kei, 1977: 70; see also Koo, 1981a: 65–67).[15]

RIGHTS TO ORGANIZE

Labor unions were formally protected by South Korea's labor laws. Initially set up under the U.S. military government and modeled on U.S. labor law, Korean law permitted trade unions, collective bargaining, and strikes. A labor union obtained legal recognition only if its funds came from its members, not from employers. Government Labor Committees were supposed to mediate and arbitrate labor disputes (K. Y. Lim, 1976a: 86–162; 1976b: 29–31, 35).

Despite this progressive legislation, the development of an independent labor movement was severely hampered in South Korea. One major reason was the labor policies of the Park regime. In 1972 President Park declared a state of national emergency, followed by martial law. Park's stated labor policy was to enhance mutual cooperation between labor and management in order to increase the nation's productivity. In practice, under the "Regulation of Collective Bargaining under the National Emergency," this policy permitted almost complete control of labor union activities by the government. Thus, although the right to collective bargaining was guaranteed in the South Korean constitution, it was abrogated under the state of emergency (K. Y. Lim, 1976a: 73–85).[16]

An example of such abrogation was the Small–Medium Size Firms Cooperation Law, first passed in 1961 and amended in 1963. The law exempted smaller firms from collective bargaining: "The assumption is that this will keep labor costs down in these firms, hence enabling them to grow and modernize quickly" (K. Y. Lim, 1976a: 189).

The Korean government suppressed Korean labor not only to achieve their conception of national development, but also to attract foreign investment. The government knew that Korea's principal resource was industrious low-cost labor. Thus special provisions were made to ensure that foreign investors would not suffer from labor problems. A "Special Law on Trade Unions and Mediation of Labor

Disputes in Enterprises Invested in by Foreigners," was passed in 1970, after a labor struggle in two U.S. firms. The new law put all disputes under the jurisdiction of the director general of the Office of Labor Affairs. After its passage, labor disputes in foreign firms declined sharply (Lim, 1976a: 237). *Korea Business* proudly proclaimed: "Foreign investors are given special protection from unwarranted labor disputes." [17]

Special labor conditions existed in the free export zones. In the 1970 Law on the Establishment of the Free Export Zones, Article 18 specifically limited the rights of labor to organize there. In addition, in Masan, special dormitories were built to house workers. These barracks enabled employers to gain better control over workers (Kei, 1977: 71). A description of these dormitories is reminiscent of those set up for African mineworkers in South Africa.

An intermediate stratum of Korean supervisors aided foreign firms in controlling Korean workers. According to Kei (1977: 76), these managers played an important role in the Masan free trade zone. They loyally promoted "labor-management cooperation" and rarely sided with the workers against foreign capital.

In addition to legal controls, militant Korean workers faced harassment by the Korean Central Intelligence Agency (KCIA) and police (Kei, 1977: 74). As one observer notes: "Anyone attempting to create a free labor movement committed to defending the interest of the workers must be prepared to face dismissal, arrest, imprisonment and torture" (C. S. Kim, 1977: 32–33). Kim (1977: 36) also speaks of the unity between the state and management in the suppression of labor unrest. In response to an effort to organize a textile factory, "workers not only faced obstructive company actions in the initial stage, but had to fight the police and the Korean CIA. Workers are confronted not by capital alone, but in collusion with the repressive power of the state."

Another government tactic to control labor was support of the FKTU as the sole legal trade union organization in the country. After he came to power, Park developed a "General Plan for the Reorganization of Labor Groups" providing for the development of an anticommunist labor movement that would prevent undisciplined labor disputes. The FKTU admirably served this function. Workers had no right freely to elect their own exclusive bargaining agent. As long as there were members of the FKTU in a plant it was entitled to be the exclusive representative of the workers. However, only when a majority of employees were members of FKTU did it act as the bargaining agent for all workers (K. Y. Lim, 1976a: 169–170).[18]

According to Kei (1977: 74), the FKTU supported and promoted Park's policies and possibly had links to the KCIA. With respect to foreign investment, the head of the FKTU's Foreign Facilities Trade Union Department stated:

> [FKTU] supports the effort to attract multinational corporations, and will defer the organization of a labor union for six to twelve months after the firm has arrived, limiting ourselves to setting up a vehicle for mutual understanding between labor and management. (cited in Kei, 1977: 74)

Thus FKTU acted as another Korean intermediary to control labor.

In addition to repressive government intervention, cultural and economic factors also limited the development of the Korean labor movement. Lim (1976a: 157) points out that labor relations in Korean firms were often paternalistic. Many firms were small, making relations between employers and employees personal. But even in larger firms, paternalistic labor relations prevailed, thus obviating the formation of antagonistic organizations among workers. A survey found that 21.9 percent of 379 workers believed their employer treated them like members of his own family (K. Y. Lim, 1976a: 171). Employers encouraged this attitude: "The company president likes to assume the role of 'father', referring to employees as members of the family. In speaking to employees, company presidents often advise their workers to look upon the factory and company as their own home" (K. Y. Lim, 1976a: 229).

Emphasizing respect for rank by subordinates and paternalistic obligations by those in power, the Confucian tradition helped to undermine the principle of collective bargaining and strengthened the position of management (K. Y. Lim, 1976a: 233). This precapitalist value system thus served as a cultural brake on the development of a strong labor movement.

More important in the retardation of the development of a labor movement was the level of economic development in South Korea. Jobs in the nonagricultural sector were both scarce and desirable. Workers who held these jobs were fearful that union organization would lead to their dismissal and quick replacement. Given the high level of government intervention in the economy, a discharged worker would have difficulty finding another job (K. Y. Lim, 1976a: 156—157). Hardship combined with repression to limit the ability of workers to organize.

Korean workers were, of course, neither completely docile nor wholly intimidated. Despite political repression and economic hardship workers often made efforts to improve their conditions. For instance, numerous labor disputes arose in the Masan free trade zone, many of which have never received public acknowledgement (Kei, 1977: 74—78).

Events following President Park's assassination illuminate the government's role in labor repression. The *Los Angeles Times* reported: "Sitdown strikes, walkouts, and other labor protests, some of them violent, are spreading across South Korea in a wave of workers uprisings that were never tolerated during the reign of the late President Park Chung Hee." [19] At least twenty-five companies were affected. One thousand steel workers clashed with police in Pusan. Coal miners took over the central city of Sabuk. In Seoul, 980 workers at the Ilshin Steel Company staged a sit-in where workers demanded higher wages and benefits and the ouster of promanagement union representatives put in office under elections rigged by the government. These uprisings were supported by major student demonstrations all over the country (C. S. Lee, 1981: 128—129).

The retarded state of trade unionism in South Korea affected the class consciousness of emigrants to the United States. Historical experience with trade unionism is an important factor in the price of labor. Those who have had little experience with independent unionism and who have been tied to precapitalist relations of production of a paternalistic or coercive character are more vulnerable, at least initially, to exploitation as cheap labor.

DISTRIBUTION

Apart from the direct relationship between management and workers at the workplace, labor policies can be more broadly conceived to include the way a society allocates its surplus. A prolabor policy redistributes a high proportion of social wealth to the poorer segments of the population. Progressive taxation, and public expenditures on health, education, housing, and welfare, are examples of prolabor policies in this sense. In contrast, antilabor, or procapitalist,

Table 8.   Percentage Share of Household Income by
Percentile Groups of Households: Korea and Selected
Middle-income Countries

Income Quintiles	South Korea 1976	Brazil 1972	Philippines 1970–1971	Turkey 1973	Mexico 1977
Lowest	5.7	2.0	5.2	3.4	2.9
Second	11.2	5.0	9.0	8.0	7.0
Third	15.4	9.4	12.8	12.5	12.0
Fourth	22.4	17.0	19.0	19.5	20.4
Highest	45.3	66.6	54.0	56.5	57.5
Highest Decile	27.5	50.6	38.5	40.7	40.6

Source: Robert Cassen, et al. *World Development Report 1981.* (London: Published for the World Bank by Oxford University Press, 1981), table 25.

policies include minimal state intervention in the redistribution of social wealth and the encouragement of capital accumulation in the hands of the few. The degree of equality in a society is a rough indicator of its pro- or antilabor policies.

Developing countries generally have a poor record in terms of internal equality. Economic growth has frequently been accompanied by increased inequality, especially in the rural areas. Only a few, mainly socialist countries have escaped this pattern. However, a few capitalist developing countries are also believed to have avoided excessive inequality, and South Korea (along with Japan and Taiwan) was considered by several authors (see, for example, Adelman and Robinson, 1978; Hasan and Rao, 1979; Rao, 1978) to be a prime example. These countries are sometimes referred to as the "East Asian model of development" (E. Lee, 1979: 493).

The East Asian model of development has received considerable attention: "It is seen as the vindication of the viability of the neo-classical route to development, that the free market can generate rapid growth without floundering in the impasse of growing inequality and mass poverty" (E. Lee, 1979: 493). Consequently, Korea's distribution policies and level of equality have received some attention.

If income distribution was more equitable in South Korea than in other developing countries, and some data suggest it was (see table 8), it was generally not because of prolabor redistribution policies. With the exception of a major land reform from 1945 to 1953, which

redistributed Japanese-held land in small parcels to Korean peasants
(E. Lee, 1979: 493–494; Choo, 1977: 310–317; Adelman and Robinson, 1978: 38–39), government policy favored capital accumulation
over redistribution.

Apart from supports to keep grain prices low, the Korean government engaged in little direct intervention to redistribute income. The
tax system was not progressive. Central government social subsidies
amounted to only 1.7 percent of GNP in 1975, even including the
payment to local governments for education expenditures. To the
extent that financial intervention by the government occurred, it
tended to support the growth of capital through interest subsidies
and accelerated depreciation allowances (Rao, 1978: 386–387). In
sum, "government expenditures . . . are not specifically directed to the
alleviation of poverty" (Rao, 1978: 387).

South Korea's relative social equality, it was thus argued, depended not upon direct government subsidies to the poor, but upon
its strategy of growth. Korean government support for rapid industrialization was presumed to bring with it a rise in employment
opportunities and a concomitant increase in the standard of living for
the masses (Rao, 1978: 387). By supporting capital accumulation,
everyone supposedly benefited. This is, of course, the standard conservative argument.

There is no question that employment increased in South Korea
after the emergence of the export-oriented industrialization plan.
Increasing numbers of Koreans became wage and salary earners. But
the rise in employment statistics masked other trends. One cannot
assume that the previously nonemployed were unemployed—only
that they were not employed in the capitalist sector. South Korea
was a country in transition from peasant agriculture to industrial
capitalism. Job opportunities could grow in the capitalist sector while
the peasant sector bore many of the costs of industrial growth.
Moreover, rapid growth in industrial occupations could be accompanied by high unemployment and poverty in cities when peasants
displaced from the land could not be absorbed quickly enough into
wage labor. Rao's (1978) heavy reliance on the growth of employment is thus a poor indicator of the true level of inequality and social
dislocation in South Korea.

Within the agricultural sector itself Korea appeared to be more
egalitarian than most developing societies. Unlike many developing

countries, which had a wide disparity between capital-intensive, export-oriented agriculture, and small-scale, peasant agriculture, South Korea managed to avoid this polarization. The country was, in a sense, fortunate to inherit, from the period of Japanese colonial rule, a system of surplus extraction based on high rents charged to multiple small-scale tenant farmers, rather than a system of large estates, employing masses of workers who had been alienated from the land. As a result, land reform was relatively easy to effectuate, with the removal of Japanese owners, by transforming tenants into land owners. The reforms did not alter the basic agricultural productive system. Therefore, there was much more equitable distribution of land than was found in many countries, a pattern that was reinforced by a government policy limiting land ownership to a maximum of three hectares (E. Lee, 1979: 493–496). As time progressed, however, rural inequality was increasing (E. N. Lee, 1979: 503–505).

Despite relative equality within the rural sector, capitalist development in South Korea, as in most developing countries, was accompanied by increasing disparity between urban and rural conditions. Comparable income statistics for rural and urban areas are difficult to obtain since peasant farmers acquire most of their livelihood on a noncash basis. Still, even Rao (1978: 388) agrees that the relative position of farmers was not improving, while Wideman (1974: 276) asserts that the countryside was drained of its small surpluses to subsidize industrial development, a conclusion supported by Lee (1979: 511–512) and Sunoo (1978: 330–332).

A controversial policy of the Korean government was grain subsidizing. The government bought grain from the peasants and sold it back to the urban populace at reduced prices. Rao (1978: 387–388) contends that this policy subsidized the peasants. Wideman (1974: 279–281) and Lee (1979: 511–512), on the other hand, argue that the government's purchase price was below the market price, even if the grain was sold for still less. Therefore, the grain subsidies were a tax on the peasantry. Serious grain shortages, and a rise in the country's dependence on imported grains, indicate that the subsidy did not aid the peasantry. Furthermore, the U.S. government's PL 480 grain loans to South Korea enabled U.S. farmers to dump surplus grain there, undermining Korean agricultural prices.

The net result of lack of support for agriculture was a massive outmigration from rural areas, perhaps the best indicator of rural–urban

Table 9.   Growth in the Population of Seoul, 1955–1975

	Total Population	Population of Seoul	Seoul Percent of Total
1955	21,502,000	1,574,868	7.3
1960	24,954,000	2,445,402	9.8
1966	29,160,000	3,803,360	13.0
1970	31,425,000	5,525,262	17.6
1975	34,681,000	6,889,470	19.9

Source: Republic of Korea, Economic Planning Board, *Korea Statistical Yearbook,* 1977: 35–36.

disparities. Wideman (1974: 276) estimated the annual rate of out-migration from the countryside at 300,000 per year, while Lee (1979: 496) found Korean rural exodus to be extraordinarily high relative to other developing countries. Farm population dropped from 58 percent of the total in 1960 to 38 percent in 1975. Between 1967 and 1976, an estimated 6.7 million farmers left their land (C. S. Kim, 1977: 22). By 1975, 21 percent of the total labor force, and 40 percent of nonfarm workers were wage earners in the industrial sector.

Despite rural exodus, the peasant sector continued to support some of the surplus population displaced by development. Rao notes: "It is generally accepted that there still exists some under-employment in agriculture in the sense that the numbers employed in agriculture could decline without any significant losses of agricultural output" (1978: 386). In other words, the subsistence sector absorbed a certain amount of unemployment, providing economically ineffi-cient jobs, a common pattern in developing countries when insuffi-cient social insurance is provided for workers. Reliance on the agri-cultural sector for social insurance was a hidden tax on the peasants.

Rural decline was accompanied by the rise of urban centers, nota-bly Seoul. Table 9 shows the growth in the capital's population from 1955 to 1975. Not only did the city more than triple in size over the twenty-year period, but the proportion of the country's growing population living there also increased dramatically.

Urban growth would not necessarily be associated with social inequality if accompanied by the absorption of the rising labor force in new jobs. The level of unemployment should, therefore, be an-other indicator of maldistribution. Official Korean statistics did not

Table 10. Employment Status of Korean Workers,
1970 and 1976

	1970		1976	
	Number (in thousands)	*Percent*	*Number (in thousands)*	*Percent*
Total	9,745		12,556	
Regularly Employed	2,236	22.9	2,965	23.6
Self-employed	3,331	34.2	4,263	34.0
Family Workers	2,628	27.0	3,096	24.7
Temporary Workers	520	5.3	1,086	8.6
Daily Workers	1,030	10.6	1,146	9.1
Nonfarm	4,629		6,700	
Regular	1,959	42.3	2,691	40.2
Self-employed	1,250	27.0	1,756	26.2
Family	417	9.0	473	7.1
Temporary	427	9.2	983	14.7
Daily	576	12.4	797	11.9

Source: Republic of Korea, Economic Planning Board, *Korea Statistical Yearbook*, 1977: 73.

reveal high unemployment rates, however. According to the *Korea Statistical Yearbook*,[20] unemployment was only 3.8 percent in 1977, and since 1970 it had never risen above 4.5 percent. Male unemployment was somewhat above the total, ranging as high as 5.6 percent since 1970. In 1977 it was 4.6 percent. Still, even for males, this rate was low relative to most countries. These statistics lead one to believe that South Korea was well able to absorb her growing population and displaced peasantry.

The umemployment rate alone, however, is not a good indicator of absorption capacity. As Koo (1976) has pointed out for underdeveloped societies in general, and Korea in particular, rural–urban migrants may never appear in unemployment statistics because they often employ themselves as peddlers or vendors of personal services. The size of the self-employed class serves as one indicator of the failure of the economy to absorb all the dislocated in regular jobs.

Table 10 shows the employment status of Korean workers in 1970 and 1976. Less than one-quarter of all workers were regularly employed in full-time, stable jobs. Over one-third were self-employed, and an additional quarter were employed as family workers, presumably in the firms of the self-employed. Thus over 50 percent of Korean workers were in this petit bourgeois sector. In addition, another 16 to 18 percent were temporary or daily workers, a further instance of employment instability.

Since many Koreans were self-employed farmers, the ability of the growing cities of Korea to absorb displaced peasants is better indicated by the distribution of nonfarm workers. Less than half had regular employment. Over one-quarter were self-employed, and their family employees boosted this sector to about 35 percent of all workers. In contrast to the figures for the country as a whole, temporary and daily jobs were higher in nonfarm areas, and appeared to be growing, from 22 percent in 1970 to 27 percent in 1976.

Over this six-year period, nonfarm employment grew, from 47.5 percent of total employment in 1970, to 53.4 percent in 1976, an indicator of the rapid shift away from farming. The population on farms grew 14.5 percent from 1970 to 1976, but in the nonfarm areas population grew 44.7 percent (Republic of Korea, 1977: 73). The rapidity of this shift strained the labor absorbing capacities of nonfarm areas. From these statistics it is evident that unemployment rates alone do not reveal the degree of economic dislocation that results from early capitalist development and rural displacement. In South Korea there appeared to be a substantial population that was unable to find a stable livelihood in the growing urban economy (C. S. Kim, 1977: 28–31).

The rapid growth of the urban unemployed and underemployed population contributed to the depressed wages in South Korea (Hasan, 1976: 55). Wideman (1974: 278) quotes *Korea Business*, 1972, as boasting to potential investors: "The wage scale in Korea is one of the lowest in Asia ... Unionization is not well developed in Korea because of a large reserve labor force." Low wages from urban workers were also supplemented by PL 480 grain imports from the United States, and by government's subsidy for grain prices (Kuznets, 1977: 103), a policy that, as mentioned earlier, hurt the agricultural sector to the benefit of industrial capital, including foreign investors.

Urban areas had many social and environmental problems that were not adequately taken care of by the government. These included traffic congestion and air and water pollution. As of 1974, Seoul and other Korean cities did not have sewage systems, and industrial pollution was unmonitored (Breidenstein, 1974: 245–246). Indeed, Japan exported some of its most polluting industries to South Korea the acceptance of which was one way the government could lure foreign capital (Halliday, 1980: 13).

One of the most serious social problems in Seoul was a severe housing shortage. A 1970 study estimated that 2.5 million people, half of the population of the city, lived in illegally constructed housing, much of which consisted of wooden shacks or even tents. Slum housing averaged three families per dwelling, or twelve to fifteen people in each shack. This type of housing had no water supply, no sewage disposal or garbage collection, and often no electricity. Although other Asian slums were worse, Seoul's were bad (Breidenstein, 1974: 245–247).[21] Despite the tremendous growth of industry and exports, urban poverty and squalor remained a reality.

Another type of distribution is the educational system. If a country provides widespread public education, people's earning potential ought to increase, thereby decreasing inequality, or so the theory goes. On this score, South Korea performed relatively well. Between 1953 and 1963 Korea's literacy rate rose from 30 to over 80 percent. Universal primary education was established, and secondary and higher education grew quickly. Adelman and Robinson note: "As a result by 1965 Korea's human-resource development had exceeded the norm for a country with three times its median per capita GNP" (1978: 41; see also Kuznets, 1977: 92–93).

The growth in education was not entirely a product of government policy. In fact, in the early 1960s the Korean government tried to cut back higher education. The demand for educational expansion came from the people themselves and was, perhaps, rooted in the Confucian tradition. Regardless of its causes, Koreans firmly believed education was the key to advancement (Adelman and Robinson, 1978: 41).

Despite the growth in educational opportunities, many more Korean young people desired an education than could obtain one. Until 1969 only primary education was both compulsory and free of charge. For any higher level, students' families not only had to pay increasingly high fees, but students had to compete in entrance examinations, described as "examination hell," at every level. In 1969, middle school (the three years after the first six years of elementary schooling) was made compulsory, and the entrance

Table 11.   Level of Education and Occupation of the
Graduates of 1976 (in percents)

	High School	Junior College	College and University	Graduate School
Professional and Technical	0.7	35.4	44.0	62.5
Administration	2.8	3.8	3.4	8.7
Clerical	19.4	5.0	11.6	8.7
Sales	3.8	1.1	1.6	1.6
Services	5.7	4.1	2.7	1.3
Agricultural and Fishing	4.9	3.8	1.1	1.2
Production	15.4	12.0	6.5	5.7
Other	1.3	1.2	0.8	0.6
Armed Forces	0.5	0.3	7.5	2.1
Unemployed	45.4	33.4	20.8	7.7
Total Number	(232,745)	(19,428)	(34,693)	(4,182)

Source: Republic of Korea, Economic Planning Board, *Korea Statistical Yearbook,* 1977: 372.

examination system was eliminated. However it persisted for high schools, and was even more competitive for higher education.[22]

Even for the lucky minority admitted the rewards were uncertain. Table 11 shows the employment opportunities for 1976 graduates at various levels. Rates of unemployment at the lower levels could, in part, reflect the intention to enroll at a higher level of schooling. But they also reveal the difficulty of finding employment for Korea's increasingly educated population. The fact that one-fifth of college and university graduates in this cohort did not find work again suggests the inability of Korea's expanding economy to absorb all those it had trained. Lack of employment opportunities for college graduates played a significant role in the high rate of student political protest in Korea in the 1970s (Adelman and Robinson, 1978: 41–42). It also contributed to emigration to the United States, a theme we shall develop in the next chapter.

The distribution of jobs is also of interest. During the period of our study, many high school graduates entered clerical work, yet the second largest job category for this group was production. Among junior college graduates, production jobs were also important, though the highest proportion became professionals. The fairly high levels of blue-collar employment at these educational levels may indicate an inability of the economy to make full use of its trained manpower.

At the other end of the spectrum, those coming out of graduate school were mainly entering the professions, though over one-third of them failed to do so. Indeed, fairly large percentages were found in clerical work, production, and the ranks of the unemployed, again suggesting that education was outpacing South Korea's need for educated workers.

Perhaps the most interesting distribution is that of college graduates. Over one-fifth were unemployed. More surprising, almost 12 percent were clerical workers. Adding sales and service workers, the figure for lower white-collar workers grows to 16 percent. While high school graduates may have seen these white-collar jobs as satisfactory employment, it seems likely college graduates were less sanguine.

One group of trained personnel is of particular interest, namely, health professionals. This field was rapidly expanding. In 1970, Korea had 55,642 health professionals; by 1977 the figure had jumped by 45 percent to 80,542.[23] These figures mask growth among modern health professionals, such as physicians, dentists, pharmacists, and nurses, since traditional lines, like herb doctors and midwives, were declining in number. The fastest growing of the modern health professions was nursing with a 109 percent growth in licensed personnel between 1970 and 1977. Pharmacy was second with a 46 percent growth.

Despite the expansion of education for health professionals, few health benefits trickled down to the population at large. The government had established health centers around the country, but they tended to be understaffed. Most medical care was dispensed privately and was therefore costly or inaccessible, especially to residents of rural areas; 80 percent of all doctors and 90 percent of nurses were located in urban areas. Because private practice was more lucrative than public, few good doctors were attracted to the latter. And, in the face of inadequate opportunities in private practice, many preferred to emigrate rather than move into public health centers. Indeed, in 1972 the government sent 4000 doctors and 6000 nurses abroad to earn foreign exchange, leaving Korea's own population without adequate care (Breidenstein, 1974: 251–252; Wideman, 1974: 275).

The relative health expenditure of South Korea was low compared to that of Japan and the United States. In 1974, 7.46 percent of GNP was spent on health care in the United States. For Japan the figure was 3.56 percent, and for Korea, 2.83 percent. Per capita expenditures for the same year were $492 in the United States, $130 in Japan, and $14 in Korea (C. K. Park, 1977: 242). Ninety-nine percent of Korean hospitals were private as of 1973, and there were only 12.2 hospital beds per 10,000 population, compared to 74.4 in the United States and 103.5 in Japan. Moreover, 86.7 percent of hospital beds were in urban areas in 1975, leaving only 13.3 percent for the half of the population that resided in the countryside (Park, 1977: 245–246).

Finally, one might add under the concept of distribution the level of political repression. Another resource a regime can distribute more or less equitably to its citizens is freedom to pursue their lives without high levels of government interference, and to express disagreement with, or even opposition to, policies they find detrimental to their well-being. South Korean regimes have not scored well on this dimension.

On May 16, 1961, military forces under the command of Major General Park Chung-Hee overthrew the civilian government of South Korea in a sunrise coup d'etat. Park's military junta dissolved the National Assembly, suspended the Constitution, and disbanded political parties (Banks, 1977: 219–220). Under the terms of a revised (*Yushin*) constitution adopted in October 1972 General Park took office as civilian president eligible for reelection without limit to six-year terms of office. The Yushin constitution permitted the president to appoint one-third of the membership of the National Assembly, to assume dictatorial powers in case of national emergency, to suspend the National Assembly at his pleasure, and to evade the Supreme Court by means of an appointed Constitutional Committee (Choy, 1979: 196). The Yushin constitution provided no firm guarantees of the human or civil rights of the South Korean people (Buss, 1982: 13).

Even during the years of his civilian administration, President Park ruled Korea with the open support of the military. Enjoying this support, Park was able to suppress internal political dissent, labor disturbances, intellectuals, and the socially activist segment of the Christian clergy. To this end Park created a vast internal police agency known as the Korean Central Intelligence Agency, frankly modeled upon its U.S. counterpart. The KCIA managed and probed every corner of South Korean life in a daily round of surveillance and detentions without trial or charge. Episodes of corruption and political kidnapping occasionally captured headlines in the world press. Of these the most sensational was the KCIA's kidnapping of Kim Dae-Jung, opposition political spokesman, from a Tokyo hotel in 1973, and the Koreagate bribery scandal that exploded in Washington in 1977.

Ultimately the police apparatus claimed the life of its creator. On October 26, 1979 President Park was assassinated by Kin Chae-Kyu, head of the KCIA (Sung, 1982: 103). Commander of the Armed Forces Security Command, General Chun Doo-Hwan was thereupon appointed to investigate Park's assassination. Shortly after, on May 3, 1981, Chun was himself inaugurated President of the Republic of Korea, replacing Park. With support of the military, Chun suppressed the worker and student demonstrations that had plagued Park in the last year of his administration. Pledging loyalty to the repressive, export-oriented polices of his predecessor, Chun's government subsequently followed the same political and economic lines as Park, utilizing the same methods of police surveillance and dictatorship.

Korea's political leaders ignored the democratic process. When constitutional limitations stood in their way, they changed the constitution. When the legislature opposed their policies, its members were threatened or imprisoned. They used the army, police, and KCIA to ensure their power. And they used the threat of invasion from the North to justify the continued participation of the military in politics (Palais, 1974). Thus there was considerable political inequality in South Korea.

In sum, the benefits of Korea's economic development were not evenly distributed. The contrast between rich and poor was stark. Even though Korean statistics revealed greater income equality than most developing countries, government policy was not calculated to increase or even maintain that degree of equality. Indeed Koo (1983a) finds that, during the decades of the 1960s and 1970s, income inequality increased in South Korea. The Gini Index fell from .448 in 1960 to .389 in 1980. Apart from "corporatist control of labor organizations," Koo (1983a) contends that this result is not surprising, given government polices that favored big business at the expense of small business, inflationary financing that hurt those on fixed incomes, and a generally regressive tax policy.

Baldwin (1974: 22) thinks that U.S. and Korean economic planners may not have been completely cynical, however. They were "confident that development must precede such political questions as the equitable distribution of wealth. They argue that the pie must be baked before there can be discussion of who gets how many slices." Development strategy was aimed at supporting business in order to accelerate the accumulation of capital so that productivity could grow. Once the economy became industrialized, emphasis would shift (according to these planners) to more concern for social welfare. In part this switch would arise as a product of "natural " economic forces: the demand for skilled labor would climb, leading to increasing emphasis on education; a condition of labor scarcity would push wages up; and the government would find it necessary to correct gross injustices in the distribution of wealth in order to maintain social stability (Baldwin, 1974: 23).

Baldwin (1974: 23–24) believes this model of development was unlikely to emerge in South Korea, for the following reasons: labor could not organize and effectively pressure the regime from below; all political opposition had been quelled; and perhaps most important, "foreign interests are in South Korea because labor costs are low ... and they will not approve of tax or welfare policies that reduce profits." He predicts that Korean workers and farmers "will be caught in a police state vise, working long hours for low wages, while the profits go to foreign capitalists and a small ruling elite."

NATIONALISM

A third aspect of South Korea's labor policy, broadly defined, concerns government efforts to mobilize workers and induce them to accept low wages. Not only did the Korean government use coercion to keep its workers in line; it also used persuasion. Nationalism was one method of persuasion. The government invoked national solidarity or the national interest in order to urge the workers to accept sacrifices. People must be self-disciplined, it was argued, and willing to give up immediate benefits for the long-range good of the whole. Only by accepting such temporary sacrifices could the nation industrialize, and all would eventually reap the benefits of a higher standard of living. Meanwhile, the government presented the populace with constant evidence that conditions were improving, GNP was rising, and more people were becoming middle class, suggesting that, very soon, they too would share these benefits.

The following quote from a speech by President Park captures the flavor of this appeal. It specifically deals with the issue of labor relations, but there are many other illustrations of this kind of appeal to national belt-tightening at a more general level:

> Cooperative relationships between labor and management are an important factor in strengthening the international competitiveness of our country on the world business scene. Even more harmonious industrial relations are called for at this time, not only for further success in export promotion, but also for speedier normalization of domestic economic conditions and greater improvement in the living standards of the people. I ask all employers of the country to make sincere voluntary efforts this year to further improve the welfare and working conditions for their employees ... At the same time, I would like to ask the workers of the country to understand more clearly the nature of the difficult economic problems now confronting the nation, and to display a greater spirit of cooperation in seeking smooth solutions of various labor–management issues, even though they may be faced with many problems involving their welfare.[24]

Accompanying the reprinting of this speech were several industrial photographs. One picture portrayed crowds of well-dressed, middle-class people, walking down an urban street. The heading read: "All Korean people benefit from the nation's increased economic welfare."[25]

Subsequently, Korea's chief economic planner since Park's death, Lee Hahn Been, stated that Korean workers would have to accept a reduction in their real income for 1980. Inflation threatened to reach 40 percent but the government adopted wage guidelines limiting increases to 15 percent. Lee called a meeting with the FKTU to persuade them of the necessity of accepting these policies:

> We are saying, "be patient this year ... We will suffer this year," Lee said ... Labor's cooperation in the [government's] program is crucial, he said. Without that cooperation, he added, higher wages could nullify the progress achieved by ... the effort to restore South Korea's exports to a competitive position.[26]

In an effort to mobilize the nation behind his development program, President Park launched the New Community Movement (*Saemaul Undong*) in 1971. Mainly begun as a rural development program, it was later extended to urban areas to become "a nationwide movement of nation-building activities" (Ban, 1977: 208). Park termed the movement a "spiritual revolution," but Wideman (1974: 294) considered it to be "a last-ditch effort to use coerced labor power in place of government investment for the improvement of agricultural production. " The movement was government-induced even though it praised self-help, and, while expressing concern with raising the standard of living of the peasantry, attempted to achieve this less through the transfer of capital to the villages, than through efforts to get the villagers to work harder (Ban, 1977: 212; Wideman, 1974: 294—296).[27]

A part of the Saemaul movement involved building factories outside of the major urban centers. One of the goals of such construction was as follows: "They aim at making the nation an Export Industrial Zone through enabling villages to become industrialized with export industries as a backbone."[28]

The Saemaul movement was used in the free export zones themselves. According to Kei (1977: 72), the movement there inculcated the idea of labor-management cooperation. Extra hours of unpaid work in the Masan free trade zone were authorized in the name of the movement, for example (Kim, 1977: 33). In other words, Saemaul Undong was an ideological tool to tame labor demands. This effort, by the way, had the full support of Korea's anticommunist labor organization, the FKTU, which placed high priority on total cooperation with the Saemaul movement (Kei, 1977: 75).

Whatever the defects of the South Korean government, its nationalist appeal contained a sufficient element of truth to make it convincing to many. In fact, Korea's success in attracting foreign capital, and in the export field, did depend upon the cheapness of her labor. If workers' demands were given priority before the foundations of industrialization were laid, the competitive edge of Korean products would disappear. As it was, Korea participated in a fiercely competitive world market, in which still poorer, less-developed countries with even cheaper labor threatened to undercut her: "South Korea's manufactured goods are competitive only as long as her workers' wages remain extremely low" (Breidenstein, 1974: 241).

Workers in South Korea faced a grim choice. They could either demand better wages and work conditions now, and see many jobs disappear, or they could accept poor conditions now, but watch industrial jobs expand. Given that rural decline was well under way, and many people had no alternative to industrial employment, the acceptance of short-term deprivation to secure employment seemed like the best alternative.

Of course, other options were possible. Korean workers could have overthrown the current regime and instituted a completely different development strategy, based, for instance, on self-sufficiency. However, most people did not see such an option as readily available and felt compelled to choose between the alternatives that were immediately presented.[29]

The nationalist plea was effective in part because some of the promised rewards were in fact forthcoming. Industrial job opportunities were expanding (Watanabe, 1972a). The country appeared to be well on its way to industrialization. Whether it would be able to move out of the pattern of manufactured exports and into a well-rounded industrial economy remained to be seen, for only if this transition was made would South Korea escape the cheap labor role. In the meantime, as long as industrial growth continued, people could be persuaded that, in serving the national interest, they were ultimately serving their self-interest as well.

In persuading as well as coercing Korean workers to accept low wages and poor working conditions, the Korean government performed a useful service for both its own ruling elite and for international capital. Foreign investors, subcontractors, and exporters to foreign markets reaped the benefits, too. In essence, the Korean government played a kind of middleman role, helping to keep Korean labor cheap and docile by invoking nationalism. As we shall show later, this role has parallels in the immigrant community.

CLASS CHARACTER OF THE KOREAN STATE

We have treated the Korean government as if it were an independent actor, apart from the class structure of Korean society. There is some truth in this approach since the Korean state was very strong, even by Third World standards, and played a crucial role in directing the development strategy of the country (Koo, 1983b). Still, no government is independent of class forces, and the Korean government was no exception. However, class forces were complicated in a society such as South Korea because the state played an active role in creating certain class segments that in turn provided the major backing for the government.

In a general sense, the class character of the Korean state was unambiguous: it was capitalist, supporting the interests of capital over labor. However, certain sectors of capital appeared to receive more support than others. Most supported was the export sector with links to international capital. Sectors less well served included agricultural capital and internal-oriented capital. In agriculture, the cheap-labor policy necessary for competing in the world market was supported by cheap food, which was sustained at the expense of capital accumulation in the rural sector. In the latter case, the national bourgeoisie, oriented towards internal development independent of international capital, was at odds with government policy. According to Sunoo (1978: 324), many locally oriented textile, lumber, mining, and construction firms were forced to suspend or drastically reduce their operations in the face of international competition.[30]

Although linked to international capital, the dominant class in South Korea was not totally dependent on it. True, they depended upon infusions of foreign capital, imports of raw materials and components, and access to foreign markets. But the strict subordination to the dictates of foreign capital of the sort characterizing the comprador class of colonial days was not applicable to modern South Korea (Halliday, 1980: 5,11). Korea's internationally oriented capitalist class, and the state that supported it, cooperated with international capital but were not ruled by it. They exercised considerable control over their own affairs. including controlling their own working class. They had, in other words, chosen for themselves a development strategy that linked them to international capital rather than having such a strategy simply imposed from outside (Rhee, 1979).

CLASS AND NATION

As discussed in chapter 2, the American working class saw itself as hurt by the rise of manufactured exports in Third World countries, based on cheap labor. The gross discrepancy in the price of labor, fostered by their own capitalist class as well as the ruling classes of the countries in question, created a complex set of relationships among the major classes in the two groups of nations. These are summarized in figure 2. Needless to say, this bare-bones sketch could

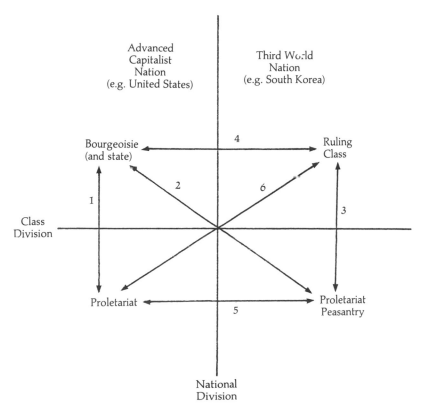

Figure 2 National and Class Relations between Advanced Capitalist and Third World Nations

be elaborated by the introduction of intermediate classes, intraclass conflicts, governments, and so forth.

In figure 2, we start with arrow 1, class relations within the advanced capitalist countries. As capitalism advances, the price of labor tends to rise, for several reasons, including the increase in the dependence of workers upon commodities, the emergence of powerful trade unions, and the development of welfare state provisions, which set a floor for labor standards (Bonacich and Cheng, 1984).[31] The higher the price of labor, the lower are potential profits for capital investment. In addition, businesses in advanced capitalist countries become vulnerable to competition from firms in Third World countries which can produce at much lower costs, especially labor costs.

As a consequence, capital in advanced capitalist countries is attracted to cheaper Third World labor (arrow 2), a process facilitated, in part, by the state, as we saw in chapter 2. Labor is cheap in the so-called developing Third World countries in part because of the early stages of their development. Displacement of the peasantry, for example, creates a so-called surplus population, which has little alternative other than to sell their labor-power cheaply. And transitional phases between precapitalist and capitalist productive systems permit some of the costs of reproduction of labor-power to be borne by the precapitalist sector. Thus, peasant families cover some of the subsistence costs of wage workers and their families, freeing capitalists from having to bear these costs.

The cheapness of Third World labor, however, is not only a product of level of development. The ruling classes in those countries that permit penetration by foreign capital often play a pivotal role in keeping their labor forces cheap (arrow 3). Many Third World countries are under the domination of highly dictatorial and repressive, often military, regimes. These regimes have established labor policies that help to keep labor costs down by open repression, the destruction of leftist elements, the encouragement of paternalistic labor relations, and a state-controlled labor movement. Furthermore, they utilize nationalistic sentiment to gain worker cooperation in their development plan, fostering the idea that low wages and poor working conditions are a necessary but temporary expedient for attracting capital, hence development.

The ruling class of many of these Third World countries is not merely an independent, self-generated class. Their governments were often created with advanced capitalist nation (particularly U.S.) backing (arrow 4). The military character of many of the regimes suggests their lack of popular support, and several of them, including that of South Korea, were created out of wars with leftist elements who were ultimately vanquished, or forced to establish themselves in a divided territory.

The ruling class of Third World nations plays a pivotal, middleman role between international capital and domestic workers. They help to keep their workers suppressed, in part for the benefit of international investors. Instead of international capitalists having to engage directly in processes of labor control, a task rendered especially difficult by the connotations of foreign domination, the ruling class of these nations performs many of the functions of labor control for them. This is seen in the many indirect ways in which foreign capital is utilized in Third World countries, such as subcontracting or importing.

One should note that not all segments of the ruling class of Third World countries favor the intrusion of foreign capital. For example, the national bourgeoisie may find its endeavors thwarted by the much more powerful international capitalist class. Such capitalists may push for nationalist takeovers or severe restrictions on the role of foreign capital in their country

Relations between the two groups of workers (arrow 5) become strained as a result of these processes. Capital's attraction to the cheapness and repression of Third World workers both directly displaces workers in the advanced capitalist countries and indirectly puts curbs on hard-won labor standards. In the face of cheap goods based on cheap labor, labor in countries like the United States faces an eroding job base and declining real wages. Efforts to protect against these processes, however, threaten to limit the flow of capital and technology to the Third World, where workers and expeasants desperately need jobs. The two groups of workers are thus pitted against one another in a competition for jobs, a fact that international capital exploits to increase its bargaining power relative to labor, hence its profits.

Finally, the working class of advanced capitalist countries finds itself at odds with the ruling class of Third World countries specializing in manufactured exports (arrow 6). This is true regardless of their strategy towards the workers of the poorer countries. If the workers in countries like the United States pursue a course of international labor solidarity and attempt to help organize Third World workers, the right-wing ruling classes in those countries would be threatened. On the other hand, if the workers respond with protectionist strategies, they threaten the development plan of those ruling classes which depends upon the inflow of foreign capital and access to the markets of the developed capitalist world.

Out of the configuration of interests described so far, we come full circle back to the class relations between capital and labor in the advanced capitalist countries (arrow 1). The system subverts the class struggle within the advanced capitalist nations, forcing labor organizations to make concessions to capital in the form of wage decreases and declining labor standards. Other forms of capitulation include the willingness to support a military build-up as a means of obtaining jobs.[32] Supporting militarism is likely to have adverse consequences for Third World workers who face the veiled or not-so-veiled threat of U.S. military intervention in support of their repressive ruling classes.

The model presented in Figure 2 has two axes: the vertical axis represents national solidarity across class lines, while sources of division occur between national groups. The horizontal axis represents class solidarity across national boundaries with the chief source of division and conflict lying between the major classes.

Most Marxists would predict that the axis of class solidarity and conflict ought to predominate over nationalism. Generally speaking, nationalism can be seen as an irrational sentiment that calls upon presumed primordial ties. The capitalist class is already internationalizing itself, and there are strong links between the bourgeoisies of many countries. One might anticipate that the world's working class, too, would see the common interests that unite them. In fact, very little progress has been made toward international labor solidarity. Protectionism, which is a form of nationalism, appears to be on the rise. And workers in both advanced capitalist and Third World countries appear to be more ready to cooperate with their bourgeoisies than with their fellow workers across national boundaries.

The predominance of nationalist outcomes, however, should not be seen as the victory of irrational primordial sentiment over rational class action. Given the tremendous discrepancy in price of labor, the structure of rational interests, especially short-term interests, leads, paradoxically, toward nationalist alliances. Ultimately the reason lies in the fact that the segments of the working class in advanced and Third World countries face distinctive material and political conditions. These class fragments have quite different short-term interests, given their location in the world capitalist system. Hence, despite the sharing of a general position in the working class, coordination is exceedingly difficult under current circumstances.

CONCLUSION

The cheapness of labor in South Korea did not result wholly from interventions by international capital and foreign governments. It was also determined by the policies and practices of the Korean government. True, this government was partly a construct of the United States and Japan, and might well have fallen if it had not received their continual support. But it also had a degree of autonomy to pursue policies that did not necessarily please its foreign supporters. Paradoxically, while the United States was critical of the authoritarianism of the Korean government, that government in fact served U.S. business interests well by keeping Korean labor subdued. *Fortune* captured this paradox well, pointing out that, although the U.S. public was critical of human rights violations in South Korea, businesses and banks were continuing to invest there, being delighted with the hardworking Korean people. As one Korean economic planner put it: "Businessmen abroad never ask about human rights" (cited in Rowan, 1977: 174).

4

Emigration From South Korea

The international system described in the previous chapters sets the context in which Koreans emigrated to the United States during the late 1960s and 1970s. It is our contention that there was a link between U.S. involvement in South Korea and the movement of Koreans to the United States. Our purpose in this chapter is to attempt to identify that link.

The United States was not the first territory to which Koreans emigrated. Before and during World War II several million Koreans moved to Japan and Manchuria. This movement was associated with Japanese colonial domination of the Korean peninsula and had many of the same world system sources as the later Korean emigration to the United States.

In this chapter we confine ourselves to postwar emigration from South Korea, attempting to evaluate its linkage to Korea's position in the international capitalist system. We start by describing the pattern of emigration as it developed after World War II. Then we move on to examine the causes of this emigration as they relate to U.S. influence in that country. And finally, we consider what little is known about the class character of the emigrants.

PATTERNS OF EMIGRATION

In describing the movement of Koreans abroad one must distinguish between emigrants proper, that is, people who plan to settle abroad, and people who leave temporarily for a variety of reasons, including working abroad or engaging in overseas trade. The analytic distinction is important but, in practice, the categories are often indistinct. Available statistics typically combine the two major types of movement. Futhermore, real emigration can arise in the context of the other types of movements: temporary workers and traders chart a

102

pathway for settlers or choose themselves to remain in their new location. Meanwhile, those who apparently had intended to leave for good sometimes aspire to return or do return to their homeland at some later date when conditions there have changed, or when they have achieved goals abroad, such as accumulating capital, which alters their position in the homeland.

In the first fifteen years after World War II few Koreans left their homeland. For instance, in 1957, only 4,855 Koreans emigrated (in the broad sense of the term). The next few years showed a slight increase, with 5,960 leaving in 1958; 8,903 in 1959; 7,856 in 1960; and 11,245 in 1961 (Republic of Korea, 1962: 30).

In late 1961, 97.4 percent of all overseas Koreans resided in Japan. The second largest settlement was the United States, with 2.2 percent. Otherwise, the number of Koreans who had moved abroad as of this date, was tiny and scattered. In addition, a few thousand students were abroad: 4771 in Asia, 4186 in the Americas, and 541 in Europe. Clearly the immediate postwar period was not a major time of Korean emigration.

In 1962 the South Korean government passed an Overseas Emigration Law to encourage emigration as a means of controlling population, alleviating unemployment, earning foreign exchange, and acquiring knowledge of advanced technology (Nishikawa, 1981: 3; I. Kim, 1981a: 52–53). In December of that year, the Ministry of Public Health and Social Affairs set up an emigration section, which encouraged seventeen families, encompassing ninety-two individuals, to move to Brazil. Furthermore, 157 people emigrated individually, or married or were adopted by foreigners. In 1963, the number of such emigrants rose to 2190 but the majority (65 percent) left through marriage to foreigners.[1]

In addition to encouraging emigration, the Korean government began to organize the export of Korean labor under contract to various countries in 1963. Again, the purpose was to earn foreign exchange and to acquire training in advanced technology. The first group of 280 workers went to West Germany in December 1963 to work in the coal mines. They were sent under a three-year contract specifying that they would work a seven and a half hour day for a monthly salary of $170.[2] Soon to follow were nurses, nurses aides, and household workers. Between 1963 and 1974 about 17,000

Table 12.   People Leaving South Korea, 1972–1977

	Total	Males per 100 Females	Percent Increase per annum	Percent Increase from 1972
1972	84,245	211.5		
1973	101,295	204.2	20.23	20.23
1974	121,573	214.4	20.02	44.31
1975	129,378	217.7	6.42	53.57
1976	164,727	265.8	27.32	95.53
1977	209,698	396.7	27.30	148.91

Source: Republic of Korea, Economic Planning Board, *Korea Statistical Yearbook,* 1978: 68–69.

Korean nurses and miners went to West Germany (I. Kim, 1981a: 53–54). Construction workers, doctors, pilots, and sailors were sent to various other countries, such as Thailand, Uganda, and Malaysia.[3] By 1970, over 45,000 Korean workers had been exported under the "overseas contract" program. About 25,000 of these were sent to Vietnam during the war there (I. Kim, 1981: 54). With the U.S. pullout, the number of Korean workers in Vietnam declined.[4]

Labor export continued into the 1970s with the addition of the Middle East as a major new source of employment. In 1976, the first year in which this new source is mentioned, Korea planned to send 37,000 workers to Middle Eastern countries and hoped to earn $194,000 in remittances from them.[5] By the end of the decade over 50,000 Korean construction workers had been sent to the Middle East and were working on projects run by South Korean firms (I. Kim, 1981: 57).

The number of Koreans leaving the peninsula for any reason continued to rise during the 1960s. In 1962, 10,242 persons exited. By 1965, the figure had risen to 19,796.[6] Table 12 shows the exodus in the mid-1970s and, as can be seen, it exceeded the earlier figures. Those leaving included diplomats, businessmen, and visitors, as well as true emigrants. The number leaving rose at a rate of about 25 percent per year, more than doubling from 1972 to 1977. The sex ratio was heavily male, with about two men leaving for every woman, a figure that rose to almost four to one in 1977.

The major countries of destination for people leaving South Korea

Table 13.   People Leaving South Korea by Country of
Destination, Selected Years (in percents)

	1971	1975	1977
Japan	33.8	42.5	29.7
United States	27.6	35.5	26.0
Vietnam	11.8	0.0	0.0
Germany (FRG)	4.8	2.6	1.7
Saudi Arabia	0.0	3.0	19.5
Iran	0.2	1.8	3.4
Kuwait	0.0	0.0	2.7
Hong Kong	2.6	1.8	1.9
Taiwan	2.3	1.7	1.6
Paraguay	0.0	0.8	1.0
Spain	0.7	1.2	1.7
Other	16.2	9.1	10.8
	100.0	100.0	100.0
Total Number	(76,701)	(129,378)	(209,698)

Source: Republic of Korea, Economic Planning Board, *Korea Statistical Yearbook*, 1972, 1976, 1978.

in the 1970s are shown in table 13. Japan attracted the largest number while the United States was a close second. Together these two countries accounted for over half the people leaving Korea. Indeed, in some years they made up over three-quarters.

The table reveals the decline of Korean emigration to Vietnam since the U.S. evacuation. West Germany, Spain, Hong Kong, Taiwan, and Paraguay were relatively steady recipients of Koreans, although for different reasons. Germany and Spain both received Korean workers, whereas businessmen were the most important category going to Hong Kong and Taiwan. In contrast, Paraguay received mainly emigrants. Movement to Saudi Arabia, and to a lesser extent, Iran and Kuwait, rose sharply in the late 1970s. Koreans who went to these countries were almost exclusively males, who relocated under the category "employment."

The reasons given for leaving South Korea, as collected by the government for 1977, are shown in table 14 for the two major countries of destination: Japan and the United States. The first three columns show the distribution of reasons by country of destination. The largest number of Koreans (42 percent) left for temporary em-

Table 14.   People Leaving South Korea for Japan and the
United States, by Purpose of Leaving, 1977

	Percent			Males per 100 Females		
	Total	Japan	U.S.	Total	Japan	U.S.
Diplomatic	0.9	1.0	0.6	216.3	202.5	197.4
Official	3.0	3.6	3.3	725.3	698.6	1,095.3
Military	0.0	0.0	0.0	—	—	—
Business	20.2	43.8	11.5	3,800.7	5,479.8	4,839.4
Journalism	0.0	0.0	0.0	—	—	—
Study and Training	0.1	0.2	0.0	270.0	230.0	—
Employment	41.7	28.9	5.4	3,989.5	3,061.3	5,377.8
Emigration	21.0	1.7	64.8	74.6	30.8	76.0
Visit	8.0	12.9	9.8	65.6	80.1	53.6
Culture, Religion, and Sports	5.0	7.4	4.5	397.5	409.2	332.5
Other	0.1	0.4	0.0	136.1	142.0	70.0
	100.0	100.0	100.0			
Total	209,698	62,380	54,529	396.7	691.6	121.9

Source: Republic of Korea, Economic Planning Board, *Korea Statistical Yearbook*, 1978:
68–69.

ployment abroad, and another substantial proportion (20 percent),
for business. Only about one-fifth were emigrants. Those whose
destination was Japan or the United States deviated from the total
pattern. Koreans who went to Japan did so for business more than
any other reason (44 percent). A smaller proportion of Koreans went
to Japan for employment than was true for the total number of
people leaving the country (29 percent compared to 42 percent). And
only 2 percent emigrated to Japan.

Among those going to the United States, the pattern was almost
the opposite. By far the largest category, 65 percent, left Korea for
emigration. Business and employment, and indeed all other categories, were underrepresented in comparison. Thus, the total number
leaving for each of these countries masked very different kinds of
movements.

The last three columns of table 14 show the sex ratio of those
leaving. The higher the number, the more imbalanced in favor of

Table 15.   Emigrants to the United States from
South Korea, Selected Years

	Total Emigrants	Emigrants to U.S.	U.S. Percent of Total
1971	17,922	12,992	72.5
1975	35,642	29,711	83.4
1977	43,996	35,362	80.4

Source: Republic of Korea, Economic Planning Board, *Korea Statistical Yearbook*, 1972, 1976, 1978.

males, with 100.0 representing parity. Among all leavers, regardless of destination or reason for leaving, there were four men to every woman. The sex ratio leaned much more toward males among those going to Japan (close to seven to one), while it was almost at parity for those whose destination was the United States. These totals reflect, to some extent, the different reasons for leaving, since, within each reason, the sex ratio was similar regardless of country of destination. Thus, among those leaving for business or employment, the sex ratio was heavily skewed towards males. Emigrants and visitors abroad, in contrast, tended to be somewhat more famale than male. Since the United States drew emigrants, while Japan drew businessmen and employees, their total sex ratios were naturally very different.

True emigration, as opposed to leaving the country for diverse reasons, also rose over the years, though not as steadily (see table 15). Emigration almost doubled from 1971 to 1975 and rose another 35 percent in the following year, only to decline a bit in 1977. Emigration to the United States followed a similar pattern. Table 15 reveals a startling fact: while the United States accounted for slightly over one-third of the numbers leaving South Korea for all reasons, it accounted for over 80 percent of all real emigrants. In other words, the United States was by far the major destination of Koreans who wanted to leave their homeland on a permanent basis.

In sum, the post-World War II movement of Koreans abroad was a phenomenon that began as a trickle in the mid-1960s and grew massive in the 1970s. Between 1962 and 1979, 376,000 Koreans left their homeland. By 1982, approximately 10 percent of the world's Koreans resided abroad (Chol, 1982). Some of this movement was

encouraged by the Korean government in the form of labor exporting. Much of it reflected Korea's increased involvement in the world
economy, with a rise in business-related travel reflecting the shift.
True emigration also rose dramatically over the period, and the large
majority of emigrants moved to the United States. For the remainder
of this chapter we narrow our focus to emigrants proper, particularly
emigrants to the United States, in an attempt to understand why
people emigrated and who the emigrants were.

CAUSES OF EMIGRATION

Our theory leads us to predict that U.S. economic, political, and
military involvement created important dislocations in the South
Korean political economy, inducing certain classes of people to seek
to emigrate. Readiness to emigrate, however, was by no means the
only qualification for actually leaving. Legal constraints on both sides
of the Pacific determined which of those desiring to leave would
ultimately emigrate. Korean emigration law and U.S. immigration
law formed an overlapping grid through which the potential emigrant had to squeeze, and many who would have left if they could
were screened out by one or the other set of legal constraints.

Only certain classes of Koreans could obtain an immigrant visa to
the United States. The U.S. immigration system, and its effects on
Koreans, is described in detail in chapter 5. Very briefly, U.S. law
severely restricted the number of annual entrants per country of origin. Among those permitted to enter, U.S. law showed preference for
professionals and skilled workers in short supply in the United States
and particularly favored relatives of U.S. citizens and permanent
residents. Unskilled laborers were admitted only when the preferred
categories had not exhausted the quota. Thus, even though U.S.
involvement in South Korea may have helped to create a large pool
of dislocated peasants who sought to emigrate to the United States,
they could not, by and large, gain entrance to the United States.

Korean emigration law was far less restrictive than U.S. immigration law. Nevertheless, the Republic of Korea regulated emigration
to some extent. In addition to limits on draft resisters (I. Kim, 1981:
42), convicts, diseased persons, and so forth, the Korean government
prohibited emigration for two "social" categories. First was the
elite—former National Assembly members, military officials above
the level of colonel, government bureaucrats above the position of

bureau director, and persons with personal property valued over $100,000. Currency restrictions, limiting emigrants to taking only $2,000 per adult and $1,000 per child, further aimed to restrain the exodus of the prominent and wealthy. The second major restricted category was political dissidents and/or those who might injure the national reputation abroad. In both cases people who might otherwise want to leave, such as disaffected capitalists or critics of the government, were excluded from the pool of potential emigrants.

Despite these efforts, many prominent and wealthy Koreans managed to emigrate to the United States and many smuggled out considerable sums of money (I. Kim, 1981: 64–69; Koo and Yu, 1981: 22). One sensational example of money smuggling occurred in 1981 when the President of the Korean Association of Southern California was arrested at the airport in Seoul for carrying $158,000 in $100 bills in his luggage.[7] South Korean newspapers developed a special disparaging term for these prominent emigrants, calling them "runaways" (I. Kim, 1981: 37).

In contrast, political dissidents apparently had a more difficult time obtaining permission to emigrate. In our interviews we heard stories of people denied passports because relatives were critical of the Park regime. Some Korean emigrants probably left their homeland for political reasons, but few were willing to admit it. The very desire to leave may have muted criticisms. Thus the recent exodus did not have a frankly political character.

In sum, in looking at emigration patterns we note that a particular social system may squeeze certain segments of a population, and these ought to be the most ready for emigration. But simultaneously, the legal stipulations set by population-exporting and -importing countries may permit only some of the affected to relocate. Actual emigration will thus bear only partial resemblance to homeland dislocation. In the remainder of this section we focus on dislocation rather than on actual emigration. Our goal is to uncover who the potential Korean emigrants were, even if not all of them were legally able to move.

DISLOCATION

While individual Koreans may have wanted to emigrate for a whole host of idiosyncratic reasons, as with other major migrations, there were also systemic reasons why Koreans left their homeland to settle in the United States. These reasons involved massive dislocations in a changing South Korea such that some individuals and families found their situation there increasingly untenable. Dislocations arose in Korea for two major reasons: internal economic development, and Korea's position in the international system we have described in previous chapters. Since the international system largely fed into internal development, and vice-versa, we shall not attempt to disentangle them here. Rather, our goal is to examine their joint impact on dislocation. Since we are talking only of potential and not actual emigrants, our analysis is largely speculative.

Within South Korea, dislocations can be divided into two broad types: economic and political. We start by examining each of these, then proceed to show how these dislocations were not fortuitous, independent factors, but were, in fact, linked to the entire pattern of U.S.–Korean relations.

Economic Dislocations

Dramatic population growth was a central cause of economic dislocation in South Korea. Between 1949 and 1975, the Korean population grew 72 percent, an average of 2.8 percent yearly. At the end of the 1960s, Clare and associates (1969) already declared that the population of South Korea was "in excess of the support capability of Korea's resources." Between 1970 and 1975, the population increased at an annual rate of 1.8 percent. However, compared to other developing countries, South Korea did not have an extraordinarily high rate of population increase. For instance, Brazil's growth rate was 3.0 percent per annum, while Mexico's was 3.5. On the other hand, compared to developed countries like the United States (0.8 percent) or Japan (1.2 percent), South Korea's population was growing rapidly (Republic of Korea, 1977: 542–543).

The true significance of Korean population growth resided in density rather than growth rate. By 1975, South Korea was one of the most densely populated countries of the world, with a population of 351 per square kilometer. In comparison, the United States had 23 residents per square kilometer, the USSR had 11, Brazil had 13, and Mexico, 30. Even India had only 182. South Korea was comparable in population density to the countries of Western Europe, such as the Netherlands (334), Belgium (321), and to a lesser extent, Britain (229), and West Germany (249). Even Japan had a lower density (298 per square kilometer) than Korea.[8] While overpopulation can only be gauged relative to a territory's resources and economic development, at least on the surface it appears that Korea had a population problem. Population growth could spur emigration. Of course we should recognize that population growth was not independent of modernization; also, population growth reflected the general trend in so-called developing societies.

As we saw in chapter 3, capitalist development in South Korea, as in many Third World countries, was accompanied by rural decline. The capitalization of agriculture led to a concentration in landholdings, while government price controls on agricultural products made farming less viable to the small peasant (Chong, 1975: 7). Consequently, segments of the rural population were forced off the land and into the cities in search of a livelihood.

The result of rural exodus to the cities, as elsewhere in the Third World, was unemployment, underemployment, a swollen service sector, and metropolitan shanty towns. In chapter 3 we saw that, despite official government statistics, which claimed a very low unemployment rate, high proportions of Koreans who were being displaced from the rural areas could not find stable employment in the urban economy. Many of these people were likely to contribute to the pool of potential emigrants.

Another aspect of South Korea's economic development was a large increase in general level of public education. Between 1970 and 1977 the number of junior college, college, and university students increased 12.1 percent yearly.[9] In roughly the same period, the nation's population increased only 2 percent yearly. As discussed earlier, by the 1970s South Korea had a population whose educational level was exceptionally high relative to the economic development of the country. Un- and underemployment was common among college graduates. In particular, Korea had difficulty absorbing the rapidly expanding numbers of health professionals produced in her own schools and hospitals.

The production of highly trained professionals in Third World countries who then move to the advanced capitalist countries was part of a widely recognized phenomenon, the "brain drain" (Glaser, 1978; Oh, 1977; Portes, 1976; Portes and Walton, 1981: 37−41). The reasons for this exodus were complex, but apparently connected to the workings of the world capitalist system. Thus, part of the reason for a boom in the training of health professionals in countries like South Korea was the establishment of training facilities under Western influence or with Western aid. The training provided, however, followed a model more suitable to conditions in advanced capitalist countries than in poor, developing societies. For instance, doctors sometimes received training in the use of advanced technology that hospitals in the home country could not afford, or they were socialized to value research that their country could not sustain.

The distribution aspects of Korean society exacerbated this condition, by funding little but the most routine health care to the masses of the population. Thus, a discrepancy arose between the aspirations of newly trained professionals and their prospects for putting their training into practice. That salary discrepancies between the home country and countries like the United States were also huge merely added to the attractions of emigration.

Finally, another class that was likely to be experiencing economic dislocation was the national bourgeoisie, or indigenous capitalists oriented to the national market. This class was hurt by foreign investment and foreign competition, especially when foreign firms received special breaks from the government. Similarly, the advantages given to entrepreneurs who produced for export were likely to be harmful to those who concentrated on the national market. While selective benefits for exporters may have led some capitalists to switch, others may have been unable to enter the export trade (Breidenstein, 1974: 239).

In sum, South Korea was experiencing economic dislocation as a result of internal capitalist development, as well as participation in the world capitalist system. The classes most likely to be dislocated, and therefore to have most incentive to emigrate, were: capitalists who produced for the local market and who had to compete with foreign investors, educated white-collar workers who could not find jobs commensurate with their training, and the urban underemployed who ran marginal businesses, worked irregularly or not at all, and who probably included a sizable group of displaced rural people who had recently moved to the towns and cities.

Apart from dislocated persons, one would expect that South Korea's position in the international system itself would spur emigration. That Korean wages and work conditions were kept artificially low was an important source of worker discontent. The contrast with the high wage levels and favorable work conditions in the United States was striking and served as a lure to Korean workers. As we have seen earlier, this wage discrepancy was not fortuitous: U.S. capital was active in helping to keep Korean labor cheap relative to U.S. labor. A paradoxical consequence was that at least some workers wished to move from one country to the other.

Political Dislocation

Several aspects of South Korea's political situation stimulated Korean emigration (Han, 1973: 5). The most obvious was the questionable future of an independent, noncommunist country. The fact that the country was divided, that both sides were armed, that there had been a war in the past, that U.S. military support occasionally wavered, and that the country was located in a region where noncommunist regimes had been toppling led many South Koreans to doubt the country's future as a noncommunist state. Indeed, many residents of South Korea were refugees from North Korea. In 1977 North Korean exiles made up about 14 percent of the South Korean population. According to Illsoo Kim (1981: 35), North Korean refugees would have special motives for wanting to emigrate: they were more fearful of war than most, and they had weaker kinship and other ties to the South where they were now residing. However, for all South Koreans regardless of origin, the threat of war would be an important motivation to emigrate.

The dictatorial character of the Park regime also contributed to emigration. We have little firm evidence on the point but can speculate which types of people would suffer most. First would be professionals and students, or the intelligentsia, who valued civil liberties highly. South Korea had experienced major student uprisings, a testimony to the discontent of this class. Another group likely to resent the dictatorship was independent capitalists. The Park regime was a kind of state capitalism, intervening heavily in the economy, rewarding political allies, and punishing political foes by denying business opportunities. Those who resisted government intrusion were likely to face ruin and might consider emigration.

Park's state capitalism probably hurt not only the independent capitalists, but also classes from the previous mode of production.

We have seen that numerous peasants were dislocated. So too were major landholders and their families. Although this category would fall under economic dislocation as well, we regard it as primarily political because it represented a change in the ruling class, mediated by the state. The Park government's actions took power away from the landed aristocracy and granted it to capitalists, and in so doing, stripped the landlords of their patriotism.

Another category of potential political emigrants were Christians.[10] Park's authoritarian regime encouraged reform of the country's Confucian traditions, thought to inhibit industrialization, but Park also opposed Westernization, and in particular, liberal Christianity. For their part, the liberal clergy were among the most outspoken of Park's critics, and while our research was in progress dozens were incarcerated for political crimes (S. Kim, 1975). A Korean clergyman in Los Angeles explained that Park objected to activist Christianity, but was prepared to tolerate evangelical religion free of political content. None of the Koreans we interviewed complained of religious persecution in South Korea. Nonetheless, Christians had a motive for leaving a society in which their religion was officially disapproved, in favor of the United States where their religious affiliations were mainstream. In 1976, 22 percent of Koreans residing in South Korea were Christian, and this percentage was twice as high as a decade earlier.[11] In the same year, 50 to 80 percent of Koreans residing in major U.S. cities were Christians, an indicator of overrepresentation and self-selection of Christians for migration to the United States.

Finally, the most politically dislocated class was the working class. Denied the right to organize freely to protect themselves, and kept in the position of cheap labor, many Koreans workers must have been eager to escape from a regime that suppressed them. Of course, the cheap labor role acted as a curb on emigration, too, because workers often lacked the resources for international relocation.

The United States must have been an especially attractive destination for the politically dislocated because it apparently represented the polar opposite of South Korea, politically. There was no prospect that the U.S. government would fall or that the country would be seriously threatened with a communist invasion. Civil liberties were more protected, and there was generally a greater air of freedom, including religious freedom. Labor was free to organize politically to protect itself. All these features would lead those classes most hurt by

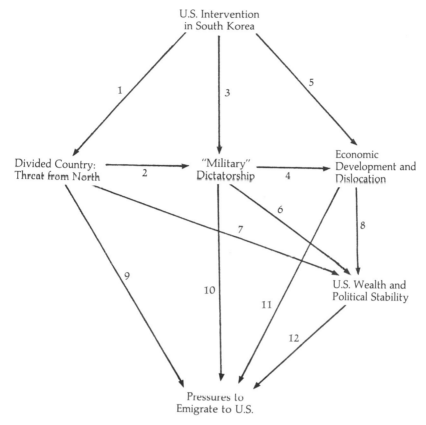

Figure 3 Causes of Emigration from South Korea to the United States

these issues in South Korea to view the United States as a political haven.

THE INTERNATIONAL SYSTEM AND EMIGRATION

So far economic and political dislocations have been treated as more or less discrete factors contributing to the potential emigration of Koreans to the United States. Figure 3 shows how these forces were interconnected and grew out of the relations between the two countries within the international capitalist system.

In figure 3, we start with U.S. intervention in South Korea at the end of World War II (arrow 1), leading to the creation of a divided country and the continuing possibility of war between the two Koreas. The dangerous position of South Korea helped justify a military takeover and dictatorship (arrow 2), and even though the Park regime lost its overt military character towards the end, it retained dictatorial control—justified, in part, by the need to deal quickly and effectively with the threat from the North. The regime was also bolstered by the United States (arrow 3) as we have examined at length in chapter 2, in part to make use of Korea's cheap labor.

The Park government was, of course, very active in developing South Korea economically, along capitalist lines, with resultant dislocations of certain classes in Korean society (arrow 4). These dislocations were exacerbated by the activity of foreign capital in the country (arrow 5).[12]

Perhaps the most controversial aspect of the international system was its impact on the United States. A case can be made that both the economic advantages of living in the United States, and some of its political features, such as stability and democracy, were dependent upon their negation in countries like South Korea (arrows 6, 7, and 8). This is perhaps clearer on the political side, where the propping up of a military dictatorship on one of the frontiers of communism (arrow 3) provided the United States with a buffer against having to face a frontier itself (arrow 7), thereby allowing it considerably more internal flexibility. On the economic side it can be argued that imperialist activity in South Korea (arrow 5) earned U.S. capitalists huge profits, some of which made the United States a wealthier, more desirable society in which to live (arrow 8).[13]

Several features of this system generated pressures toward emigration. First of all, military threat from the North (arrow 9) made living in South Korea potentially dangerous. Second, the dictatorial aspects of the regime made it politically oppressive to live there (arrow 10). Third, economic development and foreign imperialism drove some people to seek to leave (arrow 11). And finally, to the degree that the international system provided benefits to the United States, so it would attract residents from countries like South Korea who sought to escape the very conditions on which U.S. wealth and political freedom depended (arrow 12).

Not all emigration from South Korea was of a negative character. Not everyone was "escaping from" or "fleeing to." Some Koreans left for positive reasons, though their migration was also generated by the international system. For example, the tremendous growth in trade between the two countries led some Koreans to move to the United States to promote and take advantage of trading opportunities.

Regardless of the detailed intervening processes that led to a rise in Korean emigration to the United States, one cannot but be struck by the coincidence of the rise in manufactured exports from South Korea to the United States and the rise in emigration. Both shifts began in the mid-1960s and rose rapidly thereafter. Many explanations can undoubtedly be adduced to account for this coincidence. In our view, both processes were rooted in the emergence of a proletariat (that is, free wage labor) in South Korea and reflect U.S. capitalist efforts to make use of this labor force. This emergence was partly a product of internal development in South Korea, but U.S. capitalist involvement there (backed by political and military involvement) contributed substantially to the process of proletarianization and thus to the loosening of Koreans for work in U.S. invested plants and firms specializing in manufactured imports, and for emigration. Finally, the U.S. presence contributed to the harsh conditions of political and economic life in the republic, which made it both a fertile ground for profitable investment and trade and provided an impetus for emigration.

CLASS BACKGROUND OF THE EMIGRANTS

So far we have considered those classes in South Korea which experienced dislocations as a result of internal economic development and imperialist involvement in their country. These dislocated people, we have argued, were the most likely candidates for emigration. In this section we briefly examine the class character of the people who actually made it to the United States. As mentioned before, only a select group of the potential pool of emigrants were able to work their way through the legal barriers set up on both sides of the Pacific.

The U.S. Immigration and Naturalization Service (INS) collected information on the occupation of immigrants on arrival. Unfortunately, INS data were limited to persons with immigrant visas, thus missing a segment of the emigrant community. Moreover, their question failed to differentiate between occupation in the homeland and intended occupation in the United States. Besides, since many people arrived under quotas specifying relatedness to U.S. citizens and permanent residents, they had no motive for revealing their occupation. Thus, INS data are of limited value in examining the class background of the emigrants. Nevertheless, we shall examine these data in chapter 5 when we consider U.S. immigration policy and practice.

To our knowledge, no systematic study has been conducted on the class background in Korea of the emigrants to the United States. However, based on impressions, newspaper accounts, a few surveys of the immigrant community, and faulty INS data, several beliefs about the character of the emigrants have emerged. For instance, it is believed that most immigrants were highly educated; that many were originally refugees from North Korea who fled South during the Korean War; that a sizable proportion came via other countries (notably West Germany and Vietnam) where they had been working as miners or nurses; that most were urban dwellers, especially from Seoul; that they tended to be professionals in South Korea; that most came with some money; and that a higher than average number were Christian. It has also been widely asserted that their principal goal in coming to the United States was to provide their children with educational opportunities. Generally, they were not believed to be political refugees so much as people concerned about the future stability of the country given the threat from the North. And they were viewed as largely permanent immigrants rather than sojourners, planning to return to Korea to live only if conditions proved to be unbearable here.

An example of the common wisdom comes from an article in the *San Francisco Chronicle*:

> The Korean population in Los Angeles County consists principally of two categories of immigrants. The first group includes many middle-class and upper-class Koreans seeking better economic opportunities here. Many were related to Korean war brides, and some had fled the Park regime. The second and more recent group includes many well-to-do Korean businessmen who do not necessarily oppose the current government but are seeking a refuge for money because of fears that the Park regime might collapse or that there might be a Communist takeover of South Korea.[14]

The article cited "banking officials and other people" who claimed that hundreds of wealthy Koreans were smuggling money out of South Korea and purchasing real estate worth over $100,000 per transaction with cash, sometimes out of a paper bag.

Although systematic data are unavailable on these questions, we did conduct a telephone survey of business owners (appendix 1) in which a few questions were asked regarding background in Korea. Our data must be viewed with caution since they do not represent a random sample of the Los Angeles Korean community. Rather, they represent people whose businesses were listed in the yellow pages of the Korean community's telephone directory, and who were willing to talk to our interviewer. Apart from possible errors introduced by nonresponse, and by incomplete listing by the directory, the survey only aimed at business owners and managers and excluded employees.

Allowing for these deficiencies, our respondents revealed the following background characteristics. Out of 152 who answered the question, 97 percent came from Seoul. We did not ask how many originally derived from North Korea, but we did inquire if they had lived in another country before coming to the United States. Twenty-three said yes but, contrary to the common wisdom, seventeen of these came from Latin American countries. The remainder came from Vietnam, Germany, Japan, and Canada.

Unfortunately, we neglected to ask about their own occupation before emigration, except to inquire whether the respondent had owned a business in South Korea. Of 177 who answered this question, 18 percent answered yes, a level that indicates that most of the emigrants were not entrepreneurs in their homeland. Since the question was only addressed to people who were currently engaged in small business, it is likely that they had a higher rate of entrepreneurship in their homeland than the average Korean immigrant. In any case, even among Korean small businessmen here, 82 percent did not have a business background in South Korea. Of those who did own a business in Korea, we asked whether that business had employed more than five workers. Of twenty-three who answered, twelve (52 percent) had employed under five, while the remainder had employed over five. In the main, a business background in South Korea meant small, perhaps marginal, business.

The business owners were asked about their fathers' occupations, a better indicator of class origins than the occupation of the emigrant, in that it indicates historic class roots. A small number (10.6 percent) were from farming or peasant backgrounds. Similarly, fathers were neither unskilled laborers nor the unemployed, and only a small proportion (12.5 percent) were skilled workers. The bulk of the emigrant entrepreneurs we interviewed were from white-collar and professional families (51 percent), confirming this common belief. That the largest occupation was "white collar" rather than professional (35.0 versus 15.6 percent) suggests that they were not from the most elite occupations. Eighteen percent came from business-owning families, a figure that corresponds exactly with the number of emigrants who themselves owned a business in Korea, suggesting a degree of intergenerational continuity. Finally, 6 percent were peddlers, an occupation that suggests an adaptation to urban unemployment. In sum, these data suggest that Korean emigrants were not displaced rural people, as were pre–World War II Chinese, Japanese, and Pilipino immigrants, but rather, were members of the urban middle class.

This result is confirmed by their level of education. In our sample, only two people had not completed high school. Three-quarters were college graduates or higher. Although some of these immigrants may have completed their education in the United States, most were probably educated in South Korea.

Respondents were asked why they had left South Korea. Some gave more than one reason and table 16 presents them all, leading to more reasons than respondents. Economic reasons predominated, constituting 42 percent of all the reasons given. In contrast, political reasons were much less articulated, making up only 13 percent of the total. This result corroborates earlier impressions that this emigration was not mainly political. We should not forget, however, that Korean emigration law prohibited the emigration of people whose departure was deemed harmful to the republic. Emigrants had a motive for minimizing their overt political dissidence, if only to escape the country. And they might continue to keep quiet about political motives for fear of repercussions for family members still living in Korea.

Compared to political motives, family reasons were highly ranked. About one-fifth of the reasons given concerned providing better advantages to their children. Unspecified in these data, conversations

Table 16.   Reasons Given for Emigrating to the
United States

Reasons for Emigrating	Number	Percent
Economic		
For a better life	96	36.6
To get rich quickly	14	5.3
Political		
Escape political repression	14	5.3
Danger from North	12	4.6
Freedom	5	1.9
Refugee	4	1.5
Family		
Children's benefit	52	19.8
To join family	31	11.8
Other		
To study	31	11.8
To visit	2	0.8
To escape religious persecution	1	0.4
Total	262	100.0

Source: Appendix 1.

with Korean immigrants suggested that better advantages mainly meant educational opportunities. Finally, the "other" category included students and visitors who apparently decided to remain as immigrants after their initial goals had been achieved.

As stated earlier, we had inferred that this was not a sojourning immigration and that most Koreans who came here planned to settle permanently. We were, therefore, surprised to discover in interviews that this was not fully the case. Asked if they intended to return to Korean, 20 percent said yes, and another 17 percent planned to go back to visit. Only 33 percent replied that they definitely did not plan to return, while a rather high 30 percent had not made up their minds. If we combine the definite "yes" with the "don't know" responses, well over half of the sample could return to South Korea.

In sum, according to this limited evidence, emigrants from South Korea who came to the United States were mainly from the urban middle class, primarily seeking economic betterment for themselves and their children. They may have had political reasons for leaving as well, but these were likely to be under the surface, and they did not prevent a substantial proportion from contemplating an eventual return to South Korea.

It would appear that there is only a moderate correspondence between the dislocations caused by South Korea's position in the world capitalist system and the emigrants who actually emigrated to the United States. From the limited evidence we were able to collect, no firm conclusions can be drawn that prove our hypothesis. Nevertheless, there is some correspondence between the character of the emigrants as far as we were able to ascertain it and the classes dislocated by world capitalism in Korea.

First, at least some Korean immigrants came to the United States with considerable amounts of money. Part of the bourgeoisie was leaving its homeland. Whether these people were more likely to be members of a disgruntled national bourgeoisie who felt they were being displaced by the international orientation of their government we cannot say. The point deserves further investigation.

Second, it appears that the bulk of the emigrants were from the urban middle class. As we noted above, several forces were exerting pressure on this class in South Korea. Some were receiving training in the health professions and similar service occupations for which there were not sufficient positions commensurate with their training. This lack of positions, as we saw in chapter 3, was related to the Korean government's policies of social distribution, as well as to U.S involvement in the creation of educational institutions with training programs more appropriate to the needs of more advanced capitalist countries.

Another pressure on the urban middle class was the lack of civil liberties under authoritarian, militaristic regimes. Many emigrants had received a college education in South Korea, where they had been exposed to a student movement calling for the institution of democratic government. The educated and professionals were more likely to chafe under the political restrictions that were a concomitant of South Korea's position as a repository of cheap labor for international capital.

Finally, even though middle-class Koreans were economically better off than many of their compatriots, the discrepancy between what they could earn in South Korea and what they could earn in the United States was vast. Apart from the most wealthy stratum, the whole Korean economy was relatively depressed in its wage and salary level. As we have tried to show, this was a product not only of the internal level of development, but was also artifically created through repression.

Two dislocated classes significantly absent from the emigrants were impoverished workers and peasants. These were the classes most severely affected by the role South Korea had chosen to play in the international economy. One would expect them to be the most likely of all to try to escape through emigration. Certainly there are many historical instances of migration by these classes from Third World countries. But in Korea's case at least two forces prohibited it. First, the impoverished typically lack the wherewithal to migrate overseas no matter how much they want to. In the present day, with exceedingly costly means of international transportation, the ability to move is confined to those who can raise the cash. Of course, if American entrepreneurs wanted to import Korean workers in large numbers, they would find a way to finance the movement. However, the second force limiting this particular movement was U.S. immigration law. The poverty-stricken were simply not permitted entrance into the United States. That U.S. capital tolerated such a law and did not actively seek to evade it in the case of Koreans can perhaps be attributed to the fact that employers received an adequate supply of impoverished labor from south of the border. U.S. immigration law was unable to prevent displaced peasants and unskilled workers from entering the country from Latin America, but it could stop such immigration from elsewhere in the Third World.

Nevertheless, once a Korean professional stratum had established itself in the United States, the law was more easily manipulated. Family preferences allowed less-educated and less-middle-class Koreans to join their more established relatives as the immigration process wore on. Thus it is likely that at least some of the dislocated poor were able to make their way to the United States by the end of the 1970s.

Despite their predominantly middle-class origins, people leaving South Korea were still a type of cheap labor migration to the United States. In part four we shall examine this aspect in detail. For now let us simply note that the tremendous discrepancies in wages and salaries, hours of work per week, level of unionization and strike activity, paternalistic ties to employers, fringe benefits, social welfare programs, and government support of labor organization between the two countries meant that emigrants from South Korea came to the United States with very different experiences and expectations than the average U.S. worker. Korean experience would lead them to expect hard work, and even low U.S. wages and salaries looked relatively desirable. This discrepancy was an important part of the lure of this country to Korean emigrants. Yet the discrepancy also gave immigrants an orientation to work that differentiated them from native workers, long exposed to the benefits of an active labor movement. In this sense, Korean immigrants were the kind of workers U.S. capitalists were likely to welcome. Just as Korean labor was cheap and desirable to U.S. capital on Korean soil, so the same workers were cheap and desirable in this country.

CONCLUSION

When one examines emigration from South Korea to the United States, one fact is clear: the emigration, which began in the mid-1960s and grew to large proportions in the 1970s, was paralleled by a simultaneous growth in South Korean integration in the world capitalist economy. The United States was one of the foremost nations active in bringing Korea into the orbit of world capitalism. Through trade, investment, and economic and military aid, the U.S. played a vital role in shaping Korean development. The Korean government itself was, of course, the direct creator and implementor of most policies. Yet U.S. aid and involvement in the peninsula helped to mold the kind of regime established there.

It is our hypothesis that emigration from South Korea to the United States in the late 1960s and 1970s was causally connected to Korea's involvement in world capitalism. In particular, the economic and political consequences of Korea's role as a producer of cheap manufactured exports led to the dislocation and discontent of certain classes. Those who emigrated derived from these dislocated classes. We recognize that we have not proven this case beyond doubt. Our evidence is admittedly circumstantial. Still, our argument explains the basic paradox of Korean emigration: its tremendous growth even at a time when all economic indicators appear to have pointed to considerable Korean economic development. Hundreds of thousands of Koreans uprooted themselves to come and live in the United States during the period 1965–1980. They obviously did not do so only for personal reasons. Something systemic was going on. Our circumstantial evidence suggests what it was.

The most interesting aspect of our hypothesis is that it lays ultimate responsibility for the emigration at the door of the United States. The United States plays an important role in driving immigrants to its own doors. When the United States shuts its doors to certain kinds of immigrants, it often is imposing a barrier against a movement that the United States itself stimulated. This point extends beyond South Korea, of course. In any case, immigration policy does not exist in a vacuum—much as politicians would like to keep it there. It is intimately tied to foreign policy, including economic aid, trade, cultural influence, military assistance, and political interference. U.S. foreign policy in South Korea (as in many other countries) has a direct and indirect impact on the migration of peoples to this country.

PART THREE

KOREAN BUSINESS IN LOS ANGELES

5

Immigration And Settlement

Prior to 1965, U.S. immigration law favored applicants from northern and western Europe. The countries of Asia, including Korea, came under continuing restrictions reflecting a century of exclusionary legislation. This legislation began with the exclusion of Chinese in 1882. There followed a gentlemen's agreement negotiated with Japan in 1907–1908 that limited Japanese emigration to the United States and the establishment of a "barred zone" across much of Asia in 1917. Exclusionary policy toward Asian immigration prior to World War II came to fruition in 1924 (Garis, 1927: 128–130, 286–354; Bennett, 1963: 15–29). Also known as the Oriental Exclusion Act of 1924, the Johnson-Reed Immigration act set quotas for most nationalities but specifically declared natives of the Asian barred zone to be inadmissible as immigrants.[1] With a minor modification in 1952, exclusion remained U.S. policy until 1965.

EARLY KOREAN IMMIGRANTS

Despite legal restrictions, some Koreans entered the United States prior to 1965. Starting in 1883, the first Koreans to come were diplomats, political refugees, students, and merchants.[2] No more than fifty Koreans came in the nineteenth century. Larger-scale immigration began in 1902. Between 1902 and 1905 some 7000 Koreans were brought to Hawaii as plantation laborers, 1000 of whom subsequently moved to the mainland.[3]

The immigration of Koreans ended when Japan first invaded, then annexed, Korea in 1910. Japan denied passports to Koreans wishing to emigrate to the United States (Warren Y. Kim, 1971: 4; Melendy, 1977: 126–127), although Japan did permit over 1000 picture brides to join their husbands, mainly in Hawaii, between 1910 and 1924 (Melendy, 1977: 127–128; Moon, 1976: 120–131). Between 1905

Table 17.   Koreans in the United States, California, and
Los Angeles: 1910–1980

	U.S.	California		Los Angeles	
		Number	Percentage	Number	Percentage
1980	354,529	103,891	29.3	60,618	17.1
1970	69,510	15,909	22.9	8,811	12.7
1940	1,711	1,088	63.6	482	25.1
1930	1,860	1,097	59.0		
1920	1,224	772	63.0		
1910	462	104	22.5		

Sources: U.S. Bureau of the Census, *U.S. Census of Population, 1920,* vol. II, *General Report and Analytical Tables* (Washington, D.C.: USGPO): 107; *U.S. Census Population, 1930,* vol. II, *General Report, Statistics by Subjects* (Washington, D.C.: USGPO): 98; *U.S. Census of Population, 1940,* vol. II, *Minor Races in Cities over 100,000* (Washington, D.C.: USGPO): 14; *U.S. Census of Population, 1970,* vol. II, *Subject Reports, Japanese, Chinese, and Filipinos in the United States* (Washington, D.C.: USGPO); *1980 Census of Population, Supplementary Reports, PC 80-3. Race of the Population by States, 1980* (Washington, D.C.: USGPO, 1981): table 7.

and 1909 Japan denied passports to nonimmigrant Korean students who wished to study in the United States. Japan suspected that the expatriates would foment anti-Japanese agitation. However, after 1909, Japan permitted a few students to study in the United States. In addition, about 500 political refugees came without passports between 1910 and 1918, helping to form a core of anti-Japanese activism in the United States (Melendy, 1977: 128–129; Choy, 1979: 78–79, 141–189; Lyu, 1977). The total number of students and political refugees entering before World War I did not exceed 900 (Yu, 1977: 118–119).

Ironically, Koreans in the United States were treated as Japanese and subjected to anti-Japanese agitation. Founded in 1905, the Asiatic Exclusion League was first known as the Japanese and Korean Exclusion League (Daniels, 1966: 27, 126). The presidential order of 1907, the gentlemen's agreement, and the 1924 Oriental Exclusion Act—all measures aimed primarily at the Japanese—restricted Korean immigration too. As result, only a small Korean community was established in the United States prior to the World War II. The number of Koreans on the mainland never exceeded 2000 and declined after 1930, presumably as a result of return migration (table 17). Koreans on the mainland clustered on the Pacific Coast, particularly in California. However, Hawaii remained the major Korean concentration, with four times as large a Korean population as the entire mainland.

Turn-of-the-century Korean immigrants on the mainland worked primarily in farm labor, construction, and mining. Some became independent farmers despite Alien Land Laws, which denied land ownership to "aliens ineligible for citizenship," a legal category reserved for Asian immigrants. A small urban population emerged, particularly in Los Angeles, which quickly became the American center of Korean concentration. The census counted 14 Koreans in Los Angeles in 1910, 84 in 1920, 345 in 1930, and 482 in 1940. These figures probably undercounted Koreans since Givens' (1939: 31) study of the Los Angeles Korean community enumerated 650 Koreans. Some urban Koreans can small businesses (Yim, 1981; Choy, 1979: 129–133; Moon, 1976: 15–200). In Los Angeles, Givens (1939: 48) enumerated seventy-three such enterprises, of which thirty-three were fruit and vegetable stands.

The McCarran-Walter Immigration and Nationality Act of 1952 reformed immigration Law. Reformed law granted Asian immigrants the right to naturalization. National origins quotas were retained, but all countries, including those of Asia, received an annual minimum of 100 immigrants. However, although quotas were charged to the country of birth of an alien, in the case of the "Asia-Pacific triangle," which encompassed all countries from Pakistan to Japan and Pacific islands north of Australia and New Zealand, an alien's race was taken into account. If 50 percent or more of his or her ancestors derived from a triangle country, the immigrant was charged against the small quota allotted to his or her country of ancestry, regardless of place of birth.[4]

Despite the limitation, the Korean War (1950–1953) introduced some Koreans under special statuses. Between 1950 and 1964, an average of 2834 Koreans entered the United States annually of whom 35.4 percent were immigrants (H.-C. Kim, 1977: 111). Most immigrants were military wives or war orphans. Both categories were treated as immediate relatives of U.S. citizens and thus not subject to quota exclusion (B.-L. Kim, 1977, 1978; D.-S. Kim, 1978; Hurh and K. Kim, 1980: 28–29). Nonimmigrants included an estimated 6000 students (Melendy, 1977: 130; Hurh and K. Kim, 1980: 47), as well as political refugees and visitors. An unknown number of nonimmigrants shifted their status to immigrant.

IMMIGRATION ACT OF 1965

The 1965 Immigration and Nationality Act overturned the discriminatory aspects of the McCarren-Walter Act, abolishing the Asia-Pacific triangle and all other differentiation based on national origins. In their place, the 1965 Act distinguished between the Eastern and Western hemispheres, the latter encompassing the Americas, and the former all else. An annual limit of 170,000 immigrants was established for the Eastern hemisphere, and 120,000 for the Western. Eastern hemisphere nationals were subject to an eight-level preference system, whereas Western hemisphere residents were accepted in order of application. In addition, the 1965 legislation gave each country in the Eastern hemisphere an annual limit of 20,000.[5] In 1976 Congress amended the law again to bring the Western hemisphere in line with the Eastern, and to impose a preference system in the Western hemisphere too. Since Korea falls within the Eastern hemisphere, the 1976 amendments did not alter the situation of immigrants from Korea. Finally, a 1978 amendment abolished the distinction between Eastern and Western hemispheres and set a worldwide ceiling of 290,000.[6]

Why was the immigration law changed at all and why in 1965? Promoting Korean immigration was not a consideration. Politics was. The political roots of policy change antedate 1965, coinciding with the emergence of the United States as the world's leading power after World War II. Although the McCarran-Walter Act perpetuated a discriminatory immigration policy, political opposition to this policy had already surfaced in 1952. Indeed, President Truman vetoed the McCarran-Walter Act on the grounds that it was discriminatory—but Congress overrode Truman.[7] Between 1952 and 1965 Congress passed numerous exceptions to the law so that the national origins principle remained more alive in law than in practice. For instance, testifying before a House subcommittee, Secretary of State Dean Rusk (1964: 388) pointed out that, despite discriminatory quotas, in the period 1953–1963, fully 119,677 immigrants had arrived from China, Japan, and the Philippines. Nonetheless, "national origins" remained official U.S. policy. When the civil rights movement grabbed world headlines in the early 1960s, domestic racism tarnished the United States' image abroad. In the Cold War context, loss of reputation abroad was embarrassing, and politicians jettisoned racist immigration laws in order to halt the embarrassment (Trussell, 1964a, 1964b).

The war in Vietnam increased the urgency of immigration reform. As the United States waded into a lonely and unpopular war against an Asian adversary, the racist implications of the immigration law provided arguments for Hanoi's propagandists. At the Congressional hearings of 1964 and 1965, prominent witnesses stressed the undesirable foreign policy consequences of the McCarran-Walter immigration law. According to Secretary of State Dean Rusk (1965: 88): "We are concerned to see that our immigration laws reflect our real character and objectives because what other people think about us plays an important role in the achievement of our foreign policies." Rusk (1965: 90) singled out the Asia-Pacific triangle as the most discriminatory aspect of the law, finding it "indefensible from a foreign policy point of view."

Manpower considerations also encouraged liberal amendments of the immigration law. Confronting increased competition in world markets, the United States experienced shortages of skilled workers in technical occupations. On the one hand, manpower experts claimed that "the slackening of expansion" in Western European countries had resulted from "manpower shortages." On the other hand, the experts foresaw "a substantial increase in demand" for "workers in the professional, technical, and managerial groups" (Walter and Wolfbein, 1962: 14, 28). In the wake of the 1957 Sputnik alarm, Congress concluded that the immigration of professional and technical workers would bolster the nation's military and industrial capability. In this sense, the importation of skilled foreigners was the counterpart to domestic programs intended to support education and training of the native born.

THE NEW IMMIGRATION

The 1965 immigration law dramatically affected immigration from Asia (table 18). In 1965, Asians comprised only 7 percent of all immigrants. Between 1965 and 1968, the transition period during which the law was eased into full effect, Asian immigration almost trebled. Thereafter, growth was steady both in absolute numbers of annual entrants and in the proportion of the total coming from Asian countries. By 1974, one-third of new immigrants came from Asia.

Table 18. Korean, Asian, and Total Immigration to the United States for Fiscal Years Ending June 30, 1965–1975, and September 30, 1976–1981

Year	Total	Asia	Korea	Asian Percent of Total	Korean Percent of Asian	Korean Percent of Total
1965	296,697	20,683	2,165	7.0	10.5	0.7
1966–1970	1,871,365	332,429	25,618	17.8	7.7	1.4
1971–1975	1,936,281	611,810	112,493	31.6	18.4	5.8
1976–1980*	2,557,029	1,001,990	159,463	39.2	15.9	6.2
1981	596,660	264,343	32,663	44.3	12.4	5.5
Total	7,258,032	2,002,256	332,402	27.6	16.6	4.6

*In 1976 the end of the fiscal year was changed from June 30 to September 30, thus the 1976 figures include an extra quarter. In all subsequent tables, unless otherwise stated, 1976 runs from July 1 to September 30.

Source: U.S. Department of Justice, Immigration and Naturalization Service, Annual Reports, 1965–1981, table 6.

Immigration from South Korea increased faster than Asian immigration in general. Table 18 shows that Korean immigration increased fifteenfold between 1965 and 1981. The Korean proportion of Asian immigrants also grew to the point where Koreans constituted about one-fifth of Asian entrants. Indeed, in between 1971 and 1981, Koreans were the fourth largest immigrant group to the United States, behind only Cuba, Mexico, and the Philippines.[8]

The distribution of Korean immigrants by preference category from 1966 to 1981 appears in table 19. Levels 1, 4, and 7 were hardly used. The exempt category declined, but levels 2 and 5 (spouses and siblings) grew dramatically, especially level 5. In contrast, the occupational quotas (3, 6, and nonpreference) showed gentler growth and tapered off after 1975. Indeed, nonpreference visas ceased to be available for Koreans.[9] Of course, the larger an immigrant group, the more relatives there are in the homeland who can take advantage of kinship preferences.

The annual immigration reports of the INS present information on the "major occupation group" of immigrants.[10] Table 20 presents these data for Koreans, 1966 to 1981. Move than seven in ten Korean immigrants were housewives, children, or had no occupation, a proportion that remained stable until 1977 and was high relative to other immigrant groups. However, among those who did report an occupation, professional, technical, and kindred workers were initially three-quarters of the Korean immigrants, compared to only one-quarter of all immigrants. After 1966, the proportion of professionals among the Koreans dropped whereas the proportion of professionals among all other immigrants remained approximately the same. Therefore, by the early 1980s, Korean immigrants included a slightly smaller proportion of professionals than did the entire population of immigrants.

In contrast, the proportion of managers, officials, and proprietors among Korean immigrants consistently increased after 1966. Though, only 3.8 percent of immigrants who declared an occupation in 1966, managers, officials, and proprietors had become 18.6 percent of Korean immigrants in 1982. In the same period, the managers' share of the United States' entire immigrant population increased from 5.3 to 10.0 percent. Therefore, Koreans were initially less frequent in the managers category than were all immigrants but, be-

Table 19. Percentage Distribution of Korean Immigrants by Preference System, 1966–1981

	1966–1968	1969–1971	1972–1974	1975–1977	1978–1980	1981	Total
Percent Exempt from Quota	62.9	43.3	30.9	34.0	37.7	39.1	37.7
Total	10,259	29,656	69,834	96,969	90,856	32,663	127,202
Preference Level (in percents)							
1. Unmarried adult children of citizens	0.08	0.2	0.1	0.1	0.2	0.2	0.1
2. Spouses	15.7	14.3	18.5	20.8	29.1	45.4	25.7
3. Professionals	55.8	10.6	11.5	13.4	5.0	4.9	10.4
4. Married children of citizens	1.3	0.4	0.3	0.4	0.9	2.6	0.8
5. Siblings	9.1	22.2	28.9	54.1	58.4	38.2	44.8
6. Skilled	17.3	16.7	8.6	4.7	3.3	8.7	7.0
7. Refugees	0.0	0.0	0.0	0.0	0.0	0.0	0.0
Nonpreference	0.8	35.4	32.2	11.3	1.8	0.1	12.1
Total	100.0	100.0	100.0	100.0	100.0	100.0	100.0
Number	(3,806)	(16,997)	(48,371)	(63,268)	(56,235)	(19,901)	208,578

Sources: U.S. Immigration and Naturalization Service, *Annual Reports*, 1966–1977: tables 6 and 7A; U.S. Immigration and Naturalization Service, *Statistical Yearbook of the Immigration and Naturalization Service*, 1979–1981: tables 1A, 7A (1979); tables 5, 6 (1980); tables 5, 6 (1981).

Table 20. "Major Occupation Group" of Korean Immigrants on Arrival, 1966–1981

	1966–1968	1969–1971	1972–1974	1975–1977	1978–1980	1981
Housewives, Children, No Occupation (in percents)	75.4	72.1	73.4	74.3	66.6	54.1
Number	(10,259)	(29,656)	(69,834)	(90,082)	(57,397)	(13,258)
Those Reporting an Occupation (in percents):						
Professional, Technical, Kindred Workers	75.2	70.1	50.6	38.4	26.8	21.1
Farmers and Farm Managers	0.1	0.1	0.1	0.4	0.1	0.0
Managers, Officials, Proprietors	3.8	5.2	12.4	12.8	18.4	20.7
Other White-Collar	8.0	6.6	7.0	14.2	14.2	13.1
Craftsmen, Foremen, Kindred Workers	1.9	6.6	14.7	13.6	11.9	10.5
Other Manual	11.0	11.3	15.0	20.5	28.3	34.7
Total	100.0	100.0	100.0	100.0	100.0	100.0
Number	(2,521)	(8,239)	(18,591)	(23,094)	(19,172)	(6,080)

Source: U.S. Immigration and Naturalization Service, Annual Reports, 1966–1977: table 8; Idem., Statistical Yearbook, 1978: table 8; 1979: table 26; 1980: table 8; 1981: table 26.

tween 1967 and 1976, they caught up with and surpassed the general immigrant population. In the next decade, 1972–1982, Korea's immigrants always contained a higher share of managers, officials, and proprietors than did the rest of the world's immigrants.

The changing occupational profile of Korean immigrants suggests the process whereby immigrant employability in American labor markets reached back to affect the immigration choices of persons still in the Korean labor force. Although U.S. law awarded preference to immigrant professionals, a decade's experience showed that American labor markets absorbed entrepreneurs more easily than salaried professionals and rewarded them better. As the news leaked back to Korea, the occupational profile of Korean immigrants changed in response to America's economic reality. At the same time, the proportional preponderance of managers, officials, and proprietors among Korean immigrants probably helps to explain the Koreans' margin of entrepreneurial superiority relative to other immigrants. The Korean immigrant labor force included a higher proportion of experienced entrepreneurs than did the rest of the world's immigrant labor force.[11]

Yet, this preponderance was not wholly the product of American economic conditions that offered, after all, the same entrepreneurial opportunities to all the world's immigrants. Korea's entrepreneurial preponderance reflected as well uniquely Korean social conditions that governed the availability for immigration and underlying supply of entrepreneurs. Although the world's cohorts of immigrants all began to shift toward experienced entrepreneurship in the 1970s, Korea's cohorts shifted more than the rest, a presumptive reflection of Korea's responsiveness to entrepreneurial opportunity in the United States. Moreover, Korea's immigrant cohorts always included a higher proportion of women and of persons reporting no prior occupation than did the rest of the world's. Even in 1982, when experienced entrepreneurs were almost 19 percent of Korean immigrants with occupations, 55 percent of Korean immigrants reported no occupation, compared with only 34 percent of all immigrants. Women also usually demonstrate lower rates of entrepreneurship than do men, and in the 1970s about 60 percent of Korean immigrants were women. Admittedly, some women immigrants and persons with no occupation stayed out of the labor force when in the United States, but many did not. As inexperienced workers and women filtered into the Korean labor force in the United States, they diluted the pool of experienced entrepreneurs, thus reducing the Korean immigrants' preponderance in respect to entrepreneurial experience.

NONIMMIGRANTS

More Koreans entered this country as nonimmigrants (that is, as tourists, students, representatives of the Korean government, agents of Korean businesses, and so forth) than as immigrants. Some nonimmigrants were able to adjust their status to immigrant once in the United States. Such adjustments reached a peak of 4238 in 1972. Students and tourists were the largest two categories of adjusters; visitors for business, and treaty traders and investors occupied third and fourth place respectively.[12] Adjusters were counted in the regular immigration statistics. Adjusters reflected movement between nonimmigrants and immigrants, suggesting that at least some nonimmigrants remained in this country even when their temporary visas expired (Yu, 1977: 118).

A few Koreans were in the United States illegally (Lee and Wagatsuma, 1979: 10–11). Unlike Mexican illegals, who evaded border controls, Asian illegals tended to be "visa abusers." Visa abusers entered the United States with nonimmigrant visas, then violated the terms of their visa by overstaying or working. Between 1970 and 1980 the Immigration and Naturalization Service (INS) apprehended 109,190 Asians illegally in the United States. Of these, 43 percent were visitors and 30 percent were students. Because INS allocated only a small staff to the nonborder area, apprehended illegals were only a fraction of the illegal population. INS reported that about one-fifth of Asian illegals were Chinese and another fifth were Filipinos, but INS did not provide a profile of other Asian nationalities (North, 1979: 238–241). However, an instance of illegal Korean immigration came to light when newspapers reported that five Los Angeles-based Army recruiting officers had enlisted 102 Korean illegal aliens over a fourteen-month period. In the Hollywood and Crenshaw recruiting stations, 71 of 342 Korean enlistees were found to have no legal residence. Most were here on nonimmigrant or student visas, but 12 came on a fraudulent scheme.[13]

Table 21.   Korean Population for Regions and Selected
States, 1970 and 1980

	Number		Percent Distribution		Percent Change: 1980/1970 × 100
	1980	*1970*	*1980*	*1970*	
Northeast	68,152	13,908	19.2	20.1	390
New York State	34,157	6,607	9.6	9.6	417
North Central	62,149	13,172	17.5	19.1	372
Illinois	23,980	3,673	6.8	5.3	553
South	70,375	12,594	19.9	18.2	459
West	153,853	29,456	43.4	42.6	422
California	103,891	15,756	29.3	22.8	559
Hawaii	17,948	8,656	5.1	12.5	207
United States	354,529	69,130	100.0	100.0	413

Source: U.S. Bureau of the Census, *1980 Census of Population. Supplementary Reports,
PC80-3. Race of the Population by States, 1980.* (Washington, D.C.: USGPO, 1981), table 7.

REGIONAL SETTLEMENT

Between 1970 and 1980 the Korean population of the United States
grew from 69,130 to 354,529. Of the 285,399 additional Koreans
enumerated in 1980, about 10,000 resulted from natural increase and
275,000 from immigration. Naturally, some regions and localities
increased faster than the national average and some slower. Table 21
shows that the Korean population of the South and West increased
faster than the national average, whereas the Northeast and North
Central regions increased more slowly. Of four major states containing Korean population, California and Illinois increased by more than
the national average; New York and Hawaii by less. As a result of
differential growth, the South rose from fourth to second rank in
respect to Korean population. Conversely, the Northeast declined
from second to third rank and the North Central from third to fourth
rank. The West ranked first in respect to Korean population in both
1970 and 1980 with approximately 43 percent of the national Korean
population residing in the West.

Koreans clustered in selected regions and localities rather than
fanning out evenly over the entire United States. Comparing the
percentage distribution of Koreans in 1980 with that of the entire

United States (table 22), one finds Koreans underrepresented in seven regions, at parity in one region, and overrepresented in one region. For example, only 2.4 percent of Koreans resided in New England, but 5.5 percent of the United States population resided there. Koreans were underrepresented in New England, the East North Central, the West North Central, the South Atlantic, East South Central, West South Central, and Mountain regions. The Middle Atlantic Region contained 16.8 percent of Koreans and 16.2 percent of all Americans, approximate parity. However, the Pacific region contained 39.7 percent of Koreans, but only 14 percent of all Americans.

Koreans were more dispersed around the United States than were Asians and Pacific Islanders (API) in general. For example, 12.6 percent of Koreans resided in the South Atlantic region in 1980, but only 7.4 percent of API. This pattern was repeated in every region of the United States, except New England where API–Korean parity prevailed. Even the Pacific region, their heartland, contained only 39.7 percent of Koreans compared to 56.6 percent of Asians and Pacific Islanders.

Comparison of 1970 and 1980 population distributions offers some basis for explaining API–Korean differences. First, Koreans were already more dispersed than API in 1970. In 1970, 68.7 percent of API resided in the Pacific region whereas only 39.4 percent of Koreans did so. Second, the dispersion of Koreans in 1970 probably reflected cultural conditioning leading to readiness for assimilation. The Christianity of Korean immigrants is an obvious point. Barkan and O'Brien (1981: tab. 2.4) also reported that in the period 1950–1978 a higher percentage of Koreans obtained naturalization than did either API or all immigrants. Barken and O'Brien treated the naturalization rate as an index of assimilation. Third, Korean dispersal reflected the many war orphans and soldiers' brides among the small Korean population, still unswollen by the mass migration of the 1970s. These Koreans assumed membership in their adoptive families, fanning out over the United States in consequence. In contrast, the API population arose as a result of labor immigration with the usual formation of immigrant centers in the course of migration. Therefore, API population was more concentrated in the Pacific region than was the Korean population in 1970.

Finally, because of inherited dispersion, growing Korean populations in the 1970s built upon existing nuclei rather than further

Table 22. Percentage Distribution of Population by Regions for the United States, Koreans, and Asian–Pacific Islanders in 1980

	All Persons 1980	Koreans		Asians and Pacific Islanders*	
		1970	1980	1970	1980
Northeast					
New England	5.5	3.6	2.4	2.3	2.3
Middle Atlantic	16.2	16.5	16.8	10.9	13.7
North Central					
East North Central	18.3	13.9	12.9	6.4	8.6
West North Central	7.6	5.2	4.6	1.8	2.5
South					
South Atlantic	16.3	11.5	12.6	4.6	7.4
East South Central	6.5	2.3	1.9	0.8	1.2
West South Central	10.5	4.4	5.3	2.0	4.8
West					
Mountain	5.0	3.2	3.7	2.5	2.8
Pacific	14.0	39.4	39.7	68.7	56.6
Total	100.0	100.0	100.0	100.0	100.0
	226,504,825	69,130	354,529	1,538,721	3,600,636

* Asian and Pacific Islander (API) includes: Japanese, Chinese, Filipino, Asian Indian, Korean, Vietnamese, Hawaiian, Samoan, Guamian.
Source: U.S. Bureau of the Census, 1980 Census of Population. Supplementary Reports, PC80-S1-3. Race of the Population by States: 1980. (Washington, D.C.: USGPO, 1981), tables 1, 30.

deconcentrating in search of economic opportunities. As a result, the clustering of Korean population changed little in the decade despite quadrupled population. In contrast, API responded to slower population increase by reducing Pacific Coast concentration, a process that brought them into closer alignment with the 1970 Korean distribution. In the period 1970–1980, API expanded their population percentage in every region except the Pacific, where API population declined from 68.7 percent of the national to 56.6 percent. Assuming also that the adjustment of the API population in the decade of the 1970s represented a response to new economic opportunities beyond the Pacific region, Koreans required less adjustment to take advantage of such opportunities because their initial population distribution was more dispersed.

Two regression analyses support this interpretation of Korean settlement patterns in the 1970s. We tested the extent to which one could explain Korean population growth in the 1970s by either population growth of fifty states and the District of Columbia on the one hand, or by Korean population in 1970 on the other. If Koreans settled wherever economic growth was most rapid, Korean population change in the decade ought to correspond to the overall population change of each state. Conversely, if Korean population change arose by chain migration, building on existing nuclei, than growth between 1970 and 1980 would be proportional to the 1970 Korean population of each state.

Table 23 reports the results of both regression analyses. Equation 1 first regressed the 1980 Korean population (KOPOP80) on the 1970 Korean population (KOPOP70). The effect was very strong with $R^2 = .89$. This result indicates that Korean population in 1970 closely corresponded with Korean population in 1980. Equation 2 then introduced control variables representing 1970 and 1980 state population (STPOP70, STPOP80). When state population in 1970 and 1980 were introduced, a slight reduction occurred in the standardized regression coefficient of KOPOP70. Additionally, R^2 was increased from .89 to .92, a modest improvement. This result indicates that state population in 1970 and 1980 did not add much to our explanation of Korean population distribution in 1980, nor seriously amend an explanation based upon Korean population in 1970.

Similarly, equation 1 regressed the change in Korean population in the decade 1970–1980 (KOCHG) upon Korean population in 1970 (KOPOP70). The effect was powerful with $R^2 = .85$. This result

Table 23.   Growth of Korean Population of Fifty States
and the District of Columbia, 1970—1980:
Standardized Regression Coefficients

Independent Variables:	Dependent Variable: KOPOP80	
	Eq 1	Eq 2
KOPOP70	.94	.78
STPOP80		.45
STPOP70		−.23
R^2	(.89)	(.92)

	Dependent Variable: KOCHG	
	Eq 1	Eq 2
KOPOP70	.92	.75
STPOP70		−.21
STCHG		.44
R^2	(.85)	(.88)

All coefficients $p < .01$.
Source: U.S. Bureau of the Census, *1980 Census of Population,* PL-80-S1-3 (Washington, D.C.: USGPO, 1981), p. 13.

indicated that growth in Korean population in the decade 1970—1980 probably took place by proportional increase in size of existing nodes. Equation 2 then introduced state population in 1970 (STPOP70) and change in state population 1970—1980 (STCHG) to test this explanation. The two control variables caused a reduction in the coefficient of KOPOP70 from .92 to .75. They also produced a slight increase in R^2 from .85 to .88. This result confirmed the results of the first analysis: Korean population in 1970 offered the most reliable guide to growth in Korean population in the next decade. Growth of state populations in the decade provided little improvement in explanatory power, nor reduced greatly the explanatory share of KOPOP70.

IMMIGRATION PREFERENCES AMONG KOREANS

United States immigration statistics offer additional evidence of chain migration among Koreans. This evidence derives from the categorical system of preference which U.S. law imposed (table 19). The three kinship categories (exempt, 2, and 5) were 66 percent of all immigrants in 1967, but increased to 92 percent in 1981. This growth was unsurprising because the number of overseas kinspeople eligible for immigration preference increased as the naturalized population in the United States increased. The first immigrants brought over their foreign kinsfolk. Once established, foreign kinspeople brought over their own kinspeople, also relatives of the first immigrants admitted. And so the process continued.

Often chain migrations arise just because kin help kin. Green (1977) and Lim (1976) described the rural–urban migration of Koreans to Seoul in this manner. However, U.S. immigration law channeled immigration into kinship chains that might not otherwise have been so pronounced (Hong, 1982). The joint effect of Korean preference and U.S. law was a preponderance of kin of previous immigrants among those admitted to the United States.[14] According to INS *Annual Reports*, kinship claimants were 87.9 percent of the Korean immigrants admitted between 1966 and 1981.[15] Every one of the kinship claimants thus admitted had proved to the satisfaction of INS officials that he or she had a *bona fide* kinship relationship with a U.S. citizen or permanent resident alien.

KOREANS IN CITIES

In 1980 about 47 percent of U.S. Koreans resided in seven cities (table 24). By contrast, the same seven SMSAs contained only 14.4 percent of total U.S. population. The threefold overrepresentation of Koreans in these seven SMSAs exceeded their overrepresentation in the Pacific region. Compared to API, Koreans remained less concentrated in these seven SMSAs, but their margin of dispersion was much less than among regions. In 1980 just over 50 percent of API resided in the seven SMSAs compared with 47.1 percent of Koreans. Compared to API, Koreans were, moreover, overrepresented in five SMSAs: Los Angeles–Long Beach, New York, Chicago, Washington, Anaheim–Santa Ana–Garden Grove. They were, conversely, underrepresented relative to API in Honolulu and San Francisco–Oakland. In all, Koreans clearly selected different SMSAs for residence than did API, but their preference for these seven SMSAs together was little different from that of API in general.

Asked why they migrated, Korean business owners in Los Angeles mentioned economic reasons more frequently than any other (see

Table 24. U.S. SMSAs with 10,000 or More Koreans in 1980

SMSA	Koreans		Asian & Pacific Islanders		All Persons	
	Number	Percent	Number	Percent	Number	Percent
Los Angeles–Long Beach	60,618	17.1	434,914	12.4	7,477,657	3.3
New York	28,531	8.0	271,044	7.7	9,119,737	4.0
Chicago	21,020	5.9	141,339	4.0	7,102,328	3.1
Washington, D.C.	17,306	4.9	82,147	2.3	3,060,240	1.4
Honolulu	16,880	4.8	456,873	13.1	762,874	0.3
Anaheim–Santa Ana–Garden Grove, Ca.	11,339	3.2	86,876	2.5	1,931,570	1.4
San Francisco–Oakland	11,250	3.2	325,759	9.3	3,252,721	1.4
Total, 7 SMSAs	166,944	47.1	1,798,952	51.4	32,707,127	14.4
Total, USA	354,529	100.0	3,198,681	100.0	226,504,825	100.0

Sources: U.S. Bureau of the Census, *1980 Census of Population, Supplementary Reports, PC80-S1-3* (Washington, D.C.: USGPO, 1981), table 7; Idem., *1980 Census of Population, PC80-S1-5. Standard Metropolitan Statistical Areas and Standard Consolidated Statistical Areas: 1980* (Washington, D.C.: USGPO, 1981), table 4.

table 16). But economic motives are incompatible with heavy selection of just these seven SMSAs for Korean settlement. In the decade 1970–1980 these seven SMSAs increased their aggregate population by only 2 percent whereas aggregate population of all U.S. SMSAs increased 10 percent in the same period. If economic growth of SMSAs attracted Korean settlement, these seven SMSAs ought to have been among the last chosen. Indeed, in the period 1970–1980 the population of the United States increased 15 percent so, on this basis alone, Korean immigration ought to have settled outside of SMSAs and certainly outside the lackluster seven in which heavy overrepresentation of Koreans in fact developed.

LOS ANGELES–LONG BEACH

The same issues arise in the specific case of Los Angeles–Long Beach, the residence of 17 percent of total Korean population, far the largest Korean settlement in the United States. Los Angeles turned in a lackluster economic performance in the decade of the 1970s. A gross measure of economic expansion is population change. In the period 1970–1980 the population of Los Angeles–Long Beach increased 6.2 percent whereas the population of the United States increased 15 percent. The stagnation of Los Angeles population in this period occurred despite net migration of some 50,000 Vietnamese and an unknown net immigration of illegal aliens, mostly Mexicans (Light, 1987).

Other economic indicators tell the same luckluster story. In the period 1974–1982, the labor force of Los Angeles County increased less than did the labor force of San Francisco–Oakland or of San Diego; gross employment also increased less; and unemployment increased more than in San Francisco–Oakland or San Diego, major cities in California.[16] Comparing Los Angeles County to the State of California for the period 1970–1978, we find that every industry in Los Angeles County increased less than the state average.[17] A more detailed analysis compares the County and City of Los Angeles in just those seven selected industries in which Koreans most strongly entrenched themselves.[18] County and city retail sales in every industry (except gasoline service stations) declined as a percentage of California's total in the period 1970–1979. Second, in all but food stores, change was more unfavorable in the City than in the County, yet Korean business concentrated in the City. Since even these heavily Korean industries were in decline during most of the 1970s, there is no evidence here that industrial niches Koreans occupied were outstandingly attractive in economic terms. On the contrary, the problem is rather to explain why people who traveled so far would choose to locate in a deteriorating economic environment when they might have selected so many more prosperous local economies in the United States.

LOS ANGELES' THRIVING KOREAN ECONOMY

Notwithstanding the lackluster economic performance of Los Angeles County, Los Angeles' Korean economy was the most thriving and profitable Korean economy anywhere in the United States during the 1970s. This singular fact offers an obvious economic explanation for the Koreans' perference for Los Angeles as a place for settlement. Table 25 shows that Korean firms in Los Angeles represented 26.0 percent of all Korean firms in the United States in 1977 even though Los Angeles contained only 17.1 percent of the nation's Korean population in 1980. Additionally, the Koreans firms in Los Angeles reported gross dollar receipts that represented 37.1 percent of all receipts obtained by Korean firms in the United States. Average gross receipts of Korean firms in Los Angeles were $92.9 thousand in 1977 whereas Korean firms in the United States grossed on the average only $65.1 thosuand in that year. Korean firms in Los Angeles exceeded 17.1 percent of all Korean firms in the United States—their expected share—in every industry except transportation and public utilities. In manufacturing, Korean firms in Los Angeles were 49.2 percent of all Korean firms in the United States. The gross receipts of Korean firms in Los Angeles exceeded their expected share of the gross receipts of all Korean firms in the United States in every industry except service. In manufacturing, their star performer, Korean firms in Los Angeles earned 63.3 percent of the gross receipts of all Korean manufacturing firms in the United States.

Although census statistics record a slight deterioration of the Los Angeles Korean economy's relative position in the five years 1977—

Table 25. Gross Receipts by Industry of Korean-owned Firms in the United States and Los Angeles, 1977 with Comparison of Totals for 1982

	United States			Los Angeles		
	Number of Firms	Gross Receipts ($1000)	Average Gross Receipts ($1000)	Number of Firms	Gross Receipts ($1000)	Average Gross Receipts ($1000)
Construction	267	7,235	27.1	70	1,856	26.5
Manufacturing	191	23,639	123.8	94	14,974	159.3
Transportation and Public Utilities	210	5,207	24.4	19	1,114	58.6
Wholesale Trade	209	35,503	169.9	58	12,774	220.2
Retail Trade	3,766	341,478	90.7	1,089	144,773	132.9
Finance, Insurance, and Real Estate	235	4,161	17.7	87	1,695	19.5
Service	3,286	126,001	38.4	693	23,726	34.2
Other	131	2,471	18.9	50	629	12.6
Not Classifiable	209	8,345	39.9	52	4,011	77.1
TOTAL, 1977	8,504	554,040	65.1	2,212	205,552	92.9
TOTAL, 1982	31,769	2,677,063	84.3	7,906	916,637	115.9

Source: U.S. Bureau of the Census, 1977 Survey of Minority-Owned Business Enterprises: Asian American, American Indian, and Other. MB77-3. (Washington, D.C.: USGPO, 1979), table 4; Idem, 1982 Survey of Minority-Owned Business Enterprises: Asian Americans, American Indians, and Other Minorities. MB82-3 (Washington, D.C.: USGPO, 1986), pp. 5, 133. The 1982 survey did not provide the industrial distribution of Korean firms in Los Angeles.

1982, the Los Angeles economy's superiority was still great in the latter year. In 1982, after having increased threefold in number since 1977, the Korean firms in Los Angeles still represented 24.9 percent of all Korean firms in the United States. Sales of Los Angeles Korean firms were still 34.2 percent of gross sales of all Korean firms in the United States (table 25).

THE GARMENT INDUSTRY

In the import/export trade and in garment manufacturing, the Los Angeles Korean economy did benefit from a favorable industrial context. The garment industry in Los Angeles registered stronger than average growth in Los Angeles County during the 1970s. Moreover, strong growth in this industry was already apparent in the period 1969–1973, well before the peak of Korean immigration. Koreans have been overrepresented in the garment industry as workers and contractors. Since garment industry growth anticipated the peak of Korean immigration, this industry's growth was a specific inducement causing Koreans to overselect Los Angeles for residence.

Korean directories reported eleven garment manufacturing firms in 1975 and sixty-one in 1979, a fivefold increase. In 1975, the eleven garment factories accounted for nine-tenths of 1 percent of Korean firms; in 1979 sixty-one garment factories accounted for 2.3 percent of Korean firms. Although they made up only 2.3 percent of all firms listed in the 1979 *Korean Directory*, garment contractors were bigger employers of Korean labor than were Korean firms in general so their representation in the business population understated their job-generating importance in the Korean community of Los Angeles. Jin (1981: 20–21) estimated that the Korean garment firms employed 5400 Korean workers in 1979. These Korean garment workers represented 18.5 percent of Korean labor force of Los Angeles. Of course, Los Angeles was not the only city in the United States whose garment industry was expanding in 1970s (Waldinger, 1987: chs. 1, 2; Day and Wong, 1979). Nonetheless, garment industry growth represents a case in which a one-to-one connection can be made between industrial opportunities in Los Angeles and Korean overselection of that city for residence.

THE IMPORT/EXPORT INDUSTRY

Some Koreans selected Los Angeles for residence because they found employment in the Korea–United States import/export industry (Choy, 1979: 133). This presumption is strengthened by the slight imbalance that existed in Los Angeles between Los Angeles' share of the United States Korean population (17.1 percent) and its share of Korean exports to the United States (22 percent). It is possible that some overselection of Los Angeles by immigrant Koreans resulted from the city's pivotal role in the Korea–United States import/export trade.

Our proprietors' survey (Appendix) turned up some evidence bearing on this issue. We asked Korean owner-respondents to indicate what percentage of their suppliers were Korean. Those who indicated that between 66 and 100 percent of their suppliers were Korean implicitly identified themselves as participants in a vertical distribution network that might originate in South Korea. Twenty-nine percent of owner-respondents did so indicate. This proportion was high, thus suggesting that the distribution of Korean-made goods was a major industry of Korean store owners. In the retail wig business 95 percent of owner-respondents were wholly dependent upon Korean suppliers, and the wigs they sold were, in fact, manufactured in South Korea. Wholesale trade also evidenced a higher than average proportion of Korean suppliers, although the number of interviews was skimpy. In the service sector, no one was dependent upon Korean suppliers.

A simple procedure estimates the maximum extent to which garment manufacture and/or the import/export trade in Los Angeles might account for the superior number and receipts of Korean firms in Los Angeles county. By assigning Korean firms in Los Angeles their expected share (17.1 percent) of the nation's Korean firms in their industry and the average gross returns of all Korean firms in their industry, we project the expected number and receipts of Korean firms in any Los Angeles industry as if these were equivalent to national averages. These calculations project 152 firms in these two industries instead of the 400 observed. Additionally, these 152 firms would have grossed only $17,634,000 instead of the $27,747,000 observed. As expected, this statistical exclusion reduces the number of Korean firms in Los Angeles from 26 to 25 percent of the national total of Korean firms. Additionally, it reduces the gross receipts of Korean firms from 37.1 to 33.9 percent of the national total. This result means that if the Los Angeles Korean economy had obtained only an average performance from its manufacturing or wholesale sectors, its overrepresentation in firms and average receipts would have been only slightly reduced.

NONECONOMIC CAUSES OF KOREAN IMMIGRATION

Having examined the industrial attractions of Los Angeles County, we turn to the County's noneconomic attractions. Likely candidates, commonly mentioned by Koreans, were political democracy, peace, military security, educational opportunities for their children, and religious freedom (Han, 1973: 5). We agree that peace, freedom, and domocracy encouraged Koreans to emigrate to the United States. However, these blessings were equally available everywhere in the United States so they cannot explain overselection of Los Angeles.

Koreans valued higher education, which was difficult to obtain in Korea because places were limited and access required success in competitive examinations. Since many students failed these examinations, many Korean families of the middle or higher status looked enviously at the United States where an educational second chance was available.

California's attractiveness to Korean immigrants is partially explained by reference to the Golden State's system of public higher education. After all, California's state university and college system was larger than that maintained by any other American state, educational quality was superior, and fees low. On one hand, we cannot rule out this possibility, and we consider it likely that California's public colleges and universities attracted Korean immigrants to the state. On the other hand, this attraction in no way explains the Koreans' overselection of Los Angeles for residence. Los Angeles public schools were in turmoil as a result of white flight, bussing, teacher turnover, and fiscal crisis (Boyarsky, 1977). There was nothing in the city's educational system to bring people from Seoul to obtain it. There was also no reason to settle in Los Angeles if access to California's universities was desired.

CHAIN MIGRATION

Chain migrations arise when newcomers settle in the same locality as did kinspeople or friends who preceded them (Light, 1983: 275–277). Common in Korea (Green, 1977: 96), chain migrations place new population where population has already settled. Chain migrations are noneconomic insofar as settlers made their locational decision on the ground of kinship rather than jobs. Chain migration could explain the Korean immigrants' overselection of Los Angeles when other explanations cannot: Koreans overselected Los Angeles because their kinspeople already resided there (Portes and Bach, 1985: 10).

Koreans acknowledged (Ahn, 1975: 17; Han, 1973: 50–51) the importance of chain migration in residential selection, and Koryo Institute's (1978) workshops heavily stressed this theme. As one observer notes: "Almost all [Koreans] have contacted relatives or friends in the United States in order to find jobs and housing in the regions where they intend to reside" (I. Kim, 1981: 25). But quantitative evidence of chain migration is fragmentary. Since the 1970 census published the Korean population of only four cities, we cannot employ a statistical approach to assess the correspondence between the Korean population of an SMSA in 1970 and its growth in the next decade. However, one may cite the historic preference for Los Angeles among Koreans on the North American mainland. Moon's (1976) history of Korean immigration mentions this preference, but the only census documentation is 1940. In 1940, California contained only 5 percent of the United States population but 63.6 percent of Korean population (table 17). In the same year, Los Angeles contained 25.1 percent of Korean but 2 percent of national population. In 1970, California's share of the Korean population (22.9 percent) had dropped back to twice her share of the United States population. But Los Angeles still manifested a fourfold overrepresentation of Koreans. This persistence establishes the preference of Koreans for Los Angeles as early as 1940, and therewith the possibility that chain migration explains Korean overselection of Los Angeles ever since. Of course, table 17 also indicates that Los Angeles' relative attraction to Koreans *declined* between 1940 and 1970 and increased between 1970 and 1980. Since chain migration implies continuity, chain migration cannot explain why Los Angeles' percentage of the U.S. Korean population was 17.1 percent in 1980 rather than only 12.7 percent, the 1970 level. Therefore, chain migration plausibly explains the residential settlement of 12.7 percent of immigrant Koreans, but the Korean economy in Los Angeles might residually account for why an additional 4.4 percent of immigrant Koreans chose to locate in Los Angeles.

WAS CHAIN MIGRATION NONECONOMIC?

Newcomers in a strange land welcome the social support that friends and relatives bestow. Social reassurance is a strictly noneconomic consideration. However, newcomers also need help. For example, newcomers speak no English; hence, they need access to Korean-speaking people who can translate for them—and relatives provide this service. Relatives also offer a place to stay until one has found an apartment of one's own (Han, 1973: 50–51). Relatives help a newcomer to obtain a driver's license in California, lend money, give advice, and steer a person to a job. These kindnesses confer economic benefits on their recipient. Therefore, settling near relatives permitted a newcomer to obtain economic benefits as well as social support.[19]

When we consider the economic constraints upon Korean newcomers in the United States, the economic benefit of chain migration becomes clearer. The principal constraint was inability to speak English (Hong, 1975; Yu, 1982b: 70). So long as this constraint persisted, a Korean could not function in American labor markets. Hence, he or she was restricted to earning opportunities in the Korean-speaking economy. In general, therefore, job opportunities confronting a new Korean immigrant depended upon the size of a Korean-speaking economy. Los Angeles had the largest Korean economy in the United States, and Los Angeles was in this sense the most economically attractive place for a new Korean immigrant to settle. The fact that the general economy of Los Angeles was stagnant was of indifference to Korean newcomers because Koreans were restricted to the Korean economy anyway. When we take into account the nepotistic employment practices in the Korean firms, their training and sponsorship functions, the one-to-one connection between kinship propinquity and economic opportunity becomes more evident (Harris, 1983: 196). In an extreme case, a new immigrant could *only obtain work* in a business a kinsperson owned (H.-S. Lim, 1976: 11).

Koreans whose kin already resided in Los Angeles had the easiest choice. If they chose Los Angeles, they obtained access to the social reassurance and economic assistance their kinsfolk provided. They also gained access to the largest Korean-speaking economy in the United States. Koreans whose kin lived in smaller Korean centers faced a more difficult choice. These newcomers had to choose between the social reassurance and economic assistance their kinspeople could bestow and access to a larger Korean-speaking economy. For example, a Korean settling in San Jose could expect his relatives there to help him. But the Korean community was small; hence, jobs open to non-English-speaking Koreans were scarce. Ironically, a Korean who settled in thriving San Jose chose a less favorable labor market than did a Korean who settled in stagnant Los Angeles.

SUMMARY AND CONCLUSION

The concentration of Koreans in Los Angeles was chiefly the result of that city's historic attraction for Korean people. As a result of chain migration, Koreans already in Los Angeles attracted newly arrived friends and relatives. However, chain migration cannot provide a fully satisfactory account of Korean overselection of Los Angeles because Los Angeles contained a larger proportion of the United States' Korean population in 1980 than it had in 1970. Therefore, it appears that the thriving Korean economy of Los Angeles added about one-third additional Korean population to what chain migration alone produced. Indeed, in view of the higher-than-average gross returns that Korean firms earned in Los Angeles, chain migration to other localities in the United States possibly impeded the saturation of economic opportunities in the Los Angeles economy by causing some Koreans to select for residence U.S. cities in which Korean firms earned lower rates of return than they did in Los Angeles. Before concluding that chain migration was a sentimental influence on Korean settlement, one needs, however, to recall the economic benefits that migration chains confer upon participants. These benefits are sufficiently important that they might explain why still more Koreans did not settle in Los Angeles despite the objectively superior earning opportunities available in Los Angeles' thriving Korean economy.

6

Entrepreneurs and Firms

Until the appearance of the salariat around the turn of the century, entrepreneurship simply defined the American middle class. To be an entrepreneur was to be middle class because entrepreneurs possessed property, which set them above wage earners (Mills, 1951: 5–6). Some entrepreneurs inherited wealth, but immigrant entrepreneurs usually started at the bottom. Additionally, at least after 1880, the foreign born were consistently overrepresented among the nonfarm self-employed so, as a mobility channel, entrepreneurship was more important among immigrants than among the native born (Light, 1984: 198). Insofar as American society depended for legitimacy upon a vision of free and equal opportunity for all, immigrant entrepreneurs propped up her parliamentary democracy and free enterprise system (Mayer, 1953).

America's historic celebration of immigrant entrepreneurship naturally cast the Korean immigrants in the classic role: Korean entrepreneurs were individual successes, and the high rate of entrepreneurship among Koreans betokened a high rate of success for the whole Korean minority, a demonstration of the continued openness of the market system, and a vindication of the American Dream (K. Kim and Hurh, 1983). Although plausible, this popular conclusion depends on many issues of fact of which the first is the true rate of entrepreneurship among Koreans. That estimate depends importantly upon how one defines entrepreneurs, since a generous definition admits owners of the smallest businesses to the entrepreneur population, and some of these entrepreneurs do not qualify as successful people. Second, rate of entrepreneurship is too crude a measure of a group's business stature. Korean business stature obviously depended upon the average size and earnings of the Korean-owned firms as well as upon the rate of Korean self-employment. Third, as Min and Jaret (1984), Yu (1983), and Kim and Hurh (1983) have claimed, Korean entrepreneurs did not always receive material rewards commensurate with middle-class status. Insofar as Korean entrepreneurs worked harder and earned less than non-Koreans, the Korean entrepreneurs' material rewards fell short of the American Dream. Entrepreneurship alone does not prove middle-class status independent of evidence showing that the entrepreneurs actually enjoyed middle-class rewards.

WERE KOREANS ENTREPRENEURS?

Acknowledging "considerable overlap" between entrepreneurship and small business ownership, Carland and associates (1984: 357) nonetheless concluded that many small business owners were insufficiently innovative to quality as entrepreneurs. The position is attractive because economists have traditionally distingusished entrepreneurs from managers on the basis of innovative function. Expressing the standard view, Leibenstein (1968: 75; see also Baumol, 1968: 66) defined entrepreneurs as individuals or groups who connect markets, fill gaps to correct market deficiencies, complete factor inputs, or create or expand firms. On this view, entrepreneurs assemble the factors of production, compensating from personal resources the market failures they confront.

However, Leibenstein (1968: 74) stressed that gaps in markets were "inherent in all cases" to greater or lesser degree. Therefore, Leibenstein's distinction does not permit the exclusion of any active owner-managers of business firms from the class of entrepreneurs on the grounds that they neither founded nor expanded their firms, never completed factor inputs, and confronted no market imperfections. Virtually every active owner-manager accomplishes one of these entrepreneurial functions in some degree.

Sociological definitions of entrepreneurship have come to a similar conclusion. Kilby (1971: 29) defined entrepreneurship as "... performance of services that are required but not available in the market." Listing the functions of entrepreneurs, Kilby (1971: 27–28) identified thirteen, such as perception of market opportunities, purchasing inputs, managing human relations within the firm, and quality control. Since owner-managers of business firms always assume responsibility for each of Kilby's thirteen entrepreneurial functions, Kilby's list provides no basis for excluding any active owner-manager from the class or entrepreneurs.

Wilken (1979: 60) defined entrepreneurship as a social role involving the combination of factors of production to initiate qualitative or quantitative changes in production of goods or services. However, Wilken immediately encountered the problem of measuring the degree, number, and rate of innovation. That is, innovations may be big or small, one or many, rapid or slow. Following Wilken, any quantitative or qualitative innovations qualify as entrepreneurship, no matter how small, how few, or how slow. As Wilken (1979: 71) explained, big, numerous, and rapid innovations have greater economic consequences than one small innovation. Nonetheless, by introducing a graduated scale of entrepreneurship along three dimensions, Wilken eliminated the capacity for excluding from the class of entrepreneurs active owner-managers with any claim to any innovation, no matter how slow, how small, or how few their innovations. Additionally, Wilken (1979: 71) acknowledged that some types of entrepreneurship were "impossible to measure" and others were impractically difficult to measure. As a result, even Wilken's determined effort provides no means for reliably excluding any owner-managers from the class of entrepreneurs nor for distinguishing more entrepreneurial entrepreneurs from less entrepreneurial entrepreneurs.

MEASURING THE ENTREPRENEUR POPULATION

In view of these problems, the best available measure of Korean entrepreneurship is Korean representation in the population of business owner-managers. Therefore, the first task is to define the business population of which Korean firms constituted a segment. The business population of an area consists of all firms located in the area, but what is a firm? On a narrow definition, firms are permanent economic actors with sales, assets, capital equipment, premises, employees, fixed hours of operation, and established reputation. Any such definition narrows the business population to substantial firms. On a broad definition, firms offer goods or services for sale, and there is no requirement that firms employ labor, make sales, have assets or equipment, occupy premises, or demonstrate regular work habits (Sethuraman, 1976). In an extreme case, a vagrant offering apples for sale from a bag is one grocery firm and Safeway Corporation is another. Admittedly, the vagrant is not wealthy, but lack of wealth does not bar access to the class of firms whose owner-managership is the most common mode of entrepreneurship.[1] Additionally, Aldrich and Weiss (1981: 288) specifically tested the hypothesis that firms without employees did not belong to the capitalist class. Finding no size-adjusted differences in owner income, they concluded that firms without employees were simply the smallest capitalists and "should be assigned to the owner class in future research."

Because enumeration of entrepreneurs requires a broad definition of a firm, official documents utilizing a narrow definition are inadequate. U.S. documents omit and undercount firms that should be enumerated in any survey of entrepreneurs. Among firms typically omitted are no-employee firms, firms engaged in illegal or secret activities, tax evading firms, firms without a business address, and parttime firms with negligible sales. In view of the obvious difficulty of locating and enumerating such firms, their absence from official documents is understandable, possibly unavoidable. Additionally, the smallest firms make negligible contributions to industrial output so their enumeration is inessential from an economic perspective. This consideration explains the reluctance of census enumerators to search out the smallest firms, but it does not diminish the difficulty of attempting to establish the true population of entrepreneurs from published data. In fact, the inadequacy of "the small business data base" is less serious than the inadequacy of the entrepreneur data base.[2]

Koreans were more numerous among entrepreneurs than they were among owners of big businesses. To document the discrepancy, we discuss and contrast the major sources of information on the Los Angeles and Korean business population, showing how each represented the true entrepreneur population. In general, enumerators counted firms or they counted the self-employed. Enumerations of firms found fewer businessess than did enumerations of the self-employed. The discrepancy arose because enumerations of firms excluded or overlooked small firms whose owner-managers turned up as self-employed in surveys. Since Koreans owned a smaller proportion of big firms than of marginal firms, counts of Korean firms underestimated Korean representation in the population of entrepreneurs.

Table 26.   Korean and All Business Establishments in
Los Angeles County, 1977 and 1980

	L.A. County,* 1980		Koreans,** 1977		Index [100 = Expected]
	No.	%	No.	%	
Agriculture	1,228	0.7	0	0	0
Mining	264	0.2	0	0	0
Construction	9,738	5.9	70	3.2	102
Manufacturing	18,509	11.2	94	4.2	121
Transportation, etc.	4,907	3.0	19	0.9	48
Wholesale Trade	14,823	9.0	58	2.6	49
Retail Trade	36,433	22.0	1,089	49.2	374
Finance, etc.	16,359	9.9	87	3.9	66
Services	53,651	32.4	693	31.3	161
Not Classifiable	9,540	5.7	102	2.4	
All Industries	165,362	100.0	2,212	100.0	167

*U.S. Bureau of the Census, *County Business Patterns, 1980, California* (Washington, D.C.: USGPO, 1982): Table 2.

**Idem., *1977 Survey of Minority-Owned Business Enterprises: Asian American, American Indians, and Other* (Washington, D.C.: USGPO, 1980).

THE SURVEY OF MINORITY-OWNED BUSINESSES

In order to compare the total business population with the Korean business population, we developed two estimates of the population of Korean firms in Los Angeles County. The first was based upon the Census Bureau's *1977 Survey of Minority-Owned Businesses*. Published as part of the economic censuses, the *Survey of Minority-Owned Businesses* compiled information from government and nongovernment sources, published and unpublished. In determining specific Asian ethnicity, the survey compilers used Social Security files to canvass firms identified as "other," that is, neither black- or white-owned. The economic census was then used to flesh out a portrait of these firms.

Table 26 shows the industrial distribution of Korean business enterprise according to the *1977 Survey of Minority-Owned Business Enterprises*. The survey enumerated firms rather than entrepreneurs, and some firms might have been partnerships. Unfortunately, the survey did not disaggregate legal form of business by detailed ethnicity. However, among Asian-Americans, 90.5 percent of all enumerated firms were sole proprietorships, 7.3 percent were partnerships, and 2.2 percent were corporations.[3] Projecting this distribution upon Koreans, we estimate that 621 Korean-owned firms in Los Angeles were partnerships, slightly raising the number of Korean entrepreneurs.

Table 26 also compares the percentage distribution of the 2212 Korean firms with the 165,362 firms in Los Angeles County. Just in percentage terms, Korean were underrepresented in every industry except retail trade in which they were massively overrepresented. The index norms the number of Korean firms observed against their expected share (0.8 percent) of the County business population. A score of 100 indicates that the Korean share of this industry was exactly proportional to their share of the labor force. A score less than 100 indicates statistical underrepresentation; and a score above 100 indicates overrepresentation. The index shows that Koreans were overrepresented in manufacturing, services, and retail trade. They had their approximate share of firms in construction. However, Korean firms were less numerous than expected in agriculture, mining, transportation and public utilities, wholesale trade, and finance. Overall, Korean-owned firms comprised 167 percent of the business firms that would have been expected on the basis of chance.

KOREAN DIRECTORIES

In 1975, a local Korean firm, Keys Advertising and Printing Company, published the *Korean Directory of Southern California*, which listed the name, address, and telephone number of Koreans in the region and also provided a yellow pages section of Korean businesses. In 1976 Keys published a supplement. Then in 1977 another directory appeared, followed by others in 1979, 1980, and 1982. Keys' directories were valuable sources of business information. Yu (1982), Hurh and Kim (1984), and Lee and Wagatsuma (1979) relied on Keys' white pages for lists of Korean households. We used Keys' yellow pages to estimate the Korean business population. No other published source provided so detailed a listing of Korean enterprises, and no other source gave firm addresses, permitting us to plot the distribution of Korean business throughout Los Angeles County.

Despite these advantages, the Keys directories' white pages

Table 27.   Korean Businesses in Los Angeles, by Industry,
1975–1982

	Percent			
	1975	1977	1979	1982*
Agriculture	0	0	0	0.1
Mining	0	0	0	0
Construction	0.9	1.0	1.7	4.3
Manufacturing	2.7	2.6	2.5	3.4
Transportation and Public Utilities	2.4	2.1	2.4	1.3
Wholesale Trade	8.6	9.1	7.1	8.5
Retail Trade	45.3	45.0	43.7	39.7
Finance, Insurance, and Real Estate	4.5	5.1	5.5	6.1
Service	35.6	35.1	37.1	36.5
Total	100.0	100.0	100.0	100.0
Number	(1,277)	(2,268)	(2,671)	(4,266)

*Figures for 1982 from M. David Oh, *An Analysis of the Korean Community in the Mid-Wilshire Area*, pt. II (Los Angeles: Office of Economic Opportunity, State of California, 1983), table II-1A, p. 9.
Source: *Korean Directory of Southern California* (Los Angeles: Keys Advertising and Publishing Co., 1975, 1977, 1979, 1982).

missed many Kims listed in the general telephone directories as Yu (1982a: 30) discovered. Further, many Korean businesses failed to list in the yellow pages, even though listings were free. The Keys directories probably contained a bias in favor of businesses serving a Korean clientele, since the directories were circulated in the Korean community. Hence, Koreatown firms were probably well covered, whereas firms outside Koreatown were underenumerated. Finally, some businesses owned by Koreans were not owned by Korean immigrants. This problem particularly affected trading companies, but it also affected large firms, such as banks, airlines, and newspapers. Some Korean businesses were owned in South Korea and operated in the United States by nonimmigrant managers rather than by immigrant entrepreneurs.

Table 27 presents the industrial distribution of Korean firms in the Keys directories. Building upon our earlier results, David Oh (1983: pt. 2, 9) coded the 1982 Keys directory. Juxtaposed with ours, his results provide a longer view of the growth of Korean enterprise. In this seven-year period, the Korean business population more than tripled. Naturally, one cannot be certain that all the apparent growth was real—rather than the result of fuller enumeration in the Keys directories. In fact, we believe that later editions of the Keys directories achieved worse coverage of the Korean business population because the 1977 keys directory enumerated 98 percent of the total of Korean firms also enumerated in the *1977 Survey of Minority-Owned Business Enterprises*. In contrast, the 1982 Keys directory enumerated only 54 percent of the total of Korean firms also enumerated in the *1982 Survey of Minority-Owned Business Enterprises*.

Census Data on Self-Employment

The 1980 U.S. Census enumerated the self-employed in Los Angeles County. The self-employed are persons working on their own account as sole proprietors or partners. The self-employed need not employ wage or salary workers, and about one-third of the self-employed were solo proprietors working alone.

The 1980 census reported 165,362 establishments and 235,754 self-employed in Los Angeles County. Since the establishments included corporations, and some of the self-employed were partners in a single venture, the discrepancies need not represent enumeration error. On the other hand, establishments excluded no-employee firms, the modal class among self-employed persons. If no-employee firms had been included, the number of firms would have been increased and the population of self-employed and of establishments brought into closer alignment.

Although the 1980 census did not publish Korean self-employment for Los Angeles County, the unpublished, 5 percent public use sample of the 1980 census did enumerate Korean and non-Korean self-employment in the County. Table 28 shows that the census found 16.8 percent of Koreans were unincorporated self-employed compared to 6.4 percent of non-Koreans. Additionally, 4.0 percent of Koreans were employees of their own corporation whereas only 1.9 percent of non-Koreans employed themselves in this manner. Finally, 2.2 percent of Koreans were unpaid family workers, and only 0.4 percent of non-Koreans reported that occupation. Combining the three categories, we find 22.6 percent of working Koreans in the self-employment sector and 8.7 percent of non-Koreans. Therefore, in 1980, Koreans represented 0.76 percent of Los Angeles County's

Table 28.   Class of Workers Aged 16 Years or Older
in Los Angeles County, 1980, for Koreans and non-Koreans

	Korean		Non-Korean	
	Number	*Percent*	*Number*	*Percent*
Wage and Salary Workers	22,515	77.0	3,480,411	91.3
Unincorporated Self-employed	4,912	16.8	243,972	6.4
Employee of Own Corporation	1,170	4.0	72,429	1.9
Unpaid Family Worker	643	2.2	15,248	0.4
Total	29,240	100.0	3,812,060	100.0
Number	(1,462)		(190,603)	

Chi-square = 446, df = 3, $p < .001$
Source: U.S. Bureau of the Census, *Census of Population and Housing, 1980 (USA), Public Use Microdata Samples* (Ann Arbor, MI: Interuniversity Consortium for Political and Social Research, 1983).

labor force, but 2.0 percent of the County's unincorporated self-employed, 1.6 percent of employees of their own corporation, and 4.0 percent of unpaid family workers.

Koreans were more prominent among the self-employed than they were among business establishments. Table 29 compares the industrial distribution of the self-employed Koreans with that of all the self-employed in Los Angeles County in 1980. The index shows Koreans overrepresented in eight industries and underrepresented in one, finance. In contrast, the comparison of Korean and all business establishments (table 26) shows Koreans overrepresented in only four industries and underrepresented in five. Similarly, the comparison of Koreans with all self-employed persons in table 29 shows an overall self-employment index of 288 whereas comparison of Korean and all business establishments (table 26) produces an index of only 167. In Los Angeles County, establishments constituted 51 percent of the self-employed. However, among Koreans, establishments were only 36 percent of the self-employed. These discrepancies suggest that census enumerations of establishments missed a higher proportion of Korean firms than of non-Korean firms. This undercount arose because of the greater marginality of Korean firms, and the much greater difficulty of identifying them. Since the self-employed provide the best available measure of entrepreneurs, enumerations of establishments systematically underestimated Korean entrepreneurship.

Table 29.   Industrial Distribution of Self-employed*
in Los Angeles County for Koreans and All Persons, 1980

	L.A. County		Koreans		Index
	Number	Percent	Number	Percent	
Agriculture	15,000	0.5	160	2.6	164
Mining	380	0.1	20	0.3	810
Construction	34,380	10.6	360	5.9	161
Manufacturing	34,020	10.5	680	11.2	308
Transportation	10,020	3.1	120	2.0	184
Wholesale Trade	15,760	4.9	440	7.2	430
Retail Trade	57,380	17.7	2,540	41.8	681
Finance, etc.	25,480	7.8	40	0.7	24
Services	132,380	40.8	1,720	28.2	199
All Industries	324,800	100.0	6,080	100.0	288

*Includes employees of own corporation.
Sources: U.S. Bureau of the Census, *Census of Population and Housing, 1980 (USA), Public Use Microdata Samples* (Ann Arbor, MI: Interuniversity Consortium for Political and Social Research, 1983).

ASSESSING KOREAN-OWNED FIRMS

Mean Receipts

Assessing the relative size of Korean-owned firms, table 30 compares mean receipts of Korean firms in the United States with mean receipts of all proprietorships and of all firms in the United States for 1977. In both the United States and in Los Angeles, mean receipts of Korean-owned firms exceeded mean receipts of U.S. proprietorships—but fell short of means receipts for all U.S. firms. Since the "all firms" category included corporations as well as proprietorships, the basis of comparison with Koreans is obviously different in the two cases. In general, Korean-owned firms obtained twice the gross receipts of the average American proprietorship but only one-fifth or one-third of the gross receipts of all U.S. firms. Therefore, Korean-owned firms actually fell between proprietorships and big business in terms of gross receipts. Korean firms were small, but not the smallest firms in the U.S. economy.[4]

When industries are compared, Korean-owned firms assume the same middling position except in construction and finance, insurance,

Table 30.   Average Gross Receipts of Korean-owned
Firms in Los Angeles and the United States Compared with
Average Gross Receipts of Proprietorships and All Firms in
the United States, 1977

Industry	Average Gross Receipts ($000s)			
	Koreans*		United States**	
	U.S.	Los Angeles	Proprie-torships	All Firms
Construction	27.1	26.5	48.0	802.1
Manufacturing	123.8	159.3	49.1	945.5
Transportation and Public Utilities	24.4	58.6	35.8	692.5
Wholesale Trade	169.9	220.2	120.3	1,161.4
Retail Trade	90.7	132.9	71.2	321.1
Finance, Insurance, and Real Estate	17.7	19.5	20.9	260.8
Service	38.4	34.2	20.9	68.5
Other	18.9	12.6		
Not Classifiable	39.9	77.1		
TOTAL	65.1	92.9	40.6[†]	298.4

[†]Nonfarm industries only.

Sources: *U.S. Bureau of the Census, *1977 Survey of Minority-Owned Business Enterprises: Asian American, American Indians and Other. MB77-3* (Washington, D.C.: USGPO, 1979), tables 1b, 4.
**Idem., *Statistical Abstract of the United States: 1980* (Washington, D.C.: USGPO, 1980), table 929, p. 557. U.S. Internal Revenue Service, *Statistics of Income 1978. Sole Proprietorship Returns.* (Washington, D.C.: USGPO, 1982), table 6. IRS results include firms without adjusted gross income.

and real estate. In construction, Korean-owned firms in the U.S. and in Los Angeles were smaller than the mean of U.S. proprietorships, indicating Koreans were operating very small construction firms. In finance, insurance, and real estate, Korean firms were about the same size as U.S. proprietorships. In transportation and public utilities, Korean-owned firms in Los Angeles were larger than the average U.S. proprietorship, but Korean firms in the U.S. were smaller (table 30). Since these results exclude the nonemployer self-employed, the results do not warrant the interpretation that Koreans had higher average gross receipts than did non-Koreans in 1977. Rather, the top one-third of the Korean distribution earned more than the top half of the general distribution, a result whose implications for size are more ambiguous.

Table 31.   No-Employee Firms by Industry among
Korean-owned Firms of Los Angeles and U.S. Firms, 1977

Industry	Koreans in Los Angeles, 1977	U.S. Firms, 1977
	Percentage of Firms No Employees	Percentage of Firms No Employees
Construction	94.3	65.5
Manufacturing	33.0	11.2
Transportation and Public Utilities	68.4	
Wholesale Trade	70.7	6.1
Retail Trade	63.4	43.9
Finance, Insurance, and Real Estate	98.9	
Service	80.1	68.9
All Firms	71.5	53.7
Number	(2,212)	(5,589,806)

Sources: U.S. Bureau of the Census, 1977 *Census of Minority-Owned Business Enterprises: Asian Americans, American Indians, and Others* (Washington, D.C.: USGPO, 1979), table 4; Ronald Reagan, *The State of Small Business: A Report of the President Transmitted to Congress March, 1982.* (Washington, D.C.: USGPO, 1982), Table A1.26, p. 211.

EMPLOYEES AND PAYROLL

Number of employees provides a more accurate estimate of business size than gross receipts. All studies asked this question, but they reported different results. The *1977 Survey of Minority-Owned Business Enterprises* probably assembled the most accurate estimate because its sample is so much larger than other efforts. The survey distinguished employer and nonemployer firms among Korean businesses in Los Angeles.[5] It reported that 71.5 percent of Korean firms were nonemployer firms in 1977. This percentage exceeds the percentage of nonemployer firms that the U.S. president reported for the entire United States in the same year.[6] Table 31 shows that in every industry for which data were available, the percentage of nonemployer firms among Koreans in 1977 was greater than the percentage of nonemployer firms in the United States. On this basis, one concludes that an appreciably higher percentage of Korean than of American firms had no employees in 1977. However, were Korean firms compared with U.S *proprietorships*—rather than with all businesses—the discrepancy would be reduced.

Comparing Korean-owned firms with all firms produces a frame of reference in which Korean firms appear diminutive. This result arises because most tabulations excluded the smallest proprietorships most comparable to Korean firms, thus giving a misleading impression of scale to the general business population. To correct this distortion, table 32 compares mean annual payroll per firm among Koreans in Los Angeles and California proprietorships in 1977 and 1978 respectively. In 1977, 77 percent of all U.S. firms were sole proprietorships, and these proprietorships were the smallest class of firms as well as the most numerous. Since proprietorship data were assembled from IRS records, they represent the most accurate account of the entire small business population, especially its smallest sector. Juxtaposing Korean firms in Los Angeles and California proprietorships, one finds comparability of mean annual sales per firm—except in manufacturing in which Korean garment factories produced a larger than average annual payroll. As a result of manufacturing's larger payroll among the Koreans, the all-industry mean among Koreans slightly exceeded the all-industry mean among California proprietorships. However, differences were not great. These results indicate that Korean firms in Los Angeles were of average size for proprietorships except in manufacturing where Korean firms were larger than average.

WAGES AND WORKING CONDITIONS

Both Korean and American newspapers claimed that Korean proprietors worked long hours making extensive use of unpaid family labor. Journalists also reported that employees of Korean-owned firms, mostly coethnics, had to work long hours for wages lower than the prevailing standands in their industry, and often below the statutory minimum (Chaneka, 1980; S. Kim, 1981). Min (1984b: 344–345) reported that Korean entrepreneurs in Atlanta worked longer hours than American entrepreneurs and employed more family labor, a result confirmed also by Hurh and Kim (1984: 111). Interviews we conducted with Koreans and knowledgeable non-Koreans confirmed this conclusion. For example, an oil company vice president claimed that Korean owners kept their gas stations open around the clock, utilizing family labor for the purpose. Investigations by state labor standards enforcement agencies documented massive violations of

Table 32. Mean Annual Payroll (in thousands of dollars) per Firm: Koreans, 1977, and Sole Proprietorships in California, 1978, by Industry

	Koreans: Los Angeles, 1977		California: Sole Proprietorships, 1978	
	All Firms	Employer Firms Only	All Firms	Employer Firms Only
Construction	$ 1,886	$ 33,000	$13,248	$31,089
Manufacturing	68,479	102,174	10,938	28,866
Transportation and Public Utilities	3,474	11,000	6,473	21,305
Wholesale	6,535	22,294	5,180	17,693
Retail	6,395	17,454	6,498	18,810
Finance, Insurance, and Real Estate	NA	NA	604	11,117
Services	3,665	18,406	3,735	17,159
All Nonfarm Industries	8,165	26,345	5,028	20,497
Number of Firms	(2,023)	(627)	(1,171,779)	(287,470)

Sources: U.S. Bureau of the Census. 1977 Survey of Minority-Owned Business Enterprises: Asian Americans, American Indians, and Others. MB77-3. (Washington, D.C.: USGPO, 1979). table 4, p. 89. U.S. Internal Revenue Service, Statistics of Income 1978. Sole Proprietorship Returns. (Washington, D.C.: USGPO, 1982), table 4, p. 57.

wages and working laws in the garment and restaurant industries—important Korean industries—but enforcement officials refused to divulge national origins of owners cited for violations. Yu (1982b: 57) found that "a large proportion" of Korean workers in Los Angeles worked more than eight hours daily, but Yu did not isolate the working hours of Korean proprietors.

Fortunately, the *1977 Census of Minority-Owned Business Enterprises* reported total payroll for Korean-owned firms in the United States and in Los Angeles. Dividing total annual payroll by total employment provides the mean wages of employees in Korean firms in 1977, and these wages can be compared with mean wages for all firms (table 33). In 1977 the mean wages of employees of Korean-owned firms in Los Angeles were $6,400 whereas the mean wages of employees in all Los Angeles firms were $11,364. Therefore, mean wages of Korean firms' employees were only 56 percent of mean wages in all Los Angeles firms. The same disparities in wages recurred when Korean employer firms were compared with all employer firms in respect to mean wages: employees of Korean firms earned 48 percent of what employees of American firms earned. Comparing specific industries, we find that the greatest discrepancy in wages occurred in finance, insurance, and real estate. In this industry employees of Korean firms earned only 47 percent as much as employees of all firms. The smallest wage discrepancy occured in retail and service industries. In both of these industries, employees of Korean firms earned 81 percent of the general wage rate for their industry.

Unfortunately, interpretation of table 33 is cloudy because the publication *County Business Patterns* excluded nonemployer firms. Since three-quarters of Korean firms were nonemployer, the comparison of Koreans and *County Business Patterns* skews one's frame of reference. It would be desirable to know whether Korean mean wages by industry were also lower than mean wages of general proprietorships. Unfortunately, the U.S. Internal Revenue Service excluded number of employees from its proprietorship tabulation so that direct evaluation of this comparison is impossible.[7] Lacking this direct comparison there is no hard evidence Korean firms were undercutting wage rates among proprietorships, the most marginal and numerous segment of the business class. However, Koreans certainly increased the number of proprietorships in California and

Table 33. Mean Annual Earnings per Employee by Industry: Korean Employer Firms and All Employer firms, 1977

Industry	Korean Firms, 1977		All Firms, 1977	
	Los Angeles	United States	Los Angeles	United States
Construction	$7,765	$8,200	$15,106	$17,756
Manufacturing	6,754	7,000	13,662	13,743
Transportation and Public Utilities	NA	8,200	15,220	17,427
Wholesale Trade	6,891	8,400	13,780	14,946
Retail Trade	5,685	5,300	6,985	7,951
Finance, Insurance, and Real Estate	NA	5,800	11,491	12,329
Services	7,384	6,500	9,171	11,413
Non Classifiable			12,821	13,092
All Industries	6,400	6,100	11,364	12,512

Source: U.S. Bureau of the Census, 1977 Survey of Minority-Owned Business Enterprises: Asian Americans, American Indians, and Others. MB77-3. (Washington, D.C.: USGPO, 1979), table 4; Idem., County Business Patterns, 1977. United States. CBP77-1. (Washington, D.C.: USGPO, 1979), table 1A; Idem., County Business Patterns, 1977. California. CBP77-6 (Washington D.C.: USGPO, 1979), table 2.

Table 34.   Mean Hours Usually Worked per Week for
Employed Koreans and Non-Koreans in
Los Angeles County, 1979

| | Mean Hours Worked Weekly | |
	Koreans	Non-Koreans
Not Self-employed	38.6	37.7
Unincorporated Self-employed	46.2*	39.8
Employee of Own Corporation	43.4	44.9
Unpaid Family Worker	40.7	33.3
All Classes	40.1*	37.9
Number	(1,462)	(190,603)

*Difference of means t test: $p < .01$.
Source: U.S. Bureau of the Census, *Census of Population and Housing, 1980 (USA), Public Use Microdata Samples* (Ann Arbor, MI: Interuniversity Consortium for Political and Social Research, 1983).

Los Angeles, thus reducing mean wages of all firms by increasing the proportion of low-wage firms in the total.

HOURS OF LABOR

Korean entrepreneurs worked longer hours than did non-Koreans. Table 34 displays the weekly hours usually worked in 1979. Employed Koreans averaged 40.1 hours of work weekly whereas employed non-Koreans averaged only 37.9, a difference of 2.2 hours weekly. However, among wage and salary workers the difference between Koreans and non-Koreans was only 0.9 hours weekly. Conversely, among the unincorporated self-employed, Koreans reported 46.2 hours of labor in an average week and non-Koreans reported 39.8, a difference of 6.4 hours weekly. In an average week, Korean proprietors worked 16 percent longer than did non-Koreans. Korean unpaid family workers probably logged more hours than did non-Korean family workers. Table 34 shows that Korean family workers reported 40.7 hours of weekly labor in 1979 whereas non-Korean family workers reported only 33.3 hours, a difference of 7.4 hours, but the difference was not statistically significant.

Since unpaid family workers were 2.2 percent of employed Koreans but only 0.4 percent of employed non-Koreans, the Korean family workers' longer hours of labor accentuated the difference in the extent to which Korean and non-Korean proprietors had access to unpaid labor. Koreans had more unpaid workers who worked longer hours. Among Koreans, 643 unpaid family workers logged 26,170 hours of unpaid labor every week. If divided equally among the 6,080 Korean self-employed in Los Angeles County, this unpaid labor would have provided each entrepreneur with 4.3 hours of unpaid labor, nearly 10 percent of his or her own weekly hours. Conversely, among non-Koreans 15,242 unpaid family workers produced 507,559 hours of weekly free labor. If equally divided among the 316,404 self-employed non-Koreans in Los Angeles County, this volume of unpaid labor would have provided only 1.6 hours of unpaid labor for each entrepreneur. Thus, Korean entrepreneurs probably obtained 2.7 times more unpaid family labor than did non-Korean entrepreneurs.

If we sum the average hours of labor of each entrepreneur plus the average hours of unpaid labor each enjoyed, we compound the Korean's margin of overtime. That is, Korean entrepreneurs worked 46.2 hours weekly, and each one enjoyed an average of 4.3 hours unpaid family labor each week. Therefore, the average Korean entrepreneur disposed of 50.5 hours of weekly labor, his own and his unpaid family workers. In contrast, the average non-Korean entrepreneur worked 39.8 hours, and tacked on 1.6 hours of unpaid family labor, a total of 41.4 hours weekly. Therefore, the average Korean business family probably worked 9.1 hours longer every week than did the average non-Korean business family. In all, Korean business families contributed 23 percent more labor time to their family firm than did American business families.

RETURN ON HUMAN CAPITAL

Human capital is an entrepreneur's investment in training. The best measure of return on human capital is annual self-employment income in dollars per year of education. This return measures the extent to which Korean entrepreneurs were obtaining as favorable returns on their educational investment as were non-Koreans. After all, if Koreans received lower returns on human capital, as several authorities suppose (Chung, 1979; Yu, 1983; Hurh and Kim, 1983), then the Korean entrepreneurs were not as successful in business as were comparably educated American counterparts.

Table 35.   Mean Years of Schooling and Mean Dollar
Income per Year of Schooling for Korean and Non-Korean
Workers, Aged 18–64, by Class of Worker for
Los Angeles County, 1979

	Mean Dollar Income per Year of Schooling		Mean Years of Schooling	
	Koreans	Others	Koreans	Others
Self-employed	$1246*	1352	14.8*	13.7
All Other Workers	763*	1096	13.3*	12.2
All Occupations	864*	1140	13.7*	12.4
N	(1,252)	(151,333)	(1,252)	(151,333)

*Difference of means t test $p < .01$
Source: U.S. Bureau of the Census, *Census of Population and Housing, 1980 (USA), Public Use Microdata Samples* (Ann Arbor, MI: Interuniversity Consortium for Political and Social Research, 1983). Table includes only persons in the labor force who were not attending school.

Utilizing the public use sample of the 1980 census we obtained estimates of money returns on human capital (table 35). The census reported that in 1980 Korean entrepreneurs aged eighteen to sixty-four in Los Angeles County averaged $1246 for each year of education whereas comparable non-Koreans averaged $1352. Hence, Korean entrepreneurs' return on their human capital was only 92 percent of that of non-Korean entrepreneurs. Admittedly, the gross income of the two groups was almost identical: Korean entrepreneurs averaged $18,441 whereas non-Koreans averaged $18,522. However, because the Koreans' mean schooling was 1.1 years higher than that of non-Koreans, the Korean's mean self-employment income represented a lower average return on the Koreans' human capital investment.

Nonetheless, the situation of Korean entrepreneurs was more favorable than that of Korean wage and salary workers. Korean wage and salary earners also averaged 1.1 years of education more than non-Korean wage and salary workers. However, the Korean workers' mean return on their educational investment was only 70 percent of that obtained by non-Korean wage and salary workers. As a result, the better-educated Korean wage and salary workers actually earned an average wage ($10,148) that was only 76 percent of the non-Korean average ($13,371), even though the Koreans reported 8 percent more schooling than did the non-Koreans. This imbalance of remuneration persisted among both men and women workers except that relative to non-Korean men, Korean men earned an even lower average wage and a lower return on schooling than did Korean women relative to non-Korean women.

However, the Korean self-employed also worked 16 percent longer hours than did self-employed non-Koreans. In contrast, wage-earning Koreans worked no longer hours than did wage-earning non-Koreans. Adding the unpaid household labor to the labor surplus among the self-employed, we found that Korean households might have contributed 23 percent more labor to their firms than did non-Korean business households. Therefore, not only did Korean entrepreneurs earn a lower return on their human capital than did the non-Koreans, the Korean entrepreneurs and their family helpers worked longer hours to obtain that lower return. Possibly the longer hours of the Korean entrepreneurs reflected only their beginner status: perhaps when their period of getting underway is completed, Korean entrepreneurs will work no longer than non-Korean counterparts and will receive the same return on human capital. Conceding the possibility, one has nonetheless to observe that in the initial phases of their business history in Los Angeles, Korean immigrant entrepreneurs worked harder than non-Koreans to earn a lower return on human capital. In this compound sense, Korean entrepreneurs earned a 24-percent lower rate of return on their human capital than did non-Korean entrepreneurs. Those who receive a lower-than-standard return on their labor are cheap labor, a categorization that fits the Korean entrepreneurs almost as well as the Korean wage earners (Chung, 1979).[8]

SUMMARY AND CONCLUSION

Overrepresented in the entrepreneur population of Los Angeles County, Koreans tended to operate small firms without employees. As a result, Koreans were almost twice as numerous among the self-employed as among the owners of business establishments. Census surveys of business establishments systematically undercounted the true Korean business population, two-thirds of which consisted of firms too small to notice. Admittedly, these surveys also undercounted marginal non-Korean firms, but since, except in services, a higher proportion of Korean firms were marginal, census enumerations of establishments concealed more Korean than non-Korean firms. We also suppose, but cannot prove, that even the census sample of self-employed undercounted the Korean entrepreneurs because of unmeasured parttime, illegal, underground, and barter-only enterprises.

Korean firms were small, but they were larger in respect to both payroll and gross receipts than the average of American proprietorships. Korean firms reported fewer employees than did all firms, but had it been possible to norm the Korean firms against proprietorships, this difference would have been attenuated. In general, Korean firms were average or above average among American proprietorships in terms of their size. However, the Korean firms paid below-average remuneration to employees and employers alike. First, employees of Korean firms received lower wages in every industry than did employees of all firms, a difference which might, it is true, have been attenuated had it been possible to norm the Korean firms against proprietorships only. Second, the Korean entrepreneurs and their families worked longer hours to earn a lower return on their human capital than did the non-Korean entrepreneurs. In sum, the Korean immigrants built an impressive network of proprietorships, but they did so on the basis of low wages for employees and long hours and low returns for the proprietors and their families.

Even so, elements of the Korean story vindicate the Horatio Alger imagery that has attached itself to their entrepreneurship. Just starting a business permitted a Korean immigrant to increase his money return on human capital by 63 percent and to increase his income by 82 percent. Korean entrepreneurs earned as much in self-employment as did non-Korean entrepreneurs. Among Koreans and non-Koreans alike, entrepreneurs were better educated than wage and salary workers, and they also earned higher returns on human capital as well as higher incomes. However, the disadvantage of Korean workers in the general labor market was so extreme that self-employment conferred upon Koreans a much more favorable relative dollar return than it did upon non-Koreans who increased their income only 39 percent by starting a business. Obviously, this more favorable return encouraged Korean entrepreneurship and, in this sense, the Korean experience confirms the contribution of labor force disadvantage to immigrant entrepreneurship (Light, 1984; Min, 1984a: 344). At the same time, relatively more favourable does not mean equal. Because Korean entrepreneurs worked longer hours than non-Korean entrepreneurs yet obtained a lower return on their human capital, they accepted remuneration standards lower than those prevailing among non-Koreans. Korean wage earners were cheap labor as employers had only to pay them $763 to rent the human capital for which non-Koreans charged $1096. But the same was in principle true of Korean entrepreneurs who also undersold the market. Therefore, one may accurately characterize Korean entrepreneurs as cheap labor albeit less cheap then Korean wage and salary workers.

7

Class and Ethnic Resources

Koreans built their small business network from resources at their disposal. These resources included the money, human capital, materialistic values, and business skills bourgeoisies normally possess. To this extent, class background successfully accounts for Korean entrepreneurship, which had, however, a cultural as well as a material side. That is, the vocational socialization of bourgeois youth in Korea equipped some Korean immigrants with knowledge, motivations, attitudes, and values required for successful entrepreneurship in Los Angeles. Without this vocational endowment in class culture, the immigrant Korean bourgeoisie would have been unable to utilize its inherited wealth for entrepreneurship.[1]

However, in point of fact, Korean entrepreneurs were an ethnic bourgeoisie, not just a bourgeoisie because in addition to class resources, they also utilized ethnic resources in the construction and management of their small business network. *Ethnic resources* are sociocultural features of the whole group which coethnic entrepreneurs utilize in business or from which their business benefits (Light, 1984: 201).[2] Thus, ethnic resources include orthodox cultural endowments, acculturation lags, reactive solidarities, sojourning orientation, and all other group and individual manifestations of ethnic influence upon behavior. Ethnic resources endow an entire group, not just its bourgeois class. This chapter examines the industrial clustering and industrial organization of Korean entrepreneurs in Los Angeles in order to supplement conventional class analysis with a detailed account of the ethnic resources Koreans also employed in entrepreneurship.

EMPLOYMENT OF EXTENDED KIN

Our telephone survey asked Korean entrepreneurs about extended kin in their employ. The percentage of firms employing extended kin was 20.7. Among those firms that employed extended kin the average number of kin employed was 2.4 per firm. One cannot assume that the firms that employed nuclear relatives were not the same firms that also employed extended kin, but one can combine these two pieces of information to obtain a sense of the outside limit of the number of Korean businesses utilizing family labor: among all Korean firms, 56.8 percent reported nuclear or extended kin at work.

We asked entrepreneurs whether any workers were unpaid. About one-third reported some use of unpaid workers all of whom, we assume, must have been family members of one kind or another. Ninety percent of firms reporting the use of unpaid labor said there was only one such worker in their business. However, 10 percent of businesses reported more than one unpaid family worker.

Business owners were also asked about nonkin employees. Forty-five percent reported none. For the remainder, the average number of employees was 3.6, with five firms employing over 10 nonkin employees. However, the bulk clustered in the one- or two-employee level. Asked about the ethnicity of their paid workers, 37.4 percent reported that they were all Korean, 20.6 percent that they were "American," 19.6 percent Mexican, and the remainder other Asians, blacks, and various combinations. If we add firms employing Koreans among the others, we find that 52.3 percent employed nonkin co-ethnics. Since Koreans in Los Angeles constituted only 0.8 percent of the labor force but 37.4 percent of nonkin employees, nonkin co-ethnics were represented in the work forces of Korean-owned firms forty-seven times more frequently than would have been expected by chance alone. As for extended kin Koreans, these represented no more than 0.8 percent of the Los Angeles labor force, but 20.7 percent of employees of Korean-owned firms. Hence, Korean extended kin appeared among the work force of Korean-owned firms at least twenty-six times more frequently than would have been expected on the basis of chance alone. These results are unsurprising, and we suppose they are characteristic of ethnic small business in general. Nonetheless, they strikingly measure the impact of ethnicity and kinship in the recruitment of labor among Korean firms.

INDUSTRIAL CLUSTERING

Industrial clustering is overrepresentation of Korean firms in certain industries and under- or nonrepresentation in others. Industrial clustering is already visible in table 29, which juxtaposes the per-

Table 36.   Distribution of Korean-owned Businesses in
Los Angeles County by SIC Level

Classification Level	Number of L.A. County Industries	Percentage of Industries With any Korean Firms		
	1975	1975	1977	1979
One-digit	9	77.8	77.8	77.8
Two-digit	59	62.7	64.4	57.6
Three-digit	275	30.2	25.8	35.3

Source: *Korean Directory of Southern California*, 1975, 1977, 1979 editions (Los Angeles: Keys Advertising and Publishing Co.).

centage distribution of Koreans self-employed by industry with that of Los Angeles self-employed. Further to assess the extent of industrial clustering among Korean firms, we compared the representation of Koreans at one-, two-, and three-digit SIC levels with county totals (table 36) utilizing the Keys directories for this purpose. When all Los Angeles businesses are grouped into one-digit SIC classes, there were nine classes in all, and Koreans appeared in seven (77.8 percent) of these nine. This percentage suggests an even dispersion of Korean firms among Los Angeles County industries. However, more refined analysis produces the opposite impression. Grouping the County's business population into two-digit industrial classes produced fifty-nine groups, and Koreans participated in 62.7 percent. In 37.3 percent of industries, no Korean firms appeared. At the most precise, three-digit level of classification, Koreans participated in only 30.2 percent of the 275 industries. In other words, 100 percent of Korean firms clustered in 30.2 percent of industries, and 69.8 percent of Los Angeles County industries sustained zero Korean participation. We repeated this analysis with 1977 and 1975 directory data. In every year, Korean participation in County business took the form of an inverted pyramid: a wide base of participation at the one-digit level narrowing to specialization as additional layers of refinement are added.

Continuing this inquiry, we prepared a three-digit and a one-digit list of unrepresented, underrepresented, and overrepresented Korean industries in the 1980 Public Use Sample of the U.S. Census (table 37). Unrepresented industries were those in which no Korean firms participated. Underrepresented industries were those in which

Table 37.   SIC Categorization of Korean Representation in
Los Angeles Industries

| One-digit SIC | Public Use Sample | | | |
| | Industries | | Self-employed | |
	Number	Percent	Number	Percent
No Koreans	0	0	0	0
Underrepresented	0	0	0	0
Overrepresented	9	100	304	100
Total	9	100	304	100
Three-digit SIC	*Number*	*Percent*	*Number*	*Percent*
No Koreans	143	68.4	0	0
Underrepresented	13	6.2	21	6.9
Overrepresented	53	25.3	283	93.1
Total	209	100.0	304	100.0

Chi-square $= 295.13$, $df = 2$, $p < .01$
Sources: U.S. Bureau of the Census, *Census of Population and Housing, (USA), Public Use Microdata Samples* (Ann Arbor, MI: Interuniversity Consortium for Political and Social Research, 1983).

Korean firms constituted more than zero but no more than 0.9 per-cent of all Los Angeles county firms engaged in this trade. Over-represented industries were those in which Korean firms numbered more than 0.9 percent of the county total. Table 37 shows how the census categorized the industrial distribution of self-employed Koreans at the one-digit and the three-digit SIC levels. At the one-digit level, the census found Koreans overrepresented in all industries, including agriculture and mining in which the Korean directories had reported no Korean firms. All the Korean firms in the census sample operated in overrepresented industries, suggesting a uniform dispersion of Korean self-employed throughout the indus-tries of Los Angeles County. However, at the three-digit level, the finest the census permitted, the characteristic clustering of Koreans becomes apparent again. In 68.4 percent of Los Angeles County industries, the census detected no self-employed Koreans. Koreans were underrepresented in 6.2 percent of industries and overrepre-sented in 25.3 percent. Ninety-three percent of self-employed Koreans clustered in the fifty-three industries in which Koreans were overrepresented. Only 6.9 percent of self-employed Koreans worked

Table 38.   Korean Representation in Employment
and Self-employment: 232 Industries of
Los Angeles County, 1980

Industries	Korean Workers				Total
	Employees		Self-employed		
	Number	Percent	Number	Percent	
No Koreans	82	35.3	166	71.6	248
Less than 1% Korean	3	1.3	18	7.8	21
More than 1% Korean	147	63.4	48	20.7	195
Total Industries	232	100	232	100	464

Chi-square = 89.427, $df = 2$, $p < .01$
Source: U.S. Bureau of the Census, *Census of Population and Housing, 1980 (USA), Public Use Microdata Samples* (Ann Arbor, MI: Interuniversity Consortium for Political and Social Research, 1983).

in the twenty-one industries in which Koreans were underrepresented. In the twenty-one underrepresented industries, Koreans were 0.5 percent of the total self-employed in the industry. In their fifty-three overrepresented industries, Korean self-employed were 3.7 percent of total self-employed in the average industry. If the Koreans had been equally distributed among all industries, they would have represented 0.8 percent of each and every County industry.

The significance of industrial clustering depends upon the extent to which self-employed Koreans were more clustered or less clustered than Korean wage and salary workers. To assess this issue, we analyzed the 1980 Public Use Sample of Los Angeles County. First, we distinguished three industrial classes depending upon the proportion of Koreans in the total industry: industries with no Koreans, industries with less than 1 percent Koreans, and industries with more than 1 percent Koreans. Second, we distinguished between Koreans who were self-employed and those who were wage or salary workers. Table 38 shows the quite divergent distributions that resulted. Among employees, 35.3 percent of industries reported no Koreans. Among the self-employed, 71.6 percent of industries reported no Koreans. Conversely, Korean employees were more than 1 percent of total employment in 63.4 percent of the industries whereas the Korean self-employed were more than 1 percent of the total self-employed in only 20.7 percent of industries (table 38). In short, 100 percent of Korean employees worked in 64.7 percent of industries, but 100 percent of Korean self-employed worked in only 28.5 percent of industries.

A second and finer assessment utilized the index of dissimilarity (ID) to compare the industrial distribution of self-employed Koreans with that of self-employed non-Koreans and of wage- and salary-earning Koreans with wage- and salary-earning non-Koreans. "The most widely used measure of residential segregation," the ID can also measure industrial segregation, the subject of this inquiry (Lieberson, 1981: 61). The ID compares two percentage distributions in order to measure the extent to which either must change in order to obtain perfect conformity with the other. The ID ranges form 0 (perfect integration) to 100 (perfect segregation).

At the one-digit SIC level, the ID for Korean self-employed was 28.0 and for Korean wage and salary workers 10.8. This result indicates that Korean self-employed were more industrially segregated than were Korean wage and salary earners. At the three-digit SIC level, the ID for Korean self-employed increased to 54.9 and the ID for Korean wage and salary earners increased to 33.0 Never before reported in the sociological literature, this result shows that industrial clustering of the self-employed was more extreme than that of wage- and salary-earning Koreans. Additionally, the increased ID at the three-digit SIC level reaffirms that clustering becomes more visible as our information increases.

CAUSES OF INDUSTRIAL CLUSTERING

Why should Korean businesses cluster in a handful of heavily Korean industries rather than fan out evenly across the industrial spectrum? This question concerns the manner in which Koreans achieved integration into the business population. The first issue concerns the extent to which Korean ethnicity played any role in this process. In an economistic model, ethnicity plays no role: industrial clustering arises because calculating individuals reached the same decisions independently. The assumption is plausible. Especially since Koreans entered Los Angeles County's economy at approximately the same moment in history, all confronted the same industrial opportunities, and simple economic rationality might have been enough to lead calculating, independent entrepreneurs to the same industries.

Additionally, Koreans entered the Los Angeles economy with similar class resources. Class resources include money to invest, educational background (human capital), bourgeois skills, bourgeois values, and credit ratings. In previous sections we saw that Korean-owned firms in Los Angeles were small firms characterized by low receipts; long hours of labor; a high proportion of no-employee firms; low hourly wages; much use of coethnic, kin, and unpaid family labor; nonunion labor; and low annual payrolls. Possibly these characteristics of the Korean firms also explain the industries in which Koreans located since Koreans could only enter those industries in which small firms could successfully compete. Hence, we suppose that, in addition to perceived growth prospects, Koreans selected for entry those industries in which they had the money, experience and education to establish themselves. These requirements limited their choice to industies in which small business was viable.

Industrial growth and class resources define an individualistic explanation of industrial clustering which falls, however, short of adequacy. That is, insofar as Koreans utilized only class resources to select promising industries, they entered industries on the basis of independent choices, each one shrewdly sizing up the market and striking out for himself or herself. In this sense, any heterogeneous aggregation of newcomers entering Los Angeles at that moment in history and with identical class resources would have clustered in exactly the same industries as did the Koreans. Missing from this conception of industrial process is any reference to *ethnic facilitation*, the utilization of ethnic resources to solve problems of entrepreneurship. Yet, insofar as Koreans informed, assisted, educated, supported, and protected one another in business enterprise, their entrepreneurship reflected ethnic facilitation in many forms.[3] But any aggregate of like-resourced but heterogeneous newcomers would, by definition, lack ethnic ties so they could not utilize ethnic resources in entrepreneurship and would have to rely wholly upon class resources. Since Koreans did help and inform one another, they operated as a group rather than as isolated individuals. For this reason, a complete explanation of industrial clustering needs to take account of ethnic resources as well as of class resources.

ETHNIC FACILITATION

Three sources of evidence underscore the importance of ethnic facilitation in Korean industrial choice: studies of kinship and coethnic labor, classified advertising, and Korean directories.

Table 39.   Regressions of Korean Wage and
Salary Employment (KWSE) on Independent Variables,
Dependent Variable: Korean Wage and Salary Employment

Independent Variables	Eq 1		Eq 2	
	B	Beta	B	Beta
Korean Self-employment (KSE)	1.6	.52	1.08	.36
Non-Korean Wage and Salary Employment (NKWSE)			.56	.63
Non-Korean Self-employment (NKSE)			−.14	−.19
R²	.27		.57	
Constant	2.80		.14	

All coefficients: $p < .01$, and exceed three times their standard error.
Source: U.S. Bureau of the Census, *Census of Population and Housing, 1980 (USA), Public Use Microdata Samples* (Ann Arbor, MI: Interuniversity Consortium for Political and Social Research, 1983). N = 232 industries.

KINSHIP AND COETHNIC LABOR

First, the extensive use of kinship and coethnic labor suggests that Korean employers selected workers nepotistically in order to minimize search costs. Working in a shop owned by a kinsman or coethnic, Koreans learned skills their employer knew. Having mastered these skills, Koreans had learned how to function in their employer's industry and later opened their own shop in this industry. In this manner, Koreans created an "entrepreneurial chain" that eventuated in massive overrepresentation in heavily Korean industries and absence from others (Werbner, 1984).

The Public Use Sample of the 1980 U.S. Census permitted an indirect estimation of the extent to which Korean employers preferred coethnic employees. The U.S. Census did not distinguish non-Korean and Korean employees of Korean firms. However, providing nearly the same information, a simple regression model permits us to evaluate the relative importance of the Korean and non-Korean economies in respect to the wage and salary employment of 22,460 Koreans in the Los Angeles County labor force. Table 39 regresses Korean wage and salary employment among 232 industries in Los Angeles County on three economic variables. Our objective in this table is to ascertain whether the general economy or the Korean ethnic economy better explains the wage and salary employment of Koreans in each of the 232 industries. Korean self-employment (KSE) is the number of Koreans self-employed in each industry. It includes employees of their own corporation. KSE measures the impact of Korean employers upon the industrial employment of coethnics. Non-Korean wage and salary employment (NKWSE) is the number of non-Koreans employed for wages or salaries in each of the same 232 industries. Non-Korean self-employment (NKSE) is the number of non-Koreans self-employed in each industry. NKWSE and NKSE measure the impact of the non-Korean economy upon wage and salary employment of Koreans. In an extreme case, if there were no Korean economy, and if Koreans fanned out equally among County industries, NKWSE and NKSE would completely explain the wage and salary employment of Korean workers. Conversely, if Koreans obtained wage and salary employment only in Korean-owned firms, KSE would completely explain their industrial employment.

Equation 1 shows that KSE alone explained a little more than one quarter of the variation among industries of the Korean wage and salary workers (table 39). Equation 2 drops NKWSE and NKSE into the model to ascertain their simultaneous effect upon Korean employment net of KSE. This intervention reduces the standardized regression coefficient of KSE from .52 to .36 while increasing explained variation from .27 to .57. Indeed, NKWSE emerges as the first-rank predictor of Korean employment by industry, beta = .63. The coefficients of NKSE are small but negative in direction. Negative direction is awkward to interpret, but it certainly offers no evidence that the non-Korean self-employed were significant employers of Korean wage and salary workers.

Table 39 confirms the first-ranking importance of non-Korean employment as a predictor of Korean wage and salary workers by industry. This result is unsurprising. Since the Los Angeles County economy contained 3.4 million wage and salary workers and only 6080 self-employed Koreans, one cannot wonder that the non-Korean labor market accounted for more wage or salary jobs (excluding upaid family workers) than did the tiny Korean economy. Rather, the relative impact of these two unequal factors provides the surprise. The tiny Korean ethnic economy explains 57 percent as many Korean jobs as does the huge labor force of Los Angeles County. This result could only occur if Koreans' employment chances were much better in the Korean economy than they were in the general labor market, a phenomenon incompatible with the assumption that

Koreans obtained jobs in the Korean economy on the same basis on which they obtained jobs in the general labor market. However, extended kin and coethnic preferences in employment are fully compatible with the results of this regression analysis.

CLASSIFIED ADVERTISING

Classified advertising offers additional evidence of ethnic facilitation. Korean-speaking people subscribed to Korean newspapers in which were listed "business opportunities" for sale. Reading the Korean language press, Koreans linked themselves into an information system that channeled them into those industrial niches already dominated by coethnics. The massive effect of this informational linkage is evident in table 40, which compares the "business opportunities" listed in the *Los Angeles Times* on May 13, 1981 and May 13, 1982 with those listed the same day in the *Korea Times*. With a population less than 1 percent of Los Angeles county, Korean readers found 573 businesses listed for sale in the *Korea Times* compared to 615 in the *Los Angeles Times*. The obvious discrepancy indicates that relative to their scant numbers, readers of the *Korea*

Table 40.   Combined "Business Opportunities"
Advertising on May 13, 1981, and May 13, 1982

	Korea Times*	*Los Angeles Times*
Fast Food or Coffee Shop	128	45
Liquor Store or License	87	42
Grocery Store	79	12
Dry Cleaning	63	9
Ready-to-wear Clothing	34	4
Restaurant	14	14
Dairy	14	2
Oriental Restaurant	14	1
Motel and Hotel	10	0
Gift Shop	10	5
Garment Factory	10	0
Nursery	5	1
Gasoline Service Station	9	9
Bar	7	16

Table 40. (continued)

	Korea Times*	Los Angeles Times
Jewelry	4	8
Photography	7	2
Hardware	3	5
Shoe Store	5	0
Maintenance	5	0
Beauty Shop	5	3
Amusement Arcade	2	6
Stereo, Phonograph, TV	3	3
Gardening	2	2
Wigs	3	0
Trucking	1	2
Auto Repair	8	33
Catering	2	2
Luggage	1	0
Farm	2	0
Ice Cream Parlor	1	3
Childrens' Wear	2	0
Car Wash	2	15
Doll Factory	3	0
Automobile Wrecking	1	1
Bowling Alley	1	0
Cigars and Cigarettes	1	2
Cosmetics	1	0
Shoe Repair	3	1
Fresh Fish	1	0
Health Foods	6	1
Pet Shop, Aquarium	4	1
Sports Wear and Equipment	1	4
Stationery	1	1
TV Repair	3	0
Travel Agent	1	2
Video	2	3
Personal Loans	2	1
Total Above	573	261
All Other	0	354
	573	615

*Translated from Korean by Hye-Kyung Lee
Chi-square $= 641.78$, $df = 47$, $p < .01$

Times found more listings than did readers of the *Los Angeles Times*. Additionally, the 573 Korean-language listings concerned 47 industries in which the *Los Angeles Times* listed only 261 businesses for sale. Therefore, Koreans had more choices in these 47 industries than did readers of the *Los Angeles Times*, the County's largest daily. Finally, the *Los Angeles Times* listed 354 businesses for sale in industries wholly ignored by the *Korea Times*. Therefore, a reader of the *Korea Times* could not apply to purchase businesses in these ignored industries but would be constrained to buy businessses listed in the Korean-language newspaper. To buy a business in one of these ignored industries, a potential business owner needed to read the *Los Angeles Times*, an English-language publication. As Korean immigrants reported little exposure to American magazines or newspapers, their dependence upon business opportunities advertised in the Korean-language press was great (Won-Doornink, 1985).

Another informational resource appeared in the *Joong-ang Daily News* on September 23, 1983. The article listed sixteen small businesses and indicated a formula according to which a purchaser could compute the expected purchase price of a small business. For example, a purchaser would expect to pay four to five times monthly gross sales for a liquor store. The effect of this information on Korean commerce is apparent. First, the information provided a rule-of-thumb for calculating a reasonable buying price, thus reducing uncertainty between Korean buyers and sellers. Second, the table listed only sixteen industries, thus channeling Korean buyers into these already heavily Korean industries. Finally, no comparable information appeared in the *Los Angeles Times*—so a person had to read the *Korea Times* in order to get this lesson in small business acquisition and disposal.

Another Korean-language newspaper, the *Hankook Ilbo* ran a "business information" series in 1977. On sixteen successive dates, the *Hankook Ilbo* produced a feature article about a selected industry. These series provided detailed information about how to buy and manage a small business enterprise in that industry. For example, on November 1, 1977 the *Hankook Ilbo* concentrated on retail shoe stores. The newspaper explained there were forty Korean-owned shoe stores, and experience was needed to start one. Start-up cost were $50,000 in the central business district, less elsewhere. On other dates the *Hankook Ilbo* covered realtors, florists, laundry and dry cleaners, groceries, jewelry stores, construction and architecture, auto body repair, night clubs, liquor stores, food wholesaling, restaurants, automobile dealerships, printing, and gift shops (E.-J. Lee, 1984). The newspaper also kept its readers informed about research in Korean business. Articles described the findings, including the number and distribution of Korean firms in various industries, the start-up cost, profitability, and typical problems. Learning of our research, the *Korea Times* invited Ivan Light to lecture on his results, and the story was covered in the *Korea Times* as well as the *Hankook Ilbo* on April 15, 1977.

KOREAN DIRECTORIES

Third, when quantitatively analyzed in conjunction with county business statistics, Korean business directories show a process of self-reproduction compatible with the ethnic facilitation hypothesis. That is, the 1975 Korean business directory listed Korean firms by industry. This listing proved an exellent predictor of Korean business growth by industry (KOCG) in the period 1975–1979—even when the influence of alternative predictors was controlled. Since this kind of analysis has never been completed before, we describe it in detail.

Attempting to explain the industrial distribution of Korean firms as these were listed in the Korean directories, we extracted six economic variables from the U.S. Bureau of the Census' (1975, 1979) *County Business Patterns*. This document recorded conditions in sixty-three two-digit SIC industrial categories in Los Angeles County. Thus, in table 41 EST75 represents the number of establishments in every industy in 1975, EST79 represents the same for 1979. MPAY75 represents mean pay in every industry in 1975, and MPAY79 represents the same for 1979. %SML75 references the percentage of firms in every industry which reported one to four employees in 1975, and %SML79 the same for 1979. KO75 recorded the number of Korean-owned firms in every one of the sixty-two SIC industries as reported in the Keys Publishing Company (1975) yellow pages. KO79 reported the same for 1979. KOCG indicates the difference when the number of Korean firms in 1975 in each industry is subtracted from the 1979 number. Thus KOCG is a measure of change in number of Korean firms between 1975 and 1979.

Table 41.   Predictors of Korean Business Firms in Two-
Digit SIC Industries: Standardized Regression Coefficients

Independent Variables:	Dependent Variables:		KOCG	
	KO75	KO79	Eq 1	Eq 2
EST75	.46		.58	.47
MPAY75	−.22		−.22	−.16
%SML75	.03		.02	NS
KO75				.24
R²	.34		.46	.50
EST79		.58	.57	.41
MPAY79		NS	.02	.04
%SML79		.13	.14	.11
KO75				.36
R²		.36	.35	.45

All coefficients: $p < .01$; N = 63 industries
NS = Not Significant
Sources: U.S. Bureau of the Census, *County Business Patterns 1975, California* (Washington, D.C.: USGPO), table 2; *County Business Patterns 1979, California,* table 2; *Haninrock, the Korean Directory of Southern California* (Los Angeles: Keys Publishing Co., 1975 and 1979).

Observing a correlation matrix, we found a statistically significant correlation ($r = .56$) between KO75 and KOCG. The correlation beteen KO75 and KOCG stands for the ethnic facilitation hypothesis according to which Korean industrial clustering followed the channel already in existence. To test this ethnic facilitation effect, table 41 displays the results of a regression analysis. The first problem was to explain Korean industrial clustering as well as possible from *County Business Patterns* data. The first column shows that three CBP variables (EST75, MPAY75, and %SML75) explained 34 percent of variance in KO75. These three variables also explained 46 percent of variance in KOCG (equation 1). However, when we dropped KO75 into equation 2 the coefficients of all CBP variables were reduced while variance explained increased to 50 percent. KO75 emerged as the second-ranking variable in terms of its effect upon KOCG.

Continuing this line of inquiry, we regressed KO79 on EST79, MPAY79, and %SML79, obtaining results quite similar to those achieved with KO75. When KOCG was regressed on these three variables, no improvement in R^2 (.35) was achieved. However, dropping KO75 into the equation raised R^2 to .45 while reducing the standardized regression coefficients of EST79 and %SML79. Again KO75 emerged as the second-ranking predictor of Korean industrial distribution.

Summarizing this analysis, we found that the 1975 industrial distribution of Korean firms was a moderate predictor of Korean industrial growth in the period 1975–1979—even when the influence of mean pay, proportion of firms small, and general industrial population was controlled. These data do not permit one to exclude the hypothesis that Koreans operated as individual entrepreneurs utilizing class resources. Rather, these results indicate that simple economic rationality and class resources cannot fully explain the industrial growth of Korean firms in the period 1975–1979. The total explanation is enhanced and the share attributable to class resources reduced when we consider the channeling effect of ethnic facilitation. These statistical results confirm the analysis based on information costs and nepotism in their suggestion of a social contagion process by which coethnics selected industries for entry and overrepresentation.

INDUSTRIAL COOPERATION

Wherever business owners collaborate in restraint of trade, they can drive prices and profits above the levels obtained under competitive conditions. Naturally, the business owners' ability to cooperate encounters the problem of market competition, an insuperable barrier in at least some cases. That is, those entrepreneurs wishing to cooperate must sanction those who choose to compete. Unless the cooperators introduce effective sanctions, nonconforming competitors may compel them to join the general competition, abandoning hope for industrial cooperation.

Because Korean enterprises clustered in heavily Korean industries, Korean entrepreneurs confronted a paradoxical situation. On the one hand, many business competitors were coethnics, thus introducing competition in what "ought" to have been a relationship of ethnic solidarity (Yu, 1983: 67). Among the Los Angeles Korean proprietors we interviewed, 70.1 percent reported they had business competition, and of these about 38 percent indicated their "principal competitors" were fellow Koreans. For example, in the wig trade, 78.1

percent of competitors were Koreans. In their survey of Korean retailers in South Chicago, Kim and Hurh (1984: 47) also found that 50 percent of Korean store owners identified other Koreans as their "major business competitors." Intraethnic business competition extended to lease renewals, payment of goodwill in purchasing a continuing business, relations with suppliers, diversification of merchandise stocks and, of course, prices. Asked to identify the consequences of business competition, Korean merchants in Chicago mentioned prices so low as to threaten the survival of their firms.

On the other hand, precisely insofar as competitors were coethnics, Korean entrepreneurs could appeal to ethnic solidarity in the interest of regulating competition (I. Kim, 1981: 117).[4] In this sense, Korean ethnicity offered a social vehicle potentially capable of restraining business competition. Obviously, ethnic appeals could not be completely effective because in most trades no more than half of competitor firms were Korean-owned. Even in the Los Angeles wig industry, as close to a Korean monopoly as any, only 70.1 percent of competitor firms were under Korean ownership. Thirty percent were not. Assuming furthermore that all Korean-owned firms cooperated in restraint of trade, non-Korean firms in the industry would have prevented Koreans from obtaining monopoly power on the basis of appeals to Korean ethnic solidarity.

Nonetheless, the clustering of Koreans in industries conferred a potential for moderating competition, exchanging information, and mutual aid. Since this potential would have been absent had Koreans been evenly distributed among County occupations and industries, clustering provided Koreans with a resource non-Koreans proprietors lacked except, of course, insofar as non-Korean proprietors too had ethnic resources upon which to draw. In this sense, ethnic clustering of the Koreans created an industrial situation that increased the likelihood of Korean cooperation in business. Admittedly, coethnic cooperation required work and could not extend to monopolistic control of any industry. Nonetheless, between the extremes of control and powerlessness Koreans influenced the industries in which they participated, thus translating ethnic solidarity into a business resource.

Koreans cooperated in formal and informal ways. Informal cooperation involved mutual aid in social as well as business roles (Yu, 1983: 67). Formal cooperation involved the creation of Korean trade associations and chambers of commerce with elected leadership, a mailing address, and dues-paying membership. Additionally, a Korean caucus within non-Korean professional or business associations could influence the behavior of those. To investigate the extent to which Koreans developed or utilized trade, business, and professional associations, we examined the Keys directories for 1975, 1978, and 1980 under the heading "Non Profit Organizations." The 1980 directory listed twenty-four associations of which eleven had been listed also in both the 1975 and 1978 directories, ten had been listed also in the 1978 directory, and three were listed for the first time in the 1980 directory. Additionally, the 1975 and 1978 Korean directories contained thirteen associations that were unlisted in the 1980 directory, presumably having failed in the interim. In all, the three Korean directories listed twenty-one business and sixteen professional organizations. Among the professional organizations 43.7 percent were listed in all three directories; only 19 percent of business organizations demonstrated this longevity.

The extent to which Koreans actually exerted the potential economic power that their industrial clustering bestowed is difficult to ascertain and should not be exaggerated. However, there is enough evidence that Koreans did exert some industrial leverage that one can safely reject the supposition that Koreans made no use of ethnic solidarity in business (McMillan, 1984). Exertion of industrial leverage benefited Koreans in two basic ways. First, inhibition of competition increased the money returns and reduced the labor of all proprietors in a trade, Korean and non-Korean, thus improving the attractiveness of the trade. Second, Korean mutual aid increased the number of Koreans who could operate firms at all. Since the ability of Koreans to accomplish these objectives depended upon coethnic solidarity, it is apparent that some portion of Korean overrepresentation in self-employment resulted from this ethic resource.

One way to assesss the extent of busesss and professional associations among Koreans is to compare their numbers with the listing of "membership organizations" which *County Business Patterns* collected. Table 42 juxtaposes data obtained from the 1978 *County Business Patterns* with comparable results from the 1978 Korean directory. The percentage distribution of results from the two sources shows that Koreans were heavily invested in civic and social, political, and especially religious organizations when compared to Los Angeles

Table 42. Nonprofit Membership Organizations in Los Angeles County: Koreans and All Persons, 1978

| | Los Angeles County, 1978 | | | Korean Directory, 1978 | | |
	Number	Percent	Rate*	Number	Percent	Rate*
Business Associations	336	10.4	.5	18	5.0	3.0
Professional Associations	123	3.8	.2	14	3.9	2.3
Labor Organizations	462	14.4	0.7	2	0.6	.3
Civic and Social	851	26.4	1.2	133	37.2	22.1
Political Organizations	30	0.9	.4	6	1.7	1.0
Religious Organizations	1,258	39.1	1.8	178	49.7	29.7
Membership Organizations	153	4.8	.2	7	2.0	1.2
Total	3,219	100	4.6	358	100	59.7

*Per 10,000 population

Sources: U.S. Bureau of The Census, County Business Patterns 1978, California CBP-78-6 (Washington, D.C.: USGPO, 1980), table 2; Haninrok, the Korean Directory of Southern California (Los Angeles: Keys Publishing Co., 1978).

County in general. The comparative organization rate per 10,000 population suggests still bigger differences. In general, the Koreans' rate was thirteen times greater than that of County residents. The Koreans' rate of religious organizations was nearly seventeen times higher than the general rate. More to the point, Koreans formed six times more business organizations, and eleven times more professional organizations than did County residents in general. However, in proportion to population, Koreans only formed half as many labor organizations as did County residents.[5] This evidence indicates that Koreans were better endowed with business and professional organizations than non-Koreans and presumably benefited from such market power as these organizations conferred.

The ability of Korean business organizations to exert power depended upon the percentage of Korean traders they enrolled, as well, of course, as the discretionary authority the organizations obtained from members. We interviewed thirteen spokesmen of Korean business and professional organizations. Nine interviews yielded the impression that the organizations existed mostly on paper, lacking real membership support. The president of the Korean Food Association (defunct in 1980) explained that his organization had thirty-eight members in 1977. Since the 1977 Korean directory identified 221 Korean grocery stores, the association's membership was only 17.2 percent of the total. The president complained that his association members were "friendly at meetings, but [they] hurt each other after the meeting." An attempt to create a group purchasing plan had failed. In point of fact, members of the association were waging a price war at the time of the interview, and the president bewailed the saturation of opportunities in the grocery trade. In response to a direct question, he indicated that grocers worked hard, thought only of themselves, and did not cooperate much.

The president of the Petroleum Dealers Association (also defunct in 1980) gave an equally gloomy report of his association's activities. The association had begun in 1972 with 40 members, and in 1977 claimed a membership of 80 from an estimated Korean dealer population of 200. The president, an accountant, ran the association as a "one man show" to benefit his clients, about half of whom were gasoline station operators. However, the last previous meeting of this association had been two years earlier and none of the eighty members bothered to pay the $10 annual dues. The president explained that his members understood the potential benefits of co-operation in trade, but were "too tight" to spend the dues money that would be required to establish a viable dealer organization. As a result, they tended to compete with one another.

Koreans came closest to an ethnic monoply in the retail wig industry, and it was not surprising, therefore, that a serious attempt at price conformity occurred in this trade. The president of the Korean Hair Products Association explained that his organization enrolled wig importers, not retailers. Its U.S. membership was eighty-one, of whom twenty-one resided in Southern California. The Hair Products Association had formed in 1972 when importers decided their industry contained "too much competition." With the assistance of the Korean government, the Hair Products Association attempted to set minimum prices for retailers, to control dumping, and to curtail direct sales to street peddlers (I. Kim, 1981: 134–135). However, a dealer complained to federal authorities, who initiated an antitrust action. On June 24, 1975 the U.S. District Court in the Southern District of New York enjoined the Korean Hair Products Association from furnishing Korean wig exporters "any list of the importers' trade association members or information concerning pricing or sales practices of any person." Additionally, the court required the Hair Products Association to admit to membership "any applicant who met reasonable and nondiscriminatory requirements" consistent with industrial competition. Finally, the court required the Hair Products Association to maintain minutes of meetings in which there was discussion of member complaints, commercial disputes, market conditions, distribution channels, advertising policies, sales practices, or relations between the Korean and U.S. wig industries.[6] The decree ended the Hair Product Association's efforts to impose price conformity upon retailers. However, South Korean continued to help the overseas wig dealers and had imposed a quota in 1977. The quota had not helped much, and the president of the Hair Products Association was pessimistic about the future of this industry in view of the excessive competition in it.

The Korean Business Women's Association was founded in 1976 and had enrolled sixty members by 1977. The association enrolled women business owners in many fields, especially liquor stores, restaurants, bars, clothing stores, shoe stores, and trading companies. The association offered membership to women aspiring to open stores as well as to those already self-employed. The president was also active in her high school alumnae association and a member of the Wilshire Chamber of Commerce, an area merchants group serving Koreatown and vicinity. The women members had not known one another before joining the association, she claimed. The association offered several services to members: it counseled members about how to purchase a business, it had translated the liquor law into Korean, and it had sponsored a trade show.

The general secretary of the Korean Christian Businessmen's Committee owned a travel agency and served the Businessmen's Committee without remuneration. In 1977 the committee enrolled thirty-seven Christian business owners. The board of directors screened applicants to verify character. Formal goals of the committee were Bible study, prayer, friendship, and charity. However, the general secretary acknowledged that between two and three members visited his office every day for business discussions. Additionally, members used the general secretary's travel service when they planned trips; and he used their businesses when in need of a product or service they sold.

Four Korean trade associations showed evidence of exerting power. The Korean Traders' Association of America enrolled fifty members in 1977. However, its membership list included some large firms in the import/export trade between Korea and the United States. The Traders' Association contained members representing a battery of specific trading interests of which the largest was garment manufacture followed by wigs, luggage and hand bags, shoes, and hardware. The Traders' Association published a weekly business news service receiving its daily information from the Korea Trade News Service in Seoul. The Traders' Association also organized member travel to Seoul's annual trade fair. The president explained that most of his daily activities involved answering questions of the membership on such subjects as regulations, tariffs, quotas, and so forth. In fact, the Traders' Association had come into existence in response to the need of Korean exporters and importers for accurate information about technical and legal requirements.

In 1979 the Korean Sewing Contractors Association shared offices with its president's garment factory in the heart of the Los Angeles garment district. The Sewing Contractors enrolled 160 Korean members, about 46 percent of the Koreans thought to be operating garment factories in Los Angeles and 8 percent of all firms in the industry. A few years later, the Sewing Contractors changed their organization's name to the Korean American Garment Industry Association and moved its headquarters to an office suite. By 1986, the KAGIA claimed 400 members, 57 percent of the 700 Korean sewing contractors thought to be active in Los Angeles. Although possibly the largest, the Korean contractors' association was not the only ethnic trade association in the garment industry in 1986. In fact, four ethnic trade associations existed in this industry: Chinese, Korean, Latin American, and American (mostly Jewish) These four sometimes combined into an umbrella organization called the Confederated Clothing Contractors of America. However, according to officials of the Korean garment association, the Conferederated Clothing Contractors met infrequently and then only in response to specific problems.

Growth of the KAGIA owed a lot to the state's Concentrated Enforcement Division, whose investigative sweeps multiplied its membership roll. The director of the enforcement program called Koreans "very well organized," crediting their high educational background. The president of the KAGIA claimed that his association's purpose was "to help each other and to understand the labor law." [7] Prior to the association's formation, he had not known the other officers. He agreed that the state's enforcement drives had stimulated his organization's growth, supposing that labor unions were probably behind the drive. As far as the contractors were concerned, the president explained with heat, the main problem was powerlessness. Because their industry was so competitive, contractors had to accept low-priced contracts that they could not fulfill without the use of undocumented workers paid less than the statutory minimum wage. The contractors devoutly wished to establish a pricing standard that would permit them to operate within the labor code. To accomplish this objective, the contractors needed solidarity. The president pointed out that the contractors' association had also held many seminars for members on the subject of their obligations under the labor code. An officer had even translated sections into Korean. The association also provided legal and business advice over the telephone. It offered a group insurance plan. "We don't make any big effort to get members," said the executive director. "Koreans need our association's help."

Jin (1981: 75) surveyed 153 Korean sewing contractors. Asked to evaluate the KAGIA, almost 30 percent thought that exchange of information and of techniques was the organization's most important service. Another 24 percent thought that the "role of the association was to end the excessive competition among the Korean sewing contractors." A fifth thought collective bargaining was the organization's chief service. Only 2 percent thought the organization was useless. As Jin noted: "This means that a clear majority of contractors surveyed acknowledged the need for the ... Korean Sewing Contractors Association to support their business activities" (1981: 77).

The Southern California Korean Grocery and Liquor Retailers Association (SCKGLRA) began in November 1982 with 47 charter members. Four years later the association had 1089 members of whom 729 operated groceries with a liquor license and 360 operated groceries without a liquor license. Annual gross sales of the membership totaled $1 billion in 1985. According to the president, the association's members were 39 percent of all Korean dealers in the five-county Southern California region. Koreans turned over 40 percent of all industry sales in 1985. Therefore, the Korean association enrolled about 16 percent of all grocery and liquor dealers in Southern California. The association attracted membership by its bulk-buying program, thus obtaining a discount price on some staple items, especially soft drinks. The association inserted a Korean-language page in the *Beverage Bulletin,* a trade periodical, and also published a monthly bulletin and newsletter in Korean. Additionally, the association assisted members in "establishing good relations" in black and Mexican neighborhoods where many Korean stores operated, even "acting as a liaison if needed." Finally, the association lobbied major beverage manufacturers to open more "dealerships or distributorships" to Korean entrepreneurs.[8]

Of all the Korean business associations, the Korea Town Development Association (KTDA) had assembled the most successful record of political action. Originally an association of real estate developers and traders, the Korean Town Development Association engineered the creation and recognition of Koreatown. It accomplished this task by publicizing in Seoul information about Los Angeles' small Korean community, so that new immigrants would know where to locate when they reached Los Angeles—driving up Koreatown rentals and property values in the process. The association also pursued publicity and political contacts in Los Angeles. In February 1973 the association offered free business signs in the Korean language for any persons requesting the service. The offer produced sixty acceptances and Koreatown obtained immediate visibility (Smith, 1976: 34). Additionally, the Development Association sponsored the first annual Korean-American parade in 1975. This parade attracted 100,000 spectators in 1982 as well as the mayor, the governor, and the chief of police. As a result of KTDA efforts, the City of Los Angeles installed street signs proclaiming the area "Koreatown," and the California Department of Transportation installed a "Koreatown" exit notice along a highly traveled freeway. This notice brought business to Koreatown merchants. When street crime became a problem in Koreatown, the KTDA complained to police, and, when their complaints were ineffective, took up a collection from area merchants to pay for a "Koreatown substation" from which two uniformed officers operated for about one year. The KTDA also orchestrated a large, if unsuccessful, protest of City Hall's redistricting plan (Decker and Simon, 1986).

The KTDA explained its purposes in a number of public statements to the press. On one occasion, the president told fellow Koreans that "prosperity of shops" was the motive propelling the social development of the whole Korean community. To this end, he explained, the KTDA attempted to attract new Korean firms to Koreatown, sponsored seminars on business problems, and urged "prevention of overheated competition among Korean business firms." The KTDA also sponsored a "Buy Korean" campaign intended to encourage Koreans to patronize stores owned by coethnics.[9] On another occasion, the Orange County Korea Town Development Association sponsored a meeting of Korean grocery store owners at which business owners discussed "various ways to avoid excessive competition among themselves."[10] They decided to close stores every Wednesday, reduce their throat-cutting price competition, and stop offering gifts to customers.

This review establishes a context for evaluating the extent to which Korean trade associations were exerting market power. Most Korean trade associations were weak. Only the KTDA, the Korea Traders, the Grocery and Liquor Retailers, and the KAGIA had achieved tangible benefits resulting from cooperation. These benefits were important, and they prove that Koreans utilized formal institutional arrangements to coordinate economic activity. Indeed, on the one hand, without the Korea Town Development Association, Koreans in Los Angeles would have lacked a central residential community—as Koreans in New York City lacked it. On the other hand, the benefits of institutional coordination were not so great as to justify the claim that Korean overrepresentation in commerce depended upon institutional coordination.

Our research occurred in an early phase of Korean business development, and one would expect formal trade associations to consolidate power after the Korean business population peaked. Koreans understood the desirability of coethnic solidarity in trade and took every opportunity to remind one another of it as well as to reassert the low value Korean culture places on competition. For example, at a meeting of fifteen Korean chambers of commerce and business associations from all across the United States, one association president reported that all participants "held the same feeling that we must unite ourselves to promote and protect our ethnic interests in the mainstream." [11] As the recession deepened in 1980, the Korean Chamber of Commerce and Industry (of Southern California) urged Korean business owners throughout its region to undertake "more cooperation ... in economic activities."

Given their industrial clustering, Koreans found coethnics overrepresented among their business competitors, a situation they deemed humiliating because, as Yosup Lee (1982) observed, "competition is not held in high esteem in the Korean speaking world." This humiliation explains the despair implicit in Sunny Kim's analysis of her failure to organize Korean boutique owners. Kim had wished to "see a cooperative organized among Korean boutique women" so that all could "survive" (K. Lee, 1980)

> But everybody says it will not work. I get discouraged by their saying Koreans are always fragmented. It is very sad. (K. Lee, 1980)

However, shame caused Koreans to strengthen ethnic solidarity. For this reason, solidarity and solidarity-building were Korean preoccupations.[12] This preoccupation emerges clearly from Hwa Soo Lee's (1982: 192) survey of 118 voluntary associations among Los Angeles Koreans. Lee found numerous small, poorly attended associations that concentrated upon "members' immediate interests or community affairs." Leaders felt their associations were making contributions to the Korean community, but bewailed the low solidarity in the Korean community. Regarding their own achievements, the leaders of Korean voluntary associations identified enhancement of coethnic solidarity and community services. Church and alumni association leaders also regretted inadequate solidarity among coethnics, but congratulated themselves for having strengthened fellowship among members. Many recounted incidents that epitomized the mutual aid they encouraged. For example, the president of a high school alumni club had assisted eight alumni in job searches. In his opinion, Koreans helped each other because of a norm of mutual aid formed in Korea's long history of external oppression. Asked why they had formed an alumni club in the first place, officers explained the purpose was to bring together people who had the old school in common. A puzzling, bland response, this answer actually reflected an underlying consensus upon the desirability of enhanced solidarity.

Numerous instances of mutual aid among business owners surfaced in these interviews. One alumni president told us about a businessmen's committee composed of ten to fifteen friends who gathered to "talk" about business problems. If a gas station owner found his trade too slow, he would ask around for a brisker trade, soliciting the help of the circle's accountant in evaluating his capital adequacy. Clearly, these business conversations were understood as byproducts of the more basic purpose of the alumni groups and churches: promotion of solidarity.

SUMMARY

Class theory advances an individualistic explanation of overrepresentation in business and industrial clustering: both arise as a result of independent calculations by persons equally endowed with money and human capital. This chapter supports some aspects of class theory. First, regression results are compatible with the claim that Koreans entered the general business population as resource-endowed individuals, a process independent of ethnicity. Second, Koreans apparently utilized class resources of money and education to effect this entry.

However, we also found evidence of ethnic facilitation, a process less understood than class theory and stressed for this reason. Ethnic facilitation involves the entrepreneurial utilization of collective resources. Insofar as they reflected a cultural orientation, hard work and the willingness to take low wages were also ethnic resources. But we also found evidence of nepotism and chauvinism in hiring—which are resources because of the diligent labor force they provided at low search cost. Additionally, information channels structured the access of Koreans to business information, simultaneously reflecting the present and producing the future. A regression analysis found that Korean industrial distributions reproduced themselves to an extent that could not be explained by control variables. Finally, Koreans cooperated formally and informally to exert market power and improve their chances in competition—while making embarrassed efforts to raise the community's level of social solidarity.

Class and ethnic resources coproduced the Korean business population. On the one hand, Korean business owners invested and calculated in a typically bourgeois manner. On the other hand, Korean business owners had access to ethnic resources that they utilized in furtherance of business objectives. Therefore, Korean business was the creation of an ethnic bourgeoisie, not just a bourgeoisie.

8

Business Location

Thus far we have examined the number of Korean firms in Los Angeles County, their industrial distribution, and their characteristics. In this chapter we turn to the spatial distribution of Korean firms in Los Angeles County. Korean business firms were not evenly distributed in Los Angeles County nor did their actual distribution correspond closely with the general distribution of business firms (Holley, 1985). This uneven and unique territorial arrangement permits inferences about the extent and form of Korean integration in the business population. First, territorial distribution and clustering of Korean firms implies their likely customers. Second, it betokens the probable source of their principal business competition. Third, changes in territorial clustering and distribution are important because of the corresponding changes in clientele, competition, and residence which they suggest.

METHODS

Using the Keys' Korean directories for 1975, 1977, and 1979, we coded Korean-owned businesses by industry and zip code. In addition, we obtained zip-coded data on useful social indicators from the United Way, an umbrella organization of private charities. The Los Angeles County Departments of Regional Planning and Community Development provided tabulations of business enterprises in the country by zip code and industry for 1973.[1] Juxtaposing these three data sources, we were able to examine the distribution and growth of Korean business by industry and to make inferences about their clientele and competition in each postal zip code.

Using zip codes as the major unit of analysis poses two problems, one minor and one severe. The minor problem is that the post office occasionally changed zip codes, redrawing boundaries or adding new numbers. In coding Korean businesses we used zip codes as currently listed in each directory. The second, more serious problem is the hazard of ecological correlation. Strictly speaking, one cannot infer the clientele of Korean retail and service businesses from the socioeconomic characteristics of the zip codes in which those businesses were located. After all, the clients of Korean businesses might have only been those with nondominant characteristics such as, for example, eccentric millionaires who lived in slums. Obviously it would be preferable to have direct data on who were the customers of Korean-owned businesses but since, except for our proprietors' telephone survey, we do not have that information, we must utilize ecological correlation accepting the known hazard of generalization from such data.

This chapter is divided into three sections, each of which utilizes a slightly different approach to the spatial characteristics of Korean business sites. The first section emphasizes the changing distribution of Korean firms within and outside of Koreatown. Our purpose is to assess the extent to which Koreatown had a peculiar mix of businesses and industries because of its heavily Korean clientele. Underlying this approach is the crude division of Los Angeles County into two areas: Koreatown and outside Koreatown. The second section abandons this dualism, examining instead the location of Korean firms within five socioeconomic areas of Los Angeles County. This section retains the assumption that Koreatown was economically unique, but distinguishes areas within the remainder of the County, showing that Korean participation varied in quality and volume in the zones. Finally, we abandon areal categories in favor of socioeconomic analysis of zip codes in which Korean businesses located. This approach treats Los Angeles County as a mosaic of 251 zip codes whose socioeconomic characteristics affected the number and industry of Korean firms located in them.

KOREATOWN AND OTHER AREAS

Unlike New York City, Koreans in Los Angeles had a residential and commercial center (I. Kim, 1981: 315–316). They called this neighborhood "Koreatown." Basing their designation on Korean residential population, Lee and Wagatsuma (1979) defined Koreatown's constituent zip codes: 90006, 90004, 90005, 90007, 90019, and 90020. Although not a residential area, Wilshire Boulevard (90010) runs

Table 43.   Korean and General Population of Los Angeles
County by Areas, 1977 and 1979

Area	Korean Population, 1977		All Persons Los Angeles County, 1979	
	Number	*Percent*	*Number*	*Percent*
Koreatown	20,308	34.8	92,599	1.3
Area 5	7,023	12.0	1,372,880	19.5
Areas 1–4	31,090	53.2	5,566,596	79.2
Total	58,421	100.0	7,032,075	100.0

Source: Changsoo Lee and Hiroshi Wagatsuma, "The Settlement Patterns of Koreans in Los Angeles." Paper presented Asian Studies Association Annual Meeting, Los Angeles, CA, March 30, 1979.

through these zip codes and can reasonably be assigned to Koreatown. Lee and Wagatsuma also listed five heavily Korean zip codes on the periphery of central Koreatown. Although the peripheral zip codes are dispersed, we defined the 1979 Koreatown as the seven core zip codes plus the five peripheral ones.

Of an estimated 58,421 Koreans in Los Angeles County in 1977, approximately 35 percent resided in Koreatown (table 43). Another 12 percent resided elsewhere in the United Way's area 5, a distressed central city district within whose northwestern border Koreatown actually is situated. The remaining 53.2 percent of Koreans resided in United Way areas 1 through 4, which included near suburbs and nonghetto city neighborhoods. The territorial concentration of Koreans within the County's five regions appears strongly when contrasted with the territorial concentration of all persons. Koreans were 22 percent of persons within the twelve Koreatown zip codes, 0.5 percent in area 5, 0.6 percent in areas 1 through 4, and 0.8 percent in Los Angeles County.

The zip codes that became Koreatown were not distinctively Korean in character in 1969 and 1970 because the migration from Korea was only beginning in those years. Nonetheless, one can infer the character of the district from comparision with other areas of Los Angeles in 1970. Although technically within the northwest sector of the United Way's area 5, the County's most distressed central portion, Koreatown escaped the depressed conditions existing in the core of area 5. One sign was the intermediate proportion of black and

Table 44.   Korean Firms by Industry Inside and Outside of
Koreatown, 1975 and 1979

	1975		1979	
	Number	*Percent*	*Number*	*Percent*
Koreatown				
Agriculture	0	0.0	0	0.0
Mining	0	0.0	0	0.0
Construction	3	0.7	15	1.5
Manufacturing	14	3.1	7	0.7
Transportation, Public Utilities	16	3.6	24	2.5
Wholesale Trade	38	8.5	45	4.6
Retail Trade	140	31.3	364	37.4
Finance, Insurance, Real Estate	31	6.9	66	6.8
Service	206	46.0	451	46.4
TOTAL	448	100.0	972	100.0
Outside Koreatown				
Agriculture	0	0.0	0	0.0
Mining	0	0.0	0	0.0
Construction	9	1.1	30	1.8
Manufacturing	20	2.4	59	3.5
Transportation, Public Utilities	15	1.8	39	2.3
Wholesale Trade	72	8.7	147	8.7
Retail Trade	438	52.8	803	47.3
Finance, Insurance, Real Estate	26	3.1	80	4.7
Service	249	30.0	541	31.8
TOTAL	829	100.0	1699	100.0
COUNTY TOTAL	1277		2671	

Source: Haninrok, the Korean Directory of Southern California (Los Angeles: Keys Publishing Co., 1975, 1979).

Hispanic persons in Koreatown. Higher than the Los Angeles County average, this percentage was appreciably lower than the black and Spanish proportion of the rest of area 5 (table 44). An area in transition, Koreatown was actually losing white population when the migration of Koreans began. This migration stabilized the neighborhood's total population and middling socioeconomic character. In the late 1970s, Koreatown remained an ethnically mixed area in which

Koreans represented approximately 22 percent, blacks and Hispanics 39 percent, and other Asians and whites 39 percent.

Table 44 shows the distribution of Korean firms by industry in Koreatown and the rest of Los Angeles County in 1975 and 1979. About 46 percent of Koreatown's businesses were in service industries, a proportion that remained stable despite growth in absolute numbers. The second most important industrial concentration in Koreatown was retailing, accounting for about one-third of all businesses. In contrast to services, the proportion of retailing grew rapidly. Retail and service firms represented more than three-quarters of all Koreatown enterprises. Retail and service were equally significant outside Koreatown, but their proportions were reversed. Outside Koreatown retail predominated, accounting for about half of all Korean enterprise. In contrast, services made up less than one-third of the total. Although the retail sector showed a proportional decline, retail trade remained the predominant activity of non-Koreatown entrepreneurs.

This contrast between Koreatown and outside Koreatown makes linguistic sense. Service industries require more English-language skills than do retail. As the center of Korean community in Los Angeles, Koreatown provided Korean-language services for immigrants.[2] The distribution of the remaining business lines showed no striking contrasts between the two areas. True, manufacturing and wholesale were more stable outside Koreatown, though their proportions of the total were roughly similar. Finance, insurance, and real estate were slightly more prominent in Koreatown. But, generally, the levels of representation of remaining industries were similar.

The outstanding economic characteristic of Koreatown was industrial diversity. As the residential center of Los Angeles' 58,421 Koreans, Koreatown offered an institutionally complete business environment in which Koreans could buy a wide range of goods and services from coethnics (Breton, 1964). The *Los Angeles Times* estimated that 70 percent of customers in Koreatown's Korean stores were Korean, 10 percent were other Asians, and 20 percent were non-Asian (Holley, 1985). On the other hand, outside Koreatown, Koreans in business needed to obtain non-Korean customers, competing in the process with non-Korean sellers. As a result, Korean business outside Koreatown sought the benefits of industrial specialization.

These conclusions emerge from table 45, which compares indus-

Table 45.   Percentage of Korean Firms in Each Industry
Class by Location for 1975 and 1979

Location		Korean Firms in Industries of Los Angeles County			
		Few	Some	Many	Total
1975	Koreatown	48.4	42.9	25.9	34.5
	Other Areas	51.6	57.1	74.1	65.5
	Total	100.0	100.0	100.0	100.0
		(384)	(140)	(753)	(1277)
1979	Koreatown	67.0	37.6	25.4	34.9
	Other Areas	33.0	62.4	74.6	65.1
	Total	100.0	100.0	100.0	100.0
		(460)	(487)	(1734)	(2681)

Source: *Haninrok, the Korean Directory of Southern California* (Los Angeles: Keys Publishing Co., 1975, 1979). Data for 1977 were deleted to economize space.

tries with few, some, or many Korean firms in respect to the firms' location inside or outside of Koreatown. Firms per industry means the number of Korean firms identified in a two-digit SIC category. Thus, in few-firm industries, 48.4 percent of Korean firms were located in Koreatown and 51.6 percent outside Koreatown in 1975. By contrast, in many-firm industries, 25.9 percent were located in Koreatown and 74.1 percent outside Koreatown in the same year. These results are reproduced for 1975 and 1979, demonstrating considerable stability. In industries with many Korean firms, three-quarters of firms were located outside Koreatown, the saturated core. In contrast, in few-firm industries, half or less than half located outside Koreatown. In the few-firm industries, the saturation of Koreatown's market was incomplete so a higher proportion of firms could locate there.

In view of the 78 percent non-Korean composition of Koreatown, the contrast of Koreatown and other areas must not be mistaken for a contrast of a strictly Korean clientele and a strictly non-Korean clientele. Many Korean firms in Koreatown had non-Korean customers; some Korean firms outside Koreatown had Korean customers. Nonetheless, grosso modo, the contrast of Koreatown and other areas does reflect the specialization of Koreatown in Korean clientele and of other areas in non-Korean clientele. This underlying ethnic specialization tilted the many-firm industries toward other areas and the few-firm industries toward Koreatown.

FIVE SOCIOECONOMIC AREAS

Koreatown created a unique business enviroment with a high density of Korean firms in an institutionally complete ethnic economy. However, two-thirds of Korean-owned firms were located outside of Koreatown. Roughly speaking, this two-thirds of firms participated in the general economy and was responsive to it. One evidence of this responsiveness is enhanced specialization outside the enclave (table 45). Another evidence is the specialized socioeconomic niches in which Korean firms predominated. Constituting 80 percent of the Korean business population, service and retail firms tended to locate in nonwhite, low-status, and low-income areas. In such areas competition from big business was minimal, and the resources of Korean entrepreneurs were most effective.

Table 46 divides Los Angeles County into five socioeconomic areas distinguished by the United Way (Bonacich and Jung, 1982: 86–88). Comparing the five areas with respect to average standing on five indicators of economic hardship and crime, we find that area 5 was consistently worst. That is, area 5 ranked higher than any other in respect to percentage of labor force unemployed, percentage of population in poverty, percentage of population receiving public assistance, and juvenile arrests per 10,000 youths; and it ranked lower than any other area in respect to average family income. Additionally, area 5 ranked worse than the County average on each of the above indicators of economic deprivation and crime. Finally, when areas with Korean firms are compared with County means, one finds Korean firms consistently located in areas with higher than average crime and economic hardship.

Admittedly, these results are complicated by the location of Koreatown in the northeast corner of area 5. It is desirable to distinguish Korean firms located in Koreatown from Korean firms elsewhere in area 5 (table 49). The Korean firms located in area 5 but outside Koreatown represented 31.8 percent of all Korean firms in 1979, and firms located in areas 1 through 4 represented 26 percent of the total. Yet area 5 contained 19.5 percent of Los Angeles County population in 1970 whereas areas 1 through 4 contained 79.2 percent

Table 46. Social Indicators by Areas of Los Angeles County and United Way Areas of Korean Business Concentration, 1970

	United Way Areas:					LA County		Weighted Mean: Zipcodes with Korean Firms
	1	2	3	4	5	Total		
Average Annual Family Income	10,597	10,111	9,972	10,720	7,783	9,756		8,454
Percent Labor Force Unemployed	6.1	5.1	5.6	5.9	8.0	6.2		7.3
Percent Population in Poverty	5.1	6.1	6.0	5.5	14.7	7.9		10.1
Percent Receiving Public Assistance	3.2	3.7	3.7	3.2	8.5	4.7		6.7
Juvenile Arrests per 10,000 Youths, 11–18 Years Old	121.6	149.3	142.5	156.5	269.6	169.5		181.8

Source: United Way of Los Angeles, *Los Angeles County Social Status Report* (Los Angeles: Uni-Parc, 1973).

Table 47.   Korean Retail and Service Firms in Zip Codes
by Region, 1979 (in percentages)

Korean Firms in Zipcodes	Koreatown	Area 5	Areas 1–4	Total
Retail				
No Korean Firms	0.0	4.2	40.3	31.5
1–10 Korean Firms	25.0	62.5	59.2	58.2
11 or More Korean Firms	75.0	33.3	0.5	10.3
Total	100.0	100.0	100.0	100.0
Service				
No Korean Firms	0.0	22.9	46.6	39.8
1–10 Korean Firms	16.7	66.7	52.9	53.8
11 or More Korean Firms	83.3	10.4	0.5	6.4
Total	100.0	100.0	100.0	100.0
N (= zip codes)	(12)	(48)	(191)	(251)

Source: *Haninrok, the Korean Directory of Southern California* (Los Angeles: Keys Publishing Co., 1979).

of total population (table 43). Obviously the Korean-owned firms had formed a secondary cluster, inferior only to Koreatown itself, in the downtrodden central portion of Los Angeles County (Light, 1987).

Additional confirmatory evidence appears in table 47, which shows Korean retail firms per zip code for socioeconomic regions in 1979. The density of Korean retail and service firms was greatest in Koreatown where three-quarters of twelve zip codes contained eleven or more firms, one-quarter of zip codes contained one to ten firm, and no zip code lacked Korean-owned firms. In area 5, one-third of forty-eight zip codes contained eleven or more Korean-owned firms, 62.5 percent contained one to ten Korean firms, and 4.2 percent contained no Korean firms. Finally, in areas one through four, only 0.5 percent of 191 zip codes contained eleven or more Korean firms, 59.2 percent contained one to ten firms, and 40.3 percent contained no Korean firms. A similar distribution is apparent in services.

The tripartite areal division of Los Angeles County provided an unusual opportunity to check the accuracy of Korean business data derived from Korean directories. This accuracy was uncertain because of unknown errors arising from possibly more thorough coverage of within-Koreatown than outside-Koreatown business enterprises.

By good luck and the intervention of Mayor Tom Bradley of Los Angeles, we obtained a microfiche copy of the February 1980 business tax license roll for the City of Los Angeles. This roll registered all licensed firms doing business in the City of Los Angeles. The City of Los Angeles is an incorporated area with a population of approximately 3 million, wholly enclosed within the large County of Los Angeles whose 1980 population was approximately 7 million. Since this roll listed licensees alphabetically, we were able to extract licencees named Kim from the total roll. Tae-Hwan Jung inspected the Kim roll, and purged it of non-Koreans, leaving 1,865 Koreans named Kim as a 22 percent sample of the Korean business population of Los Angeles (Shin and Yu, 1984). Since the tax roll included the zip code of each licensee's business address, we could establish the socioeconomic zone of every Kim-owned business in the City of Los Angeles. Unfortunately, a business tax roll is not a business roll because some firms (such as grocery chains) bought a license for each outlet, and some firms bought a license for each taxable activity. Therefore, we could not validly juxtapose the Kim roll with the directories to obtain an independent estimate of the absolute size of the Korean business population.

Two information sources indicate that the distribution of Korean-owned firms among the three socioeconomic areas diverged from that of all firms. The first source is the business license tax roll for the City of Los Angeles in February 1980. Representing about 1 percent of the population of the City of Los Angeles, Koreans held 4.9 percent of all business licenses in 1980. Table 48 juxtaposes the areal distribution of business licensees named Kim with a one-in-sixty systematic sample of the business license tax roll of the City of Los Angeles in 1980. Comparing the percentages of both populations in the three socioeconomic areas, we find that 39.5 percent of Kim licensees were in Koreatown compared to 13.5 percent of general licensees. Thirty-nine percent of Kims indicated an area 5 address compared with 35.6 percent of all licensees. Finally, 21.2 percent of Kim licensees reported addresses in area one through four whereas 50.9 percent of all licensees did so. Although unequally distributed among the three socioeconomic areas, Kims were actually overrepresented in each. That is, Kims were 14.4 percent of all licensees in Koreatown, 5.4 percent of all licensees in area 5, and 2.0 percent of licensees in areas one through four.

Table 48.   Korean and General Business Licensees and
Firms in the City and County of Los Angeles, 1980
(percentages)

	City of Los Angeles		County of Los Angeles	
	*Kim**	*All Licensees***	*Korean*[†]	*All Firms*[††]
Koreatown	39.5	13.5	42.4	6.5
Area 5	39.3	35.6	31.8	31.5
Other	21.2	50.9	26.0	62.0
Total	100.0	100.0	100.0	100.0
Number	(1865)	(2869)	(2658)	(129,348)

 * All Korean licensees named Kim. Estimated size of Korean licensee population =
1865/.22 = 8477 or 4.9% of total licensees.
 ** 1-in-60 systematic sample of approximately 172,000 business licensees in the City
of Los Angeles, February 1980.
 [†] Data from *The Korean Director of Southern California* (Los Angeles: Keys Publishing
Co., 1979).
 [††] Data from Los Angeles County Departments of Regional Planning and Community Development, *Industrial-Commercial Employment Project* (Los Angeles: County Board
of Supervisors, 1973).

As we have pointed out, the City of Los Angeles is wholly
encompassed by the surrounding County of Los Angeles—of whose
population the City contained 40 percent in 1980. Koreatown is situated wholly within the City of Los Angeles, but parts of area 5 and
much of areas one through four are County territory. Yu (1982a: 30)
estimated that 54 percent of Los Angeles' Koreans resided in the City
of Los Angeles in 1977–1980. The balance resided in Los Angeles
County. Table 49 compares the Korean and general business population of the County of Los Angeles. We derived the Korean estimates from the 1979 Korean directory. To obtain areal estimates of
the general business population, we utilized Los Angeles County's
own sample survey of the business population in 1973.[3] Again, the
evidence indicates unequal distributions of the two business populations among the three socioeconomic areas. Forty-two percent of
Korean firms in Los Angeles County were located in Koreatown
compared to only 6.5 percent of all County firms. In area 5, about
one-third of the Korean and the general business population reported
addresses in area 5. In area one through four, we identified only 26.0
percent of Korean firms compared to 62.0 percent of all firms.
   Comparing County estimates and City estimates, we note that,

Table 49.   Korean and General Business Firms by Area
and Industry (in percentages)

	Korean Firms, 1975	Korean Firms, 1979	Los Angeles County Firms, 1973
Koreatown	42.9	42.2	6.5
Area 5	37.5	31.8	31.5
Areas 1–4	19.6	26.0	62.0
Total	100.0	100.0	100.0
Number	(1266)*	(2658)*	(129,348)**
Area 5	65.2	55.0	33.7
Areas 1–4	34.8	45.0	66.3
Total	100.0	100.0	100.0
Number	(728)*	(1535)*	(120,893)**
Retail Trade	46.0	43.9	17.3
Services	34.8	35.2	32.3
All Other	19.1	20.8	50.2
Total	100.0	100.0	100.0
Number	(1266)*	(2658)*	(157,046)†

Sources: * The Korean Directory of Southern California, 1975, 1979; **Los Angeles County,
Departments of Regional Planning and Community Development, *Industrial-Commercial
Employment Project* (Los Angeles: County Board of Supervisors, 1973); † U.S. Bureau of
the Census, *County Business Patterns, 1978: California* (Washington, D.C.: USGPO, 1978),
pp. 64ff.

although both indicated overrepresentation of Koreans in the business population, the Koreans' margin of overrepresentation was
higher in the City than in the County. The only exception occurred
in area 5 where neither City nor County data showed much diver-
gence between the percentage of Korean and the percentage of
general firms reporting an area 5 address (table 48). This similarity
raises the possibility that, in area 5 at least, Koreans were simply part
of the general business population. We evaluated this possibility by
comparing the percentage of Korean firms to total firms in all industries and retail industries among the three socioeconomic areas. If the
percentages were the same in each industrial category, that identity
would indicate that Korean firms were members of the general business population in area 5. However, in all of the socioeconomic areas,
Koreans domonstrated a higher representation in retail trade than in
all industries. Even in area 5, where the percentage of Korean firms

did not depart markedly from the general percentage of firms, Koreans were 5.4 percent of all retail firms but only 2.1 percent of all firms. Therefore, Korean firms in every zone represented an *industrially specialized* component of the business population. Outside Koreatown, their specialization was retail trade in the most distressed socioeconomic area of Los Angeles County.

INDUSTRIAL GROWTH AND CHANGE,
1975–1979

Korean firms clustered in identifiable regions and industries of Los Angeles County. Clustering implies segregation from the general business population in terms of location as well as of industry. Assuming that Koreans will one day break out of the institutionally complete enclave economy, as they have every business motive to do, their business future lies in integration into the mainstream. Integration would eliminate the locational and industrial clustering of Korean firms leaving them, in the extreme case, with exactly the same locational and industrial characteristics as the general businesss population to which they would, indeed, belong.

Although limited, data do suggest that in the period 1975 to 1979, Korean firms had begun to break out of the *territorial* segregation that distinguished them from the general business population. But *industrial* segregation persisted. In table 49, note the comparison of three county regions in terms of the percentage of Korean firms located in each in 1975 and 1979 on the one hand, and, on the other, the percentage distribution of all county firms among the regions in 1973. Obviously, Koreans remained overrepresented in Koreatown where 42.2 percent of their firms were located in 1979 compared to only 6.5 percent of general firms. On the other hand, Koreans reduced their overrepresentation in area 5 and reduced their underrepresentation in areas one through four. This change emerges more clearly when Koreatown is removed, and Korean firms' percentage distribution is examined for area 5 and areas one through four only. In area 5 the percentage of Korean firms declined from 65.2 to 55.0 in this four-year period. Conversely, the percentage of Korean firms in areas one through four increased from 34.8 to 45.0 in the same period, thus moving closer to 62.0 percent, the County all-firm statistic. Similarly, the Korean percentage of firms in areas one through four increased

Table 50.   Koreans as a Percentage of Business Tax
Licensees in the City of Los Angeles by Date of
First License and Area, 1980

Area:	Date Licensed:			Total
	to 1970	*1970–1975*	*1976–1980*	
Koreatown	3.4	7.2	23.6	13.8
Area 5, Except Koreatown	1.3	3.1	10.5	6.0
Areas 1–4	0.8	0.9	3.8	2.3
City	1.4	2.5	9.1	5.4
Number	(38,274)	(45,333)	(74,184)	(157,791)*

*Excludes cases for which no zip code information was in file.
Source: City of Los Angeles, Business License Tax Roll for February 1980.

from 34.8 to 45.0 in the four-year period, thus bringing the Korean alignment into closer approximation with the County's.

On the other hand, data bearing on industrial segregation show scant decline from initial concentrations. Comparing retail trade, services, and all other industries, the bottom section of table 49 detects only a 2 percent increase in the underrepresented "all other" industries and a 2 percent decrease in the overrepresented retail trade. This modest change left the Korean industrial distribution skewed and abnormal when compared to the general county pattern.

Table 50 offers additional evidence bearing upon territorial clustering of the Korean business firms. Based on our samples of the 1980 business license tax roll of the City of Los Angeles, table 50 shows the percentage Korean of all business licensees in the three areas as of February 1980. However, table 50 also groups the licensees on the basis of the inception date of their license: 1969 and before, 1970 to 1975, and 1976 to 1980.

Although this procedure exposes the chronological age of survivor firms in the three areas, its unit of analysis is the City of Los Angeles rather than the County of Los Angeles as in table 49. Since the City of Los Angeles included less of areas one through four than did the encompassing County of Los Angeles, table 50 minimizes the true ringward shift of Korean firms, thus imposing a severe test of the suburbanization hypothesis. Nonetheless, the data confirm a relative shift of Korean business firms toward areas one through four in the period 1976 to 1980. As a percentage of the entire population of business tax licensees in the City, Korean licensees increased in all three areas in both 1970 to 1975 and in 1976 to 1978. However, in 1970 to 1975, the Korean percentage of all area 5 (except Koreatown) licensees increased 1.8 percent whereas the Korean percentage of all area one through four licensees increased only 0.1 percent. Conversely, in the period 1976 to 1980, the Korean percentage of area 5 licensees increased only 7.4 percent whereas the Korean percentage of area one through four licensees increased 2.9 percent.

ZIP CODE ANALYSIS OF KOREAN
BUSINESS LOCATIONS

Taken together, tables 49 and 50 depict expansion outside of Koreatown, especially in areas one through four, as well as liquidation of concentration in the central city, but stability in industrial distribution: in other words, Korean firms were practicing the same trades in nicer locations. One interpretation is upward mobility.[4] Korean business registered upward mobility when its center of gravity shifted from the depressed central city toward the suburbs. A grocery store in Pasadena was safer, cleaner, and more prestigious than a grocery store in Watts. Alternatively, boundary crossings might represent continuation of prevailing business styles in the low-income neighborhoods of areas one through four. After all, area 5 did not contain *all* of Los Angeles' poor neighborhoods. If new Korean retail and service firms opened in the shabbiest neighborhoods of areas one through four, this growth would represent radial expansion of the same barrel-scraping industries rather than upward mobility. Of course, these interpretations need not exclude one another. It would be possible for some boundary-crossing retail and service firms to move up and out while others merely moved out. But it would be desirable to know what was the balance between upward mobility and radial expansion.

To assess these possibilities, we switched the unit of analysis from five United Way areas to 251 postal zip codes. With zip code as the unit of analysis, correspondences between socioeconomic characteristics of a locality and number of Korean businesses provide a closer reflection of the socioeconomic environment of Korean firms. To measure socioeconomic environment we selected two items from the

Table 51.   Zero-order Correlations Between
Socioeconomic Indicators and Number of Korean Firms
in Zip Codes

	All Firms		Retail Firms		Service Firms	
	1975	1979	1975	1979	1975	1979
Los Angeles County						
Family Income	−.19*	−.17*	−.23*	−.19*	−.13	−.10
Low Education	.22*	.20*	.26*	.22*	.14	.10
Areas 1−4 Only						
Family Income	−.05	−.05	−.08	−.15	.01	.05
Low Education	.15	.20	.13	.26	.03	.05

*$p < .01$

Source: United Way of Los Angeles; *The Korean Directory of Southern California*, 1975,
1979.

United Way data set: family income (FAMINC) and percentage of
adult population with no more than eight years of education (LOED).
Table 51 shows the zero order correlations of these two socioeconomic indicators with the number of Korean firms in 1979 and
1975. Additionally, table 51 compares Los Angeles County with
areas one through four, excluding area 5 and Koreatown. In each case
the larger areal units consisted of grouped zip codes, and correlations
represent the correspondences between socioeconomic conditions
and number of Korean firms in member zip codes.

Looking first for evidence of social mobility in a business context,
we compared 1975 and 1979 in Los Angeles County. In both years,
low education and low family income were significantly associated
with Korean firms in total and with Korean retail firms, but not
with Korean service firms. Comparing 1975 and 1979 in areas one
through four, we find no significant associations between socioeconomic characteristics of zip codes and number of Korean total,
retail, or service firms. The result is compatible with the supposition
that Korean firms in Los Angeles County occupied zip codes with
lower socioeconomic status than did Korean firms in areas one
through four, the ring. In this sense, movement from core to ring
would normally signify some improvement of socioeconomic characteristics of firm zip codes, a result compatible with the mobility
hypothesis.

KOREAN POPULATION AND BUSINESS POPULATION

In evaluating the mobility hypothesis, socioeconomic characteristics of zip codes are essential, but a balanced explanation of firm location requires attention to alternative factors affecting it. Korean residential population and general business population are important alternatives. First, Korean residential population obviously affected Korean business concentration in and around Koreatown, and it would be valuable to learn to what extent Korean residential population continued to affect Korean business location outside Koreatown. Second, Koreans in business presumably responded to the same economic incentives that shaped the locational distribution of business in general. Therefore, the extent of and variations in correspondence between Korean and general business distributions might indicate how much integration Korean firms achieved in the general businesss population.

To assess the relative power of alternative determinants, we completed a regression analysis of four variables in three conditions and two years. Table 52 displays the standardized regression coefficients and R^2 resulting from this analysis. The four explanatory variables were Korean population in 1977 (KOPOP77), Los Angeles County retail firms in 1973 (LACRET), Los Angeles County service firms in

Table 52. Standardized Regression Coefficients of Korean Business Locations: Los Angeles County Zip Codes, 1975 and 1979

Korean Business Firms in County, CEK, and Areas 1–4	Dependent Variable:		
	County*	CEK**	Areas 1–4
Retail, 1975			
KOPOP77	.66	.28	.39
LACRET	.13	.19	.21
LOED	.09	.14	.05
FAMINC	−.10	−.15	−.06
R^2	.58	.33	.30
Retail, 1979			
KOPOP77	.75	.24	.40
LACRET	.04	.21	.23
LOED	.09	.22	.16

Table 52. (continued)

Korean Business Firms in County, CEK, and Areas 1–4	Dependent Variable:		
	County*	CEK**	Areas 1–4
FAMINC	−.06	−.15	−.07
R²	.64	.37	.37
Service, 1975			
KOPOP77	.86	.21	
LACSER	.08	.21	
LOED	.04	.10	
FAMINC		−.06	
R²	.77	.13	.00
Service, 1979			
KOPOP77	.66	.38	.48
LACSER	.21	.43	.35
LOED		.14	
FAMINC	−.05	−.08	
R²	.53	.44	.41
Firms, 1975			
KOPOP77	.81	.37	.43
LACTOT	.08	.12	.27
LOED	.09	.21	.05
FAMINC	−.05	−.12	−.04
R²	.71	.28	.35
Firms, 1979			
KOPOP77	.79	.32	.49
LACTOT	.07	.17	.35
LOED	.08	.24	.07
FAMINC	−.04	−.10	
R²	.67	.29	.50

All coefficients: $p < .01$ and exceed three times standard error.
*Los Angeles County, N = 251 zip codes
**Los Angeles County Except Koreatown, N = 239 zip codes
Variable Key:
KOPOP77   Korean population of each zip code, 1977
LACTOT   All business firms, each zip code, Los Angeles County, 1973
LACRET   All retail firms, each zip code, Los Angeles County, 1973
LACSER   All service firms, each zip code, Los Angeles County, 1973
LOED   Percentage of adult population with 0–8 years education, each zip code, Los Angeles County, 1970
FAMINC   Mean family income, each zip code, Los Angeles County, 1970
Sources: United Way of Los Angeles; Los Angeles County, *Industrial–Commercial Employment Project*; *The Korean Directory of Southern California*, 1975 and 1979; Lee and Wagatsuma, "Settlement Patterns of Koreans in Los Angeles."

1973 (LACSER), Los Angeles County firms in 1977 (LACTOT), percentage of residential population with less than an eighth-grade education (LOED), and mean family income (FAMINC). In general, Korean residential population (KOPOP77) emerged as the consistently strongest performer, far outdistancing the three others. Second ranking were three measures of general business population in retail (LACRET), service (LACSER), and total (LACTOT) industries. Third ranking were family income (FAMINC) and low education (LOED), both socioeconomic indicators of zip code ambiance. However, FAMINC and LOED represented dimensions of an underlying variable, socioeconomic status, so it is appropriate to add the coefficients to obtain a unitary measure of the underlying variable. When LOED and FAMINC coefficients are summed, the total exceeds the coefficients of the general business population in nine of eighteen conditions. In this sense, socioeconomic status of zipcodes and general business population tied for second rank as predictors of Korean business.

Regression results also display interesting patterning when year, industry, and area are compared. Comparing first the effects of KOPOP77, we note that, with one exception, the KOPOP77 coefficient is highest in the County, lowest in CEK (the County except Koreatown), and intermediate in areas one through four. The only exception occurred in 1975. In that year, none of the explanatory variables had *any* effect on Korean business population of area one through four services. However, in 1979 both LACSER and KOPOP77 registered huge increases, reflective, we believe, of an influx of Koreans into suburban service industries. The KOPOP77 improvement implies that suburban business growth was more attributable to residential suburbanization of Koreans than to joining the general business population, although both factors were at work. Koreans moved to the residential suburbs and opened businesses near their suburban homes.

Supporting this inference is the relative magnitude of KOPOP77 compared to LACSER, LACRET, and LACTOT. KOPOP77 exceeded LACRET, LACSER, and LACTOT in fifteen of eighteen cases, suggesting that where Koreans lived was a more important determinant of where they located their businesses than was the location of County businesses. In County zip codes, the effect of KOPOP77 was maximal, sometimes tenfold greater than the effect of business population. Naturally, this amplitude reflected the inclusion of Koreatown in the County, and the powerful concentration of Korean business and population in that neighborhood. On the other hand, differences in magnitude between KOPOP77 and business population were minimal in the County except Koreatown (CEK). Indeed, in 1979 service firms of CEK were *more* affected by business population (LACSER) than by Korean residential population (KOPOP77), a reversal of the prevailing relationship. Especially in the light of other results, this pattern suggests that Korean owners of area 5 stores were less likely to live near their stores than were Korean owners of either Koreatown or areas one through four stores: Koreans worked in area 5, but they frequently did not live in it.

When we examine socioeconomic coefficients, the presumptive causes of this perference emerge. Although generally the third-ranking variable, the two socioeconomic indicators are largest (mean = .29) in the CEK and smallest (mean = .09) in areas one through four zip codes. This pattern interacts with industry such that CEK retail firms operated in the worst neighborhoods whereas areas one through four service industries operated in the best. When areas are held constant, service firms selected higher-ranking neighborhoods for location than did retail firms. The reasons for this are that low-income people consume fewer services on the one hand, and, on the other, because Koreans avoided service industries in lower-status neighborhoods, possibly because of high risks associated with transportation to work sites in dangerous neighborhoods (Bloom, 1970: 40–41).

The magnitude of KOPOP77 requires discussion. Studies of Indian and Pakistani business in British cities (Aldrich, Jones, and McEvoy, 1984: 198–199; Aldrich et al., 1981) reported correlations of .61 between Asian population and Asian business in heavily Asian districts. Large correlations supported the claim (Cater, 1984: 222), buttressed by survey data, that Asian shops catered to Asian customers and could not, therefore, be understood as middleman enterprises. Since this British result was limited to heavily Asian areas, however, Aldrich (et al., 1981: 180) acknowledged that the ethnic demand explanation could not be demonstrated.

On first approach, the heavy effect of KOPOP77 upon Korean business locations in CEK, County, and areas one through four underscores the conclusions earlier advanced by British research. Indeed, the Los Angeles findings are more compelling than the British because industry was controlled, two observations were collected at separate moments, and the whole of the SMSA was subjected to analysis. Nonetheless, it would be untenable to conclude that ethnic patronage explains the magnitude of KOPOP77's effects. First, unlike Hindus and Pakistanis in Bradford, Ealing, and Leicester, (Aldrich et al., 1981: 171–173) Koreans in Los Angeles were *overrepresented* in retail and services trades. Given this overrepresentation one can rule out an ethnic market explanation of business location because eight-tenths of 1 percent of population could not very well support 4 percent of Los Angeles' retail and service proprietorships. Additionally, our telephone survey of 213 Korean-speaking proprietors (appendix 1) disclosed that fully 49.5 percent reported zero Korean clientele, and the mean was 23.3 percent Korean customers. Finally, Korean business locations make most sense when understood in the context of the Koreans' suburbanization. During the 1970s, suburbanization was permanently underway among Los Angeles Koreans who began their acculturation in Koreatown then relocated to suburbs as soon as income and language skills permitted (Hurh and Kim, 1984: ch. 3).[5] The percentage of Korean households in the City of Los Angeles declined from 70.1 in 1972 to 50.1 percent in 1979. The percentage of County Koreans who resided in Koreatown declined from 37 percent in 1977 to 29 percent in 1981 (Yu, 1983: 32). Indeed, Yu (1982a: 37) reported that 94 percent of Koreatown's residents in 1972 had relocated to suburbs by 1977. Like others, Koreans wished to work near their homes, and they satisfied this preference so long as they did not have to reside in central city neighborhoods. Central city stores were frequently worked by nonresidents who commuted to their business. Therefore, because Koreans preferred to work near their residences, Korean-owned stores were located in the vicinity of Korean settlements—but this connection does not prove that Korean stores depended upon the patronage of coethnics.

SUMMARY AND CONCLUSION

Between 1975 and 1979, Koreans continued to concentrate in retail trade in central Los Angeles. However, in this period, Koreans also achieved some residential social mobility. As Koreans settled in the suburbs, they opened businesses near their new homes. The result was suburbanization of Korean business and possibly reduction of the margin of ethnic patronage on which Koreatown firms depended for economic viability. However, Korean population remained a powerful influence on Korean businesses even in the suburbs because, like others, Koreans preferred to work in the vicinity of their stores. For this reason, Korean firms in the center zip codes depended to a larger extent than other Korean firms upon commuting proprietors who preferred not to live in the slums they serviced.

9

The Retail Liquor Industry

The retail liquor industry of Los Angeles consists of firms licensed to resell alcoholic beverages to the public for consumption on or off the premises. The structure of the retail liquor industry is simple: package liquor stores, grocery stores, taverns, and restaurants. Because Koreans have been active in each of these four, the retail liquor industry provides a microcosm of Korean enterprise in the County. Additionally, the State of California has imposed licensing requirements upon all retail liquor firms. Therefore, liquor licenses have created an archive of unparalleled accuracy and comprehensiveness permitting a case study of Koreans in commercial industry.

Table 53 indicates the number and percentage of Korean-owned liquor stores, grocery stores, and eating and drinking places in 1979. The 466 Korean-owned firms in the retail liquor industry constituted 17.4 percent of all Korean firms; among County firms in general, the 13,370 firms in the liquor industry constituted only 8.1 percent of total firms. Korean firms represented 3.5 percent of firms in the County's retail liquor industry even though Koreans were only 0.8 percent of County population in 1980. Hence, the Korean representation in the liquor industry was 438 where 100 was expected. Within the liquor industry, Koreans were most heavily represented in grocery stores and liquor stores; their ownership of bars and restaurants was below their average for the liquor industry as a whole.

METHOD OF ANALYSIS

This chapter analyzes public documents recording transfers of ownership of liquor licenses within the City of Los Angeles in 1975 and 1977. Specifically, this archive contains all acquisitions or sales of liquor licences in two of the five regulatory districts that constitute the City of Los Angeles. Since the California Constitution requires every liquor business to obtain a license, we have a comprehensive

Table 53. Korean Representation in the Los Angeles Retail Liquor Industry, 1979

	Establishments, 1979		Korean As Percent L.A. County	Index of Korean Representation [100 = Expected]
	L.A. County*	Korean**		
Liquor Stores	1,657	91	5.5	688
Grocery Stores	2,189	206	9.4	1,175
Eating and Drinking Places	9,524	169	1.8	225
Total	13,370	466	3.5	438

Sources: *U.S. Bureau of the Census, County Business Patterns 1979: California CBP-79-6 (Washington, D.C.: USGPO, 1980), table 2, p. 66ff.; **The Korean Directory of Southern California 1979 (Los Angeles: Keys Printing, 1979).

list of all acquisitions and transfers of liquor licenses. As such our data base is not a sample but the universe of all those who obtained or divested licenses in the given year within the regulatory districts studied. This comprehensiveness renders our data uniquely compelling as far as they go, but the data include no estimate of the underlying population of owners. That is, we obtained information about all licenses whose ownership was acquired or transferred—but we obtained no information about licenses that underwent no change of ownership. Since liquor businesses changed hands once every four years on the average, we estimate our universe included one-fourth of the license population in both of the targeted districts, but we have no knowledge of the representativeness of the known fourth. Obviously County data provide helpful estimates (table 53), but County boundaries include the City of Los Angeles, an autonomous chartered community occupying only one-quarter of the County's area. Therefore, one cannot be certain Koreans were 3.5 percent of liquor industry firms in the City of Los Angeles as well as in the County of Los Angeles.

The Department of Alcoholic Beverge Control (DABC) entered every liquor license modification in a daily ledger. The daily ledgers of the Hollywood Division of the DABC recorded 1420 administrative actions in 1975. Nearly 60 percent of actions concerned new license applications or transfers of a liquor license from one owner to another. DABC criteria also distinguished 31 additional actions, and the remaining 40 percent of ledger entries concerned these. To simplify we reduced the 31 residual categories to two: administration and sanctions. Administration consisted of routine approvals for changes in business license not involving transfer of license ownership. Withdrawals and temporary surrender of license were the most frequent cases. Sanctions—or punishments for rule violations—represented 4.4 percent of Hollywood DABC ledger entries in 1975, administration represented 36.1 percent, and ownership acquisition or transfer 59.2 percent. Comparable information was not sought in the Inglewood DABC ledgers from which we extracted only new applications and transfers of ownership.

The California Constitution (Art. XX, Sec. 22) assigns the regulation of the liquor industry to the state's Department of Alcoholic Beverage Control. Five DABC offices regulated Los Angeles' liquor industry. Of these five we obtained the file of "transfer sheets" from the Hollywood District for the whole year 1975 and from the Inglewood District for the whole year 1977. Each transfer sheet listed *all* the ownership transfers of liquor licenses that the DABC office approved on a single working day.

The Hollywood District and the Inglewood District derived their names from the place-named communities they served, but DABC boundaries did not correspond exactly to juridical boundaries. Both districts were big. The Hollywood Division encompassed 112 square miles including the northeast quadrant of the City of Los Angeles. The Inglewood Division encompassed almost as large a district abutting Hollywood on the north and extending as far as Downey to the south. Population composition of the two districts differed importantly. As the name implies, Hollywood contained the cinematic industry at its core, and therefore included a residential population of middle- and upper- income whites and white ethnics, artists, bohemians, and middle-status Asians. Chinatown, Little Tokyo, and Koreatown lay within the southern portion of the Hollywood Division. Inglewood contained the international airport and some heavy and light manufacturing industry. Its residential community consisted of mixed black, Mexican, Asian, and poor white people. Since our research interest initially focused on recent Asian immigrants, we selected the Hollywood Division for analysis because this division contained the most Asian firms. Later we decided to add a low-status, inner-city division for purposes of comparison, and selected the Inglewood Division as most closely approximating this condition.

To infer ethnicity we relied upon owner's surname using given name as a clue when surname was uncertain. Thus, Robert E. Lee was coded Anglo whereas Lim P. Lee was coded Chinese. The surname method of coding requires coders to recognize the ethnicity of surnames: Takahashi = Japanese; Kim = Korean; Lopez = Hispanic, and so forth. In our preliminary analysis we distinguished twenty-two ethnic categories. However, it appeared later that the categories were of unequal validity and reliability, so we reduced them to five only: Chinese, Japanese, Korean, Hispanic, and other. In these first four cases, we concluded, coders were reliably identifying ethnicity of surname. In addition we flagged problem cases in our analysis and these were personally completed by a senior investigator, from superior knowledge where possible and, when necessary, on the basis of random assignment.

The method of inferring ethnicity from surname has obvious limitations. Blacks are undetectable because their surnames are Anglo-American. White ethnics often carry modified Anglo-American surnames that mask cultural origins. Married women usually take the surname of their husband regardless of their own ethnic origin. Spanish surnames include a bewildering array of Hispanic minorities and would fail in New York City. However, in Los Angeles, Mexicans were 85 percent of the Spanish surnamed (Pilipinos ranked second) so we deemed the error tolerable. Of all groups East Asians were among the easiest to identify by surname, and with slight practice one can reliably distinguish Chinese, Japanese, and Korean surnames. Especially in the case of recent Asian immigrants who still bear unanglicized patronymics, the method of inferring ethnicity from surname is reliable and fast. Nonetheless, our method did not produce an error-free reproduction of the ethnic components of the districts' liquor industry. In all probability we undercounted the true ethnic component by tending to exclude the anglicized segment of each ethnic group. Therefore, we counted the most ethnic of the ethnics, a selectivity that might have affected our results.

Multiple ownership of firms posed a special coding problem. Multiple-owner firms consisted of firms listing two or more owners or, in the case of corporations, two or more officers. The ethnicity of multiple-owner firms was uncertain because surnames did not always agree. That is, a firm owned by Lopez and Gomez is unambiguously Hispanic, but a firm owned by Lopez and Chang is ethnically mixed. Of 2218 new applicants, buyers, and transferrers in the Hollywood District, 848 or 38.2 percent were coowners of multiple-owner firms. Of these 848 multiple owners, only 9.6 percent were coowners of an ethnically heterogeneous firm. Ninety percent of multiple-owner firms were ethnically homogeneous, a result wildly in excess of chance expectations.[1] Heterogeneous multiples amounted to 3.7 percent of all licensees in the Hollywood Division. To control the problem of mixed ethnicities, we utilized the concept of *predominant ethnicity*. To make an assignment of predominant ethnicity, we counted the majority ethnicity in three or more owner firms, the ethnicity first appearing in two member firms, and the ethnicity of the highest-ranking officer in the case of corporations. In this manner we were able to assign every license holder to a single ethnic category, reserving the analysis of mixed cases for later.

RESEARCH RESULTS

The basic structure of the retail liquor industry was simple, but the licensure system was complex. The DABC issued forty-four different licenses. Each license authorized a specific, legally defined business activity, and DABC personnel referred to each type of license by its number. For example, number nine was a beer and wine importer, number thirteen a distilled spirits importer, and number fifty-eight a caterer. Most retail outlets had only one license, but a minority owned more than one. Retail liquor outlets were complexly differentiated in terms of whether or not consumption was permitted on the premises, whether food was sold, whether children were permitted, and what beverages were sold in what manner. According to the DABC, the seven most common licenses made up 96.4 percent of all alcoholic beverage licenses valid on April 1, 1977. But these seven constituted a somewhat smaller proportion of the new applications and personal transfers we examined, suggesting less turnover in the largest licensure categories. Even so, the seven major licensure categories constituted about 90 percent of all the licenses processed in the two years we examined.

There were only two ways to acquire a liquor license in California: by purchasing one from its present owner or by applying to the DABC for a new license. In some categories (notably liquor stores and taverns) California law had established a fixed ratio of outlets to local population, so that issuance of new licenses ended when this ratio was attained. Since this maximum had been attained long ago, the DABC issued no more liquor licenses for package stores or saloons, and newcomers could enter either business only by purchasing a license from a holder at the market price. On the other hand, California law authorized expansion of the population of licensed grocery stores and restaurants in response to demand. In the period 1970 to 1979, the number of grocery licenses in Los Angeles county increased 28 percent and the number of restaurant licenses increased 56 percent.

As expected, ethnic groups displayed distinct profiles of participation in the retail liquor industry. Asians in general and Koreans in particular were heavily overrepresented in this industry. Indeed, the Southern California Retail Liquor Dealers Association translated its informational literature into Korean and Japanese in order to reach

Table 54.   Predominant Ethnicity of New Liquor License
Applicants, Buyers, and Sellers: Hollywood, 1975 and
Inglewood, 1977 (percentages)

	New Applicants	Personal Transfers		Total
		Buyers	Sellers	
Hollywood, 1975				
Korean	13.8	16.1	11.7	12.2
Chinese and Japanese	6.0	12.9	8.0	9.4
Hispanic	3.3	2.6	3.0	2.9
All Others	83.8	68.3	77.3	75.5
Total	100.0	100.0	100.0	100.0
Number	(344)	(496)	(436)	(1276)
Inglewood, 1977				
Korean	2.4	5.5	3.3	3.9
Chinese and Japanese	3.3	7.3	5.9	5.9
Hispanic	10.1	7.3	8.0	8.2
All Other	84.3	80.0	82.9	82.0
Total	100.0	100.0	100.0	100.0
Number	(377)	(619)	(614)	(1610)

Source: Daily ledgers of the Department of Alcoholic Beverage Control, Hollywood
Division and Inglewood Division.

Asian dealers. In the Hollywood District, we found Koreans were
13.8 percent of new applicants, 16.1 percent of buyers, 11.7 percent
of sellers, and 12.2 percent of all three classes combined (table 54).
However, Koreans represented about 0.8 percent of Los Angeles
County population in 1980. Representing about 5.8 percent of Los
Angeles County population in 1980, Chinese and Japanese combined were 9.4 percent of new applicants, buyers, and sellers. Conversely, Hispanic-surnamed owners were 2.9 percent of Hollywood
applicants, buyers, and sellers even though Hispanic-surnamed persons accounted for 27.6 percent of Los Angeles County population
in 1980. On the other hand, in Inglewood, less-imbalanced ownership patterns appeared. Chinese and Japanese accounted for 5.9 percent, Koreans for 3.9 percent, and Hispanics for 8.2 percent of all
owners. We suppose the interdistrict contrasts resulted from the
residential concentration of Asians in Hollywood and of Hispanics in
Inglewood. However, residence obviously leaves some intergroup
difference unexplained. Cultural causes cannot be ruled out but

should not be assumed either: recent Asian immigrants were well educated, and they frequently brought big money to the United States. Mexican migrants were unskilled and had low income. Hence, class resources of Asians presumably accounted for much if not all of the intergroup differences in liquor industry participation.

Evidence of the dual influence of ethnic and class resources also appears in table 54. In general new applicants were applying for cheap licenses to operate lunch rooms, groceries, and sandwich shops. These premises were also cheap to buy. On the other hand, buyers were acquiring expensive licenses to operate package liquor stores and cocktail lounges whose premises were also expensive. Hence, new applicants were generally buying lower-cost small businesses than were license buyers. The balance of new applicants versus license buyers roughly indicates the economic level of each group's business acquisitions. Asians and Koreans in particular were overrepresented in new applicants as well as in license buyers, but the balance of overrepresentation was greater among the license buyers. This imbalance suggests Asians were purchasing more expensive businesses. Conversely, among Hispanics in Hollywood and in Inglewood, underrepresentation prevailed, but the margin of underrepresentation was greater in the buyers group. This balance suggests Hispanics were buying cheap businesses, a reflection of their lower economic level. However, the margin of Asian overrepresentation dropped off in Inglewood whereas the margin of Hispanic underrepresentation decreased in Inglewood. This contrast presumably reflected residential concentration of Asians in Hollywood and of Hispanics in Inglewood.

Another test is the percentage of each group buying or selling package liquor stores. This license was the most expensive of any, and cost according to the DABC about $22,000 in 1975, with inventory extra of course. Table 55 shows that each of the three Asian surname groups was appreciably more represented in liquor stores than were Hispanics, thus tending to confirm the lower economic level of the Hispanic business population. Summing both districts, we find Asians bought 203 package liquor licenses, 80 percent of those transferred. Conversely Hispanics bought 14 package liquor licenses, 5.5 percent of the total transferred.

Ethnic groups displayed different profiles of participation in the different lines of the retail liquor industry. Table 55 shows the pre-

Table 55. Ethnicity of New Applicants and Buyers by Licensure for Hollywood, 1975 and Inglewood, 1977 (in percentages)

Type of License	Hollywood, 1975					Inglewood, 1977				
	Korean	Chinese	Japanese	Hispanic	All Groups	Korean	Chinese	Japanese	Hispanic	All Groups
Grocery Store	43.1	19.2	6.8	21.1	20.2	52.8	18.5	11.1	22.0	18.1
Liquor Store	18.3	17.9	27.1	10.5	9.2	25.0	11.1	61.1	3.4	16.1
Sandwich Shop	7.2	16.7	3.4	21.1	18.8	2.8	7.4	0.0	32.2	17.9
Restaurant	15.7	24.4	33.9	5.3	18.7	8.3	37.0	11.1	23.7	19.2
Beer Bar	2.0	0.0	10.2	10.5	8.5	0.0	0.0	0.0	3.4	3.8
Saloon	11.1	14.1	8.5	7.9	8.9	8.3	25.9	16.7	1.7	12.6
Cocktail Lounge	0.0	2.6	8.5	13.2	5.5	0.0	0.0	0.0	6.8	4.4
All Other	2.6	5.1	1.7	10.5	10.2	2.8	0.0	0.0	6.8	7.7
Total	100.0	100.0	100.0	100.0	100.0	100.0	100.0	100.0	100.0	100.0
Number	(153)	(78)	(59)	(38)	(1445)	(36)	(27)	(18)	(59)	(745)

Hollywood: Chi-square 92.92, df 21, p < .01

Inglewood: Chi-square 87.83[a], df 21, p < .01

Source: Department of Alcoholic Beverage Control.

dominant ethnicity of firms in the seven principal trades for both Hollywood and Inglewood. The various ethnic groups did not participate equally in each trade but tended to cluster in some, neglecting others. For example, in Inglewood, the modal trade of Koreans was grocery stores, of Chinese restaurants, of Japanese liquor stores, and of Hispanics sandwich shops. Because each group produced a distinctive trade profile, chi-square tests were highly significant, a finding that was also replicated among sellers, although for economy of space, the sellers' table has been omitted.

LEGAL FORM OF ENTERPRISE

Studies of Japanese and Chinese enterprise have commonly stressed the economic contribution of cohesive nuclear and extended families (Bonacich and Modell, 1981: 15, 187–195; Bonacich, 1975: 104; Benedict, 1968: 2–11; Dewey, 1962: 179). A sociological feature of East Asian culture, cohesive kinship groups have naturally affected the business style of Asian immigrants, tending to stimulate their use of multiple-ownership firms. Admittedly, family firm and family farm have been basic units of small business in the American business tradition too, so there is nothing uniquely East Asian about a "mom and pop" store. On the other hand, when cultural traditions keep together a large proportion of husband–wife families, they lay the basis for a greater number of mom and pop stores than do cultural traditions that do not equivalently stress nuclear family cohesion. Additionally, extended families, characteristic of Chinese and Japanese family systems, give easier access to kinship pools whose members may share ownership in a family firm. In the Anglo-American cultural context, father-and-son firms extend ownership intergenerationally within a nuclear family, but linking cousins of the same generation is rare in Anglo-American culture although common in East Asian cultures.

Table 56 compares the legal form of business ownership among Koreans, Chinese, Japanese, and Hispanics in Hollywood. On one hand, in a simple sense, these tables vindicate the earlier literature because Chinese and Japanese displayed appreciably higher rates of two-owner and three-or-more owner firms than did business owners in general. This pattern of multiple ownership is compatible with the claim that kinship cohesion and extension affected the legal organi-

Table 56. Legal Form of Business Ownership by
Predominant Ethnicity of Firm: Hollywood, 1975*

Legal Form of Business	*Korean*	*Chinese*	*Japanese*	*Hispanic*	*All Groups*
Corporation	5.5	13.3	11.7	21.0	10.3
One Owner	42.0	36.1	36.4	33.9	52.7
Two Owners	50.2	43.8	45.5	41.9	33.7
Three Owners or More	2.3	6.7	6.5	3.2	3.3
Total	100.0	100.0	100.0	100.0	100.0
Number	(219)	(105)	(77)	(62)	(2115)

*Includes buyers, sellers, new applicants, and administrative.
Chi-square $= 19.769$; df $= 9$; $p < .05$
Source: Department of Alcoholic Beverage Control, Hollywood Division.

zation of Japanese and Chinese business enterprises. This ethnic resource was a cultural endowment whose effect was visible even when demand was held constant.

On the other hand, table 56 also exposes unexpected complexities. First, Chinese and Japanese showed representation just above parity in corporations. If we assume that corporations mainly reflected class resources, then the top of Chinese and Japanese liquor industry consisted of corporations whose owners had shifted away from dependency upon ethnic resources impressively utilized at lower levels of the Asian business structure (Thompson, 1979). This shift implies an increasingly bourgeois business style as generations ascended the socioeconomic hierarchy. We have no evidence of how ethnic or class-based were the resources actually employed by Chinese and Japanese corporations. But even if it is assumed that all corporations were wholly individualistic and bourgeois, an unwarranted simplification, the preponderance of firms of two and three or more owners among Chinese and Japanese still bespeaks the persistence of ethnic resources cultural in origin. If the corporation sector were eliminated from the Chinese and Japanese business populations—but were retained in the general business population—the result would be augmented overrepresentation of Chinese and Japanese in two- and three-owner firms. This thought experiment reproduces the prewar business population in which Chinese and Japanese did not operate business corporations in anything approaching the general rate. In sum, the postwar development of a corporate small-business sector among Chinese and Japanese has probably tended to reduce—but still has not eliminated—their overrepresentation in multiple-owner firms.

Existing literature offerred no guidance to Koreans and Hispanics in business so there was no basis for comparing our results with earlier ones (Oh, 1983: Vol. 1, 24). However, as East Asians, Koreans might be expected to share that region's predilection for mutiple-owner firms. Actual results were only mixed. On the one hand, Koreans showed more than the expected number of two-owner firms and fewer than their expected number of one-owner firms. On the other hand, Koreans had relatively fewer three-or-more owner firms than the general business population, and one-half the percentage of Chinese and Japanese. These mixed results lend uncertain support to the simple claim that East Asian family patterns produce multiple-owner firms. On the one hand, nationality origin seems to affect East Asian business style. Changsoo Lee and De Vos (1981: 370) have reported that Korean culture is more individualistic than Japanese culture, an observation compatible with our results. On the other hand, Korean–Japanese and Korean–Chinese contrasts might result from the groups' respective stages of mobility in the United States. Unlike Chinese and Japanese, Koreans are more recent immigrants whose small business system had not matured. As one result, Koreans are still located in lower-ranking niches of the business population. Two measures of business rank are legal incorporation and number of partners. Koreans in the period of our study were appreciably lower than Chinese and Japanese on both measures, thus suggesting Koreans ranked lower in business. Possibly economic mobility will increase Korean representation in larger firms, therewith increasing the proportion of corporations and three-or-more owner firms among Koreans. In this case, Korean ownership style would attain closer approximation to the other Asians without any cultural change.

ETHNIC HOMOGENEITY OF LIQUOR LICENSE TRANSFERS

DABC files provided a complete record of every transfer of liquor license in each district within the specified year. Most transfers of liquor licenses transpired in the context of business sales in which

Table 57.   Ethnic Homogeneity of Liquor License
Transfers* in Hollywood, 1975 (in percentages)

Buyers	Sellers					Total
	Korean	Chinese	Japanese	Hispanic	All Other	
Korean	80.4	19.0	21.4	25.0	7.5	17.6
Chinese	7.8	66.7	0.0	0.0	3.6	6.9
Japanese	3.9	0.0	50.0	8.3	3.0	4.6
Hispanic	0.0	0.0	7.1	25.00	2.1	2.5
All Other	7.8	14.3	21.4	41.7	83.8	68.3
Total	100.0	100.0	100.0	100.0	100.0	100.0
Number	(51)	(21)	(14)	(12)	(334)	(432)

Chi-square = 395.8; df = 16; $p < .01$; lambda = .28
*Includes only buyers and sellers.
Source: Department of Alcoholic Beverage Control, Hollywood Division.

sellers unloaded their premises, fixtures, inventory, goodwill, and license for a single price. However, DABC ledgers only recorded the legal transfer of license ownership— they did not record a sale price nor any terms of license transfer. Nonetheless, the ledger archive permitted us to examine the ethnic homogeneity of license transfers, an examination the like of which, so far as we know, had never before been completed.[2] When coethnics buy and sell to one another, their transaction is ethnically homogeneous. When ethnics buy or sell to outsiders, their transaction is ethnically heterogeneous. Thus, when Korean sells to Korean, the transaction is ethnically homogeneous, but when Korean sells to Chinese (or vice versa) their transaction is ethnically heterogeneous.

DABC ledgers indicated that the number of ethnically homogeneous license transfers was wildly in excess of chance expectations. Tables 57 and 58 show the homogeneity of license transfers in Hollywood and Inglewood. Homeogeneity occurred along the diagonal in each table, and we have italicized the appropriate cells to facilitate comprehension. In both districts, the italicized transactions occurred much more frequently than would have been expected on the basis of chance. For instance in Hollywood, Korean sellers found Korean buyers in 80.4 percent of transactions even though Koreans were only 17.6 percent of all buyers. Hence, Korean–Korean homogeneity was 4.6 times greater than chance levels. Similarly, Hispanic

Table 58.　Ethnic Homogeneity of Liquor License
Transfers in Inglewood, 1977 (in percentages)

Buyers	Sellers					Total
	Korean	Chinese	Japanese	Hispanic	All Other	
Korean	60.5	11.1	10.5	2.0	3.1	5.5
Chinese	10.0	77.8	0.0	2.0	2.1	4.5
Japanese	0.0	0.0	68.4	0.0	1.0	2.9
Hispanic	5.0	0.0	0.0	53.1	3.5	7.2
All Other	20.0	11.1	21.1	42.9	90.3	79.9
Total	100.0	100.0	100.0	100.0	100.0	100.0
Number	(20)	(18)	(19)	(49)	(515)	(621)

Chi-square = 849.854; df = 16; $p < .01$; lambda = .23
Source: Department of Alcoholic Beverage Control, Inglewood Division.

sellers found Hispanic buyers in 25.0 percent of cases even though Hispanic buyers were only 2.5 percent of all buyers. Hispanic homogeneity was ten times greater than chance.

Why should small business owners prefer to sell to and buy from coethnics? The literature suggests three explanations. A utilitarian explanation would cite convenience and cheapness of ascription (Mayhew, 1968; Wilensky and Lawrence, 1979). That is, ethnic business owners participate in social circuits where they contact coethnics. These circuits include the reading of foreign language newspapers in which businesses are offered for sale in classified sections. Therefore, it is both easy and inexpensive to locate a buyer or seller by utilizing one's ethnic connections.[3]

We have presented evidence of information networks in Table 40. When summed, liquor stores, grocery stores, bars, and restaurants represented 21.2 percent of firms advertised for sale in the *Korea Times* but only 11.9 percent of those for sale in *Los Angeles Times*. Therefore, anyone reading the *Korea Times* had access to more liquor industry advertising than a reader of the *Los Angeles Times*—but only persons able to read Korean could obtain this superior information.

A Durkheimian explanation is mutual trust (Foster, 1974; Macaulay, 1963). Buying a business is risky. The Bank of America (Jones, Walker, and Reed 1973: 5) advised prospective buyers of liquor stores to "watch for tricks played by some disreputable retailers" who inflated gross receipts in order to jack up the selling price. The outsider is always a stranger about whom lingering stereotypes and fears persist. People trade with those they trust, especially in risky business affairs. Stories circulated in the Korean community about swindlers who had sold businesses to inexperienced Koreans for much more than their true value by deceptive and unethical accounting and sales practices (Young, 1983: 68b). Fear induced Korean buyers to favor coethnic sellers. "Mutual trust seems to be the most important prerequisite to the creation of any business association among Koreans" (Oh, 1983: 17–18).

Related to trust is ethnic chauvinism, a third possibility. Chauvinism may reflect frank hostility to out-groups or simply the desire— fortified by social control—to bolster the coethnic economy by keeping one's trade within the coethnic orbit. Although no evidence indicates Koreans were more chauvinistic than others, undertones of economic chauvinism appeared in Korean publications.[4]

> Many Korean firms tend to promote the "buy Korean" concept: I am Korean and you are Korean; therefore, you should buy from me. Though not openly promoted and admitted, the "buy Korean" expectation on the part of Korean firms [is] especially prevalent among those located in Koreatown. (Oh, 1983: Vol. 1, 37)

These explanations need not exclude one another. An obvious problem is to disentangle, test, and weight each. A basic issue is possible spuriousness. Perhaps homogeneity of transaction spuriously reflected the prior clustering of coethnics in one or another line of liquor business? Thus, if all grocery store owners were Korean and all grocery store buyers were also Korean, all grocery store sales would be ethnically homogeneous, but one would not need to invoke cheapness, trust, or chauvinism to explain the homogeneity. To test this possibility, we mechanically held constant licensure groups and calculated lambda for each group. Lambda is a "measure of association for cross tabulations based on nominal-level variables" (Nie, et al., 1975: 225). If within-license clustering produced ethnic homogeneity of license transfers, lambdas should decline and change direction when licensure groups are mechanically controlled. However, table 59 shows that lambdas are unaffected by controls, thus indicating that licensure clustering does not explain the homogeneity of transaction reported in tables 57 and 58. This result does not prove no clustering existed. Rather, the persistently high levels of

Table 59.   Zero-order Buyer/Seller Lambdas by
Licensure Groups: Hollywood and Inglewood

Licensure Group	Hollywood, 1975		Inglewood, 1977	
	Lambda	Number	Lambda	Number
All Groups	.28	432	.23	621
#20	.32	112	.48	60
#21	.19	54	.24	117
#40	.23	91	.08	87
#42	.50	28	.25	14
#47	.73	29	.38	82
#48	.0	18	.50	32

Source: Department of Alcoholic Beverage Control, Hollywood and Inglewood Divisions.

lambda in the licensure groups indicate that coethnics preferred one another in business sales even *within* licensure categories.[5]

CONCLUSION

Utilizing official archives of the Los Angeles retail liquor industry, we have obtained evidence showing the coexistence of ethnic and class resources in business. Class resources affected which industries ethnic groups could afford to enter, how many entered, and how they organized themselves. Ethnic resources affected the same outcomes but in different ways. An important class resource, money limited Asians and Mexicans to industries that they could afford to buy into. But their access to these industries also depended upon ethnic homogeneity in business transfers, which tended to advantage coethnics while excluding outsiders. The ethnic linkage arose from cheapness, trust, and chauvinism, characteristics independent of money resources or class membership.

Our analysis of the cultural division of labor in Los Angeles' liquor industry turns up may obvious points of similarity with the invasion–succession cycle in residential housing.[6] That is, the creation and maintenance of ethnically homogenous industries is analogous to the creation and maintenance of ethnically homogeneous neighborhoods: ethnic homogeneity of transfer governs both. Ethnic neighborhoods arise from buying and selling of housing. Ethnic industries arise from the buying and selling of firms.

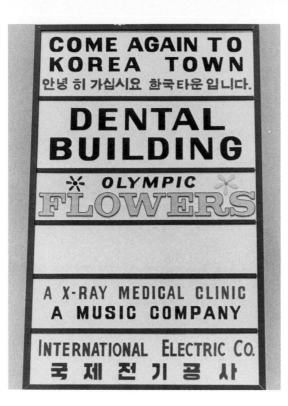

Korea Town did not exist until the Korean Chamber of Commerce invented the term, and encouraged Korean merchants to put up signs in Hangul lettering. Popularization of Korea Town as place and as concept is a basic, often overlooked achievement of the Korean Chamber of Commerce.
Source: Asian American Studies Center, University of California at Los Angeles. Photo credit: Alan Ohashi.

This advertising section is sponsored by the Korea Traders Association and other participating advertisers, and their cooperation is gratefully acknowledged.

The Republic of Korea owes its survival to American and other United Nations fighting men. That help has not been forgotten. Today's Korea, recovered from war, is working for partnership with the United States, not dependence.

Korea wants a long-term, expanding, balanced trade relationship with the U.S., with mutual benefit for both sides. Korea welcomes the normalization of relations between the U.S. and China, and unreservedly supports American policy in Asia.

Korea sees a harmonious trade and cultural relationship with the U.S. growing deeper in the years ahead. In good times and bad, Korea is a stable and reliable friend.

PARTNERSHIP
REPUBLIC OF KOREA–UNITED STATES

The Korean Traders Association sponsored this advertisement in recognition of the political, cultural, and economic impact of the United States on Korea, and in hope that future relationships would be based on partnership, "not dependence."
Source: The New York Times Magazine, July 15, 1979, p. 45. Reproduced by permission.

Kim is the most common surname in Korea. Twenty-three percent of
Koreans bear this name.
Source: Asian American Studies Center, University of California at Los
Angeles. Photo credit: Alan Ohashi.

A wholly owned branch of the Korean government, the Korea Exchange Bank made loans to Korean small business firms in Los Angeles. The prominence of the Bank gave rise to speculation that KEB loans bankrolled the Korean entrepreneurs in southern California. But the KEB's role was in fact a modest one, and by no means accounts for the dramatic overrepresentation of Koreans in business.
Source: Asian American Studies Center, University of California at Los Angeles. Photo credit: Alan Ohashi.

The retail liquor industry sold soft drinks too.
Photo credit: Steve Gold.

Some businesses require the customers to wait while their product is prepared to order.
Photo credit: Steve Gold.

Koreatown corner, 1977.
Photo credit: Alan Ohashi.

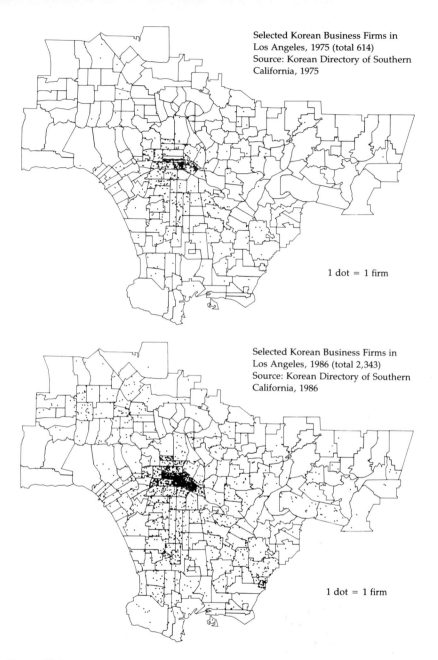

Selected Korean Business Firms in
Los Angeles, 1975 (total 614)
Source: Korean Directory of Southern
California, 1975

1 dot = 1 firm

Selected Korean Business Firms in
Los Angeles, 1986 (total 2,343)
Source: Korean Directory of Southern
California, 1986

1 dot = 1 firm

Dong Ok Lee's maps depict the development of Korean firms between 1975 and 1986. However, these maps actually underestimate the true number of Korean firms as they were developed from data published in the Korean telephone directories yellow pages. Additionally, the maps include only firms in selected service and retail industries. Nonetheless, the Koreatown center and subsequent process of suburbanization are both clearly visible in these maps.

Credit: Dong Ok Lee, "Spatial Patterns of Korean Small Business in Los Angeles," paper presented at the Annual Meeting of the Association of American Geographers, Portland, Oregon, April 22, 1987. Reproduced by permission.

10

Raising Capital

To open a business, Koreans require capital. This money buys the equipment, inventory, licenses, and premises that permit the business to open and then to weather the phase of getting underway. Start-up costs depend upon the industry, but minimum costs of even modest businesses are appreciable. For example, during the period studied, the Bank of America (Eagen and Cingolani, 1977) estimated the opening costs of a table-service restaurant with 3000 square feet of floor space were $150,000 to $242,000. In addition, operating costs of the first three months added between $44,000 and $52,000, so the required net investment ranged between $194,000 and $294,000. A four-chair beauty salon required capital investment of $15,400 to $28,950 to open and remain afloat for three months (Rowe, 1975: 12). In 1978, the minimum cost of a gas station franchise in Los Angeles county was $16,000 for a nonservice facility. Service bays added $30,000 to start-up cost. Additionally, service station franchisers needed to lay out $15,000 to $24,000 for operating expenses in the first three months. The most cheaply entered business was garment manufacturing. Many garment shops opened on only $2000—basically the cost of six sewing machines.

Because start-up costs varied, a novice could enter the small business hierarchy at the bottom, then move up by selling an improved business for a profit and buying into a higher-cost trade. A career in business among Los Angeles Koreans often took this form, so that the success of one's career was measured by the distance between starting point and finishing point as well as the speed of one's climb. As a result, Korean owners often held onto a business one to six years before selling it and trading up to a better one. Since the entire business population was in turnover, getting capital together for new business ventures was a continuous preoccupation in Koreatown. Moreover, start-up was not the only occasion on which business owners needed capital. Seasonal peaks, cash flow, and acquiring new equipment and facilities were other problems that compelled owners

243

to borrow money (Stern, 1976). Especially becasue of the high level of self-employment among Los Angeles Koreans, business capitalization emerged as a recurrent and widespread problem that required regular and methodical provision.

One possibility is that Koreans faced the credit problem as isolated individuals, each one turning for assistance to outsiders. Alternatively, Koreans might have met their credit need from ethnic institutions and resources. These resources would include rotating credit associations, informal loans, and Korean-owned financial institutions serving Korean customers. Finally, Koreans might have employed both outsider institutions and ethnic resources to supply their credit needs. In this case, their solution to the credit problem would blend class and ethnic resources. Class theory would provide a fully satisfactory explanation of Korean credit only in the first case. That is, insofar as Koreans supplemented class resources with ethnic resources, class theory falls short of a full explanation of their capitalization strategy.

ROTATING CREDIT ASSOCIATIONS

A rotating credit association consists of a group who pool their funds on a regular basis then rotate the pool around the group until all members have received it. In this manner, all but the last receive an advance upon their saving. The organizer receives the first fund, which is also the maximum credit this form permits. Rotating credit associations represented an ethnic response to individual money problems. Prewar Chinese and Japanese immigrants made extensive use of rotating credit associations for the purpose of capitalizing small- and medium-business enterprise as well as for consumption (Light, 1972: ch. 2; Woodrum, Rhodes, and Feagin, 1980: Table 8). Moon (1976: 192) reported that between 1903 and 1918 Koreans on the Pacific Coast and in Hawaii also utilized *kye*, the Korean rotating credit association, for business capitalization.

ROTATING CREDIT ASSOCIATIONS IN
SOUTH KOREA

The rotating credit association has a long history in Korea. Koreans call this institution *kye*. Hoon Lee (1936: 250) called the kye (pronounced "kay") "an old-fashioned Korean cooperative society." He reported that "the first known" record of kye occurred in a census book of 1663. Kennedy (1973: 21) found "no indication" of kye before 1500 but thought the institution was probably ten centuries old anyway. Oh (1972: 12) simply declared the kye "hundreds of years old." Either way, this cooperative financial institution had a firm place in the cultural history of Korean people. We expected to learn that the ancient kye was tapering into oblivion in South Korea as a result of modernization. In reality, kye became more prominent after the Korean War. According to Mintz (1980) "most Koreans" belonged to "at least one kye—men with their own cronies, women separately with theirs." Growth of kyes was so strong that the Korean government and Korean banks regarded their proliferation as an obstacle to economic development. Several surveys documented the renascent popularity of the kye in South Korea *especially* among urban and educated people (Kennedy, 1973: 120). A 1959 survey of 2691 Korean families found that 60 percent were in debt. Of these, two percent had borrowed funds through *mujins*, related to kye but incorporated. Eight percent were in debt to banks. The remaining 90 percent had borrowed from "relatives and acquaintances" and "it is believed that most of these loans were obtained through kyes ... " (Cambell and Ahn, 1962: 55). A 1963 survey disclosed that 43.7 percent of Korean households were members of one or more kyes. Oh's (1972: 12) sample survey reported that 65.8 percent of households contained active kye members. Only 18.8 percent of Korean households had never been kye members. Member households invested approximately 26 percent of their monthly incomes in the kye, an astounding rate of saving (Kennedy, 1973: 21; cf. Bonnett, 1976: 38). A 1969 survey by the Bank of Korea reported that 72.3 percent of adult respondents were active kye members. To offset this competition for depositors' funds, the Bank of Korea devised "kye-like savings plans," and mounted a publicity campaign on their behalf (Kennedy, 1973: 121). Kennedy's research found that Koreans with higher education and income were more likely to belong to kyes than were lower status persons. However, multiple-kye membership was the standard practice of all strata of Korean society. Since higher-status Koreans were overrepresented among immigrants to the United States, the heaviest users of kye in Korea were precisely the strata from which immigrants were recruited.

Kennedy (1973: 27) distinguished five types of kye. One was work-sharing and nonfinancial. Two involved mutual aid for consumption, especially weddings and funerals. The "industry kye" and the "money-making" kye involved the payment of interest within the membership group and the investment of portions in farm or business. Oh (1972: 30) found that 40.5 percent of kye members utilized their share for investments of various kinds. The majority utilized their share for consumption, and the modal use (40 percent) was tuition payment. Memberships in a kye usually numbered about thirty, and as elsewhere members were typically kinsmen, friends, neighbors, or alumni. Kennedy attributed this "tendency to core" to the institutional necessity for mutual "trust which is the key to success."

The revival of kyes in South Korea is an important datum. Campbell and Ahn (1962: 62) attributed the revival to rates of interest in the kyes that were " much higher than those paid on the more liquid deposits in Korea's commercial banks and government credit institutions." Oh (1972: 3–9) even claimed that negative real interest rates prevailed in mainstream financial institutions of South Korea in the 1960s. Additionally, capital was in short supply in South Korea, a reflection of the country's forced industrialization and diversion of credit to this end. The predictable result was shortage of credit for individual consumption and small business. This context, Oh (1972: 84) reasons, revived kyes and other institutions of the informal financial sector. Oh's conclusion is compatible with Cole and Lyman (1971: 178–179) who observed that informal credit institutions in South Korea were "not subject to the interest rate ceilings and could afford to pay interest rates well above the prevailing rates of inflation." By the mid-1960s, informal credit institutions had become "the main source of readily available funds, and most businesses depended on them to some degree."

The influence of economic conditions on the revival of kye in Korea is unmistakable, and Korea's case leaves no doubt that kyes can remain of value in modernization. The flourishing rotating credit associations in President Park's South Korea were not just an archaic survival dependent upon sentimentality or ignorance. However, the revival of the kye was only possible so long as rotating credit associations remained latent in Korean culture. It is unclear whether economic conditions alone would have reanimated rotating credit associations among a population who no longer retained a cultural memory of kye.

External economic conditions governed kye formation in South Korea such that the rate of kye formation varied inversely with availability of consumer and small business credit in mainstream institutions. In the Park era institutional credit in Korea was tight, and kyes proliferated. The opposite situation would be one of abundant institutional credit and diminished kye formation. In such a period, the role of sentiment and ignorance in kye formation would increase as the kye receded into cultural latency. Centuries-long nonuse of kye would then cause the rotating credit institution to pass from latency to nonexistence such that kye could no longer be retrieved should economic conditions once again turn favorable.

ROTATING CREDIT AMONG KOREANS
IN LOS ANGELES

Koreans in Los Angeles were familiar with kye and continued to use it for social and business purposes.[1] All Korean interviewees indicated familiarity with kye. The vice president of a Korean bank said kye was "widely used" for business capitalization and for social needs. Among the latter he mentioned a "diamond kye" whose members used their proceeds to purchase wedding and engagement rings. When one sees a large party in a Korean restaurant, he observed, the group is usually a kye. In his opinion, churches and alumni clubs were the usual organizers of kyes (Interview 92). Two presidents of high school alumni associations were members of kyes operated among alumni. The first participated in a kye of fourteen members, each of whom contributed $250 monthly toward a fund of $3500. The second participated in a kye of thirteen alumni who contributed $100; this was only one of several kyes operated by the alumni club, and the respondent indicated he was also participating in another kye organized among members of a Korean dentists' association. A college student reported that his mother participated in one alumnae kye and his sister in another. He distinguished big kyes and small kyes. Big kyes were business oriented; small ones were social in nature. He knew a big kye involving twenty-one people and a fund of $10,000. A CPA knew of a kye whose ten members subscribed $1000 monthly for a fund of $10,000. Kye was useful as "forced saving" in this respondent's opinion (Interview 13). An economist reported that kye was very popular in Korean but was only "emerging" in popularity among Los Angeles Koreans. He thought kyes typically included ten to fifteen persons, met in restaurants, and raised between $1000 and $10,000 at every meeting.

Other Koreans knew about kye but were uncertain or dubious about its prevalence among Koreans in Los Angeles. A Baptist pastor "did not see" any kye among his congregants, noting that kye participants engaged in drinking and merriment in restaurants, activities of which Baptists disapprove; he thought kye was only for "secular people." Another minister indicated kye was popular in Hawaii, but he was uncertain how prevalent the institution was in Los Angeles. A social worker thought kyes mainly occurred in churches, but he asserted that kyes were much more prevalent in Korea than in Los Angeles. In Korea, he explained, people needed kyes because banks were useless, but in America people could obtain loans from banks. A journalist thought that kye was popular in Los Angeles, but doubted its importance for capital accumulation in business. Most Koreans brought money with them from Korea—so they did not need kyes here.

To expand this interviewing effort, we employed two Korean-speaking graduate students with funds subscribed by the UCLA Asian-American Studies Center. Edward Chang (1983) interviewed kye members in three settings: a church, an alumni club, and a garment factory. In the garment factory workers were listening to gospel songs when Chang arrived. Of ten Korean workers on the premises, four refused to answer any questions, and four indicated they never participated in kye because they were Christians. One indicated she had belonged to a kye but was not now enrolled. One worker reported she was currently enrolled in a sequence kye for $4000 running over twelve months. Chang's church kye enrolled eighteen members for a fund of $5000. Chang called it a "friendship kye." Chang interviewed five kye members, all women.[2] Four had been in the United States for ten years or more; one for only three years. "All of them had borrowed" from banks more than once. Two of the women asserted that more than 80 percent of their neighbors, friends, and relatives participated in kyes. Two indicated only 50 percent participated, and one said only 30 percent. The alumni association Chang studied had a "friendship kye" of $600 among six women, all wives of classmates. All their husbands were graduates of the high school's class of 1968. Two women also participated in a second kye operated outside the membership circle of the alumni association. All the women believed the kye was more popular in Korea than in the United States.

Chang also inquired about kye among his own circle of friends and associates. Because these people knew and trusted him, Chang reported, their answers were more candid than those of other respondents. One interviewee was Mrs. L., a kye organizer. She ran a kye with fifteen members generating $5000 every month for twenty months. Most kye members were middle class. She believed kye members used their fund for "various purposes such as to start a small business, to pay for children's educational expenses, to purchase durable goods, and to prepare for marriage ceremony" (Chang, 1983: 11). Claiming that kye was widespread among Koreans in Los Angeles, Mrs. L. was defensive about the safety of kyes in general and her own in particular.

B.'s mother participated in three kyes—two auction kyes for $30,000 and one friendship kye for $5000. The first auction kye was formed by three organizers each of whom had recruited ten members. The other auction kye operated in the same manner, but B.'s mother had joined for only a one-third membership, a fund of $10,000. Most members of the first auction kye worked at Todd Shipping Company in San Pedro. Chang also interviewed C., a loan officer at a big Korean-owned bank. This banker thought "just about everyone is a participant in a kye." He guessed that most small business operators used both kye and bank loans to capitalize business enterprises. The advantage of the kye was speed, flexibility, and nonrequirement of collateral. A loan officer at an American bank, Ms. L., told Chang that kye was useful because it is fast, requires no collateral, and is easy to organize. However, she thought kye use had declined among Los Angeles Koreans since the Mine's Restaurant defalcation became headline news.

Mrs. Y. was a participant in the ill-fated Mine's Restaurant kye. She had been introduced to Mine's kye by her husband's elder sister who was operating a small business near the restaurant. She joined a $30,000 kye with several organizers each of whom assembled her own members. Her kye ran from April 1979 until January 1983. Members gathered weekly at Mine's Restaurant; that week's fund recipient was responsible for the restaurant bill, usually $300. Some members of the kye lost more than $50,000 in its bankruptcy. Working in a cosmetic shop, Mrs. Y. though most of her women customers were kye participants. The advantage of kye was speed and ease of acquiring "lump sums of money which are essential to one's business success" (Chang, 1983: 22).

Mrs. P. was a kye organizer who operated a sequence kye with seven members and a fund of $2500. This kye met monthly, but Mrs. P. indicated that daily kyes were very popular "among waitresses and nightclub hostesses."

Eun-Jin Lee (1984) conducted a series of interviews about kye with persons to whom he was referred along a friendship network. L.'s mother was a member of a kye with thirty members and three organizers. Most members were kinsmen. "The kye circulated a rotating fund of $20,000 among thirty members each of whom contributed $667 monthly." L.'s father ran a small apparel shop that utilized the proceeds of this fund. A friend's mother had organized a bidding kye. She had run a grocery store and currently ran a sewing factory. However, she refused to discuss further details. A UCLA graduate in engineering, M.'s mother earned $40,000 a year working for Hughes Aircraft Corporation. In addition to their regular jobs, she and her husband sold at swap meets for extra income. She organized a sequence kye, using the money to retire a bank loan. All kye members were UCLA alumnae. Next she organized a $10,000 sequence kye, and used her fund as downpayment on a house, a common use of kye money according to her.

Mrs. S. had graduated from nursing school, then migrated to the United States. Her husband currently worked as a car salesman, but they hoped to open a small clothing shop and planned to utilize their kye fund for this purpose. Mrs. S. held two memberships in a single kye. She said other kye members used their money for downpayments on houses or for business investments.

Sun-Hee's aunt organized a kye for $20,000. She had recently bought a liquor store in which she worked with her husband and sister.

Lee interviewed "Michael's mother" at the home of Mr. Wang, a mutual friend. Mr. Wang and Michael's mother were graduates of the same Korean university. Both were about thirty years old at the time of the interview. Michael's mother had been in the United States about six years. Her first business was a liquor store; to purchase it she had borrowed money form her father. Currently she held membership in two kyes. The first was a one-and-a-half membership in a $20,000 fund with twenty-five to thirty members in a variety of occupations. She mentioned owners of sewing factories, small business operators, and seamstresses. As a result of this diversity, the financial status of kye participants was quite different. She also participated in a second kye for $30,000 in which she held one membership. All members were small business operators. They knew one another very well, but she did not indicate the nature of the social connection. As a result of participation in two kyes, she paid $2000 monthly. She indicated that auction prices in kyes depended upon bank interest rates, and had been higher a few years ago when interest rates were also higher.

Mr. Kim was vice-president of a big high school alumni association. He operated a small gasoline service station and body shop in an affluent black neighborhood. Introduced to Lee by a mutual friend, Mr. Kim was receptive to an interview because Lee hailed from his home town and Lee's brothers were alumni of its high school. Kim explained that his alumni association was one of the largest in Los Angeles with 150 members. They had raised $10,000 at their annual party, a feat of which Mr. Kim was proud. Kim had immigrated to Los Angeles in 1974. At first he had expected to go to New York City, but a relative in Los Angeles was successful in the service station business, and he persuaded Mr. Kim to open a service station in the same city. In the first seven months Mr. Kim learned how to operate a service station while working at his relative's operation. He saved the "start-up money" for his own station from wages, then earned a lot of money in the 1979 gasoline shortage. Mr. Kim explained that he was not a kye subscriber although he saw many small business operators enrolled in kyes. Mr. Kim thought the kye was risky and, in view of his ability to secure loans from American banks he declined to take risks.

Chang and Lee also scanned the Korean language press for articles dealing with kye. They found many articles dealing with kye defalcations, and two survey articles describing the kyes in Los Angeles. On March 17, 1977, the *Hankook Ilbo* published a feature article describing the numerous kyes in Los Angeles, Chicago, and New York. The newspaper declared that kyes were "thriving" in Los Angeles, and estimated their number at 350 to 500 with funds ranging from $1000 to $50,000. Kyes were usually organized among co-workers, neighbors, alumni, and church members, the newspaper explained. Currently a boom in kyes was underway. As one indication, the money invested in kyes was much greater than just a few years earlier. The *Hankook Ilbo* declared that the kye had become one of the main sources of capital among Korean immigrants as the rotating credit associations nearly equaled the amount of money borrowed from banks. The newspaper quoted a kye organizer who claimed most kye members were small business operators. A hamburger stand owner observed that kye was the only way for a Korean immigrant without established credit to obtain business capitalization.

The *Korea Times* published a feature article about kyes in Los Angeles.[3] The *Times* estimated that the number of kyes in Los Angeles was "at least 1,000." Despite the $100,000 default of a kye only one month earlier, the *Times* believed kyes would "continue to grow in the Los Angeles Korean community." The newspaper distinguished eight types of kye in popular use. Funds ranged from $500 to $100,000. Garment workers were supposed to be heavy users of kye. However, the kye was also "widespread among shop owners in Koreatown." Many owners engaged simultaneously in more than one kye.

Newspaper reports of kye defalcations provided additional information about rotating credit associations in Los Angeles and other cities. When a Hawaiian kye organizer defaulted in 1979, he owed $16 million to 1100 creditors, many of whom were Korean.[4] Some victims of this fraud had been paying as much as $200,000 monthly into this fund. In another incident, the Korean Chamber of Commerce of Northern California undertook an investigation when a Korean kye went into defalcation leaving $400,000 in unpaid debts and 100 creditors.[5] Los Angeles' biggest kye defalcation occurred in 1983 when Mrs. Mine Kim, a leading businesswoman, was unable to meet the debts of a kye meeting in her restaurant. "The loan club went bankrupt when some members wrote dishonored checks, and Mrs. Kim had to assume the entire responsibility as the club principal" (Yun, 1983). Los Angeles police arrested Mine Kim for failing to pay $30,000 owed to kye members. This kye had thirty-one members, one of whom sued the organizer for restitution. Months later Korean newspapers reported police were investigating three additional fraud cases involving kyes.[6]

Terry and Stull (1975: 37—38) found that the kye was "used frequently" by Los Angeles Koreans for "a variety of reasons." They mentioned two Buddhist temples that used the kye for socioreligious purposes. However, they indicated (1975: 38) that kye was "also utilized by organizations, individuals, and associations for the development of business." Won H. Chang (1977: 147) reported that Los Angeles Koreans formed kyes to provide "banking, wedding, funeral, and other services for everyone in the community."

A UCLA anthropologist, Kunae Kim (1982) undertook an ethnographic investigation of Korean rotating credit associations in Los Angeles. Alerted to this phenomenon by newspaper stories describing defalcations, Kim (1982: 2) found the safety of kyes was a "matter of general concern among Koreans in Los Angeles." Starting with a friendship circle of nine young couples united by alumni ties, Kim (1982: 17) followed outward the social network that radiated from this nucleus. She thus assembled seventy-seven Korean informants whom she categorized as regular practitioners of kye, occasional practitioners, past practioners who would not repeat, and never-practitioners. She found sixty regular practitioners, one occasional practitioner, two past practitioners, and fourteen never-practitioners. Of the 80 percent who were regular practitioners of kye, Kim (1982: 21) observed:

> Their involvement in the kye constitutes a significant part of their strategies for "making it" in the United States. There is a heavy representation of small business enterprise in their occupational choice. About 70 percent of them have chosen or will choose self-employment as their major career.

The fourteen nonparticipants were salaried professionals. These Koreans viewed the kye with suspicion because of well-publicized cases of the "breakdown and abuse" of kyes as well as from a philosophical antipathy toward utilizing "human connections for economic ends."

Kim distinguished three types of kye, differentiated according to their purpose: social, mutual aid, and commercial profit. Social kyes knit together people whose primary purpose was sociability, not gain. Mutual-aid kyes emphasized "individual economic betterment" without, however, losing track of the sense of mutuality and sharing. "To such participants, the kye usually occupies a significant position in their economic adaptation to host society" (Kim, 1982: 26). Commercial profit kyes stressed "self-centered calculation of monetary gain" rather than mutual assistance. Kim claimed her distinctions were real rather than analytic as participants themselves distinguished the three types in this way. Fixed kyes predominanted in social and mutual-aid groups; auction kyes were the typical form of commercial profit groups. Small-fund kyes were social; intermediate-size funds were for mutual aid; and large funds were oriented toward commercial profit.

Regarding use of the kye fund, Kim (1982: 30) found that social kye members had no objective in mind when they joined. One member could not remember how she had spent her $5000 fund. Mutual-aid kye members mentioned purposes such as business purchase, real estate purchase, or consumption. Seven of the nine borrowers in Mrs. Park's mutual-aid kye "utilized their funds for the purchase and improvement of their business activities" (Kim, 1982: 31). Funds drawn in commercial profit kyes were mainly "used for larger investment and speculative ventures." For instance borrowers used the fund to extend private loans to other Koreans or to invest in real estate. Again, the monthly payment they owed the kye was covered by the interest they earned from investment of their kye funds. Some paid obligations to one kye with funds drawn from another. Kunae Kim (1982: 3) found that the kye was a controversial institution among Koreans, "at once the symbol of their ethnic solidarity and the object of ridicule."

> At one end I have seen its positive aspects being stressed by its participants who are proud of their unique cultural heritage. These people evaluate the institution as an ideal and effective mechanism of mutual help and social solidarity and attribute their relative socio-economic success in America to its existence. At the other end, some—most often non-participants—emphasize its ... risk ... and are critical of the kye for being "backwark," "stupid," and the "cancer of our society."

SURVEY STUDIES OF KYE

The ethnographic and newspaper evidence uniformly suggests that kyes were prevalent among Los Angeles Koreans and widely utilized for business capitalization. If the estimate of the *Korea Times* is accepted, there was one kye for every sixty Koreans in Los Angeles.

Table 60.   Sources of Business Capital Among 213 Korean
Proprietors in Los Angeles, 1977

	Bank	SBA	Kye	Own Savings	Friends or Family
Percentage Using Any	36	4	1	80	15
Median Percentage Of Total Start-Up Capital	0	0	0	51	0

Source: Telephone survey, 1977.

However, survey research failed to confirm the extent to which the kye was used for business capitalization as opposed to real estate investment or consumption. David Kim (1975) carried out an enumeration of 278 Hangul storefronts in Los Angeles' Koreatown. He asked business owners to check off their sources of capital from a list of eleven alternatives, among which kye was covered only in the residual "other" category. Kim reported that "own savings" was by far largest source of business capital, followed distantly by bank loans and Small Business Administration loans. He made no reference to rotating credit associations.

Hyung-Chan Kim (1977: 97, 104) compiled a nonrandom list of fifty-two Korean firms in four American cities. Only one owner acknowledged using kye as a source of capital for business investment: "Evidence indicates an awareness of the traditional ... kye among Korean immigrants in America. However, they did not use kye as a means of creating business capital."

Our telephone survey of 213 Korean proprietors in Los Angeles also included questions about source of business capital (table 60). "Own savings" was unambiguously the leading source, and this accounted for approximately one-half of all business capital. The rest was borrowed, mostly from banks, friends, and family. Only 1 percent of respondents mentioned any use of kye for business capitalization.

Young (1983: 56–57) interviewed forty Korean business owners in New York City during the summer of 1981. Shown an article about the research in a Korean language newspaper, respondents were said to have been cooperative. However, when asked about kye, only one acknowledged participation. Nonetheless, twenty-one knew of other Koreans who had "received at least some help from these associations."

Kwang Kim and Hurh (1984) interviewed 94 Korean business owners on Chicago's South Side, a predominantly black area. Operating from an initial list of 100 business owners provided by the Korean Chamber of Commerce of Chicago, Kim and Hurh inquired about sources of business capital. Thirty-four percent of respondents indicated that they had "accumulated some of their own capital through the rotating credit system" (1984: 35). Most of these respondents had used kye-subscribed capital for operation of their current business. However, one-quarter had used kye-subscribed capital for their first and second business or for their first business only. A third of the Chicago business owners believed that rotating credit was "widely used" among Korean entrepreneurs as a method of capital formation.

Assessing all the evidence regarding kye use among Korean business owners, we find a confusing range of results. Kim and Hurh's (1984) Chicago survey reported much more frequent kye use among Korean entrepreneurs than did either Hyung-Chan Kim (1977), Young (1983), or our telephone survey. The ethnographic results of Chang, Lee, and Kunae Kim uniformly reported more kye use than did any of the surveys. Since results do not agree, the problem arises of how to reconcile differences. One solution would be to conclude, following Illsoo Kim (1981: 211), that Korean kyes in the United States were widespread but primarily oriented toward consumption rather than investment. After all, the three surveys inquired into kye utilization for business capitalization. They did not inquire into prevalence of social kyes in the Korean community. Conversely, when Kunae Kim (1982) reported that 94 percent of business owners were kye participants, she did not specify what proportion of kye users invested some or all of their fund in their business. Therefore, the likelihood arises that kye use was more frequent than even Hurh and Kim reported, but that only about one-third of kye users invested funds in business enterprises.

But this solution is only plausible because important methodological issues remain. Hyung-Chan Kim's sample was the smallest of any of the three surveys and was assembled, moreover, in a haphazard fashion. Our 1977 telephone survey contacted the most Korean entrepreneurs, but telephone surveys are notoriously unsuccessful in eliciting candid answers to sensitive questions. Since Kim and Hurh's interviewers visited the Korean stores, they might have been more successful in obtaining respondent candor. Addressing this problem of interviewer rapport, Kunae Kim (1982: 13) complained that surveys "could not elicit intimate and honest response regarding the kye from respondents." In her view, the ethnographic results were more credible than the survey results because they were obtained in a climate of rapport. Although Kim and Hurh's results appeared two years after Kunae Kim expressed this doubt, the issue of respondent candor is important for two reasons. First, our Korean-speaking research assistants encountered reluctance to discuss kye participation even on the part of informants to whom they had been referred along kinship and friendship networks (Chang, 1983: 2):

> I tried to get as many references as possible from my relatives and friends. But it wasn't easy. Some of them showed a great deal of anxiety, and were reluctant to introduce another person. Some refused to do so. Workers were very suspicious of me and reluctant to talk to me. Instead they stressed that kye is a good thing for the Korean community.

Second, as Chang observed, Koreans believed kye was illegal in the United States, a misconception that explains their reluctance to discuss participation. Newspaper stories encouraged this erroneous belief. Following the defalcation of the Mine's restaurant kye and prosecution of the organizer, the *Korea Times* (Yun, 1983) reported that Mine Kim's "troubles began in 1981 when she organized a kye ... which is prevalent among women in Korea (outlawed in the United States)." Early in 1983 the Los Angeles police arrested several kye organizers for fraud. The *Korea Times* again reported that "kye itself is illegal according to American banking law," an error of fact that corresponded to popular belief.[7] The police officer to whom the *Times* attributed this statement told Edward Chang (1983) that he had been misquoted in the Korean press. In reality, the officer claimed, he had not stated that kyes were illegal, only that kye *fraud* was illegal and would be punished under American law. But Los Angeles police were not the only authorities involved. Seeking ways to avoid high interest rates, American real estate promoters turned to the *pandero*, a Brazilian rotating credit association. House buyers joined the promoter's pandero. However, the U.S. postal authorities intervened to close down this rotating credit association, sending an additional message of doubt to Koreans about the legality of kye under federal law (De Wolfe, 1982).

Some Koreans employed their kye draw to finance usurious loans to nonmember Koreans. A loan obtained from an auction kye for 12 percent could be retailed at 40 percent to a needy immigrant.[8] Additionally, the informal banking system among Koreans in Los Angeles reminded the immigrants of South Korea's own "curb money market," a flamboyantly illegal institution in their homeland.[9] Finally, Koreans were sensitive to questions about money because so large a proportion of them had sneaked money out of South Korea in defiance of currency laws (I. Kim, 1981: 66–67; Yoshihara, 1976:1).

An unresolved question concerns the manner in which Korean business owners interpreted our survey questions about kye. Our question asked proprietors for the source of the money they had invested in their business; Kim and Hurh (1984: 88) asked about use of "money obtained from " a kye. Possibly respondents understood our question to mean direct investment of kye funds received in advance of subsequent repayment. But direct investment was, after all, only one way in which kye could have been useful to Korean business owners. If entrepreneurs used kyes to enhance personal saving, then drew upon personal savings to capitalize their business, the entrepreneurs indirectly utilized kye in capitalization of their business; however, respondents might have answered "own savings" when asked to identify the immediate source of money invested in their business. Therefore, it is possible that the large "own savings" category actually included persons whose savings had been amassed through kye participation. This issue underlines the motivational utility of kye in the Korean community, possibly its most important contribution to Korean enterprise. As Myers (1983: 86–97) emphasized, kyes provided social status and recognition to participants who also had fun participating. However, the price of admission was regular and strenuous saving. Just as Weight Watchers clubs encourage people to diet, a troublesome accomplishment, so kyes encouraged Koreans to save, something they might have done without the club—but probably would not have achieved alone.

In view of Kim and Hurh's Chicago results, the ethnographic and newspaper evidence, possible lack of candor on the part of survey respondents, and the uncertain interpretation survey respondents made of questions asked, we conclude that our telephone survey probably underestimated the true utility of kye in promoting business capitalization (Goozner, 1987). The extent of this underestimate

Table 61.   Proportion of Business Capitalization from
Personal Savings and Bank Loans, 1977

	Own Savings	Bank Loan
Total Workers	−.12*	.14*
Business Volume	−.15*	.19**
Korean Clientele	.08	−.12*
White Clientele	−.05	.22**

*p < .05; **p < .01
Source: Telephone survey, 1977.

is unknown. At the very least, however, kye was a popular thrift institution that made a serious contribution to Korean enterprise in Los Angeles. The evidence gathered permits rejection of Reitz's (1980: 242) claim that rotating credit associations "cannot raise the substantial funds needed today to launch and expand small businesses." This evidence also discredits Kurtz's (1973) claim that rotating credit associations represent an "adaptation to poverty" since Korean kye users were richer at the end of their kye cycles than at the beginning—and not poor at the beginning.

CREDIT OR SAVINGS?

When did Koreans borrow and when did they rely upon their own savings to finance business ventures? Our proprietors' survey turned up three variables governing this balance. The first was the size of the respondent proprietor's business. Both business volume and total employment were positively associated with percentage of capital borrowed and negatively associated with percentage of capital taken from the proprietor's own savings (table 61). This relationship indicates that proprietors borrowed when their own savings were insufficient to finance a business. Thus, "own savings" was the first resort and borrowing the second.

Ethnicity of business clientele also affected the savings–borrowing ratio. Firms reporting a heavily Korean clientele tended to report a high percentage of intitial capitalization from own savings. Conversely, firms reporting white clientele were borrowers (table 61). There was no association between saving or borrowing and percentage of Afro-American clientele. The connection between ethnicity of clientele and the borrowing–savings ratio of a business was related to business size. Korean-clientele firms tended to be small, so the proprietors' own savings sufficed to capitalize them. Non-Korean-clientele firms required larger capital so their owners needed to contact external lenders for supplementary funds.

A third variable affecting saving or borrowing was an owner's personal wealth. Start-up costs being equal, wealthy Korean owners could finance business enterprises without borrowing whereas poor owners needed to borrow. Many Korean immigrants brought money to the United States and, for this reason, borrowed little. The Korean consul general has asserted that the U.S. military defeat in Vietnam had produced political uncertainties in South Korea, precipitating a flight of rich Koreans from their homeland. Anticipating an invasion by the People's Democratic Republic of Korea, wealthy South Koreans decided to leave their homeland before war broke out, the republic collapsed, and communists came to power. According to the consul general, the South Korean government responded by strict currency laws aimed at preventing rich people from removing their assets, impoverishing the country, and creating a climate of pessimism. These laws set the stage for the currency violations in which wealthy refugees thereafter engaged.

During the period studied, rampant evasion of South Korean currency regulations was common knowledge among Korean and informed non-Korean respondents alike. Only one Korean denied any knowledge of currency violations among Korean emigrants. The Korean consul general evidenced on two occasions total ignorance of any currency violation among Koreans in Los Angeles. However, among others in a position to know, we found universal agreement that many Koreans in business had violated South Korean currency regulations in order to bring to this country the capital sums with which they opened business enterprises. As one result, American banks soliciting Korean accounts stressed their "confidentiality" and vigilance "against any possible information leak" (Y. Y. Lee, 1981; Berkman, 1984).

We interviewed a Korean employed by the Office of Minority Business Enterprise in the capacity of minority business specialist (Interview 32). In his opinion Korean businessmen arrived in the United States with "five-figure sums," often $50,000 or $60,000. They "laundered" this illegally exported money by investing it small business enterprises. Among the 100 Koreans this specialist had assisted, the average "injection" was $70,000 on a $100,000 investment. Because downpayments were big, the SBA found Korean loan applications easy to approve. A Korean social scientist also reported that intricate international networks existed among Los Angeles Koreans by means of which those already here could, with the contrivance of friends or relatives still in Korea, sneak additional capital sums out of South Korea, possibly by way of Europe or Southeast Asia. This was also the opinion of an influential Korean realtor who claimed that the typical Korean business person brought $20,000 to $30,000 from Korea, most of it in violation of Korean law. A non-Korean business analyst also stated that Koreans smuggled capital out of their country, importing it via Vietnam or Germany. The sales director of a multinational petroleum corporation indicated that Korean franchisees invariably put up $15,000 to $45,000 for initial capitalization. Koreans told him they had smuggled this money out of South Korea in violation of Korean law.

CHOOSING A LENDER

Institutional lenders in the United States have never been satisfactory sources of capital for new small businesses (see Light, 1977b; Light, 1972: ch. 2).[10] This situation still prevailed in the 1970s (Burrell, 1977). Even the Bank of America (Stern, 1976: 1) acknowledged that "small or embryonic companies" were "at the bottom of the financing totem pole" because banks preferred to lend to the "big boys." Indeed, the problems of small business finance have been so severe that American owners were eager to sell to cash-rich foreigners the businesses for which they themselves were unable to obtain adequate finance (Anderson, 1978).

In prewar Asian communities the shortage of institutional finance contributed to informal credit systems, and the shortage might have produced the same consequence in the 1970s. However, the borrowing position of Koreans in this decade was in reality superior to that of prewar Asians—and even superior to that of non-Asians. One reason was the augmented supply of mainstream credit to non-white small businesses (Kobelinski, 1977: 22). Stung by charges of racism and redlining, white-owned banks were more responsive to minority borrowing needs than in the past. Additionally, a number of minority-owned banks and savings and loan institutions existed in this period, and these institutions extended credit to coethnics.[11] In fact so many Chinese-owned savings institutions had come into existence already that, in 1978, San Francisco Chinese protested against the attempt to open another Chinese-owned savings and loan association in Chinatown.

Many Asian banks opened full-service branches in California during the 1970s. The number of Asian banks opened in this period was so great that in 1977 the U.S. Senate restricted the criteria for entry. A Korean banker claimed that the proponents of this legislation were American banks unhappy with the competitive pressure of Asian banks.[12] Our research disclosed no grounds for supposing that Asian borrowers were racially disadvantaged in private credit markets during the 1970s.[13] In historical perspective, this absence of disadvantage represented an important step forward. Of course, absence of discrimination did not create problem-free financing for Asian business owners because all small business owners suffered the indifference of mainstream financial institutions. Hence, relative improvement in access to venture capital did not eliminate financial obstacles to Asian business, even though it eliminated discriminatory obstacles.

A few Asians were beneficiaries of preferential treatment by state and federal agencies in the 1970s. This they received under programs intended to stimulate minority business enterprise. Initially launched by the Nixon administration in response to black pressure, these programs included all nonwhite minorities by the early 1970s. Three public authorities carried on programs to benefit minority business owners. Minority Enterprise Small Business Investment Companies (MESBICs) "were introduced in 1969 to serve only those small businesses owned by minority group members ..." (Stern, 1976: 10). In 1975 California became the thirty-third state to legislate the existence of MESBICs. Thus, both state and federal MESBICs assisted minority business people after 1975. Federal MESBICs supplied equity financing and long-term debt financing; by law they might assist only small businesses owned by nonwhites. A second public lender was the Small Business Administration. Under its Operation Business Mainstream and Economic Opportunity Loan programs, the SBA made direct loans or guaranteed bank loans for nonwhite owners of small businesses. Four percent of Korean respondents in our proprietors' survey acknowledged borrowing money from the SBA (table 60). The third authority was the U.S. Department of Commerce's Office of Minority Business Enterprise (OMBE). OMBE funded local business development organizations (BDOs) in which coethnics managed the federal loan fund for the benefit of their people. The principal BDO servicing Asians in Los Angeles was the Asian American National Business Alliance (AANBA). A representative of this organization stated that Koreans did not use AANBA's facilities much, even though these were free. AANBA had no loans to Koreans outstanding in 1975.

Although Korean immigrants benefited from public loan programs directed to nonwhites, the benefit was modest. First, government loan programs were generally unhelpful, ineffective, and unnecessary (Blaustein and Faux, 1972: 248). According to Mitchell Kobelinski (1977: 15) administrator of the U.S. Small Business Administration, the "vast majority" of small businesses did not need SBA loans. If creditworthy, they could secure loans from banks; if not creditworthy, loans were not the proper mode of government assistance for them. After their review of government loan programs for minority business enterprise, Knight and Dorsey (1976: 167) also concluded that their impact was negligible.

Second, Asian-American sources agreed that federal and state loan programs had contributed little to Asian business in the decade of the 1970s. According to the director of Asian-Pacific Business Services, a packager of section 8(a) loans for the Small Business Administration, "Historically Asian business owners haven't benefited from government programs that help small business." [14] The director of California's Office of Small Business Development claimed that "not one" Korean had approached her agency in the first two years of its operation. [15] Only Amsun Associates (1977) attempted to assess the impact of government programs on Asian enterprise. According to Amsun (1977: 75) Asians were short-changed, receiving less than their expected share of assistance specifically targeted for minority entrepreneurs. Under the procurement program administered by SBA between 1968 and 1975, Asian firms received only 135 contracts whose total valuation was $12.7 million. Amsun (1977: 77) claimed this figure was unfairly low relative to other minorities.

The fragmentary character of statistical evidence is unfortunate, but federal documents were almost useless for evaluating the contribution of federal loan programs to Asian enterprise. Lamenting this situation, the Office of Manpower and Budget complained that "information on Federal assistance does not tell us how these programs affected the number or viability of minority-owned businesses."[16] Nonetheless, utilizing SBA annual reports, we pieced together evidence that can be adjusted to provide estimates of probable effectiveness (table 62). In the period 1975–1979 Asians in the United States received 791 Economic Opportunity Loans (EOLs) from the Small Business Administration. Assuming generously that none of these 791 firms failed, they constituted less than one-tenth of one percent of the 110,837 Asian-owned business firms enumerated by the U.S. Bureau of the Census (1979). Similarly, in Los Angeles, the SBA made 176 loans to Asians between 1975 and 1981. Assuming that one-half of these loans went to Koreans, and that none of these firms failed, the EOL-sponsored Korean firms amounted to 4 percent of the 2212 Korean-owned firm enumerated in Los Angeles County by the U.S. Bureau of the Census. Obviously, these generous estimates do not permit the conclusion that EOL loans provided more than a minor proportion of the capitalization of Korean enterprises in the United States or in Los Angeles.

However, David Kim uncovered SBA data that suggest a bigger role for the agency in Los Angeles. Kim (1975: 77) obtained the help of SBA staff who compiled from their records an exact enumeration of SBA loans to Koreans in the period 1971–1974. Kim's (1975: 42) results indicated that Koreans in Los Angeles obtained 101 SBA loans in this period with a mean loan size of $102,000. Of these loans, 33 were for liquor stores, 18 for grocery stores, and 15 for restaurants. The loan figures Kim provided included directly subscribed SBA capital as well as SBA-guaranteed loans. Assuming none of these SBA-sponsored firms failed, they represented 4.5 percent of the 2212 Korean-owned firms enumerated in Los Angeles by the census.

We brought David Kim's statistics to the attention of a Korean loan-packaging officer employed by the Business Development Center of Southern California, an OMBE affiliate. This officer claimed to have counseled about 100 Korean loan applicants in the period 1976–1979. He thought that Kim's estimate of 4.5 percent was about right for direct loans to Koreans. However, he observed that SBA also made indirect loans in the form of guarantees. He thought SBA's

Table 62. Economic Opportunity Loans to Asians from the U.S. Small Business Administration, 1975–1981

	1975	1976	1977	1978	1979	1980	1981
Number of Loans	148	186	194	132	131		
Percent of Total	4.0	5.1	5.1	4.0	4.6		
Dollar Amount (thousands)	3,684	5,315	6,263	5,083	5,635		
Percent of Total	4.8	6.2	5.6	5.0	5.6		
8(a)* Loans in Los Angeles	22	25	27	28	29	15	30

*"Under the authority of section 8(a) of the Small Business Act, the SBA serves as prime contracor for selected federal procurement requirements, then subcontracts to firms owned and controlled by socially or economically disadvantaged persons." Small Business Administration, *Annual Report 1976* (Washington D.C.: USGPO, 1976), p. 46.
Source: U.S. Small Business Administration, *Annual Reports* (Washington, D.C.: USGPO, 1975–1981).

indirect and direct loans would affect more than 4 percent of Korean firms in the County, but he declined to offer firmer evidence, declaring that no statistics could be released. Underscoring the refusal, his supervisor invited us to leave the premises.

KOREAN BANKS IN LOS ANGELES

The government of the Republic of Korea provided a second source of financial support for Korean-owned businesses in Los Angeles county. Several informants mentioned this financial support. One was the Korean consul general. He stated that the South Korean government supported Korean business in Los Angeles by means of the Korea Exchange Bank (KEB), a wholly owned entity of the Republic of Korea (see also Jo, 1982: 206; I. Kim, 1981: 231). A bank manager expanded on this relationship. In 1975, the KEB's annual loan volume was $100 million and the KEB offered full-service banking. Most customers were Koreans. Most of the business of the Los Angeles branch was with Korea in the export–import trade. Two lines of trade predominated: human-hair wigs and clothing. In the period 1967–1972 human hair wigs were "a high-class decoration for whites." Korea exported 70 percent of the world's human-hair wigs. Wigmaking is a labor intensive industry, and labor was cheap in Korea, the banker stated. Korean women did the work, earning about $100 a month. He estimated that Koreans operated 200 wig shops in Los Angeles County in 1975. However, by 1975 the wig business had gone into eclipse as a result of style changes, and stores were shutting down.

The clothing industry was the second major recipient of the Korea Exchange Bank's capital. This industry was much larger in 1975 than wigs in terms of employment and total capital investment. About 20 percent of U.S. clothing imports came from South Korea at this time. An example of a successful clothing importer was Zion Industrial Company. Only three or four Korean garment firms had achieved its size. The KEB had loaned Zion more than $3 million. A few Korean garment importers were branch offices of Korea-based corporations, but most were independents incorporated in the United States.

The KEB also helped Korean immigrants to open gas stations and restaurants. Gas station owners and restauranteurs might receive a cash loan from the KEB of 20 to 50 percent of their downpayment.

However, this loan had to be repaid within a year, a ruling imposed by Seoul. Additionally, Seoul had imposed a $3000 limit on loans for any business lacking a letter of credit. In 1975, this limit was raised to $5000 without a letter of credit and $20,000 with it. The figure was too small. Korean customers who visited the KEB commonly needed more than $20,000, and it was hard to repay this amount in one year. The KEB had repeatedly requested Seoul to authorize more liberal terms, but these requests had been denied. The banker indicated that KEB loans to Koreans in America were interest-bearing at the full market rate. In contrast, he observed, the U.S. Small Business Administration offered loans at below-market cost, and Koreans preferred SBA terms.

We also interviewed the general manager of the Hanil Bank, Ltd. of Seoul, Korea. Unlike the KEB, the Hanil Bank was privately owned. In the period 1975–1978 three privately owned Korean banks had opened agencies in Los Angeles. In addition to Hanil Bank, these were the Korean Commercial Bank and Korea First Bank. Since KEB continued to operate, altogether four Korea-based banks were doing business in Los Angeles in 1978. However, the private banks had experienced difficulty in obtaining licenses to operate in the United States. The business of the Hanil Bank was import-export and foreign exchange. The latter involved remittances by individuals of U.S. currency to Korea as well as corporate finance. Most of the Hanil's business in the United States was conducted with 100 Korean corporations that imported goods from Korea for sale in the United States. Among the 100 were ten "general trading corporations" modeled on Japanese *zaibatsu*. The Hanil Bank made no loans to small businesses or consumers and neither, according to the general manager, did the other two privately owned Korean banks operating in Los Angeles.

The KEB incorporated a subsidiary, the California Korea Bank, in 1974.[17] The California Korea Bank (CKB) was incorporated in California and licensed to do a full-service business. In 1978 U.S. legislation prohibited the formation of domestic subsidiaries of foreign corporations, but California Korea Bank predated this legislation and so was unaffected. The KEB manager provided estimates of the KEB's and CKB's outstanding loans in Los Angeles: Korean corporations, 56 percent; Korean residents of Los Angeles, 40 percent; non-Koreans, 4 percent. These figures indicate that Los Angeles Koreans were important consumers of Korean capital in 1978. The major source of these loans was the California Korea Bank. Since the CKB was a subsidiary of the Korea Exchange Bank, itself a wholly owned subsidiary of the South Korean government, CKB loans to Koreans in Los Angeles actually represented intervention by the government of South Korea on behalf of Koreans abroad.

Of course, these loans were for consumption as well as for business. We obtained no basis for estimating the relative importance of consumption or business in the CKB's loans to Korean individuals. The KEB had experienced problem of loan defalcations. The banker claimed these defalcations had been mainly due to "ignorance," and, we suspect, the bank's ignorance was as much a factor as borrowers'. The California bankruptcy statute had come as an unwelcome surprise to the KEB whose debtors were able by means of this statute to escape repayment of loans. The problem of loan defalcations was now under control, the banker insisted. However, the KEB's defalcation problem was front-page news in Koreatown. A news article stated that the KEB had reluctantly decided to turn its debtors, all Korean nationals, over to a collection agency.[18] The KEB's loan crisis began in 1972 when it unwisely advanced money to Korean nationals, about a hundred of whom failed to repay. As a result of the loan crisis, the KEB's general manager was arrested in Seoul. By 1978 only twenty debtors were still outstanding and their total of unpaid principal was $50,000. "Stern measures" to collect past-due principal represented a reaction to excessively liberal loan terms offered in the past. Korean-Americans had coined a maxim in this period: "You are a fool if you are unable to borrow money from the [Korea] Exchange Bank. More foolish are those who repay."

The loan defalcation crisis was mute evidence that the Korea Exchange Bank had made loans to Koreans on terms too liberal for the California market. This liberality suggests that the Korean government was pressing the bank to help Koreans in Los Angeles, and the bank issued easy credit as a result. We do not believe, however, that the "severe measures" represented a repudiation of this liberal policy, but rather that government and bank had learned how to function more effectively in California.[19] The government of Korea still wanted the KEB to assist nationals in Los Angeles, but this assistance was expected to pay its own way. In 1978 the KEB's interest rate on business loans was 13.5 percent, somewhat lower than major American banks, but no gift.

KOREAN-AMERICAN FINANCIAL
INSTITUTIONS

Korean-Americans opened several financial institutions during the 1970s. One institution was a finance company operated by the Na U Club. Our first reference to this club was a Korean accountant. This informant stated that his business consisted of "external audits" of firms of which 85 percent were Korean owned. He mentioned that in 1967 the Korea Exchange Bank had helped ten Koreans start in business. These ten became his clients. In 1972, KEB policy hardened and the defalcation crisis ensued. In that year the accountant claimed to have lost "about fifteen clients" with sales of $500,000 or more. The KEB was still very "lenient" to fellow Koreans, and the respondent thought this leniency was the best example of fellow-feeling among Koreans.

Asked about rotating credit associations, he acknowledged their existence but deprecated their business importance. However, the Na U Club (of which he was a former officer) had a working capital of approximately $600,000. Its members were all business people who met together to decide how to invest the fund. Thus, the Na U Club was not a rotating credit association. Rather, this informal organization was an "investment club." As such its resources were actually quite slender, he conceded.

The president of the Na U Club had cofounded the organization in 1973. Na U Club's membership was forty-five in 1978. All members were "leaders" in the Korean community. The chairman was representative of this leadership. The accountant himself was an officer in the Korean Association of Southern California, the Korean Chamber of Commerce, and a member of the Bicentennial Committee of the City of Los Angeles and advisor to a Korean-student association. He claimed at-large membership in a variety of other community organizations. Membership in the Na U Club was selective. Applicants were required to have "much prestige in the Korean community." Five judges screened applicants and recommended their choices to the general membership. As a result, the Na U membership was an elite, and members often were past or present officers of major Korean organizations. On the membership list in front of him our respondent ticked off six current presidents of community organizations. Once admitted, Na U members could be expelled for nonattendance or for developing a "bad reputation" in the Korean community.

Every Na U member was required to contribute monthly to the club's capital fund. In addition the Na U Club required a monthly contribution to pay for the monthly meetings held at restaurants in Los Angeles. The club sponsored seminars on how to get SBA loans. Its current speaker was a Bank of America executive, non-Korean, who was running for public office. With $100,000 the Na U Club was beginning a "finance company" to serve the Korean community.

The *Korea Times* described the Na U Club as "a fraternity of Korean businessmen in Los Angeles."[20] This fraternity had decided to establish the finance company "with an eye to helping the Korean immigrants operate small and medium size business firms in the United States." The club's spokesman expected the finance company to provide loans for "settlement of new-coming Korean immigrants and operation of their business firms."

A year and a half later, the *Korea Times* reported the inauguration of a savings and loan fund in the Los Angeles Korean community.[21] Eleven founders were pledged to obtain 40 stockholders each. These 440 stockholders were to subscribe the $2 million needed to open a federally chartered institution. Described as "the first of its kind to set up by Koreans in the United States," the projected association was "pushed ahead to help the economic development of Korean community." Spokespersons promised to hire Korean experts in banking and law. Of the five founders listed by name, all were past presidents of officers of major Korean community organizations. Global Oriental Savings and Loan opened for business in 1981, bringing this plan to fruition.[22]

Three additional financial projects deserve mention. Twelve Korean-American businessmen bought the ailing Bank of Finance in 1982. Its main offices located near Koreatown, the Bank of Finance had opened in 1963 as a black-owned bank. When the bank ran into "financial difficulties," four Koreans on the board of directors recruited eight others; this group bought 83 percent of stock and then elected themselves directors.[23] Another group of Korean businessmen established the Korean Community Bank in 1979 "to serve Korean business circles."[24] A joint venture with non-Koreans, the Wilshire State Bank began in 1981 on South Vermont Avenue. Four of fifteen directors were Korean, and Koreans were 31 percent of those subscribing capital for the new bank.

Like the kyes and private loans, the Korean-Americans' banks were self-help institutions of the Korean community. However, these formal institutions were built around self-conscious elites of business people whose subscribed capital was loaned to coethnics for profit. This pattern reflected bourgeois social stratification as well as ethnic solidarity. However, all these institutions did depend upon Korean ethnicity in the sense that a random group of equally wealthy business people would not have subscribed capital specifically to service the *Korean* community. Being Korean, the subscribers knew about the financial need of coethnics and how to service it.[25] Additionally, the banks all stated that their purpose was to provide capital for the Korean community, a benevolent objective. After all, subscribers might have invested in triple-A-rated corporate bonds had they only desired to maximize safety and yield. That they choose instead to establish banks in Koreatown is evidence that the profit motive was guided to this particular employment by ethnic feeling and ethnic information channels, as well as by the self-interested calculation of financial advantage.

CONCLUSION

Korean capital came from many sources. Some were external to the Korean community, but most were internal. Complex as a proper evaluation of financial sources may be, the evidence readily permits rejection of the null hypothesis (that is, no ethnic agencies existed to assist Koreans so every Korean was strictly on his or her own when it came to finding business capital). Even if it were conceded that Korean proprietors' own savings were the principal source of business capitalization, they were not the only source. Koreans also borrowed from friends and relatives, utilized kyes, founded their own thrift institutions, and borrowed money from California branches of Korean banks. Since all these sources were broadly ethnic in character, a class interpretation of Korean capitalization distorts by omission. Additionally, personal savings was not merely a class category, important as was the exported capital of wealthy Koreans. First, personal savings reflected the propensity to save of Korean immigrants, and this propensity surely reflected ethnic values and need dispositions. Second, kyes assisted thrift, thus obtaining an indirect role in promoting savings, the direct source from which start-up capital was most frequently derived.

Two external sources of financing require special comment because of the misconceptions to which exaggeration of their importance has given rise. First, Korean banks supported Korean-owned enterprise in Los Angeles, but their total effect was modest. It would be an exaggeration to suppose that Korean banks caused the high rate of entrepreneurship among Koreans in Los Angeles. Similarly, Koreans did obtain loans on favorable terms from agencies of federal and state government. These loans helped Korean entrepreneurship even though, as chapter 13 observes, the government's trend throughout the decade of the 1970s was toward ever less favorable treatment of Korean loan applications. However, it would represent a great exaggeration to claim that Korean entrepreneurship in Los Angeles occurred *because* agencies of government pressed low-cost money upon them.

Assessing the evidence, we find that that Koreans in Los Angeles participated simultaneously in two financial systems, one ethnic and one nonethnic. The ethnic financial system consisted of intracommunal lending and saving agencies such as kyes, private lenders, loan sharks, loan clubs, Korean-American thrift institutions, and American branches of Korean banks. The ethnic system also provided the motivation underpinning the frugality that distinguished Koreans from other Los Angeles residents. The nonethnic financial system included government bureaus and American banks, as well of course as the public school system, advertising media, the money supply, tax laws, and other agencies shaping the general population's motivation to save. The money Koreans brought with them from overseas is harder to classify in these terms. On the one hand, it represented a class resource. On the other hand, the Koreans' cultural background, immigration plans, and social networks shaped the accumulation and export of this capital. Insofar as capital imported from Korea permitted the accumulation of capital in Los Angeles, capital beget capital—a process requiring no assistance from ethnicity to explain. However, insofar as the ability of imported capital to beget capital was enhanced by Korean ethnicity, then the process of accumulation in Koreatown was not one which simple class theory wholly explains.

11

Sources of Entrepreneurship

Asked to explain the overrepresentation of coethnics in business, Koreans advanced a variety of causes. Naturally many mentioned the Koreans' educational background and the money Koreans brought with them. An equally common theme, however, was their countrymens' willingness to work hard, to save money by thrifty living, and to enroll family members in the business. Sometimes informants put such remarks in a comparative framework, observing that Koreans worked harder, were thriftier, and were more family oriented than Americans:

> They are diligent, compared to Americans and other minorities. They work harder and longer.
>
> —Korean diplomat

> Koreans are not more business-minded than others, but they work very hard at it.
>
> —Korean professor

> Koreans are highly motivated and willing to work hard.
>
> —Korean realtor

> Koreans prefer family-oriented businesses. These require sixty to seventy hours of work a week. The work is hard, but one can make a good living in the United States if willing to work hard.
>
> —Korean banker

> Our people tend to work harder than other people.
>
> —Korean pastor

Korean sources reported the same comments from their own Korean respondents. Terry Chang (1980) analyzed sixteen Korean-language autobiographies published in the *Joong-ang Daily News* as part of a prize contest. Admittedly, the winning entries had been selected for readability by the newspaper. Nonetheless, the cultural themes in these autobiographies were resonant with the newspaper's conception of what would interest their immigrant readership. Amid the themes of loneliness, betrayal, divorce, role conflict, and cultural shock, these autobiographies depict struggling people who believe their bottomline resource is willingness to work hard.

> My husband had to get up at 5:30 am, and only came back after 7 pm. Even Sunday ... (he still had to work.... My husband said he could survive this kind of hardship because he was athletic.... I opened a restaurant ... in Redondo Beach. In my restaurant I hired two people, and two of my children helped, too.... The amount of work I do has never been reduced since I worked at Andy's ranch [e.g. 81 hours a week]. (Life History 2)

> I always dreamed about opening my own market or having my own business.... I decided to become a butcher.... Physically working with Americans was very hard for me because I had to cut up 200- to 400-pound slabs of meat all by myself. I just didn't have that kind of strength. I became exhausted. (Life History 15)

> Immigration.... This word gave me the power to survive hardships. I always remind myself: work hard, don't ever forget sweat and endeavor in your life. (Life History 12)

> It was January, 1978. Our hardships really started now. My husband could work at a gas station or as a janitor, but his biggest hope was to find a secure job in his skill and eventually to open his own jewelry shop.... Our future hopes are: we want to have a small house of our own and expand his new business. I believe no matter what kind of hardship you go through if you depend on each other and try harder you will succeed. I also thank God who helped our family all the time. (Life History 5)

> Dad worked in the gas station 6 am through 12 pm at night. I worked 3 pm to 7 am. Although it was hard and tiring, we thought since we had an opportunity, we ought to work hard.... So finally we got the gas station on our own account. We started our own business for the first time. That night my husband and I couldn't sleep. We cried for a long time and promised each other that we would work harder. We didn't even have a bed so we were sleeping on the floor. (Life History 1)

Korean newspapers often published biographies of Korean entrepreneurs, cultural heroes among their own people. In these biographies, the theme of hard work surmounting obstacles recurred whether as editorial interpretation or direct quotation from the autobiographical subject. The following are representative synopses:[1]

> Dorothy Kim operated a Regal Liquor Store in Culver City.... Her clientele was 50-percent black, 50-percent white. Armed robberies were frequent, and Kim prayed daily to Buddha for the courage to

stand behind her counter. A college-educated school teacher in Korea, Kim had no previous business experience when she opened her liquor store. Hours of operation were 13 hours daily and 15 hours weekends.

Philip Hwang invested $9,000 in 1975 in his own company, TeleVideo Systems, Inc. In 1981 Hwang's firm grossed $35 million. Nonetheless, Hwang and his wife "still fret over the cost of heating" their home. Hwang employs 100 "young Koreans" some of whom "will learn the secret of success from their boss and achieve similar success in the future." "Enterprise, challenge, and improvement make this a great country" says Hwang.

Mun Ung Kang founded a food importing concern "whose products dot the tables" of Koreans in Los Angeles. Kang started as a coal miner in West Germany earning $300 a month in 1964. The Germans taught him the meaning of hard work says Kang. Kang opened a small grocery in Los Angeles in 1971. "We worked 16–18 hour days." Kang still does not "shy away from work."

In 1976 David Kim opened a corner grocery store in Spanish Harlem. He worked 12–14 hours a day. After a year, he sold the grocery store, and bought a bigger one in a better neighborhood. In 1980 Kim was President of the Korean Chamber of Commerce of New York, and his store grossed $200,000 yearly. "The Koreans are showing that the way to honorably succeed in America is through the old-fashioned virtues of toil and self-sacrifice."

Young Whan Cho arrived in Los Angeles with $200 in 1976. In 1980 Cho owned two restaurants and was President of the Ventura County Lions Club. On arrival in the US, Cho lived with his brother while he studied English and worked nights as a warehouse clerk. He saved enough money to buy a hamburger stand; in 10 months he and his wife tripled the stand's business, sold it, and bought a snack shop. Cho warns his countrymen they must be prepared to swallow their dignity, start at the bottom, and work hard to obtain material success.

Kim Chong-So hanged himself under the pressure of business debts in 1977. Kim arrived in the United States in 1966, and made a good start in business "due to faithfulness and diligence." However, Kim's business failed, and he was saddled with debts he could not repay. Kim was the son of a prominent Christian pastor in Korea.

President of a food store in Los Angeles, Kim Young-Gil, died of high blood pressure in 1978. "In 1975 he was interviewed by *Newsweek* which highly praised the diligence and hard work of Kim." Kim was 52.

As these synopses indicate, Korean entrepreneurs suffered mental and physical health problems as a result of overwork. Korean newspapers, noticing this problem, called their countrymens' attention to the dangers of neglecting their health and their childrens' welfare in devotion to the almighty dollar.[2]

Allusions to Korean diligence, thrift, and hard work were almost as common among non-Koreans as among Koreans. We encountered these allusions in two situations. First, we questioned non-Koreans knowledgeable about Korean business activities, and these informants mentioned the hard work of the Koreans when listing their business talents. Second, journalist's accounts of Korean life referred to their phenomenal business success, often mentioning the Koreans' proclivity for hard work in explanation. Admittedly, diligence and thrift were mentioned alongside educational background, money, and labor-force disadvantage. In fact, Americans emphasized money, education, and labor-force disadvantage more than did the Koreans, in whose version long hours of labor bulked larger.

The American publisher of an apparel-industry newspaper assured us that garment manufacturing was so unpleasant no one would do it whom circumstances did not compel. Blacks would not take this work, he said, because the welfare state relieved them of economic desperation. As a result, only Koreans and other foreigners would perform "this hard, honest work." The retail sales manager of a major oil company said his company had forty-five Korean gas station franchises in Los Angeles, about 10 percent of the company's dealer force. He called Korean dealers "aggressive businessmen," noting that family members "took shifts" working the station so their stations stayed open longer. As a result, Korean-owned stations "did more business" than non-Korean stations. Americans did not want to manage gasoline stations because Americans were "lazy" and fearful of robbery. Having experienced hard times in their country of origin, Koreans were prepared to work harder than Americans. An American service station operator in Koreatown agreed that Koreans sold more gasoline than non-Koreans. In his opinion, Koreans achieved higher output by accepting low profits, employing family members, and cooking on hotplates in the rear of their stations. On a visit to the Small Business Administration, we interviewed a minority small business specialist who had worked closely with "a number of Korean clients." Acknowledging that Koreans laundered money earlier sneaked out of Korea, he nonetheless felt that the "Korean impact" on business depended upon "their work ethic." "Koreans are willing to toil harder."

American journalists frequently put Korean business success in the framework of our Horatio Alger tradition (Wyllie, 1954). According to *Newsweek* (Dotson, 1975), Los Angeles' Koreatown "abounds with Horatio Alger success stories." *Newsweek* mentioned the career of Hi-Duk Lee; he arrived in California with $50, then built up a thriving real estate, restaurant, and nightclub business in Koreatown. Discrimination was part of the explanation, according to *Newsweek*, since unemployed and underemployed Koreans had little alternative to self-employment. Nonetheless, the magazine found evidence of "pluck" in the Korean character and noted the immigrants' reputation for thriftiness and cleanliness. *Westways* (Smith, 1976: 38) admitted that Korean entrepreneurs had found "devious ways" to sneak capital out of their homeland. Nonetheless, *Westways* concluded, their success derived from "such old-fashioned American virtues as industry, thrift, dependability, and enterprise." The *Los Angeles Times* (Yoshihara, 1976) also returned to the case of Hi-Duk Lee, probably because, as president of the Koreatown Development Association, Lee greeted the parade of reporters inquiring about his fellow Koreans. Noting that many smuggled money out of Korea in excess of the legal maximum, the *Times* also insisted that "in most cases the [Koreans'] money has been accumulated here through sheer hard work, sacrifice, and determination." Within two years, such families had accumulated a "modest bankroll" permitting them to purchase a grocery store, liquor store, gas station, or restaurant.

Another *Los Angeles Times* report (Overend, 1978) started with the story of Byung Min who had $5 in his pocket when he landed in Los Angeles in 1972. "Now he owns an apartment building and supermarket on Alvarado Street." The article quoted Sonia Suk, a Korean-born real estate tycoon; in her opinion, the prevailing idea among her countrymen was to "work hard, save money, and educate the children." In Overend's estimation as well "it all boils down to hard work." In the typical case, a Korean immigrant of professional background would start his American work life with a job as a gas station attendant or store clerk while his wife worked as a seamstress. Within two years—"working six or seven days a week and ten hours or more a day"—the couple had accumulated $10,000, approximately half their gross earnings in the period. This money they then invested in a small business, the first rung on the ladder of success.

Sherman (1979) provided a harsher account of Korean entrepreneurship. In her story an experienced broker described Koreans as "dynamic, aggressive, ruthless people" whose acquire-at-any-price determination had driven property values up along Olympic Boulevard. "Prices are being driven skyhigh overnight" according to the broker who also observed that Koreans overpaid for properties in their acquisitive rush. Price was no object because "unlike other ethnic groups," Koreans had entered the United States with money. In its editorial judgment of the city's "new middle class," the *Los Angeles Times*[3] deemphasized the Koreans' initial capital and higher education, quoting a Korean engineer to the effect that hard work was the key:

> Frankly, I don't see Caucasians who work hard. That gives us [Koreans] more chance. Time was my capital. [My wife and I] opened at 7 am and closed at 10 at night, I slept in the back of the garage for a while.

Our 1977 telephone survey of Korean proprietors asked 213 respondents to indicate the hours and days of operation of their businesses. The wording of this question was unfortunate (because answers referred to stores rather than to individuals) so we could not ascertain how hard Korean proprietors were working individually. Nonetheless, in view of the fact that most Korean businesses were mom and pop operations, the respondents' answers are of some assistance in estimating working time for the owners. Among 197 proprietors who responded, average hours of store operation were 12.5 daily. Only 23 percent reported 8 hours of store operation daily. Eleven percent reported 24-hour operation. Mean days of operation were 6.3 weekly. Ten percent opened their stores only 5 days weekly; 50 percent opened 6 days; and 41 percent opened 7 days weekly. In sum, the average Korean-owned store was open 79 hours a week.

CHARACTER OF KOREAN
ENTREPRENEURS

In view of the impressionistic and statistical evidence assembled above—plus the statistical evidence cited in table 34—we conclude that Korean proprietors in Los Angeles worked longer hours than non-Korean ones. Since the long hours contributed to the survival and success of Korean firms, the Koreans' willingness to work these long hours emerges as a specific resource upon which Korean entrepreneurs drew.

Illsoo Kim (1981: 299, 300) has advanced a characterological explanation of his countrymens' business drive. According to Kim (1981: 299, 300) the "character of Korean immigrants" was formed in a historical process which blended Confucian and Protestant religious ethics:

> As far as the socioeconomic adjustment of Korean immigrants is concerned, there is a value congruence between Confucianism and the Protestant ethic in the sense that both of them are directed toward self-control and self-abnegation.

> Confucian values correspond to white, middle-class Protestant values such as emphasis on work, politeness, family authority, diligence, cleanliness, and neatness.

Kim claims (1981: 297–298) that the "central values in the Korean personality" became work and economic mobility. As a result of these internalized cultural values, Koreans in the United States worked hard in business, saved, looked for advancement, avoided public welfare, and "attached themselves" to their families. In this sense, Kim's explanation for the Koreans' entrepreneurship was the character structure of the immigrants, an ethnic resource imported from Korea.

Kim's characterological interpretation of Korean entrepreneurship is plausible and compatible with what many Koreans and non-Koreans alike believed. However, proof of any such claim is difficult because the mere presence of entrepreneurial behavior in a population leaves unexplained why or how the behavior arose (Wilken 1979: 60–68). National character is a possibility, but alternatives are wider. Indeed explanatory combinations are dismayingly complex. At present, explanations of entrepreneurship in a population fall into three broad classes: cultural, social movement, and situational. Only some of the explanations require any assumptions about culturally derived character structure. In this chapter we treat only cultural and social-movement sources of the Korean work ethnic, leaving situational and acculturational sources to part four.

CULTURAL THEORIES

Cultural theories explain entrepreneurship by referring to prior socialization (Jenkins, 1984: ch. 13). This socialization may induct into ethnic or class cultures (Thompson, 1979). True, primary socialization is only the first stage and is later supported by institutions and life styles that control adult conduct. Nonetheless, primary socialization is an indispensable prerequisite of any cultural theory; all who share an entrepreneurial culture do so because they earlier learned the values, attitudes, motives, information, and skills of this culture in the course of socialization. Thus, Waterbury (1972: 44, 48, 188) found that Berber toddlers in Morocco were already imbued with the commercial skills and attitudes of their parents. Similarly, De Vos (1973: 3) declared that "to be ethnically Japanese" is to have undergone socialization into an achievement-oriented culture whether one resides in Japan, North America, or Brazil. What is more, patterns once internalized are "not easily modified by adult experience" (De Vos, 1973: 3). In these terms, the explanation for the entrepreneurship of any Japanese is prior socialization in the course of which the person acquired a Japanese character.

A class interpretation of entrepreneurship is also possible. Occupational inheritance is pronounced in any occupation involving the transmission of property—such as a business or farm (Hall, 1975: 154). Insofar as a bourgeoisie introduces its youth into business, entrepreneurship is the cultural aspect of intergenerational transmission. That is, the bourgeoisie turns over to its children the means of production, a material transfer. However, the bourgeoisie also turns over to its children the entrepreneurial values, motivations, and skills requisite to reproducing the private economy. This is a cultural transmission. In this sense entrepreneurship is an essential part of the class culture of a bourgeoisie (Robinson, 1984). Naturally, a class effect is compatible with an ethnic effect. For example, in their panel study of self-employment among ethnic groups in Providence, Rhode Island, Goldscheider and Kobrin (1980: 176) found large, persistent intergroup differences with Italians and, especially, Jews much overrepresented. At the same time, they found that, holding ethnicity constant, father's self-employment increased self-employment among sons, a class effect. In the Providence data, then, both class and ethnic differences combined to explain self-employment of younger generations.

These results are compatible with Marxist sociology too. Soviet Marxists have long treated deviance in their socialist society as the expression of residual bourgeois culture lagging behind material change (Connor, 1972). Additionally, they have discriminated against persons of bourgeois origin on the ground that primary socialization lays down cultural styles hostile to socialism. This discrimination is a backhanded acknowledgement that bourgeois culture exists, is communicated in primary socialization, and affects adult performance.

The boundary between class and ethnic culture depends upon how generally entrepreneurial values, motivations, and skills are distributed among a population. Ethnic cultures are entrepreneurial when they distribute entrepreneurial motivation and skills among all socioeconomic levels. At least among classic middleman minorities, entrepreneurship is a part of the ethnic culture. Thus, Sway (1984) has shown that Gypsy culture bestows upon all Gypsies, rich or poor, the ambitions and skills requisite to self-employment. Conversely, a class culture of entrepreneurship limits entrepreneurial values, motivations, and skills to the bourgeoisie. Sometimes class and ethnic cultures interpenetrate, especially when a dominant bourgeoisie imposes its entrepreneurial culture upon subordinate classes. In the United States, for example, faith in the enterprising individual varies with socioeconomic status. Higher-status people explain individual success in terms of effort and preparation whereas lower-status people emphasize luck and connections (Huber and Form, 1973: ch. 5). In this sense, the culture of entrepreneurship belongs more to the bourgeoisie than to other social groups. On the other hand, Lipset and Bendix (1959: 102–103, 177–181) showed that American workers cling to aspirations for self-employment, a value impossible to explain as the class culture of the bourgeoisie. In point of fact, the culture of entrepreneurship flourishes most in the American bourgeoisie, but it has significantly affected all social strata.

ENTREPRENEURSHIP AS SOCIAL MOVEMENT

Social movements resocialize and mobilize adults in the interests of social change. In some instances social movements have championed entrepreneurial values, motivations, and skills, thus promoting entrepreneurship among movement adherents and, depending upon their effectiveness, in society generally.[4] Weber's (1958a, 1958b) Protestant sectarians are the most famous example. Admittedly, Weber's sectarians were a segment of the occidental bourgeoisie, an ethnic as well as a class linkage. However, as Weber stressed, admission to any sect was voluntary in principle. Sects rejected infant baptism on the grounds that only those old enough to make a mature commitment were eligible for membership. Naturally, this rejection was unrealistic in the historical long run because adherents' children sought membership for themselves as a matter of birthright. Nonetheless, Weber's argument demonstrates that in the short run a religious movement can induct, reeducate, and mobilize adults whose commitment to the values, motivations, and skills of entrepreneurship do not depend upon primary socialization. In this sense, sectarians displayed the Protestant ethic because they had joined the religious movement rather than because they had been born into an ethnic or class culture of entrepreneurship.[5]

CULTURAL SOURCES OF KOREAN
ENTREPRENEURSHIP

The ethnic culture of Korea might explain the entrepreneurship of Koreans in Los Angeles. But a cultural explanation must meet two tests. First, a cultural explanation must address enduring themes in Korean culture rather than transient ones. Unless a cultural explanation accepts this discipline, results explain behavior by itself. For example contemporary residents of Seoul buy frankfurters at fast-food stands. A cultural explanation might be: Koreans like frankfurters. The obvious difficulty is the recency of frankfurter eating among Koreans. Frankfurters are not a classic part of the Korean diet. However, Osgood (1951) noted that Koreans are "omnivores" who for centuries have evidenced willingness to eat a wide variety of foods. Some of these (dog meat, undrained intestines, spicy pickles) are unpalatable to non-Koreans, but the proclivity of Koreans to enjoy a wide variety of foods is of sufficient vintage to qualify as a genuinely cultural trait of this people (Brown, 1919: 50). From this starting point, one might explain the swift integration of frankfurters, a nontraditional dish, into the Korean diet by referring to the Korean willingness to accept a wide variety of foods. This is a legitimate cultural explanation.

Second, cultural explanations of Korean enterprise in Los Angeles must address the state of Korean culture a generation ago. The reason is the requirement of primary socialization in cultural explanations. Korean business people in Los Angeles experienced primary socialization a generation ago. Therefore, the Korean culture they learned is already a generation old. Yet Korea has been undergoing rapid social change since the Korean War. Therefore a Korean who behaves in a manner appropriate to a prior generation would be an old-fashioned person today (Park, 1975). But an objection to this idea signals the limits of socialization explanations of adult behavior: adults keep abreast of cultural change, and in doing so they undergo continuous resocialization. Social movements are one source of resocialization, and a fluid culture must contain the motivation for its own rejuvenation. Still, a genuinely cultural explanation needs to fasten upon something in the Korean culture of a generation ago rather than something strictly contemporary.

During the Yi dynasty (1392–1910) Confucianism was the official religion of Korea. However, the culture of Yi-dynasty Korea actually had two poles: the official Confucianism of the elite, and the folk collectivism of the peasantry (Brandt, 1971: 240). Both were anti-bourgeois, albeit in different ways. Confucian thought distrusted merchants. In Korea, merchants remained "an inferior class without political rights or social status, and a complete ban on innovations and inventions was imposed upon them" (K. Kim, 1977: 13). Jones and Sakong (1980: 210–211) have called attention to the obstruction that Confucian culture provided entrepreneurship:

> The emergence of a thriving entrepreneurial class in Korea is particularly intriguing since it runs counter to the traditional value system. Confucianism places commerce and industry at the bottom of the ... status hierarchy.

Confucianists also regarded manual labor and commerce as degrading. A proper gentleman eschewed money counting, displaying instead literary refinements born of a cultivated use of leisure. Japanese colonial occupation (1910–1945) encouraged Korean Confucianism whose emphasis upon hierarchical obedience was supportive of Japanese domination (Park, 1975: 58). Official support for Confucianism finally ended in 1972 when the government of Park Chung-Hee restricted official Confucian ceremonies, declaring them unproductive and contrary to the national goal of rapid economic development (Park, 1975: 59–60).

But Confucian attitudes "still linger" (see Choi, 1965). South

Koreans regard entrepreneurs as dependent beneficiaries of government largesse (Juhn, 1977: 8; K. D. Kim, 1976). Unfavorable public attitudes were strikingly indicated in 1983 when the founder-president of Daewoo Industrial Company, Korea's second-largest conglomerate, protested against public disesteem for businessmen noting that entrepreneurs had done "as much" for Korea as professors or the clergy (Jameson, 1983). Park (1975: 33–34) found that Korean families "still retain many values from the past because the primary socialization agent ... is the family unit. The parental and grandparental generations pass on the traditional cultural values and behavioral norms." Among Koreans in the United States Oh (1975: 221) found residual differences in attitudes toward work among Confucianists and Christians. Christians placed a higher value on work than did the Confucianists, but Confucianists were more oriented to upward social mobility than were Christians. Confucianists fancied high rank without the indignity of work. But, Confucians were willing to *study* hard in order to gain high status; indeed, study and self-improvement is a requirement of Confucian ethics. Only manual labor and money-counting are despised, and these are what "work" means to Confucianists.

Peasant collectivism paid lip-service to official Confucianism but peasants made no effort to live a gentleman's life. Osgood (1951: 65) described cultivation and harvesting as "a cooperative affair." Villagers raised as much as they needed for self-sufficiency and taxes; then they relaxed. The harvest gathered, Korean villagers turned to feasting and dancing with "abandon." Osgood (1951: 331, 333) also noted the peasants' "tremendous interest in drinking and eating." Drunkenness was institutionalized in this culture. Another entertainment was stone-throwing between teams of men. Fatalities were expected consequences of this brutal sport. This is how Korean peasants once lived; whatever this lifestyle was, it was not bourgeois.

Folk collectivism in Korea receded under the twin pressures of urbanization and industrialization. Nonetheless, as late as 1966, Brandt (1971: 15) found "the traditional social system was still largely intact" in the village of Sokp'o. Economic activities in Sokp'o were cooperative: "Cooperative labor is customary for house building, transplanting rice, threshing grain, moving, hauling boats, and on ceremonial occasions" (Brandt, 1971: 70). Cooperation also appeared in response to any emergency. "The typical villager cannot be seen simply as an individual competing with his neighbors in order to maximize material possessions." On the contrary, Brandt (1971: 76) found that subordination of individual goals and satisfactions to the group was "nearly automatic, while excessive individualism stands out and is likely to be criticized." One such issue was working too hard. Sokp'o villagers did not work hard. Men quit work in midafternoon and spend the remainder of a nice day gossiping and drinking beer around a work site.

In the eighteenth and nineteenth centuries, Korea's banking and commerce were appreciably less developed than China's or Japan's, nor were there cities in Korea comparable to the manufacturing and commercial centers of Osaka or the lower Yangtze river (Mason et al., 1980: 69). Koreans have not had the reputation for hard work, thrift, and commercial acumen that early writers ascribed to their Chinese and Japanese neighbors, nor have they always been regarded as very intelligent. On the contrary, a generation ago America's leading Korea scholar, Cornelius Osgood (1951: 337), explained Korea's economic and social stagnation on the basis of the cultural backwardness of the Korean people.

Osgood's opinion of Korean culture was the prevailing one. A decade earlier, Givens (1939: 14) had asserted defensively that "some people believe" Los Angeles' Koreans must be "backward and unprogressive" because of their country's reputation as the "hermit kingdom." Damning with faint praise, she concluded this was "not true in all respects." Still earlier treatments of Korean national character minced fewer words. According to Brown (1919: 44) "no other people in Asia have been so contempuously characterized." George Kennan called Koreans "lazy, dirty, unscrupulous, dishonest, incredibly ignorant ... the rotten product of a decayed Oriental civilization" (Brown, 1919: 45). And Brown declared:

> They lack the energy and ambition of the Japanese; thrift, industry, and strength of the Chinese.... Indolence is a national characteristic. The Koreans take life as easily as possible. (Brown, 1919: 46)

The only virtue Brown found in Koreans was their ability to "learn readily under favorable conditions" and then to "develop rapidly."

Koreans long accepted this judgment of their traditional work ethic. Oh (1975: 214) writes:

> There is a self-recognition among Koreans that they do not work as methodically as Europeans or Americans do; this conduct is taken as laziness to some extent.

Korean spokespersons we interviewed accepted with some satisfaction our inquiries into their compatriots work ethic, feeling the inquiry was flattering in implication. However, a few noted that a reputation for hard work had never been characteristic of Koreans, and was, in fact, a reversal of the usual stereotype. Korean scholars even complained to the press that Korean-Americans were treated as money-grubbing workaholics, thus ignoring the cultural, religious, and artistic dimensions of their lives. Of course, this objection is valid in its own terms. Still, the necessity to raise it signals a reversal of the world's opinion of Korean culture. In one generation, the idle grasshopper became the industrious ant, and—although neither stereotype was ever accurate—the direction and abruptness of change is unmistakable. This abrupt change of the Korean image is hard for a cultural explanation to account for because a change cannot be explained by a constant. Accordingly, we conclude that the traditional culture of Korea does not provide a satisfactory explanation of Korean hard work in Los Angeles.

CLASS CULTURE

Class culture of Korean immigrants might explain their entrepreneurship in Los Angeles. This explanation would be valid if evidence indicated Koreans once bourgeois in Korea had stayed bourgeois in Los Angeles. This situation turned up among East African Gujerati in Britain. Aldrich, Jones, and McEvoy (1984: 18) found Gujerati entrepreneurship in Britain was fully explained by Gujerati entrepreneurship in Africa, generations earlier. "For African Gujeratis, the shop in England is a means of reerecting an existing family tradition." Since Korean immigrants were highly educated and possessed capital, an element of international class continuity leaps out. However, one must distinguish class culture from other class resources, especially human capital, property, and money. True, class culture and material resources are empirically linked because culturally bourgeois people usually have the other resources of their class. Nonetheless, resources and culture are analytically distinct, and only class culture is at issue here, the contribution of human capital and money having been already conceded.

The contribution of class culture to Korean entrepreneurship depends upon how class is defined. A Marxist definition centers upon ownership of productive property. This is a narrow conception of class, and evidence supporting this explanation is thin. Dearman (1982: 178) found that three-quarters of Korean Christians in Los Angeles were either born in North Korea or had parents born in the North. Since about half of the Koreans in Los Angeles were Christians, Dearman's estimates imply that about 38 percent of Los Angeles Koreans had northern antecedents. Illsoo Kim also stressed the importance of northern origins among Koreans in New York City. According to Illsoo Kim (1981a: 35) North Korean refugees constituted 14 percent of the South Korean population in 1977—but a larger percentage of the country's commercial class. In their study of entrepreneurship in South Korea, Jones and Sakong (1980: 218) also found that northerners were impressively overrepresented in business. "More than one-third of northerners' fathers had been engaged in some form of trade as opposed to only one-seventh of the southerners." A "subordinated group" in the south, the Christianized northerners utilized entrepreneurship as a reactive means for obtaining social mobility in the South. In view of the conspicuous entrepreneurship of northern Christians in South Korea, the entrepreneurship of the same people in Los Angeles and New York City suggests an international transfer of cultural heritage. True, this mercantile group did not encompass the entire Korean population in either New York or Los Angeles. On the other hand, approximately a third of Koreans in these cities did have this antecedent, thus defining a significant minority with a firm cultural credential for entrepreneurship.

Previous ownership of a business in South Korea would, however, provide a firmer link to class culture than northern origin. Studies found no evidence that more than one-fifth of Korean business owners in America had, in fact, owned businesses in South Korea prior to emigration. Hyung-Chan Kim (1977: 102) completed an informal survey of fifty-two Korean business owners in four cities. None of his respondents indicated their "former profession in Korea" had been business. Twenty-five percent indicated they had been unemployed in Korea. Our 1977 telephone survey found only 15 percent of proprietors who reported prior self-employment in Korea. This percentage is significantly below the urban Korean average (over 30 percent), indicating that Los Angeles proprietors were recruited from social groups less likely than most to be self-employed in Korea. Moreover, only 18 percent of business owners indicated that their father was or had been a business owner. Hong (1982: 102) found that only 10 percent of Korean immigrants had been managers or proprietors in Korea. Yu (1982: table 13) also found that 18 percent of Kim's sample had been business owners in Korea whereas 34 percent were business owners in Los Angeles. Since there were more proprietors in Los Angeles than in Korea, prior history of business self-employment falls short as an explanation of Korean entrepreneurship in Los Angeles. Moreover, only one-fifth of Korean proprietors in Los Angeles had self-employment experience in Korea (Yu, 1982b: 60).

When class is interpreted as socioeconomic status, a stronger connection appears between social origins in Korea and entrepreneurship in Los Angeles. Korean immigrants were heavily recruited from the white-collar stratum of college-educated Seoul residents (Choy, 1979: 133–134). The 1970 census reported that 36 percent of Korean-Americans over age twenty-five had completed at least four years of college compared to 12 percent of white Americans. Among persons twenty-five years of age or older, the 1980 U.S. Census reported that 10.7 percent of Americans had completed four years of college. In contrast, 15.8 percent of the foreign born in the United States had completed four years of college, and of this group, 35.9 percent were Asians and 54.6 were Koreans.[6] Kim and Wong (1977: 230–231) found that 58 percent of Los Angeles Koreans eighteen years of age or older had completed a four-year college degree. Ninety-three percent had completed college in Korea. Moreover, percentage of college graduates in the population of Korea is lower than the American percentage, so the Korean immigrants were relatively more elite in Korea than in the United States. Hong (1982: 103) reported that 62 percent of Korean men in Los Angeles were graduates of four-year colleges, whereas only 15 percent of native-born white Los Angeles men had completed that much education. Of the business owners we interviewed by telephone in 1977, 69 percent indicated they were graduates of four-year colleges. Table 35 shows that self-employed Koreans in Los Angeles had 1.1 more years of formal education on the average than did self-employed non-Koreans.

Korean immigrants had held white-collar, salaried jobs in Korea. Hong (1982: 102) reported that 46.7 percent of Koreans in Los Angeles had "professional and technical" backgrounds compared to 52.8 percent of adult Korean immigrants (excluding housewives) who indicated this socioeconomic level in the period 1959—1976. Hurh and associates (1978) found that 65 percent of Koreans in Chicago were last employed in Korea in white-collar jobs, 8.5 percent in professional jobs, and only 1 percent in blue-collar jobs. The percentage of agricultural workers was negligible even though South Korea's population is predominantly agricultural. Korean immigrants regarded themselves as middle or upper-middle class in social origin. Comparing three generations, Park (1975: 1137) found that "the major portion" of each "perceived themselves as being middle class."

These middle-class Koreans did not know how to run business enterprises when they arrived in Los Angeles. Korean informants often mentioned how serious was the problem of inadequate business skills among their self-employed compatriots. Jin's (1978: Table 6) survey of 1132 Korean small business owners identified "lack of management knowledge" as the number one problem the business owners reported. To remedy this situation the Korean Association of Southern California and the Korean Chamber of Commerce held numerous conferences at which experts in business administration lectured the membership. The trained ability to understand such lectures—and to profit from business experience—was the greatest intellectual resource of the Korean immigrants. In this sense, the immigrants' higher educational background provided them with the intellectual flexibility needed to acquire business skills, a capability that was highly significant to their business achievement in Los Angeles. Middle-status Koreans had valued education for their children and inculcated this value in the course of primary socialization. Education equipped the immigrants with cognitive skills adaptable to running a business in Los Angeles. Therefore, the social values of the parental generation ultimately placed the children in the American class structure. Koreans themselves believed this; we have no evidence they are wrong, and agree that intergenerational value transmission played a role in the process.

SOCIAL-MOVEMENT SOURCES OF
KOREAN ENTREPRENEURSHIP

Just before World War II approximately 5 percent of Koreans were Christians. But the percentage was much higher in the north, especially in Pyongyang, which had more Christians than any other city in Asia (McCune, 1966: 93). By the early 1970s, approximately 10 percent of Koreans were Christian, and their percentage was increasing as a result of proselytism (Guillemoz, 1973: 12). In 1982 the Republic of Korea's Ministry of Culture indicated that 19.9 percent of the country's population were Christians.[7] Of the Christians, 84 percent were Protestants, the remainder Roman Catholics. Korean Christians were religiously observant. A 1982 survey of Christian lay people found that 43 percent attended church four or more times a week.[8] Oddly, Koreans reported one of the world's smallest percentages believing in God. In a 1982 survey only 42 percent of Koreans acknowledged belief in God compared to 95 percent of Americans.[9] Presumably Korean Christians were more theistic than Korean non-Christians, for 92 percent of Christian lay people in Korea reported that they believed in the dogmas of the Bible among which, one supposes, the existence of God must be included.

Christians were overrepresented among Korean immigrants in Los Angeles. Rev. Shim (1977: 36) concluded only that "many, perhaps the majority" of Korean immigrants in Los Angeles were Christians. Dearman (1982: 170) tabulated the congregations of sixty-five Korean churches that responded to his survey. On this basis he estimated the Christian church-member population of Koreans in Los Angeles as 25,000, about half the area's Korean population. Won (1977: 56) sampled the *Korean Directory of Southern California*. Of 151 respondents, he found 46 percent were Christian, 28 percent Buddhist, 6 percent Confucian, and 20 percent other. Won's is the most exhaustive study of Los Angeles, but studies of Koreans in other American cities have also found overrepresentation of Christians. Sanglio Kim (1975) collected data on Chicago's Koreans in 1967–1968. He found that 84 percent were Christian, and the community's leadership was exclusively Christian. Also in Chicago, Hurh, Kim, and Kim (1978: 24) reported that 69 percent of Korean immigrants were Christians. Hurh, Kim, and Kim (1978: 24) also found that the number of Christians among the immigrants had been only 53 percent in Korea, then increased to 69 percent after debarkation in the United States.

Counting churches is easier than counting Christians, and available studies indicate Korean churches are overrepresented (Min, 1982). The 1979 Korean Directory of Southern California listed 189 churches (Dearman, 1982: 168). In proportion to Korean population during the period studied, this number was six times greater than the number of "religious voluntary associations" supported by all residents of Los Angeles County in 1979. Terry and Stull (1975: 11) counted 120 Christian churches and 2 Buddhist churches in Southern California. *The Korea Times* reported 218 Korean Christian churches and 300 pastors in Southern California. The Christianity preached from Korean pulpits was conservative and evangelical in character.[10] Dearman (1982: 169) found that 86 percent of pastors classified themselves as evangelical or conservative whereas only 1.6 percent called themselves liberals. The Reverend Sun Moon's Unification Church provided a caricature of Korean religiosity that Korean clergy eschewed, claiming Moon's followers were non-Koreans. Some clergy claimed Moon was a paid agent of the Korean Central Intelligence Agency. True, Moon's extremism placed him on the fringe of Korean Christianity, but there is no denying that Korean Christians had "a reputation for religiosity" (Shim, 1977: vii), and this religiosity expressed itself in fundamentalist Christianity.

The prevailing Christianity of Korean immigrants was chiefly the result of selective migration. Christianity in Korea was strongest among the urban intelligentsia. Cole and Lyman (1971: 15) point out that between 1952 and 1962 Christians provided 41 percent of South Korea's cabinet members, assemblymen, and senior officials. The Korean immigrants have been recruited from this modernizing class. For example, Hyang Tae Kim (1966: 62) reported that Korean students in the United States came from the upper-middle class in Korea and "the dominant religious background of the students is the Christian religion." Admittedly, church participation of Koreans increased one-third after debarkation in the United States (Hurh, Kim, and Kim, 1978: 24; Han, 1973: 73). Christian clergy were aware that many parishioners became devout when they discovered a need for the social services Christian churches delivered (D. C. Lee, 1977: 160; J. S. Park, 1975: 70). Critics of Christianity made similar allegations in Korea where "the dollar religion" was a sneer directed to the alleged opportunism and materialism of Christians (Sanglio Kim, 1975: 19–26). Naturally, this critique reflected the competition of Christianity and Asian religions for adherents, and the bitter resentment of non-Christians at the proselytic success of the Christians. The terms of the indictment (opportunism, materialism) are also suggestive of this contest because adherents of traditional religions were proud of their cultural fidelity (the opposite of opportunism) and their spirituality (the opposite of materialism). Becoming a Christian they perceived as a strategy to help a selfish person make money in ways destructive of Korean culture.

Christianity in Korea has been a powerful force for modernization in the last century. Protestant missionaries brought Christianity to Korea in the 1880s. The missionaries founded fifty-three high schools and seven universities where the modernizing segment of Korean society obtained education (McCune, 1966: 93; S. Kim, 1975: 19–26). "Korea's modernization can never be understood apart from her relations with American churches" (H. T. Kim, 1966: 3). Christianity in Korea has been for a hundred years a social movement encouraging modernization, secularism, equality, individualism, and nationalism (H.-C. Kim, 1977: 55; Oh, 1975: 2400). Christians also discouraged fortune-telling and ancestor veneration while preaching "the sacredness of work." Such themes have been missing from the teachings of Buddhism and Confucianism. Won (1977: 82) observes that Christians in Korea "are always distinctly identifiable because of their adherence to Western values." The "modern values" of the Christians he contrasts with Buddhism and Confucianism, which came under attack from Korean intellectuals who argued that "disruption of the social order is necessary ... for the modernization of Korea" (see also J. S. Park, 1975: 60).

The equating of Christianity and modernization in Korea raises the possibility that Koreans who emigrated to the United States brought along a Protestant work ethic that triggered their business success. Illsoo Kim (1981: 206) has championed the view that Korean churches inculcated "their version of the Protestant ethic of nineteenth-century America" in the Korean population. In point of fact, Korean evangelists taught that Koreans were the latest Puritans. According to Rev. Chung Kuhn Lee (1982), for example:

> We Koreans have come to this new continent as the "Oriental puritans" in the most positive sense. God has called us to restore the puritan spirit which was once the invisible foundation shaping this young nation. On the verge of desolation of the spirit, God has sent the Oriental puritans to this land to revive it.... God, through Koreans, is directing the expansion of His kingdom to the end of the world.

Korean scholars agree that the immigrants' Christianity encouraged their migration and reduced cultural shock, but they are divided about the extent to which religious differences produced life-style differences among Korean Christians, Buddhists, and Confucianists. Oh (1975) compared child-rearing attitudes of Korean Christians and Confucianists. One issue was whether there were any life-style differences among Koreans of matched socioeconomic status who differed in religious preference. Oh (1975) found Christians slightly more likely to favor autonomy as a socialization goal, more likely to use material rewards to obtain conformity, more likely to support equality of the sexes, individualism, transcendentalism, and this-worldliness. Confucianists scored slightly higher on punitive child-rearing techniques and fatalism. Won (1977) found that Christians and Confucianists were assimilators in the United States, Buddhists were bicultural, and adherents of other religions were nonassimilating. Differences were, however, small. Moreover, J. S. Park (1975: 91) found no difference between "behavioral norms and patterns" of Korean Christians and Korean non-Christians in Los Angeles.

If Christianity caused business success, Christians ought to be more represented in the Korean business population than in the general Korean population. Data on this point are scant. Our 1977 telephone survey of Korean business owners found that 38.5 percent identified themselves as Christians, but a whopping 54.5 percent refused to answer so our result is uninformative. Won (1977) found that 46 percent of persons listed in the *Korean Directory of Southern California* were self-declared Christians. On one hand, these results provide no evidence that Christians were more numerous in the business population than in the general Korean population of Los Angeles. On the other hand, the data do indicate that Korean Christians were four times more likely than Korean non-Christians to wind up running small business enterprises in Los Angeles.

Was this a generational phenomenon? J. S. Park (1975) gathered evidence on "generations and psychosocial adjustments among Korean immigrants in Los Angeles." He distinguished three generations: persons socialized during the Yi dynasty, those socialized during Japanese colonial occupation (1910–1945), and those socialized since 1945. Park's research assessed the extent to which generations reflected "varying commitments to both the traditional Korean value system and the contemporary American value system." Park (1975: 5) found that youth and education were negatively associated with traditional Korean values on filial piety, the position of women, and familial continuity. Conversely, younger and more educated persons were more modern and individualistic in social attitudes. In the concluding opinion of Park (1975: 60), the source of the intergenerational contrasts was the "apparent irreconcilability between a system of social value based on kinship" and a modern, industrial society requiring "the cooperative interaction of autonomous individuals." The pace of industrial change in modern Korea had been so rapid that intergenerational "tensions" arose in reflection of cultural lag.

The evidence reviewed above is impossible to summarize in a simple formula. On the one hand, Christianity was strong among Los Angeles' Koreans, and Christianity was associated with modernization in Korea. On the other hand, no evidence proves Christians were overrepresented in the Korean business population, and there is no evidence their values or attitudes differed much from non-Christian Koreans in Los Angeles. Generation was a more significant division among Koreans in Los Angeles than was religion. We are, therefore, compelled to agree with Oh (1975: 244) who speculated on the "interesting possibility" that Christianity had so deeply affected Korean culture that its influence was found even in individuals who had not made "any explicit acceptance of Christian faith."

South Korea has for some time been a society undergoing momentous and rapid cultural change. Immigrants to Los Angeles emanated from the most modernizing strata of urban Korean society. They had their modernizing, materialistic, individualistic character before they emigrated, and there is ground for supposing that this modernizing cultural endowment contributed to the number of businesses they opened in Los Angeles as well as to their individualistic style of business management. With no evidence to disprove this contention, we believe the modernizing cultural endowment of Korean immigrants encouraged their enterprise in Los Angeles. For purposes of explaining the Korean business enterprises in Los Angeles, the modernizing cultural endowment of the Korean immigrants (not the traditional ethnic culture of Korea) appears as an independent variable of significance.

SOJOURNING

Bonacich (1973) has identified sojourning as a key situation producing self-employment among middlemen minorities. As Werbner (1984: 167) observed of Pakistanis in Britain, "being in the society but—as strangers—not of it," Koreans were "freed from the constraints of their hosts' frame of reference, and thus able to pursue a way of living which is ... particularly supportive of entrepreneurs." Sojourners have little motive to learn English or otherwise acculturate. Therefore, they retain the situational motive for self-employment that linguistic disadvantage bestows (Tienda and Neidert, 1984). True, sojourning ends when sojourners repatriate. However, insofar as repatriated sojourners are replaced by new sojourners, the number of sojourners in the population remains the same even when personnel change.

Sojourning can be cultural or situational. It is cultural when generations of expatriates carry abroad a repatriation ideology such that their normal life plan includes eventual return to their homeland. Among overseas Chinese a repatriation ideology accompanied actual repatriations. As a result, turnover in Chinese colonies was always high with newcomers replacing those who, their sojourn over, were returning to China. Among Jews, repatriation turned into a ritual promise of "next year in Jerusalem." However, until the Zionist movement of the twentieth century, the Jews of the world had no real intention to return to Jerusalem nor any practical possibility of so doing. In the preceding centuries of diaspora, the repatriation myth was a strictly cultural phenomenon, intimately connected with the religious expression of the Jews and their continued sense of peoplehood (Light, 1979: 33–34).

In 1981 nearly 4 million Koreans lived abroad. These expatriates were almost 10 percent of the population of the Republic of Korea. Of Koreans living abroad, 46 percent resided in the People's Republic of China, especially Manchuria; 11 percent in the Soviet Union; and 43 percent in ninety-eight noncommunist countries. The 1980 Korean population of the United States was 354,529, only 10 percent of the world's overseas Koreans. The numerous Koreans abroad give the impression of a national *Wanderlust* that might be genuinely cultural and, if so, connected with a persistent repatriation myth. However, the uninterpreted statistics exaggerate that impression.

Korea does not have an ancient history of sojourning. During the Yi dynasty (1392–1910) Koreans did not venture abroad in great numbers as did the Chinese. Indeed, the hermit kingdom derived its sobriquet from the lack of interest its inhabitants showed in the outside world. Koreans on the Asian mainland migrated between 1916 and 1940 or are themselves the descendants of those migrants.

The working-class exiles carried abroad a lively Korean nationalism and contributed to anti-Japanese agitation, propaganda, and armed resistance. However, liberation achieved, Koreans on the Asian mainland did not massively repatriate as one might have expected had a repatriation ideology existed. Admittedly, 2 million Koreans returned to Korea from Japan in the early 1950s. But these repatriates nursed specific grievances against Japanese society; they did not actualize a repatriation myth that they had carried with them from Korea and kept alive in exile (Mitchell, 1967).

Of Koreans abroad in the noncommunist world, 80 percent left Korea for temporary work assignments, a classic sojourn. But, as table 16 shows, this sojourning pattern was specifically reversed among Koreans preparing to enter the United States, among whom 65 percent were self-declared immigrants and only 17 percent temporary workers or business travelers. Hence, if there is any sojourning ideology by overseas Koreans in the noncommunist world, the United States is apparently its least active site. Nonetheless, whatever their repatriation intentions upon departure, Koreans in the United States shared a situational motive to be thrifty and to work hard. The source of this motive was the favorable exchange of currencies. Because Korean wages were only one-eighth of American wages, a day's work in the United States earned the money equivalent of ten days' work in Korea. If a Korean worked five years in Los Angeles and saved 50 percent of his wages, he returned to Korea with the money equivalent of twenty-five years full-time Korean wages. Given this exchange ratio, it is no wonder Koreans came to the United States to sojourn, and while here, worked as hard as they could, saving every penny by dint of severe frugality. But this is a strictly situational—not a cultural or characterological—explanation of the Korean work ethic.

Evidence bearing on the extent of sojourning is mixed. Choy (1979: 217) acknowledged that "early residents" were sojourners, but insisted "the new immigrants are here to stay and to start a life for themselves and their children." The balanced sex ratio among Korean immigrants was a point in favor of Choy's claim since sojourning migrants usually leave wives and children behind. On the other hand, other studies reported extensive sojourning among Korean immigrants. J. S. Park (1975: 145) indicated that "thinking often" about repatriation to Korea was the modal response of Korean immigrants he interviewed. Rev. Shim (1977: 45–46) commented on the extensiveness of sojourning orientation among Koreans in Los Angeles. Hurh, Kim, and Kim (1978: 41) found that 66 percent of Chicago Koreans indicated they would probably or certainly retire in Korea. A Korean-language newspaper (Jo, 1982: 204) completed a survey of 500 Korean residents in twelve cities of the United States. When asked of which country, Korea or the United States, they regarded themselves as citizens, 78 percent chose Korea. Additionally, 62 percent indicated they would like to return to Korea for good some day. In 1978 the Korea Overseas Development Corporation conducted a survey of 400 immigrants about to embark for any foreign country. Their survey revealed that 52 percent intended to return to Korea for retirement, and 45 percent expected to visit frequently. Our telephone survey of Korean proprietors asked respondents to indicate their intention of returning to Korea. Of 174 who answered, 20.1 percent indicated that they intended to return to Korea to live, 17.2 percent planned to visit Korea, and 29.9 percent were uncertain. Only 32.8 percent expected never to return to Korea.

Although sojourning declined in the 1970s (Choy, 1979: 217), our review indicates that sojourning was always significant among Koreans. Various efforts to measure the extent of sojourning found that between one-fifth and two-thirds of Koreans expected to return to Korea for retirement. Admittedly, their life plan was different from the three- or four-year sojourn typical of sojourners in the first half of this century. Nonetheless, sojourning it remained. We have, however, no evidence that sojourning was higher among proprietors than among nonproprietors, so we cannot produce firm evidence that sojourning was productive of entrepreneurship.

CONCLUSION

In this chapter we have assembled evidence bearing on cultural and social-movement explanations of why Koreans are entrepreneurial. Table 63 summarizes our results. In each case we have indicated whether evidence permits an assessment of a source as likely, unlikely, or uncertain. Two sources have been declared unlikely. Korean traditional culture was probably not part of the explanation of Korean entrepreneurship in Los Angeles. Bourgeois culture explains the work motivation of a fifth of the Korean entrepreneurs but does

Table 63.   Likelihood of Sources of Korean
Entrepreneurship in Los Angeles

	Likely	Uncertain	Unlikely
Ethnic Culture			
Korean traditional culture			×
Cultural change in Korea	×		
Sojourning		×	
Class culture			
Commercial skills, bourgeois values			×
Cognitive skills, modern values	×		
Social Movement			
Christianity	×		

not explain the whole self-employed group. However, cognitive skills and "modern" values, cultural change in Korea, and Christianity were identifiable sources from which Koreans probably derived entrepreneurial enthusiasm. Sojourning was characteristic of a minority and was situational rather than cultural in origin. We have been unable to prove that sojourning specifically affected Korean entrepreneurship, but neither can we rule out the possibility.

The exclusion of ethnic culture and commercial background from the explanation of Korean entrepreneurship distinguishes Koreans from classic middlemen minorities. For example, Jews and Chinese both relied upon cultural repertoires supportive of shopkeeping, and took with them their business skills whenever they changed countries. But most Koreans in Los Angeles had little prior business experience, depending upon values and cognitive skills associated with the modernizing intelligentsia of South Korea. In this sense, the business activities of Los Angeles' Koreans actually depended upon skills and values distorted by immigration from their expected articulation with social structure.

Our results indicate how complex is the explanation of Korean entrepreneurship. Cultural and social-movement sources contributed to entrepreneurship among Los Angeles' Koreans. In principle, a simple cultural or social-movement explanation would have been possible. Cultural and social-movement explanations of entrepreneurship are not incompatible in principle, and they are likely to be jumbled together in most empirical situations (Turner and Bonacich, 1980: 148). This is a major conclusion, and one unlikely to be revised were the research evidence available to make firm assignments of the source we have labeled uncertain in its effects.

For these reasons, we partially disagree with Illsoo Kim's (1981: 299, 300) attribution of Korean entrepreneurship to Korean national character. Traditional culture did not bestow entrepreneurial character. Additionally Kim's formulation overlooks the independent contribution of Korean Christianity, still a minority religion in South Korea. Granted, Christianity influenced Korean national culture, but it influenced Christians the most. Insofar as Christians formed a distinct status group in South Korea, the work ethic of this status group shared responsibility for the entrepreneurship of Korean immigrants in Los Angeles. Additionally, Kim's national-character formulation overlooked the bourgeois cultural sources from which about a fifth of the Korean entrepreneurs presumably derived their work ethic. Here then are two class resources that Kim's formulation overlooked. Finally, Kim ignored the sojourning attitudes that might have encouraged Koreans to work harder in the United States than they worked in Korea. At that juncture, class and ethnic culture interacted with American society to generate altogether novel (if possibly transitory) work motivations. As a matter of empirical fact, the work ethic of the Korean immigrants in Los Angeles derived from a pastiche of analytically distinct sources. As such, the Korean case is among the more complex in the literature of ethnic entrepreneurship.

12

Reaction and Solidarity

Especially in periods of high and rising unemployment, a rapid influx of immigrants promotes resource competition with residents, some of whom regard immigrants as competitors for jobs, housing, and social services (Light, 1983: chs. 12, 13). Since the self-employed do not participate in the wage labor market, they do not, it might be supposed, compete with native wage earners. Unfortunately, the literature of middleman minorities (see Bonacich and Modell, 1981: ch. 2; Porter, 1981; Zenner, 1977) offers international evidence of the social conflicts that have repeatedly enveloped entrepreneurial minorities (Turner and Bonacich, 1980: 146). Those initiating complaints are typically customers, business competitors, organized labor, or all three, but the antimiddleman attack brings uninterested groups into the hostile alliance.

Confronting the hostile alliance, entrepreneurial immigrants increase internal solidarity in self-defense. Turner and Bonacich (1980: 154) even propose that "the greater the level of hostility in the receiving society," the more likely are beleaguered middlemen minorities to "develop or maintain distinctive cultural and organizational forms." Ironically, defensive reaction exacerbates the original tension by increasing the economic competitiveness of the middleman and encouraging outsiders to denounce their clannishness (Bonacich, 1973). For this reason, middleman minority theory predicts a self-reinforcing spiral of hostility and solidarity in the course of which what began as rational, interest-centered objection winds up as furious, irrational hatred.

REACTIONS TO KOREAN INFLUX

On the basis of middleman minority theory, we predicted in 1975 that Korean entrepreneurs would experience defensive, even hostile reactions to their entrepreneurship, thus stimulating the Korean

300

population to increase its solidarity in response.[1] Response to the Korean influx in the next decade was more tranquil than expected, but it was not completely tranquil. From a methodological standpoint, our problem was to measure low-intensity social conflicts resulting from Korean immigration. Additionally, we had to distinguish conflicts that arose from the entrepreneurship of Koreans from conflicts into which Koreans were pulled for no reason related to their own entrepreneurship.

To this end we compiled a catalog of American responses to Korean influx. Some responses originated in Los Angeles; most originated outside. The catalog shows that scattered reactions had invariably the effect of limiting the number, profitability, or safety of Korean business enterprises. True, frank gook-baiting was infrequent, but intensity of reaction is only one issue. *Direction* is another. Mild in intensity, American reaction to Korean entrepreneurship was uniformly to restrict Korean access to business opportunities.

For the most part, Americans' reactions reached Koreans via the political system. Therefore, some reactions originated in Sacramento, some in Washington, and some in Los Angeles City Hall. As for the Koreans, confronting restricting reactions by American authorities, they banded together in defensive solidarities. Some of the solidarities they employed were all-Korean. Some involved joining with other Asians. Some involved coalitions with persons sharing common interests. Nonetheless, Korean penetration of the American economy produced social responses that compelled the Koreans to intensify their solidarities—in order to protect their economic niche.

PURCHASE PRICE OF SMALL BUSINESSES INCREASES

An immediate result of the proliferation of immigrant businesses was a rise in the sale price of small business enterprises in Los Angeles county (cf. Russell, 1984: 81). Anderson's (1978) survey of business brokerage firms in Los Angeles found that the proportion of business owners who "appear to be foreign" had sharply increased and that, as a result, the price of small business enterprises had increased much faster than inflation. Every industry in Los Angeles County was affected.

The increased selling price of small businesses was the automatic response of the market to an influx of business-oriented immigrants among whom Koreans were just one component. The price increase was not anti-immigrant or anti-Korean, even though its effect was to render the acquisition of business enterprises more difficult, thus inhibiting further growth of Korean enterprises.

However, the unorganized market was not the only regulator governing the size of the business population in Los Angeles County. At numerous points, public and private agencies also intervened to inhibit Korean business growth. The political interventions were not so even-handed as the unorganized market, which raised the price of businesses to immigrant and nonimmigrant alike on an equal basis. On the contrary, social agencies intervened to change the composition of the business population by rendering it increasingly difficult for Koreans in particular or immigrants in general to flourish in commerce.

THE LIQUOR INDUSTRY

When the influx of Korean entrepreneurs began, Southern California's liquor market was a "fair trade" zone in which state law regulated the minimum price of alcoholic beverages. Fair trade laws had been passed in 1939 in expectation of reducing consumption of liquor by supporting its price. Fair trade worked to the advantage of small business owners because chain stores were unable to employ volume purchasing power to cut prices. However, as liquor industry sales expanded, dissatisfaction with fair trade increased. Large chains argued that fair trade laws cost consumers millions of dollars. Their argument prevailed in the State Supreme Court which repealed fair trade laws in 1978. The *Los Angeles Times* (Cannon, 1976–1979) reported the general expectation of small dealers that repeal would subject them to merciless competition from big chains. The Korean community shared this concern.

Koreans viewed fair trade's repeal as an American reaction to the money immigrant entrepreneurs were making in the liquor trade. The *Joong-Ang Daily News* interpreted the repeal movement as "white liquor stores" attempting to "stir up latent prejudice against Orientals" (Lee, 1977: 48). The actual effectiveness of repeal was uncertain. A spokesperson for the Southern California Retail Liquor Dealers Association complained, on one hand, that "predatory pricing" by supermarkets forced many small owners out of business in the first year after repeal. On the other hand, the editor of *Beverage Beacon* knew of "not one retailer" going broke as a result of free market competition. In the immediate wake of repeal Koreans newspapers expressed fear of the economic damage repeal would inflict upon Korean stores, but in subsequent years they dropped reporting of this issue, suggesting that expected damage did not materialize.

Whether or not repeal had anti-Asian overtones, as Koreans suspected, the legal change dealt a blow to an ethnic community heavily dependent on peddling beer, wine, and liquor. In class terms, big business rallied behind repeal in order to obtain a bigger share of a lucrative trade in which immigrant small business was making profits. In this sense, the success of the immigrant small businesses in the liquor trade encouraged a reaction by big business that utilized legal changes to bolster its market share at the expense of small fry.

A second hostile reaction to proliferation of liquor industry businesses centered around black and Spanish neighborhoods in central Los Angeles (Durant, 1977). According to the California Black Commission on Alcoholism, a private organization, the ratio of liquor stores to population in the ghetto was nearly twice the ratio in white neighborhoods, and in excess of the legal limit. The commission maintained that this high ratio had resulted from proliferation of liquor stores in the black neighborhoods, largely as a result of immigrant entrepreneurship. The California Commission on Alcoholism for the Spanish Speaking concurred. Conducted in the twelve largest counties of California, their research disclosed that of thirty zip codes with the highest concentration of alcoholic beverage licenses, on-sale and off-sale, 60 percent were areas with Spanish population above the state average, 27 percent were zip codes with black populations above the state average, and 90 percent were zip codes with median family income below the statewide median.

Opponents of the liquor industry also claimed that overconcentration of liquor licenses in minority districts encouraged high crime rates (see Rabow and Watts, 1982: 799). The California Department of Alcoholic Beverage Control held public hearings on this question in 1977. A succession of police and minority spokespersons testified to concentrations in excess of the legal limit and to the undesirable social effects of this concentration.

The director of the Alcoholism Council of South Central Los

Angeles did not know "where Koreans fit in the picture," but acknowledged much community awareness of the "high presence of Orientals in all phases of the black community," especially the liquor industry. This person wondered whether the Tong-Sun Park bribery scandal in Washington did not explain "how Koreans are acquiring these licenses." These were not in his opinion acquired from blacks, but from "previous Anglo or 'Anglo-Judean' owners," a belief that Cleaver (1983b) confirmed. Another spokesperson for the council confirmed its concern that "outsiders" were opening too many liquor stores. The outsiders were "whites and Asians" who controlled half the business while blacks controlled the other half. Black liquor dealers also complained of unfair competition from Asian competitors who had access to low-interest federal money, charged cut-rate prices, and hired industrial spies (Cleaver, 1983a, b, c).

The wrenching changes in the liquor industry promoted dealer solidarity, especially since independents confronted the stormiest changes. The nonimmigrant sector of the liquor trade tried to bring immigrants into existing trade associations. The Southern California Retail Liquor Dealers Association (SCRLDA), (1978) explained that dealer solidarity had been necessitated by changes in SBA loan policies. Previously, SBA had refused to lend money to liquor businesses, but this policy changed, and immigrants crowded into the liquor industry as a result: "It soon became evident that the largest trade association in the county, in order to preserve our liquor licenses for small independent retailers, would have to guide and teach any and all people who wanted to learn how to be successful in liquor retailing." Therefore, the SCRLDA opened a trade school for prospective liquor store owners in 1978. This school taught applicants how to prosper in the liquor industry, and education was a force for dealer solidarity independent of ethnic connections. Another evidence of the SCRLDA's openness to Korean dealers was a seminar the association conducted on the threat of price deregulation. One hundred fifty Korean liquor store owners attended this meeting.[2]

Nonetheless, SCRLDA failed to obtain Korean participation. In 1982 Korean liquor dealers established the Southern California Korean Grocery and Liquor Retailers Association with an initial membership of 47. By 1986 this organization had recruited 1089 members, about one-third of the Korean dealer population in Southern California. To its great chagrin, the SCRLDA had negligible Korean membership in the same year. Koreans explained that they found SCRLDA unresponsive to the distinctive problems Korean dealers experienced as a result of their central city locations. Additionally, SCRLDA did nothing to protect Korean liquor dealers in conflict with nationalist blacks. Finally, the Koreans explained, SCRLDA had no Korean directors and they simply despaired of influencing SCRLDA policies by action from within (Interview 108).

Since two-thirds of Korean dealers remained independent, the threats to Korean livelihoods in the liquor industry had obviously been insufficiently challenging to force their entire dealer population into a trade organization. At the same time, however, the threats *increased* Korean solidarity in the liquor industry, an increase the more noteworthy in that Koreans deliberately selected ethnic solidarity in preference to class solidarity despite their explicit recognition of the competitive threat posed by "giant supermarkets and chains." [3] That is, the Koreans started their own, all-Korean retailer organization rather than joining the existing industry-wide trade organization, the SCRLDA.

THE GARMENT INDUSTRY

Large manufacturing firms were the controlling powers in the Los Angeles garment industry. These big businesses subcontracted the actual work procedures to small firms.[4] Garment contracting was competitive. Before the 1970s Los Angeles garment contractors had been heavily Jewish. However, as Jews moved out of the garment industry, they were replaced by Latin Americans, Chinese, and Koreans. By 1979, Jews, Latin Americans, Chinese, and Koreans had effectively divided the garment contracting industry among themselves. The Korean Sewing Contractors Association estimated that there were 350 Korean contractors, approximately 9 percent of the total contractor population of Southern California in 1979. By 1986 the same organization estimated that 700 Korean contractors were working in Southern California. These Korean contractors represented 19 percent of the total contractor population.

The heterogeneity of the garment industry entrepreneurs shielded Koreans from being identified with numerous garment industry evils and abuses that investigations brought to public attention. The first

of these investigations occurred in 1973 when the California Industrial Welfare Commission (IWC) initiated criminal prosecutions
against nineteen garment firms accused of "flagrant violations of
California labor laws" (Bernstein, 1973: 1). These violations involved
substandard working conditions, failure to pay the minimum wage,
and destruction of records to conceal fraudulent practices. In 1976
the County's Occupational Health Office conducted a health and
industrial sanitation survey of the garment industry in the "central
region of Los Angeles." Of 840 factories surveyed, 32 percent were
in violation of sanitation standards. In 1978 worker complaints compelled another comprehensive survey, in the course of which 575
garment plants were surveyed. Of these, 67 percent were found in
violation of one or more sanitation standards. Investigators found rat
feces and urine on garment bundles, soiled toilet paper and sanitary
napkins on the floor of bathrooms, and so on. Another investigation
began in May 1979 when the Los Angeles County Board of Supervisors found sanitary violations in 72 percent of 662 garment industry plants inspected.[5] The City Attorney's Office began yet another
"crackdown" on garment "sweatshops" in September 1979; this time
ten garment contractors were fined a total of $17,825 for violations
of the health code. Of the ten, two were Korean (Farr, 1979).

Beset by complaints of systematic violations of wage and working
conditions in the garment industry (Entin, 1979), California established a Concentrated Enforcement Program. The Los Angeles task
force was under the command of Joe Razo, an attorney of Mexican
descent. Razo's force raided 1083 garment factories in 1978. It found
92 percent in violation of state minimum wage and overtime laws.
Violations of records, IWC orders, and labor code were found in 99
percent of factories. Workers affected by these violations were 73
percent "Spanish" (mostly Mexican), 15 percent "Asian," and 12
percent "other." Commenting on these rampant violations, the *Los
Angeles Times* declared editorially that "many employers prefer to
hire illegals ... because such employees are not likely to protest
substandard wages and working conditions."[6] This was also the
opinion of Razo and all trade unionists we interviewed. Even industry spokespersons acknowledged this preference.

In Razo's opinion, the ultimate beneficiaries of stricter enforcement
of labor standards were the garment *contractors* as well as workers.
Competition forced contractors to pay workers less than the mini-

mum wage and to reduce working standards correspondingly. As matters stood, only violators of labor standards could bid low enough to obtain contracts from the big manufacturers (Subber and Tchakalian, 1976: 2). As evidence for his conclusion, Razo pointed out that one year's persistent enforcement of labor law in the garment industry had already encouraged the formation of contractor groups and the merger of separate groups. Prior to enforcement, only one group, the Southern California Garment Contractors, had existed, but enforcement compelled contractors to band together for self-protection.

One group was the Korean Sewing Contractors Association of California. We interviewed officials of this group in 1979 and 1986 (the association changed its name to Korean American Garment Industry in 1982). All agreed that labor law enforcement had compelled their group's formation. Indeed, before the enforcement effort, the three spokespersons had not been personally acquainted. They claimed that as of February 1979 their association had secured the membership of 46 percent of the 350 Korean sewing contractors in Southern California. In 1986, KAGI officers claimed a membership of 400, 57 percent of the Korean contractor population in Southern California and 11 percent of the total industry. The main purpose of the contractors association was to "know each other and learn more about this business from each other." Translating the labor code into Korean was an important priority. To this end they had invited a Korean-speaking representative of the Concentrated Enforcement Division who lectured the membership on their obligations under the labor code.[7]

Korean contractors felt themselves to be in a competitive squeeze. "If you don't take their [manufacturer's] price, they will get someone else bidding for their work." As a result, "[contractors] are compelled to pay below the minimum wage ... because in order to survive they must seek violations." We later interviewed a member of the Korean Sewing Contractors Association (KSCA) in his factory. Of the thirty-six workers on his floor, most were Mexican women. Of these only 25 percent were in the United States legally. He felt the formation of the KSCA had benefited the Korean industry. Before this association was formed, Korean contractors "wouldn't even say 'hi' to each other" because they were so "suspicious" and competitive. Now the Association brought the Korean owners together to share information. The Strike Force's director, Joe Razo, had an even more positive view of the Korean Association, which he described as "very well organized." Their biggest coup was hiring away the ILGWU's capable attorney to represent their interests. The director also regarded the Koreans as ingenuous, contrasting them with other contractors who had learned better how to "cook" their books. (However, Koreans were learning how to fake their books, he added.)

Contractors treated the manufacturers' price as a grabbing game among competing ethnic groups. "If we don't accept the price," said a Korean, "they [Chinese, Latins] will get it." Another Korean contractor felt that Koreans could get business away from Jews provided their bids were lower. However, bids being the same, a Jew would prefer a Jew to a Korean. Similarly, enforcement personnel stated that Korean employers preferred Korean workers because of the improved social relationship shared ethnicity permitted. Some Korean contractors scoffed at this idea, noting they preferred "skilled workers" whatever their ethnic background.

At the level of contractor organization the same tension between ethnicity and class recurred—but ethnicity predominated. In addition to the Korean Association we learned of an American (mostly Jewish) contractors' association, a Latin American one, and a Chinese association. These four met occasionally in response to crises as an umbrella association known as the Confederated Clothing Contractors of America. But Confederated meetings were infrequent. The routine business of the garment contractors was strictly in the hands of the four ethnic associations. In the opinion of the Korean contractors, the state's regulation of their industry had benefited the association since Korean contractors often needed the association's help to pass the required contractors' examination.

REAL ESTATE

When Koreans began to develop the Olympic Boulevard Koreatown as a business and residential center for their immigrant community in Southern California, the neighborhood had been an underused, low-density residential quarter catering to working-class whites, blacks, and Hispanics. A decade's Korean influx changed the character of this neighborhood and compelled Koreans to organize in response to political reactions to their entrepreneurship. Efforts to promote

Koreatown had involved concentrated investments by Korean real estate operators in one neighborhood. Here the visibility of a specifically Korean invasion was high. There was adverse public reaction to Koreatown's growth (Dotson, 1975). Korean influx caused rental and land prices to increase, especially on commercial property (Yu, 1985: 42). Non-Korean merchants in the area feared that the Korean influx threatened their economic viability. Non-Korean residents complained about business signs in Hangul as well as the encroachment of Korean business firms into formerly residential areas (Holley, 1985). The numerous Korean stores also increased traffic congestion on the streets, and promoted a shortage of parking places.

As the Korean merchants reached out to attract tourists to Koreatown, non-Korean residents of Koreatown felt themselves "squeezed out and with no place to go" (Kaplan, 1979). In 1980, the 213,898 non-Korean residents of Koreatown still represented 93 percent of the neighborhood's population (Yu, 1985: 38). Many of these people had resided in the neighborhood before immigrant realtors declared it "Koreatown," and, from their point of view, Koreatown's commercial expansion was imperialistic and undesirable. Under the circumstances, racial tension reached a critical level, and municipal redevelopment agencies intervened to regulate growth in the public interest (Yu, 1985: 43). Existing Korean organizations lacked the cohesion to represent the Korean interest to municipal planners. Accordingly, six Korean organizations coalesced to form the Committee for Koreatown Community Planning, obtaining an initial grant of $100,000 from the Los Angeles City Council. The committee was expected to work with outside private and public organizations in the framing and implementation of plans for Koreatown's orderly expansion.

Although the Committee for Koreatown Community Planning arguably represented the long-range best interest of Korean business interests, the need for its formation emerged in response to social and political problems triggered by Korean capitalism. Happy about the tax revenues Koreatown generated, the City of Los Angeles, nonetheless, had politically to regulate the traffic congestion, parking shortages, and ethnic tension that Korean entrepreneurship had generated in the Olympic area. At least in part the City's intervention in Koreatown represented an external, political demand that Koreatown's future expansion be regulated in the public interest, thus offering a political voice to non-Korean residents of Koreatown. Additionally, since regulation required Korean participation, the City's intervention compelled Koreans to increase and to improve their own ethnic organization in response. In this sense, Koreatown's entrepreneurship proceeded just so far on the basis of laissez-faire before social problems triggered a regulatory response that, in turn, required Koreans to enhance their ethnic solidarity.

CRIMINAL VICTIMIZATION

As Koreans moved behind retail counters in the central city, they moved into an occupational role subject to criminal victimization (McCall, 1975: 1). The immigrants had located in a high-crime zone where they were subject to purse snatching, burglary, armed robbery, and rape. The usual perpetrators of these crimes were youthful blacks who had learned that Koreans carried cash on their person (Yu, 1986: 34). The Korean press carried much crime news; and crime in Koreatown was a regular topic of conversation among Koreans.[8]

Admittedly, the occupational roles and central-city location of Korean immigrants simply exposed them to criminal attacks. No data indicate that criminal victimization rates increased in areas of Korean residential settlement nor that Korean store owners were more often victimized than other store owners. Rather, Koreans had accepted the challenge of living and making a living in the central city. This challenge more comfortably situated predecessors had declined— thus creating a niche for Koreans to occupy. Only persons who tolerated crime could occupy central Los Angeles neighborhoods or stand behind store counters in the danger zones. Black store owners had long referred to this necessity as a "ghetto tax," and Korean immigrants had to pay it too.[9]

In response to crime the Korean press demanded enhanced organization for self-defense:

> Call Los Angeles Korea Town a Vietnam for those helpless immigrants who must live and eke out a living there. Hundreds have been mugged, robbed, burglarized, raped, and slain in recent stormy years. Yet the Korean community remains unorganized and unprepared for this murderous assault.[10]

Koreatown organizations enhanced their authority in response to the peoples' need for protection. First, the Korea Town Development

Association began to operate "its own patrol car" in response to the crime problem.[11] Second, the *Korea Times* held a seminar for business people on the subject of preventing criminal attack.[12] The newspaper invited police to advise business owners on robbery prevention and survival. Third, the Korean Association of Southern California demanded more police protection for Koreatown. Finally, the Korea Town Development Association raised money to pay for a Los Angeles police "outpost" in Koreatown. Staffed by uniformed police, the outpost's premises and Korean interpreter were paid for with funds privately subscribed by Koreatown merchants and bankers.[13] According to the president of the Korea Town Development Association, the outpost was necessary because merchants and customers were afraid—so business was declining in Koreatown. Koreans' demand for augmented police protection thus permitted Korean associations to increase their political power in the community and to strengthen their political connections with City Hall. Without the criminal attacks of non-Koreans, these solidarity-enhancing activities would never have occurred; thus criminals may claim partial responsibility for strengthening the institutional power of Korean associations.

CIVIL AND CRIMINAL LAW VIOLATIONS BY KOREANS IN BUSINESS

Cryptic notices of law violations by Koreans in various trades appeared during the late-1970s in the Korean press. In 1977 the California Public Utilities Commission investigated Korean packing companies. These were allegedly "doing business without a license" and charging customers "less than the legitimate minimum fee."[14] In 1978 city inspectors found Korean restaurants in Los Angeles in violation of sanitary requirements. Insects were present, and employee hygiene was below standard. In addition Koreans were preparing food on the floor rather than on tables as required by law; they were also marketing food without trademarks.[15] The Concentrated Enforcement Division (CED) of the California Division of Labor Standards also staged many sweeps of the restaurant industry; it reported that of 1374 restaurants investigated, 64 percent were in violation of minimum wage laws, 79 percent in violation of record-keeping requirements, and 100 percent in violation of the state labor code. The CED's director claimed that Koreans were overrepresented in restaurant work and as culpable as the rest of the industry—but he released no more detailed statistics. Nonetheless, many references indicated that labor conditions in Korean restaurants were chronically in violation of law; and a strike of Korean waitresses brought the issue of low wages to public attention.

The Police Commissioner's Office conducted an investigation of sixty Korean-owned massage parlors in June 1979.[16] The commissioner's office indicated that Koreans operated approximately 12 percent of the 500 licensed massage parlors then existing in Los Angeles. Closely regulated by law, massage parlors commonly served as fronts for prostitution. The police commissioner declined to indicate why Koreans were singled out for investigation, but the presumption must be that prostitution was suspected. No convictions resulted, but in 1981 undercover police arrested seventeen masseuses who were charged with prostitution; seven were Korean.[17] In April 1984 a Superior Court judge held two Koreans in contempt of court and fined them $1000 for employing ex-prostitutes in their massage parlor (Oliver, 1984).

Police investigations of organized crime in Koreatown also turned up four extortion gangs. According to police, a "favorite" business of Korean gangs was to extort protection payments from operators of massage parlors. A vice squad detective alleged that by 1984 Koreans owned "just about all the massage parlors in Los Angeles." In 1981 the Los Angeles chief of police charged that a Korean godfather operated an organized crime syndicate with 400 thugs on its payroll. However, police made only three arrests and never identified the alleged crime boss.[18]

Korean violations of business law had in common a willingness to evade legal requirements in order to gain industrial footholds. This willingness reflected saturation of business opportunities—and the consequent necessity to risk legal sanctions. That is, in many cases Korean entrepreneurs had to shave legal corners in order to squeeze into crowded industries. In the same sense, the overrepresentation of Koreans in the massage parlor business resulted from their dependence upon self-employment and the subsequent, uncomfortable necessity for accepting the legal challenges of operating firms even in a sleazy industry. In all these cases, economic survival necessitated violation of legal standards. The response of law enforcers to these violations reflected the interests that had earlier written their labor, sanitary, and moral standards into law. No laws directly attacked Korean enterprise. However, as Korean entrepreneurs packed and then overflowed their industrial niches, survival required noncon-formity with existing labor, sanitary, and moral standards. At that point police took over the task of restricting the number of Korean firms.

SMALL BUSINESS ADMINISTRATION

Federal government policies were important to Korean business in Los Angeles. In two important cases changes of federal law produced adverse changes in the status of Korean business. Both issues were financial in character, threatening Korean businesses by attacking their sources of credit. The first case arose when the House of Repre-sentatives briefly deleted "Asians and Pacific-Americans" from the list of minorities authorized for affirmative-action preference under Public Law 507. This exclusion applied only to the SBA's 8A Program under which the agency procured minority-owned firms to complete federal construction contracts. The excluding law indentified blacks, Hispanics, and Native Americans as "disadvantaged" but deleted Asians, thus eliminating their claim to affirmative action priority (Overend, 1979).

The cause of the brief deletion was never fully established, but one legislator remarked that his Japanese friends were too rich to deserve minority status. We found no evidence of anti-Asian propaganda by any interest bloc except blacks, who complained about the "ease with which Asians obtained loans to purchase businesses in the black community" (Cleaver, 1983c). Whether black complaints received attention in Congress or not, some force triggered an adverse change in laws governing Asian eligibility for governmental subsidies, thus threatening to set in motion other, more restrictive reactions by the federal government.

The administrator of the Small Business Administration, A. Ver-non Weaver (Springer, 1979), had maintained that Asians had to accept some responsibility for deletion. In Weaver's opinion Asians needed to become "better organized and less fragmented" if they wished to obtain benefits from the federal government. Weaver's candor was not wasted upon the Asians. The repeal campaign required Asians of different nationalities to work together. This stimulated a new all-Asian solidarity, rather than a specifically Korean, Chinese, or Japanese solidarity. Indeed the deletion itself had ignored these national subgroups, eliminating them all without distinction by striking the works "Asian and Pacific peoples" from the designated list. The federal government thus lumped a multiplicity of Asian nationalities into a common category for administrative convenience. The need to aggregate Asian nationalities derived from the small size of Asian national contingents. For this reason, Asian nationalities found it necessary to reach for a higher level of ethnic awareness when seeking to obtain political recognition. Because political defense required it, adverse societal reactions to Asian business encouraged the creation of a new and untraditional ethnic awareness in Koreatown: all-Asian solidarity. Thus, unfavorable reactions to Asian business success triggered a solidaristic response in Koreatown (Fong, 1987). However, the response was Asian, not specifically Korean; the Korean ethnic associations had to share their constituencies with non-Korean Asians who proclaimed a continental rather than a national loyalty.[19]

INVESTOR'S EXEMPTION

In 1976 the Immigration and Naturalization Service abruptly raised the ante for the investor's exemption from $10,000 to $40,000. As a result, persons wishing to enter the United States via the investor's priority had to put up $30,000 more, thus restricting the utility of this exemption to a wealthier class. Naturally this change applied equally to immigrants of all nations; it was not directed in reprisal to Koreans. Nonetheless, as an entrepreneurial minority, Koreans felt the adverse impact more than most immigrant nationalities. As a consequence of the higher investment requirement, fewer Koreans could qualify for the investor's exemption, so fewer could obtain entry in this manner.

OMBE CENTERS

In 1978 the Office of Minority Business Enterprise (OMBE) announced changes in funding policies to create a "one-stop" service center for all minorities—rather than a plurality of centers catering to distinct minorities. Winner of the OMBE contract was a black-operated business organization; Asian, Inc. lost its existing contract in the interdepartmental reshuffling.[20] For a while, the loss of this federal connection seemed to threaten the survival of Asian, Inc., but diversification permitted the agency to rebound. Nonetheless, Asians complained that blacks had wrested an important federal contract from them thanks to superior political organization, visibility, and influence in government.

These threats shaped the outlook of Korean and other Asian businesss owners. Six Asian-American delegates were designated for the White House Conference on Small Business in 1980. Spokespersons for the Asian delegation stressed the desirability of a coordinated Asian "strategy" to assure that Asians achieved recognition by federal agencies. Other delegates commented that Washington bureaucrats were "insensitive to the needs of Asian-Americans" who were "not politically visible." Delegates were encouraged to imitate blacks whose political strength had permitted them to wring material benefits from the federal government.[21]

IMMIGRATION REFORM AND CONTROL ACT OF 1986

After years of debate, the proposed Simpson-Mazzoli immigration reforms became law with the passage of the Immigration Reform and Control Act of 1986. This legislation tightened enforcement of existing immigration controls and introduced employer sanctions for hiring undocumented workers. Although the implementation of employer sanctions was successively delayed, in response to anguished pleas by affected industries, Korean entrepreneurs had reason to fear the employer-sanctions provision of the new law. As employers of undocumented labor, Korean entrepreneurs confronted the criminalization of their normal business practice.

INS raids of Korean firms in Los Angeles during 1982 afforded Korean entrepreneurs a foretaste for the possibly bitter consequences of employer sanctions. For example, INS officers surrounded a Korean-owned body shop on Vermont Avenue, searched the premises, and arrested three Latino workers.[22] Under existing law the Korean owners were not chargeable for employing illegal workers— but under the later Immigration Reform and Control Act they would be (Yun, 1983).

BANKING LAWS

Korean business owners in Los Angeles made some use of Korean banks for business capitalization. Federal measures to restrict the activities of foreign banks operating in the United States therefore threatened sources of capital upon which Koreans drew. These federal restrictions became law in the International Banking Act of 1978.[23] This law extended federal jurisdiction to foreign banks and compelled them to accept limits on their lending. The restrictions imposed were two. First, foreign banks were prohibited from establishing either federal or state branch banks outside of a home state without permission of the Federal Reserve Board. Second, the 1978 law required foreign banks to accept reserve requirements equivalent to those imposed upon American banks. Thus the effect of the law was to equalize competition by eliminating advantages that U.S. law had formerly bestowed upon foreign banks.

Korean banks mounted no ethnic defense against banking reform. Instead the foreign banks coordinated a joint defense via the Institute of Foreign Bankers. The institute represented 142 member banks from thirty-five countries. Congress waved aside the institute's arguments; nonetheless, the bankers' lobby reflected the financial interest of foreign capital rather than the parochial interest of any one nation's banks. Although this federal attack on foreign banking had a modest affect on Korean business in Los Angeles, there was no evidence of ethnic solidarity in the Korean response to it. (Obviously a go-it-alone reaction would have been ineffective, for events showed that even the concerted opposition of the foreign banks was unable to stop this legislation.) Still, the events in Washington indicate the complexity of the international trade issues whose effects trickled down to Los Angeles.

VIOLENCE AGAINST ASIANS

In the late 1970s a mood of public hostility toward immigrants spread in the wake of deteriorating economic conditions (Viviano, 1979; Oster, 1979). First, public opinion polls reflected growing tension. The proportion of the U.S. public favoring a decrease in legal immigration rose sharply between 1965 and 1981 (Cornelius, 1982: 9; California, 1982a: 52). Fifty-two percent of Californians agreed that immigrants took jobs from Americans in a 1982 poll organized by the Field Institute (1982). Sixty-five percent also agreed that illegal immigration was a serious problem. Opposition toward immigrants was not, however, directed equally toward all groups. Between 1975 and 1979 the percentage of Californians opposing additional influxes of Vietnamese refugees rose from 49 to 72 percent (Cornelius, 1982:12). A survey of San Diego County found that 40 percent of respondents believed Mexican immigrants had a negative impact on the city, 36 percent thought Asians had a negative impact, but only 17 percent thought Western Europeans had a negative impact (Cornelius, 1982: 16).

Second, violent outbreaks betokened a movement from unfavorable attitudes toward frank hostility. The basic tension was perceived to be economic competition between native-born Americans and immigrants. Vietnamese fishermen faced violence in Northern California and in Texas.[24] A state commission in Seattle reported that Asians in Washington had experienced harassment of "very serious proportions" at the hands of native workers who believed that the state's Asian population deprived them of jobs and that Asians obtained preferential treatment from government agencies.[25] In California a Governor's Task Force compiled a list of 450 instances of racial, ethnic, and religious violence in 100 cities throughout the state (California, 1982: 26). Most incidents cited by the task force occurred in the period of January 1979 to July 1982; its witnesses testified "over and over again" that the "threat to racial peace" stemmed from economic competition in a context of increasing unemployment, inflation, and high interest rates (California, 1982: 119).

Los Angeles County was the scene of several incidents involving Asians.[26] In 1983 the Los Angeles County Human Relations Commission initiated hearings on "anti-Asian bigotry" in the wake of a "widespread perception" that intolerance was rising.[27] According to the Commission's chairman: "Hostile bumper stickers, negative incidents of varying intensity, racial name-calling, and violent acts against Pacific-Asian persons seem to be occurring with increasing frequency."[28]

A series of murders also suggested that public hostility toward Asians was moving into the realm of the irrational. The most sensational murder occurred in Detroit in 1982. Two white men murdered Vincent Chin, beating him with baseball bats after a barroom altercation in which they had called Chin "a Jap." His murderers blamed Chin, a Chinese-American, for Japan's market-grabbing automobile exports and the resulting unemployment among American automobile workers (Smollar, 1983). Although premeditation was proved, the judge imposed only a $3000 fine on the murderers and released them on parole. The lenient sentence horrified Asian communities, who read in it official condolence of anti-Asian violence (Wong, 1984). Alarm spread when other murders followed. White youths murdered a Vietnamese student in Davis, California; a demented white pushed a Chinese woman in front of a subway train in New York City; and a Vietnamese woman was murdered in a racial altercation with whites in Boston. In the general context of deteriorating intergroup relations, Asians understood these murders as symptomatic of a hostile climate of opinion.[29] Concerned Asians in Los Angeles formed the Asian Pacific-American Roundtable, to demand justice in the Chin case and to stem the trend of homicide they perceived in the country at large (Justi, 1983). In the climate of fear Koreans and other Asians became sensitive to veiled attacks, insults, and incitements they perceived in the mass media's, coverage of Asian communities (Tokunaka, 1983; Yun, 1983; Wong, 1984). Korean entrepreneurship did not cause this general anti-Asian violence; however, Koreans had no choice but to concern themselves with a hostility that implicated them. This concern required organization.

BLACK–KOREAN TENSIONS

As Koreans continued to buy existing or establish new businesses in predominantly black communities, Korean stores encountered the long-standing antipathy of blacks toward commercial outsiders. First, ghetto mercantilists accused Korean store owners of retreating after business hours to their suburban homes, thus removing their day's business receipts from the black community in which they were earned (Eng and Sargent, 1981; McMillan, 1985). Second, blacks accused Koreans of giving hiring preference to coethnics over black applicants. Third, blacks complained of disrespectful treatment by Korean owners whom they suspected of racial prejudice. Finally, blacks resented Korean commercial success, regarding Korean stores as insults to black aspirations and obstacles to black commercial progress (I. Kim, 1981: 138, 318).

Black–Korean tensions arose for similar reasons in Baltimore, Washington, New York, Philadelphia, and Los Angeles (I. Kim, 1981: 157–259; Yoo, 1981).[30] Although possibly less severe than in New York City, Korean–black tensions were serious in Los Angeles. As in New York, the *Los Angeles Sentinel*, the city's black newspaper, accused Koreans of greed, overwork, not hiring blacks, and failing to contribute to the black community. The newspaper's series on the subject exposed the underlying tensions between black customers and Korean merchants. Although the author initially targeted "Asian-owned" gas stations and convenience stores, he (Cleaver, 1983a–f) later acknowledged he had not at first understood that Koreans were involved since neither he nor other blacks could distinguish Koreans from other Asians. By the end of his series, however, Cleaver (1983f) had specifically identified Koreans as the source of the "Asian problem" in central Los Angeles. Subsequently *Money Talks News* advised readers "not to give those Koreans a dime of your money" (McMillan, 1985). In general, blacks complained that after Koreans took over from Jewish store owners, their stores raised prices and fired black employees previously on the payroll, replacing them with Koreans. Additionally, Koreans expressed a pettyfogging determination to extract every nickle the traffic would bear at whatever expense in customer goodwill.[31] In the same vein, the *Los Angeles Sentinel* declared that employers were "letting it be known" they preferred Asian workers to black workers because Asians "would do anything to please" (Robertson, 1981; Baker, 1980).

Koreans in Los Angeles tried to improve relations with blacks. One method was to conclude a cooperative agreement with the Watts Labor Community Action Committee, a major black organization operating several businesses in the ghetto. This agreement included signing a "treaty" in which the Korean Association of Southern California and the Watts Labor Community Action Committee mutually pledged cooperation and exchange of human and material resources.[32] How much the treaty mitigated grass-roots tension it is impossible to ascertain, but four years later Koreans in Baltimore also resorted to the same intercommunal treaty in an effort to improve relationships with blacks (Ogburn and Butler, 1983).

Another way to mend fences with blacks was to alter one's business policies to comply with their demands. A few Korean business owners utilized this method. Chung Lee ran a market in Watts. To reduce tensions, Lee shared his Korean meals with customers, kept track of customers' family affairs, donated to local charities, gave free candy to children, extended liberal credit, and hosted a free barbecue party for some 200 neighborhood residents. Lee refused to sell Zig-Zag cigarette papers (used for rolling and smoking marijuana) even though this item was profitable. Rather than raise his own hand, Lee relied upon customers to apprehend and punish shoplifting youths in his store. Lee's store stood in a high crime zone where two Korean store owners had earlier died of gunshot wounds (S. Kim, 1983). When outside area youths burglarized Lee's store in 1982, neighbors called the police. Known as "Brother Lee" in the neighborhood, Chung Lee (1984) scolded other Korean merchants for failing to take a position of civic responsibility in the black community.

MIDDLEMAN MINORITIES IN THE WELFARE STATE

Although reaction to Korean influx was comparatively mild, three features of the American response are noteworthy. First, all the responses were restrictive—that is, no agency attempted to make more business opportunities available to Koreans. Rather, all reactions limited the business resources Koreans utilized or the freedom with which they had conducted business affairs. By 1982 the American public and government officials had moved closer to the view that the economy contained enough Korean businesses; therefore, political supports for expansion of Korean small business were redundant or unfair.

A second feature of American reaction was its administrative and anonymous character. With the exception of the International Banking Act of 1978 and (arising after the period of this study) the Immigration Reform and Control Act of 1986, adverse legal sanctions affecting Korean enterprise did not require changes in statutory law. Law enforcement agencies rousted Korean entrepreneurs in the garment industry, the massage industry, the restaurant industry, and the packing industry. Police exercised their administrative judgment to determine when violations of industrial law warranted enforcement drives. Similarly, changes in the INS's investor's exemption and the SBA's loan policies occurred when administrators decided to alter agency practices in ways adverse to the interest of Koreans. These alterations were within the scope of their legal authority.[33] Neither agency held public hearings in which those demanding social control were required to surface as moral entrepreneurs. In effect, aggrieved interests enjoyed anonymity because their protection was written into law or informally understood by the law's administrators. Police, the INS, and the SBA interpreted existing law in ways hostile to Koreans but helpful to the interests that had written the legislation in the first place (Dror, 1959).

A third feature of American reaction was phased correspondence between short-run and long-run sanctions. Requiring no changes in statutory law, police and administrative sanctions provided speedy responses to abuses. These administrative responses were first-phase sanctions. Even as they unrolled, adverse changes in public opinion supported still more drastic revisions of immigration law, threatening second-phase damage to Korean enterprise. However, since the statutory changes depended upon prior changes in public opinion, second-phase sanctions took longer to mature. That is, the elapsed time between the public's perception of a problem and its remedy was longer in the case of statutory law than in the case of police or administrative sanctions. In this sense, short-run, administrative sanctions anticipated long-run sanctions—and possibly reduced their urgency by reducing the problem. Conversely, long-run changes in law would only be required insofar as administrative and police sanctions proved incapable of controlling a problem.

This point implies a major difference between the manner in which the welfare state managed Korean immigration in 1985 and the manner in which the "Chinese problem" had been managed under a regime of laissez-faire in 1885 (Saxton, 1971). Because the welfare state was in place in 1985, Koreans encountered regulatory laws prohibiting low wages, dirty kitchens, substandard working conditions, low prices, and the like. Laws also regulated the place and manner in which Koreans could sell liquor, operate massage parlors, sew garments, pack food, or maintain eating places. The welfare state even made business capital available to Koreans disadvantaged because of their race. Because these welfare measures existed, police and administrators had the authority to punish Koreans for competitive economic practices. Natually, in a laissez-faire context, such laws would not have been in force, and it would have been the responsibility of grievants to abate Korean enterprise by means at their disposal. Insofar as these means could not include legal restraint, grievants would have confronted the Korean nuisance by force or boycott. Therefore, the more tranquil reception of Los Angeles' Korean immigrants than of turn-of-the-century Asian immigrants owed something to the welfare state. In this altered context, police had the responsibility for protecting the industrial status quo, thus relieving injured parties of the necessity for identifying themselves in public demonstrations against immigrant competitors.

The seeming exception to this generalization was the conflict between Koreans and blacks. In this conflict, blacks identified themselves as complainants and pressed their claims with vigor. But the apparent exception really confirms the generalization because blacks stood outside the circle of those whose interests were protected by American law. In the liquor-industry controversy, blacks asked for the restriction of beer, wine, and liquor vendors operating in their neighborhoods, petitioning police to undertake more vigorous suppression. In this case, blacks claimed officials were not according them the protections from competitive business practices that they merited under existing law. But other black grievances had no remedy at law. Law permitted Koreans to operate stores in black neighborhoods while living elsewhere, to fire black employees, to refuse credit to black customers, to treat black customers like potential shoplifters, to make no contribution to black charities, and to look down upon black people. Therefore, blacks had no recourse at law for their complaints —and had to press them by violence, boycott, or threats (Harris, 1980).

REACTIVE SOLIDARITIES

The sanctions confronting Korean enterprise (table 64) in the early 1980s originated in three contexts. First, Koreans sometimes experienced hostile responses to their entrepreneurship in a context of what Yen Espiritu (1987) has called "ethnic categorization," the simplistic but authoritative identification of a newcomer ethnic group. Standard business competition with non-Koreans was the unorganized form of this response, but Korean entrepreneurs also confronted organized challenges. Only the anti-Korean movement among inner-city blacks originated as a specific response to Korean entrepreneurship, but the massage parlor investigations almost met

Table 64. Threats to Korean Business Enterprise in Los Angeles

Threat	Character of Threat	Korean Response
Garment Industry Sweeps	Law enforcement	Korean solidarity plus class solidarity
Massage Parlor Investigation	Law enforcement	Unknown
Restaurant Industry Sweeps	Law enforcement	Unknown
Packing Industry Sweeps	Law enforcement	Unknown
Criminal Victimization of Koreans	Law violations	Korean solidarity
Liquor Industry Protests	Law enforcement	Korean solidarity
Repeal of Fair Trade Law	Statutory law change	Korean solidarity
Investors Regulation	Administrative change	Unknown
SBA: 8A deletion,	Administrative change	Asian-American solidarity
International Banking Act of 1978	Statutory law change	Class solidarity
Immigration Reform and Control Act	Statutory law change	Asian-American solidarity
Violence by Americans	Law violations	Asian-American solidarity
Black Grievances	Boycott	Korean solidarity
Purchase Price of Business Increases	Market	Unknown

this condition because Koreans were so dominant in the massage industry. In both these cases, sanctions meted out to Koreans corresponded to what sanctioners perceived as Korean misdeeds. Whether Korean entrepreneurs merited these sanctions is, of course, unclear and of no consequence here. Evidence suggests, indeed, that blacks exaggerated the economic conflict of interest between themselves and Korean entrepreneurs.[34] Nonetheless, their objections to Korean entrepreneurship were based on what Koreans themselves were alleged to have done, a characteristic not shared by most objections to Korean entrepreneurship.

Most of the hostile sanctions affecting Korean entrepreneurs originated against an economic category in which Koreans represented only a minority. In the garment industry sweeps, the liquor industry protests, the investor's exemption amendments, the SBA policy changes, and later in the 1986 Immigration Reform Act, Koreans were members of a class under political attack, but they did not constitute the whole of that class. For example, the Immigration Reform Act sanctioned employers of undocumented workers, and Koreans were among this group. But Koreans were not the only employers of undocumented labor and were, in fact, a small proportion of the offending group.

When Korean entrepreneurs provoked reprisals for their own real or alleged misbehavior, Koreans suffered the consequences of their own actions. But racism and deteriorating public attitudes toward Asians and immigrants also caused Koreans to suffer sanctions for no behavior of their own. Because the public could not distinguish Koreans, Chinese, Japanese, Vietnamese, or Filipinos, hostilities directed at any one of these groups affected the others as well. The absurdity of this situation is reflected in some public disputes in which Koreans were involved. In one instance, Korean golfers on a public course engaged in a club-swinging fracas with off-duty police who had identified them as "dumb Japs." [35] In another, black teenagers in Los Angeles chanted "chink" in front of Korean-owned stores (see also Harris, 1983: 196). In yet another episode, vandals painted "Nip go home" on a Korean storefront. Few Californians cared that Koreans must be called "gooks" rather than "chinks," "nips," or "Japs" if an accurate epithet is wanted (Allen, 1983: 62).

Although the inappropriate insults were ludicrous, the racism behind them complicated the Koreans' adjustment problems beyond the simplicity of middleman theory. In theory, middleman minorities suffer reprisals for their own entrepreneurial success—not for the activities of others who resemble them. Insofar as Koreans experienced sanctions directed at their race, not at their entrepreneurial success, the sanctioning afflicted them for no instrumental reason. Distinguishing the etiology of any sanction is difficult for Koreans as well as for sociologists. Motives were often mixed so that sanctions presented as wholly or partially responsive to Korean misdeeds often carried a racist message too. In the specific case of the Immigration Reform Act, for example, the unfavorable law materialized in small part because of what Koreans had done, but much more because of what others had done. Moreover, protestations of innocence not-withstanding, public support for immigration reform included a component of racism. Therefore, the actual sanction confronting Koreans was more responsive to the misbehavior of others than it was to Korean misbehavior. Since the same observation applies to most other sanctions Koreans confronted, it is generally true that the sanctions exceeded any economic misbehavior for which Koreans were responsible. In this sense, middleman theory does not offer a wholly successful explanation of why Koreans experienced so much sanctioning.

This theoretical problem is partially resolved if one thinks in terms of a middleman function rather than in terms of a middleman minority. Unlike Poland in the interwar period, Los Angeles did not have a unitary middleman minority with a firm ethnic boundary (Andreski, 1963). Instead, a plurality of immigrant and ethnic minorities occupied fragmentary niches that, taken together, constituted a middleman economic function. Since public outrage was directed at this ethnic spectrum, crystallization around a unitary target was difficult—but anit-Asian sentiment came nearest the mark (Fong, 1987). For its part, each ethnic middleman confronted the necessity of forming alliances in response to outgroup hostility. Middleman theory makes no reference to alliances because middleman theory assumes a unitary minority under attack because of its own economic success. In urban black communities, a specifically anti-Korean challenge materialized and, as Illsoo Kim (1981: 259) observed, black hostility promoted "a deeper and greater ethnic solidarity" among the Koreans. However, most attacks housed Koreans within a broader spectrum of attacked groups so that specifically Korean solidarity was too limited a response to be wholly effective.

In response to attacks, Korean leaders, newspapers, and intellectuals strove to raise ethnic solidarity at every level (I. Kim, 1981: 318; H.-C. Kim, 1977: 80). The United Korean Community of California federated the seven major Korean associations in the state (Lee, 1980). He-In Kim (1982) advised fellow Koreans to fight discrimination by behaving in ways that brought credit to the Korean community. Even Korean should "realize that his manner and actions will reflect upon the character of all Koreans and thus will directly influence the ... attitude and opinions American society will form of Korean-Americans in general." Others encouraged organizational affiliation and utilization of bloc power. Sonia Suk urged her compatriots to "raise their voice as a political pressure group" in emulation of better-organized Chinese and Japanese.[36] But realizing that Korean solidarity was inadequate to the challenges, Korean spokespersons also sought to reach out to non-Koreans, especially other Asians, whatever the barriers posed by historical rivalries, dislikes, or resource competition.[37] In this manner, Korean ethnic consciousness and its attendant collective action became, under the force of necessity, a panethnic consciousness enrolled in a panethnic movement (Espiritu, 1987; Olzak, 1986: 21; Light, 1972: 179).

Koreans simultaneouly activated three levels of solidarity in response to external threats: Korean, Asian-American, and class. Asian solidarities arose when Koreans joined with other Asians in defensive alliances. Class solidarity involved common cause with any persons, regardless of race or ethnicity, who shared an industrial interest with Koreans. Class solidarity was the least common mode of association and, when it did occur, did so as a coalition of Korean groups with non-Koreans. Korean solidarity meant the grouping of Koreans for self-defense. For example in the garment industry Koreans formed a contractors' association in response to enforcement sweeps. This was Korean solidarity. Confronting the SBA's removal of "Asians" from its affirmative-action list, Koreans joined forces with other Asians. This was an Asian-American response. In both the food and liquor industries, Koreans cooperated with non-Korean trade associations in defense of small dealers against economically powerful rivals and external interference. This was a class response.

The complexity of this web of reactive affiliations is an important finding that amplifies conventional middleman theory (Lyman, 1974). Koreans adapted their defense to the threats they confronted and, as these threats were more complex than middleman theory assumes, the response was more complex too. When Koreans were under attack for their own entrepreneurship, as in the black communities, Korean solidarity was a satisfactory defense. When Koreans came under attack because of their membership in a larger class of entrepreneurs, Koreans joined with non-Korean trade associations in defense of small business, a nonethnic class response. When Koreans came under attack because of their race, their response was Asian-American solidarity, an ethnic solidarity encapsulating Korean solidarity in a larger vehicle. In the complex, pluralistic Los Angeles setting, Koreans picked whichever solidarity best defended their interest and put most weight behind this coalition. Korean ethnic solidarity was a resort to which Koreans turned when circumstances isolated them from allies. One can imagine a situation in which Koreans, stripped of allies, would be compelled to organize their social life around all-Korean groups. This is the extreme scenario developed in the literature of pariah capitalism. But this isolation had not by the mid-1980s arisen in Los Angeles. Moreover, the ability of Koreans to form class and Asian solidarities created alliances that inhibited the isolation and scapegoating of Koreans as a middleman minority. The pluralism of social associations posed a barrier to making true middlemen of Koreans. Conversely, attacks on Korean capacity to obtain allies would set in motion a process of stigmatization and isolation from which would ultimately emerge the pariah solidarity described in the literature of middleman minorities.

The macroliterature of sociology often gives the impression that class and ethnic solidarities are opposed polarities: people have either a class or an ethnic consciousness. Thus, Hechter (1978: 367) claimed that ethnics "must choose between" ethnic and class identities. Obviously Koreans failed to make that tidy choice. First, where they came into play at all, class solidarities required multiethnic coalitions as a condition of their existence. Second, the best interest of Korean owners was to form a web of associations (Korean, Asian, and class) linking them simultaneously to many levels of defense. A proprietor felt most safeguarded in his material interest when he had connections with class, Asian, and Korean solidarities; and stripping any defenses rendered him more insecure. True, a polarization of events could compel Koreans to stress one solidarity—but this they would only do when so compelled, and given the opportunity they would quickly revert to the web of affiliations from which the strongest social support was derived.

PART FOUR

KOREAN SMALL BUSINESS IN AMERICAN CAPITALISM

13

The Protection of U.S. Labor Standards

Korean immigrant small business can be seen as a form of "cheap labor." In part two we discussed the movement of U.S. capital abroad in search of cheap labor whether by importing the products of such labor or by establishing plants overseas. An alternative to moving capital abroad is moving cheap labor to the United States through immigration.

Cheap labor immigration serves the same purposes as cheap imports and the runaway shop. It lowers the cost of production to business enterprises, enabling them to be more competitive and to earn higher profits. In addition it helps the capitalist class to undermine local labor standards. U.S. labor has continuously pressed for improvements in wages and working conditions. The immigration of cheap labor enables capital to circumvent local high-priced labor, while implicitly threatening those who remain employed with displacement if they become too militant or costly.

Cheap labor immigration is not a new phenomenon, and its role in capitalist development has been widely recognized. Less recognized is the idea that immigrant cheap labor need not be employed directly in a simple wage relationship. Immigrant small business can also be a form of cheap labor utilization by U.S. capitalists, even though the employment of the labor is indirect.

Part of the reason for Korean concentration in small business lies in the fact that direct access to immigrant cheap labor is limited in the United States. Through a long history of struggle over the cheap labor issue, U.S. labor has managed to forge protections against easy displacement by cheap labor. Immigrant small business can be seen as a means of circumventing these protections, since the utilization of cheap labor indirectly, through the small business form, is not well covered by the protections.

In this chapter we examine the legal system built up by U.S. labor to protect itself against undercutting by capitalists with cheap labor, as of 1980. These protections were not evenly spread across the whole industrial spectrum. The porous nature of the protections helps to account for the industrial concentrations of immigrant small business. Where protections of U.S. labor standards were weak, immigrant cheap labor could more easily be utilized.

The protection of U.S. labor standards has generally increased over the years, particularly since the New Deal, although this trend may have come to a halt in 1980. Immigrant small business predates the New Deal. Late nineteenth- and early twentieth-century Jewish and Asian immigrants, for example, showed a heavy propensity to run small businesses based on cheap labor long before the emergence of the welfare state. Early Jewish and Asian immigrants created their own cheap labor enclaves, as do today's Korean immigrants. Nevertheless, we contend that increased protection of U.S. labor standards helped to channel immigrants into small business by confining capital's ability to employ cheap labor directly.

The phenomenon of immigrant small business can be placed in a larger context of dual or segmented labor markets. Korean enterprise falls squarely in the "secondary labor market" (or periphery or competitive sector). Authors writing in this tradition tend to explain segmentation by the characteristics of industries or firms in themselves, with large, monopolized, capital-intensive industries producing durable goods requiring certain work-force characteristics, and vice versa for small, competitive businesses.[1] The analysis tends to be static and ahistorical, taking the division for granted. To the extent that the creation of dual labor markets is studied, the focus tends to be upon the monopoly sector, treating competitive small business as a residual category. The study of the creation of Korean enterprise can thus contribute to our understanding of the creation of dual labor markets and, particularly, the production and reproduction of the competitive sector.

For the remainder of this chapter we focus on the law as the chief mechanism for the protection of U.S. labor standards. The historical struggle by labor to protect itself against undercutting has often been fought in other arenas, including the streets; but in the 1970s the major arena was the legal system. Our purpose is to examine the structure of the law as it protected workers from being undercut by the use of cheap labor. The pertinent laws can be divided into three types: labor laws, welfare laws, and immigration policy. We plan to show how the structure of these laws left loopholes where labor standards could be undercut. These loopholes helped to determine where cheap labor would be employed, namely in certain industries and in small businesses.

The federal government and the State of California each had laws to protect labor standards. To a large extent they overlapped and duplicated each other, though in some cases one was stronger than the other. For instance California had its own minimum wage and its own enforcement of the minimum wage laws. We have chosen to by-pass state legal structure in any detail and to focus on the federal standards, mainly to avoid tedious repetition. Themes were generally the same at both levels, even if specific details varied.

LABOR LAWS

Labor laws can be divided into two broad classes: those establishing labor standards, and those that recognize trade union rights.

LABOR STANDARDS

One of the principal protections against the use of cheap labor, or undercutting, was the federal Fair Labor Standards Act (FLSA). First passed in 1938, the law was subsequently amended six times, as of 1980, each time changing—generally extending—the law's coverage. The FLSA set minimum wages, overtime pay, equal pay, and child labor standards. Each of these can be seen, in part, as an attempt to prevent undercutting.

The minimum wage provision attempted to establish a floor below which compensation for labor would not sink. It aimed at preventing employers from hiring cheap labor.

The overtime pay section of the law set maximum hours considered to be a normal workday. If people worked over this standard they were to be paid at least time and one-half. The standard workweek was set at forty hours. The purpose is clear: to prevent employers from overworking their employees.

The Equal Pay Act was passed in 1963, amending the FLSA. It provided that employers should not pay one sex less than the other for equal work requiring substantially the same skills, effort, and responsibility, when working in the same establishment. While partially aimed at preventing the exploitation of women, its purpose can also be to prevent male workers from being undercut by employers seeking to use cheaper female labor.

Child labor poses a similar problem to female labor in that both have been historically cheaper (more exploitable) than adult male labor. This section of the FLSA set the basic minimum age for employment at sixteen years, thereby preventing employers from using cheap child labor.

Despite these intentions, the FLSA has been subject to numerous exemptions. The most important, from the point of view of Korean small business, was that the law only applied to wage and salary workers. The 7.9 million self-employed and the 0.8 million unpaid family workers (a figure that is probably an undercount) as of September 1978 were not protected. Of the remaining 87.6 million members of the civilian labor force, only nonsupervisory workers came under the law. Thus we arrive at a total of 57.6 million, or about 60 percent of the work force covered.[2]

Even within this eligible pool, various exemptions have been set up. These have changed over time. When first passed, the law only covered workers who engaged in interstate commerce or who produced goods for that commerce. The 1961 amendments—the most far-reaching of six amendments—extended coverage to all employees of an enterprise if some of the employees were engaged in interstate commerce, and if the enterprise met certain minimum dollar-sales criteria.[3] For example, retail and service enterprises, including gas stations, hotels, and restaurants, required an annual gross sales volume of at least $250,000 to come under the act. In other words a size criterion was built into the law: small businesses were more likely to be exempt.

In 1977 new amendments raised the minimum gross sales volume for retail and service establishments. They would only be covered under the FSLA if they had a gross annual volume of at least $275,000 beginning in July 1978, at least $325,000 from July 1980, and $362,000 after December 1981. Thus the member of workers covered by FSLA might be expected to shrink over time.

The effect of exemptions from minimum wage coverage for different industries, as of 1978, is shown in table 65. Omitted from the

Table 65. Workers in the Private Sector Exempted from Minimum Wage Provisions of the Fair Labor Standards Act, by Industry Division, September 1978

	Total Nonsupervisory Employees* (in thousands)	Number Not Subject to Minimum Wage (in thousands)	Percent Not Subject to Minimum Wage	Industry Percent of Total
Agriculture	1,518	965	63.6	10.0
Mining	792	4	0.5	0.0
Contract Construction	4,122	21	0.5	0.2
Manufacturing	17,828	502	2.8	5.2
Transportation and Public Utilities	4,344	33	0.8	0.3
Wholesale Trade	3,396	859	25.3	8.9
Retail Trade	13,114	2,695	20.6	28.0
Finance, Insurance, and Real Estate	3,221	975	30.3	10.1
Service	12,184	2,894	23.8	30.1
Private Household Service	1,845	665	36.0	6.9
TOTAL	62,364	9,613	15.4	100.0

*Includes only employed wage and salary workers in the civilian labor force who are not executives, administrators, professionals, or outside salespersons.
Source: Adapted from U.S. Department of Labor, Employment Standards Administration, Minimum Wage and Maximum Hours Standards under the Fair Labor Standards Act: An Economic Effects Study Submitted to Congress, 1979: 63–64.

table are the automatically exempt, namely self-employed and supervisory personnel, as well as public-sector employees, many of whom worked at the state and local level and were not covered by the federal statute. As table 65 shows, almost all workers in mining, construction, manufacturing, and transportation were covered. In contrast substantial proportions of workers in agriculture, trade, finance, and service were not covered by federal minimum wage provisions. Looked at another way, over one-quarter of workers not covered were concentrated in retail trade and the service industries; together these two industries accounted for close to three-fifths of exempted workers.

Exemptions from the requirement to pay premium overtime wages were more numerous than those for minimum wage. Twenty-two percent of private-sector, nonsupervisory workers were exempted from this provision as of 1978, compared to a total of 15.4 percent exempted from minimum wages. The industrial distribution of exemptions from overtime differs somewhat from minimum wages, but generally the same industries were protected: mining, construction, and manufacturing. Again agriculture, trade, finance, and services received much lower levels of federal protection. And half of all workers not covered were employed in the retail and service sector.

The equal pay provisions of the FLSA were vulnerable to no exemptions, other than the general limitations of coverage with respect to size of enterprise. In contrast the child labor laws had several exemptions. For instance, children aged fourteen and fifteen were permitted to work in agriculture and a variety of nonmanufacturing jobs outside of school hours. In addition a few specified jobs could be performed by even younger children; particularly important was an exemption for children who worked for their parents in agriculture and in non agricultural occupations other than mining or manufacturing.

Exemptions to the FLSA help to explain how dualities in the labor market arose, and how they were distributed across industries. Big business was forced, under the law, to pay minimum wages and overtime, whereas small business, especially self-employed small business, was not. Mining, manufacturing, and construction were consistently prohibited from using cheap labor, while agriculture, retailing, and services received numerous exemptions. It is hardly surprising, therefore, that low-wage jobs tended to be concentrated in these sectors.

But how and why did this particular pattern of exemptions get written into the law? Some may argue that they reflected the differential needs of various industries: big, monopoly industries did not require cheap labor and so could afford a protected work force. While there may be some truth to this, we doubt that industrial need is the major reason. The very fact that protections were written into law and had to be enforced suggests that there were pressures to act against the law's mandates. And indeed the law was continually being broken.

Responsibility for enforcing the FLSA lay with the Wage and Hour Division of the Employment Standards Administration. Most of their activity was in response to complaints. Although there was no statutory requirement that they respond to all complaints, they attempted to do so. In 1978 they received 48,893 complaints, had a backlog of 24,487 from the previous year, and investigated 61,239 cases. That year they disclosed a total of $91.7 million in unpaid wages, of which $40 million was in violation of the minimum wage provision and $51.7 million was for underpayment of overtime wages. Altogether 542,000 workers were affected. Under the equal pay provision, 18,376 employees were declared underpaid by a total of nearly $16 million, while child labor violations were found in the cases of 14,603 workers.[4]

The FLSA was also enforced through litigation, especially in cases where voluntary compliance was refused. Some of these suits were against the nation's largest corporations, such as TWA in 1978.[5] In 1978 the Wage and Hour Division actively investigated industries known to hire undocumented immigrant workers. Uncharacteristically, they took the initiative in this investigation rather than responding to complaints.[6] (Generally, the division only responded to complaints, so many violations probably went undetected.)

If the nature of the industries themselves does not fully explain the pattern of protection, then what does? We believe that pattern rested on a combination of enforceability and the relative strength of contending forces. On the first point, small business tended to be exempted because of the tremendous policing problems it posed. Authorities probably assumed that if they could control big businesses, the small ones would follow. And in any case, since they could not possibly investigate every business, they should pursue those accounting for the largest number of workers.

Regarding the second point, it seems likely that the pattern of protection mainly reflected the differential strength of the working class by industry. In industries where labor was highly organized, workers were most able to win legal protections, whereas unorganized industries fell prey to the special pleadings of capital for exemptions. For example, when the FLSA was first passed in 1938 it only covered an estimated 11 million workers, or one-fifth of the labor force. Of these, only about 300,000 (3 percent) were at the time being paid below the minimum wage. The law avoided those sectors of the labor force where wages were lowest and child labor most prevalent (Grossman, 1978: 29), still somewhat the case even in 1980. This avoidance would appear to be a response to political realities, that is, the balance reached in the class struggle at that point in time.

Within a capitalist society it is in the interests of labor to expand the protection of labor standards to all segments of the work force and to all industries, so that one cannot be used to undercut another. On the other hand, the capitalist class tries to weaken or abolish such principles as the minimum wage. For example, congressional hearings were held in 1977 over a proposed amendment to the FLSA that called for indexing the minimum wage to 60 percent of the average wage in manufacturing (a measure that would raise minimum wages) and for the abolition of "tip credit" to employers of workers who earn tips (making employers comply with a full minimum wage). The AFL-CIO and the Women's Union testified on behalf of the bill, H.R. 3744. Testifying in opposition were representatives of the following organizations: the National Association of Retail Grocers, the U.S. Industrial Council (an organization of business and industrial firms employing over 4 million workers), the American Hotel and Motel Association, the National Federation of Independent Business (with 491,000 members), the National Restaurant Association, the National Association of Convenience Stores, the Food Service and Lodging Institute, the American Farm Bureau Federation, the U.S. Chamber of Commerce, and a few economists.[7] The particular mix of businesses that testified probably reflects the particulars of this bill, but it also demonstrates clearly how the interests align.

The 1977 amendments to the FSLA marked some major victories for capital and a shift from earlier amendments that had generally strengthened coverage (Elder, 1978: 10). In particular the indexing proposal failed, and while tip credit was lowered from 50 to 40 percent, it was not abolished. As we have seen, the minimum size for retail and service establishments to come under the act was raised. Although labor made a few gains—such as the abolition of a special lower minimum wage in agriculture and for Puerto Rico[8]—on the whole 1977 was capital's year. Regardless of the details, the legal protection of labor standards remained an arena of constant struggle. Segmentation reflects, at least to some important extent, the particular balance reached at each historical moment.

Trade Union Rights

Another means of protecting labor against undercutting is the recognition of the rights of workers to form independent trade unions, to bargain collectively, and to engage in strikes without punitive retaliation. These rights can be seen as protection against undercutting since it was a common practice in the past to use cheap labor as strikebreakers, thereby driving down the price of labor and undermining the bargaining power of workers. The right to form independent unions and to strike prohibits the employer from engaging in these kinds of tactics.

The National Labor Relations Act (NLRA) or Wagner Act, first passed in 1935 and subsequently amended, is the major law addressing trade union rights. The main purposes of the act at its inception were: to define and protect the rights of employees to bargain collectively with representatives of their own choosing; to set up a National Labor Relations Board (NLRB), which would conduct secret ballot elections to ensure that workers could freely elect their own representatives without employer interference; and to specify certain practices of employers or unions as "unfair labor practices."[9]

The NLRA has many specific provisions of no concern here. The main point is that the protection provided by the law has been incomplete, leaving loopholes where capital can still have access to cheap labor. Thus, the law only covers "employees," and certain workers are exempted from this designation: agricultural laborers, domestic servants, any individual employed by a parent or spouse, independent contractors, supervisors, individuals subject to the Railway Labor Act, and government employees.[10] Of most relevance to Korean small business are exemptions for self-employed and family workers.

Apart from these exemptions, the NLRB has the authority to regulate labor—management relations in all enterprises that "affect commerce." Although commerce is defined as interstate trade, traffic, transportation, or communication, the term "affect" can be interpreted to cover almost any enterprise. For example, a local manufacturer who sells goods to a wholesaler who then ships a proportion of them out of state, would fall within the definition. However, strictly local enterprises would not be covered.[11] It is reasonable to assume that such local enterprises are likely to be small. Thus, some small business escapes the NLRB by being purely local.

In addition, the NLRB does not act in all cases definable as "affecting commerce." The board exercises discretion, limiting its jurisdiction to cases involving enterprises whose affect on commerce is "substantial." The NLRB sets up "jurisdictional standards" that specify the yearly amount and type of business that must be conducted for the board to consider the case. These standards vary by type of enterprise. For instance newspapers (as of July 1976) had to have a volume of business totaling at least $200,000, while symphony orchestras had to receive at least $1 million in gross revenue from all sources. During the period studied, the specifications most relevant to us were: retail enterprises, which had to have a total annual business volume of at least $500,000; and "nonretail business"— which, despite its name, did not cover everything else, since special terms were set for transportation enterprises, health care facilities, and so on—which required at least $50,000 per annum of direct or indirect sales or purchases in other states. Finally, even if a labor dispute occurred in a company falling within its jurisdictional standards, the NLRB could exercise discretion in not looking into the matter if deemed insufficiently substantial.[12]

In sum, only some employees during our study period fell under the NLRA by law, and only larger enterprises tended to fall under it by NLRB practice. The effects in terms of industrial coverage are shown in table 66. The first two columns report all cases received by the board in 1978, including both elections and charges of unfair labor practices. The second two columns show the distribution of completed elections. Comparable data were not provided for unfair labor practices. Although the distribution of cases does not reveal the number of workers involved, in cases both submitted and acted upon, manufacturing loomed large. Given that manufacturing work-

Table 66.   Industrial Distribution of Cases Received and
Representation Elections Held by the National Labor
Relations Board, 1978

	Cases Received		Elections Held	
	Number	*Percent*	*Number*	*Percent*
Agriculture	0	0.0	0	0.0
Mining	916	1.7	105	1.3
Construction	4,729	8.9	205	2.5
Manufacturing	23,038	43.3	3,565	43.3
Transportation and Public Utilities	6,496	12.2	892	10.8
Wholesale Trade	3,044	5.7	844	10.2
Retail Trade	5,413	10.2	1,079	13.1
Finance, Insurance, and Real Estate	787	1.5	155	1.9
Services	7,586	14.2	1,385	16.8
Private Household	0	0.0	0	0.0
U.S. Postal Service	1,212	2.3	3	0.0
Public Administration	40	0.1	7	0.1
TOTAL	53,261	100.0	8,240	100.0

Source: Adapted from National Labor Relations Board, *43rd Annual Report for Fiscal Year Ending September 30, 1978*: 248–249, 276–277.

ers constituted less than 30 percent of all civilian, nongovernment employees (see table 65), and that average manufacturing establishments were likely to be larger than average retail and service establishments so that each manufacturing case probably covered more workers, the protection provided by the NLRB was apparently quite heavily skewed.

Even apart from considerations about the impact of size or advanced technology on union organization, this pattern of legal protection would lead us to expect that unionization would be more advanced in large plants and in industries that had a high degree of capital concentration. Small businesses—and industries with a high proportion of small businesses, such as retail and service—ought to have shown low levels of union membership, since efforts to unionize the small business sector received little federal backing.

The effect can be seen in union membership statistics. While there are numerous problems with the data, a rough estimate can be made

Table 67.   Union Membership of Private Sector Workers,
by Industry, 1974

	Total Employed (in thousands)	Union Members* (in thousands)	Percent Unionized
Agriculture	1,314	36	2.7
Mining	694	372	53.6
Construction	3,957	2,738	69.2
Manufacturing	20,046	9,144	45.6
Transportation and Public Utilities	4,696	3,258	69.4
Wholesale and Retail Trade	17,017	1,329	7.8
Finance, Insurance, and Real Estate	4,208	32	0.8
Services	13,617	1,665	12.2
TOTAL	65,549	18,574	28.3

*Omits 91,000 unclassified nonmanufacturing union members.
Source: Adapted from U.S. Department of Labor, Bureau of Labor Statistics, *Handbook of Labor Statistics, 1978, 1979*: 134, 150, 502–503.

of unionization by industry. Union membership data for the 1970s was collected in 1974. Using 1974 data on the number of people employed in the major industrial categories, table 67 presents the percentage of workers unionized by industry. Unfortunately, the union membership figures include some international unions with members in Canada, but since their proportion was about 7 percent overall, the degree of error introduced is fairly small. As can be seen, the least-unionized industries were agriculture, wholesale and retail trade, finance, and services.

Note that the points of weakness in the legal structure of protection overlap. Self-employed and family workers were covered neither by the FLSA or NLRA. Similarly, retail and service workers were among the most poorly covered by both laws. And small business, overrepresented in the above categories, tended not to fall under the scrutiny of federal laws because of its smallness. Thus, while efforts were made to protect labor from undercutting by these laws, their coverage was incomplete, helping to explain the emergence of dualities.

How certain exemptions and standards got established in law and practice is, again, a topic we cannot examine in depth here. But it seems likely that pressure groups played a significant part. Thus the exclusion of agricultural labor from protection under the NLRA would seem to have been a product, at least in part, of the political strength of farmers' lobbies and of the lack of organization (at least until recently) of farm workers.

Protective legislation for labor unions is subject to continual struggle. Labor keeps pushing to extend coverage while business tries to reduce or eliminate it. New laws are proposed by each camp and are either passed, modified, or rejected. For instance the Labor Reform Act of 1977 was proposed to strengthen the NLRB and prevent businesses—especially in the South where the problem was most severe—from delaying union elections and engaging in other tactics to curb unionization. Again this can be seen as an effort to prevent undercutting, in that the South had become an attractive region for industries because of its dual (and linked) advantage of low wages and weak unionization. Labor wanted to plug this particular loophole by upgrading southern labor standards so that they matched the rest of the nation.

Although the 1977 Labor Reform Act failed to pass, hearings held on it are instructive. Organizations speaking against it included the National Association of Manufacturers, the American Retail Federation, the Council of State Chambers of Commerce, and the National Small Business Association, among others. In other words capitalists, both big and small, were aligned against it. On the other side were such labor organizations as the AFL-CIO and the United Auto Workers and representatives of several individual unions. Significantly, the NAACP testified on behalf of the bill.[13] Given high unemployment levels in the black community, the NAACP might have taken a position that favored opportunities for blacks to undercut organized labor. Instead they chose to join with labor in pushing for stronger government protection.[14] Overall, the pattern of testimony leaves little doubt about the class alignments on this issue.

In sum, labor legislation served as a battleground for continued class struggle. Whether large or small, business wanted to keep labor costs down, undermine protections for workers, and weaken or destroy labor unions. Labor, on the other hand, wanted to push up wages, improve work conditions, and extend coverage to all workers, so that one segment could not be pitted against another in an effort to undermine them all. The outcome was a legal maze in which some workers were better protected than others. The loopholes allowed capital to continue to use cheap labor but only in restricted segments of the economy, such as small business and the retail and service sectors. Thus were dualities created.

WELFARE

Another protection against undercutting labor standards is the system of providing public support for the unemployed or disabled. The welfare system obviously has many functions (Piven and Cloward, 1971); one is protecting people against the desperation of having to sell their labor at any price under any conditions. Welfare curbs the reserve army of the unemployed, who could be used by capital against employed workers to drive down their wages and undermine their organizations. Thus welfare bolsters labor standards in ways not dissimilar to minimum wages. It sets a floor under which no one should be permitted to sink; it aims at eliminating desperate poverty.

Perhaps the clearest instance of this meaning of welfare is unemployment insurance. Without such insurance, an unemployed person would be desperate for a job and forced to take anything that came along. By receiving such insurance coverage one can look around for another job, avoiding the most exploitive offers. But all forms of welfare share this quality. People faced with the choice of a cheap labor job or no job at all can resist the former because of welfare. Thus welfare cuts down on the cheap labor supply.

The principal piece of federal legislation dealing with welfare is the Social Security Act, first passed in 1935. Since then, numerous amendments have been passed and new programs created to the point that welfare has become a very complex system. As of 1980, programs established under the act were administered by the Social Security Administration (SSA). These included Old Age, Survivors, Disability and Health Insurance (OASDHI), popularly known as "Social Security"; Medicare; Supplemental Security Income (SSI), which provided aid in conjunction with states to the needy aged, blind, and disabled; and Aid to Families with Dependent Children (AFDC), under which the federal government provided grants to states.[15]

Coverage under OASDHI was generally compulsory for the self-employed as well as for employees. According to the Social Security

Administration's 1977 Annual Report,[16] "more than nine out of ten people in paid employment and self-employment are covered or eligible for coverage under the social security program." The 1975 *Social Security Bulletin Annual Statistical Supplement* defined who was not eligible:

> In some occupations, employees and self-employed persons are covered only if certain conditions defined in Title II of the Social Security Act are met. These conditions mainly involve meeting minimum earnings requirements or choosing elective or optional coverage. The larger groups affected are (1) self-employed persons (especially farm operators), (2) farm employees, (3) household workers, (4) employees of non-profit organizations, (5) employees of state and local governments, (6) members of religious orders subject to a vow of poverty, (7) persons in family employment, and (8) American citizens working abroad.

As is stated, some of these categories came under optional coverage. But it is significant that the same categories of poor coverage reappear here, namely, farm workers, household workers, the self-employed, and family workers. People working in these lines were again most vulnerable to being forced to sell their labor cheaply.

Apart from Social Security, we have not been able to determine whether any occupational categories were especially likely not to be covered by the various types of welfare. In a sense the occupational distribution of the covered is irrelevent, since at the time of coverage recipients were mainly unemployed. Welfare basically provided aid to the national reserve army of labor who might otherwise be forced to sell their labor cheaply, especially, the aged, women and childen who lacked a male breadwinner, and disadvantaged minorities (for instance, 44.3 percent of families supported on AFDC in 1977 were black, 39.9 percent were white, and 12.2 percent Hispanic,[17] indicating that minorities were heavily overrepresented). Still, it is likely that coverage for these especially vulnerable groups was incomplete and that many of them were forced to accept cheap labor jobs. For those it did cover, welfare provided protection not only to the people who received the aid but also to the employed, who otherwise would have had to compete with the desperately poor.

The welfare system meant that capitalists had difficulty acquiring cheap labor within the nation's border. It therefore served as an incentive for capital to move overseas in its search for cheap labor. Consequently, unemployment tended to grow among the local underclass pushing more and more of them to depend upon welfare. This was the price the U.S. working class (including the subproletariat itself) paid for protecting labor standards, and it was a heavy and growing one.

Immigrant workers occupied a special position in this situation. Regarding OASDHI, many immigrants entered the labor market at such an age that they lost retirement coverage from their home country (if such existed) while not being able to accumulate enough benefits here. Indeed, a representative of the American Committee on Italian Immigration testified before the U.S. House Ways and Means Committee to this effect,[18] urging that international agreements be established so that benefit credits could be transferred across national boundaries. The significance of this loophole extended beyond what happened to the immigrant and his family upon retirement. It also affected their choices while still employed. Knowing they would be poorly covered in case of accident or upon retirement, they would be forced to take actions now that would ensure their own "social security." Establishing a family business, without a forced retirement age, and with the ability to sustain a wife and children even if something should happen to the husband, was one such option.[19]

AFDC also tended to discriminate against immigrants. In 1973 a federal regulation, based on a Supreme Court decision, required that states grant eligibility only to U.S. citizens and permanent residents.[20] Given that many immigrants entered the United States in a variety of other legal capacities, sometimes without legal standing, many were not covered. Thus immigration, especially from cheap labor countries, could serve as another means by which capital circumvented the inaccessibility of its own reserve army of labor and looked overseas. One would thus expect that immigrants from poorer countries would be overrepresented in secondary labor markets.

Welfare acted as a differentiator between local and immigrant poor. On one hand it enabled locals to resist, at least to some extent, the cheap labor role. But it also supported a permanently depressed subproletariat locked into high unemployment. Immigrants who could not get welfare benefits, on the other hand, were forced to become cheap labor. For many this was just another dead end, but in some cases it could, ironically, provide the means for escaping from the underclass in which welfare recipients were trapped. At least this may have been the case for some immigrant Korean small business owners.

Welfare legislation was another arena of class struggle. Capital had an interest in reducing benefits, thereby decreasing their own expenditures and increasing the supply of labor willing to work for low wages at depressed conditions. Numerous examples could be adduced of efforts by business groups to reform the welfare laws and essentially throw people off welfare and back into the labor market where they could be forced to work cheaply. For instance, in September 1977 the Senate Finance Committee voted in favor of a provision to let states force welfare clients to work off their benefits at special jobs paying below the federal minimum wage in many cases.

Labor's position on welfare was more ambivalent than capital's. On the one hand, they had an interest in preserving the system as a protection against undercutting. On the other hand, welfare payments were costly, and workers resented the taxes they entailed. From labor's perspective, full employment at above minimum wages was far preferable to having to support an underclass.

In sum, the welfare system contributed to the creation of dualities in the labor market by providing differential protection for different categories of people. Especially vulnerable were some immigrants, and probably also important segments of the local poor. Although we have been unable to obtain data on who exactly is not covered by the complex welfare system, it would seem that such information would go a long way toward revealing who works in the cheap labor sector, or secondary labor market. Without an available labor force, such a sector would of course cease to exist.

IMMIGRATION LAW

The issue of capital's undercutting labor standards has probably most frequently been confronted in the area of immigration. The uneven development of capitalism, compounded by the underdeveloping consequences of imperialism, led to the impoverishment of many nations; the populations of these Third World countries were willing and sometimes eager to move to wealthier nations to take advantage of job opportunities. And capital in the more developed societies was more than willing to encourage their immigration, sometimes even going so far as to actively recruit immigrant workers.

Not all immigrant workers are cheap labor. Immigrants from developed countries who have needed skills, or who have had experience with labor organizing, are unlikely to constitute cheap labor. However, the very fact of immigration acts as a damper on the price of labor, both for the immigrants themselves and for the labor market as a whole. In the former case, adjustment problems such as language difficulties or job discrimination may lead immigrants, at least temporarily, to accept wages and work conditions they might otherwise reject. And in general an increase in supply drives the price of labor down—and the larger the flow of immigration, the greater will be the negative impact on wages.

For these reasons one would expect that, within a capitalist system, local workers would have an immediate interest in controlling immigration. By restricting the growth of the labor force they could boost their own wages and work conditions. Capital, on the contrary, should generally support immigration as a means of preventing the upgrading of labor standards.

These natural interests of capital and labor regarding immigration become exaggerated when the immigrants come from impoverished backgrounds, have little familiarity with labor organizing, or are bound by contracts. Cheap-labor immigrants are especially attractive to capital since they can be used to drive the price of labor below the normal level. In addition they can be used to undermine labor organizations among local workers. Differences among immigrants in terms of cheapness have thus differentiated the responses of local classes: the cheaper the immigrants, the more likely is capital to favor their entrance, and labor to favor their exclusion.

Admittedly, this picture is somewhat oversimplified. Neither capital nor labor is completely monolithic in its interests regarding immigration, so that segments of each may take opposing positions for a variety of reasons. For instance, particularly politicized segments of the working class may feel that opposing immigration divides the world's working class and, thus, undermines the long-term interests of labor in overthrowing capitalism as a system. Also, changing economic conditions may sharpen or cool the intensity with which the general interests are pursued. In times of depression, local labor is more likely to push for strictures than in times of prosperity, while capital may be more willing to tolerate exclusion movements under the former condition in order to avoid paying subsistence for the jobless. Despite these refinements and exceptions, the general rule under capitalism is that capital favors immigration, and labor opposes it.

Immigration policy has thus been an arena in which the class struggle between capital and local labor over access to cheap labor has been waged. The history of U.S. immigration law and policy reveals the scars of this struggle. For instance, the Chinese Exclusion Act of 1882 was fought for by local workers and opposed by capital (Saxton, 1971). Similarly efforts to exclude immigrants from Japan at the turn of the century received strong labor backing (Daniels, 1966: 16–30).

Recent U.S. immigration policy appears to favor the interests of local labor over capital. The 1965 Immigration and Nationality Act set severe limitations on the number of immigrants permitted to enter the country. A total of 290,000 per year were allowed in under a quota system. In addition certain classes of people, mainly immediate relatives of U.S. citizens, were exempt from numerical limitations, bringing the total who actually entered up to almost 400,000 each year by the late 1970s. The annual absorption rate relative to the U.S. population was about 0.18 percent, compared to a rate of 1.2 percent at the turn of the century (North, 1971: 4). Thus, in terms of rate of entry, the law favored tight controls.

The law established seven ranked preference categories (see chapter 5). As we saw before, the first-, second-, fourth-, and fifth-preference categories dealt with relatives of U.S. citizens and permanent residents. Apparently humanitarian in purpose, the reuniting of families also had implications for the price of labor. It discouraged the entry of single, young adult men who were cheap in part because the employer (and state) did not have to provide for their families, or the reproduction of the work force (Burawoy, 1976: Castells, 1975). The emphasis on families in the U.S. law underscored labor's desire to prevent this kind of immigration.

Only two of the seven preference categories explicitly admitted workers: the third and sixth levels. For most of the preference levels, "fall-down" to the next preference was permitted if the category was not filled. This was not the case for the third and sixth preference; their numerical ceiling was set strictly. Furthermore, family members were included in the quota of 58,000. If we assume that each immigrant worker headed a family of four, the total number of workers permitted to enter drops to 14,500 per year. Clearly vast numbers of workers were not being encouraged to enter this country.

A way that immigrant workers could circumvent these restrictions was by coming in as nonpreference immigrants. This category was made up entirely of fall-down from higher categories and thus was not a reliable method of ensuring the entry of laborers.

Even those workers who were admitted under preference-levels three and six were subject to careful controls. Third preference visas were restricted to people of exceptional ability in the professions, sciences, and arts whose services were "sought by an employer in the United States," while sixth-preference visas were given only to persons capable of performing specified jobs "for which a shortage of employable and willing persons exists in the United States."[21] The two classes above and nonpreference immigrant workers were required to obtain a labor certificate from the U.S. Labor Department ensuring that they would not undermine the local labor force. Labor certificates were issued only if "there are not sufficient workers in the United States who are able, willing, qualified, and available" to do the work, and if "the employment of such aliens will not adversely affect the wages and working conditions of the workers in the United States similarly employed."[22] Adverse effect was determined by whether the wage offered by the prospective employer was lower than the prevailing wage.

Despite protection for local labor standards in immigration law, there were many legal (as well as illegal) loopholes. For instance, while the labor certification program aimed at preventing undercutting, nonquota immigrants and those coming in under relatives' preferences did not require a labor certificate. Moreover, large numbers of nonimmigrants entered each year, some of whom worked but did not come under the labor certification program. As few as one in thirteen entering alien workers who were here legally acquired a labor certificate (North, 1971: 61–62), making the provision largely ineffective in terms of actually preventing labor competition.

Apart from legal entrants, cheap labor continued to enter the country in the form of undocumented workers. Their illegal status itself contributed considerably to their cheapness, making them easy prey to extreme exploitation. It is not difficult to demonstrate that segments of the U.S. capitalist class have an interest in the perpetuation of this immigration while local workers, especially those most directly in competition with immigrants, would generally like to see greater restrictions. Perhaps vacillating policy and practice regarding control of the U.S.–Mexican border reflected these cross-pressures, though that very inconsistency served capital's interests to some extent by maintaining the illegality—hence ultraexploitability—of these workers. Needless to say, this "loophole" in the structure of legal protection for labor standards provided many of the workers for the secondary labor market. In other words, the presence of cheap labor immigrants permitted the development or persistence of a cheap labor sector.

CONCLUSION

This legal review has shown how efforts to protect labor standards and to prevent capital from using cheap labor have been promulgated in U.S. law. But legal protection was incomplete, leaving numerous loopholes in the law permitting the utilization of cheap labor. These loopholes help to explain where cheap labor concentrated in the economy.

We found that weaknesses in legal protection tended to overlap and to concentrate in certain sectors. The most vulnerable industries were agriculture, retail, service, and private-household service. And the most vulnerable form of enterprise was small business, especially those firms relying on family labor. The reasons for poor protection of these sectors are complex, but they probably include a legacy of weak labor organizing, meaning workers in these sectors could not push as hard for protections. Once unprotected, an industry tends to recruit the most vulnerable, unorganized workers, enabling it to maintain its unprotected status. A vested interest develops on the part of employers to keep their industry low-wage since they have not been required to develop the technology to compensate for rising labor costs. Thus a vicious circle develops that keeps an industry reliant on cheap labor.

The existence of protective legislation has led capital to seek out ways of circumventing the protections. These have been multiple, including moving to states where legal protections (and unionism) are weak or fleeing overseas to cheap labor countries. Another re-

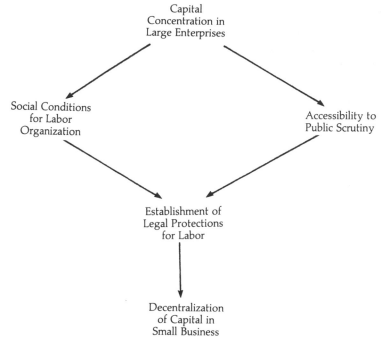

Figure 4 Forces Creating the Concentration of Cheap Labor in Small Businesses

sponse, given the loophole in the law for small business, has been to decentralize. If big capital runs many small businesses instead of a few large, centralized plants, it can avoid the creation of social conditions that promote a strong labor movement, while simultaneously avoiding close legal scrutiny. Decentralization permits big capital to take advantage of the cheapness of labor in the small business sector, and permits some of the surplus generated in that sector to be extracted by big business. Figure 4 summarizes the major processes that have led to this result. Needless to say, once labor becomes aware capital is using this loophoole, it is likely to make efforts to plug it.

The gaps in the grid of protection for U.S. labor standards provided a framework into which immigrant cheap labor could be pushed. In this chapter we have presented a possible motive for such pushing by the U.S. capitalist class: to circumvent high local labor standards. But a reasonable motive does not ensure that that action will be taken. In the next three chapters, therefore, we try to demonstrate that Korean business—during the period of this study—was indeed utilized in the suggested manner. In chapter 14 we establish that Korean small business was a form of cheap labor; chapter 15 examines the ways in which U.S. big business made use of Korean enterprises; while chapter 16 presents evidence to support the contention that Korean concentration in small business was, to a certain extent, a product of efforts to push immigrants into a particular type of economic adaptation. We do not mean to suggest that there was a vast conspiracy against Korean immigrants to make them entrepreneurs against their will. But neither was their entrepreneurial concentration strictly a matter of free choice or cultural proclivity. The social system in which they found themselves exerted subtle influences such that their choices were channeled in one direction rather than another.

14

The Cheapness of Korean Immigrant Small Business

We have suggested that Koreans, along with other immigrants, played the role of cheap labor in the United States. We have also suggested that the small businesses operated by the immigrants disguised the cheap labor role but nevertheless permitted that role to be played in an otherwise protected U.S. labor market. In this chapter we focus on these issues by addressing three interrelated questions: First, how can small business be seen as a form of cheap labor? Second, why was Korean immigrant labor cheap? And third, why did immigrants, as opposed to locals, tend to run cheap small businesses? The data in support of much of the argument put forth in this chapter have already been presented in previous chapters. Our purpose here is to synthesize the Korean information into a coherent argument.

SMALL BUSINESS AS A FORM OF CHEAP LABOR[1]

It is unusual to think of small business as a form of labor. One usually thinks of businesses as employing labor, but not the business itself or the entrepreneur who runs it as a form of labor. In contrast we contend that the entire makeup of the small business—including the entrepreneur and his/her employees—constitutes a form of labor and that the small business form in particular makes that labor cheap.[2]

Let us start by analyzing the role of the entrepreneur or business owner-operator. In many big businesses the owner is a shadowy figure or set of figures who have invested their capital and expect a return on it based on the labor of others. Investors of this sort definitely do not constitute labor. But in the case of small business, the chief investor is typically also the manager of the business. He/she works there and contributes to the labor effort that earns profits.

As we have seen in chapter 7, three-quarters of Korean businesses employed no wage labor; they were entirely run by the owners. Thus the whole labor component of a firm was handled by the entrepreneur and his or her family. The labor of the entrepreneur can be examined like any other job in terms of labor standards. For instance, we can assess the equivalent of wages by examining how much the entrepreneur earns per hour as take-home pay. We can assess hours of work, fringe benefits—such as medical coverage, Social Security benefits, unemployment coverage—health and safety standards, and so forth connected with the entrepreneur's job.

Without repeating data already covered in chapters 7 and 11, it is evident that the labor standards under which the typical Korean entrepreneur operated were low relative to the average U.S. worker. The Korean entrepreneur tended to work long hours. He/she earned a low profit margin, or wage equivalent, particularly if one takes into account the family members who worked in the shop. We cannot make a precise estimate of the hourly earnings of an individual Korean immigrant shopowner working in a typical store but, from all the evidence we have presented, it was probably below minimum wage. Furthermore, the owner did not earn overtime pay for the long hours he/she put in. And fringe benefits were spotty or nonexistent.

Put another way, running an owner-operated small business of the type run by Koreans was a form of dirty work (Oppenheimer, 1974). It was hard and tiring. It demanded many long and tedious hours of work, day in and day out. It entailed great risks, with little of a cushion of security if one failed. Merely looked at as a form of labor, running a small owner-operated business was an undersirable job by U.S. labor standards.

To see the owner of a small business as a worker implies that there was an employer who made use of this labor. It suggests that the hard work, long hours, and low pay of the entrepreneur benefited others. This, we shall argue, was indeed the case, even though the employer–employee relationship was hidden in the small business form. Instead of openly employing the small business owner as a wage worker, where the surplus earned by the investor from the labor of others was open and evident for all to see, the small business form masked the fact that others benefited from the entrepreneur's hard work. The ways in which Korean small business enhanced the profits of others will be thoroughly explored in the next chapter.

The fact that small business owners were apparently independent, with the fruits of their hard labor evidently only accruing to themselves, spurred entrepreneurs to worker harder and accept worse conditions. As long as they did not realize that they were being exploited by others, they would put out a maximum of effort. They would work much harder than the average wage-earning employee, who clearly saw that his or her extra effort mainly benefited the boss.

Finally, the apparent independence of small businesses made it exceedingly difficult for the owners to organize to protect themselves against exploitation.[3] Small business owners were ununionized workers. Their conditions of work discouraged the formation of unions, since they were dispersed and rarely had an opportunity to come together to compare grievances. Furthermore, the masked nature of their exploitation hindered their ability to perceive it, hence to see the necessity for forming protective alliances. In other words the small business form politically subdued its chief workers, the owner-operators. Their hidden employers could take advantage of these unorganized workers in a way that was impossible with unionized wage labor.

Apart from entrepreneurs, Korean businesses sometimes employed other workers. These can be divided into two categories: unpaid family labor, and paid wage labor. In both cases the small business form contributed to the cheapness of these employees.

Unpaid family labor reveals with stark clarity the cheapness of labor associated with the small business form. Unpaid family workers simply shared the profits of the business, adding to the number of hours of work put into it. The "wage rate" of small business owners therefore must be calculated on the basis of family labor as well, reducing the hourly earnings still further. The unpaid family worker was an ideal employee. He or she identified completely with the business owner and served as a loyal and hard-working contributor to the firm. Unionizing family workers was, of course, out of the question. Their primary loyalty was to the family and its business.

No doubt unpaid family members sometimes chafed under the domination of the business owner. The children who worked in the business (a situation that benefited from exceptions in the standard child labor laws) may have wished their parents would give them more spending money and let them work fewer hours in the family business. They may have contrasted their hard work with their age-peers whose parents did not run small businesses, and resented the demands placed upon them. But the discontent was unlikely to take the form of business—labor relations. The conflict between employer and employee was submerged in the conflict between parents and children. The open antagonism of interests between capital and labor was lost in the obvious commonality of interests between members of the same family.

Small businesses varied in the degree to which their paid employees resembled unpaid family workers, ranging from a totally objective capital—labor relationship much like that found in big business to a close, paternalistic relationship in which employees were treated almost like family. Many of the firms classified as small business by the U.S. government clearly fell at the capital—labor end of this continuum. With a hundred or more employees they were really "small" big businesses, run exactly like larger enterprises but on a lesser scale.

In the Korean immigrants' world, most businesses were at the most miniscule end of the continuum, as we saw in chapter 8. However, there was some variation in terms of number of employees. Generally we expect that the smaller the number of employees, and the more similar they are in ethnicity to the owner, the more paternalistic or familistic will be the labor relations in the business.

In Korean businesses where wage labor was employed, the small business form served to cheapen labor. Employees in such firms tended—like the owners—to work long hours for little remuneration, with few fringe benefits and under substandard work conditions. They were also very unlikely to be members of labor unions or to engage in militant action. The acceptance of such conditions was partially a product of the small business form itself.

The conditions of wage labor in small business were unconducive to the development of class consciousness and class conflict. When only a handful of employees worked in a business, they tended to develop personal relationships with the employer. They saw how hard the owner and his family worked, and they worked alongside them as fellows. Personal knowledge encouraged loyalty and bonds of mutual obligation, making it very difficult for employees to place themselves in conflict with employers. Besides, with no union protections, conflict would have led to a quick firing and replacement by someone eager to take the job who would not complain.

Just as the owners of small businesses were dispersed and unable to compare grievances, so were employees. Employees of small businesses rarely had an opportunity to meet with one another as a group. They were not in a position to develop the bonds and friendships that could develop among fellow workers of a large factory. The personal relations developing out of the work situation were vertical (between owner and employee) rather than horizontal (among employees). Thus a shared class consciousness as employees was unlikely to develop. Hence unionism was virtually nonexistent in small businesses of the Korean type.

Ethnic homogeneity contributed to the blurring of class antagonisms. Korean owners of small business could call upon common ethnicity as a kind of primordial tie, similar to the family tie, to encourage worker loyalty and extra effort. Since both employer and employee were members of the same ethnic community, they both had an interest in seeing its businesses flourish. On the one hand, the working class of the ethnic community was more likely to find jobs there than anywhere else, and business owners were likely to put whatever charitable contributions they made into ethnic community well-being. On the other hand, the ethnic small-business owner could call upon nationalistic loyalties, much as did President Park in South Korea, to get the working class to accept temporary sacrifices for the good of the ethnic community.

Non-Korean employees of Korean firms, in contrast, were much more likely to be treated strictly as employees. In this case one would anticipate that class antagonisms would be more likely to arise. However, the dispersion of firms and isolation of employees from one another would still curb the development of class consciousness even among this stratum.

Apart from the internal dynamics of small business, the legal milieu in which they operated (described in chapter 13) contributed to low labor standards in small businesses. Workers in such firms were less protected than were workers in larger firms. Thus any efforts made by small business employees to organize and develop class consciousness faced special obstacles. Their unions could more easily be crushed by employers without recourse to the courts. Besides, the very smallness and dispersion of such firms made them more difficult to police for violations of labor standards.

Another way to look at immigrant small business of the Korean variety is to see it as a kind of precapitalist enterprise embedded within capitalist America. Its labor intensity, its small size, its paternalistic ties between employer and employee, its use of unpaid family labor, and its lack of clear class delineation bespeak a bygone era or earlier mode of production. The lack of class consciousness and formation of class organizations reflected the level of development of the Korean firm. The structure of these firms and their internal dynamics resembled more closely businesses in the preindustrial United States than they resembled the modern capitalist corporation. These premodern characteristics help to explain the cheapness of small business. Proletarian consciousness and the protection of labor standards are outgrowths of capitalist development. Korean small business had not reached that stage.

The use of ethnic and family bonds as a means of labor control, along with other uses of ethnicity to run businesses more efficiently, was another way in which Korean enterprise retained precapitalist features. Instead of utilizing universalistic principles as the basis for business decisions, ethnic particularism was employed—and ironically, found to be more efficient and cheaper. Of course it was no accident that ethnic business tended to concentrate in those sectors of the economy that were least developed, least rationalized, and least mechanized—namely, retail and services. Premodern business practices suited the least-modernized sectors and even had advantages there. The cheapness of the small business form, and especially of ethnic small business, thus suited well the niche it occupied in the economy.

THE CAUSES OF KOREAN "CHEAPNESS"

So far we have suggested that small business can be seen as a form of dirty work or cheap labor. Our next task is to explain why immigrants, and Koreans in particular, constituted the kind of cheap labor that would fill this dirty-work role. Then, in this chapter's final section, we consider the problem of why locals tended not to fill this role.

Immigrants from countries like South Korea were cheap labor for three interrelated reasons. First, conditions in their homeland led the immigrants to leave with certain customs and expectations that conditioned their attitudes toward work. Second, the immigrant situation played a part in shaping their choices. And third, the concentration in ethnic small business itself acted as a depressant on immigrant labor, helping to maintain its cheapness. Let us consider each of these in turn.

Conditions in South Korea

Part two described the situation of labor in South Korea. During the 1970s, South Korean workers earned about one-tenth of U.S. workers' wages. They worked an average of ten extra hours per week. And they were much less likely to belong to labor organizations and to engage in strikes. To some extent these features were a product of level of development, reflecting the early stages of transition to capitalism. And to some extent they were a product of political repression.

Many people left South Korea precisely because of the low wages and poor working conditions there. The United States was seen as a land of opportunity, where wages were high and work conditions far superior. Immigrants came here because of their dissatisfactions with the homeland's conditions, eager to better their situation.

A large discrepancy in accustomed labor standards, however, could make a difference in the conditions people were willing to tolerate. Obviously people do not set an upper ceiling on the material well-being they are willing to accept. No doubt most people would like to be as rich and do as little work as possible. But on the other end of the scale, there may be differences in the minimal standards of living and labor people are willing to tolerate. What is intolerable to those who have lived in a society where the minimum wage is $3 an hour may seem very attractive to someone who comes from a society where the average wage is $3 a day.

Because of the conditions in their homeland, Korean immigrants were no strangers to hard work at low pay. They were used to it. They expected it. They might be eager to escape it as an inevitable feature of life for themselves and their children, but they also had the experience to know they could survive it, if necessary.

Korean immigrants thus entered this country with an orientation toward work that was different from most locals. They were willing to work very hard in the short run in order to escape the necessity of having to work hard all their lives, or especially of their children having to do so. While short-term sacrifice entailed in this kind of behavior might, in fact, mean that the immigrants worked harder for a period than they had ever had to in South Korea, nevertheless the discrepancy between their immediate past and the present was not so great as it would have been for a local worker. An immigrant shop-keeper might extend his workweek from fifty to sixty hours after arriving here, a 20 percent increase. But for a local person used to working forty hours a week, the jump to sixty hours would represent a 50-percent increase.

We do not suggest that the past experience of hard work and low wages in South Korea entirely explains Korean entrepreneurship. Clearly this is not the whole story, since immigrants from some other cheap labor backgrounds did not necessarily transform their willing-ness to work hard into entrepreneurship. Many simply worked as cheap labor in the employ of others. But a recent history of hard work and low wages was a contributory factor to entrepreneurship since it was a necessary ingredient of it. Korean immigrants may have had other necessary ingredients as well, but without this one, the dirty work of the small shop would not have been acceptable to them.

There was, in other words, a congruence between the labor standards brought by the immigrants from their homeland and the labor standards demanded by small business. That the immigrants slipped themselves into this particular niche was, therefore, not too surprising.

THE IMMIGRANT SITUATION

The immigration process itself contributed to the cheapness of Korean labor in several ways. First of all, most came with a severe English-language handicap. Needless to say this greatly restricted their job opportunities, not only directly by limiting the number of jobs they could reasonably do, but also indirectly by limiting access to job-placement agencies. Many new immigrant groups suffered from this handicap, but Koreans were among the worst off. Filipinos and Indians, for instance, typically knew far more English on arrival, while the lengthy presence and size of the Mexican minority meant that Spanish had some recognition as a semiofficial language. The newness of Korean immigration and the absence of any links between Korean and local languages added to the difficulty of adaptation.

Another disadvantage coming from immigration itself was plain discrimination. Some employers were reluctant to hire people they viewed as foreigners, an issue that was exacerbated by Koreans also constituting a racial minority. Parlin (1976), for example, has demonstrated that even Asian immigrant professionals who were educated in the United States suffered some job discrimination.

Worse still was the built-in discrimination of California's licensing procedures. The California Advisory Committee to the U.S. Commission on Civil Rights investigated licensing boards in the four health professions (pharmacy, medicine, nursing, and dentistry) in which Korean immigrants were most likely to have been trained. In the case of pharmacists the foreign-trained were not even permitted to take the licensing examination, while in the others command of English played the most critical role in determining one's chances of passing. Consequently, many Korean immigrants were unable to practice the profession for which they were trained.[4]

As a consequence of language disability and job discrimination, Korean options were severely limited. There were only a few jobs for which immigrants could apply with any hope of success. As a result they were crowded into a narrow, highly competitive labor market, driving down the price of their labor.

Apart from restricted opportunities, immigrant status legally weakens a person's bargaining power with employers and thus is likely to depress wages. Immigrants must undergo a probationary period before they can become citizens, during which they are under considerable pressure not to make trouble. For the Korean immigrants of our study, a potential threat of deportation hung over their heads and served to subdue their expressions of anger at exploitive conditions.

Being an immigrant weakens one's position in terms of welfare laws as well. The Immigration and Nationality Act states that persons likely to become a public charge should not be granted admittance to the United States. In addition if any immigrant becomes a public charge within five years of admittance—for causes that could be shown to have arisen before the immigrant's entry—he/she is subject to deportation. While often unobserved, in part due to peculiarities in the law, this feature puts an unusual pressure on immigrants to find work. Unlike indigenous minorities and the local poor, immigrants can be forced to accept bargains out of desperation. The absence (or weakness) of the welfare alternative, therefore, serves to depress the price of immigrant labor.[5]

Apart from the negative aspects of immigration, there is also a positive inducement to work hard and make sacrifices in the short run, in order to get established in the new life. Immigrants typically undergo considerable sacrifice in order to come to a new country. They are eager to set themselves up. They have made a positive choice about where to live and do not usually come ready to criticize, to cause trouble, and to join opposition movements. The authoritarian character of the South Korean state perhaps enhanced a wariness with respect to complaining about conditions. For these reasons also, recent Korean immigrants were unlikely prospects for joining unions or making demands to improve their work situation.

The low price of labor arising out of the Korean immigrant situation itself was also an aid to entrepreneurship. Because of the lack of viable or attractive alternatives for the immigrant, self-employment would often appear to be his or her best choice. Certainly many disadvantaged populations—such as Third World urban migrants who have been displaced from peasant agriculture—engage in various forms of self-employment such as peddling or service work in order to survive. Similarly, the so-called irregular economy in black neighborhoods often entails forms of self-employment in the absence of adequate job opportunities. Self-employment among Korean immigrants may have had some of the same roots. Because they could only get the most undesirable jobs (or no jobs at all), the dirty work of small business was relatively attractive to immigrants.

In addition, rather ironically, entrepreneurship may have provided more security for Korean immigrants than would regular employment. For locals self-employment seemed to be the riskiest of fields to enter, while wage and salary work appeared to promise greater security. But for immigrants—whose job options tended to cluster in occupations of highest turnover—self-employment probably represented greater security. Furthermore, as suggested earlier, Koreans like other immigrants could not easily transfer social security and other old-age benefits with them to their new homeland. Since small business did not have a mandatory retirement age, and since a business could be passed on to one's children who might aid in one's support, a small business could provide better coverage for old age. Besides, it could provide security and immediate job opportunities for one's relatives who were also likely to face disabilities in the job market.

The low price of immigrant labor also enables immigrant entrepreneurs to have access to a cheaper-than-average labor supply, giving them an edge against nonimmigrant competitors in terms of labor costs. Given that immigrants often face job discrimination or the absence of job opportunities, they are likely to be funneled into the ethnic job market, leading to crowding and lowered wages.

In sum the immigrant experience itself, irrespective of prior standards of living and labor in the homeland, can serve to cheapen labor, mainly through the special disadvantages faced by immigrants. As a result, the low labor standards of small business can appear attractive relative to the real options immigrants confront. The long hours and low profit margin of a small store will look good compared to working as a sewer in a garment factory having unpredictable hours, no promise of a raise, and no security in one's old age.

If we combine the two causes of cheapness discussed so far we find that they complement one another. Labor standards in South Korea set a cultural backdrop to the willingness of immigrants to live with standards unacceptable in the United States. However, many immigrant Korean entrepreneurs found they had to work even harder here than they had in Korea. This extra workload can be attributed to the demands and disadvantages of the immigrant situation.

CONCENTRATION IN ETHNIC SMALL BUSINESS

A third source of Korean immigrants' labor cheapness was the fact that they concentrated in ethnic small businesses. We have already discussed how the small business form itself served as a type of cheap labor. And we have suggested that ethnicity could be used to heighten certain of the cheap features of small business, by calling upon ties of loyalty. Thus the ethnic small business was a particularly efficient mechanism for employing people to work hard for low remuneration.

That Korean immigrants concentrated in small business, then, acted as an additional factor in keeping their labor cheap for longer than one might otherwise expect. People who come from countries with low labor standards are likely to adjust these standards upward reasonably quickly in the new environment. Immigrants can overcome some of their initial disadvantages in the labor market, acquire citizenship rights, and approach equality with local workers. And they can come to learn of the local labor movement, join unions, or form labor organizations of their own. But participation in small business tends to retard these processes.

Concentration in small business encouraged immigrant Koreans to work especially long hours, to sacrifice for their families, and retarded the development of class consciousness. In addition the very isolation of workers in small shops, separated from the mainstream of American workers, maintained in the immigrants a special attitude regarding acceptable labor standards. The result was that concentration in ethnic small business probably kept Korean labor standards low for longer than they might otherwise have been. The form of small business itself served as a depressant and helped to keep immigrant labor cheap.

There was thus an interaction between small business and cheap labor. On the one hand, small business was dependent on cheap labor. If Korean immigrant labor was not cheap, Koreans would not have had this prerequisite for successfully establishing small businesses. On the other hand, small business helped to keep Korean immigrant labor cheap by the retention of precapitalist forms, including paternalism. Cheap labor was both the cause and effect of Korean concentration in small business.

In conclusion Korean immigrant labor was cheap for three reasons: (1) labor standards in their homeland, (2) disabilities associated with immigrant status (compounded by being a racial minority), and (3) their concentration in small business. The cheapness of Korean labor in turn helps to explain why Koreans concentrated in small business. Cheap labor (willingness to work long hours for low remuneration) was a necessity for the kind of businesses Koreans operated.

We do not mean to suggest that Koreans entered small business only because their labor was cheap. Nor do we imply that they were merely pushed into small businesses against their will. As discussed in chapter 11, Koreans recognized positively the advantages of their orientation to work. They saw local residents as lazy and unenterprising.

Thus Koreans eagerly seized an opportunity to which locals seemed blinded. The drive toward entrepreneurial success was facilitated by the cheapness of Korean labor, but it is not fully explained by it. Nevertheless, that cheapness was a necessary component of entre-

preneurship without which Koreans would surely have been unable
to run small businesses.

LOCAL WORKERS AND THE AMERICAN DREAM

Owning a small business is the American Dream. It represents an
opportunity to escape from the position in society one was born into.
It is an avenue out of the working class, an opportunity to make
money and even possibly to become a millionaire. With a small
investment, an entrepreneur with a good idea and some luck may hit
it big and transform his life. The belief in this possibility has always
been a feature of American society. This belief curtails discontent in
its lower echelons and gives the impression that the United States is
a land of opportunity where gigantic leaps on the social scale are still
possible. Small business is seen as an important gateway to social
mobility. The opportunity to engage in it suggests that the United
States is still an open society, without rigid classes from which one
cannot escape.

We are faced with a paradox. Although some Americans of the
late 1970s still continued to pursue the American Dream of running a
business of their own, the figures indicate that the vast majority did
not. Disadvantaged minorities, the sector of the population most in
need of social mobility, had a lower-than-average business concentration. But even working-class and lower-middle-class whites, whom
one would presume might have the wherewithal to start a business,
showed low rates of entrepreneurship.

Some might argue that the American Dream was dead. With the
massive concentration of the economy in giant corporations and
government bureaucracies, the opportunities for social mobility via
small business had dried up. The Dream had retreated to the status of
a myth, describing bygone patterns rather than current realities.

The paradox is this: at the same time that native-born Americans
had largely given up on the American Dream, immigrants arriving
from certain countries like South Korea were pursuing the Dream
with enthusiasm and not infrequent success. They entered small
business in much higher proportions than did native-born residents.
They believed in this avenue to social mobility, and they were
willing to put in the investment of savings and effort necessary to
make it work.

If immigrants managed to find the opportunities to engage in small business, then obviously these opportunities still existed, even in a highly concentrated economy like the United States. The puzzle we must confront is, if the opportunities for small business in this country were not dead, why did local residents—including local minorities—not take advantage of them? Why was the American Dream left to non-American immigrants?

The answer has several facets. First of all, small business was not the great opportunity it was assumed to be for most who entered it. The failure rate was high, estimated at 50 percent in the first five years. Undoubtedly, the smaller the business, the higher was the likely failure rate. For most people with little capital, entrepreneurship was a gamble that they were likely to lose. Why bother to take the chance?

Second, as we have already suggested, small business was a form of dirty work. It entailed considerable hardship. Most native-born workers were unwilling to put in the long hours of tedious labor for low remuneration necessary to make a success of a small business. The low labor standards of the job were unacceptable.

Nor was it necessary for most local residents to accept this form of dirty work. Most had other job opportunities that paid better, had shorter hours, and provided greater security. True, on one hand, by sticking to a regular wage or salary job the worker limited his or her opportunities for becoming very wealthy. But on the other hand, one also did not risk one's shirt nor the possibility of working oneself to death in the process. The average American worker might wistfully long for greater independence, and wish he or she could make a million dollars in a clever business venture, but most were accommodated to the reality that these were longshots, with a heavy price to be paid.

Put another way, the average American worker had been thoroughly proletarianized. They had come to accept the inevitability of the dominance of capitalism and of capitalist productive relations. And they had fought to better their condition within those relations rather than outside of them. As a result work conditions, including pay and hours, had improved over the years within the capitalist labor market. The choice to enter small business meant foresaking these benefits. Most local workers were not willing to pay the price. And because most of them had reasonable jobs, they had no need to.

A substantial segment of the local population, however, did not

have good jobs. This segment included the local poor, welfare recipients, disadvantaged minorities, the unemployed, and low-paid
employees in the competitive sector. Why did these populations not
follow the route charted by groups like the Korean immigrants?

In part the answer lies in degree of disadvantage. The local poor
were likely to have less capital and less education than the immigrants. There may also have been cultural and experiential differences such that the immigrants were more familiar with the
requirements of running a business enterprise. However, on top of
this, we suspect that the motivations of the local disadvantaged were
closer to local nondisadvantaged workers than they were to the
immigrants. Like their better-employed compatriots, the local poor
had a certain conception of the length of a reasonable workday, of
how hard they ought to expect to work, of how much leisure time a
good life entailed, and so forth. The local poor had similar aspirations to the regular workers. They were equally proletarianized.
Their goal was not risky self-employment but a good-paying, secure
job with decent labor standards.

Also in contrast to immigrants, the local poor had alternatives
enabling them to avoid the dirty work of running a small business.
Welfare, unemployment insurance—indeed the whole apparatus of
support for the poor under the welfare state—gave the local poor a
choice. It would appear that more people preferred to receive state
payments than to accept the high risk and poor work conditions of
small business enterprise.

Not only did immigrants suffer relative handicaps in terms of
good alternatives to self-employment; they also enjoyed positive
benefits when it came to small business. Some came with capital, a
decided advantage in getting established in entrepreneurship. But
even for those who came with little or no capital, ethnic solidarity
(including access to a cheap and reliable group of employees) could
play a substantial role in minimizing the risk of small business. For
immigrants with a strong ethnic community, the failure rate for small
business was much lower than it was for the average local resident.
An increased probability of success, of not losing one's life savings,
made entrepreneurship a more attractive option to an immigrant. The
risks were less.

Another factor that might enter the equation features prominently
in middleman-minority theory. Local residents, whether employed in

Table 68.   Forces Propelling Immigrants Versus Locals to
Enter Small Business

	Korean Immigrants	*Local Workers*	*Local Poor*
Negative inducements			
Alternative Jobs	No	Yes	No
Welfare Support	No	Yes	Yes
Proletarianization	No	Yes	Yes
Positive Facilitators			
Capital	Yes	Yes	No
Ethnic Support	Yes	No	No
Low Labor Standards	Yes	No	No
Stranger Status	Yes	No	No

good jobs or not, have bonds to the local community that make it difficult to engage in commercial relations with them. Most people do not like to have to "sell," particularly to their friends and neighbors. By being outsiders to local social relations, immigrants are relatively immune from the discomforts of commerce.

By way of summary, table 68 presents an assessment of the key factors that either push people into small business (negative inducements) or make it easier for them to enter it (positive facilitators). Generally local residents, whether regularly employed or poor, came up short on both sides, although each group's reasons differed somewhat. Regularly employed local workers probably could acquire capital at least as easily as the Koreans, which was not the case for the local poor. Yet, the local poor were less diverted from small business by the attractiveness of other current job opportunities. Still, overall one can see that a combination of weak negative inducements and positive facilitators made entrepreneurship an unattractive choice for locals.

The payoffs shown in table 68 might alter under changing economic conditions. With a major recession, the quality of alternative jobs and even welfare support could decline, leading small business to appear relatively more attractive to local residents. Indeed it has been widely observed that self-employment is inversely related to economic conditions. The reasons are clear: negative inducements rise during periods of economic decline. Of course, the fact that positive facilitators do not increase suggests that the new small businesses are also likely to show a high failure rate, no doubt exacerbated by the hard times.

There is a final paradox in all this. Some Koreans were very successful in small business and proved that the hard work and willingness to invest in it paid off. The American Dream, a faded illusion for most locals, truly worked for some immigrants. As a result a certain amount of resentment was stirred up among local residents, who saw the immigrants as grabbing opportunities and attaining the kind of social mobility they could not. Immigrants leapfrogged over locals. Success in small business brought its own price: hostile relations with the surrounding community.

CONCLUSION

In this chapter we established that Korean-immigrant small business can be seen as a form of cheap labor, or dirty work. We argued that even the entrepreneur in a small business can be seen as a type of worker, and that he or she works under conditions lower than those generally acceptable by U.S. standards. Employees, including family members of the owner, also generally work under conditions of low standards, making the immigrant shop as a whole a cheap operation.

We considered why immigrants—and Koreans in particular— might be available to play a cheap labor role, concluding that conditions in South Korea, the immigrant situation, and the organization of work around small business all play a part. Important in our analysis was the idea that Korean small business represents a precapitalist form in certain respects. We contrasted the condition of immigrants with that of the U.S. working class, including its impoverished sector, in order to explain why Koreans and others like them pursue the "opportunity" for social mobility afforded by small business when locals do not. Among our major conclusions was the idea that local workers are not willing, and do not need, to accept the work conditions and high risk associated with small business. More proletarianized than immigrants, native-born workers would rather improve conditions within capitalist social relations than move outside them to return to a petit bourgeois form.

15

The Use of Korean Small Business by
U.S. Capital

In the previous chapter we looked at Korean immigrant small business as a form of labor, suggesting the existence of a hidden employer who took advantage of the cheapness of the Korean shop. In this chapter we want to pursue that theme by examining who such an employer might be. We contend that sectors of the U.S. capitalist class have had direct and indirect linkages to small business of the Korean type; thus they have been able to take advantage of the cheap labor found in these firms.

The relationship between U.S. big business and Korean immigrant small business can be seen as an instance of the articulation of different modes of production. Korean enterprise was essentially a precapitalist form, or a form with major precapitalist features, depending as it did on ethnic and paternalistic rather than contractual bonds. Instead of such precapitalist firms failing to survive in capitalist America because of being outmoded, they survived surprisingly well. Far from destroying all precapitalist forms, capitalism appears to adapt to such forms and take advantage of them.

The observation that capitalism does not necessarily destroy all precapitalist forms has been widely recognized in the Third World. Capitalist soical relations coexist with peasant agriculture. Capitalist firms use the subsistence sector as a way of cheaply reproducing the labor force. Indeed, it has been contended that capitalist ruling classes sometimes actively recreate (or even newly create) precapitalist social relations in order to be able to take advantage of their cheapening features. The system of apartheid and migrant labor in South Africa is a clear instance of maintaining and actively resuscitating a precapitalist subsistence sector as a prop to capitalism.

This idea also applies to one of the most advanced of capitalist countries, the United States. The presence of a precapitalist small business sector could be made use of by elements of the big business sector. Thus, instead of disappearing under the apparent domination and superiority of giant corporations, these small businesses have been not only permitted to survive but even subtly cultivated and encouraged.

Underlying all the particular ways in which Korean enterprise has been made use of by U.S. capital is cheapness. Because of its precapitalist features, the Korean small shop during the time of this study was run exceedingly cheaply. It was a haven of cheap labor. The very organization of this labor in diffusely distributed small businesses with precapitalist relations kept the labor cheap. If Korean immigrants had been simply absorbed into the regular U.S. labor force, they would have quickly lost their cheapness. Because of labor law, described in chapter 13, employers could not readily employ Korean at lower-than-average rates. And the conditions of their work would have led the immigrants to begin to demand fair treatment in line with their fellow workers.

The segregation of Korean immigrants in a precapitalist sector thus kept their labor cheap for a longer period. The immigrant small business sector was an island of cheap labor, cut off from the mainstream of the American working class. Just as U.S. capital could take advantage of precapitalist social relations in the Third World, so it could do so on its own soil. The relations between U.S. capital and immigrant small business can be seen as having reproduced the relations between the U.S. and South Korea on a very reduced scale, within the political jurisdiction of the United States.

With the articulation of modes of production, U.S. capitalists did not directly employ the immigrants who worked so hard in their small businesses. Nevertheless, through various linkages between big business and small business sectors, some of the benefits of the cheap labor of the Korean firm worked their way up (one might say "trickled up") to the big business sector in the form of enhanced profits. In this sense, segments of the U.S. big business community exploited the labor of immigrant entrepreneurs and their families.

By any standards, the Korean immigrant small-business community was a tiny drop in the bucket of U.S. capitalism. It had little detectable impact on the GNP. Thus the reader might wonder whether the profits to be earned by large corporations from the Korean business sector were of any significance. We would agree that Koreans, by themselves, probably had little impact on corporate profits. But when we consider that Korean immigrants were not alone in engaging in ethnic enterprise based on cheap labor, the significance of the phenomenon grows. Immigrants from other Far Eastern countries, from South Asia, from the Middle East, from Cuba, and so forth swelled the ranks of precapitalist small business. In assessing the impact of Korean enterprise, we need to place it in this broader context.

One can ask whether all U.S. small business, nonimmigrant as well as immigrant, should be seen as a precapitalist form that articulates with the more developed corporate sector. Perhaps it should be. However, we contend that immigrant small business has had special features that make it more suitable for the purpose. These features have included: the greater initial cheapness of immigrant labor based on homeland conditions and immigrant status, and the greater ability of immigrants from certain countries to make use of strong ethnic communal ties to keep labor cheap. Although all small business may be exploited by big business, immigrant small business has been more vulnerable to exploitation. Thus it has occupied a distinctive position in the U.S. political economy.

This chapter is divided into three sections. In the first two sections we examine two clear cases of direct linkage between big and small businesses: franchising and subcontracting. The third section considers some other ways in which Korean small business has been made use of by local big business, even when no direct linkages exist between the two groups.

FRANCHISING

Franchising is a system that permits corporations to make direct use of small business. Indeed it has been described as "corporate small business." While there has been considerable concern over potential and actual fraud and corruption in this relationship,[1] even the normal, legal franchising relationship can be seen as a form of exploitation similar to the normal relationship between capital and labor.

Franchising began with automobile and truck dealerships, gasoline service stations, and soft-drink bottling. These so-called traditional fields have continued to dominate franchising, accounting for almost 80 percent of sales in 1976.[2] However, new franchising lines have been emerging and growing fast. These include a variety of retail and service industries.

Table 69.   Types of Franchised Business, 1975

	Sales (in thousands of dollars)	Number of Establishments
Automobile and Truck Dealers	90,538,000	31,846
Gasoline Service Stations	43,895,000	189,480
Fast Food Restaurants	12,261,964	42,983
Retailing (Nonfood)	9,031,073	37,179
Soft Drink Bottlers	6,998,000	2,398
Automotive Products and Services	5,006,200	47,454
Hotels and Motels	4,539,904	5,413
Convenience Stores	3,905,600	13,513
Rental Services (Auto-truck)	1,474,597	6,490
Retailing (Food other than convenience stores)	1,445,290	11,761
Business Aids and Services	1,396,966	22,159
Construction, Home Improvement, Maintenance and Cleaning Services	639,128	10,821
Laundry and Dry Cleaning	214,209	3,170
Educational Products and Services	172,694	1,304
Recreation, Entertainment, Travel	162,265	3,410
Rental Services (Equipment)	156,619	1,436
Campgrounds	60,954	1,014
Miscellaneous	414,464	2,707
Total	182,312,927	434,538

Source: U.S. Department of Commerce, *Franchising in the Economy, 1975–77*, 1976: 41.

Table 69 shows the kinds of businesses that were being franchised in the mid-1970s, their sales volume, and the number of establishments. As can be seen, franchising had become a multibillion dollar business. It accounted for about 12 percent of the GNP and almost one-third of all retail sales.[3] It employed 3.5 million people including proprietors and part-time workers.[4] Indeed franchising had become a multinational enterprise. In 1975, 222 franchisors had almost 11,000 outlets in foreign countries.[5]

Both dollar volume and number of franchise establishments grew dramatically in the 1970s. In 1969 there were about 384,000 establishments making approximately $120 billion in sales. In 1977 there were over 450,000 outlets, bringing in over $253 billion in sales.[6] This represented a 15 percent increase in number of establishments and over a doubling in dollar volume of sales.

Franchising was a concentrated industry. In 1975 among 1115 nontraditional franchisors, only 45 companies (4 percent) accounted for 58 percent of outlets (122,069 establishments) and 50 percent of sales ($20,471,200).[7] Concentration was also prevalent in the traditional lines.[8]

Not only was the industry concentrated, it was also being acquired by large U.S. corporations. According to Timothy H. Fine, general counsel for the National Franchise Association Coalition, testifying before the U.S. Senate Committee on Commerce:

> Today franchisors are big business—including many conglomerates. They read among *Fortune's* 500 largest corporations. As examples the following large diversified corporations purchased successful franchising systems:
>
> (1) United Fruit has purchased both A&W Root Beer and Baskin-Robbins Ice Cream;
> (2) Great Western United, the Colorado-based conglomerate, has purchased the large Shakey's Pizza franchise system;
> (3) Consolidated Foods has purchased Chicken Delight franchise system;
> (4) General Foods has purchased Burger Chef;
> (5) Pillsbury has purchased Burger King;
> (6) Pet, Inc. has gained control of Stuckey's;
> (7) Union Tank Car has absorbed the Lindsay chain; and
> (8) Household Finance has purchased the Ben Franklin system, White Stores, and the National Car Rental franchise system.[9]

As a government report stated: "Established companies are ... turning to franchising as means of expanding their distribution systems by either converting their wholly owned outlets or by launching new programs."[10] Franchising thus has not been a backwater of the U.S. economy. It has become a way in which big capital can intrude into the retailing and service sectors while taking advantage of the small entrepreneur.

The chairman of a House investigating committee succinctly described the nature of the exchange between the franchisor and franchisee: "Big business usually supplies the know-how and marketing expertise while small business supplies the labor and capital."[11] Franchisors typically provide at least some of the following services; advice on location, store design, equipment and inventory, established reputation, mass advertising, standardized accounting and operating procedures, and tax information.[12]

On the other side, the franchisee provides the franchisor with several tangible and less tangible benefits. First, the franchisee invests his own capital in the business and bears the risks of failure. Second, of more direct benefit, the franchisee usually agrees to pay the franchisor a percentage of gross sales and/or to purchase equipment and inventory from the franchisor. In 1975, nontraditional franchisors sold about $4 billion worth of products and services to their outlets,[13] a figure that would rise enormously if traditional lines were included.

Each franchise had its own rules. A common franchise in which Koreans participated, 7-Eleven convenience stores (run by Southland Corporation) required an initial cash payment of $5000 for "training and store set-up," plus purchase of the entire inventory valued at $20,000, though the franchisee could retire this debt gradually.[14] In addition Southland Corporation took 55 percent of the store's gross profit, claiming that this charge covered overhead, advertising, most property taxes and the like. Payroll and other "in-store controllable expenses" were deducted from the franchisee's gross profit.[15]

Less tangible benefits included the following: The franchise system enabled corporations to penetrate difficult markets including high-crime areas (such as ghettos and barrios) or low-volume markets (such as the corner "dribble-in" trade). The franchisor benefited from the willingness of the small entrepreneur to work long hours and to make use of unpaid family labor without having to pay directly for that labor itself. The franchisor could also take advantage of the labor-management and control features of small business, thereby avoiding the dangers of unionization in its outlets.

For instance, one informant told us that service stations in Los Angeles used to be unionized. The oil companies had been forced to pay union wages as well as fringe benefits. Franchising placed the burden of wages and benefits on the franchisee, who was only required to pay minimum wage. And service stations were only required to pay overtime wages if they had a volume of trade in excess of 240,000 gallons. Unpaid family labor was permitted. Thus franchising enabled big companies to circumvent statutory labor standards.

The cheapness of labor in a franchise outlet was of benefit to the franchisor in that its profits depended on their success. The more cheaply they could operate, the more competitive they would be; hence, the greater would be the franchisor's volume and profit. This relationship was most evident and direct when franchisors took a percentage of gross sales. But even the selling of inventory to outlets depended on their ability to turn it over quickly, which in turn depended on long hours and low prices.

Franchising faced some legal challenges in the 1970s. One important issue was the repurchasing of franchised stores by the parent company so that they were operated by employee managements rather than by independent proprietors. Of 434,538 establishments, 80,561 or 19 percent were company-owned in 1975. Franchisors and suppliers were accused of wanting to take over distribution "now that they have accumulated the capital, generally from the efforts of franchisees."[16] Franchisors were said to have repurchased the most successful stores, leaving marginal and poorly located shops to the franchisees.[17] After 1975 the trend toward franchisor takeovers was reversed and an increasing number of outlets were converted from company ownership to franchise ownership.

Interestingly, the difference between owners and managers of franchise outlets was minimal. The manager still had to bear the financial risk, still paid for the business license and taxes, and his or her salary depended on the profits of the outlet. The only difference was that managers lost some control.[18] This similarity points up the degree to which the franchisee could be seen as a kind of "employee" or "labor" for the big companies.

Another aspect of the franchisee-as-labor theme was the gross disparity in power between franchisor and franchisee.[19] By being able to threaten termination (firing), franchisors had the ability to force unfavorable terms on their outlets, including requiring them to purchase franchisor-sponsored products at noncompetitive prices, and so on.[20]

The power imbalance encouraged franchisees to organize around their common interests. The National Franchise Association Coalition brought together such groups as the McDonald's Operators' Association, the Kentucky Fried Chicken National Association, and the American Association of Independent Newspaper Distributors.[21] Some franchisee groups were independent, but others were organized by the franchisor in order to avoid confrontation.[22] These can be seen as the equivalent of company unions.

Perhaps most indicative of the labor aspect of franchising was the fact that efforts were made by government agencies to require franchisors to bargain collectively with their franchisees. Franchisors bitterly resisted such a requirement, for obvious reasons. Yet the fact that it was raised suggests the degree to which the relationship can be, and has been, seen as one resembling labor and management.[23]

In sum, we contend that franchising was a say in which big business made use of the labor of small proprietors. Even though the relationship was formally a contract between two independent business owners, in fact, the imbalance of power, the flow of profits, and who did the work made the situation remakably like an employer–employee relationship, but without the benefits of unions for the employees.

KOREANS IN FRANCHISING

Koreans have been active in franchising, but their exact involvement is difficult to measure. Using the 1977 Korean directory, we counted franchises listed at that time. Our count probably understates the true extent of Korean franchising for several reasons. First, we did not have a master list of franchisors with which to compare Korean stores.[24] Second, the name of an outlet did not necessarily reveal its legal status. For example, a news agency could have been a franchise of one newspaper but not reveal this in its name. Third, there could be franchiselike relationships that would not be well known to the public, as in a restaurant setting up one or two new outlets. Fourth, on one hand, franchises were among the businesses least likely to appear in the Korean directory because they were least likely to be oriented to a Korean clientele. On the other hand, Korean ethnic food stores, which had a high probability of being listed in the directory, were not franchised, or at least not by U.S. companies.

These difficulties aside, we found some evidence of franchising by Korean business owners. By far the most important form was gasoline service stations. Thus there were 44 Shell stations, 33 Union Oil, 29 Mobil, 21 Texaco, 8 Arco, 4 Exxon, and 2 Chevron dealerships for a total of 141 Korean service stations in the directory. In addition Koreans ran 8 auto supply outlets for Shell, Texaco, Union Oil, and Mobil.

Next in importance numerically were insurance salespeople. It is not clear that insurance was, strictly speaking, franchised, but it had the characteristic of corporate small business. In any case, forty-two

Korean insurance officers were linked to the names of giant corporations. These included nine Prudential insurance salespersons, nine Equitable, eight California Western, six New York Life, four John Hancock, three Metropolitan, and one representative each of State Farm, Occidental, and Massachusetts.

Third in importance were American-food restaurants. Koreans operated twenty-nine known outlets, franchising from Altadena Dairy, Orange Julius, Der Wienerschnitzel, Foster's Freeze, Winchell's Donuts, and some others. In addition they operated some grocery stores, the most important of which were 7-Eleven convenience stores. Nine 7-Eleven outlets were listed in the directory, though we have reason to believe this was an undercount. The parent corporation of 7-Eleven, Southland Corporation, had a total revenue of over $2 billion in 1976 and net earnings of over $40 million (Southland Corporation, 1977: 13).

Apart from these major franchise lines, the directory listed nine Korean automobile dealers (for example, Chrysler Plymouth). There was one Avon dealer, a Hallmark gift shop, several hotels (Hilton, Sheraton, Travel Lodge), a few real estate outlets (including five Red Carpet offices), and some other scattered franchises.

These examples of franchising did not represent the bulk of Korean enterprise in the Los Angeles area. But they do show that segments of Korean small business were linked to corporations that are among the biggest and most powerful of U.S. big businesses.

The gains to be had from franchising by the franchisor are not restricted to immigrant entrepreneurs. Most franchisees have been white Americans.[25] Still, immigrants have made a difference in two respects: they are more available as franchisees than the average citizen, and they are especially desirable as franchisees.

Our strongest evidence that Korean immigrants were so perceived by franchisors comes from an interview with a sales manager from Shell Oil Company, who was responsible for selling distributorships in the central section of Los Angeles. He reported that there were forty-five Korean dealers for Shell (as of September 1978) and that they constituted between 5 and 10 percent of Shell's total dealers in Los Angeles County. He made it clear that Shell considered Koreans to be desirable dealers and that the company recruited as many Koreans as it could obtain.

Several reasons for a preference for Koreans were mentioned.

These included the fact that they were "aggressive businessmen" and were "not shy." ("They want to make money.") In addition, they were seen to represent the company well by being honest, clean, and personable. The key to a preference for Koreans, however, appeared to lie in two characteristics: their willingness to work hard, and their willingness to accept dealerships in the inner city or black areas of Los Angeles.

On the question of hard work, the sales manager noted that service station hours were regulated by the California Franchise Law and federal Petroleum Marketing Act. These laws were aimed at protecting dealers from having to keep stations open twenty-four hours a day. At the time of the interview, gasoline franchisors could only require stations on major arterial routes to stay open twenty-four hours; others had a limit of eighteen hours, from 6:00 A.M. to 12:00 P.M. Shell could, of course, keep its stations open for shorter hours; but they preferred to have fewer stations and keep them open for longer hours.

The willingness and ability of Korean dealers to keep their stations open long hours was attractive to Shell. The sales manager recognized the importance of Korean unpaid family labor in this regard. As he put it: "Koreans operate a family business whereas Anglo dealers hire employees." Among the Koreans, family members took shifts working the station. Koreans operated most of Shell's twenty-four-hour stations, he reported. "They do more business than non-Korean dealers." When we asked why local people did not take more dealerships he replied: "Americans are lazy." He attributed the difference to a lower standard of living in Korea. We should note that Korean willingness to work long hours undercut the standards set by the law, standards that were presumably established to protect the gas station franchisee. Koreans were being used by Shell to bypass this legal standard.

The sales manager pointed out that most Korean Shell dealers clustered in central Los Angeles, Inglewood, Compton, and Downey, areas with high concentrations of black population. We inquired whether Shell assigned Koreans to these locations. He replied that they did not. Under the California Franchise Law dealers could buy and sell their own franchises to whomever they pleased. Koreans bought dealerships from Anglo owners in the inner city who were vacating them.

Despite the fact that Shell was not actively involved in this transition, the company appeared to promote it indirectly. The number of gasoline service stations in the inner city had been declining. According to the sales manager, the chief reason for this decline was the rise in crime in inner-city locations. Shell wanted to keep dealerships open there because "we know that the volume and profit potential are still there." Indeed, Shell's average volume of sales was "substantially higher" there than elsewhere. "The inner-city gas stations are the most profitable ones Shell owns."

The sales manager perceived Koreans as actively pursuing inner-city dealerships. Koreans were willing to accept the greater risk of crime in exchange for a high volume of business. He quoted a Korean Shell dealer, a leader in the Korean community, who stated that Shell had more Korean dealers than other companies because of Shell's concentration in the inner city. Shell dealerships were therefore especially attractive to Koreans.

Whether Shell favored Koreans because of their willingness to locate in high-crime areas, or Koreans favored Shell for this reason, is immaterial. The point is there was a congruence of interests that joined Shell to Korean dealers in the inner city. Shell clearly benefited from the arrangement, and the company acknowledged its gains.

Ethnic linkages played a role in Korean acquisition of Shell service stations. According to this sales manager, Koreans acquired business experience by working for a relative, frequently another Shell dealer, before opening their own station. Korean Shell dealers then recommended their kin to Shell for dealerships and, in some cases, even helped to finance them. Although this arrangement was clearly of benefit to Korean entrepreneurs, it also aided Shell in acquiring experienced managers with adequate financing. Once a Korean acquired a Shell dealership, observed the sales manager, "it stays in the family forever." A particular Korean might move to another field, but he would pass his station on to a relative. Thus we discovered a process of ethnic succession, as in the liquor industry, with Koreans buying businesses from Anglos and retaining them in the Korean community.

The revelations of this important interview were confirmed and complemented by interviews with Koreans. One informant said that Koreans were desired by the oil companies because they sold a larger volume of gasoline than non-Koreans. They accomplished this by underselling Anglo competitors. This was achieved by accepting a lower profit margin (perhaps as low as $400 or $500 a month), using unpaid family labor, and eating cheap meals cooked on hot-plates at the station.

Another informant, president of the Korean Petroleum Dealers' Association, told us that Korean dealers were located mainly in the black section of the city. They began leasing stations in appreciable numbers after the Watts riots, when whites did not want to run stations there and blacks were unwilling to patronize white stations. Black entrepreneurs might have stepped in; but—according to the interviewee—they were considered dishonest by clients, who felt they were likely to overcharge, especially on mechanical work. Koreans benefited from stereotypes of Oriental honesty and efficiency. According to this man, Shell gave Koreans a discount on their dealerships in order actively to encourage their application.

In sum, the franchise arrangement clearly benefited the franchisor, regardless of the ethnicity of the franchisee. However, Koreans (and certain other immigrant groups, such as Iranians, Chinese, and Vietnamese) were especially desirable as franchisees because of their willingness to work hard and make use of unpaid family labor, their effective use of ethnic linkages, and their willingness to deal with difficult markets such as the inner city. These characteristics made them more profitable to employ than local people.

Franchising has much in common with ethnic enterprise. It grows by creating branches instead of by increasing the division of labor. It frequently makes use of spacing and pricing agreements. It depends on risk taking, hard work, and thrift. It minimizes real risk by collective means. And, as a labor-intensive line, generally, it benefits from cheap labor. It is thus not surprising that immigrant entrepreneurs and franchisors should have found one another. In a sense, big capital simply took advantage of features the Koreans brought with them.

SUBCONTRACTING

The clearest example of the equation between immigrant small business and cheap labor is found in subcontracting. Here, the small business contracts to perform a job for a larger firm and employs immigrant workers as laborers to perform the work. In other words, subcontracting shops use labor in the standard, wage-earning sense.

However, the small business form intervenes between the worker and the chief employer—the big business that subcontracts the job out—since the small entrepreneur acts as the direct employer. The small business owner serves as a middleman between the employer and the worker, much like the labor contractor of old.

The immigrant subcontractor plays an important role in keeping labor cheap, for all the reasons discussed in chapter 14: small shops are dispersed and therefore difficult to unionize; owners have a personal and paternalistic relationship with workers; owners provide workers with the few jobs available to new, non-English-speaking immigrants and thus can set the terms of employment; and owners can call upon ethnic loyalty and the business interests of the ethnic community as a whole to keep employees working at low wages. Thus subcontractors perform an invaluable function for the large enterprise, which can reduce its costs and avoid unionization.

Unintentionally—from the point of view of the subcontractor—subcontracting increases the level of competition in an industry, driving down prices for big business. In addition it permits big business to limit risk and the impact of fluctuations in demand by maintaining direct control only over the most stable and predictable sectors of an industry, while leaving the least predictable to the small subcontractors who must bid for the work (Waldinger, 1984). Thus the system of subcontracting can be highly beneficial to big businesses. Indeed, even the public sector is beginning to engage in this practice on a widening scale as a way of dealing with budget crises and spiraling costs. International subcontracting, discussed in part two of this volume, is another part of the general trend toward increasing this profitable process.

In the Korean community, subcontracting arose most prominently in two types of businesses: garment factories and maintenance companies. Interestingly, each of these tended to be specialized by gender: garment factories mainly employed women whereas maintenance companies employed men.

Forty-four maintenance companies were listed in the yellow pages of the 1977 Korean directory. We did not investigate them or the industry in any detail. Apparently they provided janitorial services to large office buildings in downtown Los Angeles. They thereby enabled these offices to avoid hiring their own cleaning staff, saving them the cost and trouble of labor management and control (as well as the cost of the most up-to-date equipment). Presumably the Korean firms could do the job at a lower cost than could the building management by hiring their own employees directly.[26]

There were an estimated 350 Korean garment factories in Los Angeles in 1979, employing 18.5 percent of Korean wage workers. Given the significance of this industry among Koreans we decided to examine it in more detail, to see where Korean subcontracting fit inside the larger picture.

THE GARMENT INDUSTRY

According to the 1977 Census of Manufactures, there were in that year 26,505 establishments engaged in the manufacturing of apparel and other textile products in the United States. These establishments accounted for 7.4 percent of all manufacturing firms. They employed 1.3 million workers, or 6.8 percent of the nation's manufacturing work force.

The apparel industry was divided into nine major subcategories, the largest of which was Women's and Misses' Outerwear. The average apparel firm employed 50.3 workers in 1977, a figure quite comparable to the 54.4 average for all manufacturing establishments in the country. However, within the apparel industry, firm size varied greatly by product. The average women's outerwear firm employed 37.8 workers per factory, compared to 121.0 for men's and boys' furnishings.

The American garment industry was not evenly spread among the fifty states. As measured by number of establishments, New York was the largest center, with 7797 firms. In 1977 California ranked second with 4288 establishments, followed by New Jersey and Pennsylvania with almost 2000 firms apiece. Garment firms were increasingly located in the South, particularly in North Carolina, Georgia, Tennessee, and Texas. According to United California Bank[27] Tennessee had especially large manufacturing units, with over one-third employing 250 or more workers per unit. These firms were producing for such manufacturers as Jonathon Logan, Genesco, and Levi-Strauss, as well as for big chain stores like J. C. Penney, Sears, and Montgomery Ward. These garment firms had become "runaways" to the cheap-labor South.

As of 1977 women's garment production was still largely concentrated in the mid-Atlantic states and in California. Of the 11,834 firms enumerated, 4043 or 34.2 percent were in New York. California had 2656 or 22.4 percent. These two states thus accounted for over half of the women's garment factories in the country.

The Census of Manufactures[28] reported 3073 apparel factories in Los Angeles in 1977, making up 71.7 percent of the state's total. Women's apparel factories were even more concentrated in Los Angeles, with 2118 of 2656 firms (79.7 percent) found in the County. Most of Los Angeles' garment factories, indeed close to 70 percent, were thus in the volatile women's outerwear field. (*County Business Patterns, 1977*,[29] reported lower figures in each case, but the pattern was basically the same.) Los Angeles was clearly a major center, both in the state and the country, for the production of women's clothing.

The garment industry was fiercely competitive. According to the Bank of America,[30] no single company monopolized the industry. Indeed, the four largest dress manufacturers accounted for only 7 percent of the total volume of production. *County Business Patterns, 1977*,[31] reveals that 30 percent of apparel firms in Los Angeles employed between one and four persons. Another 33 percent employed between five and nineteen, leaving only 23 percent with over twenty workers. The industry was dominated by small, competitive firms.

If a firm bought fabric, designed, and sold clothing to a retailer, it was considered a manufacturer regardless of who did the labor. In the garment industry there were "inside shops" that did their own cutting and sewing and "outside shops" for which the sewing, and sometimes the cutting, was done by a contractor who produced goods to the manufacturer's specification.[32] Sometimes different terminology was used; for instance, the U.S. Economic Development Administration[33] used "manufacturer" to refer only to shops doing their own sewing, distinguishing them from "apparel jobbers" who contracted out the work. The term "contractor" was also ambiguously used, sometimes referring to the owner of the cloth and sometimes to the sewing-shop owner. To avoid confusion we use the term "manufacturer" to mean the owner of the cloth. Manufacturers may "contract out" the sewing to a "subcontractor."

Contracting was most prevalent in the more volatile and lower-quality branches of the industry, such as women's and misses' outerwear. Bank of America[34] reported that contractors probably produced half of all women's apparel, while the U.S. Economic Development Administration[35] stated that "within the women's and misses' dress group, contractors are the most numerous type of employer." Indeed this was probably the most competitive sector of the entire industry. And it was here that minorities and immigrants were most likely to be found.

Part of the attraction of garment industry subcontracting lay in the ease of entry. Necessary start-up capital was minimal. No special space or lay-out was required to set up sewing machines; an old abandoned building would suffice. Machines could be rented or purchased on installment. The materials being processed were owned by the maufacturer so one need not invest in inventory. Even wages did not need to be on hand before the first consignment: workers were paid when the work was completed and claimed by the manufacturer, who was obliged to pay the subcontractor—by the piece—on delivery. Thus the amount of capital required to open a garment factory in the late 1970s could be as little as $200, according to a Labor Standards Enforcement investigator.

The power relationship between the manufacturer and subcontractor heavily favored the manufacturer. He or she determined everything about the garment, including design, material, and sales. Only the labor of actually making the garment was in the hands of the subcontractor. Given that many subcontractors competed with each other, there was a tendency for the price of subcontracting to be driven down. The U.S. Economic Development Administration[36] stated: "Competition is very intense.... The major form of competition is in pricing and a difference between competitors of a few cents on the cost of processing can result in the loss of business. Contractors are always trying to cut costs."

One important consequence of price competition between subcontractors was that it drove down the price of labor in the industry. Even looking only at firms that were easily accessible to public scrutiny—that is, those enumerated in the *California Labor Market Bulletin*[37]—garment industry wages were found to be among the lowest in California. We interviewed several members of the Korean Sewing Contractors Association of California, a group which was attempting to counter the devastating effects of competition by providing some coordination among subcontractors. One member made this statement:

> Contractors have to pay below minimum wage. In order to survive, they must seek violations. If you don't accept the manufacturer's price, someone else will bid for the work. Contractors have no power.

Another member of the association pointed out that manufacturers set their rates according to the productivity of a highly skilled worker, who could sew up to fifteen dresses a day. Inexperienced workers could sew perhaps two dresses a day. By setting the rates on the assumption of maximum productivity, the subcontractor was compelled to pay inexperienced workers less than the minimum wage.

Jin (1981: 46–47) found that many Korean subcontractors had problems finding experienced workers. Fifteen percent listed "difficulty in obtaining skilled sewing workers" as their most difficult problem; 27 percent listed this as their second most pressing problem; and 12 percent as their third. Korean subcontractors hired many unskilled immigrants and provided them with training. But in the process, they could not meet the standards set by the manufacturer. The discrepancy probably accounted for the prevalence of piece-rate payments among Koreans (and in the industry at large) as subcontractors tried to limit wages to productivity.

Another problem mentioned by members of the Korean Contractors Association was that the contract price for the same style of clothing had not kept pace with inflation. A $4 dress in 1976 still only brought $4 in 1979, the time of the interview. Manufacturers were thus able to pass on the negative impact of inflation to the subcontractor while they took advantage of rising prices. Again the subcontractor was pushed into labor law violations.

On top of these difficulties, Korean subcontractors felt that they faced unique problems arising from their ethnicity. The language handicap made it harder for them to deal effectively with hard-bargaining manufacturers. One association member believed that manufacturers favored giving the first bid to whites, putting Koreans at a disadvantage and forcing them to reduce their bids (and concomitantly, their labor standards).

The Korean Contractors Association favored regulating the industry by making the manufacturer pay an hourly wage for sewing rather than a contract price for a certain number of garments. This meant the association itself realized that what Koreans were providing to the manufacturer was mainly labor rather than products. The myth that the manufacturer was purchasing a product from an independent business, rather than purchasing labor, enabled the manufacturer to ignore the labor-standards implications of his pricing policies, thus leaving the subcontractor to bear the risk of evading the law. In a sense the manufacturer was paying a piece rate for labor by purchasing by the load, yet only the subcontractor was held liable for the resulting labor-standards violations. Caught between manufacturers and state inspectors, the Korean subcontractors had an interest in demystifying the relationship.

The subcontractor occupies a classic middleman position: on the one hand, trying to make the lowest bid to the manufacturer in order to get the work; and on the other, trying to placate the workers even though their wages were necessarily low. This problem could be dealt with by various means. One common solution in the industry was the hiring of illegal aliens; afraid of being turned over to the immigration authorities, they were unlikely to complain about low wages and poor work conditions.

Another solution, undoubtedly more common in the Korean case, was the use of paternalism and ethnic ties to keep workers loyal to the firm. A statistical description of Korean garment factories was presented in Jin (1981). These figures were consistent with the idea of ethnic paternalism. A study of Chinese garment factories in Los Angeles (Li, Wong, and Kwan, 1974), based less on statistics and more on in-depth interviews and direct observation, found considerable evidence of paternalism. Workers were frequently relatives of the owner. Owners would give their employees small gifts or do favors for them. One important favor was allowing the workers to set flexible hours or to take the work home. Women with small children were especially grateful for this arrangement, even though it violated state labor law. It is highly likely that similar employer–employee relations obtained in Korean factories, too.

Subcontractors in the garment industry routinely violated statutory labor standards during the period under study. Violations included below-minimum-wage payment schedules, nonpayment of mandatory overtime, nonpayment of Social Security tax, industrial home work, and substandard working conditions. Taken together these violations define classic garment industry "sweatshops." Recognizing the substandard conditions that existed in this industry, the California Division of Labor Standards conducted surprise raids or "sweeps" of the industry on several occasions in the 1970s (see chapter 12). Results of the first set of sweeps were described as follows in the 1976 *Annual Report of the California Department of Industrial Relations*[38]

> The division [of labor standards enforcement] established in 1976 a "task force" approach to correct widespread violations in the garment manufacturing industry. Investigating teams with bilingual abilities concentrated on that industry for six weeks. During that time, 271 investigations were made, 622 violations affecting over 3,000 employees found and corrected; 5,000 articles being manufactured in illegal homework confiscated; and 48 criminal complaints filed.

An article from that year in the *Los Angeles Times* quoted state .commissioner of labor James Quillin as saying: "We found that illegal homework in the garment industry is a widespread practice and it is rampant. The violations pervade all levels of the industry, although it is most prevalent among small or marginal operators."[39] The same newspaper article reported that most of the charges involved failure to pay minimum wages or failure to keep records of pay, required by law to ensure compliance with minimum wage regulations. Industrial homework was also described as "a device for avoiding state labor laws."

In April and May of 1978 the Division of Labor Standards Enforcement, under the federally funded Concentrated Enforcement Program, conducted a second sweep of the garment industry, this time confined to Los Angeles. They investigated 310 firms and found more than 500 violations. In the 1976 sweep only 2 percent of the workers were found to be Asian. But by 1978 the Asian proportion had risen to 20–30 percent, many of whom were Korean, according to an official involved in the investigation whom we interviewed. Althouth Korean firms were involved in violations of labor standards, their workers were rarely undocumented, in contrast to Hispanic firms or firms employing Hispanic workers.

Another indicator of Korean involvement was an earlier levying of fines by the Division of Labor Standards Enforcement against thirty-two Korean garment factories in April 1974. These subcontractors were charged with intentionally deleting wage records and number of hours worked, giving homework, and unsanitary working conditions. Thirteen of the fined firms were in Los Angeles, the remainder in San Francisco.[40]

An official of the local International Ladies Garment Workers Union (ILGWU) told us there was no pressure on the subcontractor, given the absence of unions, to pay more than minimum wage. Garment manufacturing was mainly a piecework industry. Yet employers set a rate for the piece often forgetting that they were obliged to pay a minimum hourly rate, regardless of what the workers earned per piece. Since there was no negotiated rate for a particular piece, the employer decided the rate himself and, in some cases, never paid the workers at all. In this official's words: "Nonpayment and the payment of less than minimum wages is no small potatoes." He reported that the Labor Commissioner's office, using only unsolicited complaints, had estimated the "rip-off"—in terms of wages not paid—within a ten-mile radius of Los Angeles' city hall; it amounted to a minimum of $1 million per week, or $50 million a year.

"They treat bodies the same way," the union official also stated, meaning that working conditions were as bad as pay. When they ran out of toilet paper, he said, subcontractors supplied newspaper. If a fan broke, they did not bother to repair it. Health and sanitary conditions deteriorated, "all for the worship of the god profit."

This union official saw the subcontractor as caught in a tight situation, with the real power lying in the hands of the manufacturer. The big shopowner was technically supposed to ask for bids and arrive at a mutually agreeable deal. The bid would presumably take labor costs adequately into account. In fact, the manufacturer simply offered a price to the subcontractor on a take-it-or-leave-it basis. The subcontractor then paid his/her workers next to nothing and skimmed what was left off the top.

The union was prohibited by law from involving itself in the price paid by the manufacturer to the subcontractor. Such involvement was seen as restraint of trade. They were only permitted to deal with the issue of wages and work conditions within the subcontractor's shop itself, assuming of course it was a union shop. This is a very important point, as it shows how the small business form could be used to subvert labor standards. "Restraint of trade" could be invoked because the subcontractor was technically an independent businessperson. But in fact, by preventing collective bargaining over the price paid by the manufacturer to the subcontractor, a ceiling could be placed upon the parameters within which the price of labor was determined. In this way, small business helped to provide big business with a terrific reduction in labor costs.

Unionization was weak and declining in the women's garment industry in the late 1970s. ILGWU had 404,914 members in the United States at the end of 1973.[41] But by the end of 1977 U.S. membership had dropped by 74,550—or over 18 percent—to 330,391.[42] Most ILGWU members were congregated in the Northeast. Only 8475, or 2.6 percent of members, were found in the Western States Region in 1977. This number represented a decline from 9381 members in 1973. (Los Angeles accounted for 4048 of the 1977 membership.) According to the 1977 Census of Manufactures, the women's apparel industry employed about 48,100 workers. Thus less than 10 percent of them belonged to the union. Furthermore, since about 22 percent of the nation's women's garment factories were located in Los Angeles, the city was grossly underrepresented in terms of unionization in this industry. Los Angeles may well have represented another "runaway" region from the more unionized Northeast.

Needless to say, the low rate of unionization in Los Angeles contributed to poor conditions in the garment industry. But the state of the industry—including the multiple small shops, dispersed and hidden around the city and run by paternalistic and/or intimidating employers who themselves earned minimal profits—also contributed to the low rate of unionization. Thus immigrant small business played an important role in keeping labor cheap and unorganized, to the benefit of big capital in the garment industry.

Subcontracting is not confined to the garment industry, and our main point regarding it is not limited to that industry. We are suggesting that subcontracting was a disguised form of labor exploitation whereby big business used the independent entrepreneur to keep wages especially low and undermine labor organizing, thereby undercutting local labor standards. In this way, big business made use of the independent entrepreneur and had an interest in fostering entrepreneurship. Since immigrants were especially effective at maintaining the cheapness of the small shop, big business had a special interest in fostering immigrant entrepreneurship.

INDIRECT BENEFITS

Both franchising and subcontracting represent fairly unambiguous links between segments of U.S. capital and Korean immigrant small business. In both cases U.S. capital could take advantage of the cheapness of Korean immigrant labor through the interposition of a Korean middleman or small entrepreneur. The middleman not only helped to mobilize this labor for big capital; he/she also helped to keep it cheap, by its dispersal into small shops, making difficult the evolution of class consciousness among workers and the enforcement of labor standards by public authorities.

However, as we have seen, most of Korean small businesses in Los Angeles were neither franchises nor subcontractors. The most common enterprise was an independent retail or service shop, with no direct ties to a U.S. big business. Were these of any interest to U.S. big capital, or did they merely arise in the face of indifference by the capitalist class?

It is our contention that even nonlinked stores were of value to U.S. capitalists in certain ways. Thus, even if corporations did not actively encourage them, they would be happy to see them spring up. The act of not seeking to have them destroyed may signify that big businesses did perceive that they benefited from the presence of a multitude of immigrant small shops.

Korean retail and service shops in the 1970s served several indirect functions for big business. These included (1) the distribution of U.S. corporate products, (2) the lowering of costs related to reproducing the labor force, (3) the reduction of labor standards and undermining of class struggle, (4) pioneering, (5) unequal exchange, and (6) certain ideological benefits. Let us consider each of these in turn.

Distribution of U.S. Corporate Products

Even though many Korean retailers were not formally dependent on U.S. big businesses, they could still play an important role by helping to distribute their products more effectively. For instance, a Korean liquor store would be of direct relevance to a liquor manufacturer as a means of selling his or her product.

The establishment of a finer network of small stores all over Los

Angeles was of advantage to producers in that it provided more thorough market penetration. Small retail stores can be likened to the capillaries in a blood circulation system. They provide detailed and immediate contact with all points in the market. In a sense Korean small enterprises were akin to the middlemen of colonial regions, such as the Chinese in Southeast Asian and Indians in East Africa. The colonial corporations allowed the local trade to these middlemen while confining themselves to the major import-export trade.

The advantage of using immigrants for small-scale retailing in Los Angeles lay in their willingness to do it at all, and cheaply to boot. The small corner store often had a relatively low volume of trade and typically had to be kept open for long hours, and on weekends and holidays, for it to be profitable. It was a labor-intensive operation. If big producers had had to hire people to sell their products, they would have had to pay hourly minimum wages and overtime, as well as fringe benefits and so forth. The presence of an immigrant-run small store meant that their goods could be distributed at the cost of the profit margin taken by the immigrant, plus the immigrant family's modest costs. Comparing this with hiring his own staff of retailers, the manufacturer came out ahead by using the immigrant entrepreneur. It was cheaper for all the reasons we have been discussing, including the low profit margin the immigrant entrepreneur was willing to sustain, the use of unpaid family labor, and so on.[43]

Especially useful was the reaching of relatively difficult markets. As in franchising, Korean (and other) immigrants were willing to accept market locations that larger enterprises eschewed. These included the corner dribble-in trade and low-income, high-crime, inner-city neighborhoods. These problem markets meant a lower profit margin for big retailers, so they tended to be inadequately covered, leaving "niches" for groups like the Koreans.

The ghetto and barrio are especially interesting, from this point of view, in that locating there gave Koreans the appearance of a classic middleman minority (Blalock, 1967: 79–84; Bonacich, 1973). They acted as the interface between big capital and depressed minorities, providing the latter with the goods sold by the former and bearing some of the hostility (as reflected in high crime rates) toward Anglo America. They also bore the numerous costs of dealing with an impoverished clientele, such as the necessity to extend credit and the risk of never getting repaid in full.

The Korean retail outlet in the ghetto probably made a very low profit margin, all things considered. It is for this reason that large supermarkets and chains tended to withdraw from inner-city locations, leaving them open to enterprising immigrants. But big producers, such as hard-liquor manufacturers, must have been pleased to see the growth of the liquor business among Koreans in South-Central Los Angeles. They sold their product to retailers at a standard rate, regardless of market conditions. It was the immigrant liquor store owner who bore the cost of a ghetto location.

There was an added advantage in using foreigners to run retail outlets. Much theorizing has been done on this point in connection with middleman minorities in general, and there is no need to review that literature in depth here (see Bonacich and Modell, 1980: 29–30). In brief, the point is that foreigners are not involved in local social relations and so are able to maintain a strictly business posture, making them more efficient business operators. Foreigners also tend to stay out of local political issues. For instance, during the United Farm Workers' boycott of Gallo products, Korean grocery stores continued to carry Gallo wines. So, of course, did many larger markets, but the union was more likely to protest these to get them to take Gallo products off their shelves. Partly out of ignorance, and certainly out of lack of involvement, Koreans were impervious to the boycott. This must have been of some comfort to Gallo, and others like them.

LOWERING THE COST OF REPRODUCTION[44]

While Korean retail shops helped U.S. corporations to distribute their products more effectively and cheaply, there were still at least two types of Korean small business that would not be encompassed by this benefit, namely service shops and wholesale and retail outlets for products imported from South Korea. Even these, however, could be of use to local big business in that they helped to reduce consumer costs. A reduction in consumer costs translated into a reduction in the cost of living for members of the U.S. labor force. This in turn reduced the wages large corporations had to pay their employees.

Lowering the cost of reproducing the labor force was not limited to service stores and importing. Retailers also contributed to this benefit to U.S. big business. It is noteworthy that almost all Korean enterprise in Los Angeles was consumer oriented. It concentrated in the production and distribution of goods and services that were necessary to daily life: food and drink, clothing and shoes, gasoline, health care, and cleaning. Korean immigrants were not in the business of producing heavy industrial products. They basically serviced the workers and unemployed of this society. And to the extent that they did it cheaply, they cut the costs of major private industries and also the welfare cost to the state.

REDUCTION IN LABOR STANDARDS

Even when there was no formal link between big business and small immigrant firms, the very existence of those firms tended to serve as a damper on labor standards. If wages were low and working conditions poor in immigrant firms, competing firms were pressured to lower their labor standards accordingly.

More importantly, the presence of a large small-business class served as a damper on the class struggle. A whole group of workers was essentially placed in a position where their consciousness as workers was diminished or even destroyed. Thus unionization was virtually unknown in the average Korean shop.

In a sense the existence of multiple, nonunion, small shops served a kind of union-busting purpose. Unions in industries with many immigrant firms found their membership eroding, as workers either became petty entrepreneurs or worked for petty entrepreneurs with whom they had paternalistic ties. The result was the lowering of labor conflict in that industry, the broad reduction of labor standards, and a dwindling of union membership. The unionized rump was left to fight to defend what seemed to be secure gains in the past.

The garment industry epitomized these processes well. But the effects did not depend on direct subcontracting. The mere presence of a large low-labor-standards sector depressed labor standards in the rest of the labor market, at least in comparable and competing industries. And the mere presence of large numbers of nonunionized workers weakened the labor movement and forced unions to accept concessions.

The union-busting role of small business has not gone unnoticed by the AFL-CIO. In a congressional hearing on independent contractors, dealing primarily with the tax implications of this status, an

AFL-CIO representative testified as follows:

> We strongly urge this subcommittee to sharply limit the use of independent contractor status so that employers will be discouraged from circumventing their responsibilities and contributing to the exploitation of workers. Apart from the tax equity issue, the AFL-CIO is deeply concerned that unscrupulous employers who manipulate the mere form of an employee's work relationship can benefit by having these employees classified as independent contractors. If such machinations are successful, employees will find themselves reclassified and excluded from job protections they now enjoy. For example, if reclassified as independent contractors, employees lose their eligibility for benefits under unemployment compensation program, FUTA. These workers are also required to pay social security taxes at the higher self-employed rates; they do not have withholding for income tax purposes and they lose opportunities for collective bargaining.... The history of labor law in this country is already replete with many challenges by employers on this issue.[45]

The representative went on to argue that other protections—such as minimum wage regulations, the determination of bargaining units under labor-relations law, laws protecting working conditions workers' compensation, and protection against discrimination in hiring and promotion—would all cease to apply to workers who were reclassified as independent contractors rather than employees.[46]

In sum, the AFL-CIO was aware that the substitution of small business for standard employment was a tool used by employers in the class struggle against working-class organization. While no mention was made of immigrant small business in particular, immigrant entrepreneurship necessarily participated in this larger trend.

PIONEERING

A fourth indirect benefit to U.S. capital of Korean immigrant enterprise was the ability of these firms to help chart new fields of endeavor. Koreans tended to concentrate in poorly developed business lines. They focused on industries that were competitive and labor-intensive, with low technological development and low productivity. In other words Koreans concentrated in the less-developed sectors of the economy.

There is a general tendency for newer, less-developed fields gradually to become more developed over time. New technology is invented, capital gets invested, and ownership becomes more concentrated. Small, competitive, labor-intensive firms help to open up these industries, develop a demand for them, and pave the way to later consolidation and takeover. To give a non-Korean example, small, individually owned Mexican restaurants probably laid the groundwork for the establishment of such chains as Taco Bell. Franchising is one obvious mechanism by which big capital takes over these pioneering efforts.

In our study we did not examine whether any takeovers had occurred in the Korean community. Nor did we consider which Korean industries would be especially prone to takeover. At the time of our research the pioneering benefit lay in the realm of speculation. But given that Koreans concentrated in one of the most rapidly expanding industrial sectors of the U.S. economy, the service sector, it seemed highly likely that they were taking some of the risks in charting new avenues for future big business ventures.

The pioneering benefit would not be limited to direct takeovers of particular business lines. Korean enterprise might simply penetrate a locale, increasing business activity there and contributing to a rise in real estate values. Big capital could then cash in on the higher land values. The Koreans essentially would absorb the risks of entering an untested territory. Their success or failure would then point the direction for large-scale investment.

Immigrant enterprise might also be used as a kind of holding action during a period of transition before big capital mustered for a direct takeover. In an unpublished study of Indians in the motel industry, Sucheta Mazumdar[47] found that Indians were permitted to run motels in San Francisco's rundown tenderloin district for a period. But when developers were ready to start moving in, they waged a campaign to drive the immigrants out. During the interim, the Indian entrepreneurs maintained, and perhaps even increased, the value of the property.

Koreatown is a development that has greatly increased property values and brought improvements to a previously rundown section of Los Angeles. It is not inconceivable that, at some point, big capital—either from the United States or South Korea—will develop an interest in this growing commercial region. Little Tokyo in Los Angeles found itself invaded by capital from Japan. Perhaps the small businesses of Koreatown will prove to have been a temporary phase in the transformation of the west-of-downtown sector of Los Angeles.

Unequal Exchange

Korean small business has been located in the competitive sector of what sometimes has been described as a dual economy. The other half of the dual economy has consisted of large, capital-intensive, high-wage, monopolized businesses.

When competitive-sector firms engage in market exchanges with monopoly sector firms they are at a disadvantage. Indeed, a parallel can be drawn between the relationship of monopoly and competitive-sector firms within an advanced capitalist economy and the relationship of advanced capitalist and Third World nations. Third World nations, like the competitive sector, are at a disadvantage in dealing with the more advanced and concentrated economies (Emmanuel, 1972).

The root of the disadvantage lies in the fact that competitive-sector firms depend more heavily on labor. Because of low levels of capital investment, the labor in this sector is relatively unproductive. In exchanging with firms whose high levels of capital investment make labor highly productive, the competitive firm is exchanging an inefficiently produced commodity for an efficiently produced one. Yet because they are involved in a single market, the prices of the products are equalized. The competitive firm, therefore, has to take a lower profit margin, while the monopoly firm earns a higher one. Surplus is thus drained from the former to the latter.

The long hours and hard work of competitive-sector entrepreneurs and their employees reflect an effort to make up this discrepancy, to some extent. They increase their productivity by extending the workday or by intensifying their labor.[48] But even these superhuman efforts cannot make up fully for their disadvantage, and some surplus is drained from them.

Apart from the inherent inequality residing in different levels of labor productivity, there is a large power differential between monopoly and competitive-sector firms, epitomized in the two sector labels. Although most monopoly-sector firms are not true monopolies, they often are able to exercise considerable control over their markets. Through advertising, product differentiation, market research, as well as pricing agreements, they can gain some control over their environments.[49] In contrast competitive-sector firms are thrown into ruthless competition with one another, driving down prices to their absolute minimum. Lacking the ability to cooperate with one another, competitive sector firms are at the mercy of big businesses, who can buy cheaply from them but sell them goods and services at high prices.

Unequal exchange works best under a situation in which each of the sectors specializes in certain goods and services. Thus, the competitive sector should not produce commodities that compete with those produced by the monopoly sector. Instead, it should produce complementary goods and services.

Generally this was the case for Korean immigrant firms in our study. They occupied niches in the economy not filled by big businesses. They did not compete directly with big business. Yet they had to purchase many of their supplies from big businesses at monopoly rates. These purchases included capital, real estate, business equipment, and inventory. Thus not only industrial manufacturers but also bankers, land owners, and speculators had opportunities to earn profits from hard-working Korean entrepreneurs.

It would be an interesting if difficult exercise to try to trace the flow of surplus from Korean small businesses to U.S. big businesses. This would entail a careful monitoring of all purchases and sales of the immigrant firms as well as the terms of these transactions. It would also entail the tracing of purchases by immigrant consumers to sustain their daily lives, since these were costs the immigrant firm had to bear. For example, if an immigrant garment factory sewed a blouse for $4 but the immigrant had to pay $25 for a finished blouse, some surplus was being drained from the immigrant.

IDEOLOGICAL BENEFITS

Apart from money to be made, certain less tangible benefits may also accrue to the capitalist class from the presence of immigrant small businesses. These include the ability to promote the idea that the United States is still a land of opportunity, where poor immigrants can come and rise from rags to riches. The fact that racial minorities are among the immigrant entrepreneurs permits U.S. business owners to claim that the United States is not really a racist society but instead is open to anyone with ambition and an enterprising spirit.

Perhaps the most pointed ideological message to be gleaned from the Korean experience is the importance of hard work. Koreans were touted in the media as paragons of this virtue. And they were shown as benefiting from their work ethic, by being able to climb the social mobility ladder. Needless to say, the promotion of hard work was not just value-free journalism. It carried a heavy ideological message to the U.S. working class: "Work hard and you, too, shall succeed. Don't join unions or make political demands. Don't rely on state handouts. Don't be so lazy and irresponsible. Instead, accept the values of capitalism, just like the Koreans, and you will prove that the American system works."

CONCLUSION

This chapter has attempted to show that Korean enterprise had various links to segments of the American capitalist class. Some of these links are obvious, as in the case of franchising and subcontracting. Some are less overt. But regardless of the degree of open connection, Korean small business served as a cheap labor sector from which both monetary and nonmonetary benefits could be drawn. Korean immigrant enterprise helped U.S. big businesses to earn greater profits. And these small firms helped to undermine the local class struggle. As such, the U.S. capitalist class had an interest in encouraging immigrant entrepreneurship. In the next chapter we consider whether, and how, this was actually accomplished.

16

The Making of Immigrant Small Business

In the previous chapter we tried to show how certain segments of the U.S. capitalist class might benefit from small business enterprise among Immigrants like the Koreans. Seeing a possible gain does not, of course, mean that big business necessarily had anything to do with the proclivity of these minorities to enter the small business field. Indeed there were strong internal forces at work among the Koreans that would lead them to concentrate in the petite bourgeoisie anyway. These included: the absence of good alternative employment, a propensity to be thrifty, an ability to utilize communal and familial resources to develop businesses, and the motivation to get established and be, mobile within the U.S. economy. In addition to these characteristics, which Koreans shared with earlier Asian immigrants, the more recent immigrants came with education and sometimes the capital to enable them to adapt rapidly to a modern economy.

It could be argued, then, that U.S. capital was passive in the formation of immigrant enterprise. Thus, the American capitalist class could take advantage of immigrant enterprise in certain ways, once it had developed, and was, therefore, happy to see it emerge; but U.S. capital took no active steps in its creation. Alternatively, it is possible that big business did not sit idly by but engaged in practices, or pushed for policies, to promote immigrant small business. In this chapter we assess the latter possibility by examining the way in which immigration policy appeared to encourage Koreans to enter small business quite apart from their internal reasons for doing so.

IMMIGRATION POLICY

In chapter 13 we pointed out that immigration law had many provisions in it aimed at protecting local labor standards, including the labor certification program. But at the same time, there were numberous loopholes in this protective structure that permitted, or even encouraged, cheap labor to continue to enter the country.

Most evident, in terms of public attention, was the continued influx of undocumented aliens. Not only did such immigrants not come under the labor certification program, but they were especially exploitable on several grounds, such as legal vulnerability, the tendency to be single males, and so on. Some authors (for example, Burawoy, 1976; Portes, 1977; Samora, 1971) argue that illegal immigration was encouraged by certain segments of U.S. capital and that the Immigration and Naturalization Service (INS) was responsive to their fluctuating demand for cheap labor. Thus, INS varyingly tightened and loosened its hold on the border, acting as a kind of valve that controlled the flow of cheap labor into the country. Whether this model is true or not, the fact remains that the influx of undocumented workers did mean that cheap labor continued to enter the U.S. economy, despite the protections built into the law.

Even for those who entered the United States legally, the protection of local labor standards was poorly maintained. North (1971) found that the labor certification program screened only about one in thirteen arriving alien workers. Some of those not covered were undocumented workers, but other large categories of people, here legally, either worked illegally or worked legally while not requiring labor certification. Among the latter were students (a policy that has since been tightened, perhaps in partial response to North's report), certain kinds of temporary workers, commuters, and visitors for business. Among those here legally but working illegally were non-immigrants who worked while trying to adjust their status to that of immigrant (North, 1971: 61–69).

North's estimate only applied to alien "workers." Among permanent resident immigrants, only those with a stated occupation were considered workers. Yet many legal immigrants, who did not need to state an occupation on arrival, ended up working. Only third-, sixth-, and non-preference immigrants had to be screened by the Labor Department. All relatives who entered under preferences one, two, four, and five did not require labor certification. The same was true for the immediate families of third-, sixth-, and non-preference immigrants. Thus in 1970 North (1971: 37) estimated that of 373,326 immigrants 97,093 (about one-quarter) were issued labor certificates. Of these only 55,452 (15 percent of the total) actually used them. Of course some of the noncertified immigrants were small children,

Table 70.   Percentage of Korean Immigrants Entering the
United States under Different Preference Levels,
1966–1976

Year	Relative Preferences (1,2,4,5)	Occupational Preferences (3,6)	Nonpreference	Total
1966	14.8	83.1	2.1	528
1967	24.6	74.3	1.0	1,718
1968	31.6	68.2	0.1	1,549
1969	36.9	43.7	19.3	2,883
1970	43.3	22.8	33.9	5,056
1971	33.9	24.7	41.4	9,058
1972	34.1	22.1	43.8	12,924
1973	52.9	17.1	30.0	15,703
1974	52.4	21.2	26.4	19,743
1975	67.9	21.3	10.8	19,620
1976	78.1	19.8	2.1	23,783
1977	86.7	13.2	0.2	19,865

Source: INS, *Annual Reports,* 1966–1977: table 7A.

housewives, and the elderly who genuinely had no intention of entering the labor force.

Even if immigrant workers obtained labor certification, the protection provided for local labor standards could often be short term. Since no one traced immigrants after arrival, there was no guarantee that those who took an acceptable first job would remain in it. For all these reasons the labor certification program did not provide much control on the entrance of cheap labor into the U.S. labor market.

Korean immigration showed the loopholes clearly. Table 70 presents the proportion of Koreans who came in under the seven preference levels. At the start of the "new" immigration, 85 percent of Koreans came under preference levels three and six or as nonpreference immigrants, all of which require labor certification. This left only 15 percent who came in as relatives. Actually the 85 percent included the families of people who received labor certification but did not require it themselves. In addition, for all the years, there were immigrants exempt from quota limits as well as nonimmigrants who may have worked. Thus, the proportion of noncertified workers was higher at all times than this table suggests.

As time passed, the proportion of Koreans coming in under the

occupational preferences declined, whereas the proportion coming in
as relatives of those already here expanded to well over four-fifths of
the total. Meanwhile the nonpreference category—which generally
required labor certification (a point we shall return to momentari-
ly)—rose to become the largest category in 1971 and 1972, only to
decline precipitously thereafter.

In sum most Koreans who entered this country, especially in the
the latter 1970s, did not require labor certification, yet most became
workers. Thus there were gaping holes in the protective structure of
the law even for these legal immigrants. The loopholes did not particularly encourage entry into small business, but they did allow a
continued stream of potentially cheap labor to flow into the country,
a point that was of crucial significance in providing a labor force for
small businesses.

INVESTOR'S EXEMPTION

Of most interest to our current topic was a small exemption written
into the regulations for administering the Immigration and Nationality Act (INA) known as the investor's exemption or regulation. For
those who are uninformed about U.S. law, as we were, there were
two bodies of law: legislative and administrative. The INA fell under
the legislative category. The agency designated to administer the
law, in this case the INS, then promulgated rules for its implementation. These appeared in the *Federal Register* and typically went into
effect after an allotted time for public response had passed. They
then became part of the Code of Federal Regulations, or CFR. In
contrast, legislative law appeared in the United States Code, or
USC. Administrative law had its own judicial system under which
challenges and appeals on administrative decisions could be brought.
Decisions on these cases helped to clarify procedure and presumably
influenced the process of creating new rules and regulations.

The investor's regulation exempted a prospective nonpreference
immigrant from requiring a labor certificate provided he or she invested some capital in a business here. We shall, in a moment, present
a detailed history of the evolution of this exemption and try to make
some assessment about the interests behind it. But let us first briefly
point out its significance. This exemption specifically encouraged
immigrants to enter small business as a means by which they could

get an immigrant visa. In itself, this is a noteworthy fact. But on top of that the investment in a small business was linked to the bypassing of the labor certification requirement. In other words, the impact of immigrant small business on the local labor market was purposefully ignored. The U.S. government was implicitly stating that it would not be concerned with the consequences of immigrant small business in terms of potential competition with local available workers in the same lines, or in terms of possible adverse effect on the wages and working conditions of workers in the United States similarly employed—the two provisions of Section 212(2)(14) of the Immigration and Nationality Act that defined labor certification. If immigrant small business was a form of cheap labor, the state would not be cognizant of that fact.

It seems not unreasonable to conclude that this blind eye was not accidental, rather, the exemption was developed in the knowledge that immigrant small business was, indeed, a form of labor standards violation, but one that the government was willing to let slide by. One wonders what interests might have encouraged the creation of this fascinating loophole.

The evolution of the investor's exemption through 1976 followed administrative decisions in a series of cases. There were cases (entitled "Matter of . . .") and rules or amendments to rules (entitled exactly as such). These cases were interspersed over time, suggesting an interplay among them.

Our story begins shortly after the passage of the Immigration and Nationality Act of 1965, with its new labor certification requirement. (Previous immigration law had had some protections, but this one was stronger.) A case involving a self-employed landscape gardener from Tonga (Matter of Talanoa, Int. Dec. No. 1591), which had been through several hearings over the previous few years, was decided on May 17, 1966. His lawyer contended that he did not need a labor certificate because he was an independent contractor.

INS stood firmly on the position that he did need one. In their own words:

> The statute makes no distinction between aliens who will be self-employed and aliens who will be employed by others. The test is whether the alien is seeking to enter the United states to work. It would be an obvious evasion of the intent of the new Act if the alien entered as a self-employed gardener, or as a self-employed

carpenter or painter. If the alien's primary purpose in seeking admission is to perform skilled or unskilled labor, he is within the provisions of section 212(a)(14), unless he is one of the exempt relative classes, irrespective of the entity under which he performs such labor. (*Administrative Decisions*, vol. 11: 633)

They allowed that cases might arise where the nature of the enterprise would mean that it did not fall under section 212(a)(14). However in this case, because his investment in the business was minimal (about $250), and because most of his income derived from his labor as a gardener, he was deemed more akin to a day laborer than an independent entrepreneur. His appeal was dismissed.

On July 23, 1966, an amendment to Chapter I of Title 8 of the Code of Federal Regulations was published in the *Federal Register* (31 FR 10021). Section 212.8 was added to Part 212 of Title 8, specifying categories of immigrants who were exempt from labor certification, including members of the U.S. armed forces, students, and parents and spouses of persons who were already certified or did not require certification. Among the exemptions was 8 CFR 212.8(b)(4), which read as follows:

(b) *Aliens not required to obtain labor certifications.* The following persons are not considered to be within the purview of section 212(a)(14) of the Act and do not require a labor certification: ... (4) an alien who will engage in a commercial or agricultural enterprise in which he has invested or is actively in the process of investing a substantial amount of capital. (31 FR 10021, July 23, 1966)

The announcement in the *Federal Register* did not require the usual response from the public because it was seen as strictly interpretive in nature. It was, therefore, put immediately into effect.

Why did the INS apparently change its stand on this issue? It is hard to know. Perhaps they felt that "substantial capital" guaranteed against the investor's becoming a worker him or herself. An interesting point is that commerce and agriculture were singled out. These, as we have seen earlier, were two of the weakest segments of the U.S. economy in terms of protection of labor standards. Did the framers of the exemption specify them because they felt they were not "labor"? While a case might be made for commerce, surely none could be made for agriculture. In any case, the specification of "commercial enterprise" suggests an even more pointed pushing of immigrants into the niche Koreans, and others like them, came to occupy.

The new regulation was tested on February 10, 1967, in the Matter of Finau (Int. Dec. No. 1700). In this case, the definition of "substantial amount of capital" was at issue. Finau, another Tongan, had invested over $1000 in a landscaping business in which he remodeled and decorated restaurants according to authentic Polynesian style. In deciding this case, the board of appeals took into consideration the fact that his unique skills in no way competed with local workers.

"Substantial amount of capital" was left vague. It was considered to be relative to the nature of the enterprise. Finau was viewed as having met the requirement, since, apart from the $1000 investment, he claimed to have contracts amounting to over $30,000 for future construction. He was seen to have, by then, considerably expanded his initial investment. The fact that he had the know-how, equipment, and facilities to carry on his enterprise were also taken into account.

The INS opposed his appeal on the grounds that "an alien who organizes and creates a commercial enterprise of his own with a small investment of capital that he has earned by performing skilled or unskilled labor cannot avoid the exclusion provisions of section 212(a)(14) unless the alien proves by tangible evidence that his business was established in good faith and that he has the ability and resources to continue and expand the enterprise" (*Administrative Decisions*, vol. 12: 88). They challenged Finau's testimony that he had $30,000 worth of contracts and that his investment was steadily increasing, but they lost the case.

The next case, adjudicated April 17, 1967, again concerned Talanoa. He had, in the interim, been granted another hearing under the new exemption. The major issue raised by the case was that his business had failed almost simultaneously with his hearing and he had entered regular employment. The INS challenged Talanoa's exemption on this basis, while his lawyer contended that there could be no ironclad guarantee of business success and that subsequent events had no bearing on the initial judgment, which should be based on his good-faith intention to enter business and a reasonable chance of success given his abilities and resources. The matter was resolved on the basis of another issue (having to do with changes in regulations regarding adjustment of status) so that this one remained unresolved.

On November 1, 1972, an amendemt was proposed to 8 CFR

212.8(b)(4), this time allowing twenty days for response from the public. It read as follows:

> (b) *Aliens not required to obtain labor certifications* ... (4) an alien who establishes on Form I-526 that he is seeking to enter the United States for the purpose of engaging in a commercial or agricultural enterprise which may reasonably be expected to be of prospective benefit to the economy of the United States and not intended solely to provide a livelihood for the investor and his family, and in which he has invested, or is actively in the process of investing, his own capital, totaling at least $25,000 exclusive of goodwill or personal skills. (37 FR 23274)

Form I-526 was entitled "Request for Determination that Prospective Immigrant is an Investor." Apparently the INS was trying to tighten this gap in the protective structure, making it more difficult for persons to use the exemption.

On January 12, 1973, the INS gave its determination in response to representations from "the public" and amended their proposed rule. They deleted the requirement that the enterprise "reasonably be expected to be of prospective benefit to the economy of the United States and not intended solely to provide a livelihood for the investor and his family." They deleted the words "his own" in front of the word "capital," and changed $25,000 to $10,000. They took out the phrase "exclusive of goodwill and personal skills" and added at the end, "and who establishes that he has had at least 1 year's experience or training qualifying him to engage in such enterprise" (38 FR 1379–1380). The new regulation went into effect February 12, 1973.

In other words, most of the teeth had been taken out of the amendment. Perhaps most significant is the fact that the capital did not need to be the immigrant's. One could presumably acquire advances from others, including lending institutions, that would set one up in business. The low $10,000 minimum made this option even more possible. Again, one wonders from whom the representations came that persuaded the INS to back down.

The next case (Matter of Ko, Int. Dec. No. 2201) concerned a man who ran a shoe store in which he had invested $18,000 but who also worked there as a cashier. The issue was whether or not such work constituted skilled or unskilled labor as defined by the labor certification provision. A lower level had decided it did, but this hearing reversed the decision, arguing that "it cannot be said in any real sense that the applicant's employment in a job that did not exist before he made his investment is unfairly competitive with American labor" (*Administrative Decisions*, vol. 14: 51). Thus job competition was narrowly defined to mean only direct displacement.[2] The ruling also asserted that the investor must be engaged full-time in his enterprise and not work simultaneously for another firm where his employment would violate the labor certification requirement.

The next several cases all tightened the investor's exemption, making it more difficult for persons to come in under it. Why this should have been the case we have not been able to determine from the record. Perhaps it was a response to what was perceived by the INS as excessive use. Or perhaps they felt it was being abused and needed clarification.

Matter of Heitland determined that having money in a bank account or in land speculation did not consititute an "investment" of the sort intended by the exemption. It had to entail "a business venture productive of some service or commodity" (*Administrative Decisions*, vol. 14: 566). Heitland's application predated the amendment to the regulation, therefore he could be judged on either pre- or postamendment criteria, whichever was more favorable to the immigrant. Since his investment of $3400 in a truck and two-way radio was less than $10,000, preamendment criteria were used. The legal details are unimportant for our purposes, but it is interesting to note that Heitland ran a delivery truck for a big firm that subcontracted delivery to many "independent" truckowners. The board decided that this occupation was not substantially different from labor and would thus require normal labor certification.

Matter of Lau mainly determined that the burden of proof rested on the prospective immigrant to establish that he had the required amount and type of investment. Involving a Mobil gas station "owner," Matter of Ahmad denied permanent residence on the grounds of inadequate documentation of investment and of not meeting the $10,000 minimum. Matter of Caralekas concerned a restaurant owner who had sold his business and was now living on the proceeds of the sale. The matter was left undecided, requiring more information.[3]

Matter of Lee concerned a cook in Chinese restaurant who had invested $5000 in the business and had signed a promissory note that he would put in another $5000 if he became a permanent resident. This was not considered adequate based on the amended regulation. Under preamendment conditions, which still applied to his case because of the timing of his petition, it was decided that working as a cook did compete with local labor. Matter of Takayanagi concerned a hairdresser who had bought $10,000 in shares of stock in a corporation operating a beauty salon. This was deemed not to be the kind of investment intended by the exemption, since Takayanagi lacked control over his investment and was employed as a regular worker. Matter of Chiang involved a man who had invested in a business but worked full-time as an employee in another firm. His petition was denied on the grounds that he required labor certification for his employee position.

All of these decisions suggest that the INS wanted a stringent definition of "investor" and was willing to consider small business as a form of job competition (as in Heitland and Lee). But the INS could only do so when using pre—February 12, 1973, criteria. Once the amendment was in force, the $10,000 requirement meant the agency could not take into consideration potential job competition, even in disguised form. Therefore it used such criteria as adequate documentation, or full-time work, or the dealing in commodities and services to narrow the scope of the exemption. Whatever the INS's motives were, the net effect was to push prospective immigrants into a particular kind of enterprise, namely, the owning and operating of small commercial or service shops.

In the *Federal Register*, March 10, 1976, the INS proposed a change in the rule, raising the minimum investment from $10,000 to $50,000 and requiring that the investor be the principal manager of the enterprise and that it employ persons other than the spouse and children of the alien. This time the INS gave a lengthy rationale for these changes:

> The investor exemption from the labor certification requirement provided by 8 CFR 212.8(b)(4) was not designed as, and it must not be allowed to become, a means of circumventing the normal labor certification procedure for skilled or unskilled labor. This exemption was never intended to apply to an alien anticipating an investment in an enterprise which would provide only a livelihood for himself and his family in competition with citizens and permanent resident aliens having similar investments in like enterprises. Neither was it ever intended to facilitate the entry of an alien making an investment in an established enterprise and coming to the United States as an employee in the enterprise in a position having no managerial pre-

rogatives in competition with available workers or workers similarly employed in this country. The minimum capital investment of $10,000 was designed to insure that the alien's primary function with respect to the investment and with respect to the economy would not be as a skilled or unskilled laborer. Experience has shown that a minimum capital investment is totally unrealistic and does not insure the fulfillment of the objectives for which it was created. In addition, the spiraling inflation experienced in the United States during the last three years has served to accentuate the inefficacy of the minimum $10,000 capital as a qualifying investment for purposes of the exemption. Accordingly, it is proposed to amend 8 CFR 212.8(b)(4) to provide for an investment of capital totaling at least $50,000 in an enterprise of which the alien will be the principal manager. (41 FR 10231)

Simultaneously, the Bureau of Security and Consular Affairs of the Department of State, which dealt with the issuance of visas, asked for an amendment to 22 CFR 42.91(2)(14)(d) that was indentical to the INS wording and presumably must always be so. Their discussion of the reasons for the proposed change was somewhat different from that of the INS. Regarding the original intent of the exemption, the bureau stated it was "to facilitate the issuance of immigrant visas to aliens coming to the United States primarily as self-employed investors ... without any consideration of the possible adverse affect ... on the wages, income and working conditions of persons similarly employed or self-employed in the United States" (41 FR 10230). In other words, the bureau was more positive than the INS in seeing the exemption as fostering small business regardless of any resulting competition, even with other small businesses.

Both the State Department and the INS opposed the prospective investor's putting his or her money in an established business. Perhaps they feared that aliens could thereby essentially buy a labor certificate, a point made by the Department of State but not the INS. But regardless of their reasons, a consequence was to push immigrants into entrepreneurship.

As usual, time was permitted to submit written representations concerning the proposed rule change. Since we were engaged in this project at the time, the possibility of getting copies of these representations arose. We wrote to the INS in Washington requesting copies of the pertinent correspondence. We were sent a sheaf of letters. However, the authors' names had been blotted out. We were told that we could appeal the deletion to the deputy attorney general under the Freedom of Information Act if we did so by a certain date.

We immediately sent off an appeal, only to discover that there was a tremendous backlog in the deputy attorney general's office and that they could not get to our case in the allotted time; we learned, however, that we had the right to seek judicial review. At this point, Catch-22 seemed alive and well in Washington.

Three months later we received a letter from a staff attorney assigned to our appeal in the deputy attorney general's office, informing us that she was handling our case. We wrote to her to find out what was happening and to ask if she needed any information. We never heard from her but, after another three months, a second, duplicate sheaf of the letters arrived from the INS, this time with the names left on except in the case of private individuals. Our appeal had won! (We tell this little tale as an illustration of the mysterious workings of the U.S. government, of which we caught a glimpse.)

We hoped, of course, that the letters would reveal the interest groups behind the investor's exemption. In this we were disappointed. Out of thirty-five representations, nineteen came from private law firms (three from the same law firm); six came from organizations (three from the Immigration Committee of the Los Angeles County Bar Association, one each from the headquarters and the Los Angeles chapter of the Association of Immigration and Nationality Lawyers, and one from the Michigan chapter of the National Association of Human Rights Workers); six were identical and seemed to represent a write-in campaign, all apparently from New York law firms; and the remaining four were from private individuals. What we discovered was a layer of lawyers who served as middlemen between pressure groups and the government. One needs to cut through this layer before one can get at the interests. At this point we gave up trying to pursue the matter further since it seemed very unlikely that lawyers would reveal the names of their clients.

Even though they did not provide identities, the letters the INS received tell us something about the interests at work. The following is a summary of each set of letters:

Private individuals

These were very diverse. Three of the four were handwritten. One was written in very poor English and simply asked for more information. Another supported the amendment and asked that the miminum investment be raised, not to $50,000, but to $100,000. This person contended that immigrants were cheating by using the exemption and passing on the same money to others to use again:

> Many times, U.S. residents send the money to his relative overseas and then the same relative comes to the U.S.A. as a visitor with the same money and invests the same money in the business.

He mentioned Los Angeles as one of the prime centers of such abuse.

The remaining two letters were proimmigrant and wanted to weaken the proposed amendment. One wanted to reduce the required capital to $30,000 and gave arguments for the fact that it took time to get established in a business, to grow large enough to hire American citizens, and so forth. He asked for greater leniency in these matters in order to enable immigrants to get established in business.

The last letter in this category made its case from an economic point of view. The author argued that the U.S. economy should be competitive, not protectionist, to curb inflation: "Competition in business through new investment is essential for all citizens of U.S." He contended that immigrants worked harder and their wages were closer to productivity while this was not the case for general workers "due to unholy alliance between business and unions." Imposing a requirement of employing nonfamily members was discriminatory, he argued, since that was not a condition imposed on local small business. Since the country was made up of immigrants, earlier immigrants should not be able to use protectionism against newer immigrants. He suggested that inflation had not risen 500 percent so that a reasonable minimum would now be $15,000. It is hard to assess where this carefully reasoned letter came from. It was anti–big business but also anti-labor. It seemed to stand for the small business ethic.

Write-in

This letter (of which there were six identical copies, suggesting an organized campaign) put forward a counterprosposal: the alien should establish that he had invested $5000—or warrant that he would invest it in a commercial or agricultural enterprise and that he would give a faithful performance bond of $5000 to assure the establishment of such a business within six months. If he failed, he would be subject to deportation. Evidence of the enterprise should be presented by proper documentation, including real estate ownership or a lease for over three years. The need to employ Americans was viewed as unreasonable, as was the $50,000 minimum. In other words, these six letters all wanted to make sure that the immigrant went into small business and remained there.

One of the write-in letters had a bizarre appendix, a letter from Joseph Coors, Executive Vice-President of Adolph Coors Co. (Golden, Colorado). The letter—soliciting support for something only alluded to as "CSFC"—made such statements as:

> Our system of free enterprise is being threatened. And the sad point is that our own government is causing most of our headaches. As members of the business community we have to be concerned about business legislation and regulatory policy in Washington.... The outrageous anti-business legislation being passed in Washington is written largely by professional politicians, political science professors and labor union Bosses who have never had to meet a payroll.

Was this letter appended to give a sign of the kind of backing that existed for the investor's exemption? The exemption was not even mentioned in the letter we were sent, so it is hard to tell. But the letter certainly is suggestive, and comes from exactly the kind of backing one would expect: a beer producer.

Organizations

It is interesting to note that four of the six organization letters originated in Los Angeles. The three from the Immigration Committee of the L.A. Bar Association were written consecutively. The first letter was written before the proposed rule appeared in the *Federal Register*; the association had heard about it through a variety of sources. The second letter came out after the *Federal Register*'s announcement and was almost identical to the first in its arguments. Essentially the association opposed the new provisions, arguing that they were too stringent, unreasonable, and went against the spirit of the law. It favored the continuation of the exemption. If it was being used improperly, it was not the rule that needed changing but its implementation.

The association's third letter included documentation. In an excerpt from an SBA publication, the agency showed that most new small businesses started with a capital outlay of under $3000. Those with an outlay of less than $7500 survived about 50 percent of the time, while those with an investment of over $7500 had an 83-percent chance of success. Most interestingly, the SBA also cited data from the *Franchise Opportunity Handbook*, discussing how little capital was required for certain franchises and how variable were the capital requirements. This suggests a recognition that immigrant investors might become franchisees. In sum, they supported a case by case approach.

The Association of Immigration and Nationality lawyers—as represented by letters from the headquarters in New York and the Los Angeles chapter—objected to the new rule for essentially the same reasons as the L.A. County Bar Association. In addition, they pointed out that the $50,000 minimum would favor rich immigrants over poor and was therefore discriminatory. "Unless the regulation is meant to attract capital rather than persons, the amount to be invested must fluctuate with the business." This is an important point. The purpose of the exemption was indeed to attract persons, not capital, that is, entrepreneurs who could do the *work* and not simply bring in funds. The emphasis on persons rather than capital again points to the labor aspect of this type of immigration.

The "principal manager" provision was attacked on the grounds that it unreasonably prohibited partnerships, a point that was of great relevance to Asian entrepreneurs. Having a voice in directing the operation was seen to be sufficient. (A similar point was made by the L.A. Bar Association.)

In the letter from the Los Angeles chapter of the Association of Immigration and Nationality Lawyers, the author cited a case whose investment fell in the $10,000 to $15,000 range but was a legitimate investment:

> As an example I represented an Oriental who had been living in South America who had owned a large market. He came to the United State [and] opened a market in a Mexican American neighborhood that sorely needed his experience in providing good food at a reasonable price, to a neighborhood that spoke Spanish primarily. He has provided a benefit to his community and has extended the labor market and indeed has hired an American citizen employee.

Who this lawyer was representing is unknown; perhaps only immigrants. Still, he clearly favored "middleman minorities," and believed the government would too.

The National Assoication of Human Rights Workers joined with the Interfaith Center for Racial Justice in their opposition to the new rule. They pointed out that "a $50,000 standard will discriminate against Asian applicants, tending to exclude all of them. This group seems to be the major beneficiary." They tried to obtain a breakdown of who used the exemption but could not get the cooperation of the Detroit INS office. Using indirect data, they argued that Asians (including Koreans) were probably the great majority of users. The $50,000 minimum was seen to be discriminatory because low wages in Asia made it difficult to accumulate so much capital. For instance, they estimated it would take a Korean sixty to sixty-five years to amass $50,000, even if he spent nothing on living. They used data from the Office of Minority Business Enterprise to show that the average minority business had an investment of about $10,000. Allowing for inflation, a $13,000 minimum seemed reasonable to them.

The notion that increasing the minimum investment might be an exclusionary measure against Asians is an interesting one. It certainly suggests that there was a conflict of interests surrounding this measure.

Private law firms

These representations were quite uniform. All opposed the proposed amendment, declaring it unduly restrictive. The most common arguments were the following. (1) A $50,000 minimum was unrealistic, since many small businesses were successful on a far smaller investment. (2) Raising the minimum from $10,000 to $50,000 was not reflective of the rate of inflation. (3) A $50,000 requirement let in only the wealthy. (4) The United States was built upon immigrant small business. (5) The "principal manager" provision was unduly narrow and precluded many reasonable forms of investment, such as partnerships, where the immigrant would have substantial responsibility for the business. (6) The requirement to hire Americans was unnecessary since small business was job-creating in indirect ways. (7) This requirement was unduly harsh since it was not required of local small business and could force a new immigrant investor to overextend his or her resources. And (8) small business did not compete with local labor.

One interesting point that several of the law firms made was that small business was a significant source of "consumption," by buying inventory, capital goods, advertising, utilities, and other services and by buying or renting real estate. In other words, they explicitly pointed to one of the interests mentioned in the previous chapter: those who sold goods and services to small entrepreneurs.

In sum the representations overwhelmingly opposed the INS's tightening of this regulation. While the interests behind the representation were not clearly stated, an occasional hint of business interests was suggested.

In response to the representations the INS modified its amendment, reducing the $50,000 minimum to $40,000, changing the "the principal manager" to "a principal manager," and slightly altering the wording regarding the requirement that the business employ non-family members so that one such employee would suffice. They repeated that the intent was not to create businesses that would compete with local businesses in similar lines (41 FR 37565–6). The final wording of the revised regulation was as follows:

> (b) *Aliens not required to obtain labor certifications* ... (4) an alien who establishes on Form I-526 that he has invested, or is actively in the process of investing, capital totaling at least $40,000 in an enterprise in the United States of which he will be a principal manager and that the enterprise will employ a person or persons in the United States who are United States citizens or aliens lawfully admitted for permanent residence, exclusive of the alien, his spouse, and children.

It went into effect October 7, 1976.

In order to attempt to further uncover the interests behind the investor's exemption, we interviewed the Los Angeles Director of the INS, in November 1976. When asked bluntly who was behind the investor's exemption, he replied that he could only conjecture but thought it was: "local ethnic groups, immigration lawyers, brokers who are interested in selling businesses, franchisors, and real estate agents who sell businesses." Even though this response was merely conjecture, we believe that the impressions of such a high official carry considerable weight.

The director did not favor the exemption. He believed it "generated an avenue of deception" in that immigrants used the exemption to obtain green cards, thereafter passing their businesses on to other prospective immigrants and entering the labor market as regular wage earners. Small business was thus used as a tool to evade the immigration law, rather than an end in itself. Correct in this assessment or not, the director supported the notion that the regulation pushed immigrants to obtain small businesses.

A second interview was conducted with the chairman of the Los Angeles County Bar Association's Committee on Immigration in August 1978. We asked him about the interests behind the investor's examption. He replied that it was a compromise based on three conflicting interests: first, there was the "real world" element, meaning that investors in small business did not compete with local labor; second, there was organized labor, which pushed for stringent control and wanted every immigrant, without exception, to be subject to labor certification; and third, there was the National Association of Manufacturers (NAM) and U.S. Chamber of Commerce, which wanted to encourage immigration. One feature of the compromise, the provision that the immigrant entrepreneur should employ at least one American worker, was negotiated by the AFL-CIO. This informant had actually met lobbyists from NAM pushing for the investor's exemption. They had exerted pressure on the Labor Department, the chief agency controlling labor certification.[4]

In 1978 there was a thirty-two-month backlog in applications for the investor's exemption, making it vitrually useless as a means to enter the country as an immigrant. A bottleneck had developed because of limiting the exemption to nonpreference immigrants. However, according to our informant, this limitation had recently been challenged, and a sixth-preference immigrant had been granted the exemption. The case, Matter of Wang-Swang, had been won in an appellate court.[5]

Our interviewee also reported that he believed virtually all nonpreference immigrants used the exemption, since it was too difficult for an unskilled worker to obtain a labor certificate. Since nonpreference immigrants were required to obtain labor certification, the only way a person who did not qualuty for immigration under a preference category could enter was by obtaining an investor's exemption.

On the recommendation of this informant we wrote to various organizations involved in the investor's exemption in one form or another: the AFL-CIO lobbyist, the National Association of Manufacturers, the local INS official who dealt with I-526 forms, a representative on the Congressional Subcommittee on Immigration, and a few others. None responded, and we gave up. We felt we had opened the window sufficiently on this interesting piece of U.S. law to reveal that it did seem to have some capitalist backing.

The Immigration and Nationality Act was amended legislatively by the Filberg Act, which went into effect in January 1977. Among many other changes, the new law tightened up the process of adjusting status to that of an immigrant by not allowing nonimmigrants to do so if they had accepted unauthorized employment while here. Such persons would have to return to their homeland and apply for an immigrant visa through normal channels. Before this, the INS had overlooked many cases of people seeking to adjust their status who could have been deported for violation of their current visa. Interestingly, prospective immigrants who claimed the investor's exemption did not fall under this new provision. Even if they had been working in a business illegally they could adjust their status without having to return home.[6] Again, small business was given a privileged status, an exemption for the exempt, thereby pushing immigrants to enter it.

Subsequent to these events two legislative actions compounded the politics of the investor's exemption. First, on December 16, 1981, Congress passed the Efficiency Package Bill, an INS-proposed measure containing numerous provisions intended to speed the operations of the INS and eliminate the applications backlog. Among the measures passed, one eliminated numerical limitations on foreign investors, thus clearing the way for the INS to authorize the wholesale admission of a large backlog of applicants under the investor's exemption. The second measure, if passed, would have contradicted the effect of the first to a certain extent. As one of the many provisions of the proposed Immigration Reform and Control Act of 1982 (the Simpson-Mazzoli Bill), the Senate suggested imposing a numerical ceiling on annual admissions under the investor's exemption, setting the limit at 7500. Additionally the Senate suggested raising the minimum exemption from $40,000 to $250,000, adding the additional requirement that any qualifying investment must create at least four full-time jobs for persons other than the immediate family of the investor. Koreans actively protested against the bill on this and other grounds (Surh, 1982).

It would be desirable to know how many Korean immigrants actually used the investor's exemption. Unfortunately the INS published no statistics on this subject. Table 70 shows the outside possibility: the number of nonpreference slots used. Koreans entering as nonpreference immigrants peaked in 1972, declining thereafter to a trickle by 1976. By that time there was a sufficient number of Koreans here to provide a base of relatedness by which more immigrants could come in as relatives, avoiding the labor certification requirement entirely. The fact that few Koreans continued to come in as nonpreference immigrants does not mean they did not continue to enter small business. But it does mean they were no longer directly pressured to do so by the immigration laws. However the possibility that a third or more of Korean immigrants between 1970 and 1973 may have used this exemption suggests a significant pressuring of the community in a small business direction during a crucial period of its growth.

In so closely scrutinizing the evolution of this exemption, one gets an impression of a series of ad-hoc decisions made in response to particular pressures. There seems to have been little grand design or clarity of purpose. Yet the net effect of all this activity was to encourage immigrants to enter a rather narrowly defined kind of enterprise, one in which they had to act as entrepreneurs (managers) whether they liked it or not. They were pushed into the petite bourgeoisie.

CONCLUSION

There is abundant evidence indicating that the U.S. government has been concerned with the preservation and expansion of small business in this country.[7] The encouragement of minority and immigrant small business needs to be placed in this larger context of national policy to foster entrepreneurship.

However, in this chapter we have suggested that government policy may have provided special encouragement to immigrant entrepreneurship above and beyond the general national fostering of small business enterprise. The motive was primarily materialistic. As we have been suggesting, immigrants could and did play a cheap labor role for U.S. capital. The small business form helped big business continue to make use of immigrant labor in this way—despite laws that protected against it—through indirect mechanisms. Under the guise of independent small business, the labor of the immigrant firm was actually being employed by sectors of the big business community. We have tried to suggest that this linkage played a part in the development of public policies, such as the INS regulations that aided and encouraged Asian immigrant entrepreneurship.

Much more research can and should be done along the lines suggested in this chapter. We have only begun to scratch the surface to learn how immigrant enterprise is shaped by outside forces and which interest groups help in that construction. We hope others will take up the challenge and dig deeper into the mysterious workings of the U.S. government.

PART FIVE

CONCLUSION

The Costs of Immigrant
Entrepreneurship

We have now completed our investigation of Korean immigrant small business in Los Angeles. That investigation took us far afield from the actual subject matter—to the Korean peninsula and the Korean War, to trade and investment patterns between developed and Third World nations, to the evolution of the American labor movement and the welfare state, and to the situation and experience of blacks and other American minorities. We believe that in order to understand a phenomenon like immigrant entrepreneurship, one cannot begin and end with the entrepreneurs themselves but must understand their position within the larger system of social relations in which they emerged and developed. In this case, given an international migration, nothing short of examining the world capitalist system will suffice if one is to achieve a comprehensive understanding.

It is necessary to examine global and national forces in order to understand the rather small phenomenon of a few thousand Koreans working as shopkeepers in a southwestern American metropolis. But that small phenomenon also provides us with an opportunity to glimpse and comprehend much larger social forces. By studying the anomalous phenomenon of a group of people (often highly educated and reasonably successful professionals in their homeland) uprooting themselves in order to set up small shops in the world's most-advanced and concentrated capitalist economy—and working harder than they ever had to before or than others around them are willing to—we can come to understand the operation of an international system that extends far beyond this small group of people.

ENTREPRENEURSHIP IN THE WORLD
CAPITALIST SYSTEM

In the 1960s and 1970s the world economy became increasingly integrated. International trade rose and tariff barriers fell. We witnessed the rise of giant multinational corporations some of which were more powerful and wealthy than nation-states, able to operate outside of the sphere of state control.

Entrepreneurship in the United States was affected by this development, generally we believe in an adverse direction. For example, the rise in oil prices in the world market had a negative impact on independent truckers in the United States, who could no longer afford to remain self-employed. On a different level, small manufacturers were hurt by competition from imports from cheap-labor countries. While large corporations were also affected by these trends, many were able to withstand them more successfully, by diversifying or moving overseas themselves. Small business was less able to adapt. Its flexibility only lay in its easy demise and rebirth in a new form under new ownership. But the individual entrepreneur was destroyed.

The effects of international trade on U.S. small business were not dissimilar to the effects of imperialism on underdeveloped countries. Just as imperialist nations were able to destroy Third World industry by undermining it with the importation of more cheaply manufactured products, so in the 1960s and 1970s the process was somewhat reversed with the rise in cheap manufactured imports to the United States from Third World countries. As a result the competitive sector in the United States was vulnerable to international competition in much the same way as were the national industries of the world's poorer countries.

Participation in the world capitalist system may have acted as a destroyer of entrepreneurship in the United States, but it also served to replenish it, through immigration. U.S. capital itself helped to create the conditions for the immigration of cheap labor to the United States, part of which came to staff needed entrepreneurial roles. U.S. activity abroad also helped to create refugees, some of whom came with the capital to move quickly into entrepreneurial roles. In other words, just as U.S. capitalism was exhausting its own supply of entrepreneurs—by the concentration of capital in fewer and fewer hands, and its inability to utilize its own reserve army of labor—it was simultaneously creating overseas some of the conditions that helped to replenish its stock of entrepreneurs.

The basic interconnections are diagrammed in figure 5. This diagram starts with the U.S. capitalist system, which generated contradictory tendencies. The system simultaneously destroyed entre-

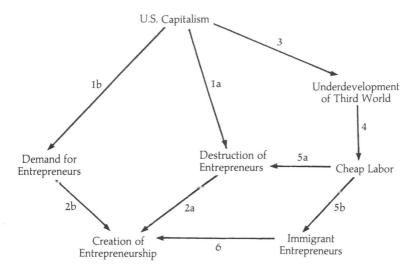

Figure 5 The Creation of Entrepreneurship in World Capitalism

preneurs (1a) yet continued to require them (1b). This duality led to efforts to stimulate entrepreneurship (2a and 2b). At the same time, U.S. imperialist activity abroad contributed to the underdevelopment of Third World countries (3) and to the reproduction and creation of cheap labor there, in part by the retention of precapitalist relations of production (4). Some of this cheap labor was used in Third World countries to produce goods that could be exported to the United States and sold below market price there. Some of this importing occurred in collusion with U.S. big business resulting in the additional destruction of entrepreneurship in the United States (5a). At the same time, in contradiction to this tendency, some cheap labor from underdeveloped countries became available for emigration (5b) and—stimulated by U.S. immigration policy—helped to replenish the declining stock of entrepreneurs in the United States (6). Thus U.S. capitalism participated in both the creation and destruction of entrepreneurship at the national and international level.

The international trade system also created another type of immigrant entrepreneur, namely those who participated in the import-export trade. These people were generally not members of the petite bourgeoisie; they were representatives of international capital. But, as we have seen, their presence may have stimulated and contributed to immgrant small business.

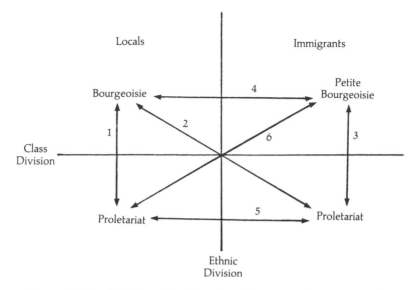

Figure 6 Class Relations Resulting from Immigrant Entrepreneurship

Korean immigrant entrepreneurship complicated the class structure of the United States, as diagrammed in figure 6. The basic class
struggle (arrow 1) leads to an increase in the price of labor. This in
turn leads capitalists to seek cheaper immigrant workers (arrow 2).
The immigrant small business owners can play a pivotal role in
keeping immigrant labor cheap (arrow 3), in part for the benefit of
American capital (arrow 4). These relationships contribute to conflict
between the local and immigrant sectors of the working class (arrow
5), as well as to local worker antagonism to the immigrant petite
bourgeoisie itself (arrow 6). Since the immigrant small business sector
often lacks clear class differentiation, and the immigrant entrepreneurs are often able to invoke ethnic loyalties, the conflicts between
local workers and immigrant small shops take on a strong ethnic
dimension. Ethnic divisions come to override class solidarities, even
though the antagonism arises because of the basic conflict between
local capitalists and workers.

You will notice the similarity between figure 6 and figure 2 (see
chapter 3). This is intentional. Part of our purpose in this book is to
demonstrate how the international system described in part two is
replicated at the local level. Cheap labor in Third World countries

becomes immigrant cheap labor, with parallel ramifications and alignments. The immigrant petite bourgeoisie plays a role that is analogous to the role of Third World ruling classes: it keeps ethnic labor cheap and docile, using "nationalistic" sentiments, ultimately for the benefit of corporate capital.

The system and processes we have described here are obviously not unique to South Korea and the Koreans, nor are they restricted to the United States. Immigrant entrepreneurs of many other nationalities abound in the United States. A similar analysis could be undertaken regarding the relationship of each nationality's homeland to this country and the impact of this relationship on emigration and the characteristics of the immigrants. Similarly, immigrant entrepreneurs are to be found in many of the countries of Western Europe, possibly performing a similar role there. This study calls for comparisons, and we hope other scholars will take up the challenge.

THE SOCIAL COSTS OF ETHNIC
ENTREPRENEURSHIP

We would like to end on a note that takes us beyond fact and theory. Knowledge is not only an end in itself, it is also a means toward achieving social progress. Thus one may ask, is ethnic or immigrant entrepreneurship a phenomenon that contributes to or detracts from the general social welfare? Is it a phenomenon that Americans want to encourage?

Ethnic entrepreneurship is often seen as unmitigatedly good. It is presumed to enable disadvantaged immigrants to escape from poverty. It permits the perpetuation of distinctive ethnic cultures, which enrich everyone through diversity. It provides relatively cheap and available goods and services to consumers, including delicious ethnic cuisines. It represents the value of pluralism and tolerance, permitting people to live as they please.

Perhaps most of all, ethnic entrepreneurship is seen as a demonstration of the benefits of the American way. It shows that the free-enterprise system works: If people are ambitious and willing to work hard, if they are willing to exercise initiative and take a few chances, they can make it in the United States. Social mobility through entrepreneurship is, in some sense, the very essence of the ideal of American capitalism. Immigrant entrepreneurs act out that ideal even better than native-born members of this society. They are symbols of what American stands for.

The touting of Asian-Americans as model minorities who have successfully adapted to the United States bespeaks these values. Although, as we have seen, Asian immigrant entrepreneurship has provoked some criticism, by and large the press coverage it has received has been favorable.

However, immigrant entrepreneurship of the Korean variety incurs some serious social costs, both to the immigrants themselves and to the society at large (Light, 1985). These costs strike at the very heart of the value system of American capitalism. Thus the evaluation of immigrant entrepreneurship is not a trivial topic but one of profound significance to the way this society operates.

COSTS TO THE IMMIGRANTS

At the most basic level is immigration itself. Migration is a wrenching, disruptive experience. It tears people from their often beloved homelands, breaks up their families, and forces them into a prolonged, sometimes lifelong period of adjustment to a strange and alienating environment. In a mass migration such as that from South Korea to the United States, a whole generation may suffer these pains of dislocation.

Many Koreans long for the comforts of home and a familiar culture and language. They would much rather live in Korea and among Koreans if that country answered their pressing economic and political needs. America may represent a certain kind of opportunity for economic advancement, but its appeal is largely confined to that narrow arena.

Part two suggested that Korean immigration is not simply a question of individual choice. It is also a product of the workings of the world capitalist system. Koreans are dislocated from their homeland in part because of the development of capitalism and imperialist penetration by Japan and the United States. Koreans have been exploited as cheap labor. The migration of Koreans to the United States and their setting up as ethnic entrepreneurs can be seen as partially responsive to the demand for cheap immigrant labor and its utilization in the small business form in this country. Thus one of the major costs of the phenomenon of immigrant entrepreneurship is that it is part of a system that forces people to dislocate themselves on a massive scale.

The most immediate cost of concentration in ethnic small business to the immigrants is the life of hard work they must endure. Immigrant entrepreneurs and their families must work much harder than other members of the society to which they have moved. They also work harder than they did in their homelands. The long hours they must put in not only deprive these people of many of the joys of life but sometimes positively threaten their health. Being an immigrant entrepreneur is a joyless existence.

Immigrant entrepreneurship creates family problems, at least in the Korean community. Instances of wife beating, divorce, child neglect, and gang warfare among adolescents are all far more common among members of the Korean community in the United States than they were in the homeland. The reasons for these breakdowns are no doubt complex, including such factors as discrepancies in cultural expectations and the clash between generations. But the immigrant Koreans' concentration in small business probably plays an important part.

Small business contributes to family breakdown in the following ways. First and foremost it typically absorbs most of the time and attention of both parents, leaving little to spare for the children. Even if parents are ostensibly pursuing small business for the goal of providing opportunities for their children, the children themselves may still suffer from immediate neglect.

Second, immigrant small business can put stress on the relationship between husbands and wives. In many instances, wives had never had to work outside the home in Korea. They had focused on the traditional female domestic roles while men had been responsible for earning the family's livelihood. Ethnic entrepreneurship pushes the woman out of the home, but typically it has not alleviated her responsibility for domestic chores and child care. The result is that women must bear a double workload, while their husbands resist taking on traditionally feminine household tasks yet see a decline in their domestic quality of life. Much friction can develop over the conflicts these changes engender.

Outside of the family, immigrant entrepreneurship frequently provokes societal antagonisms, from individual crimes to more systematic forms of anti-immigrant expression. Immigrant entrepreneurs must suffer these consequences of their economic adaptation. They can find themselves isolated in a sea of racism, unwelcome in the society where they have chosen to live.

Finally, and perhaps most important, the hardships of immigrant entrepreneurship are undertaken on the presumption that the family will accumulate capital and climb up the social ladder. Some Korean entrepreneurs no doubt will succeed in this goal. There are already a few spectacular successes in Los Angeles. But for the vast majority, the dream will never become a reality. Many Korean families will find that they have sacrificed their youth in hardship only to find that nothing but more of the same stretches ahead of them.

Immigrant entrepreneurship is risky. That is one of its essential features. It produces both success and failure, winners and losers. The failures and losers suffer the consequences of such a system. But because they are losers, because they often feel ashamed of their failure and blame themselves for it, their story rarely receives public attention. Lives dedicated to sacrifice and hardship end where they began, never having achieved the dream for which the sacrifices were made.

Costs to Society

Immigrant small business enterprise also entails certain costs to society at large. First, immigrant businesses serve as a form of cheap labor. In so doing they perpetuate a form of labor exploitation that threatens to lower labor standards in general. Unions can be undermined by the transfer of work from unionized workers to immigrants firms. In general the presence of a pocket of nonunionized firms— paying low wages, demanding long hours, and relying on unpaid wives and even child labor—serves as a depressant on the labor standards of the entire community.

The segregation of immigrant workers in ethnic small businesses is a more effective means of labor exploitation than merely hiring them directly because it inhibits the development of class consciousness. Not only are they bound to their employers by ties of ethnic and family loyalty, but they also rarely have contact with local workers who are not part of their ethnic community, except as customers. There are no opportunities for the working class to compare experiences, share grievances, or develop common values and standards, let alone engage in joint action to alleviate exploitation.

The establishment of a system of severe labor exploitation among a sector of the labor force also leads to an increasing imbalance in class forces. If, as we contend, some elements of the capitalist class are making a lot of money off the hard work of immigrant small businesses, then that accumulation of wealth at the top gives greater power to the capitalist class. Inequality in the society is exacerbated. The rich get richer while the poor are left fragmented and unable to defend themselves.

Apart from perpetuating labor exploitation, immigrant enterprise tends to create intergroup competition along ethnic lines. This group competition is not restricted to labor but, rather, encompasses all classes. Korean businesses are in competition with black, Chicano, white, and other businesses. Lines of ethnic division become deeply etched in the society.

The fact that immigrant entrepreneurship depends on the mobilization of ethnic solidarity and ethnic resources enhances this potential. Immigrant small business owners are seen to operate as a kind of collective, drawing a sharp distinction between members and nonmembers. Individualistic competition is replaced by group competition, with underlying charges of unfair business practices.

Ethnic enterprise develops the potential for what Max Weber called a dual ethic, one morality for in-group members and another for the out-group. Members of the ethnic community are granted special favors, special business privileges, while nonmembers are treated as strangers who are fair game in the capitalist market place.

A dual ethic surrounds ethnic enterprise not only in terms of the relations between business competitors. It also exists between store owners and clients. Since ethnic entrepreneurs are not part of the community they service (setting aside that minority which services their own ethnic community), they are often indifferent to the impact of their businesses on that community. The proliferation of immigrant liquor stores in black and Chicano neighborhoods is a case in point. Immigrant and ethnic enterpreneurs frequently engage in morally marginal business lines because they can maintain a stance of indifference to the effects they create on nonimmigrant communities.

In a sense, immigrant entrepreneurs act like quintessential capitalists with respect to their clients. They provide whatever service or commodity will sell, irrespective of its moral character. They are there to make money, period. The mode by which that money is made is a matter of indifference. Only market forces are considered.

When business owners are members of the community in which they do business, the pure profit motive is tempered by other considerations. There is a common moral community that sets limits on the ruthless pursuit of profit and its destructive social consequences. But with immigrant entrepreneurship, a single moral community does not exist. Instead several moral communities coexist, side by side, marked off by ethnicity, each indifferent to the concerns of the others.

This condition was observed by Furnivall when he wrote of the "plural society" (Furnivall, 1944). He pointed out that, in the capitalist homelands of Western Europe, unbridled capitalism was checked by tradition, including the institutions of feudalism, and by the existence of a single moral community that inhibited some of the worst features of the pursuit of profit. But in the colonies, where capitalism was imposed from outside, and where it was often practiced by immigrant entrepreneurs, no joint moral community was constructed, and all other values fell before the drive to accumulate wealth. (Clearly many atrocities occurred in Western Europe in the pursuit of profit, but when one compares them with such common colonial practices as outright enslavement, they pale.)

The unrestrained pursuit of profit is replicated, to a certain extent, with immigrant entrepreneurship in countries like the Untied States today. The dollar becomes the major criterion for evaluating behaviour, since few other joint values exist. Of course, the formal legal system acts as a representative of the total community, but it is remote and alienated from the cultures of the people. It is not an organic representation of common concerns but more an outside force that merely imposes what can be seen as arbitrary limits.

The law becomes the chief battleground on which the conflicts engendered by immigrant entrepreneurship get enacted, because it is one of the few arenas where disparate moral communities are brought under a single set of standards imposed by the state. There is no common community, and so informal sanctions and subtle social pressures fail to control excesses. The only recourse is the law.

In sum, because ethnic entrepreneurship, on one hand, fosters cross-class ethnic solidarities instead of cross-ethnic class solidarities, it helps to create an ethnically divided society. On the other hand, it inhibits the development of class conflict by fragmenting the working class along ethnic lines. Thus it serves as a profoundly conservative force, leaving unchecked the worst consequences of capitalist social relations.

THE MORAL LESSON

Immigrant entrepreneurs do not capitulate totally to the capitalist values of ruthless competition. Within their own communities they are often able to establish a concern for the social well-being that transcends mere profit-grubbing. Although, as we have seen, considerable exploitation occurs within these communities, still it is mitigated to a certain extent by other values. The community develops a degree of social responsibility for members of the ethnic groups.

Unfortunately, ethnic entrepreneurial communities tend to draw a tight line around their realm of social responsibility. It ends at the boundary of their ethnic community. With the rest of the world they can act as ruthless competitors. Thus they engage in a kind of group competition, using ethnic solidarity to be more effective in competing with the outside world.

Immigrant entrepreneurs are victims of world capitalism. They have been forced from their beloved homelands. They often suffer lives of great hardship and deprivation. Nevertheless, by participating in capitalism enthusiastically, and by pursuing its competitive values, they help to perpetuate the system that created their own oppression. Even if some of the members of their communities manage to escape from this oppression in this or future generations, that oppression will be replicated for others.

As victims of the system, ethnic entrepreneurs can move in one of two directions. Either they can continue to limit their vision to that of capitalism and strive to ensure their individual and group competitive advantage within it—and in so doing, threaten to engender the wrath of surrounding clients, competitors, and workers, and find themselves living in a world of insecurity and hatred. Or they can use their own experience of oppression by the system to rise above it and join together with other oppressed peoples to construct a new social order: one based on concern for the well-being of all humanity, regardless of nationality or ethnicity. They could strive to create a society that is not based on competition and exploitation, but on the value and dignity of every human being, so that no one should have to suffer what they have suffered.

Ethnic entrepreneurial communities already show their capacity for social responsibility in some of their community institutions. They have proven that they are capable of rising above individual greed and ambition. And they have proven that a collective orientation can be more efficient than individualistic competition. But it takes a leap of imagination to take these lessons beyond the boundaries of the ethnic community to incorporate humanity as a whole. Without such a vision, the world degenerates, if not into a war of all against all, then at least a war of one ethnic group against another.

Obviously it is not up to immigrant entrepreneurs alone to find alternatives to the devastating consequences of world capitalism. Other progressive forces, such as the progressive elements of the American labor movement, need to join with the immigrants and to overcome their own narrow nationalism and bigotry with respect to immigrants. All groups are responsible for developing internationalism.

Still, in the very suffering and oppression experienced by immigrant entrepreneurs and their families there lies the potential for a new idea. Others need not bring this idea to them. Rather, they have their own need, their own incentive for helping to reconstruct society in a more humanistic direction. Hopefully this study has served as a small contribution to explaining why this need exists.

Appendix: Telephone Survey, 1977

We conducted a telephone survey of Korean entrepreneurs in the summer of 1977. We based our survey on the businesses listed in the yellow pages of the 1975 Korean-community directory. A ninety-item instrument was developed and translated into Korean by Sun-Bin Yim, a graduate student in sociology at UCLA. She pretested the questionnaire and completed the interviews in the Korean language in July and August of 1977.

This telephone survey was not a random sample of Korean businesses in Los Angeles. It was based on Korean-directory listings that we knew to be incomplete but considered the best available. Rather than sampling from this directory, Ms. Yim tried to reach *all* listed businesses. She omitted banks, hospitals, newspapers, churches, and voluntary associations. In all she telephoned 1109 numbers.

As might be expected, Yim encountered an electronic nightmare of wrong numbers, lines out of service, and unexplained silences. She used every resource to locate a business listed in the directory. She also interviewed any Korean business owner who answered, regardless of whether he or she owned the business listed in the 1975 directory. This procedure yielded 325 valid telephone contacts with Korean-owned businesses. Of those business owners validly contacted, 204 interviews were completed in whole or in part. Complete interviews lasted about one hour.

One-third of valid respondents declined to answer any questions. Most said they were "too busy." But this excuse may have masked other concerns, including fear of investigation by either U.S. or Korean government officials. In the former case, people may have been concerned about the INS, the IRS, or labor standards investigators. On the other hand, the KCIA had spies in Los Angeles investigating the activities of emigrants. Wariness was common, and our interviewer had difficulty establishing rapport over the telephone. When valid contacts declined, or when busy respondents broke off before completion, the interviewer offered to call back at a more convenient time, and she was able to save a few interviews this way. In unsuccessful cases, we mailed a Korean-language copy of the questionnaire to the respondent's business address, requesting the recipient to fill out and return it to us by mail. One did so.

Our survey results build upon pyramiding layers of bias that vex interpretation. The first bias was inclusion or noninclusion of Korean businesses in the 1975 Keys directory. We only reached included firms. The second bias was survival or nonsurvival of listed businesses. Our survey only reached survivors. The third was refusal to answer. Thirty-seven percent refused. The fourth layer was respondent selectivity of questions as indicated by internal variation in nonresponse rates. The final layer was respondent candor. Notwithstanding these vexing problems, we have no reason to assume that these biases point in any particular direction. Therefore, the survey evidence ought to take its place alongside other evidence. What counts, in the final analysis, is the persuasiveness of the whole case.

Notes

1. IMMIGRANT ENTREPRENEURS

1. *Los Angeles Times*, April 13, 1980: pt. II, 1.

2. For a discussion of social problems in Los Angeles, see Ivan Light, "Los Angeles," ch. 2 in Mattei Dogon and John Kasards, eds. *The Metropolis Era*, vol. II *Mega-Cities* (Beverly Hills: Sage Publications, 1988).

3. *Korea Times English Section*, June 26, 1978.

4. Greeks operated 39 percent of pizza restaurants in Connecticut towns (Lovell-Troy, 1981a, 1981b), Dominicans were a power in New York City's garment industry (Waldinger, 1984), and Soviet Jews operated about half the taxi cabs in Los Angeles (Russell, 1984). Blackistone (1981: 1–5) identified 356 Arab-owned grocery stores in Chicago of which 195 were in predominantly black neighborhoods. Lebanese Moslems owned numerous grocery stores in Detroit and Toledo. Syrian Jews and Arabic-speaking Syro-Lebanese Christians became prominent retailers in northern New York state (Zenner, 1982: 474). In Detroit, Sengstock (1967: 112) found that among Chaldean-rite Catholics from Iraq, 54 percent of nuclear family heads were owners or part owners of grocery stores. Hong Kong Chinese doubled the number of Chinese-owned businesses in Toronto (Chan and Cheung, 1985). In Orange County, California, Vietnamese merchants created a little Saigon so large that local white merchants vainly sought to ban the posting of business signs in foreign languages (Padilla, 1981). In Sea Drift, Texas, Vietnamese shrimp fishermen provided unwelcome competition for whites (Brown, 1979; Miller, 1980).

5. See Handlin, 1959: 74; Goldscheider and Kobrin, 1980: 257; Auster and Aldrich, 1984: 39; Granovetter, 1984: 333; Hraba, 1979: 375; Reitz, 1980: 242.

6. U.S. Bureau of the Census, *Statistical Abstract of the United States: 1984* (Washington, D.C.: U.S. Government Printing Office, 1983), table 691, p. 415.

7. U.S. Internal Revenue Service, *Statistics of Income, 1979–80: Sole Proprietorship Returns* (Washington, D.C.: USGPO, 1982), table 11, p. 165.

8. U.S. President, *The State of Small Business: A Report of the President Transmitted to Congress March, 1982* (Washington, D.C.: USGPO, 1982), chapter 1.

9. Peter M. Guttman, "Statement of Peter Guttman," in U.S. Congressional Joint Economic Committee, 96th Congress, First Session, 1980, *The Underground Economy*: 26.

10. *Business Week*, April 5, 1982: 64.

11. U.S. Bureau of the Census, *Census of the Population: 1970 National*

Origin and Language PC(2)1A (Washington, D.C.: USGPO), 1973, table 16.

12. For details, see Ivan Light and Angel Sanchez, "Immigrant Entrepreneurs in 272 SMSAs," *Sociological Perspectives* 30(1987): 373–399.

13. "The essence of the American economic system of private enterprise is free competition ... The preservation and expansion of such competition is basic not only to the economic wellbeing but to the security of this Nation." Public Law 85–536, Sect. 2(a), July 18, 1958.

14. For reviews of the middleman minorities literature, see: Bonacich, 1980; Porter, 1981; Bonacich and Modell, 1980: ch. 2; see also Walter P. Zenner, "Middleman Minorities in the Syrian Mosaic," *Sociological Perspectives* 30(1987): 400–421.

15. Format follows Blalock, 1967: 21–26.

2. CHEAP LABOR IN SOUTH KOREA

1. See Bonacich (1972, 1976) for a discussion of the role of the price of labor in race relations.

2. One factor that can be omitted from the calculus of price of labor is the cost of living. While it clearly affects the quality of life to the worker, and undoubtedly plays a part in determining the level at which the wage rate can be set, it is not a direct factor in the costs of the employer. The concept "price of labor" refers strictly to employer costs, not to employee benefits.

3. Unfortunately United Nations statistics omit Taiwan, a country that ranks high among developing countries specializing in manufactured imports. This omission is a problem throughout the discussion based on the U.N. data.

4. Within the broad categories, the following commodities were especially important among South Korea's exports, as of 1978: clothing not of fur (SITC 841), accounting for $2.5 billion worth, or 20 percent of all exports; textile yarns and fabrics (65) with $1.5 billion worth; electrical machinery (72), especially telecommunications equipment (724), valued at $614 million, and electrical machinery (729), especially transistors and valves (7293), worth $372 million; transport equipment (73) valued at $1.1 billion, mainly ships and boats (735), worth $801 million; footwear (851) worth $686 million; iron and steel (67) at $577 million; metal manufactures (69) worth $525 million; and veneers and plywood (631) worth $415 million (U.N., 1978: vol. 1, 678–680). While many other items were also exported, these were the major ones, accounting for a substantial proportion of total exports. SITC or Standard International Trade Classification numbers work as follows: the first digit gives the broad commodity classification, as presented in table 6. Each successive digit provides more specificity. Thus, 841, clothing not of fur, is a subcategory of 84, clothing, which in turn is a subcategory of 8, miscellaneous manufactured goods. In this way one can tell from the first digit where this list falls in the categories presented in table 6.

5. *Los Angeles Times*, August 22, 1979.

6. *Korea Business*, special issue, no. 1, 1976: 4.

7. U.S. Senate, Committee on Appropriations, 95th Congress, First Session, 1977, *Foreign Assistance and Related Programs Appropriations, Fiscal Year 1978*: 1340.

8. Ibid., pp. 1165–1167.

9. Ibid., pp. 1301–1386.

10. *Korea Annual,* 1978 (Seoul: Hapdong News Agency, 1978), p. 210.

11. Ibid., pp. 192–197.

12. Ibid., p. 193.

13. According to Long (1977: 30), the following U.S. banks were the major lenders to South Korea through August 1975 (in millions of dollars): Chase Manhattan, $298.4; First National City Bank, $272.8; Manhattan Trust, $257.4; Bankers Trust, $226.6; Chemical Bank, $126.0; Fidelity of Philadelphia, $61.1; Irving Trust, $36.4; and Girard Bank, $30.0. These are presumably cumulative figures. Other U.S. banks had lent smaller amounts, and Long concludes that U.S. banks made 83.5 percent of the total commercial loans to Korea. This estimate does not coincide with that of the *Korea Annual* and may reflect a different definition of "commercial loan," or the effects of cumulating.

14. *Economic Statistics Yearbook* (Seoul: Bank of Korea, 1978), pp. 192–195.

15. *Korea Business,* no. 1, 1976: 6.

16. Ibid., p. 22.

17. *Korea Business,* no. 2, 1976: 9.

18. Ibid.

19. Ibid., p. 7.

20. *Korea Annual,* 1978: 477–482.

21. *Economic Factors Affecting the Use of Items 807.00 and 806.30 of the Tariff Schedules of the United States* (Washington, D.C.: Tariff Commission Publication 339, 1970), p. 9.

22. Ibid., pp. 14–15.

23. Ibid., p. 16.

24. Ibid., pp. 15–16.

25. Ibid., p. 3.

26. Ibid., p. 33.

27. U.S. House of Representatives, Ways and Means Committee, *Special Duty Treatment or Repeal of Articles Assembled or Fabricated Abroad.* Hearings before Subcommittee on Trade on Items 806.30 and 807.00 of the Tariff Schedules of the United States, March 24 and 25, 1976, p. 7.

28. Tariff Commission, *Economic Factors,* p. 6.

29. Ibid., p. 66.

30. House Ways and Means Committee, *Special Duty Treatment,* pp. 105–106.

31. Ibid., p. 107.

32. *Korea Annual,* 1978, p. 147.

33. Ibid., p. 91.

34. Ibid., pp. 91–92.

35. Overseas Private Investment Corporation, *Annual Report,* 1976: 56.

36. Ibid., p. 2.

37. For a description of OPIC's origins and goals, see U.S. Congress, Joint Economic Committee, Subcommittee on Economic Foreign Policy, 91st Congress, Second Session, 1970, *A Foreign Economic Policy for the '70s:* 739–743.

38. OPIC, *Annual Report,* 1978: 5, 12.

39. Ibid., pp. 4–6.

40. OPIC, *Annual Report,* 1976: 37.

41. OPIC, private communication.

42. OPIC was also charged with getting private insurance companies to back it up, an effort that largely failed; see U.S. House of Representatives, Committee on International Relations, Subcommittee on International Economic Policy and Trade, 95th Congress, First Session, 1977, *Extension and Revision of Overseas Private Investment Corporation Programs.*

43. OPIC, *Annual Report,* 1976: 50.

44. Ibid., p. 56.

45. OPIC, *Annual Report,* 1978: 15–16.

46. OPIC, *Annual Report,* 1976: 40.

47. See statement by Rutherford M. Poats, acting president of OPIC, House Committee on International Relations, *Extension and Revision of OPIC,* pp. 12–15.

48. OPIC, *Annual Report,* 1976: 40

49. House Committee on International Relations, *Extension and Revision of OPIC,* pp. 353–369.

50. For a review of the origins of GSP see Bell, 1972a: 354–362.

51. Most of this section is based on *Korea Business, Special for American Importers,* no. 1, 1976.

52. *Los Angeles Times,* February 5, 1979.

53. Ibid.

54. See also U.S. Department of Labor, Bureau of International Labor Affairs, *The Impact of International Trade and Investment on Employment,* 1978.

55. *The Impact of Multinational Enterprises on Employment and Training* (Geneva: International Labour Office, 1976).

56. This point was made by Elizabeth Jager of the AFL-CIO from the floor of a conference sponsored by the Labor Department (U.S. Department of Labor, *Impact of International Trade,* pp. 313–315). She contended that the sophisticated mathematical models of the economists were based on faulty assumptions, for example, that increased trade was always beneficial, as well as on inadequate data. In her view, the resulting predictions bore little relationship to reality.

57. The high price of U.S. labor, we should recall, included not only high wages, but also unionization, health and safety standards, and all other aspects of the job that increased its tolerability to the workers.

58. House Ways and Means Committee, *Special Duty Treatment.*

59. House Ways and Means Committee, *Special Duty Treatment,* pp. 168–170.

60. See, for example, Congressional Joint Economic Committee, *Foreign Economic Policy,* pp. 1425–1442; U.S. Senate Finance Committee, *Multinational Corporations: A Compendium of Papers Submitted to the Subcommittee on International Trade,* 1973: 59–84.

61. Tariff Commission, *Economic Factors,* pp. A9–A30.

62. House Ways and Means Committee, *Special Duty Treatment,* p. 96.

63. Ibid., p. 100.

64. Ibid.

65. House Committee on International Relations, *Extension and Revision of OPIC,* pp. 353–369.

66. Of course OPIC had a response to the AFL-CIO's charges, denying them all (House Committee on International Relations, *Extension and Revision of OPIC*, pp. 370—372). The retaliation was couched in the ideology of capital, as they cited studies that purported to prove that overseas investment tended to increase U.S. jobs in the long run.

67. Ibid., pp.144—145.

68. Ibid., pp.100—101.

3. THE ROLE OF THE KOREAN GOVERNMENT

1. *Korea Business*, no. 5, 1976: 37.

2. Ibid.

3. *Korean Annual*, 1978 (Seoul: Hapdong News Agency, 1978), p. 141.

4. *Korea Business*, no. 1, 1976: 36—43.

5. *Korea Business*, no. 5, 1976: 40.

6. Ibid., pp. 40—42.

7. U.S. Tariff Commission, *Economic Factors Affecting the Use of Items 807.00 and 806.30 at the Tariff Schedules of the United States*, Tariff Commission Publication 339, 1970: 146.

8. *Korea Business*, no. 5, 1976: 38.

9. Ibid., p. 37.

10. The South Korean government described its FTZs as follows;

a. The export processing zone (or free export zone) is a specifically designated industrial area where foreign-invested (as well as joint venture firms with Korean nationals as partners) can freely import raw materials or semi-finished goods, free of duty, and manufacture, process, or assemble export products.

b. The zone has characteristics of a bonded area where the application of pertinent laws and regulations is waived or relaxed, in whole or in part.

c. It is a specifically designated industrial estate where the government constructs various facilities for sale or lease, including plant sites or factory (standard type) buildings for occupant firms.

d. It is an industrial area where various privileges in legal aspects and tax incentives are provided to foreign-invested (including joint venture) firms. (cited in Takeo, 1977: 1)

11. *Korea Business*, no. 5, 1976: 25—26; see also Kei, 1977: 70.

12. *Korea Business*, no. 5, 1976: 25.

13. Ibid., p. 26.

14. Ibid., pp. 26, 35.

15. The effects of multinationals on wage levels has been studied in general (*Wages and Work Conditions in Multinational Enterprises*) (Geneva: International Labour Office, 1976). The conclusion seems to be that they sometimes did pay higher wages than local businesses as a mechanism for competing with local firms for the most skilled labor. In so doing, they helped to create an aristocracy of labor in the Third World. However, while higher wages may have prevailed in regular subsidiaries, the opposite seems to have been the case in assembly plants geared mainly to manufactured exports.

16. In the years immediately after the state of emergency, 1972 and 1973, no labor disputes were recorded in Korea (see table 5).

17. *Korea Business*, no. 5, 1976: 35.

18. This system was a legacy of the U.S. military occupation, during which no provision was made for free trade union elections because the U.S. feared that communist-headed unions would win (Lim, 1976a: 168).

19. *Los Angeles Times*, May 5, 1980.

20. Republic of Korea, Economic Planning Board, *Korea Statistical Year-book*, 1978: 83.

21. An effort to alleviate Seoul's slums was undertaken in 1969 when several thousand slum dwellers were removed to the city of Kwangju. Since jobs were not available there either, the strategy did not solve the underlying social problem and a riot broke out in the new slum city (Breidenstein, 1974: 247; Kim, 1977: 29). A 1980 uprising in that city shows that Kwangju remained an area of major disaffection from the Korean government.

22. *Korea Annual*, 1978, pp. 212—215.

23. Republic of Korea, Economic Planning Board, *Korea Statistical Year-book*, 1972: 423; 1978: 341.

24. *Korea Business*, no. 1, 1976: 17.

25. Ibid., p. 15.

26. *Los Angeles Times*, March 16, 1980.

27. A Korean journal that promoted exports to the United States and U.S. investments in Korea, described the movement in the following terms:

> The basic foundation of the Saemaul Undong is the training of rural and urban people in diligence, self-help and cooperative spirit. Diligence is the first lesson to learn. Trying to be rich without working hard is harmful to national development ... Hard work on a voluntary basis must be added to the Saemaul spirit ... Since the Saemaul Undong is dedicated to making diligence foster the spirit of saving and frugality, it avoids vanity, luxury and extravagance ... The Saemaul Undong is a movement inculcating patriotism. (*Buyers Guide*, November, 1977: 8—12)

Here again we see a nationalist or patriotic appeal to induce Korean workers to work harder to accept hardship for the sake of national development.

28. "Saemaul Movement and Saemaul Factories," *Buyers Guide*, November, 1977: 12.

29. Economic planner Lee Hahn Been expressed his confidence that Korean workers would accept a decline in their real wages. "He cited a recent newspaper poll showing that 67% of Korea's families saw themselves as either middle class or lower-middle class. These people, he said, 'feel they have something to protect.' ... Kim Key Whan, a special assistant to Lee, said that with 5.3% of the labor force expected to be out of work, 'our message is that what we need this year is more jobs, not more pay.'" *Los Angeles Times*, March 16, 1980.

Korean workers were no different from their U.S. counterparts in succumbing to this type of appeal. Several trade unions in the United States have negotiated wage decreases rather than face job reductions or the closing of plants. The option of altering the whole system of production which created plant closings and other disastrous outcomes for workers was entertained by only a tiny minority.

30. The development of internationally oriented capital at the expense of the national bourgeoisie distinguished South Korea's development strategy from Japan's, despite frequent claims that Korea was following in Japan's footsteps. Japan developed with minimal dependence upon foreign investment (Halliday, 1980: 10). Korea's heavy foreign dependence raises

serious questions about the degree to which stable industrial development was really occurring in that country (Sunoo, 1978).

31. This point will be elaborated upon at length in chapter 14.

32. "Arms Buildup Support Laid to Job Blackmail," *Los Angeles Times*, November 5, 1984.

4. EMIGRATION FROM SOUTH KOREA

1. *Korea Annual 1964* (Seoul: Hapdong News Agency, 1964), p. 309.

2. Ibid., p. 300.

3. *Korea Annual 1968*, pp. 239—240.

4. *Korea Annual 1971*, pp. 233—234.

5. *Korea Annual 1977*, p. 177.

6. Republic of Korea, Economic Planning Board, *Korea Statistical Yearbook*, 1966: 36.

7. *Korea Times*, May 29, 1981.

8. *Korea Statistical Yearbook*, 1977: 542—543.

9. Ibid., 1978: 366—367.

10. A high proportion of North Korean refugees in South Korea were Christians, leading to some overlap in these two potential emigrant categories (I. Kim, 1981: 35).

11. *Korea Statistical Yearbook*, 1977: 376.

12. While figure 3 only mentions U.S. capital, obviously the dislocations in South Korea were not limited solely to U.S. intervention. Japanese and other foreign interests also contributed to the dislocations associated with the activities of multinational corporations.

13. This does not negate the fact that elements of the American population, especially the working class, were also hurt by these developments.

14. *San Francisco Chronicle*, November 2, 1976.

5. IMMIGRATION AND SETTLEMENT

1. See U.S. Senate, Committee on the Judiciary, 95th Congress, First Session, 1979, *U.S. Immigration Law and Policy, 1952—1979. A Report Prepared by the Congressional Research Service, Library of Congress, for the Select Commission on Immigration and Refugee Policy*: 7; see also Bennett, 1963: 36—39.

2. See W. Kim, 1971: 3—4; Choy, 1979: 69—72; Hurh and K. Kim, 1980: 25.

3. See Houchins and Houchins, 1974: 553—554; Patterson and Kim, 1974: v; Shin, 1971: 200; Melendy, 1977: 121—126; Choy, 1979: 72—78; Moon, 1976: 76—82.

4. U.S. Senate, *U.S. Immigration Law*, pp. 7—8; see also Lieberman, 1968: 110—111.

5. U.S. Senate, *U.S. Immigration Law*, pp. 56—58; Abrams and Abrams, 1975; North, 1971: 34—35; North and Weissert, 1973: 9—13.

6. U.S. Senate, *U.S. Immigration Law*, pp. 62—66, 69.

7. Ibid., 5—6.

8. U.S. Bureau of the Census, *Statistical Abstract of the United States: 1984* (Washington, D.C.: USGPO, 1985), p. 86.

9. U.S. Commission on Civil Rights, *The Tarnished Golden Door: Civil Rights Issues in Immigration* (Washington, D.C.: USGPO, 1980), p. 17.

10. The accuracy and meaningfulness of these data is dubious. As Tomasi and Keely (1975: 61–65) have objected, the INS derived occupations from applications and visas, ignoring possible inaccuracies. North and Wesisert (1973) followed a sample of immigrants two years after they had applied for visas and found gross discrepancies between their current occupations and those stated on the visa application.

11. In fact, entrepreneurs were underrepresented in South Korea's immigrant population as fully 33.5 percent of the South Korean labor force was self-employed in 1980. See: Republic of Korea, Office of Prime Minister, *Evaluation Report of the Third Year Program: The Fourth Five Year Development Plan,* 1980.

12. U.S. Immigration and Naturalization Service, *Annual Reports:* 1966 to 1977, table 6C.

13. "Five Suspended by Army for Enlisting Aliens," *Los Angeles Times,* February 13, 1979: pt. I, 3.

14. *Korea Times,* August 7, 1978; INS, *Annual Reports,* 1966–1981.

15. Tables 6 and 7A. Kinship claimants include: exempt from quota and preferences 1, 2, 4, and 5.

16. California Department of Finance, *California Statistical Abstract 1978* (Sacramento: State Documents Section, 1978), p. 28; *California Statistical Abstract 1983,* p. 22.

17. Ibid., p. 19.

18. Compare California Department of Finance, *California Statistical Abstract 1971* (Sacramento: State Documents Sections, 1971), pp. 122, 126, 132; *California Statistical Abstract 1980,* pp. 135, 137, 141.

19. Green's (1977: 231) study of migration to Seoul stresses this point: "For income ... relying on the personal network is a rational choice for the migrants." She also cites Toney (1973: 96–97) to the same effect: "The benefits of social ties were economic as well as supportive, and often resulted in longer duration of residence in the receiving area, even if occupation opportunities were at low levels."

6. KOREAN ENTREPRENEURS

1. Some authors ignore this rule because of the difficulty in obtaining information about poor entrepreneurs. Thus, Saracheck "sampled" 187 entrepreneurs about whom he was able to obtain information from published biographies. Naturally, those sampled were of the stature of J. C. Penney and John Jacob Astor. Saracheck's error is to confuse entrepreneurship with easily available documentation limited to the most conspicuously wealthy among the entrepreneurs. See Bernard Saracheck, "American Entrepreneurs and the Horatio Alger Myth," *Journal of Economic History* 38(1978): 439–456.

2. See: Karsh, 1977; U.S. Small Business Administration, *The Study of Small Business,* (Washington, D.C.: Office of Advocacy, Small Business Administration, 1977); Idem., *Annual Report Fiscal Year 1979;* Idem., *The Small Business Data Base,* 1980.

3. U.S. Bureau of the Census, *1977 Survey of Minority-Owned Business*

Enterprises: Asian Americans, American Indians, and Others (Washington, D.C.: USGPO, 1980), p. 176.

4. This difference had widened by 1982. In that year, Korean firms in Los Angeles County averaged $115,941 in total receipts whereas all U.S. proprietorships averaged only $43,583 in receipts in 1981. Compare *1982 Survey of Minority-Owned Business Enterprises* (Washington, D.C.: USGPO, 1986), p. 133; U.S. Bureau of the Census, *Statistical Abstract of the United States: 1985* (Washington, D.C.: USGPO, 1984), p. 516.

5. Bureau of the Census, *1977 Survey of Minority-Owned Business*, table 4.

6. U.S. President, *The State of Small Business: A Report of the President, Transmitted to Congress, March, 1982* (Washington, D.C.: USGPO, 1982), table A1.26.

7. U.S. Internal Revenue Service, *Statistics of Income, 1979–1980, Sole Proprietorship Returns* (Washington, D.C.: USGPO, table 4.

8. Underpaid need not mean unhappy. Hurh and Kim (1984: ch. 6) found that Korean workers complained of incomes too low to support their families, and limited occupational opportunities, but nonetheless expressed high job satisfaction. This discrepancy they attribute (ch. 9) to reference group influences.

7. CLASS AND ETHNIC RESOURCES

1. Bourdieu (1977) and DiMaggio (1982) have treated "cultural resources" as aesthetic standards acquired at home in the course of primary socialization. These aesthetic standards become markers of class membership since self-made aspirants cannot know them. This conception of class culture ignores the vocational skills and attitudes of a bourgeoisie, surely more basic components of a bourgeois class. Entrepreneurship is the classic vocational culture of a bourgeoisie. In the case of Koreans in Los Angeles, Korean aesthetic standards were unimportant in reproducing class membership. Vocational culture was essential.

2. Blalock (1967: 113) defined "ethnic resources" as "actual sources of power" and "all factors relevant to the exercise of power." Unfortunately, Blalock conceived of economic competition as a strictly individualistic process, thus eliminating from consideration the collective endowments under consideration in this chapter. Blalock's conception reflects the individualistic view of entrepreneurship then current.

3. On education, see the following items in the *Korea Times English Section*: "Special Biz Classes Will Be Provided," January 25, 1977; "Underskilled Workers Must Be Given Legal Minimum Wage," May 30, 1978; "Summer School Due for Biz Managers," July 3, 1978; "Better Treatment of Employees Urged," August 7, 1978; "26 Firm Managers Complete Course," July 16, 1979.

4. See: S. Kim, "Koreans Like to Share Closeness," *Koreatown*, December 14, 1981: 11; H.-I. Kim, "Ethnic Identity Creates Obligations," *Korea Times English Section*, January 1, 1982: 5.

5. Admittedly, we have no way of comparing the methodology utilized in the original collection of these data. There is room for error if one source was more thorough than the other in admitting listees. On the other

hand, the profile of the Korean community that this comparison reveals is compatible with all the qualitative information we collected and provides a striking *Gestalt* of an immigrant community.

6. *Trade Cases, 1976* (Chicago: Commerce Clearing House, Inc., 1976), pp. 68,342—68,344.

7. In 1985, California began requiring new garment manufacturers to pass an examination on state laws and regulations affecting the garment industry. Additionally, California statutes expanded the definition of garment manufacturing while requiring bonds for any garment entrepreneur who had been cited or penalized within the prior three years. "State Laws Tighten Control on Unscrupulous Garment Manufacturers," *East/West*, January 16, 1985: 1.

8. *KRAGL, '86: The Second Annual Awards Banquet.* This is the program of the SCKGLRA's awards banquet held on September 22, 1986.

9. "Prosperity of Shops Leads Community Development," *Korea Times English Section*, November 22, 1976.

10. "Markets Agree to Cut Down on Competition," *Korea Times*, November 23, 1981: 1.

11. "Fifteen Korean Chambers Unite," *Koreatown*, November 17, 1980: 1; Y. Lee, "How Competitive Are We?" *Korea Times English Section*, May 5, 1982: 1; B.-Y. Choy, "Koreans in US Disorganized Lot," *Koreatown*, April 21, 1980: 1; "KCCI Asks Bizmen for More Cooperation," *Korea Times English Section*, February 6, 1980.

12. Ibid.

8. BUSINESS LOCATION

1. Los Angeles County, Departments of Regional Planning and Community Development, *Industrial-Commercial Employment Project* (Los Angeles: County Board of Supervisors, 1977). We thank Peter Fonda-Bernardi and Richard Platkin for making this data available.

The County subsequently learned that the ICE file contained inaccuracies. In 1981 Peter Fonda-Bernardi found large discrepancies between ICE results and census enumerations. The County of Los Angeles tried to clean up the ICE file. However, the reconstruction proving too expensive, the county abandoned the whole project.

2. For an analysis of exactly which service and retail industries were catering to the different clienteles see Bonacich and Jung, 1982: 92—94.

3. See note 1, *supra*.

4. "Minority group populations have generally expanded from clusters within the City into areas beyond Los Angeles City limits. Such movements are largely composed of the most affluent minority group members who are able to purchase residences in the non-city areas." City of Los Angeles, Department of Community Development, Community Analysis and Planning Division, *An Ethnic Trend Analysis of Los Angeles County, 1950—1980* (Los Angeles: City of Los Angeles, 1977): 37.

5. See also: "LA's Korean Population is Moving North," *Koreatown*, June 29, 1981: 1; "Many Koreans Settle in N. W. San Fernando Valley," *Korea Times English Section*, August 12, 1981: 1; "Orange County: Next Stop for Koreans," *Koreatown*, April 5, 1982: 1.

9. THE RETAIL LIQUOR INDUSTRY

1. Cobas (1987: 150) has replicated this finding in his study of ethnic homogeneity among Cuban entrepreneurs in Puerto Rico. Although Cubans were less than 1 percent of Puerto Rico's population, Cuban entrepreneurs found coethnics for partners in 70 percent of multiply owned business firms.

2. However, Zimmer and Aldrich (1987: 439) have subsequently replicated this finding in their study of business sales among Indians and Pakistanis in Britain.

3. Thus, a Korean-American college student explained how her parents had bought their food business:

> My parents currently own a fast-food restaurant in a black community. Both my parents had college educations in Korea, but because of their difficulties in English, they weren't able to apply for jobs that matched their skills. They never had the idea of owning their own business until my father's high school friend from Korea sold his fast-food restaurant to my parents.

4. S. Kim, "Koreans Like to Share Closeness," *Koreatown*, December 14, 1981: 11; H.-I. Kim, "Ethnic Identity Creates Obligations," *Korea Times English Section*, January 1, 1982.

5. Since DABC ledgers contained no selling terms, the transactions we encoded may have included noncash transfers as well as cash sales. Noncash transfers of license ownership could occur in the wake of wills, divorces, or bankruptcies. Conceivably noncash transfers were ethnically homogeneous whereas cash sales were independent of ethnicity. Prepared to agree that a two-tiered (cash and noncash) transfer system probably coexisted in these DABC data, we cannot separate the two classes of transfer. On the other hand, noncash transfers were fully as legal and essential as cash transfers. In the life of a business, necessary changes of ownership occur for various reasons, but only some require cash sales. The DABC data show that ownership changes of these liquor businesses stayed within the boundaries of each ethnic group, venturing out only rarely into the open market.

6. "Sellers selected real estate agents at least partly on the basis of a common ethnicity." Palm, 1985: 62.

10. RAISING CAPITAL

1. Koreans in other cities also used the kye. Myers (1983: 87) found kye common among Koreans in Philadelphia. Harris (1983) noted its utility in New York City where Korean greengrocers tapped this source for business loans. In Japan, overseas Koreans "usually join a mujin," a Japanese rotating credit association: "The Mujins are not limited to financial matters but also serve as social clubs" (De Vos and Chung, 1981: 239).

2. Kennedy (1973: 155) explodes the error of assuming that kyes cannot be important financial institutions because women run them. Women participated in kyes with the knowledge and consent of their husbands as part of their family's financial strategy: "The participation is part of a joint plan to obtain a lump-sum of money for some particular family need or business."

3. "Kye Widespread among Koreans in Los Angeles," July 10, 1983.

4. "16 Million Dollar Kye Fraud," *Joong-ang Daily News*, February 2, 1979: 1. Translated by Terry Chang.

5. "$400,000 Kye Broke," *Joong-ang Daily News*, February 20, 1979: 1. Translated by Terry Chang.

6. "Police Warn of Danger of Kyes and Ask People Not to Participate," *Korea Times*, August 10, 1983. Translated by Edward Chang.

7. "Police Arrest Kye Organizer," *Korea Times*, May 27, 1983; "Kye Organizer Arrested," *Joong-ang Daily News*, July 22, 1983; "Kye Fraud Case Reported to Police Again," *Korea Times*, August 1, 1983; "Police Investigate Kye for Third Time," *The Dong-a Illbo*, August 1, 1983. All articles were translated from Korean by Edward Chang.

8. "The amount of money one borrows from a private lender ranges from $2,000 to $100,000 with interest rates from 30 to 40 percent per year." "Private Lending Rampant," *Koreatown Weekly*, March 23, 1980: 11.

9. "15 Years Given to Masterminds in Loan Scandal," *Korea Times English Section*, August 9, 1982.

10. "Beginning in the 1880s, East European Jewish immigrants transported Hebrew free loan associations from Europe to America." These are philanthropic organizations intended to provide poor Jews with interest-free loans, especially for business purposes. In 1927, more than 500 Hebrew free loan societies existed in American cities, and their leadership stressed the importance of the free loan societies in helping indigent and immigrant Jews to open business firms. See: Shelley Tenenbaum, "Immigrants and Capital: Jewish Loan Societies in the United States, 1880–1945," *American Jewish History* 76(1986): 67–77.

11. "14 Minority Banks Born During 1974–75 Period," *New Korea*, Dec. 4, 1975.

12. "Asian Banks Competitive in Loan Survey," *East/West* [San Francisco] July 28, 1978: 8.

13. "'The United California Bank is keenly aware of the mushroom growth of the Korean community ... and is trying to bestow favors on Korean residents with various financial benefits including business loans,' said Ben K. Hong, 47, Asian division vice president of the UCB." "UCB Offers Benefits to Korean Residents," *Korea Times English Section*, April 28, 1980.

14. "Help for Small Businesses Available from SBA Program," *Koreatown*, November 30, 1980: 3.

15. "Businesses Ignore State Help," *Koreatown*, September 22, 1980: 1.

16. U.S. Office of Manpower and Budget, *1976 Interagency Report on the Federal Minority Business Development Programs* (Washington, D.C.: USGPO, 1976), p. 3.

17. "California Korea Bank Helps Community Grow," *Koreatown*, June 16, 1980.

18. "KEB Debtors Turned Over to Collection Agency," *Korea Times*, July 24, 1978: 1.

19. "The loan ceiling of the Korea Exchange Bank LA Agency has increased from $50,000 to $200,000 providing a bright prospect for Korean traders in Southern California districts." "FX Bank Loans Up to 200,000 Dollars," *Korea Times*, June 27, 1977.

20. "Setup of Finance Co. with $500,000 Planned," *Korea Times*, March 14, 1977. See also: "Bank of Finance is Now in the Control of Asians," *Los Angeles Sentinel*, January 8, 1981: A-1. "The bottom line here was that the bank made some loans which were not collectible."

21. "Founding of Savings, Loan Association Sought," *Korea Times*, July 17, 1978.

22. "Global Oriental Opens Office," *Korea Times English Section*, August 12, 1981: 1.

23. "Troubled Bank Taken Over by Businessmen," *Korea Times English Section*, January 28, 1982: 1; S. Kim, "Korean Woman Manager, Immigrant Businessmen Put New Life into Bank," *Koreatown*, May 17, 1982: 1.

24. "First Private Bank to be Set Up to Serve Residents," *Korea Times*, October 16, 1979.

25. "Wilshire State Bank Opens Branch To Serve LA's Korean Community," *Koreatown*, March 9, 1981: 15; "No Language Barrier in Community Banks," *Korea Times English Section*, September 29, 1981: 1.

11. SOURCES OF KOREAN ENTREPRENEURSHIP

1. See "David Kim's Life Typifies Saga of Koreans," *Koreatown*, November 17, 1980: 9; see also: S. Kim, "Irene Choi: a Great Leader," *Koreatown*, December 14, 1981: 1; S. Chaneka, "Small Savings to Multi-Million Business," *Koreatown*, July 27, 1981: 1; C. Thompson, "Korean Immigrant Turns Dilemmas to Prosperity," *Koreatown* January 11, 1982: 1; "In Dorothy Kim's Store It's Mind Over Matter," *Koreatown*, April 14, 1980: 5; S. Chaneka, "Successful Importer Claims Work, Credit Keys to Business," *Koreatown*, June 30, 1980: 7; S. Kim, "Young Whan Cho: A True Success Story," *Koreatown*, April 5, 1982: 4; "Famed Food Dealer Dies of Blood Pressure," *Korea Times English Section*, October 16, 1978.

2. Sophia Kim observes that in Korean-American families both parents worked out of a "lust for money." Sometimes grandparents were available to mind the children, often not. Left alone, Korean children got into trouble, felt lonely, and were neglected. Korean tradition denigrates social welfare, encouraging families to conceal problems. "Korean-Americans' Lust for Money: It's the Children Who Suffer Most," *Koreatown*, March 23, 1981: 1. See also "Korean Immigrants Battle Stress," *Koreatown*, July 28, 1980: 1. The debunking process had already begun, and could be found in the same publications that praised the Korean entrepreneurs for their hard work and thrift. For example, Steve Chaneka observed that Korean stores were family enterprises requiring long hours of work for small hourly returns. But the family had no leisure as a result. True, these stores earned $40,000 a year, but their owners were slaves of their loans. It's not such a great deal, Chaneka warned. "American Dream?" *Koreatown*, May 5, 1980: 12.

3. *Los Angeles Times*, April 13, 1980: pt. II, 1.

4. Hagen (1968: 225) rejects the old-fashioned view that people only work effectively to forward their personal economic interest: "The entrepreneur may act to advance himself, his family, his community, his country, some other social group, or the business organization to which he is attached."

5. Since Weber, numerous cases have come to light in which sect

adherents turned to entrepreneurship. One such was Father Divine's Peace Mission Movement, a business-oriented black sect of the 1930s and 1940s (Light, 1972: ch. 7). Cohen (1969) documented the entrepreneurial influence of the Tijaniyya cult among Hausa in Ibadan, and Stone (1974) the entrepreneurial influence of religious ethic upon the Jerban in Tunisia. In Java, Reformist Muslims introduced a "bourgeois ethic" into the bazaar economy (Geertz, 1963: 49). A nonreligious case turned up in South Africa where, according to Stokes (1974) Afrikaner nationalism encouraged whites to turn to entrepreneurship.

6. *U.S. Department of Commerce News*, CB84-179, October 17, 1984: tables 1, 2.

7. "Churches in U.S. Now Number 713," *Korea Times English Section*, April 22, 1982: 1.

8. "Church Attendance is High in Korea," *Koreatown*, April 5, 1982: 2.

9. "Survey: 42% Koreans Believe in God," *Korea News Review*, November 20, 1982: 27.

10. "Korean Churches Total 218 as of December," *Korea Times*, December 26, 1978. See also: *New Korea*, March 20, 1975; "Korean Churches," *Koreatown*, November 3, 1980: 4.

12. REACTION AND SOLIDARITY

1. "... we see potential conflict with a number of important interest groups, including disprivileged minorities who are clients and potential competitors, white small business and independent professionals, previous middleman minorities, and perhaps eventually the larger corporations. This conflict may provoke a new racism." Ivan Light and Edna Bonacich, "Recent Asian Immigrants in Los Angeles," grant application submitted to Sociology Division, National Science Foundation, 1975.

2. "Liquor Price System is Likely to Continue," *Korea Times*, January 6, 1977. See also: "Supermarkets Sell Liquor at Low Prices," *Korea Times*, July 17, 1978; "Liquor Sale Offensives Launched," *Korea Times*, June 19, 1978.

3. "This Association embodies the spirit of togetherness and of oneness in achieving worthwhile goals in business ... We represent the 'Small Guys' in this enormous industry and we assure our collective economic survival against 'Giant Supermarkets and Chains' ... We need stronger teamwork and a lasting spirit of unity." Yang Il Kim, president, Southern California Korean Grocers and Liquor Retailers Association, in the program for the SCKGLRA's Second Annual Awards Banquet, 1986, p. 1.

4. International Ladies' Garment Workers Union, *Report of the General Executive Board to the 35th Convention*, Miami Beach, May 31, 1974, pp. 51, 55–56.

5. *Los Angeles Times*, May 18, 1979: pt. II, 7.

6. "Back to the Sweatshops" (Editorial), *Los Angeles Times*, January 28, 1979: pt. V, 4.

7. "6 Employers Held for Illegal Acts," *Korea Times*, March 25, 1980; "Illegal Labor Practices Should be Eliminated," *Korea Times*, April 22, 1980; "Garment Law Compliance Mandated," *Korea Times*, July 14, 1981: 1. In January 1985, California began to require garment contractors to take and pass an examination to demonstrate their knowledge of state laws and

regulations concerning the garment industry. "This requirement is one of several changes in the California labor code passed to protect garment workers from unscrupulous employers." "State Laws Tighten Control on Unscrupulous Garment Mfrs," *East/West*, January 6, 1985: 1.

8. See the following articles in the *Korea Times English Section*: "Ex-Royal Bakery Shop Owner Shot to Death," June 26, 1978; "Shop Manager Arrests U.S. Gangster," July 3, 1978; "Patrol Car Operates to Prevent Crimes," August 7, 1978; "Two Black Youths Snatch Handbag," August 14, 1978; "Store Employee Killed in Residential District," October 2, 1978; "Crimes, Incidents Up in Korean Community," October 2, 1978; "How To Prevent Attack by Criminals Discussed," October 16, 1978; "Two Youths Steal from Grocery Shop," October 30, 1978; "Two Koreans Robbed in Koreatown," December 26, 1978; "Black Cuts Artery in Korean's Left Arm," May 7, 1979; "Criminal Acts Plague LA Korean Community," June 19, 1979; "Three Kidnappings, Rape Occur Over Weekend," June 19, 1979; "Two Armed Men Break into Korean's Market," September 4, 1979; "Anti-Crime Measures Discussed in Seminar," December 31, 1979; "Taekwondoist Knocks Down Burglar," January 22, 1980; "Rising Crimes Pose Big Threat to Koreatown," February 11, 1980; "For Crime Prevention in Korea Town," May 6, 1980; "Ways Mulled to Prevent Ever-Increasing Crime," April 22, 1981; "Gun Violence Rips Korean Community," August 28, 1981; "Couple Fatally Shot in Armed Robbery," November 17, 1982; "Koreans Urged to Help Police Prevent Crimes," May 12, 1983.

See also the following articles in other publications: "Korean Businesses Easy Prey for Criminals," *Koreatown*, February 22, 1982; "An Everyday Shooting: Korean Dilemma in Inner-City Businesses," *Koreatown*, March 8, 1982; "Crime in Korea Town: Shop Owners Learn to Live With Terror," *Koreatown*, March 22, 1982; "Coping with Crime: A Day in the Life of a Korea Town Guard," *Koreatown*, April 5, 1982; "Reliance on Police Soars in Koreatown," *Los Angeles Times*, July 23, 1982: pt. II, 1; "Korean Businesses Crime Targets," *Koreatown*, November 1982: 4; Marita Hernandez, "Tale of 2 Cultures: Murders Refocus Spotlight on Tensions between Koreans, Blacks," *Los Angeles Times*, May 18, 1986: pt. II, 1. Eui-Young Yu (1986: 34) reports that Korean newspapers tallied the ethnic/racial background of persons arrested in connection with crimes against Koreans in the City of Los Angeles during March, May, and June of 1983. About 90 percent of offenders were black.

9. "Mom and Pop Stores," *Black Enterprise* 3(1972): 17–21; "Crime Insurance," *Black Enterprise* 3(1973): 33.

10. "Inside Korea Town," *Koreatown*, February 23, 1981: 2.

11. "Patrol Car Operates to Prevent Crimes," *Korea Times*, August 7, 1978.

12. "How To Prevent Attack by Criminals Discussed," *Korea Times*, October 16, 1978.

13. See the following articles in the *Korea Times English Section*: "Community to Help Open Police Post," August 31, 1981; "Fierce Competition for Outpost Erupts," September 10, 1981; "Outpost Begins Patrol at 8th Street," September 24, 1981; "Outpost Begins Operations with Hour Long Ceremony," October 9, 1981; "Assemblyman Honors Local Businessman," December 4, 1981; "Police Center in Trouble; Kwon to Resign" July 2,

1982; "Police Outpost Launches Big Anti-Crime Programs," September 21, 1982.

14. "Korean Packing Companies to be Probed," *Korea Times*, June 20, 1977: 1.

15. "Residents Warned of Food Law Negligence," *Korea Times*, October 24, 1978; "Improvement Urged of Sanitary Conditions," *Korea Times*, November 21, 1978.

16. "60 Massage Parlors Investigated," *Korea Times*, June 18, 1979.

17. "Oriental Parlors Puzzle Police," *Los Angeles Times*, September 7, 1977: pt. II, 1; "17 Women Arrested in Massage Parlor Raids," *Korea Times English Section*, July 8, 1982; "Prostitution: The Far East Link is Growing in L.A.," *Los Angeles Times*, September 15, 1986: pt. II, 1.

18. See the following stories by Leonard Greenwood in the *Los Angeles Times*: "Police Claim Crime Syndicate Preying on Koreans in LA," June 6, 1981: pt. II, 1; "Leader of Area Koreans Arrested in Seoul Airport," June 13, 1981: pt. I, 32; "U.S. Will Probe Crime in Korean Community," July 18, 1981: pt. I, 29; "Crime Probe in Koreatown Yields Arrest," July 24, 1981: pt. II, 1. See also the following Korean reactions to these exposes: "Leaders Debate on Rhee, Crime Reports," *Korea Times English Section*, June 12, 1981; "Koreatown Reacts to 'Godfather' Article," *Koreatown*, June 29, 1981; "Task Force Names 4 Koreatown Gangs," *Korea Times English Section*, May 11, 1983.

19. "Asian American Leaders Pressure SBA for Minority Classification," *East/West*, May 23, 1979: 3; "SBA Finds Asians Eligible Socially Disadvantaged," *East/West*, July 18, 1979: 1. The formation of a federation of Minority Business Associations brought together Asians, blacks, Latins, and Indians in 1980. The federation lobbied for "stringent guidelines" to keep "front" businesses from masquerading as minority-owned in order to obtain governmental contracts awarded by preference to minority firms. See Wendy Kaufman, "4 Minority Groups Unify to Boost Business Strength," *Los Angeles Times*, May 28, 1980: pt. IV, 1.

20. "Asian, Inc. Rebounds Strongly," *East/West*, May 30, 1979.

21. "A/A delegates prepare for White House Small Business Confab," *East/West*, August 1, 1979.

22. "The largely immigrant Korean enclave seethes with rumors of impending raids on Korean-run businesses these days." "Rumors of Immigration Raids," *Koreatown*, March 8, 1982: 5. See also: Tom Suhr, "Proposed Immigration Law Would Discriminate Against Koreans," *Koreatown*, May 3, 1982: 1; Yeo-Chun Yun, "Immigration Bill Bad News for Asians," *Korea Times English Section*, January 1, 1982.

23. U.S. Congress, House of Representatives, Committee on Banking, Housing, and Urban Affairs, 95th Congress, Second Session, *International Banking Act of 1978*. Report #95-1073.

24. "Hostilities Build Between Vietnamese, White Fishermen," *East/West*, September 14, 1983: 12. See also: U.S. Congress, House of Representatives, Committee on the Judiciary, Subcommittee on Crime, 96th Congress, Second Session, *Increasing Violence Against Minorities*, 1981; U.S. Commission on Civil Rights, *Intimidation and Violence: Racial and Religious Bigotry in America*, Publication no. 77, 1983; Idem., *Recent Activities Against Citizens and Residents of Asian Descent*, Publication no. 88, 1986.

25. "Asians Harassed in Washington," *Koreatown*, January 4, 1983: 7.

26. "Chinese Americans and the KKK," *Crosscurrents* 4(1981): 13–14. Publication of UCLA Asian American Studies Department. See also: "Increasing Attacks on Minorities Cited," *Korea Times English Section*, February 15, 1983.

27. County of Los Angeles, Commission on Human Relations. "Rising Anti-Asian Bigotry: Manifestations, Sources, Solutions." Transcript of Public Hearing Conducted November 9, 1983. "Bigotry's Manifestation, Sources, and Solution Presented in LA," *East/West*, November 16, 1983: 1. See also: Penelope McMillan, "Anti-Asian Bigotry: An 'Alarming' Rise as Refugees Pour In," *Los Angeles Times*, February 4: pt. II, 1.

28. The offending bumper sticker proclaimed: "Will the Last American in Monterey Park Please Bring the Flag." A pair of slant eyes completed the thought.

29. "Asians Ready Fight Against Prejudice," *Korea Times English Section*, July 3, 1981: 1; "Trial in Boston," *East/West*, April 18, 1984: 10; "LA Coalition Forms to Combat Anti-Asian Racism," *East/West*, July 22, 1981: 3; "Asian Groups Join to Fight 'Scapegoating,'" *Korea Times English Section*, June 8, 1983: 1. The problem reached as far as Australia: John Shaw, "Return of the 'Yellow Peril,'" *Far Eastern Economic Review* 106(November 2, 1979): 38.

30. Sandy Banks, "Korean Merchants, Black Customers—Tensions Grow," *Los Angeles Times*, April 15, 1985: pt. II, 1; "Blacks Say Taxi Company Guilty of Discrimination," *Korea Times English Section*, March 29, 1983; Carl Chamberlain, "Black Cab Driver Files Discrimination Suit" *Los Angeles Sentinel*, August 6, 1981: Al. The most serious intergroup trouble occurred in New York City where Harlem's black merchants unleashed an anti-Korean boycott in 1981. The merchants called Korean competitors "vampires" sent to "suck black consumers dry" (Noel, 1981a, 1981b). See: "Boycott of Korean Merchants," *Koreatown*, January 4, 1983: 4. See also two articles by Wong Nyol Yoo in *Joong-ang Daily News*: "Why Bother Koreans in Harlem? Extended Media Coverage Disturbing," September 8, 1981: 1; also "Business Owners in New York's Harlem Struggle Against Anti-Korean Prejudice," October 19, 1981: 1; Richard Stengel, "Blacks: Resentment Tinged with Envy," *Time* 126 (July 8, 1985): 42–43. A sample of the hostile rhetoric from a black student publication at UCLA:

> These non-Blacks in the Black community have been imported into this country ... at any alarming rate. They are known to work long, hard hours for little pay. They eat sparingly and are accustomed to very little in the way of material comfort. They do not, for the most part, speak English and therefore can be manipulated much easier [sic] than Blacks. They, along with other non-Black immigrants, have been used by the U.S. to systematically replace Blacks.

See: Marlene Kelly, "We Must, I Said, We Must Be Aware," *Nommo*, May 9, 1979.

31. For example, Korean restaurateurs charged five cents for a cup of water previously given free. If blacks exceeded their cash in pumping gasoline at self-service pumps, Korean owners refused well-documented local checks for the balance, insisting that customers "leave watch" for security. Koreans also followed black customers around their stores in

obvious expectation of shoplifting. Black/Korean commercial tensions were treated on public television's (KCET) "California Stories" on January 17, 1987. This cinematic documentary provided coverage of the grievances of black consumers while developing the saccharine view that perceived conflicts of economic interest did not exacerbate any cultural conflict involved.

32. "Two Communities Seek Close Cooperative Ties," *Korea Times*, November 19, 1979. The Korean Association also concluded a mutual assistance treaty with the Jewish Federation Council of Greater Los Angeles. See *Korea Times*, December 31, 1979; John Dart, "Korean Immigrants, Blacks Use Churches as Bridge to Ease Tensions," *Los Angeles Times*, November 9, 1985: pt. II, 4; Janet Clayton, "Tenuous New Alliances Forged to Ease Korean–Black Tensions," *Los Angeles Times*, July 20, 1987: pt. II, 1.

33. Naturally, the decisions were challenged in the courts. On April 18, 1984 the U.S. Supreme Court finally upheld the INS surprise inspections of factories, concluding the tactic was an indispensable tool of law enforcement away from the border.

34. Ivan Light and Angel Sanchez examined 272 SMSAs using the 1980 Public Use Sample of the United States Census. They found that, net of five economic control variables, rate of self-employment among Koreans in SMSAs had no statistically significant effect upon rate of self-employment among native blacks nor upon mean self-employment income of native blacks. This result is not what one would expect if Korean entrepreneurs were soaking up economic opportunities that blacks would otherwise have enjoyed, yet there is a widespread belief in black communities that Korean entrepreneurs depress and inhibit black-owned business. See: "Immigrant Entrepreneurs in 272 SMSAs," *Sociological Perspectives* 30(1987): 373–399.

35. "Koreans Concerned over Name-Calling by Police," *Koreatown*, May 3, 1982: 3.

36. "Korean-Americans in LA Should Raise Voices: Sonia Suk," *Korea Times*, March 9, 1981: 1. See also Choy, 1980; Kang, 1981; Jo, 1982.

37. "Tension among Koreans, Chinese Leads to Brawls among Youths," *Koreatown*, October 19, 1981: 3; "Asians Must Work Together," *Koreatown*, December 3, 1981: 31.

13. PROTECTION OF U.S. LABOR STANDARDS

1. For a thorough review and critique of the labor segmentation literature, see Bonacich (1980). Most of the data presented in this chapter derive from that paper.

2. U.S. Department of Labor, Employment Standards Administration, *Minimum Wage and Maximum Hours Standards under the Fair Labor Standards Act: An Economic Effects Study submitted to Congress*, 1979: 61.

3. Ibid., p. 7.

4. Ibid., pp. 29, 35, 44. For a full list of number of investigations, number of workers affected, and dollar amounts for 1939 to 1977, see U.S. Department of Labor, Bureau of Labor Statistics, *Handbook of Labor Statistics, 1978*: 552–553.

5. U.S. Department of Labor, *Minimum Wage*, pp. 30–31.

6. Ibid., pp. 33–35.

7. U.S. Congress, House Committee on Education and Labor, Subcommittee on Labor Standards, 95th Congress, First Session, 1977, *Hearings on Fair Labor Standards Amendment of 1977*.

8. The equalizing of minimum wages in Puerto Rico with the mainland is a highly significant point. It can be interpreted as an effort by labor to prevent the island from being used as a cheap labor zone, hence a base for runaway shops.

9. National Labor Relations Board, *A Guide to Basic Law and Procedures under the National Labor Relations Act*, 1978: 1.

10. Ibid., p. 48.

11. Ibid, p, 45.

12. Ibid., pp. 46–48.

13. U.S. Congress, House Committee on Education and Labor, Subcommittee on Labor-Management Relations, 95th Congress, First Session, 1977, *Hearings on the Labor Relations Act of 1977*.

14. See Bonacich, 1976, for an analysis of the shift in the position of the black community from undercutting to solidarity with labor.

15. Social Security Administration, Department of Health, Education and Welfare, *Annual Report for Fiscal Year 1977*. Submitted to the House Ways and Means Committee, 95th Congress, Second Session, 1978: 1.

16. Ibid.

17. U.S. Department of Health, Education and Welfare, *Aid to Families with Dependent Children: A Chartbook*. HEW Pub. No. SSA 78-11721, 1978: 29.

18. U.S. Congress, House Committee on Ways and Means, Subcommittee on Social Security, 95th Congress, First Session, 1977, *Hearings on President Carter's Social Security Proposals*: 1013.

19. The weakness of social security converage for immigrants may help to explain their tendency to become sojourners, with plans to return to their homeland to retire, an orientation that itself encourages entry into small business (Bonacich, 1973).

20. U.S. Department of Health, Education and Welfare, *Characteristics of State Plans for Aid to Families with Dependent Children*. HEW Pub. No. SSA 78-21235: x.

21. Immigration and Nationality Act, Amendments of 1976, Section 202(e).

22. Immigration and Nationality Act, Section 212(2)(14).

14. CHEAPNESS OF IMMIGRANT SMALL BUSINESS

1. Parts of this section were presented in a paper at the annual convention of the American Association for the Advancement of Science (Bonacich, 1978).

2. Our analysis of small business as a form of labor is not completely unique. The same idea has been put forward in examining the "informal sector" and "petty commodity production" in Third World countries (see, for example, Gerry and Birkbeck, 1981; and Portes and Walton, 1981: chapter 3). To our knowledge, no one has yet considered this notion for advanced capitalist countries.

3. Chapter 16 examines efforts by Korean business-owners to do so.

4. U.S. Commission on Civil Rights, California Advisory Committee, *A Dream Unfulfilled: Korean and Filipino Health Professionals in California,* 1975.

5. In 1980 an amendment to some social welfare legislation stripped legal immigrants of access to SSI and AFDC funds by calculating their eligibility for the first three years of residence based on the income of their legal sponsors rather than their own income. This new innovation made it harder for new immigrants to find alternatives to accepting cheap-labor jobs.

15. USE OF SMALL BUSINESS BY U.S. CAPITAL

1. See, for example, U.S. Senate, Select Committee on Small Business, Subcommittee on Urban and Rural Development, *The Impact of Franchising on Small Business,* 1970; U.S. Senate, Committee on Commerce, 94th Congress, Second Session, Hearings April 7–8, 1976, *Fairness in Franchising Act.*

2. U.S. Department of Commerce, *Franchising in the Economy, 1975–77,* 1976: 2.

3. U.S. Department of Commerce, *Franchising,* p. 2.

4. Ibid., p. 40.

5. Ibid., p. 20. Franchising continued to grow into the early 1980s. In 1980 there were 442,371 franchised establishments, estimated to rise to 465,594 by 1982. Sales had gone up to $336 billion in 1980, a rise of 85 percent since 1975, and estimated sales for 1982 were $437 billion. Franchised businesses employed 4.7 million workers in 1980, expected to rise to 5 million by 1982. International franchising had almost doubled by 1980, with 279 franchisors running 20,428 units abroad (U.S. Department of Commerce, *Franchising in the Economy, 1980–82,* 1982: 1, 6, 22–24).

6. U.S. Department of Commerce, *Franchising,* 1976, p. 32; U.S. Department of Commerce, *Franchising in the Economy, 1977–79,* 1979, p. 32.

7. Ibid., p. 44.

8. Ibid., p. 1.

9. U.S. Senate, *Fairness in Franchising,* p. 60.

10. U.S. Department of Commerce, *Franchising,* 1982, p. 1.

11. U.S. House, Permanent Select Committee on Small Business, Subcommittee on Minority Small Business and Franchising, *The Role of Small Business in Franchising.* Hearings June 20–21, July 12, 1973: 1.

12. U.S. Department of Commerce, *Franchising,* 1976, p. 1. For a list of seventeen benefits to franchisees prepared by the International Franchise Association, an organization of franchisors, see U.S. Senate, *Fairness in Franchising,* p. 59.

13. U.S. Department of Commerce, *Franchising,* 1976, p. 33.

14. U.S. Senate, *Fairness in Franchising,* p. 299.

15. U.S. House, *Role of Small Business,* p. 151.

16. U.S. Senate, *Fairness in Franchising,* p. 51.

17. Ibid., p. 82.

18. Ibid.

19. Ibid., p. 17.

20. Ibid., p. 27.

21. Ibid., p. 24.

22. Ibid., p. 22.

23. U.S. House, *Role of Small Business*, pp. 29—30.

24. An effort was made to obtain such a list from the California Department of Corporations, which registers franchises under the state Franchise Investment Law. The department kindly complied with our request, but it was immediately evident that some obvious franchises, like McDonalds, were omitted. On inquiry we discovered that the law exempted companies of a certain net worth and with a specified, preexisting franchise program, from having to register. The list was, therefore, noncomprehensive. Another source we pursued was the U.S. Office of Minority Business Enterprise's *Franchise Opportunities Handbook* (1977). Approximately 750 companies were listed there, compared to 1166 franchisors enumerated in 1976 by the Department of Commerce. Gasoline service stations were one obvious omission in this source.

25. The 1980 survey of franchises conducted by the Commerce Department found 6194 units owned by minority group members, or 1.4 percent of the total units. However, thirty-nine of the largest franchisors did not maintain data on the ethnic composition of their owners. Of those outlets for which information was available, 1342, or 22 percent, of minority-owned franchises were owned by Asians (U.S. Department of Commerce, *Franchising*, 1982, pp. 7—8).

26. One wonders whether the rise of subcontracting was a response to a rise in the unionization of custodial staffs. Another interesting question is the degree to which immigrant firms bumped the employment of local minority workers, creating frictions between the different minority communities. Unfortunately, we were unable to pursue these topics. For a general description of this line of business, including its low entry capital requirements and the tendency to use relatives as employees, see Bank of America, "Building Maintenance Services," *Small Business Reporter*, 12(3) (1974): 1.

27. United California Bank, "The Apparel Industry in California" (Los Angeles, 1971), pp. 5—6.

28. U.S. Department of Commerce, Bureau of Census, *1977 Census of Manufactures—Geographic Area Series: California* (Washington, D.C.: USGPO, 1977).

29. U.S. Department of Commerce, Bureau of Census, *County Business Patterns, 1977: California* (Washington, D.C.: USGPO, 1979).

30. Bank of America, "Building Maintenance Services" p. 1.

31. Bureau of Census, *County Business Patterns, 1977*.

32. Bank of America, "Building Maintenance Services," p. 9.

33. U.S. Economic Development Administration, *Urban Business Profile: Contract Draws Manufacturing*, 1972: 2.

34. Bank of America, *Small Business Reporter*, 1971, p. 9.

35. U.S. Economic Development Administration, *Urban Business Profile: Contract Draws Manufacturing*, 1972: 3.

36. Ibid., p. 5.

37. California Employment Development Department, *California Labor Market Bulletin, Statistical Supplement (March)* (Sacramento: EDD, 1977).

38. California Department of Industrial Relations, *1976 Annual Report* (San Francisco, 1977), p. 7.

39. *Los Angeles Times*, August 21, 1976.

40. *Hankuk Ilbo,* April 8, 1974.

41. International Ladies' Garment Workers Union, *Report of the General Executive Board to the 35th Convention, Miami Beach, May 31, 1974,* pp. 218–228.

42. International Ladies' Garment Workers Union, *1977 Census Report* (New York: ILGWU Auditing Department, 1978).

43. Put another way, distribution was not a profitable enterprise to the producer of commodities. It only entailed the realization of profits rather than their generation, and its costs came out of profits. Therefore there was no advantage in hiring labor for distribution, since surplus value was not being extracted from that labor. The only consideration was that it be done as cheaply as possible. And here the immigrant retailer was unsurpassed.

44. "Reproducing the labor force" refers not only to the reproduction of the next generation of workers, but also to the daily reproduction of already employed workers. The cost of reproduction thus includes the cost of food, clothing, housing, and other essential items of consumption that keep the labor force alive.

45. U.S. House, Ways and Means Committee, Subcommittee on Select Revenue Measures, 96th Congress, First Session, 1979, *Independent Contractors*: 228–229.

46. Ibid., p. 229.

47. This untitled study remains in draft form and is only available from its author.

48. Marx called this strategy increasing absolute surplus value, as opposed to the increase of relative surplus value by improving techniques of production.

49. Obviously there were some limits to this control, especially when local "monopolies" found themselves facing new competition at an international level, as in the steel and automobile industries.

16. MAKING OF IMMIGRANT SMALL BUSINESS

1. We are indebted to Helen Chen for providing us with an initial list of relevant Interim Decisions.

2. See Bonacich, 1978, for a discussion of several other types of displacement.

3. We are missing Matter of Lui, which was unavailable in the UCLA law library.

4. At this point our funds had long since dried up and we were not in a position to open a whole new line of research. We leave anyone who decides to pursue this topic further the small legacy that they should start with the Labor Department.

Other interesting leads came out of this interview. Apparently the I-526 form filled out by a prospective immigrant who wanted to use the exemption had to be filed with INS in Washington. These forms were reputed to be in a state of chaos, hence inaccessible. However INS was in the process of computerizing their records, and perhaps these data can now be examined.

5. Here again was a level of investigation of which we had been unaware, and could not now afford to pursue, namely, Appellate Court cases.

6. *East/West*, January 12, 1977.

7. See, for example, U.S. Congress, House Committee on Small Business, 96th Congress, First Session, 1979, *Future of Small Business in America*; U.S. Congress, Joint Economic Committee, Subcommittee on Economic Growth and Stabilization, 95th Congress, First Session, 1977, *Foundations for a National Policy to Preserve Private Enterprise in the 1980s*; U.S. Senate Select Committee on Small Business, 95th Congress, Second Session, 1978, *Small Business and the Quality of American Life.*

References

Abrams, Elliott, and Franklin S. Abrams. 1975. "Immigration Policy—Who Gets In and Why?" *The Public Interest* 38 (Winter 1975): 3–29.

Adelman, Irma, and Sherman Robinson. 1978. *Income Distribution Policy in Developing Countries: A Case Study of Korea.* New York: Oxford University Press.

Ahn, Rev. Y. 1975. *Koreans in the Los Angeles Area.* Los Angeles: Korean Community Services.

Aldrich, Howard, and Jane Weiss. 1981. "Differentiation within the U.S. Capitalist Class." *American Sociological Review* 46: 279–290.

———, John C. Cater, Trevor P. Jones, and David McEvoy. 1981. "Business Development and Self-Segregation: Asian Enterprise in Three British Cities." Ch. 8 in *Ethnic Segregation in Cities* edited by Ceri Peach, Vaugn Robinson, and Susan Smith, Athens: University of Georgia Press.

Aldrich, Howard, Trevor P. Jones, and David McEvoy. 1984. "Ethnic Advantage and Minority Business Development." Ch. 11 in *Ethnic Communities in Business,* edited by Robin Ward and Richard Jenkins. New York: Cambridge University Press.

Allen, Irving Lewis. 1983. *The Language of Ethnic Conflict.* New York: Columbia University.

Amsun Associates. 1977. *Socio-Economic Analysis of Asian American Business Patterns.* Washington, D.C.: Office of Minority Business Enterprise, Department of Commerce.

Anderson, Harry. 1978. "More Foreigners Buying U.S. Businesses." *Los Angeles Times,* October 24: pt. I, 1.

Andreski, Stanislav. 1963. "An Economic Interpretation of Anti-Semitism in Eastern Europe." *Jewish Journal of Sociology* 5: 201–213.

Auster, Ellen, and Howard Aldrich. 1984. "Small Business Vulnerability: Ethnic Enclaves, and Ethnic Enterprise." Pp. 39–54 in *Ethnic Communities in Business,* edited by Robin Ward and Richard Jenkins. New York: Cambridge University Press.

Baker, Bob. 1980. "Black's Suit Charges Market Favors Asians." *Los Angeles Times* April 3, 1980.

Balassa, Bela. 1971. "Industrial Policies of Taiwan and Korea." *Weltwirtschaftliches Archiv* 106(1): 55–76.

Baldwin, Frank, ed. 1974. *Without Parallel: The American–Korea Relationship Since 1954.* New York: Pantheon.

Ban, Sung-Hwan. 1977. "The New Community Movement." Pp. 206–235 in *Essays on the Korean Economy*, vol. II. *Industrial and Social Development Issues*, edited by Chuk Kyo Kim. Seoul: Korea Development Institute.

Bank of Korea. 1978, 1979. *Economic Statistics Yearbook*. Seoul: Bank of Korea.

Banks, Arthur S. 1977. "Republic of Korea." Pp. 219–221 in Arthur S. Banks, ed. *Political Handbook of the World*. New York: McGraw-Hill.

Barkan, Elliot, and Robert M. O'Brien. 1984. "Naturalization Trends Among Selected Asian Immigrants, 1950–1976." *Ethnic Forum* 4(1–2): 91–108.

Bates, Timothy. 1985. "Entrepreneur Human Capital Endowments and Minority Business Viability." *The Journal of Human Resources* 20: 540–554.

Baumol, William J. 1968. "Entrepreneurship in Economic Theory." *American Economic Review* 58: 64–71.

Bell, Harry. 1972. "Trade Relations with the Third World: Preferential Aspects of Protective Structures." Pp. 299–334 in *The United States and International Markets*, edited by Robert G. Hawkins and Ingo Walter. Lexington, MA: D. C. Health.

Benedict, Burton. 1968. "Family Firms and Economic Development." *Southwestern Journal of Anthropology* 24: 1–19.

Bennett, Marion T. 1963. *American Immigration Policies*. Washington, D.C.: Public Affairs.

Berkman, Leslie. 1984. "Banks Catering to Asians Face a Culture Gap." *Los Angeles Times*, September 30: pt. V, 5–7.

Bernstein, Harry. 1973. "Prosecution Against 19 Garment Firms Begins." *Los Angeles Times*, November 28, 1973: pt. I, 1.

Bernstein, Sid. 1977. "Center City Poor Pay More for Food, Official Says." *Los Angeles Times*, November 1: pt. II, 1.

Birch, David L. 1981. "Who Creates Jobs?" *The Public Interest* 65: 3–14.

Blackistone, Kevin B. 1981. "Arab Entrepreneurs Take Over Inner City Grocery Stores." *Chicago Reporter* 10 (May): 1–5.

Blalock, Hubert M., Jr. 1967. *Toward a Theory of Minority Group Relations*. New York: John Wiley.

Blaustein, Arthur I., and Geoffrey Faux. 1972. *The Star-Spangled Hustle*. Garden City: Doubleday.

Bloom Gordon F. 1970. "Black Capitalism in Ghetto Supermarkets: Problems and Prospects." *Industrial Management Review* 11: 37–48.

Bluestone, Barry, and Bennett Harrison. 1982. *The Deindustrialization of America*. New York: Basic Books.

Boissevain, Jeremy. 1984. "Small Entrepreneurs in Contemporary Europe." Pp. 20–38 in *Ethnic Communities in Business*, edited by Robin Ward and Richard Jenkins. New York: Cambridge University Press.

Bonacich, Edna. 1972. "A Theory of Ethnic Antagonism: The Split Labor Market." *American Sociological Review* 37: 547–559.

———. 1973. "A Theory of Middleman Minorities." *American Sociological Review* 38: 583–94.

————. 1975. "Small Business and Japanese American Ethnic Solidarity." *Amerasia Journal* 3: 969–112.

————. 1976. "Advanced Capitalism and Black/White Race Relations in the United States: A Split Labor Market Interpretation." *American Sociological Review* 41 (February): 34–51.

————. 1978. "Middleman Minorities and Advanced Capitalism." Paper presented at the annual meeting of the American Anthropological Association, Los Angeles, CA. November.

————. 1980. "The Creation of Dual Labor Markets." Paper presented at the Structure of Labor Markets and Socio-economic Stratification Conference, University of Georgia at Athens. March 3.

Bonacich, Edna, and John Modell. 1981. *The Economic Basis of Ethnic Solidarity: A Study of Japanese Americans.* Berkeley, Los Angeles, London: University of California Press.

Bonacich, Edna, and Tae Hwan Jung. 1982. "A Portrait of Korean Small Business in Los Angeles: 1977." Pp. 75–98 in *Koreans in Los Angeles,* edited by Eui-Young Yu, Earl H. Phillips, and Eun Sik Yang. Los Angeles: Koryo Research Institute and Center for Korean-American and Korean Studies, California State University, Los Angeles.

Bonacich, Edna, and Lucie Cheng. 1984. "Introduction: A Theoretical Orientation to Labor Immigration." Ch. 1 in *Labor Immigration Under Capitalism: Asian Workers in the U.S. Before World War II,* edited by Edna Bonacich and Lucie Cheng. Berkeley, Los Angeles, London: University of California Press.

Bonnett, Aubrey W. 1976. "Rotating Credit Associations Among West Indian Immigrants in Brooklyn: An Exploratory Study." Ph.D. dissertation, City University of New York.

Bottomore, T. B. 1966. *Classes in Modern Society.* New York: Pantheon.

Bourdieu, Pierre. 1977. "Cultural Reproduction and Social Reproduction." Pp. 487–511 in *Power and Ideology in Education,* edited by Jerome Karabel and A. H. Halsey. New York: Oxford University Press.

Boyarsky, Bill. 1977. "Parents Flunk School Board." *Los Angeles Times,* August 6: pt. II, 1.

Brandt, Vincent. 1971. *A Korean Village.* Cambridge, MA: Harvard University Press.

Breidenstein, Gerhard. 1974. "Capitalism in South Korea." Pp. 233–270 in *Without Parallel,* edited by Frank Baldwin. New York: Pantheon.

Breton, Raymond. 1964. "Institutional Completeness of Ethnic Communities and the Personal Relations of Immigrants." *American Journal of Sociology* 70: 193–205.

Brown, Arthur Judson. 1919. *The Mastery of the Far East.* New York: Scribner's.

Brown, Warren. 1979. "Town in Fear Over Strife with Vietnamese." *Los Angeles Times,* August 12: pt. I, 1.

Burawoy, Michael. 1976. "The Functions and Reproduction of Immigrant Labor: Comparative Materials from South Africa and the United States."

American Journal of Sociology 81: 1050–1087.

Burrell, Berkeley G. 1977. "Testimony of Berkeley G. Burrell." Pp. 153–161 in U.S. Senate (95th Congress, 1st session), Select Committee on Small Business Advocacy, *Small Business Economic Policy and Advocacy Reorganization Act of 1977*. Washington, D.C.: USGPO.

Buss, Claude A. 1982. *The United States and the Republic of Korea*. Stanford, CA: Hoover Institution Press, Publication 254.

Buyers Guide. 1977. "Saemaul Movement and Saemaul Factories." vol. 4 (November): 8–13.

California, Governor's Task Force on Civil Rights. 1982. *Report on Racial, Ethnic, and Religious Violence in California*. Sacramento, CA: Department of Fair Employment and Housing.

Campbell, Colin D., and Chang-Shick Ahn. 1962. "Kyes and Mujins: Financial Intermediaries in South Korea." *Economic Development and Cultural Change* 11: 55–68.

Cannon, Carl. 1976. "Liquor Price Fixing Held Illegal but Faces Court Test." *Los Angeles Times*, December 3: pt. I, 1.

———. 1977*a*. "Liquor Industry in Ferment on Price Ruling." *Los Angeles Times*, December 16.

———. 1977*b*. "Fair Trade Law on Liquor Upheld." *Los Angeles Times*, March 11: pt. I, 1.

———. 1978*a*. "Alcohol Agency Watered Down?" *Los Angeles Times*, April 2: pt. VI, 1.

———. 1978*b*. "Justices Void Minimum Price Law for Liquor." *Los Angeles Times*, May 31: pt. I, 1.

———. 1978*c*. "Liquor Price War Brewing." *Los Angeles Times*, June 1: pt. I, 3.

———. 1978*d*. "State Unlikely to Fight Liquor Price Ruling." *Los Angeles Times*, June 22: pt. III, 12.

———. 1978*e*. "Liquor Consumer to Get Yule Gift." *Los Angeles Times*, July 30: pt. VII, 1.

———. 1979. "Kickbacks on Liquor Reported Spreading as Competition Increases." *Los Angeles Times*, May 13: pt. VI, 1.

Carlend, James W., Frank Hoy, William R. Boulton, and Jo Ann C. Carland. 1984. "Differentiating Entrepreneurs from Small Business Owners: A Conceptualization." *Academy of Management Review* 9(2): 354–359.

Castells, Manuel. 1975. "Immigrant Workers and Class Struggles in Advanced Capitalism: The Western European Experience." *Politics and Society* 5: 33–66.

Cater, John. 1984. "Acquiring Premises: A Case Study of Asians in Bradford." Ch. 12 in *Ethnic Communities in Business*, edited by Robin Ward and Richard Jenkins. New York: Cambridge University Press.

Chan, Janet B. L., and Yuet-Wah Cheung. 1985. "Ethnic Resources and Business Enterprise: A Study of Chinese Business in Toronto." *Human Organization* 44: 142–154.

Chaneka, Steve. 1980. "Business People Monitoring Situation." *Koreatown*,

June 12: 4.

Chang, Edward. 1983. "Korean Rotating Credit Associations in Los Angeles." Unpublished paper, Asian American Studies Center, University of California at Los Angeles.

Chang, Terry. 1980. "My Life in America: Korean Immigrants Tell Their Story." Unpublished student paper, Asian-American Studies Center, UCLA.

Chang, Won H. 1977. "Communication and Acculturation." Pp. 135–254 in *The Korean Diaspora*, edited by Hyung-Chan Kim. Santa Barbara, CA: ABC-Clio Press.

Chase-Dunn, Christopher, and Richard Rubinson. 1979. "Cycles, Trends, and New Departures in World-System Development." Pp. 276–296 in *National Development and the World System*, edited by John W. Meyer and Michael T. Hanna. Chicago: University of Chicago Press.

Choi, J. S. 1965. "Traditional Values in Korean Family." *Journal of Asian Studies* 7: 43–47.

Chol, Nam-Hyun. 1982. "Koreans Living in 100 Countries." *Koreatown* 3 (December): 37.

Chong, Gyong Mo. 1975. "South Korean Reality." Pp. 1–12 in *Aspiration of the South Korean People*. Pyongyang: Foreign Languages Publishing House.

Choo, Hakchung. 1977. "Some Sources of Relative Equity in Income Distribution: A Historical Perspective." Pp. 303–330 in *Essays on the Korean Economy* (vol. II: *Industrial and Social Development Issues*), edited by Chuk Kyo Kim. Seoul: Korea Development Institute.

Choy, Bon-Youn. 1971. *Korea: A History*. Rutland, VT: Charles E. Tuttle.

———. 1979. *Koreans in America*. Chicago: Nelson-Hall.

Chung, Joseph S. 1979. "Small Ethnic Business as a Form of Disguised Unemployment and Cheap Labor." Pp. 509–517 in United States Commission on Civil Rights, *Civil Rights Issues of Asian and Pacific Americans: Myths and Realities*. Washington, D.C.: USGPO.

Chung, William K. 1977. "Sales by Majority-Owned Foreign Affiliates of U.S. Companies, 1975." *Survey of Current Business* 57: 29–39.

Clare, Kenneth G., et al. 1969. *Area Handbook for the Republic of Korea*. Washington, D.C.: USGPO.

Cleaver, James H. 1983a. "Asian Businesses in Black Community Cause Stir." *Los Angeles Sentinel*, August 11: pt. A, 1.

———. 1983b. "Asian Attitudes toward Blacks Cause Raised Eyebrows." *Los Angeles Sentinel*, August 18: pt. A, 1.

———. 1983c. "Residents Complain about Alleged Asian Problem." *Los Angeles Sentinel*, August 25: pt. A, 1.

———. 1983d. "Citizens Air Gripes about Asians." *Los Angeles Sentinel*, September 1: pt. A, 1.

———. 1983è. "Asians May Face Lawsuits." *Los Angeles Sentinel*, September 8: pt. A, 2.

———. 1983f. "Black Agenda Hosts Korean Dialogue." *Los Angeles Sen-*

tinel, September 15: pt. A, 1.

Cobas, Jose A. 1987. "Ethnic Enclaves and Middleman Minorities: Alternative Strategies of Immigrant Adaptation?" *Sociological Perspectives* 30: 143–161.

Cohen, Abner. 1969. *Custom and Politics in Urban Africa.* Berkeley and Los Angeles: University of California Press.

Cohen, Benjamin. 1975. *Multinational Firms and Asian Exports.* New Haven, CT: Yale University Press.

Cole, David C. and Princeton N. Lyman. 1971. *Korean Development: The Interplay of Politics and Economics.* Cambridge, MA: Harvard University Press.

Conk, Margo A. 1981. "Immigrant Workers in the City, 1870–1930: Agents of Growth or Threats to Democracy?" *Social Science Quarterly* 62: 704–720.

Connor, Walter D. 1972. *Deviance in Soviet Society.* New York and London: Columbia University Press.

Cornelius, Wayne A. 1982. "America in the Era of Limits: Nativist Reactions to the 'New' Immigration." *Working Papers in U.S.–Mexican Studies* (University of California, San Diego) 3: 1–31.

Daniels, Rodger. 1966. *The Politics of Prejudice: The Anti-Japanese Movement in California and the Struggle for Japanese Exclusion.* Gloucester, MA: Peter Smith.

Day, Nancy, and Ken Wong. 1979. "Chinatown's Sewing Shops: Patchwork of Pleasure and Woe." *San Francisco Chronicle,* August 19: A12.

Dearman, Marion. 1982. "Structure and Function of Religion in the Los Angeles Korean Community: Some Aspects." Pp. 165–184 in *Koreans in Los Angeles,* edited by Eui-Young Yu, Earl H. Phillips, and Eun Sik Yang. Los Angeles: Koryo Research Institute and Center for Korean American and Korean Studies, California State University.

Decker, Cathleen and Richard Simon. 1986. "City OKs Remap Plan: Court Now to Decide Its Fate." *Los Angeles Times,* July 31: pt. II, 1.

De Vos, George A. 1973. *Socialization for Achievement: Essays on the Cultural Psychology of the Japanese.* Berkeley, Los Angeles, London: University of California Press.

De Vos, George A., and Daekyun Chung. 1981. "Community Life in a Korean Ghetto." Pp. 225–251 in *Koreans in Japan: Ethnic Conflict and Accommodation,* edited by Changsoo Lee and George De Vos. Berkeley, Los Angeles, London: University of California Press.

Dewey, Alice G. 1962. "Trade and Social Control in Java." *Journal of the Royal Anthropological Institute* 92: 177–190.

De Wolfe, Evelyn. 1982. "Fund Pools Blocked by Postal Law." *Los Angeles Times,* February 21: pt. V, 11.

DiMaggio, Paul. 1982. "Cultural Capital and School Success: The Impact of Status Culture Participation on the Grades of U.S. High School Students." *American Sociological Review* 47: 189–201.

Doerner, William. 1985. "To America with Skills." *Time* 126 (July 8):

42—44.

Dotson, John. 1975. "The Pioneers." *Newsweek*, May 26.

Dror, Yehezkel. 1959. "Law and Social Change." *Tulane Law Review* 33: 749—801.

Durant, Celeste. 1977. "Liquor Stores Come Under Attack in Black Community." *Los Angeles Times*, June 5: pt. II, 1.

Eagan, Gloria, and Melodie Cingolani. 1977. "Restaurants and Food Services." *Bank of America Small Business Reporter* 12(8).

Elder, Peyton K. 1978. "The 1977 Amendment to the Federal Minimum Wage Law." *Monthly Labor Review* 101 (January): 9—11.

Endicott, William. 1981. "Public Calls Crime L.A.'s Top Problem." *Los Angeles Times*, February 1: pt. I, 1.

Eng, Peter, and Edward D. Sargent. 1981. "A Troubled American Dream: Blacks and Asians at Odds over Money and Territory." *Washington Post*, August 17: 1.

Entin, Bruce. 1979. "Labor Law Abuse Widespread in L. A. Apparel Industry." *California Apparel News*, January 12: 1.

Ericson, Anna-Stina. 1970. "An Analysis of Mexico's Border Industrialization Program." *Monthly Labor Review* 93 (May): 33—40.

Espiritu, Yen. 1987. "Theory of Ethnicization: The Twice-Minorities." Paper presented at the Annual Meeting of the Pacific Sociological Association, Eugene, OR, March 20, 1987.

Fain, T. Scott. 1980. "Self-Employed Americans: Their Number Has Increased." *Monthly Labor Review* 103: 3—8.

Farr, Bill. 1979. "Ten Los Angeles Garment Makers Fined As 'Sweatshops.'" *Los Angeles Times*, September 26: pt. II, 1.

Fernandez, Raul. 1977. *The United States—Mexico Border: A Politico-Economic Profile*. Notre Dame, IN: University of Notre Dame Press.

Finley, Murray H. 1978. "Foreign Trade and U.S. Employment." Pp. 129—134 in *The Impact of International Trade and Investment on Employment*. Washington, D.C.: U.S. Department of Labor, Bureau of International Labor Affairs.

Flanagan, Robert J., and Arnold R. Weber, eds. 1974. *Bargaining without Boundaries: The Multinational Corporation and International Labor Relations*. Chicago: University of Chicago Press.

Fong, Tim. 1987. "Asian Small Business Growth Becomes Lightning Rod for Anti-Asian Sentiment." *East/West*, July 9: 1.

Foster, Brian L. 1974. "Ethnicity and Commerce." *American Ethnologist* 1: 437—448.

Frank, Charles R., Jr., Kwang Suk Kim, and Larry E. Westphal. 1975. *Foreign Trade Regimes and Economic Development: South Korea*. New York: National Bureau of Economic Research.

Fuentes, Annette, and Barbara Ehrenreich. 1983. *Women in the Global Factory*. New York: Institute for New Communications.

Furnivall, J. S. 1944. *Netherlands India: a Study of Plural Economy*, Cambridge: Cambridge University Press.

Gagliani, Giorgio. 1981. "How Many Working Classes?" *American Journal of Sociology* 87: 259–285.

Garis, Roy L. 1927. *Immigration Restriction*. New York: Macmillan.

Geertz, Clifford. 1963. *Peddlers and Princes*. Chicago: University of Chicago Press.

Gerry, Chris, and Chris Birkbeck. 1981. "The Petty Commodity Producer in Third World Cities: Petit Bourgeois or 'Disguised' Proletarian." Pp. 121–154 in *The Petite Bourgeoisie*, edited by Frank Bechhofer and Brian Elliott. New York: St. Martin's Press.

Giddens, Anthony. 1973. *The Class Structure of the Advanced Societies*. New York: Harper & Row.

Givens, Helen Lewis. 1939. "The Korean Community in Los Angeles County." M.A. Thesis, University of Southern California.

Glaser, William A. 1978. *The Brain Drain: Emigration and Return*. Oxford: Permagon Press.

Gold, David A., Clarence Y. H. Lo, and Erik Olin Wright. 1975. "Recent Developments in Marxist Theories of the Capitalist State, Pt. 1." *Monthly Review*, October: 29–43.

Goldfinger, Nathaniel. 1973. "An American Trade Union View of International Trade and Investment." Pp. 28–53 in *American Labor and the Multinational Corporation*, edited by Duane Kujawa. New York: Praeger.

Goldscheider, Calvin, and Francis E. Kobrin. 1980. "Ethnic Continuity and the Process of Self-Employment." *Ethnicity* 7: 256–278.

Goozner, Merrill. 1987. "Age-Old Tradition Bankrolls Koreans." *Chicago Times*, July 19: sect. 7, 1.

Granovetter, Mark S. 1984. "Small Is Bountiful: Labor Markets and Establishment Size." *American Sociological Review* 49: 323–334.

Green, Sarah Clark. 1977. "Dimensions of Migrant Adjustment in Seoul, Korea." Ph.D. dissertation, Brown University.

Greene, Richard. 1982. "Tracking Job Growth in Private Industry." *Monthly Labor Review* 105 (September): 3–9.

Grossman, Jonathan. 1978. "Fair Labor Standards Act of 1938: Maximum Struggle for a Minimum Wage." *Monthly Labor Review* 101 (June): 22–30.

Guillemoz, Alexandre. 1973. "The Religious Spirit of the Korean People." *Korea Journal* 13: 12–23.

Guttmann, Peter M. 1977. "The Subterranean Economy." *The Financial Analyst's Journal* 33 (November/December): 26–27.

Habermas, Juergen. 1973. *Legitimation Crisis*. Boston: Beacon.

Hall, Richard H. 1975. *Occupations and the Social Structure*. Englewood Cliffs, N.J.: Prentice-Hall.

Halliday, Jon. 1980. "Capitalism and Socialism in East Asia." *New Left Review* 124: 3–34.

Han, Sang En. 1973. "A Study of Social and Religious Participation in Relationship to Occupational Mobility and Self-esteem among Korean Immigrants in Chicago." Ph.D. dissertation, Northwestern University.

Handlin, Oscar. 1959. *The Newcomers: Negroes and Puerto Ricans in a Changing Metropolis*. Cambridge, MA: Harvard University.

Harris, Marlys. 1983. "How the Koreans Won the Greengrocer Wars." *Money* 12 (March): 190–198.

Harris, Ron. 1980. "Black Group Seeks More Businesses." *Los Angeles Times*, October 20.

Hasan, Parvez. 1976. *Korea: Problems and Issues in a Rapidly Growing Economy*. Baltimore: Johns Hopkins University Press.

——— and D. C. Rao. 1979. *Korea: Policy Issues for Long-term Development*. Baltimore: Johns Hopkins University Press.

Hechter, Michael. 1978. "Group Formation and the Cultural Division of Labor." *American Journal of Sociology* 84: 293–318.

Helleiner, G. K. 1973. "Manufactured Exports from Less developed Countries and Multinational Firms." *Economic Journal* 83: 21–47.

———. 1978. "Freedom and Management in Primary Commodity Markets. U.S. Imports from Developing Countries." *World Development* 6 (January): 23–30.

———. 1981. *Inter-Firm Trade and the Developing Countries*. New York: St. Martin's Press.

Henderson, Gregory. 1978. "United States Policy toward Korea in the Shadow of Vietnam: A Reassessment." Pp. 165–194 in *U.S. Foreign Policy in Asia*, edited by Yung-Hasan Jo. Santa Barbara, CA: ABC-Clio.

Higgs, Robert, 1977. *Competition and Coercion: Blacks in the American Economy, 1865–1914*. New York: Cambridge University Press.

Holley, David. 1985. "Koreatown Suffering Growing Pains." *Los Angeles Times*, December 8: pt. II, 1.

Hone, Angus. 1974. "Multinational Corporations and Multinational Buying Groups: Their Impact on the Growth of Asia's Export of Manufactures—Myths and Realities." *World Development* 2 (February): 145–149.

Hong, Heung-Soo. 1975. "L.A. Korean Community Faces Problems of Adaptation, Jobs and Leadership." *New Korea*, June 5.

Hong, Lawrence. 1982. "The Korean Family in Los Angeles." Pp. 99–132 in *Koreans in Los Angeles*, edited by Eui-Young Yu, Earl H. Phillips, and Eun Sik Yang. Los Angeles: Koryo Research Institute and Center for Korean-American and Korean Studies, California State University, Los Angeles.

Horvat, Branko. 1982. *The Political Economy of Socialism*. Armonk, NY: M. E. Sharpe, Inc.

Hossain, Mokerrom. 1982. "South Asians in Southern California: A Sociological Study of Immigrants from India, Pakistan and Bangladesh." *South Asia Bulletin* 2 (1982): 74–83.

Houchins, Lee, and Chang Su Houchins. 1974. "The Korean Experience in America, 1903–1924." *Pacific Historical Review* 43: 548–573.

Hraba, Joseph. 1979. *American Ethnicity*. Itasca: F. E. Peacock.

Huber, Joan, and William H. Form. 1973. *Income and Ideology*. New York: Free Press.

Hurh, Won Moo, Hei-Chu Kim, and Kwang-Chung Kim. 1978. *Assimilation Patterns of Immigrants in the United States: A Case Study of Korean Immigrants in the Chicago Area.* Washington, D.C.: University Press of America.

Huhr, Won Moo, Hei Chu Kim, and Kwang Chung Kim. 1980. "Cultural and Social Adjustment Patterns of Korean Immigrants in the Chicago Area." Pp. 295–302 in *Sourcebook on the New Immigration,* edited by Roy S. Bryce-Laporte. New Brunswick, N.J.: Transaction Books.

―――, and Kwang Chung Kim. 1980. "Korean Immigrants in America: A Structural Analysis of Ethnic Confinement and Adhesive Adaptation." Macomb, IL: Department of Sociology and Anthropology, Western Illinois University.

―――. 1984. *Korean Immigrants in America.* London and Toronto: Associated University Presses.

International Labour Organization. 1976a. *Wages and Work Conditions in Multinational Enterprises.* Geneva. ILO.

―――. 1976b. *The Impact of Multinational Enterprises on Employment and Training.* Geneva: International Labour Office.

―――. 1977. *Yearbook of Labor Statistics, 1977.* Geneva: International Labour Office.

―――. 1979. *Yearbook of Labor Statistics, 1979.* Geneva: International Labour Office.

Jameson, Sam. 1983. "Entrepreneur Builds Empire and Puts His Nation on the International Industrial Map." *Los Angeles Times,* October 16: pt. VI, 1.

Jenkins, Richard. 1984. "Ethnicity and the Rise of Capitalism in Ulster." Ch. 4 in *Ethnic Communities in Business,* edited by Robin Ward and Richard Jenkins. New York: Cambridge University Press.

Jin, Hyung-Ki, 1978. *A Survey of Economic and Managerial Status among Koreans in the Los Angeles Area.* Translated by Terry Chang. Los Angeles: Korean Chamber of Commerce of Southern California.

―――. 1981. *A Survey on the Economic and Managerial Status of Factories Owned and Operated by Korean Contractors in the Los Angeles Area.* Pomona, CA: Industrial Research Institute for Pacific Nations, California State Polytechnic University (Pomona).

Jo, Yong-Hwan. 1982. "Problems and Strategies of Participation in American Politics." Pp. 203–218 in *Koreans in Los Angeles,* edited by Eui-Young Yu, et al. Los Angeles: Koryo Research Institute and Center for Korean-American and Korean Studies, California State University.

Jones, Dorothy, Jenepher Walker, and Cecile Reed. 1973. "Independent Liquor Stores." *Bank of America Small Business Reporter* 11: 1–16.

Jones, Leroy, and Il Sakong. 1980. *Government, Business and Entrepreneurship in Economic Development: The Korean Case.* Cambridge, MA: Harvard University, Council on East Asian Studies.

―――. 1981. "Implication of Economic Development Planning in a 'Hard' State: the Case of Korea." Pp. 236–285 in *Modernization of Korea and the*

Impact of the West, edited by Changsoo Lee. Los Angeles: East Asian Center of the University of Southern California.

Juhn, Daniel S. 1977. "Nationalism and Korean Businessmen under Japanese Colonial Rule." *Korea Journal* 17: 4–11.

Justi, Paul. 1983. "Bay Area AAs Protest Racial Violence in U.S." *East/West*, May 18: 1.

Kang, K. Connie. 1980. "'Ugly Koreans' Live on Dole." *Koreatown*, September 28.

Kaplan, Sam. 1979. "L.A. Koreans in Search of an Identity." *Los Angeles Times*, September 26: pt. IV, 1.

Karsh, Norman. 1977. *What Is Small Business?* Washington, D.C.: Small Business Administration.

Kei, Matsuo. 1977. "The Working Class in the Masan Free Export Zone" (Special Issue) *AMPO: Japan–Asia Quarterly Review* 8(4) and 9(1 and 2): 67–78.

Kennedy, Gerard F. 1973. "The Korean Fiscal Kye (Rotating Credit Association)." Ph.D. dissertation, University of Hawaii.

Kennedy, John F. 1963. "Text of the President's Proposals to Liberalize Immigration Statutes." *New York Times*, July 24: pt. I, 12.

———. 1964. *A Nation of Immigrants*. New York: Harper & Row.

Kilby, Peter. 1971. "Hunting the Heffalump." Pp. 1–40 in *Entrepreneurship and Economic Development*, edited by Peter Kilby. New York: Free Press.

Kim, Bok-Lim C. 1977. "Asian Wives of U.S. Servicemen: Women in the Shadows." *Amerasia Journal* 4(1): 91–115.

———. 1978. "Pioneers in Intermarriage: Korean Women in the United States." Pp. 59–95 in *Korean Women in a Struggle for Humanization*, edited by Harold Hakueon Sunoo and Dong Soo Kim. Memphis: Association of Korean Christian Scholars in North America.

Kim, Chang Soo. 1977. "Marginalization, Development and the Korean Worker's Movement." *AMPO: Japan–Asia Quarterly Review* 9 (July–November): 20–39.

Kim, David S. 1975. "Koreans in Los Angeles." M.A. thesis, Architecture and Urban Planning, University of California at Los Angeles.

Kim, David S., and Charles Wong. 1977. "Business Development in Koreatown, Los Angeles." Pp. 229–246 in *The Korean Diaspora*, edited by Hyung-Chan Kim. Santa Barbara N, CA: ABC-Clio.

Kim, Kwang Chung, and Won Moo Hurh. 1983. "Korean Americans and the 'Success' Image: a Critique." *Amerasia Journal* 10: 3–21.

Kim, Dong Soo. 1978. "From Women to Women with Painful Love: A Study of National Motivation in Intercountry Adoption Process." Pp. 117–169 in *Korean Women in a Struggle for Humanization*, edited by Harold Hakwon Sunoo and Dong Soo Kim. Memphis: Association of Korean Christian Scholars in North America.

Kim, He-In. 1982. "Ethnic Identity Creates Obligations." *Korea Times English Section*, January 1: 5.

Kim, Hyung-Chan. 1977. "Ethnic Enterprise among Korean Immigrants in

America." Pp. 85–107 in *The Korean Diaspora*, edited by Hyung-Chan Kim. Santa Barbara, CA: ABC-Clio.

Kim, Hyung Tae. 1966. Ph.D. dissertation, "Relationships between Personal Characteristics of Korean Students in Pennsylvania and Their Attitudes toward the Christian Churches in America," University of Pittsburgh.

Kim, Illsoo. 1981a. *New Urban Immigrants: The Korean Community in New York*. Princeton, NJ: Princeton University Press.

———. 1981b. "The Big Apple Goes Bananas Over Korean Fruit Stands." *Asia* 4: 30–32, 50–51.

Kim, K. D. 1976. "Political Factors in the Formation of the Entrepreneurial Elite in South Korea." *Asian Survey* 16: 465–477.

Kim, Kirk Y. K. 1977. "The Impact of Japanese Colonial Development on the Korean Economy." *Korea Journal* 17: 12–22.

Kim, Kunae. 1982. "Rotating Credit Associations among the Korean Immigrants in Los Angeles: Intra-Cultural Diversity Observed in Their Economic Adaptation." M.A. thesis, Department of Anthropology, University of California, Los Angeles.

Kim, Kwang C., and Won Moo Hurh. 1984. "The Formation and Maintenance of Korean Small Business in the Chicago Minority Area." Macomb, IL: Western Illinois University.

Kim, Sanglio. 1975. "A Study of the Korean Church and Her People in Chicago, Illinois." M.A. thesis, McCormick Theological Seminary.

Kim, Seung Hee. 1970. *Foreign Capital for Economic Development: A Korean Case Study*. New York: Praeger.

Kim, Sophia. 1981. "Koreans Like to Share Closeness." *Koreatown*, December 14: 11.

———. 1982. "Korean Throws Shindig in Watts." *Los Angeles Times*, November 19 pt. II: 1.

———. 1983. "Nothing but Love and Affection for Chung Lee." *Koreatown*, January: 4.

Kim, Warren Y. 1971. *Koreans in America*. Seoul: Po Chin Chai Printing Co.

———. 1978. "The Settlement Patterns of Koreans in Los Angeles." Unpublished Paper.

Knight, Kenneth E., and Terry Dorsey. 1976. "Capital Problems in Minority Business Development: A Critical Analysis." Pp. 147–172 in U.S. Senate (Committee on Banking, Housing, and Urban Affairs; Subcommittee on Small Business—94th Congress, 2nd session), *The Role of the Small Businessman*. Washington, D.C.: USGPO.

Kobelinski, Mitchell P. 1977. "Statement of Mitchell P. Kobelinski, Administrator, U.S. Small Business Administration." Pp. 15–23 in U.S. Senate (95th Congress, 1st Session—Select Committee on Small Business), *SBA Program Authorization Levels*. Washington, D.C.: USGPO.

Koo, Hagen. 1976. "Small Entrepreneurship in a Developing Society: Patterns of Labor Absorption and Social Mobility." *Social Forces* 54 (June): 775–787.

———. 1981a. "Center–Periphery Relations and Marginalization: Empirical Analysis of the Dependency Model of Inequality in Peripheral Nations." *Development and Change* 12 (January): 55–76.

————. 1981b. "Urbanization Pattern and the Emerging Inequality Structure in Korean Development." Pp. 101–114 in *Modernization of Korea and the Impact of the West*, edited by Changsoo Lee. Los Angeles: East Asian Studies Center of the University of Southern California.

————. 1983. "Transformation of the Korean Class Structure: The Impact of Dependent Development." Unpublished paper, University of Hawaii (Honolulu).

Koo, Hagen, and Eui-Young Yu. 1981. *Korean Immigration to the United States: Its Demographic Pattern and Social Implications for Both Societies.* Honolulu: Papers of the East-West Population Institute, No. 74 (August).

Koo, Youngnok. 1975. "The Conduct of Foreign Affairs." Pp. 207–242 in *Korean Politics in Transition*, edited by Edward Reynolds Wright. Seattle: University of Washington Press.

Kujawa, Duane, ed. 1973. *American Labor and the Multinational Corporation.* New York: Praeger.

Kurtz, Donald F. 1973. "The Rotating Credit Association: An Adaptation to Poverty." *Human Organization* 32: 49–58.

Kurtz, Jerome. 1980. "Statement of Jerome Kurtz." Pp. 2–54 in U.S. Congress (Joint Economic Committee—1st Session), *The Underground Economy.* Washington, D.C.: USGPO.

Kuznets, Paul W. 1977. *Economic Growth and Structure in the Republic of Korea.* New Haven, CT: Yale University Press.

Lee, Changsoo, and Hiroshi Wagatsuma. 1979. "The Settlement Patterns of Koreans in Los Angeles." Paper presented, Annual Meeting of the Asian Studies Association, Los Angeles, March 30.

Lee, Changsoo, and George De Vos. 1981. *Koreans in Japan: Ethnic Conflict and Accommodation.* Berkeley, Los Angeles, London: University of California Press.

Lee, Chong-Sik. 1981. "South Korea in 1980: The Emergence of a New Authoritarian Regime." *Asian Survey* 21 (January): 125–143.

Lee, Chung. 1984. "Address." Seminar on Korean-American Communities in America, University of California at Los Angeles, June 2 (in Korean).

Lee, Rev. Chung Kuhn. 1982. "Oriental Puritans." *Korea Times English Section*, April 6: 1.

Lee, Don Chang. 1977. "Korean Community Structures in America." *Korea Journal*, 17: 48–55.

Lee, Eddy. 1979. "Egalitarian Peasant Farming and Rural Development: The Case of South Korea." *World Development* 7 (April/May): 493–517.

Lee, Eun-Jin. 1984. "Korean Rotating Credit Associations in Los Angeles." Unpublished paper, Asian-American Studies Center, University of California at Los Angeles.

Lee, Hoon K. 1936. *Land Utilization and Rural Economy in Korea.* Chicago: University of Chicago Press.

Lee, Hwa Soo. 1982. "Korean-American Voluntary Associations in Los

Angeles: Some Aspects of Structure, Function, and Leadership." Ch. 9 in Eui-Young Yu, Earl H. Phillips, and Eun Sik Yang, eds., *Koreans in Los Angeles: Prospects and Promises*. Los Angeles: Koryo Research Institute and Center for Korean-American and Korean Studies, California State University.

Lee, Kapson. 1980. "Sunny Park's Boutique Classy Place." *Koreatown Weekly*, April 28.

Lee, Yapson Yim. 1981. "Confidentiality, Service: Policy of Bank Manager." *Korea Times English Section,* October 14: 1.

Lee, Yosup. 1982. "How Competitive Are We?" *Korea Times English Section*, May 5: 1.

Lee, Young-Lo. 1975. "The Politics of Democratic Experiment: 1948–1974." Pp. 13–43 in *Korean Politics in Transition*, edited by Edward Reynolds Wright. Seattle: University of Washington Press.

Leibenstein, Harvey. 1968. "Entrepreneurship and Development." *American Economic Review* 58: 72–83.

Li, Peggy, Buck Wong, and Fong Kwan. 1974. *Garment Industry in Los Angeles Chinatown, 1973–1974*. Los Angeles: Asian-American Studies Center, University of California, Los Angeles.

Lieberman, Jethro K. 1968. *Are Americans Extinct?* New York: Walker.

Lieberson, Stanley. 1981. "An Asymmetrical Approach to Segregation." Ch. 3 in *Ethnic Segregation in Cities* edited by Ceri Peach, Vaugn Robinson, and Susan Smith. Athens: University of Georgia Press.

Light, Ivan. 1972. *Ethnic Enterprise in America*. Berkeley, Los Angeles, London: University of California Press.

——. 1974. "Reassessments of Sociological History: C. Wright Mills and the Power Elite." *Theory and Society* 1: 361–374.

——. 1977a. "The Ethnic Vice District, 1880–1944." *American Sociological Review* 77: 464–479.

——. 1977b. "Numbers Gambling among Blacks: A Financial Institution." *American Sociological Review* 42: 892–904.

——. 1979. "Disadvantaged Minorities in Self-employment." *International Journal of Comparative Sociology* 20: 31–45.

——. 1980. "Asian Enterprise in America." Pp. 33–57 in *Self-help in America: Patterns of Minority Economic Development*, edited by Scott Cummings. Port Washington, NY: Kennikat Press.

——. 1981. "Ethnic Succession." Pp. 53–86 in *Ethnic Change*, edited by Charles Keyes. Seattle: University of Washington Press.

——. 1983. *Cities in World Perspective*. New York: Macmillan.

——. 1984. "Immigrant and Ethnic Enterprise in North America." *Ethnic and Racial Studies* 7: 195–216.

——. 1988. "Los Angeles." Ch. 2 in *The Metropolis Era*, vol. 2, *Mega-Cities* edited by Mattei Dogan and John Kasarda. Beverly Hills: Sage.

Lim, Hy-Sop. 1976. "Values and Psychological Factors Causing Population Concentration in Seoul," *Korea Journal* 16: 4–12.

Lim, Ki Yop. 1976a. "A Comparative Study of American and Korean Labor

Laws: The Impact of the American System of Labor Law on the Development of Korean Labor Practices." Unpublished J.D. dissertation, Stanford University School of Law.

————. 1976b. "Development of Korean Labor and Practice." *Journal of Korean Affairs* 5 (January): 25–42.

Lipset, Seymour Martin, and Reinhard Bendix. 1959. *Social Mobility in Industrial Society*. Berkeley and Los Angeles: University of California Press.

Loewen, James W. 1971. *The Mississippi Chinese: Between Black and White*. Cambridge, MA: Harvard University Press.

Long, Don. 1977. "Repression and Development in the Periphery: South Korea," *Bulletin of Concerned Asian Scholars* 9 (April–June): 26–41.

Lovell, John P. 1975. "The Military and Politics in Postwar Korea." Pp. 153–199 in *Korean Politics in Transition*, edited by Edward Reynolds Wright. Seattle: University of Washington Press.

Lovell-Troy, Lawrence A. 1981a. "Clan Structure and Economic Activity: The Case of Greeks in Small Business Enterprise." Pp. 58–85 in *Self-help in Urban America*, edited by Scott Cummings. Port Washington, NY: Kennikat Press.

————. 1981b. "Ethnic Occupational Structures: Greeks in the Pizza Business." *Ethnicity* 8: 82–95.

Lyman, Princeton. 1975. "Economic Development in South Korea." Pp. 243–254 in *Korean Politics in Transition*, edited by Edward R. Wright. Seattle: University of Washington Press.

Lyu, Kingsley K. 1977. "Korean Nationalist Activities in Hawaii and the Continental United States, 1900–1945, Part I: 1900–1919." *Amerasia Journal* 4 (November 1): 23–90.

Macaulay, Stewart. 1963. "Non-Contractual Relations in Business." *American Sociological Review* 28: 55–66.

Marx, Karl. 1965. *Capital*, vol. 1. Moscow: Progress Publishers.

Mason, Edward S., et al. 1980. *The Economic and Social Modernization of the Republic of Korea*. Council on East Asian Studies. Cambridge, MA: Harvard University Press.

Mayer, Kurt. 1947. "Small Business as a Social Institution." *Social Research* 14: 332–349.

————. 1953. "Business Enterprise: Traditional Symbol of Opportunity." *British Journal of Sociology* 4: 160–180.

Mayhew, Leon. 1968. "Ascription in Modern Societies." *Sociological Inquiry* 38: 105–120.

McCall, Susan. 1975. "Crime Prevention for Small Business." *Bank of America Small Business Reporter* 13(1).

McCune, Shannon. 1966. *Korea: Land of Broken Calm*. Princeton, NJ: D. Van Nostrand.

McDonald, Richard J. 1984. "The 'Underground Economy' and BLS Statistical Data." *Monthly Labor Review* 107 (January): 4–18.

McMillan, Penelope. 1984. "Koreatown: A Struggle for Identity." *Los*

Angeles Times, June 17: pt. I, 1.

———. 1985. "Anti-Asian Bigotry: an 'Alarming' Rise as Refugees Pour In." *Los Angeles Times*, February 4: pt. II, 1.

Melendy, H. Brett. 1977. *Asians in America: Filipinos, Koreans, and East Indians*. Boston: Twayne.

Miller, Ross. 1980. "Vietnam Fallout in a Texas Town." *New York Times*, April 6: sec. VI, 39 ff.

Mills, C. W. 1951. *White Collar*. New York: Oxford University Press.

Min, Pyong-Yong. 1982. "Churches Abound in the Korean Community." *Korea Times*, October 20.

Min, Pyong Gap. 1984a. "A Structural Analysis of Korean Business in the United States," *Ethnic Groups* 6: 1–25.

———. 1984b. "From White Collar Occupations to Small Business: Korean Immigrants' Occupational Adjustment," *The Sociological Quarterly* 25: 333–352.

Min, Pyong Gap, and Charles Jaret. 1985. "Ethnic Business Success: The Case of Korean Small Business in Atlanta." *Sociology and Social Research*, 69: 412–435.

Mintz, Barbara R. 1980. "Kye is Key to Banking Korean Style." *Koreatown*, December 15: 7.

Mitchell, Richard H. 1967. *The Korean Minority in Japan*. Berkeley and Los Angeles: University of California Press.

Moon, Hyung June. 1976. "The Korean Immigrants in America. The Quest for Identity in the Formative Years," *1903–1918*. Unpublished Ph.D. dissertation, University of Nevada, Reno.

Muller, Ronald. 1975. "A Qualifying and Dissenting View of the Multinational Corporation." Pp. 21–41 in *Global Companies: The Political Economy of World Business*, edited by George W. Ball. Englewood Cliffs, NJ: Prentice-Hall.

Myers, Ronald E. 1983. "Immigrant Occupational Achievement: A Comparative Case Study of Koreans, Soviet Jews and Vietnamese in the Philadelphia Area." Ph.D. dissertation, University of Pennsylvania.

Nie, Norman, et al. 1975. *SPSS: Statistical Package for the Social Sciences*, 2nd ed. New York: McGraw-Hill.

Nishikawa, Tomoji. 1981. "Postwar Emigration from the Republic of Korea." Unpublished paper, Asian-American Studies Center of the University of California at Los Angeles.

Noel, Peter. 1981a. "Koreans Dash for Harlem Cash." *New York Amsterdam News*, July 4.

———. 1981b. "Will Black Americans Drive Koreans from Harlem?" *New York Amsterdam News*, July 11.

North, David S. 1971. "Alien Workers: A Study of the Labor Certification Program." Washington, D.C.: Trans Century Corp.

North, David S., and William G. Weissert. 1973. *Immigrants in the American Labor Market*. Washington, D.C.: Trans Century Corporation.

———. 1979. "Asia-Pacific Illegal Aliens: A Discussion of Their Status,

Limitations, and Rights under the Law." Pp. 238–244 in *Civil Rights Issues of Asian- and Pacific-Americans: Myths and Realities*. Washington, D.C.: U.S. Commission on Civil Rights.

O'Connor, James. 1973. *The Fiscal Crisis of the State*. New York: St. Martin's Press.

Ogburn, Robert, and Steve Butler. 1983. "The Tale of Three Cities Unfolds." *Koreatown*, November 12.

Oh, Francis Kyenghoan. 1975. "Impact of Religion on Individualism, Secularization of Consciousness, and Work Commitment among Korean Adults." Ph.D. dissertation, Fordham University.

Oh, Kwan Chi. 1972. "The Economics of Kye: An Informal Association of Individuals for Savings and Loans in Korea." Ph.D. dissertation, Vanderbilt University (Nashville).

Oh, M. David. 1983. *An Analysis of the Korean Community in the Mid-Wilshire Area*, vols. 1 and 2. Los Angeles: Mid-Wilshire Community Research Center Corp.

Oh, Tai K. 1977. *The Asian Brain Drain: A Factual and Causal Analysis*. San Francisco: R and E Associates.

Oliver, Melvin, and James M. Johnson, Jr. 1984. "Inter-Ethnic Conflict in an Urban Ghetto: The Case of Blacks and Latinos in Los Angeles." *Research in Social Movements, Conflict, and Change* 6: 57–94.

Oliver, Myrna. 1984. "Massage Parlor's Manager Is Fined." *Los Angeles Times*, April 21: pt. I, 18.

Olzak, Susan. 1986. "A Competition Model of Ethnic Collective Action in American Cities, 1877–1889." Pp. 17–46 in *Competitive Ethnic Relations*, edited by Susan Olzak and Joane Nagel. San Diego: Academic.

Osgood, Cornelius. 1951. *The Koreans and Their Culture*. New York: Ronald Press.

Oster, Patrick. 1979. "Indochina Refugees Face Some Resentment in U.S." *Los Angeles Times*, November 22: pt. VIII, 8.

Overend, William. 1978. "Koreans Pursue the American Dream and Find Land of Opportunity in the Southland." *Los Angeles Times*, September 10: pt. VIII, 1.

———. 1979. "Asians: Minority or Not Minority?" *Los Angeles Times*, May 17: pt. IV, 1.

Padilla, Steve. 1981. "Vietnamese Business Thriving in Southland Despite Some Opposition." *Los Angeles Times*, July 10: pt. IV.

Palais, James B. 1974. "'Democracy' in South Korea, 1948–72." Pp. 318–357 in *Without Parallel*, edited by Frank Baldwin. New York: Pantheon.

Park, Chong Kee. 1977. "The Economics of Health Care Financing with Particular Reference to Korea." Pp. 239–256 in *Essays on the Korean Economy* (vol. II: *Industrial and Social Development Issues*), edited by Chuk Kyo Kim. Seoul: Korea Development Institute.

Park, Jong Sam. 1975. "A Three Generation Study: Traditional Korean Value Systems and Psychosocial Adjustment of Korean Immigrants in Los Angeles." D.S.W. dissertation, University of Southern California.

Patterson, Wayne, and Hyung-Chan Kim, eds. 1977. *The Koreans in America.* Minneapolis: Lerner Publications.

Piven, Frances Fox, and Richard A. Cloward. 1971. *Regulating the Poor.* New York: Pantheon.

Porter, Jack Nusan. 1981. "The Urban Middleman. A Comparative Analysis." *Comparative Social Research* 4: 199–215.

Portes, Alejandro. 1976. "Determinants of the Brain Drain." *International Migration Review* 10: 489–508.

———. 1977. "Why Illegal Migration? A Structural Perspective." Duke University, Latin American Immigration Project, Occasional Papers.

———. 1981. "Modes of Incorporation and Theories of Labor Immigration." Pp. 279–297 in *Global Trends in Migration*, edited by Mary M. Kritz, Charles B. Keely, and Silvano M. Tomasi. New York: Center for Migration Studies.

Portes, Alejandro, and John Walton. 1981. *Labor, Class, and the International System.* New York: Academic Press.

Portes, Alejandro, Juan M. Clark, and Manuel M. Lopez. 1981–1982. "Six Years Later: The Process of Incorporation of Cuban Exiles in the United States: 1973–1979." *Cuban Studies* 11–12 (1981–1982): 1–24.

Portes, Alejandro, and Robert L. Bach. 1985. *Latin Journey.* Berkeley, Los Angeles, London: University of California Press.

Portes, Alejandro, and Saskia Sassen-Koob. 1987. "Making It Underground: Comparative Material on the Informal Sector in Western Market Economics." *American Journal of Sociology* 93: 30–61.

Rabow, Jerome, and Ronald K. Watts. 1982. "Alcohol Availability, Alcoholic Beverage Sales and Alcohol-Related Problems." *Journal of Studies on Alcohol* 43: 767–801.

Rao, D. C. 1978. "Economic Growth and Equity in the Republic of Korea." *World Development* 6 (March): 383–396.

Ray, Robert N. 1975. "A Report on Self-employed Americans in 1973." *Monthly Labor Review* 98 (January): 49–54.

Reitz, Jeffrey G. 1980. *The Survival of Ethnic Groups.* Toronto: McGraw-Hill.

Republic of Korea, Economic Planning Board. 1961, 1977. *Korea Statistical Yearbook.* Seoul: Republic of Korea.

Rhee, Jae-Ho. 1979. "Industrialization and Military Dictatorship in South Korea." Unpublished paper, Sociology Department, University of California at Los Angeles.

Robertson, Stanley. 1981a. "L.A. Confidential: Problems Come in Threes." *Los Angeles Sentinel*, January 1: A6.

———. 1981b. "L.A. Confidential: No Longer 'Meltingpot.'" *Los Angeles Sentinel*, January 8: A6.

Robinson, Robert V. 1984. "Reproducing Class Relations in Industrial Capitalism." *American Sociological Review* 49: 182–196.

Rowan, Roy. 1977. "There's Also Some Good News about South Korea." *Fortune* 96 (September): 171 ff.

Rowe, Janice. 1975. "Hair Grooming/Beauty Salons." *Bank of America Small*

Business Reporter 12(9).

Rusk, Dean. 1964. "Statement of Dean Rusk." Presentation by Dean Rusk, Secretary of State. In U.S. Congress (Committee on the Judiciary, Subcommittee No. 1), *Immigration, Part 2*, Washington, D.C.: USGPO.

———. 1965. "The Reform of Our Basic Immigration Law." *Department of State Bulletin* 52 (May 24): 806–809.

Russell, Raymond. 1984. "The Role of Culture and Ethnicity in the Degeneration of Democratic Firms." Pp. 73–96 in *Economic and Industrial Democracy*. London: Sage.

Samora, Julian. 1971. *Los Mojados: The Wetback Story*. Notre Dame: University of Notre Dame Press.

Saxton, Alexander. 1971. *The Indispensible Enemy: Labor and the Anti-Chinese Movement in California*. Berkeley, Los Angeles, London: University of California.

Scott, Austin. 1981. "Shopping Center Hit by Delay." *Los Angeles Times*, December 8: pt. II, 1.

———. 1983. "Watts Shopping for a Supermarket: Can't Find Any Takers." *Los Angeles Times*, June 6: pt. II, 1.

Sengstock, Mary Catherine. 1967. "Maintenance of Social Interaction Patterns in an Ethnic Group." Ph.D. dissertation, Washington University.

Sethuraman, S. V. 1976. "The Urban Informal Sector: Concept, Measurement, and Policy." *International Labor Review* (July–August): 69–81.

Sexton, Donald E. Jr. 1973. *Groceries in the Ghetto*. Toronto: D. C. Heath.

Shaw, Robert d'A. 1971. "Foreign Investment and Global Labor." *Columbia Journal of World Business* 6 (July–August): 52–62.

Sherman, Diana. 1979. "Korean Town's Extent, Population Grow Daily." *Los Angeles Times*, February 25: pt. V, 1.

Shim, Steve. 1977. *Korean Immigrant Churches Today in Southern California*. San Francisco: R and E Associates.

Shin, Eui-Hang, and Eui-Young Yu. 1984. "Use of Surnames in Ethnic Research: The Case of Kims in the Korean-American Population." *Demography* 21: 347–359.

Shin, Linda. 1971. "Koreans in America, 1903–1945." Pp. 200–206 in *Roots: An American–Asian Reader*, edited by Amy Tachiki, Eddie Wong, and Franklin Odo. Los Angeles: Asian-American Studies Center, UCLA.

Shuit, Don. 1979. "Hahn Wants Supermarkets Checked Out." *Los Angeles Times*, September 29: pt. I, 28.

Smelser, Neil J. 1976. *The Sociology of Economic Life*, 2nd ed. Englewood Cliffs, NJ: Prentice-Hall.

Smith, Adrian. 1981. "The Informal Economy." *Lloyd's Bank Review* 14: 45–60.

Smith, Jack. 1976. "L.A. with a Korean Accent." *Westways*, May: 33 ff.

Smollar, David. 1983. "U.S. Asians Feel Trade Backlash." *Los Angeles Times*, September 14: pt. I, 1.

Soja, Edward, Rebecca Morales, and Goetz Wolff. 1983. "Urban Restructuring: An Analysis of Social and Spatial Change in Los Angeles." *Economic*

Geography 59: 195–229.

Southern California Retail Liquor Dealers Association. 1978. Unpublished document describing "School for Retailers."

Southland Corporation. 1977. *1976 Annual Report: Our First Two Billion Dollar Year*. Dallas: Southland Corporation.

Springer, Richard. 1979. "Asian-American Leaders Pressure Small Business Administration for Minority Classification." *East/West*, May 23: 3.

Stein, Barry A. 1974. *Size, Efficiency and Community Enterprise*. Cambridge, MA: Center for Community Economic Development.

Stern, Susan. 1976. "Financing Small Business." *Bank of America Small Business Reporter* 13(7).

Stokes, Randall G. 1974. "The Afrikaner Industrial Entrepreneur and Afrikaner Nationalism." *Economic Development and Cultural Change* 22: 557–579.

Stone, Russell A. 1974. "Religious Ethic and the Spirit of Capitalism in Tunisia." *International Journal of Middle East Studies* 5 (June 1974): 260–273.

Subber, William G., and Edward Tchakelian. 1976. "Memorandum to State Labor Commissioner, San Francisco. Subject: Garment Industry Task Force." Interoffice memo dated July 21.

Sung, Cheon Kum. 1982. *Chun Doo Hwan: Man of Destiny* (translated by W. Y. Joh). Los Angeles: North American Press.

Sunoo, Harold Kakwon. 1978. "Economic Development and Foreign Control in South Korea." *Journal of Contemporary Asia* 8(3): 322–339.

Sway, Marlene. 1984. "Economic Versatility: The Case of the Gypsies." *Urban Life* 13: 83–98.

Takeo, Tsuchiya. 1977. "Introduction." (Special Issue) *AMPO: Japan–Asia Quarterly Review* 8(4) and 9(1 and 2): 1–5.

Tanzi, Vito. 1980. "Underground Economy Built on Illicit Pursuits Is Growing Concern of Policymakers." *IMF Survey*, February 4: 34–37.

Teitz, Michael. 1981. *Small Business and Employment Growth in California*. Berkeley, CA: Institute of Urban and Regional Development.

Terry, L. Clay, and Vincent R. Stull. 1975. "An Independent Study of the Los Angeles Korean Community and Its People." In Library of Asian-American Studies Center, University of California at Los Angeles.

Thompson, Richard H. 1979. "Ethnicity vs. Class: An Analysis of Conflict in a North American Chinese Community." *Ethnicity* 6: 306–326.

Tienda, Marta, and Lisa J. Neidert. 1984. "Language, Education, and the Socioeconomic Achievement of Hispanic-Origin Men." *Social Science Quarterly* 65: 519–536.

Tokunaka, Robert. 1983. "Anti-Korean Articles Raise Anger and Concern." *East/West*, August 24: 1.

Tomasi, Silvano M., and Charles B. Keely. 1975. *Whom Have We Welcomed?* New York: Staten Island Center for Migration Studies.

Toney, Michael B. 1973. "Social and Economic Factors at Destination: An analysis Based on Migration Histories." Ph.D. dissertation, Brown University.

Trajtenberg, Raul. 1977. "Transnationals and Cheap Labor in the Periphery." Pp. 175–206 in *Research in Political Economy*, vol. 1, edited by Paul Zarambka. Greenwich, CT: JAI Press.

Trussell, C. P. 1964a. "New Alien Quotas Urged by Kennedy." *New York Times*, July 23: 11.

———. 1964b. "Rusk Says U.S. Immigration Laws Delight Foes." *New York Times*, August 1: 2.

Turner, Jonathan H., and Edna Bonacich. 1980. "Toward a Composite Theory of Middleman Minorities." *Ethnicity* 7: 144–158.

United California Bank. 1971. *The Apparel Industry in California*. Los Angeles: Research and Planning Division.

United Nations. 1975. *Yearbook of International Trade Statistics, 1974* (2 vols.). New York: United Nations Department of Economic and Social Affairs.

———. 1977. *Yearbook of International Trade Statistics, 1976* (2 vols.). New York: United Nations Department of Economic and Social Affairs.

———. 1978. *Yearbook of International Trade Statistics, 1978* (2 vols.). New York: United Nations Department of Economics and Social Affairs.

U.S. Bureau of the Census. 1975. *1972 Survey of Minority-Owned Business Enterprises: Asian Americans, American Indians, and Others*. Washington, D.C.: USGPO.

———. 1979a. *County Business Patterns, 1977: California*. Washington, D.C.: USGPO.

———. 1979b. *1977 Survey of Minority-Owned Business Enterprises. Asian American, American Indian, and Others*. Washington, D.C.: USGPO.

———. 1983. *Statistical Abstract of the United States: 1984*. Washington, D.C.: USGPO.

U.S. Small Business Administration. 1980. *The Small Business Data Base*. Washington, D.C.: U.S. Small Business Administration.

University of California, Los Angeles. 1984. *Student Academic Services Annual Report 1982–83*. Los Angeles: UCLA.

Valence, David. 1973. "Opposition in South Korea." *New Left Review* 77 (January): 76–89.

Viviano, Frank. 1979. "Don't Give Us Your Tired, Your Poor." *Los Angeles Times*, September 26: pt. II, 5.

Waldinger, Roger. 1984. "Immigrant Enterprise in the New York Garment Industry." *Social Problems* 32: 60–71.

———. 1987. *Through the Eye of the Needle: Immigrants and Enterprise in New York's Garment Trades*. New York: New York University Press.

Walter, F. E., and Seymour L. Wolfbein. 1962. "Testimony of Francis E. Walter and Seymour L. Wolfbein." Presentation by Dr. Seymour L. Wolfbein. In U.S. Congress (Committee on the Judiciary, Subcommittee No. 1), *Study of Population and Immigration Problems: Manpower in the United States with Projection to 1970* (Special Series No. 3). Washington, D.C.: USGPO.

Watanabe, Susumu. 1972. "International Subcontracting, Employment and Skill Promotion." *International Labor Review* 105 (May): 425–449.

Waterbury, John. 1972. *North for the Trade: Life and Times of a Berber Merchant*. Berkeley, Los Angeles, London: University of California Press.

Watkins, Stephen B., and John R. Karlik. 1978. "Anticipating Disruptive Imports." Study prepared for the Joint Economic Committee of Congress. Washington, D.C.: USGPO.

Weber, Max. 1958a. *The Protestant Ethic and the Spirit of Capitalism*. New York: Scribner's.

————. 1958b. "The Protestant Sects and the Spirit of Capitalism." Ch. 12 in *From Max Weber* edited by Hans H. Gerth and C. Wright Mills. New York: Oxford University Press.

Wells Fargo Bank. 1985. *Small Business and California: a Dynamic Partnership*. San Francisco: Wells Fargo Business Marketing.

Werbner, Pnina. 1984. "Business on Trust: Pakistani Entrepreneurship in the Manchester Garment Trade." Pp. 166–188 in *Ethnic Communities in Business*, edited by Robin Ward and Richard Jenkins. New York: Cambridge University Press.

Westphal, Larry E. 1978. "The Republic of Korea's Experience with Export-led Industrial Development." *World Development* 6 (March): 347–382.

White, Robert W. 1979. "Memo to Supervisor Kenneth Hahn [Los Angeles] on Subject of Enforcement Program for Garment Industry." Office memo, May 23.

Wideman, Bernie. 1974. "The Plight of the South Korean Peasant." Pp. 271–317 in *Without Parallel*, edited by Frank Baldwin. New York: Pantheon.

Wilensky, Harold, and Anne T. Lawrence. 1979. "Job Assignment in Modern Societies: A Reexamination of the Ascription–Achievement Hypothesis." Pp. 202–248 in *Societal Growth*, edited by Amos H. Hawley. New York: Free Press.

Wilken, Paul H. 1979. *Entrepreneurship. A Comparative Historical Study*. Norwood, NJ: Ablex.

Wilson, Kenneth L., and Alejandro Portes. 1980. "Immigrant Enclaves: An Analysis of the Labor Market Experiences of Cubans in Miami." *American Journal of Sociology* 86: 295–319.

Wilson, Kenneth L., and Allen W. Martin. 1982. "Ethnic Enclaves: A Comparison of the Cuban and Black Economies in Miami." *American Journal of Sociology* 88: 135–160.

Won, Woo-Hyon. 1977. "Values and Media Preferences of Korean Immigrants." Ph.D. dissertation, Boston University.

Won-Doornink, Myong J. J. 1985. "Television and Its Impact on Assimilation of Korean Immigrants in Los Angeles." Paper presented at the 56th annual meeting of the Pacific Sociological Association, Albuquerque, New Mexico. April 17–20.

Wong, Diane Yen-Mei. 1984. "Segment on 20/20 Angers and Disappoints Korean Community." *East/West*, January 25: 1.

Woodrum, Eric, Colbert Rhodes, and Joe R. Feagin. 1980. "Japanese American Economic Behavior." *Social Forces* 58: 1235–1254.

Wyllie, Irvin G. 1954. *The Self-made Man in America.* New York: Free Press.

Yancey, William, and Eugene P. Erickson. 1979. "The Antecedents of Community: The Economic and Institutional Structure of Urban Neighborhoods." *American Sociological Review* 44: 253–262.

Yim, Sun Bin. 1981. "The Social Structure of Korean Communities in California, 1903–1920." Unpublished paper, Department of Sociology, University of California at Los Angeles.

Yoo, Woong Nyol. 1981. "Business Owners in New York's Harlem Struggle Against Anti-Korean Prejudice." *Koreatown*, October 19: 4.

Yoshihara, Nancy. 1976. "Koreans Find Riches, Faded Dreams in L.A." *Los Angeles Times*, February 1: pt. IV, 2.

Young, Frank W. 1971. "A Macrosociological Interpretation of Entrepreneurship." Pp. 139–149 in *Entrepreneurship and Economic Development*, edited by Peter Kilby. New York: The Free Press.

Young, Philip K. Y. 1983. "Family Labor, Sacrifice, and Competition: Korean Greengrocers in New York City." *Amerasia Journal* 10: 53–71.

Yu, Eui-Young. 1977. "Koreans in America: An Emerging Ethnic Minority." *Amerasia Journal* 4: 117–131.

———. 1982a. "Koreans in Los Angeles: Size, Distribution and Composition." Pp. 23–47 in *Koreans in Los Angeles*, edited by Eui-Young Yu, Earl H. Phillips, and Eun Sik Yang. Los Angeles: Koryo Research Institute and Center for Korean-American and Korean Studies, California State University, Los Angeles.

———. 1982b. "Occupation and Work Patterns of Korean Immigrants." Pp. 49–73 in *Koreans in Los Angeles*, edited by Eui-Young Yu, Earl H. Phillips, and Eun Sik Yang. Los Angeles: Koryo Research Institute and Center for Korean-American and Korean Studies, California State University, Los Angeles.

———. 1983. "Korean Communities in America: Past, Present, and Future." *Amerasia Journal* 10 (Fall–Winter): 32–33.

———. 1985. "Koreantown, Los Angeles: Emergence of a New Inner-city Ethnic Community." *Bulletin of the Population and Development Studies Center* XIV: 29–44.

———. 1986. *Juvenile Delinquency in the Korean Community of Los Angeles.* Los Angeles: The Korea Times.

Yu, Jin H. 1982. "Philadelphia's Governor Makes Koreans Welcome." *Koreatown*, May 3.

Yun, Yeo-Chun. 1983. "Mine Kim: A Success Story with Sad Ending." *Korea Times English Section*, February 7: 1.

Zenner, Walter P. 1977. "Middleman Minority Theories: Historical Survey and Assessment." Paper presented at Yiddish Studies Colloquium, Yivo and Columbia, New York.

———. 1980. "Theory of Middleman Minorities: A Critical Review." Pp. 413–426 in *Sourcebook on the New Immigration*, edited by Roy S. Bryce-LaPorte. New Brunswick, NJ: Transaction.

———. 1982. "Arabic-Speaking Immigrants in North America as Middleman Minorities." *Ethnic and Racial Studies* 5: 457–477.

Zimmer, Cathrine, and Howard Aldrich. 1987. "Resource Mobilization Through Ethnic Networks: Kinship and Friendship Ties of Shopkeepers in England." *Sociological Perspectives* 30: 422–445.

Zolberg, Aristide R. 1978. "International Migration Policies in a Changing World System." Pp. 241–286 in *Human Migration: Patterns and Policies,* edited by W. H. McNeill and Ruth S. Adams. Bloomington: Indiana University Press.

Index

Designer: U.C. Press Staff
Compositor: Asco Trade Typesetting Ltd.
Text: 11.5/13 Palatino
Display: Palatino